MEDIEVAL HUMANISM
✶
COLLECTED ESSAYS

ITALICA PRESS STUDIES IN ART AND HISTORY

THIS SERIES presents selected volumes in the art and cultural history of the Middle Ages and Renaissance, edited and written by some of the most distinguished scholars now working in these fields. Subjects include medieval and Renaissance painting, sculpture, architecture and urbanism; iconography and emblematica; cultural studies; history and historiography, philosophy and religion; manuscript studies and the history of the book.

The series aims to present the most rigorous scholarship to both an academic and a general audience with well edited and produced volumes at reasonable prices. These volumes are now available in hardcover, paperback and in a variety of digital formats, including Kindle, JSTOR and ProQuest versions. For more information see http://www.italicapress.com/index009.html.

Volumes include:

Florilegium Columbianum: Essays in Honor of Paul Oskar Kristeller
Edited by Karl-Ludwig Selig & Robert Somerville. 1987.

The Verbal & the Visual: Essays in Honor of William Sebastian Heckscher
Edited by Karl-Ludwig Selig & Elizabeth Sears. 1990.

Aldus and His Dream Book
By Helen Barolini. 1992.

Renaissance Society & Culture: Essays in Honor of Eugene F. Rice, Jr.
Edited by John Monfasani & Ronald G. Musto. 2004.

Kristeller Reconsidered: Essays on His Life and Scholarship
Edited by John Monfasani. 2006.

Rome Italy Renaissance: Essays Honoring Irving Lavin
Edited by Marilyn Aronberg Lavin. 2008.

Medieval Renaissance Baroque: A Cat's Cradle in Honor of Marilyn Aronberg Lavin
Edited by David A. Levine & Jack Freiberg. 2009.

A Scarlet Renaissance: Essays in Honor of Sarah Blake McHam
Edited by Arnold Victor Coonin. 2013.

Petrarch's Two Gardens: Landscape and the Image of Movement
By William Tronzo. 2013.

Patronage, Gender & the Arts in Early Modern Italy:
Essays in Honor of Carolyn Valone
Edited by Katherine A. McIver & Cynthia Stollhans. 2015.

The Art of Commemoration in the Renaissance
By Irving Lavin. Edited by Marilyn Aronberg Lavin. 2021.

Writing Southern Italy Before the Renaissance:
Trecento Historians of the Mezzogiorno.
By Ronald G. Musto. 2022.

More than Meets the Eye: Irony, Paradox, amd Metaphor in the History of Art.
The Mellon Lectures
By Irving Lavin. Edited by Marilyn Aronberg Lavin. 2022.

Medieval Humanism: Collected Essays.
By C. Stephen Jaeger. 2024.

MEDIEVAL HUMANISM
✶
COLLECTED ESSAYS

C. STEPHEN JAEGER

ITALICA PRESS
NEW YORK & BRISTOL
2024

Copyright © 2024 by C. Stephen Jaeger

ITALICA PRESS, INC.
99 Wall Street, Suite 650
New York, NY 10005

Italica Press Studies in Art and History

All rights reserved. No part of this book may be reprinted or reproduced or utilised in any form or by any electronic, mechanical, or other means, now known or hereafter invented, including photocopying and recording, or in any information storage or retrieval system, without prior permission in writing from Italica Press.

Library of Congress Cataloging-in-Publication Data

Names: Jaeger, C. Stephen, author.
Title: Medieval humanism : collected essays / C. Stephen Jaeger.
Description: New York : Italica Press, 2024. | Series: Italica Press studies in art and history | Includes bibliographical references and index. | Summary: "An updated collection of essays on the European cultural history of the period 950-1150, with new research and analysis, updated notes, several excursus and appendices, a comprehensive and updated bibliography, and an index"-- Provided by publisher.
Identifiers: LCCN 2024034076 (print) | LCCN 2024034077 (ebook) | ISBN 9781599104447 (hardcover) | ISBN 9781599104454 (trade paperback) | ISBN 9781599104461 (kindle edition) | ISBN 9781599104478 (pdf)
Subjects: LCSH: Humanism--Europe--History--To 1500. | Civilization, Medieval.
Classification: LCC B738.H8 J34 2024 (print) | LCC B738.H8 (ebook) | DDC 189.4--dc23/eng/20240916
LC record available at https://lccn.loc.gov/2024034076
LC ebook record available at https://lccn.loc.gov/2024034077

Cover Image: God as Architect. French, mid-13th century. Vienna, Österreichische Nationalbibliothek, Codex 2554, fol. IV.

ABOUT THE AUTHOR

C. Stephen Jaeger grew up in the San Francisco Bay area of California. He studied at Berkeley, Tübingen, and Vienna. He has taught at University of Chicago, Northwestern University, Bryn Mawr College, the University of Washington, the University of Illinois Urbana/Champaign, and as a visitor at the University of Pennsylvania, UCLA, and the Central European University. He has specialized in Germanics and Comparative Literature, among other fields.

Prof. Jaeger is the author or editor of over a dozen books and over sixty articles. His interest in the humanism of the Middle Ages extends from his first book, *Medieval Humanism in Gottfried von Strassburg's Tristan and Isold* (1977) to the present. *The Origins of Courtliness* (1985) is a study of the Latin language of courtesy, showing the connections between ancient Roman social and ethical ideals and medieval courtliness.

The structures and ideals on which humanist learning was founded are the subject of *The Envy of Angels: Cathedrals Schools and Social Ideals in Medieval Europe, 950–1200* (1994). The cultivation of an idealized form of aristocratic love that extended from antiquity to the twentieth century was the object of *Ennobling Love: In Search of a Lost Sensibility* (1999).

Jaeger's research has been supported by grants from the American Council of Learned Societies, the National Endowment for the Humanities, and the Fulbright, Guggenheim, and Humboldt Foundations. He has been a Fellow at the Institute for Advanced Study (Princeton) and the Getty Center (Los Angeles). He has lectured widely in the US, Europe, Japan, and Taiwan. His *Envy of Angels* was co-winner of the Jacques Barzun Prize in Cultural History of the American Philosophical Society (1995). In 2002 he was elected a Fellow of the Medieval Academy of America.

More recently his interests have turned to the aesthetics of the Middle Ages. He edited a collection of essays from various contributors in *Magnificence and the Sublime in Medieval Aesthetics* (2012) and has published a study of *The Sense of the Sublime in the Middle Ages* (2022).

He lives in New York City with his wife and two dogs.

✳

For Frederic Tubach
in gratitude

CONTENTS

ABOUT THE AUTHOR	VII
PREFACE	XIII
ACKNOWLEDGMENTS	XVIII
PUBLISHER'S NOTE ON THIS EDITION	XIX
ABBREVIATIONS	XX
INTRODUCTION: THE AGE OF MEDIEVAL HUMANISM	1
An Age Without a Name	1
Humanism by Acclamation	4
The Contribution (Unfinished) of Carl Erdmann	11
Cathedral Schools	12
Cultural and Intellectual History: Beyond Atomization	15
1. CATHEDRAL SCHOOLS AND HUMANIST LEARNING, 950–1150	19
Introduction	19
Cathedral Schools	22
Letters and Manners	27
The Old Learning and *Cultus Virtutum*	32
Teaching Virtue	40
The Civil Life as Productivity: Disciplina Vivendi	47
Curiales and other "New Men"	50
Old Learning vs New	60
The Schools and the Courts	69
Conclusions	79
Excursus: Reprise, 2024	81
2. PHILOSOPHY, c.950–c.1150	95
Introduction	95
Brun of Cologne	101
Gerbert of Aurillac	106
Gerbert on Reason: Philosophy Defending the Empire	112
Abbo of Fleury and Others	119
Conservative Reaction: Peter Damian	122
The Mainstream: Ciceronianism	124

PHILOSOPHIA 126
CONCLUSIONS 127

3. MEINHARD OF BAMBERG AND
EARLY MEDIEVAL HUMANISM 133
 CARL ERDMANN AND MEINHARD'S LETTERS 133
 MEINHARD AND HUMANISM: LETTER M1 TO "G" 140
 LEARNING BY IMITATION 145
 MEANINGFUL READING 148
 WHY CATHEDRAL-SCHOOL EDUCATION? 149
 PAIDEIA: FORMATION OF THE INDIVIDUAL 154
 HILARITAS 159
 LOVE AND FRIENDSHIP 166
 THE DECLINE OF THE IMPERIAL SCHOOLS 171
 APPENDIX 175

4. THE MUSIC OF HUMANITY (MUSICA HUMANA) 181
 INTRODUCTION 181
 ISOLDE'S SILENT MUSIC 182
 BOETHIUS 185
 MUSIC AND EDUCATION: TUNING THE BODY 186
 PLANETARY MOTION — HUMAN MOTION 191
 THE MUSIC OF POETRY 196
 ST. VICTOR'S SWANSONG 199
 CONCLUSIONS 201

5. ORPHEUS IN THE ELEVENTH CENTURY 203
 INTRODUCTION 203
 USEFUL POETRY 203
 ORPHEUS, THE SYMBOL OF POETRY 207
 AN ELEVENTH-CENTURY WEDDING OF ORPHEUS
  (ELOQUENCE) AND EURYDICE (WISDOM) 208
 ORPHEUS, DEFEATER OF CRUELTY, BRINGER OF COMPASSION 211
 QUID SUUM VIRTUTIS: THE MONSTERS DANCE 215
 LIÈGE SONGS: THE UNDERWORLD CIVILIZED 220
 ORPHIC DISCOURSE 222
 MYTH ANALYSES CONFLICT: WÜRZBURG VS WORMS AGAIN 223
 STARVING STUDENTS IN HELL 228
 A CRUEL BISHOP AND A MEEK ABBOT 229

A Civilizing Force: Soothing the Anger of Kings	231
Ruodlieb	237
Conclusions	241
6. HOMO PERFECTUS	**243**
Introduction	243
Microcosm–Macrocosm	244
The Hermetic Tradition: The Human Being, a "Great Miracle"	246
The Human Being as a Work of Art	248
The Dignity of Humanity (Dignitas Hominis)	249
Human Divinity	250
The Universality of the Human Soul	252
A Humanist Myth	264
7. CHARISMATIC BODY/CHARISMATIC TEXT	**267**
Introduction	267
From Bodies to Texts	270
From Real to Symbolic Presence	275
Textual Contract	277
Conclusions	287
8. HILDEBERT OF LAVARDIN ON MURIEL OF WILTON	**289**
Introduction	289
Muriel of Wilton, A Vatic Poet	289
Muriel and the Sublime	292
Hildebert's Magnificat	295
Opprobrium and Glory	297
9. JOHN OF SALISBURY, A PHILOSOPHER OF THE LONG ELEVENTH CENTURY	**299**
Introduction	299
The Metalogicon, a Catchy Title	301
The Lure of Dialectic	304
The Cure of Grammar	306
Adam of Balsham	308
William of Soissons' Logic Machine	310
The Roots of John's Humanism	316
Conclusions	322

10. PESSIMISM IN THE TWELFTH-CENTURY
"RENAISSANCE" 325
    INTRODUCTION 325
    TOPOI OF HISTORICAL CHANGE 329
    HISTORIOGRAPHY 339
    LEARNING AND STUDY 346
    THE CRITICS 349
    POETRY 359
    LOVE 365
    PESSIMISM AS A HISTORICAL CATEGORY 370
    CONCLUSIONS 374

11. VICTORINE HUMANISM 377
    INTRODUCTION 377
    MICROCOSMUS AND OTHER CREATION ALLEGORIES . 379
    THE WAYSIDE INN OF CHARITY 380
    SOCIAL IDEALS 383
    HUMANISTIC THEOLOGY 398
    RICHARD OF ST. VICTOR ON FREE WILL 409
    CONCLUSIONS 411

12. ODYSSEUS, PARZIVAL, AND FAUST 413
    INTRODUCTION 413
    THE MINIATURIZED MIDDLE AGES 416
    CHARISMATIC REPRESENTATION 418
    THE FANTASTIC 421
    STRUCTURE: THE HERO RISING 427
    DEFYING THE GODS 430
    CONCLUSIONS 433

BIBLIOGRAPHY 435
    PRIMARY SOURCES 435
    SECONDARY WORKS 447

INDEX 475

PREFACE

The studies included in this book were written over the past thirty years or so. Most have been published, some appear here for the first time, all of the former have been revised, in some cases extensively, and updated. The essays treat a wide variety of subjects in the cultural history of the period 950–1150. Looking back over related work, it seemed to me that a summing up was due. Conventional terminology and period divisions were and continue to be more of a hindrance than an aid to seeing the cultural ties that connect 950 to 1150: "Dark Age" — more recently, Claudio Leonardi's "age without a name" — followed by the "Renaissance of the Twelfth Century," Investiture Controversy and church reform — all skirt the issues of the worldly culture of the period.

"Dark age" bypasses close study and admits the irresolution of historians. "Renaissance" suggests triumphalist overcoming of an earlier obscure period by a new age of light, i.e., it accepts implicitly the stamping of what preceded as "dark." It is Burckhardtian in its magnification of the new age and the reduction of the one that it supersedes. The movements of the period that played out in monastic life and culture, the church reform and Investiture Controversy, interacted with, and in many ways were in opposition to, the trends on which these studies focus.

The worldly culture of the period 950 to 1150 is carried for the most part by secular clergy educated at cathedral schools. They filter widely through Germany, France, and England, emerging in positions that extend from parish priest to cathedral clergy, chapter and chancery, professors, worldly courts, bishops and archbishops — also prominently as "wandering scholars," poor, cold, and hungry alienated poets. They create an educated class. They draw women into that class. Women's participation in humanist culture is a rich topic now coming into prominence in the work of Alison Beach, Fiona Griffiths, Julie Hotchin, Christina Lutter.

This class reaches deep into clerical, monastic and worldly spheres. The extent to which they constitute a coherent worldly culture can be judged by seeing its poetry, art, architecture, and philosophy, and its educational, aesthetic, social, spiritual, and political ideals embedded in a shared cultural matrix in which the literature and thought of classical antiquity played an important role. Humanistic tendencies were passed on in educational traditions that disseminated social values. Those humanistic tendencies connect 950 to 1150.

A factor that encouraged that claim and a summing up is the revelation that the German historian Carl Erdmann had planned to devote his post-World War II career to what he foresaw as a multi-volume history of education and culture in early medieval Germany and France. He saw a humanism developing that connected Ottonian Germany to twelfth-century France and England.[1]

Much work in cultural history in the past three decades confirmed his views. Aldo Scaglione, Mia Münster-Swendsen, Sita Steckel, Courtney de Mayo, Martin Aurell, and Claudia Wittig have contributed important studies to developing something approaching a synthesis of European worldly culture, French, German, and English (and in Scaglione's work, Italian). As it happens it turns out to be close to the sketch that preserves Carl Erdmann's vision. My work on courtly ideals and on cathedral schools follows that same line. The present volume summarizes and adds further material.

The tenth and eleventh centuries are considerably illuminated and set in organic relation to the twelfth by regarding them as the formative period of humanistic modes of education, thought, expression, and behavior that came to dominate western and central Europe and England. This early humanism funneled into the humanism of the twelfth century and formed a matrix from which large shifts in intellectual, social, political, and spiritual life emerged.

The topic is unseasonal. We are living in a time when humanism and the humanities feel close to extinction in academic and in world culture. Recent decades have made humanism, even the human per se, into a target as a privileged form of self-aggrandizement. The post-human orientation of thought and culture invites the demolition of the human as a philosophical idea and an object of interpretation in art, literature, and critical thought. The humanism of the Middle Ages, infused with the idea of human greatness, could hardly be more at odds with that current of thought.

The antipathy of postmodernism to humanism in general makes any vision of humanism as a dominant cultural form, past and present,

1. See below, Introduction, 13–14; and chap. 3, 133–38.

appear an anomaly. In an atmosphere where capitalism reduces human individuality, positions corporate above individual identity, where technical progress diminishes individual intelligence and critical thought, creates a conflict of human with artificial intelligence, and sets the machine as the analogue to the human — such an atmosphere would seem to offer little ground for resonance with the humanism of the Middle Ages. Its exaltation of the individual, its ideals of individual genius joined to humane ethics, eloquence joined to wisdom, sociability joined to courtesy, risk seeming less genuine, less productive of human goodness, and perhaps even falsehoods complicit with hierarchic social and political structures.

But rather than a topic at odds with the world around it, humanism in its widest framing is engaged in a historical dialectic. Its curve will rise in the next decades. In each of its post-classical revivals in the West, humanism has emerged as one means by which a culture lifts itself out of catastrophes. That applies to the humanism of 950–1150, of the Italian Renaissance, of the German cultural revolution of the late eighteenth century, and of the "new humanism" that emerged at the end of WWII in many areas of European intellectual life to answer the barbarity of fascism.[2]

And now a scant three-quarters of a century after the last world war, humanism and the humanities have lost their predominant role in higher education. The democracy and liberal intellectualism of the twentieth century are destabilized by plague (Covid), shaken by political division and dissolution, by intellectual, moral materialism, and by the de-centering of truth. The culture of the present is balanced precariously between democracy and autocracy, intellectualism and anti-intellectualism, humanistic and careerist, pragmatic higher education. When the lowpoint of that trend is eventually reached, our culture may find itself in a position, as in the past, to make healing use of humanistic patterns of thought, expression, social and educational reform — and to sharpen the appreciation of them in earlier periods. Humanism recurs not as an awakening from sleep but as an endpoint of a desperate struggle against barbarity, one means among others by which a civilization digs itself out of catastrophe.

2. The new humanism post 1948 received some of its major impulses from the medievalist Ernst R. Curtius. See the discussion below, 4–5, 87–88.

It is in that sense that humanistic trends rescued the northern Europe destabilized by the collapse of the Carolingian rule from darkness and barbarity[3] and metamorphosed into a Christian-humanist culture that eventually penetrated into every area of educated society. The essays that follow here do not articulate a synthesized view of that humanism, but they offer material for one.

NOTES ON THE CHAPTERS

The following provides information on the publication history of these chapters. Chapter 1 originally appeared as "Cathedral Schools and Humanist Learning, 950–1150," *Deutsche Vierteljahrsschrift* 61 (1987): 569–616. This study appears with only minor revisions but with updated references. I have included observations on central and contested ideas and extended some arguments in an Excursus: "Reprise, 2024" after this chapter. Chapter 2 was previously published as "Philosophy, ca. 950 – ca. 1150," *Viator* 40 (2009): 17–40. Chapter 3, "Meinhard of Bamberg and early Medieval Humanism," was written for this volume, and it will appear in *Frühmittelalterliche Studien* 2024. Chapter 4, "The Music of Humankind *(Musica humana)* and its Place in Early Medieval Education," is the revised text of a lecture given at Cambridge University in July 2016 in the conference "Lost Songs of the Middle Ages c.800 to c.1200." Chapter 5, "Orpheus in the Eleventh Century," first appeared in *Mittellateinisches Jahrbuch* 27 (1992): 147–68 and is here revised with English translations of the Latin texts. Chapter 6, "*Homo perfectus*: Human Universality in the Poetry and Philosophy of the Eleventh and Twelfth Century: Prehistory and Survival of a Humanist Myth," first appeared as "Der Vollkommene Mensch in der Philosophie und Dichtung des 12. Jahrhunderts: Vorgeschichte und Nachleben eines humanistischen Mythos," in *Akademische Wissenskulturen: Praktiken des Lehrens und Forschens vom Mittelalter bis zur Moderne*, Martin Kintzinger et al., ed. (Basel: Schwabe Verlag, 2015), 225–42, revised and expanded in English. Chapter 7, "Charismatic Body–Charismatic Text," appeared first in *Exemplaria* 9 (1997): 117–37. Chapter 8, "Hildebert of Lavardin on Muriel of Wilton, a Vatic Poet: Medieval Poetry and Modern Aesthetic Response," appears here revised from its first publication as excursus 2 in *The Sense of the Sublime in the*

3. We have the term and the line of historical thought from Brun of Cologne. See below, 87–88.

★ PREFACE & ACKNOWLEDGMENTS

Middle Ages (2022): https://www.academia.edu/73053285. Chapter 9, "John of Salisbury: A Philosopher of the Long Eleventh-Century," was originally published in *European Transformations: The Long Twelfth Century*, Thomas F.X. Noble and John Van Engen, ed. (Notre Dame, IN: Notre Dame University Press, 2012), 499–520. Chapter 10, "Pessimism in the Twelfth-Century 'Renaissance,'" appeared first in *Speculum* 78 (2003): 1151–83. Chapter 11, "Victorine Humanism," was first published in *A Companion to the Abbey of St. Victor, Paris*, Hugh Feiss and Juliette Mousseau, ed. (Leiden: Brill, 2018), 79–112. Chapter 12, "Odysseus, Parzival, and Faust," originated as the Medieval Academy address at the Leeds International Medieval Studies Conference, 2004. It was first published in *Arthuriana* 16 (2006): 3–20.

THE COVER ILLUSTRATION
This is a mid-thirteenth century representation of God as architect of the universe, famous, often reprinted. Its relevance to the humanism of the tenth to the twelfth century is a case to be made. In the present context it must be left to the aesthetic authority of the image itself to argue its relevance to the topic of this book. In its cosmic sovereignty it would seem that the God of Job meets the Demiurge. But in its suffusing of divinity with humanity — or vice versa — it is indebted to trends of thought of medieval humanism, particularly the idea, recurring in the following essays, that humanity in its mastery of study, the arts, sciences, technical skills, also masters nature and achieves a form of divinity. By study humanity discovers the image and likeness of God in itself. In humanizing the creator-God, the medieval illumination invites comparison with Michelangelo's creator-God — insistently and audaciously human, muscular and with a charisma that joins king, prophet and Greek god in one — touching humanity into an already perfectly developed god-like being. The one creates an ordered universe by human technology; the other creates humanity by a human miracle. They show the two ways in which creation in "image and likeness" works: when the human is a God; and when God is human.

ACKNOWLEDGMENTS
I am grateful to those who have inspired, encouraged and improved my work over the many years of writing these studies on medieval humanism. The earliest was Frederic Tubach. His course on medieval German literature at Berkeley was my first introduction

to Gottfried's *Tristan and Isolde*. The importance of that work to medieval humanism will be evident in the chapters that follow—all of them, I believe. To Tubach I owe among other things an awareness of the imagination as a critical faculty. For that inspiration and support I dedicate this book to him. Blake Lee Spahr, my dissertation advisor, was a task-master. I am grateful to him for his hard-headed empiricism and insistence on cogent argumentation.

Early encouragement from W.T.H. Jackson at Columbia helped me take myself seriously as a scholar. The real development of the idea of medieval humanism came in a year spent at the Institutes of Germanistik and Mittelalterforschung of University of Münster. I am grateful to Friedrich Ohly for superb work conditions and for a collegial and inspiring atmosphere to Peter von Moos, Christel Meier, and Klaus Speckenbach. In later years Walburga Hülk-Althoff and Gerd Althoff again endeared Münster as a center and forum for work beyond the narrow strictures of German medieval studies. Horst Wenzel was a supporter and kindred spirit. A year at the Humboldt University Berlin resulted in *Ennobling Love*. My thanks to Walter Haug for hospitality at Tübingen and to Joachim Bumke and Ursula Peters for stimulating exchange over the years. My collaboration with Wolfgang Harms, Jan-Dirk Müller and Peter Strohschneider at University of Munich led to the establishing of a colloquium for graduate-students/young PhD's meeting in alternate years and locations at Munich and University of Washington (later University of Illinois). This proved to be a valuable locus of debate, exchange and networking. It originated in a suggestion of Ulrike Draesner.

Research leaves at the Institute for Advanced Study, Princeton, and the Getty Institute Scholar program in Los Angeles made possible completion of *Enchantment: On Charisma and the Sublime in the Arts of the West*. My thanks particularly to Giles Constable, Martin Aurell, the unforgettable Valerie Flint, and some years later, Pat Geary. University of Washington gave strong support under Dean John Simpson to Medieval Studies. Gene Vance was a close friend and collaborator. David Fowler, Miceal Vaughan, Denyse Delcourt and John Coldewey formed a uniquely engaged group of colleagues. Large debts are due to Robert Benson, Brigitte Bedos-Rezak, Sverre Bagge, John Baldwin, Robert Lerner, Barbara Newman, Brian Patrick McGuire, Michael

Allen, Teo Ruiz, Susanne Hafner, and a deep, never to be adequately repaid debt of thanks to Jerry Singerman, wise critic.

Thanks to Bonnie Wheeler, muse of American medieval studies, for her kind and generous encouragement over the years. Thanks to my colleagues at University of Illinois Urbana/Champaign, Danuta Shanzer and Charlie Wright. Members of the Shakespeare reading group helped keep the mind alive through retirement and Covid and during the preparation for this book: Randy Brown, Peter Iversen, Denice Stradling, Maurice Stephenson, Shirley Wargon, Robert Lerner, Stephen and Ona Hamilton and Celia Chazelle.

The New York Public Library with its Humanities Center and great research holdings is my current place of study. Heartfelt thanks to director Miriam Gianni.

For constant support in the very grain of life thanks to Hannah and Zoe Jaeger, and last and most to Stephanie:

> Who can find a good wife? Her value is above rubies. Strength and dignity are her clothing, and she laughs at the trials of the future. She speaks with wisdom, and the teaching of kindness is on her tongue [Prov. 31].

PUBLISHER'S NOTE ON THIS EDITION

It is the premise of this collection that the research and insights of the essays that form its core are still valid and of deep interest and importance for medieval studies today. The essays, now collected into chapters, have been edited throughout for consistency of style and language and have been updated with new research and analysis where appropriate. While the wording of several key themes has been retained in various chapters, this edition has made uniform the many styles of reference included in the original essays to conform to current usage and to make them more accessible to a contemporary readership across the various disciplines that touch on issues of humanism ancient, medieval, and more recent. This new edition includes a list of abbreviations for titles cited throughout, updated notes, several excursus and appendices, a comprehensive and updated bibliography, and an index.

ABBREVIATIONS

AB	*Analecta Bollandiana*
AHDLMA	*Archives d'histoire doctrinale et littéraire du Moyen Âge*
AHR	*American Historical Review*
CCSL	*Corpus Christianorum Series Latina*
CCCM	*Corpus Christianorum Continuatio Mediaevalis*
CSEL	*Corpus Scriptorum Ecclesiasticorum Latinorum*
CTD	Cicero, *Tusculan Disputations*. J.E. King, ed. & trans.
DMA	*Dictionary of the Middle Ages*. Joseph Strayer, ed.
EETS	Early English Text Society Publications
EHR	*English Historical Review*
ELLMA	Ernst Robert Curtius, *European Literature and the Latin Middle Ages*.
LexMA	*Lexikon des Mittelalters*
MGH	*Monumenta Germaniae Historica*
MGH, BdK	*Monumenta Germaniae Historica. Briefe der deutschen Kaiserzeit*
MGH, Poetae	*Monumenta Germaniae Historica. Poetae Latini medii aevi*
MGH, SS	*Monumenta Germaniae Historica. Scriptores* (in folio)
MGH, SSR	*Monumenta Germaniae Historica. Scriptores rerum Germanicarum in usum scholarum*
MIÖG	*Mitteilungen des Instituts für Österreichische Geschichtsforschung*
Mlat. Jb.	*Mittellateinisches Jahrbuch*
NCMH	*New Cambridge Medieval History*
NLH	*New Literary History*
PBB	*Beiträge zur Geschichte der deutschen Sprache und Literatur*
PL	*Patrologia Latina. Cursus Completus*
RE	*Pauly-Wissowa Realencyclopädie der classischen Altertumswissenschaft*
RMAL	*Revue du moyen âge Latin*
RTAM	*Recherches de théologie ancienne et médiévale*
ZfdA	*Zeitschrift für deutsches Altertum und deutsche Literatur*
ZfdPh	*Zeitschrift für deutsche Philologie*
ZRPh	*Zeitschrift für romanische Philologie*

✶✶✶

INTRODUCTION:
THE AGE OF MEDIEVAL HUMANISM

Listen now, spirit of humanity! We have written and spoken so much and so long about you; we have served you so much and in such great things; we have held you up to view for yourself, so that by seeing yourself you would know yourself, and knowing, would marvel at yourself. How could you fail to strike awe in yourself, if you see yourself as we have depicted you? Are you now waking up so that you may see yourself with open eyes? Or are you still sleeping, oblivious to all the storms that have long since swirled about you?... [The human body is the eternal habitation of God.] Because God will reside with you and through you, you will see God in your body, and it will be a participant in eternal things.... And your redeemer will reform you in and through your body "in the image and likeness" of its divinity, but also "will configure your humble body to its body of glory" [Phil. 3:21] so that you and all of humanity will be a microcosm.... But I am addressing you, human, constant in spirit and body, in one sense equal to angels by nature, in another sense superior to angels by Grace. In both ways you are in your own person united with God as no angel is; in both ways you are set above every creature, as no angel is. Not only in the masculine sex, but also — a source of greater wonder to the holy angels and the envy of reprobates— in the feminine sex.
— Godfrey of St. Victor, *Microcosmus*, "Address to the Human Spirit"

AN AGE WITHOUT A NAME

The culture of central and western Europe in the two centuries separating the Carolingian empire from the twelfth century has been studied in bits and pieces. One might assume from the current state of research that all thought and learning of secular clergy and court/secular communities was local, determined by individual teachers, writers, and poets working in isolation from each other; and that monastic Christianity was the locus of intellectual life.[1] An awkward state of affairs — and a challenge — for cultural history,

---

1. Marcia Colish, *Medieval Foundations of the Western Intellectual Tradition 400–1400* (New Haven, CT: Yale University Press, 1997), 160, finds continuity in the efforts to reform monastic life beginning with the founding of Cluny.

which tends to seek coherence among webs of ideas, forms of expression, modes of feeling and acting characteristic of a period. If the character of a given age does not somehow register in shared and debated ideas, forms, styles, and modes, intellectual history is bound to be flattened to a listing of activities, personalities, events, strings of details relevant to the mental life of a given period but without penetration, without interplay between the thought and expression of a period and its social and political life: a rehearsal of manuscript collections, book production, library holdings, genres, styles, schools, spiritual practices, works of philosophy, poetry and music — not a record of ideas and convictions and modes of behavior in dialectical engagement trying to come to terms with the contemporary world, but rather concerned mainly with the maintenance of received ideas.

Cultural history wants to see interconnectedness of forms in cultural expression. Ernst Gombrich, calling for a new cultural history beyond a reductive Hegelianism, affirms Hegel's larger claim that "any event and any creation of a period is connected by a thousand threads with the culture in which it is embedded."[2] Lacking a loom that would weave the threads of the years 950–1150 into a fabric, lacking a knowledge of its peculiar interconnectedness of cultural expression, historians have appealed to the two vital cultures embracing those two hundred years at either end: continuing Carolingian traditions in its past, and the "twelfth-century renaissance" in its future. Both sources of appeal invite the historian to understand the period in terms that apply to its past and future neighbors, not to the age as recognized in its own "essential character." That phrase may trouble acute historians with its seeming fuzzy Hegelianism, but they will be comforted by the present case, in which the current lack of a coherent overview results in cultural history by bits and pieces.

The extent to which that culture has evaded a comprehensive oversight, or even attempts at producing one, is evident in the fact that it has no name. Claudio Leonardi introduced his essay on

---

2. Ernst Gombrich, *In Search of Cultural History* (London: Oxford University Press, 1969), 30. A new cultural history was just around the corner with the emergence of Michel Foucault, the "new cultural history," cultural studies, and the New Historicism in literary studies.

INTRODUCTION ✶ THE AGE OF MEDIEVAL HUMANISM

"Intellectual Life 900–1024" in the *New Cambridge Medieval History* with just that observation:

> Period designations for 900–1024 tend to leave the tenth and early eleventh century without a name of its own except for one of the negative descriptions…'the iron age,' the "dark century." And the lack of a name suggests that it has no character of its own binding its constituent parts into a unity.[3]

The editor of this same volume of the *Cambridge Medieval History*, Timothy Reuter, can add "dark age" and "age of obscurity"[4] to the once conventional negative descriptions and extend Leonardi's misgiving to the overall conceptualizing of the period. As namelessness implies, so Reuter's line of thought, historians have not discovered "interpretative schemata" or developed "conceptual apparatus" that apply. Hence Leonardi's concern about an age without a name, and hence its intellectual history told in bits and pieces without overarching concepts that would support frameworks of analysis.

The treatment of the richer, more richly documented, and more varied intellectual life of 1028–1199 by David Luscombe[5] bears out the sense of a lack of overarching ideas or themes that could produce at least a partial synthesis for even this more vigorously studied period. The author has loosely organized his presentation chronologically by phases of education. Content is abundant and varied, the information is central and on target (the main events, trends, and personalities), but connecting ideas are absent. In terms of conceptualizing, his presentation is in the same quandary as Leonardi's, bits and pieces chronologically arranged. Both demonstrate the need for a non-reductive, cautious, and widely informed cultural history; or, if I may put it this way, an empirical cultural history, which identifies the actual dominant characteristics of the age and their interconnectedness.[6]

3. *The New Cambridge Medieval History* 3, *900–1024*, Timothy Reuter, ed. (Cambridge: Cambridge University Press, 1999), 186–211, at 186.
4. Reuter, NCMH 3:1.
5. "Thought and Learning," NCMH 4:461–98.
6. Gombrich, *In Search of Cultural History*, passim, expressed regret at the fading or discrediting of cultural history and called for a new and non-reductive form of it.

3

HUMANISM BY ACCLAMATION

My purpose in this collection of studies is to lift up "humanism" as the concept that most nearly binds the period 950–1150/1200 into something approaching a coherent whole. "Humanism" and "humanistic" have long since been applied to a swath of medieval European culture in that period — since the mid-tenth century a quickly widening swath. A scholarly consensus around the use of the term has developed over more than a century of investigation, but it is a casual and occasional consensus, attested by voices in isolation directed at diverse phenomena. The essays in this volume probe the moving forces and examine ideas developing in a shared substrate of learning, and ultimately, I hope, help define the character of the age. They deepen a sense that post-Carolingian, pre-scholastic Europe takes the coherence of its intellectual, philosophical, poetic, and musical life from impulses that can justifiably be called "humanistic." The cultural impulses operating from the tenth to the twelfth centuries continue, moving gradually into secular courts without abandoning altogether their original clerical/ecclesiastical context. This influence persists into the humanism of the Renaissance and beyond. If that map is accurate, then it argues for naming the period the "Age of Medieval Humanism."

The terms "humanism," "humanistic," "humanist," have been called on persistently to characterize aspects of pre-scholastic culture in the previous century and a half of scholarship on the Middle Ages. Hastings Rashdall (1895) gave an overview of classical studies in the twelfth century, touching on John of Salisbury and William of Conches and other "humanist philosophers," praising the high level of Latin, referring to poets and writers of the period under the influence of classical Roman literature as "humanists," while showing a brief uncertainty about the term: "humanists, if one may call them so" — a hesitation that did not prevent him from calling them so.[7] In that narrower usage, referring to the study of classical literature, others chime in: Max Manitius (1892), Ludwig Traube (1902), Eduard Norden (1909).[8] Martin Grabmann (1909) spoke of

7. Hastings Rashdall, *The Universities of Europe in the Middle Ages*, 3 vols. (Oxford: Oxford University Press, 1997), 1:66–70.

8. Max Manitius, *Geschichte der lateinischen Literatur des Mittelalters*, 1:253–55;

the *"humanistische Bestrebungen"* and *"humanistische Begeisterung"* of Hildebert of Lavardin, John of Salisbury, Peter of Blois, and others.[9] In those cases, the terms designate not an age but rather the devotion of single authors to the study of the classics in general. Ludwig Traube had ventured a period designation characterizing the tenth and eleventh centuries as an *"Aetas Horatiana"* following the Carolingian *"Aetas Virgiliana"* and preceding the *"Aetas Ovidiana."*[10] His immediate reference was verse forms favored in each period, but the terms are still sometimes cited to characterize the preoccupation with ancient literature in those three "ages."

Charles Homer Haskins' *Renaissance of the Twelfth Century* uses the terms liberally. He saw the rise of a "new humanism" in the eleventh century that, however, had exhausted its vitality by the end of the twelfth.[11] Likewise, Ernst Robert Curtius could refer to the "humanism of the twelfth century" as if it were an accepted designation for a movement. He cited the humanism of the "school of Chartres" and distinguished between the "Christian Humanism" of John of Salisbury and the "pagan humanism" of Bernard Silvester.[12] Curtius also acknowledged the broader meaning of humanism as an attitude and intellectual/spiritual orientation beyond Latin poetry. He set an obligatory school humanism over against "the real and bold

---

Ludwig Traube, *Einleitung in die lateinische Philologie des Mittelalters: Vorlesungen und Abhandlungen* 2, Paul Lehmann, ed. (Munich: Beck, 1911), 113; Eduard Norden, *Die Antike Kunstprosa vom VI. Jahrhundert vor Christus bis in die Zeit der Renaissance*, 2 vols. (Leipzig: Teubner, 1909), 2.2:680, 712–31.

9. Martin Grabmann, *Geschichte der scholastischen Methode*, 2 vols. (Graz: Akademischen Druck- und Verlagsanstalt, 1957), 2:59–64.

10. Those designations have stuck even in the broader sense of characterizing a period. For Traube they referred to metrics. Also following Traube: Ziolkowski, "Twelfth-Century Understandings and Adaptations of Ancient Friendship," in *Mediaeval Antiquity*, A. Welkenhuisen et al., ed. (Louvain: Louvain University Press, 1995), 59–81 for *aetas Ciceroniana*.

11. Charles Homer Haskins, *The Renaissance of the Twelfth Century* (New York: Meridian, 1975), 10 and chapter 4, "The Revival of the Latin Classics," 93–116, passim. On the later acceptance of the term, see below, 325–28.

12. Ernst Robert Curtius, *European Literature and the Latin Middle Ages* (Princeton, NJ: Princeton University Press, 1990), 77, 111–13.

humanism of liberal minds": "We long for a Humanism which is purged of all pedagogy (and politics!) and which rejoices in beauty,"[13] though he did not at the same time acknowledge the heightened ideal of human nature, the kindness and compassion conveyed in the medieval Latin *humanitas*.

Henry Osborne Taylor had early on (1892) understood the basis of a medieval literary humanism as an ideal of humanity:

> As century after century men grew in humanity, there came a deeper literary understanding of the classics, forming a transition to the poetic and literary reverence in which they were to be held by Boccaccio and Petrarch.[14]

Wolfram von den Steinen, Swiss historian of exceptionally broad grasp, was touched by the thinking of the circle around Stephan George. His portraits of great personalities and his search for broader chains of connections in the *"Geistesgeschichte"* of the Middle Ages are indicative of that influence. In a brief essay he depicted the "Loire Valley" poets as representatives of a "humanism around the year 1100,"[15] again referring to Marbod of Rennes, Baudri of Bourgueil, and Hildebert of Lavardin. Their poetry represented a "more refined sense of humanity" in stark contrast to the troubled political and militaristic world in which they lived and wrote. He noted in their poetry signs of a more courtly, more humane/humanistic worldly culture penetrating this world of iron sensibilities. In this early humanism he saw a partial emancipation of culture from the Church. Von den Steinen ended his essay with the thought that the Loire poets are representatives of a culture borne by poetry, arguing that the twelfth century is an age in which thought and representation of humanity and nature are based more on literature than speculative thought, an age of poetry, not early Scholasticism (*"Poetisierung"* rather than *"Frühscholastik"*).

A heightened ideal of humanity among medieval writers and poets is prominent in David Knowles' assessment of "The Humanism of

13. ELLMA, 250–51.

14. Henry Osborn Taylor, *The Classical Heritage of the Middle Ages* (New York: Columbia University Press, 1901), 48.

15. Wolfram von den Steinen, "Humanismus um 1100," *Archiv für Kulturgeschichte* 46 (1964): 196–214.

the Twelfth Century." Like von den Steinen, Knowles also saw the essence of early humanism in a certain softened, civilized, humanized spiritual/intellectual attitude (von den Steinen's *"Geisteshaltung"*) that sets it off decidedly from the intellectual world of the thirteenth century. Knowles found in the period 1050–1150 "a wide and sympathetic humanism, which anticipated to an extraordinary degree that of the age of the Medici and of Erasmus." He contrasted early humanism with the turn to scholastic philosophy and scholastic modes of thought:"

> The culture of the thirteenth century, for all its intense speculative force and abiding power [was] less universal, less appealing and, in a word, less humane than what had gone before. [That later age] lacked much of the kindly warmth and fragrant geniality of the past.... In all the qualities of self-revealing intimacy in all the arts of language, in all manifestations of aesthetic feeling or personal emotions, the great men of the thirteenth century are immeasurably poorer than those of eleventh and twelfth.... The culture of the schools of the thirteenth century was...without many of the elements that make a society fully humane.[16]

The admiration and imitation of "great men" is the chief characteristic Knowles cited in illuminating this human sensibility. It is the feature that sets the eleventh and twelfth centuries clearly apart from the following age. Abelard, Heloise, and Aelred of Rievaulx are for him the figures best representative of this quality of twelfth-century humanism. The essays that follow in this volume open to view much that resonates with the humanism Knowles observed, based on humane sensibility and individual greatness, ideals cultivated in social intercourse and study of the classics at schools and courts and expressed in a wide variety of Latin writings.

Jean Leclercq has shown that the sweep of the term "humanism" reaches well into medieval monasticism. His classic study, *The Love of Learning and the Desire for God*, ends a long chapter on "Liberal Studies" with the comment,"

---

16. David Knowles, "The Humanism of the Twelfth Century," in his *The Historian and Character and Other Essays* (Cambridge: Cambridge University Press, 1963), 16–31, at 17.

This culture...remains profoundly impregnated by literature. It is more literary than speculative. This characteristic differentiates monastic humanism from...scholastic humanism.[17]

R.W. Southern also acknowledged a "literary humanism" of the eleventh and twelfth centuries, though he introduced a concept of "scholastic humanism" that he took to be the more powerful human ideal, encompassing the great systematizing works of the thirteenth-century scholastics.[18] Southern's scheme of three major fundamental ideas constituting thirteenth-century "scholastic" humanism is illuminating for the history of humanistic thought but does not have what humanism between 950 and 1150 has: a movement with shared concepts and ideals at work socially and politically, supported by institutions, passed along, their influence filtering widely outside of academic culture and developed over the life course of the movement. Humanistic philosophical/theological ideas may make a humanist, but not a humanist movement or a humanist age. The term's historical validity is not established only by analyzing humanistic concepts, like "human dignity," human free will, the intelligibility of nature, the divinity and universality of humanity.[19] Important though such large ideas are, they are trans-historical. They set their medieval formulaters more firmly in relation with Plato, Aristotle, Boethius, Macrobius, and John Scot Eriugena than with their contemporary world. Southern's conceptualizing of medieval humanism moves away from a humanism rooted in educational, social, and political trends. Humanism of the period 950–1150 is more than an academic discourse.

An important voice was that of Peter von Moos in his 1965 study of Hildebert of Lavardin, with the subtitle: "Humanitas at the threshold of the age of courtliness."[20] Von Moos was a student

17. Jean Leclercq, *The Love of Learning and the Desire for God: A Study of Monastic Culture*, Catherine Misrahi, trans. (New York: Fordham University Press, 1961), 142.

18. Southern, "Medieval Humanism," in *Medieval Humanism and Other Studies* (Oxford: Oxford University Press, 1970), 29–60. Argued further in his *Scholastic Humanism and the Unification of Europe*, 2 vols. (Oxford: Blackwell, 1995).

19. These are the focus of both Southern's and Otten's works just cited.

20. Peter von Moos, *Hildebert von Lavardin 1056–1133: Humanitas an der Schwelle des höfischen Zeitalters* (Stuttgart: Hiersemann, 1965).

INTRODUCTION ✶ THE AGE OF MEDIEVAL HUMANISM

of Wolfram von den Steinen. His study of Hildebert showed the peculiar but powerful hybridity of a Christian and humanist cleric and bishop that was a *"Geisteshaltung"* of clergy educated at cathedral schools from the tenth to the twelfth century. Von Moos succeeded in showing the classicism and humanism of this poet-bishop, and most fruitfully he constructed in Hildebert the type of the learned cleric. This figure was the main bearer of the culture the roots of which we uncover in studying early humanism. The humanism of the age was centered in Hildebert and many others in this milieu, men and women steeped in classical traditions of poetry and prose and in Stoic and Ciceronian philosophy. Others were attracted to this intellectual/social ambience: monks, nuns, women on the margins of secular and religious communities, even whole religious communities, male and female. The learned cleric came in many forms. But it was a particular career path that was responsible for the growth of humanism as a movement, the path that led from cathedral school to positions in cathedral or monastic communities. Many became abbots or bishops, as did the major "Loire poets," Marbod, Hildebert, and Baudri.

Von Moos also probed the connection between the moral thought, the humane discretion, kindness, moderation, and restraint expressed in Hildebert's writings and sensed its connection to the moral formation of clerics actively cultivated at cathedral schools. The discipline of *mores/moralitas* would in the generation following Hildebert inform the ideal of courtly manners and ultimately chivalric knighthood. Von Moos anticipated this development by associating Hildebert with the dawning *"höfisches Zeitalter"* in which Hildebert lived.

The final word in this chorus of attesters goes to Etienne Gilson, who swept many aspects of the twelfth century into the orbit of humanism in claiming, "All those who know it admit that the twelfth century was, in its own way, an age of humanism."[21]

My purpose in this part of the introduction is not to give a review of research but rather to show the accumulated authority

---

21. Etienne Gilson, *The Mystical Theology of St. Bernard* (Kalamazoo, MI: Cistercian Publications, 1990), 7–8. His main statement: "L'humanisme médiévale et renaissance," in his *Les idées et les lettres* (Paris: Vrin, 1986), 171–96.

of the term "humanism." The chorus of voices is large,[22] but each refers to a narrow slice of the culture. The term is operative clearly in medievalist scholarship, but it operates outside of the sanction of a historical framework and an "interpretative scheme" that would make intelligible and plausible what connects Brun of Cologne and William of Conches, Gerbert of Aurillac and Thierry of Chartres, Meinhard of Bamberg, and John of Salisbury, or Hildebert of Lavardin and Peter of Blois. More is required to establish a period designation than individual studies of these figures. It is worthwhile recalling Jacob Burckhardt on "Renaissance":

> Every cultural epoch which presents itself as a complete and articulate whole expresses itself not only in the life of the state, in religion, art and science, but also imparts its individual character to social life as such.[23]

To be valuable as a period designation, terms like "humanism," "enlightenment," "romanticism," and phrases like "the character of an epoch" must penetrate and influence many facets of a culture.

THE CONTRIBUTION (UNFINISHED) OF CARL ERDMANN

The voice that might have produced a historically unifying vision of medieval humanism was that of Carl Erdmann. Alone among

22. Others deserving mention: Johan Huizinga, "John of Salisbury: A Pre-Gothic Mind," in *Men and Ideas: History, the Middle Ages, and the Renaissance*, James S. Holmes and Hans Van Marle, trans. (Princeton, NJ: Princeton University Press, 1959), 159–77, at 162: "A whole series of personalities of that century [along with John of Salisbury] — poets such as Hildebert of Lavardin and Marbod of Rennes, and not least of all Abelard — manifested a number of traits which strike us as early humanism." See also Liupold Wallach, "Onulf of Speyer: A Humanist of the Eleventh Century," *Medievalia et Humanistica* 6 (1950): 35–56; John R. Williams, "Godfrey of Rheims, a Humanist of the Eleventh Century," *Speculum* 22 (1947): 29–45; Hans Liebeschütz, *Medieval Humanism in the Life and Writings of John of Salisbury* (London: Warburg Institute, 1950); Willemien Otten, *From Paradise to Paradigm: A Study of Twelfth-Century Humanism* (Leiden: Brill, 2004); and Otten, "Medieval Latin Humanism," *Encyclopedia of Mediterranean Humanism*, Houari Touati, ed. Online at: http://www.encyclopédie-humanisme.com/Medieval-Latin-Humanism.

23. Quoted in Gombrich, 21.

INTRODUCTION ✹ THE AGE OF MEDIEVAL HUMANISM

medievalist historians, Erdmann did envision the humanism of the period as a coherent movement, unified by institutions, by a system of education, and by the ideas and cultural practices that evolved and spread from them. He saw "humanism" as the mode of thought, behavior, and action that characterizes a coherent movement that moved through Europe and flourished for two centuries. Unfortunately he died before he could articulate that vision.

Erdmann is well known to medievalists. A recent biography by Folker Reichert[24] has turned up his plans for a broad-ranging history of the intellectual and spiritual life of Europe from Saxon Germany to the "twelfth-century renaissance."[25] It was inspired by Erdmann's discovery of a sheaf of letters of Meinhard of Bamberg (d.1088) eventually published in volume 5 of the MGH series *Briefe der deutschen Kaiserzeit*. Erdmann regularly refers to Meinhard as a "humanist" and to his "humanism." He saw the centrality of Meinhard's letters within a broader history of ideas showing the roots of high medieval culture in the Ottonian/Salian period. His study would trace a path of this set of ideas and attitudes that leads into France and England, where they blossomed as twelfth-century humanism, a major component of "the renaissance of the twelfth century." It would have supplied the connections that established a humanist "movement."

The work that Erdmann planned was ambitious: an extensive history of medieval education and intellectual life, where tenth- and eleventh-century Germany, specifically the "imperial church," provided basic sources.[26] He foresaw that it would take fifteen to twenty years of work and fill several volumes. But he did not have that much time left. He died in Zagreb in 1945 on the way home from his post as translator in Albania. Fortunately, the grand lines of his study were preserved by his conversations and correspondence with Ernst Robert Curtius. Their letters are lost, but Curtius sketched Erdmann's plan in his *European Literature and the Latin Middle Ages*:

24. Folker Reichert, *Fackel in der Finsternis: Der Historiker Carl Erdmann und das "Dritte Reich,"* 2 vols. (Darmstadt: WBG Academic, 2022).
25. See below, 12.
26. Reichert, 302. For the details, see below, 11–12, 133–40.

Carl Erdmann planned a history of Franco-German culture in the eleventh century, during which French cultural primacy arose in a highly original development [while Saxon Germany lost its preeminence], and twelfth-century humanism was prepared to a far greater extent than has been recognized in previous studies. He did not live to carry out this plan.[27]

Curtius saw in Erdmann's vision a path to a "history of western culture from Charlemagne to Dante," a period that has "not yet been comprehended and presented as a coherent whole." Erdmann's biographer, Folker Reichert, predicts the probable impact of Erdmann's planned work: "Had he actually accomplished this project [it would have become] a fundamental element of the cultural history of the high Middle Ages."[28] Erdmann's vision promised what the intellectual history of the period lacks: a coherent overview.

CATHEDRAL SCHOOLS

Medieval humanism inheres significantly in social ideals in the pedagogy of the early cathedral schools beginning around 950.[29] Without a clear understanding of the character and purpose of the "imperial" cathedral schools, their spread and influence throughout Europe, the intellectual accomplishments of the age will remain in bits and pieces. The conception of the two centuries as an age of humanism depends in large part on the intellectual and social values of which cathedral schools are the matrix.

The learning of the cathedral schools introduced in the mid-tenth century[30] by Brun of Cologne in collaboration with his brother Otto I has a characteristic designation, "letters and manners" (*litterae et mores*). The term recurs frequently in a number of variants: *ingenium et mores, sapientia et mores, mores et doctrina, morum honestas et litterarum eruditio*, and others. In name and character it is based on classical, especially Ciceronian models. The formula *doctrina et mores* is also more or less interchangeable with the others just noted

27. ELLMA, 388 and n. 22.
28. Reichert, 302.
29. See below, 22–39.
30. On the role of Otto I and Brun of Cologne in designing and instituting a new kind of cathedral school, see below, 25–27, 83–88.

INTRODUCTION ✱ THE AGE OF MEDIEVAL HUMANISM

and has Christian coloring. Its absence in classical sources and its early occurrences in patristic writings mark its Christian origins. *Litterae et mores* trails classical roots. Its appearances are rare from antiquity to the late tenth century. The role of the curriculum these terms designate in the transformation of European social ideals is considerable. The term "letters and manners" is extremely rare prior to 950[31] but common by the end of the tenth century.

The subject of "letters" is better studied and understood than the discipline of "manners," also called *cultus virtutum*, though the penetration of the latter into the fabric of social life is greater and longer lasting. The fusing of the study of literature with the cultivation of ethics is a central characteristic of medieval humanism. I will refer to the curriculum of "letters and manners" and its variants as "paideic," risking anachronism rather than face the opprobrium of "pedagogy," as in its use by Curtius.[32] The provenance of the term is evident in its closeness to the Ciceronian formula, "eloquence and wisdom." In the Middle Ages as in antiquity, this double education aimed at fashioning an orator/administrator, an educated cleric capable of diplomatic missions, of representing and assisting the bishop in the "business of the church" (*rerum agendarum pericia*).

A moral education that cultivates virtue also has classical roots. However, medieval humanism is distinct from ancient in one important aspect: the glorification of humanity. The idea of divinity in humanity touches closely on the moral training of the schools, on the conception of learning, and on the ultimate goal of studies. Through learning humans can become gods or god-like. As Aldo Scaglione and Claudia Wittig have indicated, the idea is present in letters and poems, educational tracts and philosophy, German and French, since the early eleventh century to the end of the Middle Ages and beyond. It developed from modest beginnings in the language of education since the tenth century. It had its fullest expression in Victorine texts and in the *Anticlaudianus* of Alan of Lille. It was nourished by

---

31. As the title indicates, Alcuin's dialogue of instruction, *De rhetorica et virtutibus*, shares the logic of "letters and manners," but it is a work of instruction for Charlemagne, centred on "civil matters." The term does not occur in the abundant Carolingian writings on education. For more details and discussion, see below, 88–92.

32. See above, 6.

Hermetic thought and by Genesis 1:26–27, humanity made in the "image and likeness" of God. Toward the end of his allegorical epic *Microcosmus* (written in the 1180s) Godfrey of St. Victor includes an "Address to the Spirit of Humanity."[33] In it he explains his reason for composing a long, elaborate allegory dedicated to the human being as a microcosm. His purpose is to astonish humanity by revealing to them their own essential nature, their inborn divinity. The human is a microcosm, a small universe: the awareness of their identity with the universe will inevitably leave them wonder-struck, and wonder will lead to self-knowledge. In this way self-knowledge repairs the fallen state of humanity. For Hugh of St. Victor and others, learning and study are the way to self-knowledge.[34]

Much thought and expression in the period is driven by this tendency to exalt, even sanctify, humanity and the human and to envelope them in an aggrandizing conception, by which, merging with Christian values, virtually no area of the culture remains untouched, whether it generates assent or dissent.[35] It is a pedagogic/paideic value. Learning is development toward realization of the divinity implanted in each person, present in all types and stages of humanity, man and woman, body and spirit. The search for God is also self-seeking. Knowledge of God is specular — see God/see your inner God.[36] The image of God as an architect arranging the cosmos with the human tools of a draftsman on the cover of this book reiterates the vision of God suffused with humanity, or the human functioning as God, that was bred into the thought and expression of the humanist strain of culture. It is a vision of creation not, or not

---

33. *Apostrophus ad Spiritum Humanum*, quoted in part at the beginning of this introduction and discussed below in chapter 11, 399–402.

34. See the introduction by Marshall Crossnoe to *A Companion to the Abbey of Saint Victor, Paris*, Juliette Mousseau and Hugh Feiss, ed. (Leiden: Brill, 2018), 3–51.

35. See below, chapter 6.

36. The "image and likeness" doctrine stands in Victorine humanism in the position it would occupy in the Italian Renaissance: the defining element of human dignity. See Charles Trinkaus, *"In Our Image and Likeness": Humanity and Divinity in Italian Humanist Thought* (Notre Dame, IN: Notre Dame University Press, 1995).

INTRODUCTION ✶ THE AGE OF MEDIEVAL HUMANISM

only, by a miraculous speech act but by the entirely human act of setting out an edifice in "measure, number, and weight."[37]

The social context of humanist learning is social intercourse (*convictus*) of teacher and students. It aims at the development of modes of behavior both practical in civic life and personal in self-perfecting — in its highest formulation the realization of inborn divinity. This moral formation is the core towards which other aspects and characteristics of medieval humanism tend: educational, psychological, social, political.

CULTURAL AND INTELLECTUAL HISTORY: BEYOND ATOMIZATION

Recent studies have confirmed Erdmann's basic idea, that cathedral-school culture generates a humanistic movement in its earliest formation and that Meinhard of Bamberg's humanism is an early representative of a much larger movement in Germany and France, eventually also England. Sita Steckel's *Kulturen des Lehrens*, a work as scrupulous as it is voluminous, is now the standard study of education from Carolingian times to the mid-twelfth century.[38] The dissertation by Mia Münster-Swendsen[39] follows the general lines of Erdmann's view of a humanism forming a coherent element of culture in the period, as does Jaeger's *The Envy of Angels*.[40] Münster-Swendsen's work has the advantage of including conditions in

---

37. The image dates mid-thirteenth century, after the cultural turn to Scholasticism but still reiterates a long-held human idea. The translation into a visual aesthetic after fading in verbal expression is addressed in chapter 7, below. Renaissance humanism also cultivated the idea and image of the deification of the human. On the idea of God the architect, see Friedrich Ohly, "*Deus Geometra*: Skizzen zur Geschichte einer Vorstellung von Gott," in *Tradition als historische Kraft: Interdisziplinäre Forschungen zur Geschichte des früheren Mittelalters*, Manifred Balzer, et al., ed. (Berlin: De Gruyter, 1982), 1–42.

38. *Kulturen des Lehrens im Früh- und Hochmittelalter: Autorität, Wissenskonzepte und Netzwerke von Gelehrten* (Cologne: Böhlau, 2011).

39. Mia Münster-Swendsen, "Masters and Paragons: Learning, Power and the Formation of a European Academic Culture, c.900–1230" (Ph.D. diss., University of Copenhagen, 2004).

40. Jaeger, *Envy*.

Europe broadly. On the basis of these studies, it is possible to confirm the validity of Erdmann's projected work: the years 950 to 1100 were distinctly marked by a humanist movement out of which the humanist culture of the twelfth century developed.

A work that closely parallels and extends Erdmann's vision is Aldo Scaglione's *Knights at Court: Courtliness, Chivalry and Courtesy from Ottonian Germany to the Italian Renaissance*.[41] Though Scaglione's main interest is courtliness and chivalry, the length of his reach back to Ottonian Germany and forward to Renaissance Italy is an important confirmation of the influence of the learned Latin culture of clerics, both in ecclesiastical and secular courts, on the ethics of court life. The learned cleric straddling church and court, Latin and vernacular is the bearer of a culture that radiates in many directions throughout Europe but keeps many features of its classical, humanistic origins, whatever cultural setting that figure inhabits. Scaglione's sources range widely, including the Latin culture of curiales, vernacular literature, lyric and epic of France and Germany with special attention to Italian sources.

With narrower time-span but sharp focus and massive documentation, Martin Aurell can further confirm the twelfth and thirteenth century tradition of a program of manners, *mores*, *moralitas*, ancient in origin but with strong Christian coloring, passing from clerics to secular nobles, helping shape courtliness and chivalry.[42] If Scaglione's broad vision of humanism's development into courtliness and courtesy is right, if the courtly cleric in the stamp of Meinhard and John of Salisbury gradually metamorphosed into the courtier of Castiglione, then the humanist movement that began in the tenth century has powerfully influenced the social mores of the western world.

It is curious that no German historian has pursued Erdmann's line of study. Sita Steckel is the exception. Her work has been well reviewed but has to my knowledge not provoked further study or

41. Berkeley: University of California Press, 1991.

42. *Le chevalier lettré: Savoir et conduite de l'aristocracie aux XII et XIIIe siècles* (Paris: Fayard, 2011); English trans.: *The Lettered Knight: Knowledge and Aristocratic Behaviour in the Twelfth and Thirteenth Centuries*, Jean-Charles Khalifa and Jeremy Price, trans. (Budapest: Central European Press, 2017).

INTRODUCTION ★ THE AGE OF MEDIEVAL HUMANISM

revision of earlier ideas, long overdue. Of course, all the works just mentioned were written without the guidance of Erdmann's vision. The absence of interest in Germany is still curious. The brief but striking reference in Curtius might have been a facilitator but was not. The post-war period was perhaps not the optimal moment for any German to argue a leading position of Germany in the development of European cultural history. Nor is the intellectual climate of the late twentieth and twenty-first century (post-human, post-colonial, identity history, material history, etc.) favorable to a project in history of ideas and social forms arguing the coherent development of western culture "from Charlemagne to Dante." Nor are German historians since the second half of the twentieth century given to wide-ranging studies of intellectual history, as Gombrich pointed out. Perhaps Reichert's publication of Erdmann's uncompleted plans will help override whatever antipathies and hesitations hinder a broader view of the period. Lacking some breakthrough or shift in perspective, the cultural history of northern Europe from the tenth to the twelfth century will continue to be "dark," misunderstood, reduced, and atomized. If Erdmann had lived and carried out that work, it would almost certainly have borne out and extended backward in time the bold statement by Etienne Gilson declaring the twelfth century "an age of humanism."

1. CATHEDRAL SCHOOLS AND HUMANIST LEARNING, 950–1150

INTRODUCTION

The humanist strain in twelfth-century culture represented by figures like Bernard Silvester, John of Salisbury, and Alan of Lille has its roots in the late tenth and eleventh centuries. Charles Homer Haskins knew very well that the more embracing renewal he called the "renaissance of the twelfth century" grew out of developments in the preceding age, and he called the eleventh century "that obscure period of origins which holds the secret of the new movement."[1] The factor that especially favors that obscurity and guards that secret is the apparent poverty of intellectual and artistic achievement in the centers of worldly learning, the cathedral schools. The privilege that modern historians of culture give to such sources is a hindrance to understanding the vitality of the eleventh century. It directs us where there is no path and blocks the way that is open to us.[2] If we privileged intellectual and artistic achievement in judging fourteenth- and fifteenth-century Italy, then we could scrap three-quarters of Burckhardt's *Civilization of the Renaissance in Italy*, put aside his idea that the state and statesmanship can themselves be regarded as works of art, and throw out his entire notion that political conditions, court life, and the development of ideals of the individual preceded the revival of learning, art and literature, and created the necessary presuppositions of that renewal.

If we compare the visible achievements of the century-and-a-half between 950 and 1100 with its intellectual and cultural energy, the discrepancy is evident. Here are some indications that much was stirring in the period: it produced a number of eminent men praised by contemporaries for their learning and teaching: Brun of Cologne, Gerbert of Aurillac, Fulbert of Chartres, Meinhard of Bamberg, Bernard of Chartres. Yet none of them wrote any works of note, apart from their letters.

1. Haskins, 16.
2. R.W. Southern in "The Place of England in the Twelfth Century Renaissance," *History* 45 (1960): 201–16, made a fundamental point on the use of sources: that it is necessary to look behind and beyond the most prominent documents to define that place. For Europe in the late tenth and eleventh centuries, it is necessary to look behind and beyond the lack of them.

The manuscript tradition of Plato's *Timaeus* increases dramatically in the eleventh century.[3] For the period 850–900 one manuscript survives, for 900–950 two, for 950–1000 four. Then suddenly the first half of the eleventh century produces fifteen manuscripts, most of them from Germany, the second half fourteen, also largely from Germany. The preoccupation with Plato's work in that country was so intense that by the end of the century it provoked a polemic from Manegold of Lautenbach.[4] He attacks opinions and interpretations of German *philosophi*, some of which turn up a few decades later in works of Peter Abelard.[5] The thrust of the teaching that Manegold opposes is that the *Timaeus* is reconcilable with Christian doctrine. This is of course a favorite idea of the "School of Chartres." It provides the basis of Thierry of Chartres' *Hexameron* commentary.[6] And the more general problem of reconciling the ancient philosophers with Christian doctrine is the basic focus of Abelard's *Theologia Christiana*. In other words, some of the central problems that were to occupy the leading schools, or at least the leading representatives of secular philosophy in twelfth-century France, were intensely debated in

3. R.W. Southern, *Platonism, Scholastic Method, and the School of Chartres: The Stenton Lecture 1978* (Reading: Reading University Press, 1979), 14. For the list of manuscripts, see *Timaeus a Calcidio translatus commentarioque instructus*, J.H. Waszink, ed. (London: Warburg, 1975), cvi–cxxxi; Margaret Gibson,"The Study of the 'Timaeus' in the Eleventh and Twelfth Centuries," *Pensamiento* 25 (1969): 183–94. Anna Somfai corrects the view that the serious transmission of *Timaeus* and commentary began in the twelfth century. The number of manuscripts does not vary significantly from Southern's figures. Somfai does not identify national provenance. See Somfai,"The Eleventh-Century Shift in the Reception of Plato's 'Timaeus' and Calcidius's 'Commentary,'" *Journal of the Warburg and Courtauld Institutes* 65 (2002): 1–21.

4. Manegold von Lautenbach, *Liber contra Wolfelmum*, Wilfried Hartmann, ed., MGH, *Quellen zur Geistesgeschichte des Mittelalters* 8 (Weimar: Böhlau, 1972).

5. This is one of the important findings in Wilfried Hartmann,"Manegold von Lautenbach und die Anfänge der Frühscholastik," *Deutsches Archiv für Erforschung des Mittelalters* 26 (1970): 47–149, at 77.

6. Nikolaus M. Häring,"The Creation and the Creator of the World according to Thierry of Chartres and Clarenbaldus of Arras," AHDLMA 22 (1955): 137–216. The text of Thierry's tract is also published in Häring's edition, *Commentaries on Boethius by Thierry of Chartres and his School* (Toronto: Pontifical Institute, 1971), 553–75. See the comments of Southern, *Platonism, Scholastic Method*, 25–40.

CHAPTER I ★ CATHEDRAL SCHOOLS

eleventh-century Germany. The work that was to play such a major role in the philosophical commentary and poetry of France, Plato's *Timaeus*, first came to prominence in the eleventh century.[7] We know of a Manegold, a German teaching in Paris around 1080, who was the teacher of William of Champeaux and Anselm of Laon and is called *modernorum magister magistrorum*. This probably was that same Manegold of Lautenbach, himself a teacher of worldly philosophy and of the Platonic cosmology before he became an adversary.[8] Apart from the striking testimony of Manegold's polemic against Wolfhelm of Brauweiler, the writings against worldly learning by conservative monks like Peter Damian and Otloh of St. Emmeram show us a very lively academic scene, both in Italy and Germany.[9] Writings or not, there was plenty of activity. The secular courts of Germany in the eleventh century also show us a lively scene, one that deserves to be called at least "prerenaissance."[10]

7. Though it was studied intensely in commentaries on Boethius, Martianus Capella, and Macrobius from Cologne under Brun and beyond in the tenth century. This is the important find of Henry Mayr-Harting, *Church and Cosmos in Early Ottonian Germany: The View from Cologne* (Oxford: Oxford University Press, 2007).

8. For a thorough discussion and perhaps overly cautious weighing of the evidence for and against this identification, see Hartmann, "Manegold," 49–50.

9. On Otloh's opposition to worldly learning, see Helga Schauwecker, "Otloh von St. Emmeram: Ein Beitrag zur Bildungs- und Frömmigkeitsgeschichte des 11. Jahrhunderts" (Ph.D. diss., University of Würzburg 1962), 165–66. On Peter Damian, Joseph A. Endres, *Petrus Damiani und die weltliche Wissenschaft* (Münster: Aschendorff, 1910); André Cantin, *Les sciences séculières et la foi: Les deux voies de la science au jugement de S. Pierre Damien (1007–1072)* (Spoleto: Centro Italiano di studi sull'alto medioevo, 1975). On this opposition in general, Grabmann, *Geschichte*, 215–16; Pierre Riché, *Écoles et enseignement dans l'occident chrétien de la fin du Ve siècle au milieu du XIe siècle* (Paris: Aubier Montaigne, 1979), 335–44.

10. On classical revival in the eleventh century, see Percy Ernst Schramm, *Kaiser, Rom und Renovatio: Studien zur Geschichte des römischen Erneuerungsgedankens vom Ende des karolingischen Reiches bis zum Investiturstreit*, 2nd ed. (Darmstadt: Wissenschaftliche Buchgesellschaft, 1984); Reto R. Bezzola, *Les origines et la formation de l littérature courtoise en occident (500–1200)* I. *La tradition impériale de la fin de l'antiquité au XIe siècle* (Paris: Champion, 1944), 239–82; C. Stephen Jaeger, *The Origins of Courtliness: Civilizing Trends and the Formation of Courtly Ideals, 939–1210* (Philadelphia: University of Pennsylvania Press, 1985), 113–14.

These are preliminary signs of renewal, symptoms of the coming outburst of brilliant cultural achievements in twelfth-century France. The larger web of relationships in which the connections become evident has been hard to identify, partly because the rumblings occurred in Germany and the eruption they preceded occurred in France. The traditions of modern historical writing did not favor interpretations deriving the latter from the former. Drawing the lines of development in detail is not the object of this study. It aims at establishing the following points: 1) the humanism of the twelfth century has its roots in that of the eleventh; 2) there is a unity and continuity of secular learning in Germany and France in the period, which is disturbed and gradually supplanted by early Scholasticism; 3) the needs of administration at secular and ecclesiastical courts determine a humanistic curriculum, oriented strongly to *ethica*. It has its institutional accommodation at cathedral schools. This symbiosis begins to break up in the second half of the eleventh century in Germany and in the middle decades of the twelfth in France. At this point humanist learning gradually passes into the realm of the secular courts and emerges as courtly education.

CATHEDRAL SCHOOLS

The development of cathedral schools is our point of departure.[11] Episcopal schools existed since late antiquity, though they rose and fell in prominence with the coming and going of single masters. They stood in the shadow of monastic schools in Carolingian times, and indeed in the earlier period the nature of education there is hardly distinguishable from monastic education.[12] As institutions distinct from monastic schools, they appear not to have found a sustaining goal until the mid-tenth century. At that point they begin to flourish. We hear praise of

11. Gérard Paré, P. Tremblay, and A. Brunet were quite right in making this the focal point of their *La renaissance du XIIe siècle: Les écoles et l'enseignement* (Paris: Vrin, 1933). But their focus was so tightly on France and the seven liberal arts that many of the essential features of education at cathedral schools are not touched.

12. See Josef Fleckenstein, *Die Bildungsreform Karls des Grossen als Verwirklichung der norma rectitudinis* (Bigge-Ruhr: Josefs-Druckerei, 1953), 23; Rosamond McKitterick, *The Frankish Kingdom under the Carolingians, 751–987* (London: Longman, 1983), 147–48. Steckel, *Kulturen des Lehrens*, is now the standard study of Carolingian education. She confirms the near-identity of monastic and cathedral school education in the Carolingian period.

CHAPTER I ✷ CATHEDRAL SCHOOLS

the Magdeburg school in mid-century, of the great crowds of students there, of the intense interest in secular studies aroused by the "second Cicero," Master Ohtricus, a teacher of such distinction and learning that he was later to debate with Gerbert of Aurillac in Ravenna before Otto II and his court.[13] By 952, Würzburg is flourishing under an Italian master, Stefan of Novara, called to the north by Otto the Great and Bishop Poppo of Würzburg.[14] By 953, the Cologne school comes into prominence under the episcopacy of Otto's brother, Brun of Cologne, a great educator and public servant, called by his biographer a reviver of the seven liberal arts.[15] This school would produce some of the most illustrious intellectuals, statesmen, educators, and bishops of the next generation. By 954, we hear Hildesheim praised as a center of learning;[16]

13. On Magdeburg and Ohtricus, see *Vita S. Adalberti* 3, l.29–37, MGH, SS 4:582; *Brunonis vita Adalberti* 5, ll. 14–15, MGH, SS 4:597; *Annales Magdeburgenses* a. 982, ll. 40–41, MGH, SS 16:155. On Ohtricus and Gerbert, *Richeri Historiae* 3.55-65, MGH, SS 38 (Hannover: Hahn, 2000), 198-204. For some discussion of the debate, see Margaret T. Gibson, "The *artes* in the Eleventh Century," in *Arts libéraux et philosophie au moyen âge: Actes du quatrième congrès international de philosophie médiévale* (Montreal: Institut d'études médiévales, 1969), 121–26. On the Magdeburg school under Ohtricus, Franz A. Specht, *Geschichte des Unterrichtswesens in Deutschland von den ältesten Zeiten bis zur Mitte des dreizehnten Jahrhunderts* (Stuttgart: Cotta, 1885), 350–53. See also Jaeger, "Gerbert von Aurillac versus Ohtric von Magdeburg: Spielregeln einer akademischen Disputation im 10. Jahrhundert," *Spielregeln der Mächtigen: Mittelalterliche Politik zwischen Gewohnheit und Konvention (Festschrift Gerd Althoff),* Claudia Garnier und Hermann Kamp, ed. (Darmstadt: Wissenschaftliche Buchgesellschaft, 2010), 95–120.

14. See Otloh of St. Emmeram, *Vita Wolfkangi* 4–5, MGH, SS 4:528. On Stefan, see L.F. Benedetto, "Stephanus grammaticus da Novara," *Studi Medievali* 3 (1908–11): 499–508; Josef Fleckenstein, "Königshof und Bischofsschule unter Otto dem Grossen," *Archiv für Kulturgeschichte* 38 (1956): 53–54.

15. See Fleckenstein, "Königshof"; Otto Zimmermann, "Brun I.: Erzbischof von Cöln und die in den Schulen seiner Zeit gepflegte Wissenschaft" (Ph.D. diss., University of Leipzig, 1871).

16. On Hildesheim, see Specht, 343–50; G. von Detten, *Über die Dom- und Kloster schulen des Mittelalters, insbesondere uber die Schulen von Hildesheim, Paderborn, Münster und Corvey* (Paderborn: Junsermann, 1893). On the importance of Hildesheim for supplying the staff of Otto the Great, see Hans-Walter Klewitz, "Königtum, Hofkapelle und Domkapitel im 10. und 11. Jahrhundert," *Archiv*

by 956, Trier.[17] In the last quarter of the century, under the guidance of the next generation of scholars — many of them students of Brun — Worms, Liège, Mainz, Speyer, Bamberg, and Regensburg[18] come to life; in France Rheims under Gerbert;[19] and some decades later Chartres under Gerbert's pupil, Bishop Fulbert (1006–28).[20] These schools are regularly referred to as "a second Athens," the better loved teachers as

---

für Urkundenforschung 16 (1938): 102-56, at 108–22; Herbert Zielinski, *Der Reichsepiskopat in spät-ottonischer und salischer Zeit (1002–1125)* (Wiesbaden: Steiner, 1984), 1:89–91, 135–39.

17. See Emil Lèsne, *Histoire de la propriété ecclésiastique en France* 5. *Les écoles de la fin du VIIIe siècle à la fin du XIIe* (Lille: Champion, 1940), 368–69.

18. On Regensburg, see Specht, 379–87; Bernard Bischoff, "Literarisches und künstlerisches Leben in St. Emmeram (Regensburg) während des frühen und hohen Mittelalters," in his *Mittelalterliche Studien: Ausgewählte Aufsätze zur Schriftkunde und Literaturgeschichte* 2. (Stuttgart: Hiersemann, 1967), 77–115. On Bamberg, see Carl Erdmann, "Die Bamberger Domschule im Investiturstreit," *Zeitschrift für bayerische Landesgeschichte* 9 (1936): 1–46; Zielinski, *Reichsepiskopat*, 84–86, 147; Johannes Fried, "Die Bamberger Domschule und die Rezeption von Frühscholastik und Rechtswissenschaft in ihrem Umkreis bis zum Ende der Stauferzeit," in *Schulen und Studium im sozialen Wandel des hohen und späten Mittelalters*, Johannes Fried, ed. (Sigmaringen: Thorbecke, 1986), 163–201. On Liège, Charles Renardy, "Les écoles Liègoises du XIe et XIIe siècles," *Revue Belge de philologie et d'histoire* 57 (1979): 309–28; Godefroid Kurth, *Notger de Liège et la civilisation au Xe siècle* (Paris: Picard, 1905).

19. See Lèsne, 271–72; John R. Williams, "The Cathedral School of Rheims in the Eleventh Century," *Speculum* 19 (1954): 661–77; Williams, "The Cathedral School of Rheims in the Time of Master Alberic, 1118–36," *Traditio* 20 (1964): 93–114. On Gerbert, see Oscar G. Darlington, "Gerbert the Teacher," *AHR* 52 (1946/47): 456–76; Uta Lindgren, *Gerbert von Aurillac und das Quadrivium: Untersuchungen zur Bildung im Zeitalter der Ottonen* (Wiesbaden: Steiner Verlag, 1976); Hélène Gasc, "Gerbert et la pédagogie des arts libéraux à la fin du dixième siècle," *Journal of Medieval History* 12 (1986): 111–21. See also below, chapter 2, 106–19.

20. See Lèsne, 152–53; the introduction to Frederick Behrend, ed., *The Letters and Poems of Fulbert of Chartres* (Oxford: Clarendon Press, 1976); Loren C. McKinney, *Bishop Fulbert and Education at the School of Chartres* (Notre Dame, IN: Notre Dame University Press, 1957); A. Clerval, *Les écoles de Chartres au moyen-âge (du Ve au XVIe siècle)* (Frankfurt-am-Main: Minerva, 1965).

CHAPTER I ✷ CATHEDRAL SCHOOLS

"*noster Plato,*" "*noster Socrates,*" "*alter Cicero.*"[21] In a commemorative poem from c.1012, Bamberg is praised as the "city of letters [or learning], [its citizens] no wit inferior to the Stoics, greater than the Athenians."[22] In short, some twelve major cathedral schools emerged in the comparatively brief space of sixty years.[23] Clearly a sudden and dramatic growth was taking place in these centers in the second half of the tenth century, and equally clear is that the German schools preceded the French. The reasons for this renewal have been discussed by the historian Josef Fleckenstein.[24] Fleckenstein understood this development as the work of Brun of Cologne in concert with his brother Otto the Great. These two form a purposeful conception of the role of cathedral schools, and this conception raised the fate of the schools above the vagaries of what professor happens to be where. That vagary may still determine the distinction of a particular school and its power to attract students at a given time, but not its educational goal. That remains more-or-less consistent until the rise of universities at the end of the twelfth and beginning of the thirteenth centuries. The first flourishing schools were in the

21. For Regensburg as a "second Athens," Specht, 382; Liège in the first half of the eleventh century "a second Athens...in literary studies it beggars Plato's academy, in the observance of religion it leaves Leo's Rome far behind" (Gozechinus or Goswin of Mainz, *Gozechini epistola ad Walcherum* 6, Robert B.C. Huygens, ed., CCCCM 62 (Turnhout: Brepols, 1985), 15; For Hamburg-Bremen under Bishop, see Adalbert (d.1072) "a second Rome," in Adam of Bremen, *Hamburgische Kirchengeschichte* 23, B. Schmeidler, ed., 3d. ed., MGH, SSR 2 (Hannover: Hahn, 1917), 167. Tournai under Master Udo (1087–92) a "second Athens" in Paré et al, *La renaissance,* 23; Fulbert of Chartres, "noster Socrates" in letter of Adelman of Liège to Berengar of Tours, Robert B.C. Huygens, ed., "Textes latins du XIe au XIIIe siècle," *Studi Medievali,* ser. 3.8 (1967): 476-93, at 476. Ohtricus of Magdeburg "*Cicero unus*" in MGH, SS 4:597, l. 15.

22. The poem is by Abbot Gerhard of Seeon. ll. 33–34: "Non minus ista Sepher Cariath [Josh. 15:15: *Sepher Cariath = civitas litterarum*] cluit arte scienter, / Inferior Stoicis nequaquam, maior Athenis." In MGH, *Poetae* 5, 398.

23. The actual figure, mid-tenth to early eleventh century, is closer to twenty-five. Fleckenstein discussed only those that arose from the direct influence of Otto I.

24. "Königshof und Bischofsschule unter Otto dem Grossen," *Archiv für Kulturgeschichte* 38 (1956): 38–62.

episcopal centers favored by the emperor: Magdeburg, Würzburg, Cologne, Hildesheim, and Mainz. Clearly, imperial patronage was the impetus for their dramatic growth, as Fleckenstein argues. While Ruotger does not state explicitly that the two brothers collaborated on the goals of study, that connection is intuitive.

The emperor had found a purpose for the episcopal school, one it had not had before. In the Carolingian revival, the schools had taken on the role of educating laymen and clerics to read the Bible and of preparing clergymen for their pastoral and liturgical duties. The goal was correction and reformation of the religious life according to the "*norma rectitudinis.*"[25] The new purpose was to educate statesmen and administrators. The goal was not knowledge for its own sake or knowledge for the glory and worship of God, but rather knowledge to be applied in the practical duties of running the empire. Brun of Cologne as imperial chancellor was praised for transforming the royal chapel into a sort of academy of philosophy and school for imperial bishops.[26] The instruction that turned gifted young men into trained administrators and loyal supporters of the emperor originated at court, in the chapel. But it was so valuable that it spilled over the borders of that small, elite institution and sought accommodation elsewhere. This gave cathedral schools their new role. The passage of Brun of Cologne from the imperial chapel to the see of Cologne is representative for the shift: he took this particular brand of instruction with him from the court to the cathedral. This, briefly summarized, is Fleckenstein's argument. Others before him noticed that individual schools took on the task of training men for administrative and state service,[27] but Fleckenstein's study is so important because he showed

25. See Fleckenstein, *Bildungsreform*, passim; Franz Brunhölzl, "Der Bildungsauftrag der Hofschule," in *Karl der Grosse: Lebenswerk und Nachleben,* 5 vols., Bernard Bischoff, ed. *Geistiges Leben* (Düsseldorf: Schwann, 1965-68), 2:32: "Soweit das Bildungsprogramm die Schulen...betrifft, lässt es sich auf die kurze Formel bringen: 'Ziel des Unterrichts ist die Vermittlung der Fähigkeit, die Bibel zu lesen und zu verstehen; die artes liberales liefern die hierzu erforderlichen Grundfertigkeiten." This view has been considerable deepened by Steckel, *Kulturen*.

26. See the description of his influence at court by his biographer, Ruotger, *Ruotgers Lebensbeschreibung des Erzbischofs Brun von Köln* 5–8, Irene Ott, ed., MGH, SSR, n.s. 10 (Cologne: Böhlau, 1951), 6–9.

27. Klewitz, "Königtum"; and Erdmann, "Bamberger Domschule."

CHAPTER I ✶ CATHEDRAL SCHOOLS

this role to be the impetus for the rise of cathedral schools generally in the mid-tenth century, and he showed the logical integration of these schools into the Ottonian "imperial church system." Cathedral-school education became identical with preparation for service at court, be it secular or episcopal.[28] This is an insight of fundamental importance for our understanding of early medieval education and of the beginnings of the twelfth-century renaissance.

LETTERS AND MANNERS

The many studies of education in the earlier Middle Ages[29] have taught us a great deal about the curriculum. We have a good idea of the books read and the subjects taught. But it is not yet clear in what way the period 950–1100/1150 forms a unity, to what extent education at the cathedral schools in this period is distinguished from what came before, from what followed, and from what was

28. Zielinski, *Reichsepiskopat* contains an important statistical and prosopographical study of the close interrelations of cathedral school, royal chapel, and episcopate. It represents a strong confirmation of Fleckenstein's thesis: cathedral school education prepared individuals for service at the imperial court and the episcopate.

29. In addition to the major works by Specht, Clerval, Lèsne, and Paré-Tremblay-Brunet already cited, the following works deserve mention: Philippe Delhaye, "L'organisation scolaire au XIIe siecle," *Traditio* 5 (1947): 211–68; Luitpold Wallach, "Education and Culture in the Tenth Century," *Mediaevalia et Humanistica* 9 (1955): 18–22; Hans Liebeschütz, "The Debate on Philosophical Learning during the Transition Period (900–1080)," in *The Cambridge History of Later Greek and Early Medieval Philosophy*, Arthur H. Armstrong, ed. (Cambridge: Cambridge University Press, 1970), 587–610; Margaret Gibson, "The Continuity of Learning circa 850–circa 1050," *Viator* 6 (1975): 1–13; Pierre Riché, *Education et culture dans l'occident barbare, 6–8 siècles*, 3rd ed. (Paris: Editions de Seuil, 1972); Riché, *Les écoles et l'enseignement*; Cora Lutz, *Schoolmasters of the Tenth Century* (Hamden, CT: Archon Books, 1977); Zielinski, *Reichsepiskopat*; Rolf Köhn, "Schulbildung und Trivium im latinischen Hochmittelalter und ihr möglicher praktischen Nutzen," in *Schulen und Studium*, 203–84. A number of essays are relevant to our topic in *La scuola nell'occidente latino dell'alto medioevo*, 2 vols. (Spoleto: Presso la Sede del Centro, 1972). The good survey by Robert Lerner, "Literacy and Learning," is easy to overlook because of the textbook nature of the publication it appeared in: *One Thousand Years: Western Europe in the Middle Ages*, Richard de Molen, ed. (Boston: Houghton-Mifflin, 1974), 165–223.

going on at the same time in monastic schools. The tendency to see all education against the monastic model and within the scheme of the seven liberal arts is a factor that particularly obscures the role of cathedral schools. But this obscurity is hard to dispel given the nature of the sources. Writings from the monasteries are many, and writings from the cathedral communities are few. From the late tenth and early eleventh centuries we have some lists of *auctores,* some library catalogues,[30] schemes of studies, and discussions of them. We have some descriptions of education in history and biography, some school poetry, and a handful of commentaries and tracts. But deriving our understanding of education at an eleventh-century cathedral school from the authors read and the works written there is like writing history of the theater from lists of plays performed and from theoretical treatises by actors. If in a particular period the repertoire does not change much and there are no theoretical treatises (and there never are — actors do not write), then we might conclude that period was not original or productive. If from the same period that we have just judged unoriginal and unproductive, we have many rave reviews from critics, then we might say that given the lack of originality and productivity in the theater, such reviews must be taken as an indication of the low expectations and bad taste of the period.

Of course, such an interpretation is based on a fundamental misunderstanding of what a theater is and what it does. This, I would suggest, is the predicament of historians of education for the eleventh century. There is a great deal of talk about flourishing schools and great teachers, but there are no works of philosophy, little poetry, and few commentaries by masters. Therefore, the schools of Germany — and of course France, where the same holds true — must be judged to "show little vitality from within," as Haskins thought.[31]

But there is as strong a distortion in the sources as in the lack of them. To make a start in getting around it, I want to pursue the "scheme" or the framework of studies indicated in the formula *litterae et mores,* "letters" and — if I may translate it in this loose

---

30. See G. Glauche, "Die Rolle der Schulautoren im Unterricht von 800 bis 1100," in *La scuola,* 2:617–36.

31. Haskins, 16.

but convenient way — "manners."³² The phrase is very common in descriptions of cathedral school education. It occurs in a variety of forms. As schoolmaster at Trier (c.957) Wolfgang, later bishop of Regensburg, taught not only *liberales doctrinae* but also *morales disciplinae*.³³ Wazo as schoolmaster at Liège (1008–42) is said to have given instruction in the disciplines *tam morum quam litterarum*.³⁴ Bernward of Hildesheim was sent to school *litteris imbuendus, moribus etiam instituendus*.³⁵ The phrase occurs in variants like *sapientia et mores, ingenium et mores*. This is certainly not a topos without much content cribbed from ancient notions on the education of an orator. Examples outside of the standard topical section of a *vita* on the man's education show clearly the vitality of the formula.

Some students of Würzburg wrote a poem in 1031 in answer to an attack on their school by the scholars of Worms. The poem praises the virtues of their school at length and calls it a flowing spring out of which one drinks the "doctrine of eloquence and of proper conduct of life" *(recte vivendi et dogma loquendi)*.³⁶ That is, their school teaches rhetoric or oratory (proper speaking) and ethics (proper living), clearly a variant of "letters and manners." In the context of an answer to an attack, the phrase had to convey something of substance. Whether or not the school of Würzburg poured forth this two-fold doctrine as abundantly as its students claimed, such a doctrine had to exist; the students of Worms could not have been answered with an empty phrase.

32. Some observations on the formula in *Origins*, 213–19.

33. Otloh, *Vita Wolfkangi* 7, ll. 3–4: "Juvenes...non solum liberalibus exercebat doctrinis, verum etiam moralibus informabat disciplinis." In MGH, SS 4:529.

34. Anselm of Liège, *Gesta episcoporum Leodiensium* 40: "In quarum [scolarum] studio tam morum quam litterarum vigilantissime exercuit disciplinam, eos qui pro his moribus essent, licet minus litteratos, longe his anteponens, quibus, ut in plerisque solet, scientia litterarum vanae gloriae peperisset stultitiam." In Rudolf Köpke, ed., MGH, SS 7 (Hannover: Hahn, 1846), 7:210

35. *Vita Bernwardi* 1, ll. 16–17; MGH, SS 4:758.

36. *Die ältere Wormser Briefsammlung*, ll. 264–65: "istinc si discis, statim sensu resipiscis, / Recte vivendi potans et dogma loquendi." In Walther Bulst, ed., MGH, BdK 3 (Weimar: Böhlau, 1949), 119–27, at 127.

A more telling example is from a letter of the Bamberg schoolmaster Meinhard written around 1060. This letter must be considered a major text in the history of education in the eleventh century. Meinhard answers a request from his bishop, Gunther of Bamberg, for a book on the Christian faith. He complains,

> First you entangle me in all the busy cares of a headmaster, and now you are after me...for another work, a task not just arduous but downright impossible.... If the only task placed in my care were the instruction of young minds in the liberal arts — and many earlier writers argue for this single curriculum — then the rigors of the task and the reputation gained by it would be sufficient pay for me. Now however, those who are placed at the head of schools are taxed in a dual function for the profit of the Church: for they spend the first part of their fortunes in forming mores and squander the second part in teaching letters.[37]

Here "letters and manners" cannot be a topos with little content. Schoolmasters do not groan under the burden of meaningless formulae, certainly not when they explain to their bishops why they lack the time to write books. Bishops cannot be persuaded how hard their staff is working by the appeal to non-existent schemes of studies, any more than deans and provosts now can. Meinhard actually taught something called *mores*, and it took a lot of his time, time he would rather have devoted to liberal studies. Particularly interesting is Meinhard's sense of the history of this double instruction within other schemes of studies. It is comparatively recent. Earlier masters got along without it. While it is, unfortunately, not clear who or what is meant by the *studia veterum*, Meinhard knew Cicero and Quintilian well enough not to include them among the earlier

37. *Weitere Briefe Meinhards*, Epist. 39: "Cum me negociosissimi magistratus cura implicueris, urgues tamen et instas...ut novam operam, non tam arduam et difficilem quam plane impossibilem suscipiam.... Equidem si excubie nostre solis adolescentum ingeniis liberali erudicione excolendis assiderent, quod unicum curriculum pleraque veterum studia sibi vindicarunt, laboris mala fame nominisque momenta mihi pensarent. Verum nunc qui prefecti scolarum habentur, gemina pro ecclesiastico usu functione multantur: primas enim partes formandis moribus impendunt, secundas vero litterarum doctrine insumunt." In Carl Erdmann and Norbert Fickermann, ed., MGH, BdK 5 (Weimar: Böhlau, 1950), 238–39. Erdmann takes the letter to be the dedication to Meinhard's work *De fide*. See his *Studien zur Briefliteratur Deutschlands im elften Jahrhundert*, MGH, *Schriften* 1 (Leipzig: Hiersemann, 1938), 23.

CHAPTER I ✶ CATHEDRAL SCHOOLS

writers who argued for a curriculum in the liberal arts alone. In any case, it is the schoolmasters of the present (*"Verum nunc qui prefecti scolarum habentur"*), who are taxed doubly, not just in Bamberg but at schools generally. Telling also is that the instruction in letters and manners is given *pro ecclesiastico usu*, and that must mean in the midst of all this mercantile language, "to profit the Church." Why the Church? If *mores* meant proper comportment for young men and nothing more, then why not *pro scholarium usu?* I will offer some thoughts on this later.

Meinhard gives us a second telling bit of testimony to the reality of this formula. In another letter he commiserates with an unknown recipient on the death of the master of his school: now studies have died, the "light of letters" *(lumen litterarum)* is snuffed out, and "the moral discipline most excellently established and of long standing" is dead and buried. But Meinhard acknowledges with gratitude the arrival of a youth from this bereaved diocese who has been sent to the Bamberg "workshop" for an education, so that those two marks of the school's former excellence, "letters and manners," may be revived upon his return.[38] Again, an extraordinarily clear example of the real existence of "letters and manners" as a scheme of studies.

The choice of the Bamberg school as a "workshop" to prepare a master of "letters and manners" clearly made good sense. Bamberg gained a reputation for precisely this orientation of studies. We see this in a letter that the canons of Worms wrote c.1115 to their colleagues at Bamberg. They urge them to support their bishop elect, Burchard II, a former student of Bamberg (*"vestris institutis fundatus a puericia"*), "a son of Bamberg" *"in litterarum scientia, in rerum agendarum pericia, in honestate morum, in gratia discretionum."*[39] Whether this is flattery

---

38. *Weitere Briefe Meinhards*, Epist. 19: "Verum inter alia gravia et luctuosa hunc dolorem quasi capitalem deplorastis studium lumenque litterarum penitus apud vos occidisse nec minus disciplinam moralem egregie apud vos antiquitus institutam situ quodam et negligentia nunc dissolutam iam iamque obisse, immo sepultam esse. Quas ob res adolescentem vestrum officine nostre erudiendum informandumque tradidistis, ut duo pignora vestra, mores dico litterasque, per eum vobis...resuscitentur." In Erdmann ed., 213.

39. *Udalrici Codex* 172, Bibliotheca Rerum Germanicarum 5: Monumenta Bambergensia, Philipp Jaffé ed. (Aalen: Scientia, 1964), 305. Newer ed.: *Codex Udalrici* 300, Klaus Nass ed., 2 vols. (Wiesbaden: Harrassowitz, 2017), 2:505.

31

or a deserved reputation, it shows us a desirable curriculum for a school of future bishops: letters and manners, skill in governing or administering, and good judgment, presumably the kind a bishop/administrator, not an intellectual, requires.

In an earlier publication,[40] I tried to show how the educational reforms instituted at Hildesheim in the middle of the eleventh century under Bishop Azelinus (1044–54) are understandable within this same framework of studies. A conservative chronicler complained about Azelinus importing the manners of the court (*curialitas*) into the comparatively rustic diocese, and this complaint has given that bishop the reputation of an epicurean corrupter of his church. But Azelinus also hired the gifted young cleric Benno, later the second bishop of Osnabrück by that name, as *magister scholarum*, luring him from the royal court with promises of great wealth. Benno implanted in the clergy a "zeal for the study of letters" and transformed Hildesheim into a center of learning second to none in the region. We therefore have a picture of the double role of Azelinus and Benno at Hildesheim, the bishop imposing courtly *mores* on the clergy, the schoolmaster instructing them in *litterae*.

I have given a number of references, not to smother the subject in documentation, but to establish as clearly and definitively as possible the overriding importance of a formula to which I can find no reference in scholarship on medieval education. The phrase "letters and manners" occurs so often not because it was the bearer of an inherited framework of studies, but because it was a formula by which the life of the schools was organized. Whatever is conveyed in the terms *mores, recte vivendi dogma*, and others we will encounter — *forma vivendi, disciplina vivendi, studium bene vivendi* — students wanted it, and the schools had to provide it.

THE OLD LEARNING AND CULTUS VIRTUTUM

I would suggest that the formula "letters and manners," with all it implies institutionally and pedagogically, indicates to us the essential unifying element in cathedral school education in the period 950–1100/1150. It was this dual instruction that aimed at shaping the public servant/educator, that is, attaining that goal

---

40. *Origins*, 35.

that had given rise to cathedral schools in the mid-tenth century. Letters by themselves could of course be learned in monasteries. It is significant that in some of the best-known descriptions of the education of monks from the period only the term *litterae* occurs, not *mores*. Abbo of Fleury was sent to school *litteris imbuendus*, Otloh of St. Emmeram *pro litteris discendis*.[41] The study of *mores* was in part a preparation for secular administrative service, or for a secularized form of ecclesiastical service. Meinhard's statement that *mores* in the present day are added to *litterae "pro ecclesiastico usu"* makes sense only if we understand that instruction as combining the moral and ethical improvement of the individual with a preparation for service to the Church. *Mores/moralitas* could have been omitted from a monastic education, but it formed an important facet of instruction at the cathedral schools in our period. Letters had to be complemented by an ethical education[42] that could become the main goal of instruction.

Fulbert of Chartres wrote a letter to Archbishop Ebalus of Rheims in 1023 recommending a student of his who wished to transfer to Rheims for the sake of the same study that had brought him to Chartres, namely, *causa discendae honestatis*, to learn virtue or

---

41. On Abbo, see PL 139:389A; on Otloh, PL 146:38B. At Ramsey, Abbo is said to have taught *litterarum scientia*, and in a long description of his teaching no mention is made of *mores*. See PL 139:392B. Johanek, "Klosterstudien," 35–68, shows that the monasteries took a considerable interest in the teachings of the schools. But his idea of a fundamental common purpose linking education at both kinds of institutions (37) is not convincing. Neither the example of William of Champeaux continuing his teaching at St. Victor nor that of Wibald of Stablo's letter 167 to Manegold of Paderborn bear out the argument. The former fled from the threat of dialectic back to a teaching aimed at *venustas morum* (Hildebert of Lavardin, Epist. 1, PL 171:141A), that is, non-monastic. The latter gave advice appropriate to a worldly master and apologized repeatedly for stepping out of his role as monk to do it.

42. *Mores* studied along with *litterae* is another name for the discipline the sources calle *ethica* and *moralitas*. See Anselm of Laon: "Dicitur et auctor in Proverbiis ethicus, id est tractans de moribus." PL 162:1590C. The identification of the two is standard in Conrad of Hirsau's *Accessus ad auctores*, Robert B.C. Huygens, ed. (Leiden: Brill, 1970), 21 (Cato): "Ethicae subponitur, quia ad morum utilitatem nititur"; 27 (Arator): "Ethicae subponitur, id est morali scientiae, quia tractat de moribus."

morality.⁴³ The acquisition of knowledge and the study of the seven liberal arts tended toward the higher goal of an ethical education, just as all studies in Carolingian times aimed at religious perfection. The subjects studied and authors read in secular learning may have changed little, but the underlying intent of education changed or broadened considerably. Now a great intermediate object called *mores, ethica,* or *moralitas*⁴⁴ swelled the area separating the arts from theology. This explains in part the difficulty of assigning a place in earlier medieval education to the discipline called by these names. It is not an independent branch of study, even though in some schemes it may be assigned specifically to grammar or rhetoric.⁴⁵ Certainly, the association of ethics with grammar and rhetoric was a close one, hallowed since antiquity as the essence of an orator's education, cultivated and practiced in secular education in the Middle Ages.⁴⁶

43. Epist. 76: "[Hubertus]...qui de patria sua causa discendae honestatis egressus...." In Behrends ed., 136. Behrends misses the intent of the phrase, translating it, "for the sake of acquiring a sound education."

44. The strongly religious orientation of Carolingian education is evident in the following passage from the *Epistola de litteris colendis* 29: [Along with the "*regularis vitae ordo*" letters are to be studied] ...qualiter, sicut regularis norma honestatem morum, ita quoque docendi et discendi instantia ordinet et ornet seriem verborum, ut, qui Deo placere appetunt recte vivendo, ei etiam placere non negligant recte loquendo." In MGH, *Leges* 2.1:79. For commentary, see Fleckenstein, *Bildungsreform,* 52. "Right living" is taken for granted; it is not an object of education. The learned skill is "right speaking." The end of both is "pleasing God." This is very far indeed from the *utilitas, elegantia,* and *sublimitas* that Meinhard got from his studies, or from the *elegantia morum* and *dignitas vitae* that Onulf of Speyer set as the higher goal of rhetorical studies.

45. On the place of ethics in programs of studies, see the work of Philippe Delhaye, "La place de l'éthique parmi les classifications scientifiques au XIIe siècle," *Miscellanea moralia in honorem E.D.A. Janssen* (Louvain: Nauwelaerts, 1949), 19–44; Delhaye, "L'enseignement de la philosophie morale au XIIe siècle," *Mediaeval Studies* 11 (1950): 77–99; Delhaye, "*Grammatica* et *ethica* au XIIe siècle," *RTAM* 25 (1958): 59–110. It is evident from Delhaye's important works that the various subjects of the trivium could serve ethics. The latter should not be seen as a kind of pendant to the former. It was or could be the underlying motive. Observations on the dependency in Köhn, 224, 228.

46. The short work by Onulf of Speyer (1071–76), *Colores rhetorici,* Wilhelm Wattenbach, ed. (Berlin: Sitzungsberichte der Preussischen Akademie der Wissenschaften, 1894), 361–86, gives us an especially good example of the subordination

CHAPTER I ✷ CATHEDRAL SCHOOLS

Gerbert of Aurillac gave a programmatic statement of the connection in saying that he refused to distinguish the art of speaking well from the art of living well.[47] This is the formula of humanist education for the eleventh and twelfth centuries as well as for Roman antiquity. But neither of those periods necessarily confined ethical education to the disciplines of grammar and rhetoric. Education generally had the purpose not just of conveying knowledge but of forming the human being, of "attuning" one's inner to one's outer world, "composing" one's manners according to inner virtues acquired through study and practice. Speech and gesture were the activities in which inner person and outer expression met most closely, but all the disciplines and arts could serve that purpose and ideally were pursued *causa discendae honestatis*. John of Salisbury strongly stated this dominant role of ethics. In the prologue to the first book of his Metalogicon he makes this trenchant claim:

---

of rhetoric to ethics, or rather of the virtual disappearance of the discipline of rhetoric behind the ethical motive. Most of the prologue is lost. The work begins with the sentence fragment, interesting for our purpose: " ...*arti rethoricae: morum elegantiam, compositionem habitus, vitae dignitatem amplectere*" (369). A conjecture in harmony with the rest of the work would see this as completing the thought, "The art of rhetoric is not confined to the framing of speeches, but includes the cultivation of elegant manners, composed bearing and dignity of conduct." The structure of the work is the outbidding of rhetorical definitions (from the *Rhetorica ad Herennium*) with moral precepts. E.g. *complexio* is an ornament of speech, but far better and more elegant is "amorem Dei... amorem proximi complectere" (370). He wittily uses the rhetorical figure under discussion to frame the moral precept. On Onulf, see Wallach,"Onulf of Speyer;" and Carl Erdmann, "Onulf von Speyer und Amarcius," in his *Forschungen zur politischen Ideenwelt des Frühmittelalters*, Friedhelm Baethgen, ed. (Berlin: Akademia Verlag, 1951), 124–34. See also the new edition with analysis by Cornelia Linde, "Die'Rethorischen colores' des Magisters Onulf von Speyer," *Mittellateinisches Jahrbuch* 40 (2005): 333–81. Linde dates the work early twelfth century, against the mid-eleventh dating by Wattenbach and Erdmann, and sets its possible range of dating 1114 to "second quarter of the twelfth century." The arguments for this later dating seem to me too general to accept without further argumentation.

47. *Epistola* 44: "Cumque ratio morum dicendique ratio a philosophia non separentur, cum studio bene vivendi semper coniuncxi studium bene dicendi...." In *Die Briefsammlung Gerberts van Reims*, Fritz Weigle, ed. MGH, *Briefe der deutschen Kaiserzeit* (Weimar: Böhlau, 1966), 2:73

> Any pretext of philosophy that does not bear fruit in the cultivation of virtue [*cultus virtutis*] and the guidance of one's conduct is futile and false.[48]

Elsewhere, he lists and defines all the disciplines of liberal education and sums up:

> Of all these branches of learning that which confers the grace of inner and outer beauty [*decoris gratia*] in the highest degree, is ethics, the most excellent part of philosophy, without which the latter would not even deserve its name.[49]

John here is the spokesman of what I will refer to from now on as "the old learning." It is a humanistic program of education based on the integration of knowledge and wisdom, or, to use the mythographic emblem of that union, the marriage of Philology and Mercury. It dominated the cathedral schools in the eleventh century. Toward the end of the century it became locked in conflict with a new kind of learning, based on dialectic, disputation, and the systematizing of philosophical and theological problems: early scholastic philosophy, which from now on I will call "the new learning."[50] One of the essential tasks of history

---

48. *Ioannes Saresberiensis Metalogicon*, Prologus, John Barrie and Katharine Keats-Rohan, ed., CCCM 98 (Turnhout: Brepols, 1991), 11. See also Clemens J. Webb, ed. (Oxford: Clarendon, 1929), 4: "Est enim quaelibet professio philosophandi inutilis et falsa, quae se ipsam in cultu virtutis et vitae exhibitione non aperit." English text from *The Metalogicon of John of Salisbury: A Twelfth Century Defense of the Verbal and Logical Arts of the Trivium*, Daniel McGarry, trans. (Berkeley: University of California Press, 1962), 6.

49. *Metalogicon* 1.24.41-44: "Illa autem que ceteris philosophiae partibus preminet, Ethicam dico, sine qua nec philosophi subsistit nomen, collati decoris gratia omnes alias antecedit." In Hall, ed., 52; Webb ed., 55. Translation taken, with some liberties, from McGarry, 67. Cf. Abelard, *Dialogus inter Philosophum, Iudaeum et Christianum*, ll. 1263–1314, Rudolf Thomas, ed. (Stuttgart: Frommann, 1970), 88–90. Ethics, based on the pursuit of the *summum bonum* is the highest discipline, the other liberal arts merely its handmaidens.

50. The discussion of the period is getting a little crowded with "old–new" pairs, but given the transitional nature of the late eleventh and early twelfth century, the terms are useful and accurate. "Old and new learning" are consistent with the framework formulated by Gillian Evans, *Old Arts and New Theology: The Beginnings of Theology as an Academic Discipline* (Oxford: Clarendon, 1980). On the transitional nature of the period see the interesting studies by Charles Radding, *A World Made by*

of education for the tenth and eleventh centuries is to show how the *cultus virtutum* tended to penetrate into each of the seven liberal arts, to appropriate intellectual subjects for the purpose of ethical training. I pointed out Onulf of Speyer's appropriation of rhetoric for the study of *elegantia morum* and *dignitas vitae*.[51]

The subject of cosmology and astronomy as an ethical discipline is a particularly rich and important one. The connection is ancient and primitive in its origins. The Middle Ages had it most directly from Stoic philosophy, which made nature and the heavens into the pattern for humanity's moral development.[52] Cicero regarded the highest goal of moral conduct as *"naturam sequi et eius quasi lege vivere"* and formulated the pithy phrase, *"natura optima vivendi dux."*[53] John of Salisbury is fond of quoting it.[54] In the *Tusculan Disputations* Cicero traced the route by which public life leads distinguished individuals to philosophy, then to astronomy, thence to the search for the causes and origins of things, and ultimately to the good life. The Ciceronian joining of "natural science," ethics, and public service had a vital meaning for the circles of public servants/administrators in the eleventh century with whom we are concerned.[55] Boethius, in the *Consolatio philosophiae*, thanked Lady Philosophy for forming his *mores* in accordance with the celestial order

---

Men: Cognition and Society, 400–1200 (Chapel Hill: University of North Carolina Press, 1985); Radding, "Evolution of Medieval Mentalities: A Cognitive-Structural Approach," AHR 83 (1978): 577–97; and Radding, "Superstition to Science: Nature, Fortune and the Passing of the Medieval Ordeal," AHR 84 (1979): 945–69.

51. Above, n. 46.

52. See Maximilian Forschner, *Die stoische Ethik: Über den Zusammenhang von Natur-, Sprach- und Moralphilosophie im altstoischen System* (Stuttgart: Clett-Cota, 1981).

53. Cicero, *De legibus* l.21.56; *Laelius* 5.19.

54. *Johannes Saresberiensis episcopi Carnotensis Policratici sive de nugis curialium et vestigiis philosophorum libri VIII*, Clemens J. Webb, ed. 2 vols. (Oxford: Clarendon, 1909), 4.1, 1:235, l. 13; 6.21, 2:60, l. 1. See also Tilman Struve, "'Vita civilis naturam imitetur': Der Gedanke der Nachahmung der Natur als Grundlage der organologischen Staatskonzeption Johannes von Salisbury," *Historisches Jahrbuch* 101 (1981): 341–61.

55. CTD 5.24–25, 68–72, King ed., 450, 494–98. Cf. the adaptation of this passage in *Epistola* 9 of the so-called *Regensburger rhetorischen Briefe*, Norbert Fickermann ed., *Briefsammlungen der Zeit Heinrichs IV*, 316.

and the movement of the planets.⁵⁶ If the heavens are seen as a pattern for human morals, then the study of astronomy is an object of ethics. It offers an approach to forming, or re-forming, human character.

This, I believe, is one of the main impulses for the study of Plato's *Timaeus* in the eleventh century. That stern critic of *Timaeus* studies, Manegold of Lautenbach, indicated this clearly when he conceded the value of Plato's work in "moral judgment aside from questions of faith," and that means the pursuit of the virtues appropriate to the *"ecclesiastici rectores et gubernatores divine rei publice."*⁵⁷ In other words, it is fine for civil and church administrators to study the *Timaeus* within a program of moral education, but let no one confuse it with theological truth. For medieval commentators the subject of Plato's work was "natural justice," the pattern of natural law implanted in the cosmic order at its inception, upon which individuals can draw to form their own characters: "Hence the subject matter of this book," writes William of Conches in the beginning of his *Timaeus* commentary, "is natural justice or the creation of the world: for he [Plato] treats the latter by way of investigating natural justice."⁵⁸ In his glosses on Boethius, William also assigned both the *Timaeus* and *The Consolation of Philosophy* specifically to *ethica*.⁵⁹ This notion of the *Timaeus* legitimized as a work of ethics certainly helps explain its manuscript tradition. The interest in the *Timaeus* in the eleventh century coincides with the advent of a program of ethical education at cathedral schools.

56. Boethius, *The Consolation of Philosophy* 1.4, H.F. Stewart, trans. & rev. (Cambridge, MA: Harvard University Press, 1968), 142.

57. *Liber contra Wolfelmum* 22; Hartmann ed., 93–94.

58. Guillaume de Conches, *Glosae super Platonem*: "Unde possumus dicere quod materia huius libri est naturalis iusticia vel creatio mundi: de ea enim propter naturalem iusticiam agit." In *Glosae super Platonem: Texte critique avec introduction, notes et tables*, Edouard Jeauneau, ed. (Paris: Vrin, 1965), 3:59. On the origins of the idea of natural justice and its significance in the Middle Ages, see Gerard Verbeke, "Aux origines de la notion de 'loi naturelle'," in *La filosofia della natura nel medioevo: Atti del terzo congresso internazionale di filosofia medioevale*, Fernand Van Steenberghen, ed (Milan: Vita e Pensiero, 1966), 164–73.

59. Cf. Delhaye, "L'Enseignement," 83 n. 13.

The more general Stoic connection of ethics with the study of nature also had far-reaching implications for our period. The author of the *Regensburger rhetorischen Briefe* sees *honestas* as a cosmic principle without which the entire *mundana fabrica* would collapse.[60] In Alan of Lille's *Anticlaudianus*, the virtue of *honestas* teaches the new human to "love nature" and to embrace whatever nature has created.[61] Hugh of St. Victor gave the idea terse and sharp expression:

> In the meaning of things lies natural justice, out of which the discipline of our own morals [*mores*] arises. By contemplating what God has made we realize what we ourselves ought to do. Every nature tells of God; every nature teaches humanity.[62]

The root impulse for the study of the creation and of nature in the eleventh and twelfth centuries lies in this idea. Any "science" based on this conception of the universe was necessarily a "humane" science, directed towards self-knowledge and moral perfection, toward good governance of the self and the state. The idea of macrocosm/microcosm, and with it the basic form of some of the most prominent works of twelfth-century humanism, reveal this conception: William of Conche's *Philosophia mundi*, Bernard Silvester's *Cosmographia*, and Alan's *Anticlaudianus*. In each case the point of departure is the cosmos and cosmic perfection, and following upon this, humanity and human perfection. This form came from the *Timaeus*, but the idea it proclaimed was no less vivid in the mind of these twelfth-century humanists, no less vividly present in their works, than in Plato's. Eleventh- and early twelfth-century

60. *Regensburger rhetorischen Briefe* 15; Fickermann ed., 334.

61. *Anticlaudianus* 7.208–9: "[honestas monet]...ut vicium fugiat, naturam diligat.../...amplectens quidquid Natura creavit." In Alan of Lille, *Literary Works*, Winthrop Wetherbee, ed. and trans. (Cambridge, MA: Harvard University Press, 2013), 446,

62. *Hugonis de Sancto Victore Didascalicon de Studio Legendi* 6.5: "in illa [significatione rerum] enim naturalis iustitia est, ex qua disciplina morum nostrorum, id est, positiva iustitia nascitur. contemplando quid fecerit Deus, quid nobis faciendum sit agnoscimus. omnis natura Deum loquitur, omnis natura hominem docet...." In *Didascalicon de Studio Legendi: A Critical Text*, Charles H. Buttimer, ed. (Washington, DC: Catholic University Press, 1939), 123. English in text from *The Didascalicon of Hugh of St. Victor: A Medieval Guide to the Arts*, Jerome Taylor, trans. (New York: Columbia University Press, 1961), 145.

cosmology is in its basic impulse humane and ethical. The progress of science in the twelfth century towards Aristotelian empiricism, towards new Arabic astronomy, towards "natural science" in a sense approaching our understanding of the term, must be seen as a progress away from the pursuit of science in a humane, Stoic-Ciceronian sense.

TEACHING VIRTUE

How was virtue taught? Normally scholars point to the textbooks read in order to illustrate the contents of ethical instruction:[63] Cicero's *De officiis* and the adaptation of this work by Ambrose; the *Distichs* of Cato, Seneca, and medieval florilegia like the *Moralium dogma philosophorum* ascribed to William of Conches. But this does not help us distinguish the eleventh century clearly from the ninth or the thirteenth and brings us back to my comparison with theater history through lists of plays. Instruction in *mores* was vital enough to dominate studies for some two hundred years, and lists of textbooks reduce it to a collection of abstractions. What we miss and what is almost altogether unrecoverable is the life of the teacher.[64] This is the real textbook and exemplar of *mores*, and this form of instruction was conducted above all simply by *convictus*, a life shared by master and students, the imparting of the teacher's qualities to the student by force of example.[65] Meinhard of Bamberg wrote a letter to his former teacher in which he recalls nostalgically his student days:

> That way of living [*convictus*] into which you received me in so profoundly humane a manner was more free and noble, more effective and practical [*ad utilitatem efficacius*], more scrupulous in the cultivation of elegance [*ad elegantiam accuratius*], more conducive to the highest one can attain [*ad sublimitatem exquisitius*], than any other whatsoever, even if my thickness of mind deprived me of its richer fruits.[66]

63. See Delhaye, "L'Enseignement," 83.

64. Also observed by Southern, *Platonism,* 19: "In the schools it was the spoken word which was important: perhaps one should even say that it was the physical presence of the master...." Behrends, *Letters of Fulbert,* xxviii, observes, "it appears that what attracted [students] was Fulbert himself rather than the subjects which were studied."

65. See Caroline Bynum, *Docere verbo et exemplo: An Aspect of Twelfth Century Spirituality* (Missoula, MT: Scholars Press, 1979).

66. *Hannoversche Briefsammlung,* Epist. 65: "Neque enim convictu vestro, quo apud vos humanissime acceptus sum, quicquam potest esse liberalius neque studio

The fruits of *convictus* are *utilitas, elegantia,* and *sublimitas.* There is no talk of the challenges of the mind, of analysis, of knowledge gained for its own sake, no talk of learning at all but rather of the cultivation of a personal quality, called here "elegance,"[67] and of the practical benefits of a way of life shared with the master. I take the practical side of this education to be indicated directly in *utilitas* and less directly, though still distinctly, in *sublimitas,* which may mean both exquisite style or the perfect life or the highest rank or office a person can attain.

Some testimony from Fulbert's school at Chartres bears out this picture of the master's role. Fulbert was known as a teacher of "both letters and manners,"[68] and writings from his students make it clear that his instruction in *mores* was what they particularly valued. Adelman of Liège, later bishop of Brixen, wrote a poem commemorating his former teacher and fellow students, *De viris illustribus sui temporis.* He praises Fulbert with the verses,

> *Ah, with what dignity and diligence in questions of mores,*
> *With what gravity in subject matter, what sweetness in words*
> *He explained the mysteries of higher knowledge!*[69]

---

illo, tametsi mea ingenii malignitas me uberiorem eius fructum defraudavit, studio inquam illo nihil esse potest vel ad utilitatem efficacius vel ad elegantiam accuratius vel ad sublimitatem exquisitius." In MGH, BdK, 112–13. Erdmann, *Studien,* 38–39, conjectures that Meinhard's former teacher was Hermann of Rheims.

67. In general, beauty, elegance, grace — whatever the words in the context of *mores* may convey — were clearly important goals of study and learning. Recall John of Salisbury's words that *ethica,* more than any other discipline, confers *gratia decoris,* the grace of a beauty of both mind and manners (above, n. 49). Onulf of Speyer connected the study of rhetoric with *morum elegantia* (above, n. 46). On "elegant" and "beautiful manners" as an ideal of worldly clergy, see my *Origins,* 128–52.

68. Hariulf, biographer of Abbot Angelram of St. Riquier (d. 1045) says of the abbot's studies with Fulbert, *Vita Angelrani* 3: "hic ei monitor, hic tam morum quam litterarum fuit institutor" (PL 141:1406A.) An interesting bit of testimony to Fulbert's dispensing of "letters and manners" is a letter of his former student and disciple, Hildegar. In letter 95, he writes to Fulbert with two requests: to correct a little work of his [*opusculum*] and to correct his vice of anger. See Behrends ed., 172–75. Hildegar regarded both his literary and his moral improvement, his letters and his manners, the province of his teacher.

69. Julien Havet's critical edition is included in Clerval's *Les écoles de Chartres,*

Here also there is no praise of incisive intellect or of penetrating analysis, though presumably the reading of the Bible is the form of study in question. What roused this student's enthusiasm were the teacher's eloquence, gravity, and dignity.[70] The eloquence and noble bearing of the master were what students wanted from Fulbert, undoubtedly at least as much as they wanted illumination of the "mysteries of higher knowledge." Adelman praises Fulbert's student, Hildegar, for having taken over and made his own the master's facial expression, tone of voice, and manners.[71] Fulbert's personal presence was a text from which the students learned, his personal qualities a substitute for intellectual knowledge. A century

---

59–61, at 59: "Eheu! quanta dignitate moralis industriae, / Quanta rerum gravitate, verborum dulcedine, / Explicabat altioris archana scientiae!" On Adelman, see Hubert Silvestre, "Notice sur Adelman de Liège, évêque de Brescia (d. 1061)," *Revue d'histoire ecclésiastique* 56 (1961): 855–71.

70. Fulbert, letter 92, would seem to have a similar quality in mind when he refuses to send Hildegar, as schoolmaster at Poitiers, any teaching assistant who has not yet attained *gravitas morum*: Behrends ed., 164.

71. Adelman in Clerval, *Les écoles de Chartres*, 60: "Is magistrum referebat vultu, voce, moribus." Gozechin (Goswin) of Mainz praised his student Valcher for his seeming ability to transform himself wholly into his master. See *Epitola ad Walcherum* 3: "tu etiam totum magistrum in te videreris transfundere." In Huygens ed., 12. See also Hugh of St. Victor, *De institutione novitiorum* 6–7, Feiss and Sicard ed., 323–50; PL 176:932D–933C. In his adaptation of Cicero's *De officiis* Ambrose had urged young men to attach themselves to wise and prudent teachers and imitate them to the benefit of their morals and their careers, *De officiis ministrorum* 20.97: "Ostendunt...adolescentes eorum se imitatores esse, quibus adhaerent; et ea convalescit opinio, quod ab his vivendi acceperint similitudinem, cum quibus conversandi hauserint cupiditatem." In PL 16:137B. The passage is worth quoting in this context not only because of the popularity and importance of Ambrose's work in this period, but also because it is quoted along with admonitions to students to imitate their teachers and to teachers to guide the morals of their students in Manegold of Lautenbach, *Liber ad Gebehardum* 9, MGH, *Libelli de lite*, 1:327–28. "Teacher imitation" remains an important formula of ethical pedagogy into the Renaissance. See Baldassare Castiglione, *The Book of the Courtier* 1.26: "...whoever would be a good pupil must not only do things well, but must always make every effort to resemble and, if that is possible, to transform himself into his master." In Charles Singleton, trans. (Garden City, NY: Doubleday, 1959), 42.

CHAPTER 1 ✶ CATHEDRAL SCHOOLS

later, Wibald of Stablo was still speaking entirely within this conceptual framework when he urged a young master, Balderich of Trier:

> Let your mere presence be a course of studies for your students.... Your position requires more than mere teaching. You must exercise strict severity, for you are, as you know, also one who supervises the correction of conduct. This teaching and this exercise is more subtle and in its fruits more important than any other.[72]

The physical presence of an educated person possessed a high pedagogic value. One's composure and bearing, one's conduct of life, could themselves constitute a form of discourse, intelligible and learnable. Willigis of Mainz is said to have

> taught lovers of virtue how to live according to the norms of morality, not with his speech but with his actions, more with the language of his behavior than that of his words.[73]

A comment of Gozechin, or Goswin, of Mainz, gives us good reason to think that teaching merely by presence and personal authority was a recognized task at cathedral schools opposed to the comparative busy work of presenting school learning. He distinguishes between some who teach *auctoritate* and others who

---

72. Epist. 91: "Presentia tua tuis auditoribus disciplina sit.... Plus habet locus tuus quam docendi officium; nam et censoriam exhibere debes severitatem, quoniam et corrigendis moribus prefectum te esse noveris. Quae disciplina et exercitatio omnibus est subtilior et in fructu cunctis propensior." In *Bibliotheca rerum Germanicarum*, Philipp Jaffé, ed., *Monumenta Corbeiensia* (Aalen: Scientia, 1964), 1:165. Similarly his praise of a model teacher, obliquely referring to Bernard of Clairvaux, Epist. 167: "Quem si aspicias, doceris; si audias, instrueris; si sequare, perficeris." In Jaffé ed., 1:110; *Das Briefbuch Abt Wibalds von Stablo und Corvey*, Epist. 64, Martina Hartmann, Heinz Zatschek and Timothy Reuter, ed., 3 vols. (Hannover: Hahn, 2012), 1:110.

73. *Libellus de Willigisi consuetudinibus* 4, ll. 31–32: "Amatores virtutis, qualiter honesta moralitate deberent vivere, docuit in re, non ore, lingua magis morum quam lingua verborum." In MGH, SS 15.2:745. The thrust of this work (composed 1018–39) is consistently Willigis' person as an ethical curriculum: he was "vitae honestissimae speculum" (l. 35, 15.2:743); "[from his life]... possunt exempla vivendi honestissima sumere qui student honestissime vivere..." ll. 4–5, 15.2:744); "...per assiduae lectionis honestaeque moralitatis exemplum honestissimum vitam non cessavit honestare multorum" (ll. 42–43, 15.2:744). Cf. Bynum, *Docere*, 41: "life almost becomes a form (a more effective form) of speech."

teach *labore*. The former can stand the rigors of the job, "than which there is none more difficult," longer than the latter.[74]

If we can accept that the shaping of character through the person of the teacher, aided by written examples and by any of the seven liberal arts, was one of the central tasks of cathedral schools, the task indicated in the term *mores*, then we have come a long way toward understanding the nature and goal of education there and the role of *magister scholarum*, a position of incomparably greater stature than its modern counterpart, schoolmaster. It is a striking fact that the position of master is commonly a stepping stone on the way to the bishopric. A career followed by many of the most distinguished imperial bishops since Ottonian times led from student to schoolmaster to court chaplain to bishop, with perhaps stations in between as provost or chancellor.[75] Master of schools stood in a comparable relation to state service as today the law to government service. The reason for this is, above all, that the schoolmaster had to embody those qualities one was to transmit to one's students, and those qualities were ones that qualified one for royal service, for administrative and diplomatic duties, for the episcopacy.[76] Hence a good schoolmaster was an obvious candidate for the royal chapel and the bishopric. The personal charisma of the great teacher, the diplomat, the public servant, the follower of the great Roman statesmen,[77] this was the aura that surrounded the successful master at the cathedral schools, and it was the main curriculum of *ethica*.

The idea of a pedagogy of personal charisma explains the exuberant praise of masters from the period. Students were swept away by the

74. *Epistola ad Walcherum* 26: "Cuius laboris tempus, quia nichil difficilius sub sole geritur vel quod magis operarii sui vires exhauriat, a sapientibus prefinitum est septuenne, nisi de cetero is qui preest auctoritate presideat, non labore." In Huygens ed., 30. For a translation of the letter of Goswin of Mainz to Walcherus, see Jaeger, *Envy*, 349–75.

75. Cf. Lèsne, 511–12.

76. See below, 52–60.

77. One example of many that could be cited: Gerbert claims to be a faithful follower of Cicero, Epist. 158: "in otio et negotio." In Weigle ed., 187. For other examples of Roman reminiscences in the conduct of this class, see my *Origins*, 117–18.

personal magnetism of the person suited for the service of the emperor and probably destined for it. It mattered little what they taught, as long as they spoke well and exuded qualities like *gravitas, dignitas,* and *elegantia.* Recall that Abelard, a teacher in a completely different stamp from the masters of the old learning, was astonished that great crowds of students lavished devotion and respect on the venerable Anselm of Laon (whose school offered instruction in *litterae et mores*.[78]) Anselm spoke beautifully, but his thought was obscure and he could not deal with the problems of philosophy he raised:

> He had a remarkable command of words, but their meaning was worthless and devoid of all sense. The fire he kindled filled his house with smoke but not with light.[79]

A description of the lecturing style of Berengar of Tours gives us an extraordinary glimpse of this aura of the great teacher. It was recorded by one of his enemies in the Eucharist Controversy, Guitmund of Aversa:

> Whatever bespoke grandeur and distinction, he affected. This man, almost wholly ignorant, claimed to be a doctor of the arts and persuaded people of it by virtue of his pompous posing, by elevating himself above others on a platform, by simulating the dignity of a teacher in his manner rather than by the substance of his teachings, by burying his head deep in his cowl, pretending to be in profound meditation, then finally, when the expectations of the listeners had been whetted by his long hesitation, giving forth in an extremely soft and plangent tone, which was effective in deceiving those who did not know better.[80]

78. Helmold, *Chronica Slavorum* 65, ll. 8–9: "[Vicelin went to Laon to study with Ralph, Anselm's brother, where] ad ea solum enisus est, que sobrio intellectui et moribus instruendis sufficerent." In J.M. Lappenberg, ed. MGH, SS 21 (Hannover: Hahn: 1868), 47.

79. Abelard, *Historia calamitatum: Texte critique avec une introduction,* J. Monfrin, ed. (Paris: Vrin, 1959), 68. English in text from *The Letters of Abelard and Heloise,* Betty Radice, trans. (Harmondsworth: Penguin, 1974), 62; *The Letter Collection of Peter Abelard and Heloise,* David Luscombe, ed.; Betty Radice, trans. (Oxford: Clarendon, 2013), 15-17.

80. Guitmund of Aversa, *De corporis et sanguinis Christi veritate in eucharistia*: "Cujusdam excellentiae gloriam venari, qualitercunque poterat, affectabat: factumque est ut pompatico incessu, sublimi prae caeteris suggestu, dignitatem magistri potius simulans quam rebus ostendens, profunda quoque inclusione inter cucullum, ac

Berengar is a figure very much on the border between the old learning and the new. His career took him between the cathedral schools and the courts of secular lords, his personal charisma won him many enthusiastic students (Hildebert of Lavardin among them), but his use of reason and analytic thought set him sharply apart from masters like Fulbert of Chartres and Meinhard of Bamberg. He had the style of the masters of the old learning, but he combined it with probing and exacting reason. We can put aside the criticism of Guitmund, monk and student of Lanfranc, that he was ignorant. These reproaches tell us more about the categories of judgment applicable to secular masters in the second half of the eleventh century than about the quality of Berengar's learning. Probably a great many teachers could substitute personal style, intellectually unrigorous moralizing, and grand self-presentation for scholarship, and students were more than willing to accept their education on those terms.

Wibald of Stablo complains in the mid-twelfth century that students defend the sayings of their masters not because they are true, but because they love the men who pronounce them, and he sees one school set against another not in the pursuit of truth through reason but "in hate or love of individual teachers."[81] The teacher's main task, or one of them, was the cultivation of the self, of character, virtue, and eloquence in both teacher and students. This is the essence of *cultus virtutum*. Knowledge, scholarship, and rational analysis were somewhat beside the point, perhaps even dubious products of *curiositas* and the urge to novelties.

---

simulatione longae meditationis, et vix tandem satis desideratae diu vocis lentissimo quodam quasi plangore incautos decipiens, doctorem sese artium pene inscius profiteretur." In PL 149:1428B.

81. Epist. 167: "Discipuli magistrorum sentencias tuentur, non quia verae sunt, set quod auctores amant; scola adversus scolam debachatur, odio vel amore magistrorum." In Jaffé ed., 277; Hartmann, Zatschek and Reuter ed., 1:291. Cf. William of Conches' observation that students should love their teachers more than their parents: *Philosophia mundi* 4.30; in G. Maurach, ed. (Pretoria: University of South Africa, 1980), 114–15; 4.38, in PL 172:100A–B. See below, n. 66 for Abelard's statement that students should not be duped by love of their teachers into believing that they make sense.

One may well think that then as now the cult of personal manners was a substitute for genius and a sign of the mediocrity of the age. Certainly, to read what masters of the old learning did write cautions against thinking them a lot of mute inglorious Miltons. Adalbold of Utrecht's early eleventh-century commentary on Boethius' "O, qui perpetua" is wholly unoriginal. Onulf of Speyer's *Colores rhetorici* is witty and amusing, but one has the feeling that its author could have spun it out at great length with the intensity and incisiveness of table talk, requiring no particular learning or intellectual rigor. Anselm of Besate's *Rhetorimachia* shows much eccentricity and little genius.[82] Can the explanation of personal greatness possibly cover all the sins of pedantry and self-congratulation this author commits? Henry III took Anselm into the royal chapel, supposedly as a reward for the *Rhetorimachia* (though we have only Anselm's word on it). Let us hope that the emperor did it because his judgment was numbed by the spell of Anselm's personality. But a fair number of men in Anselm's position and with his ambitions were mute and glorious, whatever the quality of the unwritten works slumbering somewhere in their minds. The problem for us in the twenty-first century is to get from the muteness to the glory. Silence means obscurity, and it is a pall over the great and mediocre alike.

THE CIVIL LIFE AS PRODUCTIVITY: DISCIPLINA VIVENDI

The forum in which learning, intellect, and brilliance were to be expressed was the active life: public service, not philosophical tracts. A cleric of Worms wrote a letter to his bishop, Azecho of Worms, around 1030, in which he sets forth an ideal of public administration as the fulfillment of philosophy:

> Divine providence, in foreseeing the necessity of installing you as the governor of our republic, has placed you at the apex of pastoral care in order that you may now translate into acts of public administration those things you have learned in your private studies. The schoolmistress of all virtues [Philosophy] has taken up her abode in you,

[82]. Anselm von Besate, *Rhetorimachia*, Karl Manitius, ed., MGH, *Quellen zur Geistesgeschichte des Mittelalters* 2 (Weimar: Böhlau, 1958), 95–189.

so that in all your undertakings you may follow in her footsteps.[83]

The letter was a job application, and the applicant was not only wheedling but also putting forward his credentials by showing his mastery of Boethius and of the ideal of the learned administrator whose acts reveal the influence of philosophy. Public governance as a form of philosophy: it is a topic that would lead us back to Roman antiquity and into the heart of medieval humanism. Philosophy in the service of the *res publica* is a much cultivated educational and political ideal, one that required the alliance of schools with the apparatus of government.[84] It is a major theme of the important letter collection, the *Regensburger rhetorischen Briefe*.[85] The letters are a fictionalized, or at least partly fictionalized exchange between a cleric, in the midst of administrative duties, corresponding with friends. He asks them for advice and guidance in the trials and difficulties of public life.

The source of advice — consolation, and ministerial wisdom to which the writers regularly turn in addressing the problems raised — is, generally stated, philosophy, more specifically Cicero's *Tusculan Disputations*. The latter is a work of major importance for the cathedral schools of the eleventh century. Meinhard of Bamberg had termed it the most important work of philosophy from Roman

83. *Ältere Wormser Briefsammlung* 52: "Hinc divina providentia, cum te nostre rei publice regende necessarium previdisset, ad pastoralis cure apicem perduxit, ut quod inter secreta otia didiceras, in actum publice administrationis transferres. Magistra itaque Virtutum in te elegit sedem, ut in cunctis actibus tuis illius vestigia sequi videaris." In Bulst ed., 89. Cf. Boethius, 1.4.7: "Quod a te inter secreta otia didiceram, transferre in actu publicae administrationis optavi." Many texts on the combining of philosophy and public life in the *Regensburger rhetorischen Briefe*, e.g., 1, quoting Cicero, *Tusculan Disputations* 5.2.5: "O vite dux philosophia, o virtutis indagatrix... tu inventrix legum, tu magistra morum et discipline fuisti." In J.E. King, ed. and trans. (Cambridge, MA: Harvard University Press, 1971), 275; 22, King ed., 348–49.

84. On the combining of the intellectual and civil life in England, see Southern, "England's Place," 174–75; and Beryl Smalley, *The Becket Controversy and the Schools* (Oxford: Blackwell, 1973).

85. *Die Regensburger Rhetorischen Briefe*, Norbert Fickermann, ed., in *Briefsammlungen der Zeit Heinrichs IV*. The dating is complicated: last decades of the eleventh century. See Fickermann, ed., 268-73.

antiquity.⁸⁶ Its appeal lay in its combining of asceticism and rejection of the world with a stoically courageous affirmation of state service: persist, suffer through all the tribulations of the active life, and make the cult of virtues — identified with philosophy — into your guide. That is the thrust of the *Tusculan Disputations*, and the author of the letters makes it into his theme.

The appeal of this attitude to worldly clergy in the German empire in the second half of the eleventh century should be evident: torn between the parties in the Investiture Controversy, they could find in Cicero's work a rule of life, a philosophy that lent dignity to administrative service while at the same time casting serious doubt on it, that could idealize imperial administrators while placing the emperor in the role of Nero, Herod, and Nebuchadnezzar,⁸⁷ that reconciled *contemptus mundi* with *servitium rei publicae*. In one of the most remarkable of these letters, the author sets the trials of public life parallel with the sufferings of the martyrs and of Christ and makes the courageous facing of those trials into an act of Christian *fortitudo*. Here is a passage that shows especially clearly the odd mingling of Christian and Roman heroism typical for this writer:

> He himself [Christ] once fought for us. Should we now refuse to enter the field of battle for his sake? And would we, seeing his wounds, not suffer tribulations for his sake, having won salvation through the hate he faced? Spartan boys face tortures inflicted on them without crying out. Lacedaemonian youths in competitive fighting suffer blows and kicks and even bites but would sooner suffer death itself than admit defeat.⁸⁸

I doubt that the sufferings of Christ have ever before or since been set parallel to the training of Spartan/Lacedaemonian boys. But it shows us a central concern of this author: to legitimize and sweeten a cleric's service to the state by appeal to ancient Greek and Roman models. But our point of departure was the combining of philosophy and the active life. The *Regensburger rhetorischen Briefe* find in the

---

86. *Weitere Briefe Meinhards*, Epist. 1 (=M 1): "Unde hortor, ut Tusculanis tuis plurimus insideas, quibus Latina philosophia Cicerone parente nichil illustrius edidit." In Erdmann ed., 193.
87. *Regensburger Rhetorischen Briefe* 9; Fickermann ed., 314.
88. *Regensburger Rhetorischen Briefe* 9; Fickermann ed., 319.

Tusculan Disputations a Roman model for this combination, one that must have had a deep resonance in the schools and courts of eleventh-century Europe, at least among its administrative/intellectual class.

Cicero observed in that work that philosophy was a fairly new discipline in the Rome of his time, and he recognized the superiority of the Greeks in the writing of it. But by way of explaining this to the advantage of his compatriots, he says that if the early Romans did not write works of philosophy, it was because they were so taken up with the great tasks of running the state, and they preferred to practice "that most bountiful of disciplines, the discipline of living well" *(bene vivendi disciplina)*. They pursued this more in their lives than in their writings: "*Vita magis quam litteris persecuti sunt.*"[89] It is difficult to do justice in English to the phrase *disciplina vivendi*, and one takes recourse to spelling out its implications. It makes the conduct of public life into a form of philosophical discourse, a program of studies, a textbook. Wibald of Stablo was speaking within this trope when he urged Balderich of Trier to turn his mere presence into a discipline.[90] The example of the Roman orator/public servant who turns public life into a philosophical discipline gave allure to this substitute form of productivity: life itself could become a work of philosophy, a composition analogous to an oration or to a musical composition. This work of art, the well-composed person, was a major contribution of the eleventh century to "philosophy"[91] and to culture. It is the best answer to the question how that age could have been mute and glorious at the same time.

CURIALES AND OTHER "NEW MEN"

By its very nature, then, the product of *cultus virtutum* is lost to recovery: it is the living administrator functioning at court, expressing philosophy through acts of governing. But we can recover some literary representations of this ideal type in portraits of bishops, in descriptions of an idealized education and of particular virtues

---

89. CTD 4.3.5–6. Cf. *Regensburger rhetorischen Briefe* 1, Fickermann ed., 275; 11, Fickermann ed., 329; 12, Fickermann ed., 331–32; 13, Fickermann ed., 333; 16, Fickermann ed., 336; 22, Fickermann ed., 348.

90. See above, n. 72. Hartmann et al., *Das Briefbuch,* 1:110.

91. See below, chapter 2, passim.

within that education. The courtier and bishop embodied the ideals of a program of education in *mores* and *ethica*. *Cultus virtutum* was a preparation for those offices, and any study of qualifications for court service and the bishopric that concentrates on the conventional school subjects — letters and the liberal arts — is bound to end in uncertainty on the role of education in an ecclesiastical career. The school subjects provided the educational basis for one's advancement only in conjunction with the study of virtue. Richard of St. Victor wrote a letter to Robert of Hereford congratulating him on his promotion from schoolmaster to bishop:

> ...all your students were filled with joyful hope [at the news of your promotion], and the entire school was heartened and roused to the love of letters and the cultivation of virtue [*cultus virtutum*] through the example of your efforts and your success.[92]

Robert's promotion to the bishopric holds out hope to his and other students that the study of *litterae et mores, cultus virtutum*, is rewarded by high office, and they redouble their efforts at those school subjects in the hope of repeating his success.

The content of that program of studies registers in the idealized portraits of those pursuing that education and those ambitions. Such portraits represent an ideal of human dignity and greatness indebted — for its articulation — first and foremost to Roman antiquity, Cicero's *De oratore, Tusculan Disputations*, and *De officiis*, and Quintilian's *Institutes of Oratory*. The formation of the courtier and bishop in the eleventh and twelfth centuries was the task of the old learning. But I stress that this type, the ideal educated bishop, the courtier bishop, was in its origins a product of shaping ideas adapted to political and social circumstances. Those circumstances, created by Ottonian ideas of govenance, favored the rediscovery and revival of those ideas. An office in the Ottonian imperial church required a public servant/orator/administrator to fill it, and from that office

---

92. Epist. 1: "Magnam de promotione vestra concepit Ecclesia nostra laetitiam, et spe non modica hilarati sunt auditores vestri, tum universi scholares animati ad amorem litterarum, et cultum virtutum, vestri laboris et successus exemplo." In PL 196:1225A. On the connection between studies and promotion to the bishopric, see Zielinski, 110–11.

and its requirements[93] an educational program, the cultivation of virtues in the old learning, took its major impetus.

This program, as a survival from antiquity, had never completely died out in the earlier Middle Ages. The texts that transmitted it were a firm part of medieval education.[94] But it rose and fell in prominence, served a variety of educational goals, and maintained through all vicissitudes a fairly low profile until the end of the tenth century. Here suddenly it made itself felt distinctly — no longer just in tracts on education like Alcuin's but in the biographies of those who had received an administrator's education, imperial bishops.

I have talked elsewhere about this figure and the personal qualities requisite to this office, and I will not repeat here more than is necessary to lay the foundation for reading a few portraits. In the courtier bishop the German empire under the Ottos created a figure of great political and cultural significance. Important institutional changes took place through him and around him, the most immediate of which was the transformation of the court chapel and the cathedral schools into training grounds for future imperial bishops. This change laid the institutional groundwork for the career to which I referred earlier: from student to teacher to courtier to bishop. The position had certain personal requirements, and one of them was charisma.

There are many tales of the awe-inspiring presence of the "great man" from the episcopal milieu. William of Malmesbury tells of a bishop, the object of a murder attempt, who turns and faces his assailants, and the splendor of his presence is so dazzling to them that they drop their knives and flee. The story places us in the atmosphere of the saint's life, of the

---

93. See Jaeger, "The Courtier Bishop in *Vitae* from the Tenth to the Twelfth Century," *Speculum* 58 (1983): 291–325.

94. Alcuin speaks the language of the old learning clearly. His *Dialogus de rhetorica et virtutibus* (the connection of rhetoric and virtue already is indicative) is written for the person "qui...civiles cupiat cognoscere mores" (PL 101:919), and it ends with the master urging the pupil (Charlemagne), "Disce, precor, juvenis, motus, moresque venustos" (PL 101:950). On the civil/ethical cast of ancient and early Christian education generally, see Joseph McCarthy, "Clement of Alexandria and the Foundation of Christian Educational Theory," *History of Education Society Bulletin* 7 (1971): 11–18; McCarthy, *Humanistic Emphases in the Educational Thought of Vincent of Beauvais* (Leiden: Brill, 1976), 58–59.

miraculous, but this bishop performs a humanist miracle. He is saved by his personal qualities, by the magical spell cast by his presence, not by divine intervention.⁹⁵ A bishop had to be tall, handsome, and impressive in appearance: *"statura procerus, vultu venerandus"* are common terms of praise; *splendor* or *nitor personae* sums them up. Bishop Gunther of Bamberg (mid-eleventh century, Meinhard's bishop) was said to be so beautiful that on his crusade in Jerusalem crowds of locals gathered in front of a church he was in and prevented him from leaving, so eager were they to get a look at his fabled beauty.⁹⁶

An important ideal of this figure is borne by the phrase, "the greater we are," or "the higher we are set above other men, the more we should bear ourselves as their inferiors." It is an ideal of aristocratic deference, not Christian self-denial. The phrase is borrowed from Cicero and quoted frequently.⁹⁷ Other qualities often praised are gentleness (*mansuetudo*), affability, and popularity, if I may put it that way — being all things to all, making oneself loved of all. Particularly important is a quality called "beauty of manners" and borne by a number of terms: *elegantia morum, venustas morum, gratia morum, pulchritudo morum*. We find out-and-out reference to this virtue as a qualification for royal service and the bishopric. Meinwerk of Paderborn is said to have been judged suited for service at the court of Otto III because of the elegance of his manners.⁹⁸ Gerald of Wales complained that his Welsh nationality prevented him from receiving a bishopric from Henry II, even though he had served the king loyally and had shown the requisite learning and "grace of manners," here evidently regarded as a prerequisite for advancement from the royal court.⁹⁹ This quality forms a bridge between the teachings of

95. *De gestis pontificum Anglorum* 1.6; N.E. Hamilton, ed., Rolls Series 52 (1870), 14.
96. Cf. "Courtier Bishop," 298–99; and below, 163–65.
97. *De officiis* 1.26: "...quanto superiores simus, tanto nos geramus summissius." See *Origins*, 35–36.
98. *Das Leben des Bischofs Meinwerk von Paderborn* 59: "Meinwercus autem, regia stirpe genitus, regio obsequio morum elegantia idoneus adiudicatur evocatusque ad palatium regius capellanus efficitur." In Franz Tenckhoff, ed., MGH, SSR 59 (Hannover: Hahn, 1921), 7.
99. Gerald of Wales, *De principis instructione liber*, praef. 1: "Si quid enim gratiae morum gravitas, si quid litterae, si quid industria conferre potuit, totum id

the schools and the entrance into the service of the king or bishop. "Beauty of manners" is a subject of the study of *mores*, and at the same time a qualification for entry into the court and episcopacy.

The final quality I will mention here is one of overriding importance, though I know no name for it from the sources other than *decor*: an educated person shows the composition and harmony of their inner world by the grace, charm, poise, courtesy, and urbanity of their outward bearing, by their gait, table manners, speech, the motions of the body and limbs. Outward elegance of bearing is taken as a manifestation of *compositio morum*.[100] It might be appropriate

---

suspectum, totum infestum, totum exosum Gualliae nomen ademit." In George F. Warner, ed., Rolls Series 21.8 (London: Longman, 1891), lviii. We recognize in this triad of frustrated qualities the pair "letters and manners."

100. A history of this virtue from Cicero (who insists that outer *decorum* can never be present without inner *honestas*, nor *honestas* without *decorum*) to Shakespeare (whose Ophelia asks Hamlet, "Could beauty, my lord, have better commerce than with honesty?") would be a rewarding task. Here are a few references for our period. Ambrose, *De officiis ministrorum*, echoes Cicero in maintaining that physical beauty is a decoration to inner virtue (PL 16:48B). Poeta Saxo (888), *Annales* 5, ll. 211–20: "Interius radix operum latet exteriorum, / Mens moresque viri facta palam generant: / Qui solet esse domi constans prudensque decenter, / Perficit is crebro facta decora foris; / Intra se vitiis dominans rationeque pollens / Exteriora sibi nulla nocere sinit… / At cui mens torpet, mores neque corrigit in se, / Illum iure manet dedecus exterius." In MGH, *Poetae*, 4.1:60. Bern of Reichenau, *Vita S. Udalrici*: "…in corporis motu, gestu, incessu, foris ostendere [incipiebat], qualis habitus formaretur intus in mente." In PL 142:1186B. *Decretum* of Leo IX on the synod of Mainz (1049): "[Confirming Hugo as archbishop of Besançon, who deserves the splendid trappings of office] ut qui pollet meritorum laudabili dignitate, tam in virtutum scientia quam in morum honestate, polleat etiam ornamentorum pulchritudine in omni archiepiscopalis culminis plenitudine, semper meminerit in exteriore decore interiorem decorem procurare…." In PL 143:623D. *Vita Adalardi* 39 (1055): [though he wore vile clothes] "…non egebat aliqua corporis compositione, nihil enim sibi deerat pulchritudinis humanae, nihil etiam interioris animae." In PL 147:1059. Conrad of Hirsau, *Dialogus de mundi contemptu vel amore*: [in a discussion of the proper relation between *habitus* and *animus*] "…nihil vero prodesse cultum exteriorem virtutum gressus mentientem…iunge utrumque, et habitum et animum, et summa voti perfectionis calculo constabit." In R. Bultot, ed., *Analecta Mediaevalia Namurcensia* 19 (Louvain: Nauwelaerts, 1966), 62–63.

CHAPTER I ✷ CATHEDRAL SCHOOLS

to mention the resonance between this educational ideal and the Hellenic *kalos kai agathos*, as long as we insist that we are not dealing with a topos-like survival from an earlier culture where the ideal once was alive. It was alive in the eleventh century, and perhaps the best proof of its vitality is in a series of portraits to which we now turn.

✷

Meinhard of Bamberg writes to a friend and former student, a cleric of high nobility, who is moving to Cologne, no doubt to take up a position at the episcopal court, and who will be exposed to the dangers and temptations of that city.[101] Meinhard warns him of a war to be waged there over his soul. Two courts will fight to gain his services, to make him a member of their retinue. The one is the noble court of virtues, the other the ignoble court of vices. The court of virtues summons him as its special favorite and places the entire business of the court in his hands because of the perfection of his manners (*specimen morum*) and the sharpness of his mind (again, letters and manners, or intellect and manners as the prerequisite to court service). The other court calls to him with the allure of its "slippery, silky bodies" and tries to make him into a citizen of the second Babylon, Cologne. The allegory is a sort of psychomachia, as

---

Hugh of St. Victor, *De institutione novitiorum*: "...disciplina...est membrorum omnium motus ordinatus et dispositio decens in omni habitu et actione.... Disciplina est...frenum lasciviae, elationis jugum, vinculum iracundiae, quae domat intemperantiam, levitatem ligat et omnes inordinatos motus mentis atque illicitos appetitus suffocat. Sicut enim de inconstantia mentis nascitur inordinata motio corporis, ita quoque dum corpus per disciplinam stringitur, animus ad constantiam solidatur.... Integritas vero virtutis est, quando per internam mentis custodiam ordinate reguntur membra corporis.... Liganda ergo sunt foris per disciplinam membra corporis, ut intrinsecus solidetur status mentis." In PL 176:935B–D. See also Thomasin von Zirclaere, *Der Wälsche Gast*, ll. 912–13: "Der lîp wandelt sich nâch dem muot. / des lîbes gebaerde uns dicke bescheit, / hât ein man Lieb ode leit." In Heinrich Rückert, ed., *Deutsche Nationalliteratur* 30 (Berlin: de Gruyter, 1965), 25. See some comments on the subject in my *Origins*, 147–49.

101. *Weitere Briefe Meinhards* 1, *Briefsammlungen* M 1, Erdmann ed., 192–93. According to Erdmann, the receiver, called only "G.", was a future archbishop of Cologne on his way to be groomed for the office. See *Studien zur Briefliteratur*, 282.

Ernst Robert Curtius suggested.[102] But it is fabricated from the real situation of the competition between courts for a gifted courtier.[103] Meinhard now urges him to arm himself for this battle with the same virtues his father had possessed, whom he describes as

> a man instructed in every kind of virtue, a man who enjoyed to an astonishing degree all the charm and grace of humanity, qualities visible far and wide not only in his dazzling blaze of manners [*flagrantia morum*] but also in the bright good humor that shone most graciously from his eyes.[104]

Presumably humanity, charm and grace, dazzling manners, and gracious good humor are results of that instruction in the virtues that his father had received (*"omni genere virtutis instructus"*). The virtues are neo-classical, Ciceronian, and especially striking is Meinhard's use of *"humanitas"* in a context that shows that he understood the Ciceronian sense of the word very well.[105] It is a quality accompanied by charm and grace and one that is visible not only in his conduct and bearing but also in the joviality and charm of his facial expression. His inward qualities, a virtuous and humane disposition, shine forth outwardly like a blazing fire. We must remind ourselves that we are at a German cathedral of the eleventh century, not an Italian court of the sixteenth. It is also worth noting for our purpose that these virtues are placed exactly in the context of public life: they are what the cleric and future bishop requires to assert himself and survive in the conflicts of court life, and it is just at this point in his letter

---

102. Privately to Erdmann. See *Studien,* 282.

103. On the competition for "the sought-after" men [*viri expetibiles*]. *Origins,* 52.

104. M 1: "Est enim vir ille omni genere virtutis instructus, omni lepore humanitatis mirifice conditus, que in eo non solum flagrantia morum latissime redolet, sed ex ipsa oculorum hilaritate gratiosissime renidet. Atque sic in te animi ornamenta redundent, ut illa ocularis gratia relucet." In Erdmann ed., 193.

105. Other occurrences of *humanitas:* Weitere Briefe Meinhards 74, Erdmann ed., 122; 75, Erdmann ed., 123; 80, Erdmann ed., 130; 14, Erdmann ed., 206; 21, Erdmann ed., 216; 24, Erdmann ed., 222. Erdmann has a few comments on Meinhard's classicism in *Studien,* 61, 104–5. On *humanitas* in the Middle Ages, see Rolf Sprandel, *Ivo von Chartres und seine Stellung in der Kirchen Geschichte* (Stuttgart: Hiersemann, 1962), 9–31; and von Moos, *Hildebert von Lavardin,* 3–4, 148–49, 276–77.

that Meinhard recommends to the young man Cicero's *Tusculan Disputations*, "than which Latin philosophy has produced nothing more illustrious." This teacher of *mores* knew perfectly well that that philosophy was vital to one's entering court service.

The description is not isolated. From the eleventh century on we find "great men" said to embody virtues like these: beauty of soul, composition of manners, inner qualities that express themselves outwardly in the good-humored appearance, the graceful gait and elegant bearing of the courtier/public servant. Otto of Bamberg (d.1139) is praised by one of his biographers for manifesting his elegant breeding and his inner harmony in each and every act of the outer man, in his table manners, his speech, gestures, and dress.[106] By the twelfth century the ideal appears to have permeated the milieu of the worldly clergy in Germany, France, and England. One of the most impressive statements of it comes from Bernard of Clairvaux, certainly not the typical spokesman for external elegance, but here one of the most eloquent. He explains the line from Psalm 92, "The lord desireth your beauty," which he takes to mean beauty of soul [*decor animae*]:

> What then is beauty of the soul? Is it perhaps that quality we call ethical goodness [*honestum*]?... But to understand this quality we must observe a man's outward bearing.... The beauty of actions is visible testimony to the state of the conscience.... But when the luminosity of this beauty fills the inner depths of the heart, it overflows and surges outward. Then the body, the very image of the mind, catches up this light glowing and bursting forth like the rays of the sun. All its senses and all its members are suffused with it, until its glow is seen in every act, in speech, in appearance, in the way of walking and laughing.... When the motions, the gestures and the habits of the body and the senses show forth their gravity, purity, modesty...then beauty of the soul becomes outwardly visible.[107]

106. See *Origins*, 128–29.

107. *Super Cant. Sermo* 85.10–11: "In quo ergo animae decor? An forte in eo quod honestum dicitur?... De honesto autem exterior interrogetur conversatio.... Siquidem claritas eius testimonium conscientiae.... Cum autem decoris huius claritas abundantius intima cordis repleverit, prodeat foras necesse est.... Porro effulgentem et veluti quibusdam suis radiis erumpentem mentis simulacrum corpus excipit, et diffundit per membra et sensus, quatenus omnis inde reluceat

Bernard's description has much in common with Meinhard's. Both are using a basically Ciceronian ethical vocabulary. Both employ the image of the powerful light breaking forth from within to express the relation of inner virtue to outward grace. We see the sign of the monastic writer in Bernard's indication that "beautiful" bearing manifests not the quality Meinhard had called *lepor humanitatis* but rather a pure conscience. But we are still in a conceptual environment where behavior — speech, gesture, dress, gait — is estheticised and regarded as a visible manifestation of inward beauty and harmony.[108]

Alan of Lille's *Anticlaudianus* is a poetic summa of the old learning. At the same time, it is the highpoint of twelfth-century humanism and in many ways exemplifies the renaissance spirit of the period. Much of the work, but particularly Alan's portrait of the "new human," must be read against the background of *cultus virtutum*. Late in the poem the "new human" is equipped by a parade of allegorical virtues for his battle with the vices.[109] First comes Bounteousness *(copia)*, then Favor and Fame, then Youth and Laughter. Chastity makes him rival the patriarch Joseph. Modesty follows. She "composes" the whole man according to the law of *moderamen*, the golden mean ("*Totum componit hominem*"). She moderates his action, measures his speech and his silence, weighs his gestures, judges his bearing, and restrains his senses. She sets the tilt of his head in a middle position, not too far up towards the heavens to show scorn of the human world, nor too far down to sink into the material. Constancy comes next. She arranges his gestures and his gait, his hairdo and the style of his dress. Next comes Reason, who gives him good sense for making judgments in practical affairs, prevents him from taking any course of action hastily, teaches him to prepare all undertakings carefully, to make few

---

actio, sermo, aspectus, incessus, risus.... Horum et aliorum profecto artuum sensuumque motus, gestus et usus cum apparerit serius, purus, modestus... pulchritudo animae palam erit...." In *Sancti Bernardi Opera* 2, Jean Leclerq, et al., ed. (Rome: Editiones Cistercienses, 1958), 314.

108. Consistently *gestus, habitus, gressus* or *incessus, motus corporis, locutio* or *sermo, cibus,* and *potus* are seen as the measurement of inner virtue. These and their relation to virtue are the subject of the last chapters of Hugh of St. Victor, *De institutione novitiorum*.

109. *Anticlaudianus*, 7.74–82, Wetherbee ed., 436.

promises and give many gifts wisely. *Honestas* then gives him love of his fellows while still preserving the integrity of his inner life.

A series of recent studies has shown that the court and the civil duties of the court administrator are the context in which this description is to be located.[110] Michael Wilks calls the *Anticlaudianus* "a species of court poetry," and locates it approximately in the genre of education of princes. This seems to me accurate for one important aspect of the work, though I doubt that Alan intended a specific reference to Philip Augustus and a prediction of his victory over the Plantagenets, as Wilks and Linda Marshall argue.[111] The virtues of Alan's "new human" are a summing up of the moral instruction of the old learning. As a preparation for court life, it applied to courtiers no less than to kings. It is a preparation through civil virtues for battle against civil vices.

The gifts of Reason associate the passage especially clearly with *ethica* and *practica* and its products, the perfect public servant or courtier. Reason's gifts have to do with governing and administering, not with analysis, thought, argumentation. *Ratio* here is a virtue of the active life. It is that principle by which, according to the traditions of the cathedral schools, both the cosmos ("*O, qui perpetua mundum ratione gubernas...*") and the composed human being were governed. It is also the virtue by which individuals of well composed *mores* governed the state. The concept experienced a fundamental transformation from the civil to the intellectual realm at the hands of the early scholastics.[112] *Ratio*, in the passage just discussed, comes into effect in administrative, not intellectual, activity. None of the virtues of this parade are abstract inner qualities, cloistered, or scholastic virtues. All of their gifts aim at external perfection. What *constancia* gives is not loyalty, not faith to oaths and vows, not steadfastness, but

110. Linda Marshall, "The Identity of the 'New Man' in the 'Antidaudianus' of Alan of Lille," *Viator* 10 (1979): 77–94; Michael Wilks, "Alan of Lille and the New Man," *Studies in Church History* 14 (1977): 137–57. Also of interest is Patrick G. Walsh, "Alan of Lille as a Renaissance Figure," *Studies in Church History* 14 (1977): 117–35.

111. John W. Baldwin is also sceptical about this connection. See *The Government of Philip Augustus: Foundations of Royal Power in the Middle Ages* (Berkeley: University of California Press, 1986), 571.

112. Cf. Grabmann, *Geschichte*, 1:272–336.

an elegant gait, measured gestures, correct clothes and hairdo. The virtues do not bestow the inner qualities they govern: rather they are themselves those inner qualities, and what they bestow are the external signs of their presence. The logic at work is that of virtues made visible, beauty or harmony of soul shining forth from every action down to dress, personal grooming, and table manners.

My purpose here and throughout this section in juxtaposing texts from the eleventh and twelfth centuries, from Germany and France, was of course to suggest lines of development, perhaps even lines of dependency. The virtues of Bernard's *decor animae* and of Alan's "new human" are anticipated in the values embodied by German courtier bishops. The perfect, elegant, humane gentleman/courtier, who receives his armor from civil virtues does battle with civil vices and shows outwardly the beauty within, occurs in Meinhard's letter from the mid-eleventh century. What these common features suggest is that the fates of the old learning and twelfth-century humanism were linked, that the one was the bearer and transmitter of the other, and the institutional basis of this humanism was the cathedral school in its relation to court service. The common features of these portraits also teach us to regard the humanism of the eleventh and twelfth centuries as a more-or-less coherent phenomenon. Meinhard and Alan produced similar portraits of idealized future administrators because they taught programs of *ethica* that were not essentially different in either content or purpose.

OLD LEARNING VS NEW

Gradually in the second half of the eleventh century and precipitously in the first half of the twelfth, the masters of the old learning became threatened by a new kind of teacher offering a new kind of studies: the disputatious philosopher-scholar-teacher in the stamp of Peter Abelard. Both Italy and the north apparently bred this type, because in reports from the monastic as well as the cathedral communities we see the schools teeming with cavillers whose breasts swell with pride in their knowledge and who even contradict and show up their own teachers. Some early examples of teacher-insulting show the weakening of magisterial authority. In observing clashes between masters and bright, irreverent students we locate a fundamental characteristic of the old learning and a fundamental weakness.

The saintly Wolfgang of Regensburg, as a student at Würzburg in the mid-tenth century, had commented so astutely on Martianus Capella that his erudition became an affront to his teacher, Stefan of Novara, that Italian master called to the north by Otto the Great.[113] Stung to anger and threatened by the loss of his students, Stefan undertook to stifle Wolfgang's further progress. But the inner flame of divine erudition only burned the more brightly for the attempt to snuff it out, "as a fire flares when fanned by blasts of wind." Still, the future saint might have saved himself a lot of trouble by not giving offense at all, especially to this sensitive foreigner. Clearly some etiquette was violated here when Wolfgang complied with the request of his fellow students for a commentary on Martianus that was superior to that of their master. The incident brings us close to the circumstances in which the young Abelard outdid Anselm of Laon in explaining biblical texts.

Abelard's intellectual arrogance is foreshadowed also in the insult dealt to the clergy of Limoges by a Lombard grammarian, Benedict of Chiusa, who visited Limoges in 1028 and disputed the claim that the local patron, St. Martial, was an apostle. Our source, Ademar of Chabannes, tells the story by way of holding this pompous windbag up to ridicule. He quotes a long speech that he attributes to Benedict. In it, the latter boasts of his knowledge of grammar, claims that all of Aquitaine and most of France are ignorant of this art, that after nine years of study his own wisdom is so perfect no one under the sun can match him.[114]

The monks of St. Denis a century later would undoubtedly have liked to place such discrediting speeches in the mouth of Peter Abelard, whom, out of the arrogance of his learning, they took to be diminishing the authority of their patron.[115] It may be that Benedict

113. Otloh of St. Emmeram, *Vita Wolfkangi* 4–5, MGH, SS 4:528. In view of the fact that Stefan's countryman Gunzo had his grammar corrected by the monks of St. Gall, one wonders whether Italian masters were fair game in the North. They certainly were sensitive to contradiction.

114. *Epistola de S. Martiali*, PL 141:107–8. See Herbert E.J. Cowdrey, "Anselm of Besate and Some North-Italian Masters of the Eleventh Century," *Journal of Ecclesiastical History* 23 (1972): 115–24, at 119.

115. Cf. *Historia calamitatum*, 90, ll. 963–64.

and Abelard were entirely right in disputing the beliefs of the local monks. The validity of the claims against those beliefs, the historical truths at stake, did not matter; reasoning and proof, when pitted against venerable authority, textual or personal, were pernicious instruments of pride that invited discrediting and were seen as deserving it. But gradually in the course of the later eleventh century, knowledge, reasoning, success in disputation and in proof become ends in themselves. Grave and dignified orations were no longer the object of intellectual effort but definitions and systematizing, frameworks of argumentation, and harmonizing of inconsistencies.

The contest between old and new learning is as much a part of twelfth-century intellectual life as is the clash between the new learning and monastic orthodoxy, though the latter has commanded much more interest from historians. In many ways the old learning and monasticism were allies in opposition to the new. They had, it is true, a traditional antagonistic relationship in the eleventh century (polemics of monks against worldly professors) but at the same time an easy reciprocal relationship (many professors converted). The rise of the new learning brought their common interests and characteristics into clear focus. Representatives of both ganged up on Berengar of Tours and Peter Abelard. The intellectual world of the monasteries had much in common with that of the schools. Philosophical Realism was fundamental to both. The Eucharist Controversy showed this in the late eleventh century, the dispute on universals in the early twelfth. Also common to both was authority as the basis of argumentation and of instruction. The basic intellectual reorientation of the period has long been regarded, quite rightly I believe, as the clash between reason and authority. But some understanding of the old learning helps us to see the nature of authority in a clearer light. It does not only reside in texts and traditions. It is also a human quality, one of considerable importance both as an instrument and a goal of pedagogy.

A letter of Adelman of Liège to Berengar of Tours allows us to see this form of authority at work in the Eucharist Controversy. The letter is a trenchant rejection of Berengar's position on the divine presence in the Sacrament, but it is written in a tone of loving correction from one former student of Fulbert to another. The body of the letter is a dossier of arguments against reasoning, novelties, and heresy. Of interest to us is its introduction. Adelman evokes at length the figure of Fulbert of Chartres, their former master, and in doing so he recreates vividly and emotionally the atmosphere of the old learning:

> I have called you my fellow suckling and foster brother in memory of that sweetest and most pleasant of times we spent together, you a mere youth, I somewhat older, at the Academy of Chartres under our venerable Socrates. We have more cause to glory in the common life of studies [*convictus*] shared with him than had Plato, who gave thanks to nature for bringing him forth as a man rather than as an animal in the days when Socrates was teaching.[116]

Berengar and Adelman have experienced (*experti sumus*) the more saintly life and sound doctrine of Fulbert, and now can hope to benefit from his prayers in heaven, since the regard and Christlike charity in which he held them, as in a maternal womb, still live on. Indeed his death has only intensified them. Fulbert watches them from heaven and calls to them with his vows and silent prayers to follow him,

> entreating us through all those intimate evening colloquies he used to hold with us in the little garden next to the chapel in the city...and beseeching us, by the tears that broke forth and interrupted his lecture whenever the force of divine ardor overflowed within him, to hasten thither with all diligence, treading in a straight path the royal road, adhering with utmost observance to the footsteps of the holy fathers, lest we should be detoured, turning aside into some new and false path and succumbing to the snares of scandal....[117]

116. Ll. 3–8: "Conlactaneum te meum vocavi propter dulcissimum illud contubernium, quod tecum adolescentulo, ipse ego maiusculus, in achademia Carnotensi sub nostro illo venerabili Socrate iocundissime duxi, cuius de convictu gloriari nobis dignius licet quam gloriabatur Plato, gratias agens naturae eo, quod in diebus Socratis sui hominem se et non pecudem peperisset." In Robert B.C. Huygens ed., "Textes latins du XIe au XIIIe siècle," *Studi Medievali*, ser., 3.8 (1967): 476–89, at 476.

117. Adelman "Textes latins," ll. 14–21: "...invitat ad se votis et tacitis precibus, obtestans per secreta illa et vespertina colloquia, quae nobiscum in hortulo iuxta capellam de Civitate illa...sepius habebat, et obsecrans per lacrimas, quas, interdum in medio sermone prorumpens, exundante sancti ardoris impetu emanabat, ut illuc omni studio properemus, viam regiam directim gradientes, sanctorum patrum

In other words, Adelman conjures him by the person of their former teacher. If Berengar holds the memory of Fulbert dear, he will not deviate from the path of the fathers. These are arguments from authority, the personal authority of the "great man." He tries to dissuade Berengar from "false," at least deviant, opinions by the force and authority of Fulbert's personality by pulling him back into the orbit of the master's charisma. The nostalgia of the scene he paints — Fulbert weeping during evening colloquies, overcome by the force of divinity breaking forth in his lecture — derives straight from the rhetoric and ideals of the old learning. We see how true the statement by Wibald of Stablo rings that students defend what their teachers say because they love the men, not the truth in their pronouncements. "I conjure you by the tears of our teacher...." This is the poetry and the mood music of the old learning, unthinkable in a scholastic disputation,[118] powerful in an atmosphere where love of teacher substitutes for thought, where the teacher's person constitutes a kind of orthodoxy. For Adelman there was more truth in Fulbert's tears than in Berengar's logic.

This gives us the common strand in the examples of authority defied: the old learning responds to conflict and intellectual challenge by asserting and defending the authority of the masters. An ideal of demonstrable truth approachable through arguments represented a powerful threat to men whose instruction was based on eloquence and personality. This points up the fundamentally irrational nature of an education based on the formation of character. It relies on the personal moral authority of the teacher. Reasoning — certainly critical, independent thought — can become an offense against him, can diminish his authority. The old learning made the masters into an image of God, and the student's goal was to fashion themselves in that

---

vestigiis observantissime inherentes, ut nullum prorsus [in] diverticulum, nullam in novam et fallacem semitam desiliamus, ne forte in laqueos et scandala incidamus...." In Huygens ed., 476–77.

118. Werner of Basel's "Synodus" (mid-eleventh century) is a debate poem carried on in this climate. The Old Testament embodied debates with the New; Sophia is judge. The atmosphere is marked by harmonious intellectual exchange, loving cooperation towards a common goal. Sophia's judgment (ll. 582–85): "...vos non certastis, amici, sed bene cantastis.... / Nec clamavistis." In Pierre W. Hoogterp, ed., AHDLMA 8 (1933): 261–363, at 397.

image.[119] Disputation and reasoning are fundamentally at odds with this goal. Awe and reverence are appropriate to it.

The cult of personality in the old learning was the form of irrationality that Peter Abelard was up against long before he faced that of the Cistercians. In his early conflicts with masters of the old learning, as in so many incidents, Abelard's life is exemplary for the tendencies of the time. An entire system of education was caught in a conflict between a traditional kind of teaching that tended toward the acquisition of human qualities and a new kind that tended toward rational inquiry. This conflict forced the separation of letters and learning from manners.[120]

119. Hugh of St. Victor uses this conceit in urging students of the *schola virtutum* and *recte vivendi scientia* to imitate the examples of good individuals. *De institutione novitiorum* 7: "In ipsis [the good] siquidem similitudinis Dei forma expressa est, et idcirco cum eis per imitationem imprimimur, ad ejusdem similitudinis imaginem nos quoque figuramur." In Feiss and Sicard ed. 342–44; PL 176. 932D.

120. The letter of Goswin (Gozechinus) of Mainz to his former student Walcherus is an important document on the conflict of old and new learning in Germany. He contrasts the school of Liège where he once taught, *Epistola ad Walcherum* 6: "ad omne quod civile sit et moribus conducat informat et instruit" (Huygens ed., 14), with the schools of the present day (c.1065), which suffer from rejecting *mores* and *disciplina*. Young students, who ought to be taught beneath the rod, flee instruction on the "gravity of moral discipline" and are blown about like light chaff in the wind of every doctrine: they follow vain and pestiferous novelties and questions (27, Huygens ed., 31). Certain pseudo-masters wander about giving new readings of texts, seducing students to flee discipline and seek the levity of novelties (28, Huygens ed., 32). Since the whole Church is being poisoned by this lust for novelty and the abandoning of discipline, few can be found who will work for the true institutes of a good life (32, Huygens ed., 34). Many fine teachers, men of outstanding repute and high authority — Hermann of Rheims, Drogo of Paris, Huzmann of Speyer, Meinhard of Bamberg — have abandoned teaching for theology (33, Huygens ed., 35). The golden age of the schools, when the gravity of discipline ruled and all studies were for the utility of the republic and of *honestas*, when the beauty of virtues and the liberal arts flourished, is now past (34, Huygens ed., 36–37). The passage is full of sentiments we encounter a few decades later in John of Salisbury. It is not only an old, disillusioned teacher's empty *laudatio temporis acti*. For a translation of Goswin's letter, see Jaeger, *Envy*, 349–75.

The clash between Abelard and Anselm of Laon is a good illustration. It is as if whatever forces of history shaped the general conflict had designed Abelard and Anselm to embody it: they brewed the intellect and character of Anselm with an overbalance in favor of *mores* and eloquence (the products of the old learning). Like chemists performing an experiment, they exactly reversed the proportions in brewing Abelard. Anselm and the type he represented may have lacked penetration and analytical sharpness, but they were masters of the discipline of living well. Abelard may have known a great deal and possessed a keenly analytical mind, but he was a failure at the discipline of life.[121]

Abelard's opposition to authority was two-fold: he called it into question in its written form in his *Sic et non*, and he challenged it in its living personification by opposing, contradicting, and outdoing his own masters. Besides the clashes with Anselm and William of Champeaux, we have his written testimony to this opposition in his poem to his son, Astralabe. He prefaces the work with cautioning against some of the underlying principles of the old learning:

> Care not who speaks, but what the value of his words are. Things well said give an author his reputation. Neither put your faith in the words of a master out of love for him, nor let a learned man hold you in his influence by his love alone.

The pointedness of these precepts is quite evident against the background presented above, but Abelard accommodated the modern reader in locating the sentiments within the actual flux of trends in

---

121. Abelard came to the ethics of the old learning by betraying them. He is arguing against himself in his poem to his son Astralabe when he says, "No one becomes wise by mere sharpness of mind; character and a good life make one wise. Wisdom professes itself in actions, not in words, and the gift [of such actions] is conferred only on the good." *Carmen ad Astralabium filium*,lines 55-58: "Ingenii sapiens fit nullus acumine magni, / Hunc potius mores et bona vita creant. / Factis, non verbis, sapientia se profitetur; / Solis concessa est gratia sola bonis." In Juanita Feros Ruys, *The Repentant Abelard: Family, Gender and Ethics in Peter Abelard's* Carmen ad Astralabium *and* Planctus (New York: Palgrave, 2014), 96. Also l. 821: "Pluris sit morum tibi quam doctrina librorum...." In Feros Ruys ed., 131. On ll. 93-94 he distinguished between the philosopher, who sees the hidden causes of things, and the practical individual, who foresees the results of one's acts. In Feros Ruys ed., 97.

the schools because he immediately restated them in the formulations he had used against Anselm of Laon in the *Historia calamitatum*:
> We are nourished not by the leaves of trees but by their fruits. The meaning is to be preferred to the mere words. The rhetoric of ornate words may capture minds effectively, but true learning prefers plain speech. A wealth of words conceals a poverty of understanding.[122]

"Plain speech and ideas which bear up to criticism": the formula, combined with a willingness to contradict, to assert the truth of one's own opinion over the teacher's, was fateful for the masters of the old learning. The combination of reason and impudence answered their riddle, dissolved the magic spell of their authority. They were as vulnerable as their aura of venerability: tarnish it and they fell; contradict them convincingly and they faced early retirement. They had only faith, charisma, and tradition to fall back on, not a systematically worked-out philosophical position.

Stefan of Novara sensed that a systematic commentary on Martianus Capella, one that satisfied the intellectual curiosity of his students, was a serious threat to his authority as a teacher. William of Champeaux shows such fears to be well-founded: his teaching career was seriously deflected because he lost to Abelard in their exchanges on the nature of universals. The very foundation of the old learning, personal authority, was at the same time its Achilles heel.[123]

---

122. *Carmen ad Astralabium*, ll.7-15: "Non a quo, sed quid dicatur, sit tibi curae; / Auctori nomen dant bene dicta suo. / Ne tibi dilecti jures in verba magistri, / Nec te detineat doctor amore suo. / Fructu, non foliis pomorum quisque cibatur, / Et sensus verbis anteferendus erit. / Ornatis animos captat persuasio verbis, / Doctrinae magis est debita planities. / Copia verborum est ubi non est copia sensus." In Feros Ruys ed., 97. It is a constant theme in Abelard's works: "Do not regard the person of the teacher but the weight of his ideas; do not respect the ornament of his words, but their sense."

123. He retired from Notre Dame to found the new community of St. Victor and its famous school. But though he remained active as a teacher, he had burned his fingers on dialectic and was denied participating in the more vital life of the Paris schools. For a good summary of the founding and history of the school of St. Victor, see Stephen C. Ferruolo, *The Origins of the University: The Schools of Paris and their Critics, 1100–1215* (Stanford, CA: Stanford University Press, 1985), 27–44. See also the introduction by Crossnoe, *Companion*.

Anselm and William were not the only masters in the old tradition to suffer rough treatment. John of Salisbury tells of his own teachers, William of Conches and Richard the Bishop, who were forced to give up teaching "when popular opinion veered away from the truth" and they were "overwhelmed by the rush of the ignorant mob."[124]

John's *Metalogicon* is the most important monument to the conflict of old and new learning. The general intention of that work is to defend humanist learning against the purely scholastic and to urge an integration of the two. John sees studies and all civilized life threatened by the tendency of contemporary scholars and teachers to cultivate specialized subjects, to privilege dialectic, to separate learning from ethics and thus end the fruitful relationship between philosophy and state or church administration. In a passage that is a touchstone for these concerns, he complains about the tendency to see dialectic as separable from other disciplines and from the active life. To exercise dialectic without broad learning and a practical context for it is senseless and harmful, like a pigmy trying to wield the sword of Hercules. Learning must find its fulfillment in domestic life or at court or in the Church, not remain merely a "school" discipline. He sounds a theme central to the old learning when he asks,

> What moral philosopher does not fairly bubble over with laws of ethics so long as these remain merely verbal? But it is a far different matter to exemplify these in his own life.[125]

---

124. *Metalogicon* 1.24. 124, Hall, ed., 54; Webb ed., 57 ; McGarry trans., 71. On this passage and the "retirement" of William and Richard, see Reginald Lane Poole, *Illustrations of the History of Medieval Thought and Learning*, 2nd ed. (New York: Dover, 1920), 310–14. John says that William of Conches took over the teaching method of Bernard of Chartres. This statement and John's mention of a shift in popular opinion make William's position fairly clear: a master of the old learning has his position undermined by a new fashion. See also Barrie and Keats-Rohan ed., 51–55; and below, 71–72.

125. *Metalogicon* 2.9.34-36: "Quis ethicus morum regulis, dum in lingua versantur, non habundat? Sed plane longe difficilius est ut exprimantur in vita." In Hall ed., 70; Webb ed., 77; McGarry trans., 94.

CHAPTER 1 ✳ CATHEDRAL SCHOOLS

John's description of the teaching of Bernard of Chartres in *Metalogicon* 1.24 is a classic portrayal of the old learning. Bernard, like his predecessor, Fulbert, fit the old model in the teaching of eloquence and ethics together, in his use of the classics, in his holding of evening colloquies, in the adulation accorded him by his students, and in not producing a single written work.[126] John of Salisbury's attempt to reconcile the old and the new had no hope of succeeding. It was a conservative, humanistic, rear-guard action. The days of friendly and emotional colloquies and symposia in cloister gardens between a magisterial teacher and a handful of socially and intellectually elite disciples were past.

THE SCHOOLS AND THE COURTS

In the course of the twelfth century the old learning dwindled, collapsed, was forced out of the schools. John of Salisbury was shocked that twenty years after he had studied in Paris the learning there was merely "scholastic" and seemed to consist of abstract school exercises. Cathedrals and the new schools of Paris may have remained training grounds for administrators,[127] but they were no longer schools of virtue. The *cultus virtutum* still had life in it, as we see in the robust reception of the *Anticlaudianus* in the following centuries. But now it had to seek accommodation elsewhere, and it found it in the institution that had originally accounted for its rise in the tenth century, the prince's court. Courts secular and ecclesiastical had after all been the hidden context of the old learning for the centuries of its prominence. Cathedral schools had handled the overflow from the court chapel and had aimed at preparing men precisely for service in the chapel and what came to be called the chancellery.

The fading of the old learning at cathedral schools coincides with the rise of an education that we must now call "courtly" and no longer

126. A possible exception, his *Timaeus* commentary. See Paul Edward Dutton, "The Uncovering of the *Glosae super Platonem* of Bernard of Chartres," *Medieval Studies* 46 (1984): 192–221. But the comparative anonymity and the difficulty of the ascription tend to confirm the rule.

127. See John W. Baldwin, "Masters at Paris from 1179 to 1215: A Social Perspective," in *Renaissance and Renewal in the Twelfth Century*, Robert L. Benson and Giles Constable, ed. (Cambridge, MA: Harvard University Press, 1982), 138–64.

merely "for the court."[128] There is an old controversy on the question, whether actual schools existed at worldly courts.[129] The question to my mind is a misleading one, because as soon as we determine that in the post-Carolingian period schools at court no longer existed as institutions, we are also tempted to conclude that teachers and instruction had little role at court. The Carolingians needed court schools. They had not discovered, as their successors did, that cathedral schools could function as a more secular alternative to the monasteries. But we would shoot over the mark if we turned this around and said that the Ottonian and Salian kings did not require palace schools because the cathedral schools had taken over their function. More accurate would be: from Carolingian times on there is no useful distinction to be made between the court school and the life of the court itself. Hincmar formulated for Louis the German the ideal of the court as a school of manners:

> The king's court is indeed called a school, that is a course of studies, not because it consists solely of schoolmen, men bred on learning and well trained in the conventional way, but rather a school in its own right, which we can take to mean a place of discipline, that is, correction, since it corrects men's behavior, their bearing, their speech and actions, and in general holds them to the norms of a good life.[130]

Hincmar considered the court a school of mores, to which might have been added formal instruction in letters. This does not change in Ottonian times. The statements of Ruotger that Brun of Cologne as chancellor at Otto the Great's court rescued the seven liberal arts from

---

128. The contemporary terms are *aulica* or *curialis nutritura*. See Ferruolo, *Origins*, 215–16.

129. See Lèsne, *Les écoles*, 39–40; Fleckenstein, "Königshof," 40–41; Fleckenstein, *Bildungsreform*, 24–39; Brunhölzl, "Bildungsauftrag," 28–29; Rosamond McKitterick, "The Palace School of Charles the Bald," in *Charles the Bald: Court and Kingdom*, Margaret Gibson and Janet Nelson, ed. (Oxford: B.A.R., 1981), 385–400.

130. *Epistola synodi Carisiacensis* 12, ll. 2–6: "Et ideo domus regis scola dicitur, id est disciplina; quia non tantum scolastici, id est disciplinati et bene correcti, sunt, sicut alii, sed potius, ipsa scola, quae interpretatur disciplina, id est correctio, dicitur quae alios habitu, incessu, verbo et actu atque totius bonitatis continentia corrigat." In MGH, *Leges* 2.2:436. For other references to the Carolingian "court school," see Lèsne, 39–40.

their decline, attracted philosophers and intellectual "refugees," held philosophical disputations, improved the Latin of the court members, and served personally as an exemplar of wisdom, piety, and justice[131] cannot be emptied of their content merely because no traces of an institutionalized court school with classrooms and ranks of teachers and students can be found. Ruotger's words make perfect sense when we understand the nature and goal of the old learning and distance ourselves from a conception of education limited to notions of classroom and textbook, learned lecturing and writing. Ruotger speaks unmistakably the language of the old learning: letters are combined with manners, the person of the teacher is a large part of the curriculum; philosophy, learning, and public life are inseparable. The masters of the old learning were courtiers in their capacity as teacher, and teachers in their capacity as courtier. What need for institutionalized schools at court? The court itself was a school, where the pedagogy of personal charisma was at work more immediately and effectively than at more formally constituted schools. Every educated man at court was, ideally, philosophy embodied, translating himself into acts of public administration. What changed around 950 and in the following years is that this sort of education became more strongly oriented to classical models of the public servant and orator and was transferred out of the courts and into the cathedral schools, where hitherto secular and sacred letters had formed the curriculum. After c.1150 letters joined to manners returned to the courts secular and ecclesiastical and left the schools to "scholastic" endeavors.

The career of William of Conches is exemplary for this development. He began teaching either in Paris or Chartres or both around 1120 or 1125.[132] His student John of Salisbury tells us that he taught in the manner of Bernard of Chartres and that he had to withdraw from the schools because his students left him for other

131. *Vita Brunonis* 5. In *Lebensbeschreibungen einiger Bischöfe des 10.–12. Jahrhunderts*, Hatto Kallfelz, trans. (Darmstadt: Wissenschaftliche Buchgesellschaft, 1973), 6–9.

132. On William of Conche's career, see Jeauneau, *Glosae*, 9–10; Max Manitius, *Geschichte der lateinischen Literatur des Mittelalters* (Munich: Beck, 1973), 3:215–16; Guillaume de Conches, *Glosae in Iuvenalem*, Bradford Wilson, ed. (Paris: Vrin, 1980), 75–76. Dorothy Elford, "William of Conches," in *Twelfth-Century Western Philosophy*, Peter Dronke, ed. (Cambridge: Cambridge University Press, 1988), 308-27.

disciplines and for teachers who promised greater success with shorter studies.[133] It is a fate like the one that Stefan of Novara feared and that William of Champeaux suffered. William of Conches left the schools and consoled himself with a position as tutor to the young Plantagenet prince and future king Henry II of England. He had written his work *Philosophia mundi* under the influence of the *Timaeus* for use in the schools; he now rewrote it in dialogue form for the education of the prince and gave it the title *Dragmaticon*.

It was probably William who composed the work *Moralium dogma philosophorum*, which has stood in the center of the discussion of a "*ritterliches Tugendsystem.*" The intended audience of this work is uncertain. It is dedicated to a "*vir optimus atque liberalis Henricus,*" who may be Henry II.[134] The work is located, like William himself and like the old learning itself, between schools and secular courts. But the example of William is especially significant because his activity for worldly courts followed upon his "retirement" from teaching at schools. The new developments in the schools of France and the drift towards dialectic forced this humanist schoolmaster to transfer his pedagogy, oriented to the Platonic view of humanity and the world and to ancient Roman ethics, to a secular court, one that by no coincidence was to be closely associated with the rise of courtly literature.

133. *Metalogicon* 1.24.124: "impetu multitudinis imperite victi, cesserunt." Hall ed., 54; Webb ed., 58. Throughout his *Philosophia mundi* William's defensive posture is apparent; he was threatened with the loss of his students. See his attack on teachers who fawn on students and on students who pass judgment of their masters. See *Philosophia mundi* 4, Prol., Gregor Maurach, ed. (Pretoria: University of South Africa, 1980), 88. Also his statement that he cares not for the multitude, but only for the probity and love of truth of the few (2, Prol., Maurach ed., 41). John's notice about William's and Richard's "retirement" makes a comment by William appear especially poignant. He says that the true teacher teaches out of love of learning, not an urge for popularity. See *Philosophia mundi* 4.30: "nec, si deficiat multitudo sociorum, deficiet [*alt.* desinet]...." In Maurach ed., 114. Undoubtedly trends at the schools, new professors offering dialectic, and short periods of study cost William his students, not the attack of William of St. Thierry, as Wilson, 76, suggests.

134. John Holmberg takes this to be Henry II. See his edition of *Das Moralium dogma philosophorum des Guilaume de Conches: Lateinisch, Altfranzösisch, Mittelniederfränkisch* (Uppsala: Almquist and Wiksells, 1929), 6–7. Manitius, *Geschichte*, 3:219, disagrees.

Brun of Cologne was exemplary for the shift of court education from the chapel to the cathedral schools in the tenth century, William of Conches for its return to the courts in the twelfth.[135] Two examples of the old learning in the setting of the court will show us some of the ties between *cultus virtutum* and courtly education.

★

Thomas Becket took up a position at the court of Archbishop Theobald of Canterbury after returning from his studies in Paris. Here he worked together with many men distinguished for their learning, William Fitzstephen tells us, and while Thomas was not their equal in letters, he surpassed them all in, as Fitzstephen puts it, the far superior endeavor of *mores*. He applied himself to *moralitas* and *prudentia* and distinguished himself in this study: *"litteris adhuc inferior, moribus conspectior et acceptior...."*[136] Fitzstephen describes his character and appearance as follows:

> He was of a placid and beautiful countenance, noble in stature, his nose long and straight, his body vigorous and adept; he was skilled in eloquence, subtle in mind, great in soul, and because he tread the path of virtue in a higher sense, he showed himself amiable to all men...generous and witty [or sophisticated or courtly: *facetus*]....[137]

Upon his promotion to chancellor of England, he maintained a household that rivalled that of the king for pomp and magnificence. He loved and excelled in courtly games, especially chess, also the hunt with dogs and falcons. He gave splendid banquets where richly clothed guests ate from gold plates and drank from gold goblets. In the next chapter the biographer tells us that Becket, rich, popular, famous, and burdened with the business of state, takes over the duties of court tutor. The king places his own son and heir, Henry, in his hands, and many

---

135. Another instructive example is William of Champeaux. Forced from Paris, he founded the school at St. Victor, where a later master, Hugh, was to write important educational tracts presenting the ethical views of old learning. These writings were influential in church and monastery, but the mainstream for the future of a classically oriented ethics was at the courts, not in the Church.

136. William Fitzstephen, *Vita S. Thomae* 5, in *Materials for the History of Thomas Becket, Archbishop of Canterbury,* James C. Robertson, ed., Rolls Series 67.3 (1877), 16.

137. *Vita S. Thomae* 7; Robertson ed., 17.

princes of the land entrust their sons to his care. He prepares them for knighting.[138] This biography shows us a man who becomes a master of *mores* and *moralitas* in the schools of London, Paris, and Canterbury who then turns into an educator in *mores* at court. The moral instruction of the schools transfers comfortably to the courts; the *moralitas* of the educated cleric prepares its possessor as an educator of princes or knights.

Here we see also the successful courtier/administrator as educator. Even in the highest state office next to the king, burdened with work, Becket becomes tutor to the children of nobles. Of course, we must not imagine him holding classes in grammar, dialectic, and the classics.[139] Letters were not his strong point; *mores* were. His "students" served him (*servituros mittebant*), watched him in action, probably received an occasional lesson in comportment, possibly learned Latin names for strategies of political/social behavior, which they learned to regard as the functioning of "virtue."

The busy chancellor had little time to instruct *verbo*; but instruction *exemplo*, through the *lingua morum*, was what counted. Becket presided over this "court school" by his authority, leaving the labor to others. In his role at court, he was the perfect embodiment of what the old learning aimed at. Nothing in the text states outright that the *moralitas* Becket pursued as a young clerk at Canterbury had anything in common with the education that he gave to aspiring knights as chancellor of the king and court tutor, that moralitas and *curialitas* had approximately the same content by this time.[140] Our second example makes the connection clear.

138. *Vita S. Thomae* 12: "Cancellario et regni Angliae et regnorum vicinorum magnates libros suos servituros mittebant, quos ipse honesta nutritura et doctrina instituit, et cingulo donatos militiae ad patres...remittebat.... Rex ipse, dominus suus, filium suum...ei nutriendum commendavit...." In Robertson ed., 22.

139. It is not out of the question that such instruction took place at the court, however. William Fitzstephen tells us that Becket as chancellor had fifty-two clerics in his service, most of whom were attached to his household staff. See *Vita Thomae* 18; Robertson ed., 29. On the court at Canterbury under Becket as a school, see Jaeger, *Envy*, 301–8.

140. However Matthew Paris (mid-thirteenth century) tells that the king sent his son to Becket "to be instructed in manners and courtly ways." *Historia Anglorum (Historia minor)*: "rex filium suum...beato Thomae cancellario commisit alendum, et moribus et curialitatibus informandum." In Frederic Madden, ed., Rolls Series 44.1 (London: Longmans, 1866), 316.

CHAPTER I ✴ CATHEDRAL SCHOOLS

Gottfried von Strassburg's romance *Tristan and Isolde* is the highpoint of literary humanism in medieval Germany. The author includes a scene that is a mirror of courtly education. After Tristan, disguised as a minstrel at the Irish court, is nursed back to health from a poisoned wound, he takes over the task of educating Princess Isolde from her previous tutor, a learned courtly cleric. This scene deserves a prominent place in the history of medieval education. The princess, already instructed in foreign languages, music, and composition, learns various kinds of disciplines from him, but she devotes most of her attention to the one called *moraliteit*:

Amid this array of subjects,
he tasked her with one that we call "morality."
This is the art that teaches beauty of manners.[141]

All ladies, he continues, should occupy themselves with this "sweet discipline" from youth on. It teaches them to please God and the world, and without it they will attain neither wealth nor honor. The results of this instruction for Isolde:

from this she became well mannered,
of a beautiful and pure temperament,
her gestures were charming and proper.[142]

In the six months of her instruction she improved her "learning and comportment" *(lere unde gebare)* to such an extent that the fame of her talents spread throughout the land. When guests come to court, she entertains them with her arts: she sings, writes, and reads. Then follows a dazzling description of the "double" beauty of her singing: she not only performs a masterpiece, she herself is one. The audible beauty of her song is matched by her "unheard" song, the visible beauty of her person. The passage is one of the most sublime statements of the human presence as a work of art from the Middle Ages and beyond. There follows a final summary

---

141. Gottfried von Strassburg, *Tristan und Isold*: *under aller dirre lêre / gab er ir eine unmüezekeit, die heizen wir «môrâliteit» / diu kunst diu lêret schoene site.* Friedrich Ranke, ed., 11th ed. (Berlin: Weidmann, 1967), ll. 8002–5; Tomasek ed., ll 8002–5.

142. *...hie von sô wart si wol gesite, / schône unde reine gemuot, / ir gebaerde süeze unde guot.* Ranke ed.; Tomasek ed., ll. 8004–26.

75

of the results of this education: Tristan's instruction gave her "sweetness of mind" *(suoze gemuot)*, lent charm to her manner and her bearing. She mastered all kinds of courtly games and pastimes, could compose letters[143] and songs.[144]

It is evident against the background of our previous discussion that Gottfried speaks the language of *cultus virtutum*. Many of his terms and his turns of thought translate easily into that vocabulary: *"moraliteit"* is the art that teaches schoene site; *"moralitas est ars quae morum elegantiam docet."*[145] *"Lêre unde gebâre,"* which Gottfried also varies as *"rede unde gebâre,"* comes close to *litterae et mores*. Isolde learns many arts, but the one to which she devotes most attention is *moraliteit*. Like John of Salisbury, Gottfried sets *moralitas* as the highest goal of learning. The princess receives from this discipline beauty of mind or temperament *(schône gemuot, sueze gemuot;* cf. *decor animae, compositio morum* or *mentis)*, and both references to this "well-tempered" quality are followed by the statement that her manners and her comportment, her gestures and bearing were pleasing and charming. The implication is that her pleasant gestures are a result of her spiritual beauty. Elegant bearing expresses inner harmony.[146]

---

143. In the three translations I consulted (Hatto, von Ertzdorff, Krohn) Gottfried's phrase *brieve und schanzune* (l. 8139) is rendered as some variation of "words and songs," though neither Gottfried's usage nor any other Middle High German citation in the standard lexica justifies translating *brieve* with "song text." Gottfried's meaning is clear when we read this scene as a "mirror of courtly education": she composed letters and songs. Translating *brieve* as lyrics was the translators' means of preserving the sanctity of her artistry that would appear diminished to modern sensibilities by combining her role of siren with that of secretary. But that is what Gottfried intended: to juxtapose administrative tasks and courtly pastimes, *otium* and *negotium*.

144. Ll. 8132–33.

145. See Jaeger, "Beauty of Manners and Discipline *(schone site, zuht)*: An Imperial Tradition of Courtliness in the German Romance," in *Barocker Lust-Spiegel: Festschrift for Blake Lee Spahr,* Martin Bircher et al, ed. (Amsterdam: Rodopi, 1984), 27–46.

146. Gottfried shows his familiarity with the concept *decor* in a number of passages. See Jaeger, *Origins*, 148–49.

But what we observed first as an ethical ideal taught to aspiring worldly clerics at cathedral schools recurs here as an education in courtliness aimed at princesses and other noble ladies. Far from representing a contradiction, however, this simply shows us in a clear light what had been a feature of the old learning since its emergence in the eleventh century: that it is a preparation for court life and court service, both worldly and ecclesiastical. Here that education has shed all its religious trappings and shows the educational goal — refinement of mind and manners — as a means to wealth, honor, and reputation at court, as a prerequisite to administrative skills (reading and writing letters) and court entertainments (games, music, composing). The only remaining trace of a religious orientation of *moralitas* is the observation that it is pleasing to God and the world. But in Gottfried's romance the emphasis is decidedly on "world."

In the second half of the twelfth century a single master at the schools could still produce a grand summa of the old learning, the *Anticlaudianus*. But from the mid-century on the cult of virtues registers largely in works from the courtly milieu: tracts on the education of princes, nobles, and noble children like Gerald of Wales' *De principis instructione* and Thomasin von Zirclaere's *Der welsche Gast*. Vincent of Beauvais' *De eruditione filiorum nobilium* is a particularly rich summation of this learning and the virtues it sought to cultivate. Vincent still preserves the basic formula of that education: "...*litterarum erudicioni morum eciam instructio copulanda est*...."[147] His ethical vocabulary and concepts, though richer, still draw from the old learning and the authorities who formulated it.[148]

---

147. Vincent of Beauvais, *De eruditione filiorum nobilium* 23, Arpad Steiner, ed. (Cambridge, MA: Harvard University Press, 1938), 78. See also 63: "...congruum est, ut litteris imbuantur ct moribus instruantur...." In Steiner ed., 176.

148. See his discussion of the "two-fold discipline" of *moralis composicio*. It has an inner and an outer aspect, the inner consisting in the cultivation of virtue, the outer "*in decenti composicione membrorum*," involving "*membrorum omnium motus ordinatus et dispositio decens in omni habitu et actione.*" His best source is Hugh of St. Victor, whose *De institutione novitiorum* he quotes at great length. See *De eruditione* 31; Steiner ed., 117–18. On Vincent as an informant on courtly ideals, see Rosemary Combridge, "Ladies, Queens and Decorum," *Reading Medieval Studies* 1 (1975): 71–83.

The renaissance of the fifteenth century experienced the rebirth of an education based on the ethical formation of humanity according to classical models. In reading the humanist tracts on education that Woodward and Kallendorf have edited and translated, we encounter vocabulary and concepts familiar to us from the humanism of the eleventh and twelfth centuries: *moralitas* and *ethica* are the most important disciplines. They are "learned" by imitation of classical models and of the teacher. Philosophy is identified with the pursuit of virtue, and "school" subjects are subordinated to that pursuit.[149] Humanist education gradually moved from the courts back to the universities. In Tudor England the suppression of Catholicism rendered the dominant curriculum of canon law unimportant at the English universities and created a great space in which humanist courtier administrators could restructure university education on humanist principles.[150] When Sir Humphrey Gilbert designed an academy for courtier/statesmen for the Elizabethan government, he provided for a "reader of moral philosophy" who is to receive 100 pounds yearly salary. The reader in natural philosophy receives only 40, and

> ...shall teach civill policy and warres. By directing the Lectures to thendes afforesaid, men shall be taught more witt and policy than Schole learninges can deliver...the greatest Schole clarks are not always the wisest men.[151]

---

149. William Harrison Woodward, *Vittorino de Feltre and Other Humanist Educators* (New York: Columbia University Teacher's College Press, 1963), 221: "It is a marked characteristic of Humanism to limit Philosophy, as a serious study, to Ethics, to the entire exclusion of Metaphysic." See also Woodward, *Studies in Education during the Age of the Renaissance 1400–1600* (New York: Columbia University Teacher's College Press, 1967). For an updated collection, see *Humanist Educational Treatises*, Craig W. Kallendorf, ed. and trans. (Cambridge, MA: Harvard University Press, 2002).

150. See Joan Simon, *Education and Society in Tudor England* (Cambridge: Cambridge University Press, 1966); and Jack H. Hexter, "The Education of the Aristocracy in the Renaissance," in Hexter, *Reappraisals in History* (Evanston, IL: Northwestern University Press, 1962), 45–70. On humanist influence and the role of ethics in the founding of University of Vienna, see Jan-Dirk Müller, *Gedechtnus: Literatur und Hofgesellschaft um Maximilian* (Munich: Fink, 1982), 1:43–44.

151. Sir Humphrey Gilbert, *Queene Elizabeths Achademy*, F.J. Furnivall, ed., EETS, extra ser. 8 (London: Trübner, 1869), 3.

The formula "letters and manners" once again looms large. Castiglione writes in the *Book of the Courtier* 4.12:
> good masters teach children not only letters, but also good and seemly manners in eating, drinking, speaking and walking, with appropriate gestures.[152]

CONCLUSIONS

There is much to be said on the growth and spread of humanist learning. Here I have only been able to characterize it. I hope to have indicated where in the previous centuries the roots of twelfth-century humanism lie. The immediate social and intellectual context of the works we traditionally associate with that direction in twelfth-century culture — Bernard Silvester's *Cosmographia* and *Aeneid* commentary, John of Salisbury's *Metalogicon* and *Policraticus*, Alan's *Anticlaudianus* — is the *cultus virtutum* of the cathedral schools and its application in administrative service. The old learning flowed into and extensively informed these writings, and an acquaintance with its content and goals teaches us to regard those works as the last flowering of a movement, based on the alliance of school and court, learning and government, that preceded them by some two hundred years. The most impressive written testimony to humanism surfaced well after the establishment of humanist learning in the courts and cathedrals, the secular administrative centers of Europe. But the same sequence played out in ancient Rome and in fifteenth-century Italy: humanistic ideals were adapted as educational values and an ethic of civil life, then a social ideal of the aristocracy, finally emerged in poetry, fictional narrative, and allegory.

The continuity of secular learning in the period 950–1150 is not to be sought in texts and artifacts but in personalities and the cultivation of personal qualities. Our notions of humanism and humanistic education remain one-sided and lifeless as long as we separate the learning of the period from the lives of its educated administrators. That is a difficult fact for the historian of literature and culture to

---

152. Singleton trans., 297. For a historically and text-philologically scrupulous study of the development of courtly ideals from cathedral school to administrative service, to secular courts and chivalric milieu, see Scaglione, *Knights at Court*, whose reach is much broader than mine. He includes French, Italian, and Anglo-Norman sources and shows their derivation from Ottonian beginnings.

deal with. We interpret texts and comment on artifacts, and when we look at the eleventh and twelfth centuries, we can still read the works of Abelard and John of Salisbury, and we can still see the sculpture and architecture of the early Gothic. But the ideal of the administrators and the education that formed them are no longer visible. The ideal was as perishable as the individuals who embodied it, and it died with them, like a dance or a stage performance. Now we can only catch glimpses of its shaping ideals of humanity, deference, and elegant comportment in the writings of the schools and courts; and we can find them, sublimated, in the figure of the chivalric knight of courtly romance.

EXCURSUS: REPRISE, 2024

The commentary and notes that follow here supplement and enlarge on some of the main points and central themes of my own and others' studies on medieval humanism. I have focused on those I take to be central points that can benefit from new material or arguments or sharper formulation. The points I've chosen to reprise also are those that have broader reference across the range of medieval humanism.

Eclectic vs. Local

The main points of my book, *The Envy of Angels*, on the history and character of cathedral schools seem to me to have held up fairly well. The book was challenged for its "ecclecticism" but not, to my knowledge, its substance. One reviewer was troubled by the range of citations. For instance, I quote Bernard of Clairvaux praising a young woman (she may be fictional) living in the world, for the aura of splendor she radiates thanks to her self-mastery, discipline, beauty of motion and action — all qualities high in value in humanist ethical thought and expression of the past century. Bernard may not have spoken of himself and the monks in his authority in those terms, but he understood and mastered them and formulated them in a passage whose poetry outdoes any of his more secular contemporaries.

The title of the book was taken from that passage. The locale and social origin of the speaker played no role. It was the humanist idiom that made them relevant. It attested to shared social and intellectual values, though not his own ascetic monastic values. Beware eclecticism. This is a healthy criticism, but a firm hold on my guideline, humanist ethical concepts and language, minimized mistakes in choice of sources. The conceptual language of *mores* and *cultus virtutum* was shared by a broad community of educated men and women writing in Latin and the vernacular. That language had boundaries, and I tried to stay within them.

The language of the humanist culture is spoken by Gerald of Wales, William of Malmesbury, Hugh of St. Victor, Hildebert of Lavardin, Bern of Reichenau, the monk Jotsald of Cluny, Thangmar of Hildesheim, Ruotger of Cologne, and many others, and on occasion Bernard of Clairvaux. It is prominent in the Middle High German *Tristan* romance. Such sources must not be ruled out of court because their authors come from such varied times, locales, and backgrounds. A subject-bound discourse that develops within a shared culture is a guide to sources no matter who employs it.

The range of sources in *Envy* can be a guide to the spread of a cultural discourse. The interrelations may need close scrutiny, but the dependence on a given culture should not be doubted. When the humanist culture begins to fade in its ecclesiastical institutions, the language to describe its disappearance spreads through the lands where its influence had been strong. Hildebert laments in the first decades of the twelfth century: the loss of manners, art, and faith renders people ignorant and foolish. Thinking these values are worth something, people waste their time pursuing them. Once these values pleased, and "divine poets" were well rewarded. Now neither eloquence, genius nor honesty are of any value. The law dissolves, order perishes. (*Carmen* 17).

At the turn to the thirteenth century, Gerald of Wales laments the loss of "divine poets" and of "professors of manners." Writing prose or poetry nowadays, his lament continues, can add neither lustre nor wealth to the writer. The learned person was once a revered figure, a model for imitation and reverence. No longer. These laments surface over the entire range of humanist culture.[153]

The comparison of the two texts, Hildebert and Gerald of Wales (along with many like them) poses questions of historical change but also puts forward the shared vocabulary of humanistic cultural values. Teachers of manners, moral discipline, divine poets, genius, careers based on study of letters — these are basic elements of medieval humanist culture. The good historiographical practice of narrowing a subject in place and time occasionally needs to open up to view fully the character and spread of culture. The reach of the Latin language from 950 to 1150 sets limits, but those limits also can be too narrow.

The masters of Cambridge colleges to the present day present their graduates to the provost with the assurance, in Latin, that these students have distinguished themselves in *doctrina et moribus*. The reach of humanist language is long. The survival of that and other

---

153. See below, 362–63.

Latin academic rituals attest to that reach. "Eclecticism," like other faults and virtues of criticism, sometimes needs to be viewed critically.

Rüdiger Schnell has published a weighty treatise on aristocratic ideals of physical beauty from antiquity through the Middle Ages.[154] He produces much important and interesting material about court life and social values. But he has aimed the study at what he takes to be the central idea of *The Envy of Angels*, Ottonian origins. He argues that the social values I find in the culture of cathedral communities, being much older, cannot be seen as innovations of the Ottonian period. I answered Schnell's polemic in an article, "The Origins of Courtliness after Twenty-Five Years."[155] The single strain of ideals that he has singled out must be seen within a larger system of values that in its whole, its social-political situation and function is new. The Ottonian period was a matrix for that system of ideals, not the progenitor of all individual elements of it.

Sita Steckel is also concerned with issues of continuity and innovation. She has given a more balanced and deepened view of the entire range of issues in education from Carolingian times to the twelfth century in *Kulturen des Lehrens*. She raises two important critical points. She argues that Brun of Cologne, brother of Otto the Great (d.965), cannot be given credit for innovations that determine the character of cathedral school education after about 950. Her other critical point argues that the kind of teaching by example I call "charismatic" cannot be seen as an innovation but rather the Ottonian model adapts Carolingian forms of teaching and Carolingian curricula.

Brun of Cologne and Otto the Great as Founders

On Brun of Cologne and Otto the Great as architects of the intellectual orientation of cathedral schools, the direct connection that Josef Fleckenstein claims — and I agree — has been challenged recently. Sita Steckel understands the curriculum of imperial cathedral schools as developing gradually out of Carolingian models. Steckel cites the work of Joachim Ehlers and Ludwig Vones

---

154. Rüdiger Schnell, "Die höfische Kultur des Mittelalters zwischen Ekel und Ästhetik," *Frühmittelalterliche Studien* 39 (2005): 1–100.

155. *Haskins Society Journal* 21 (2009): 187–216.

questioning the innovative role of Brun.[156] Both Ehlers and Vones rely on a conception of teaching and learning that is irrelevant: classroom and reading material. Both overestimate the role of religious education. Vones and Ehlers base their judgments on their demonstration that Brun was never called a teacher, never appeared in the function of teacher, had no school, and wrote nothing — those are basic elements of conventional knowledge-based teaching.

The observations of Brun's biographer, Ruotger of Cologne, a near-contemporary, put forward clearly the character of Brun's person, his influence on his students, and the culture of learning at court. Here is a summary of some of his main points:

> He was gifted by God with a talent that set him apart from others. Those who knew him were astonished by his talents: highest nobility paired with humility; he had reached the pinnacle of learning and yet without arrogance; his presence exercised a salubrious influence on those around him; those who knew him were endlessly astonished at him; he surpassed his friends and relatives in every regard: physical beauty, the glory of his learning, his drive to work and perform with passion [*vivacissime*]. He cultivated peace and tranquillity, since those are the matrix in which virtue breeds. He was a "great man" [*magnus vir*]. As a boy he showed great promise; all looked on him with favor; he had a "sage genius" [*ingenio sagaci proficeret*]. No part of learning in liberal studies, in Greek or Latin eloquence, escaped the vivacity of his mind.
>
> His brother Otto I, whose glory and fame exceeded any praise that Cicero might have had to confer, called Brun to his court. He recognized in Brun a "royal priesthood sent by the grace of God to aid the empire. He combines the religion of a priest with the strength of a king. True philosophy, the mother of all the arts, nurtured him and educated him to modesty and greatness of soul."[157] The court became a haven of studies. Men of high learning and ambitions gathered there. Brun was an exemplar of wisdom, piety, and justice. God filled him with the spirit of

---

156. "Erzbischof Brun von Köln und seine 'Schule': Einige kritische Betrachtungen," in *Köln, Stadt und Bistum in Kirche und Reich des Mittelalters*, Hanna Vollrath and Stefan Weinfurter, ed. (Cologne: Böhlau, 1993), 125–37.

157. Quoting Cicero, *Tusculan Disputations* 1.26.64.

CHAPTER 1 ✳ CATHEDRAL SCHOOLS

wisdom and understanding. He himself discovered and revived the seven liberal arts, long since neglected. He discussed and analysed all things new and important from historians, orators, poets, and philosophers with utmost care in the company of scholars. He often sat in the midst of the Greek and Roman scholars most learned in philosophy. The emperor and God allmighty both observed Brun. Asked about his behavior [*mores*], his own teacher, Israel the Irish Bishop, remarked that he was a truly holy man [*sanctum adprime virum*].

He raised the level of Latin to polish and luster both in himself and many others. He arranged play readings, farce and drama, comedy and tragedy, dividing up roles and reading aloud. What mattered to him was the quality of the language, not the subject matter [*auctoritatem in verborum compositionibus pro maximo reputabat*]. He studied constantly, even when traveling. While the goal of his reading were things divine, the instrument of it were the books of the pagans [*gentiles libri*]. He was like a learned paterfamilias who kept both old things and new in his treasury. He was constantly active, either conversing with others about what was most useful or thinking for himself. In the divine service he was composed and commended himself to God in brief but pure prayers.[158]

Searching this summary for terms like "classroom," "teacher," "student," one comes up empty-handed. To conclude therefore that Brun did not teach is to be the prisoner of an irrelevant model of education. Brun was a pattern of excellence, passionate study, virtue, and learning of all kinds. The style of his compositions has a high value. Religion does not loom large. The virtues of Carolingian learning are not in evidence.

The two epithets used by Ruotger fit a pattern: *magnus vir, sanctus vir*: human greatness combined with sanctity. The virtues are largely classical. Monastic coloring is pale: intellectual acumen, affability, physical beauty, charismatic force are what matter. The biographer stresses a gift given to distinguish him from others, a criterion more aristocratic than religious.

---

158. The previous paragraphs summarize Ruotger, *Vita* of Brun, 3–9, and Otto's letter to Brun, 20.

In short, if it is difficult to carve a conventional teacher out of this description, it is because his teaching was not conventional in the sense of continuing Carolingian traditions. It is a paradigmatic case of a teacher in imperial cathedral school learning: charismatic, Ciceronian, Stoic. The stress on Otto's choice of Brun and the intellectual activities that follow him from the schools to the court and back again support the argument of collaboration between the two. So does the start-up of the first generation of cathedral schools in the immediate reign of Otto. The network of Brun's students and close associates in the episcopate stretched wide in time and space.[159] Forse's tabulation of Brun's network includes forty-five bishops during Brun's lifetime, twenty-nine with direct ties to Brun and five members of the royal family.[160] Forse's prosopographic work is a basis for further study of Brun and his influence.[161]

Descriptions of learning at court stress *conversatio*: interaction, a shared life. Learning happened in friendly gatherings, symposia, and walks in the countryside. Teaching and learning were Ciceronian, at least on the level at which Brun taught. Thangmar, the biographer of Bernward of Hildesheim, tells how the young Bernward and he "studied" an entire day while riding on horseback, spending the day reading texts as they might in school, composing verses and prose, framing arguments, or probing deep philosophical questions.[162] Needless to say, there were classrooms, books read in common, writing and declaiming exercises. But these happened at the level of rudimentary instruction, a preoccupation far behind the studies of candidates for higher office.[163]

The religious content of Ruotger's *Vita of Brun* is much reduced compared with any Carolingian biography of bishop or abbot. In

159. See James H. Forse, "Bruno of Cologne and the Networking of the Episcopate in Tenth-Century Germany," *German History* 9 (1991): 263–79.

160. For a more extensive list, see Forse, "Religious Drama and Ecclesiastical Reform in the Tenth Century," *Early Theater* 5 (2002): 47–70.

161. For questions about the range and quality of intellectual work and study in Cologne under the influence of archbishop Brun, see Mayr-Harting, *Church and Cosmos*.

162. *Vita Bernwardi Episcopi Hildesheimensis* 1, MGH, SS 4:758.

163. For some views of the distinction, see below, 150–54.

his reading, Brun was drawn to Prudentius, a Christian strongly influenced by classical style. Otherwise, his reading is of classical authors with no mention of the Bible. With respect to the books read, Ruotger makes the interesting distinction between the "instrument" of learning (books of the "gentiles") and the "goal," "things divine." His prayers were "brief but pure," a curious way of praising the devotions of an archbishop facing contemporary criticism of his preoccupation with secular and neglect of sacred issues (Ruotger answers it). In regard to the role of God and religious devotion in the writings around Brun, it can be said what one reader said of Alan's *Anticlaudianus*, that God (in the case of Alan, Jesus) is supreme, but peripheral.

Joachim Ehlers' argument that education at imperial cathedral schools prepared young men to compose documents, and that this "pragmatic orientation" determined the nature of studies under the Ottos, is based on a misunderstanding.[164] Ehlers' search for speculative reasoning and philosophizing overlooks the essentially Ciceronian-Stoic ethical orientation of learning.[165]

BRUN'S DEDICATION POEM
Brun himself composed a poem of thirty-two lines as a dedication to a copy of Frontinus' first-century *Strategemata* (*On the Art of Warfare*), a gift to his brother Otto I. Brun's poem states clearly that he and Otto regarded educational reform and intellectual renewal as an important aspect of their policies. Embedded between passages protesting humility and praising the emperor are these ten lines:

The glory, peace, decorum, and calm attained
With you as our ruler call forth a new golden age.
The study and care for the ancients, our ancestors,
Had all but collapsed
And left those dark ages
Oppressed by fierce barbarism
And stagnant ignorance.

164. See below, 140.
165. See chapter 2 passim. On Brun as instigator of cathedral schools and founder of their curriculum, see also Münster-Swendsen, *Masters and Paragons*, 100–113.

> *But where your hand holds sway,*
> *The republic enjoys safety.*
> *Once more Study sharpens her pen*
> *And bears to the throne the fruits of her work.*[166]

The poem sets classical learning in a clear historical frame. It began, or was revived from oblivion, with the reforms instituted by Otto (and, uncredited but known to anyone who might have read the dedication, Brun himself). But most important is the historical frame that the poet proposes to define this development within his own age: dark ages, blind and ignorant, are overcome by the rule of Otto. Peace and stability return to the *res publica*, the neglected study of the ancients flourishes, and a new golden age dawns.[167] The argument for the cooperation of Otto and Brun and their role as instigators of a new education is all the stronger for being stated by Brun himself.

How Ottonian were Ottonian Cathedral Schools? "Letters and Manners"

The question, whether cathedral-school learning after about 950 represented a continuation or a sharp break with Carolingian traditions receives a clear answer from a study of the term "letters and manners" and its variants. Thirty-five years ago, the essay now chapter 1 in this work[168] made the strong claim that this formula marks a sharp dividing line between the two modes of education. Now it is possible to reaffirm it. Thanks to digitalized versions of the *Patrologia Latina* and *Monumenta Germaniae Historica*, *The Library of Latin Texts*, *The Dictionary of Medieval Latin from British Sources*, and the Perseus Project

---

166. Gloria, pax, decus et requies / Aurea te duce secla refert. / Deciderat studium veterum / et vigilancia pene patrum. / Cecaque secula barbaries / Seva premebat et error iners. / At tua dextra ubi sceptra tenet, / Publica res sibi tuta placet; / Exacuit calamos studium / Fertque, quod apparat, ad solium. MGH, *Poetae* 5.1.378, ll. 19–28.

167. For a close reading of the poem with critical literature, see Jaeger, *Origins*, 119–21. On the controversy over authorship of the poem stirred by Johannes Fried, and for further literature, see Mayr-Harting, *Church and Cosmos*, 62–63, who argues persuasively for Brun as author.

168. Pages 27–32.

database of classical texts, a great deal more material is available for searching.

The provenance of the phrase, *litterae et mores*, is classical. There are clear references in Cicero, Quintilian, and Aulus Gelius. I have found no occurrences of the phrase between the fifth and the tenth century that would encourage revising that claim. A notable exception is Alcuin, and the approximation of "letters and manners" in his dialogue between himself and Emperor Charlemagne, *On Rhetoric and the Virtues*, happens fully in the context of the teaching and learning of "civil manners." This is something apart from the mainstream of Carolingian educational reform that centers on language and religious/Biblical studies and the *norma rectitudinis*.

While religious teaching is abundant in Alcuin's dialogue, the recognition that begins the work and locates it conceptually is that "the entire force of that art (rhetoric) is focused on civil questions" *(totam ejus artis vim in civilibus versari quaestionibus)*. It could well be argued that education at the royal court in the Carolingian period was on the same or similar ground as the Ottonian but has no place or usage in ecclesiastical education. "Letters and manners" does not occur in any of the abundant Carolingian writings on education. Hrabanus Maurus uses the phrase *doctrina et mores* in commenting on the gifts given to the tribe of Levi, the Levite priests, in his commentary on Joshua:[169] *perfectio doctrinae et morum* suits those in the position of masters so that their subjects can progress in their learning by their presence and their teaching. He clearly develops the concept in the context of teaching but clearly also teaching the populace, not the clergy. It is all the more telling that the phrase does not occur in his tract on clerical education, *De clericorum institutione*.[170]

The formula emerges in the early eleventh century often with reference back to the imperial churches of the late tenth. It is prominent in each of the biographies of the early, i.e. Ottonian, bishops of Liège: Eraclius (959–71), student of, and appointed bishop by, Brun, and Notker (972–1008), imperial chaplain appointed bishop by Otto I. With the patronage of Otto and Brun, these two made that Belgian city and not Cologne the "crucial center for the diffusion of the new

169. PL 108:1091D.
170. PL 107:293–420.

model of education."[171] Wolfgang of Regensburg (c. 957) instructed the youths at Trier: "He labored not only in liberal doctrines, but also in moral disciplines."[172]

The students of Würzburg, writing in the 1030s, praised their school, raised from its Carolingian obscurity by Otto I, as "a flowing stream from which one drinks the doctrine of eloquence and of proper conduct of life."[173]

Anselm of Liège (d.c.1056), historian of the bishops of Liège, looked back nostalgically c.1050 to the origins of cathedral school learning and compared those days to the early days of the schools "when in the chapels of the emperor, no less than in those of bishops, nothing more was pursued than the discipline of manners along with the study of letters."[174] This is one of many indications of decline from the mid-eleventh century. What is lost is telling, and the teaching of manners and letters is mourned.

Whatever the fate of the curriculum that the term "letters and manners" names at the German cathedral schools, the phrase survived and thrived. In the early period it can refer to a personal accomplishment and registers high praise of an individual,[175] while

---

171. Jaeger, *Envy*, 54, nn. 5 and 8. On Eradius: "Hic cum eleganti morum probitate, liberali adprime honestatis scientia,...funditus liberale studium cum memoria absolvisset, ille scolas per claustra stabilire curavit"; and Notker: "A litterali ergo scientia morum quoque ornamenta accepit et in utraque disciplina laudabiliter promotus, de scolis ad palatium transferri meruit...honestatis sue prerogativa de palatio ad regimen Leodiensis ecclesie...transierit." MGH, SS 7:201, ll. 30–32. See also Willigis of Mainz, *Libellus de Willigisi consuetudinibus* 4: "...per assiduae lectionis honestaeque moralitatis exemplum honestissimum vitam non cessavit honestare multorum." In MGH, SS 15:744, ll. 42–43.

172. Otloh, *Vita Wolfkangi*: "...non solum liberalibus exercebat doctrinis, verum etiam moralibus disciplinis." In MGH, SS 4:529.

173. "...recte vivendi et dogma loquendi." *Ältere Wormser Briefsammlung*, 127. See discussion in Jaeger, *Envy*, 54–56, 202–9.

174. "...cum litterarum studio morum disciplina." Jaeger, *Envy*, 203.

175. With reference to Anselm of Laon for the year 1117: "magister nominatissimus, litterarum scientia clarus, vir morum honestate et consilii maturitate venerabilis...." In *Sigeberti Gemblacensis Chronographia cum continuationibus*, Ludwig Bethmann, ed., Continuatio Praemonstratensis MGH, SS 6:448.

CHAPTER 1 ✳ CATHEDRAL SCHOOLS

at the same time designating an educational model as at home in cathedral schools. From the twelfth century on, it broadens into a criterion of *ideonitas*, suitability for administrative positions in courts religious and secular. It finds a prominent place in the papal language of suitability,[176] even becoming in the later Middle Ages and beyond a qualification for the highest secular honors.[177] By the end of the sixteenth century the formula had nested so firmly in academic and administrative practice and parlance that it was the language of *ideonitas* for popes, bishops, and professors.[178] It also became a formula attesting to the completion of a course of studies for a bachelor's degree.

It survives in this context to the present day at the University of Cambridge. The ritual of graduation requires masters of Cambridge colleges to lead their graduating students by hand up to the provost and give him solemn assurance in Latin that these students were qualified to advance being found in *"doctrina et moribus idoneum."*[179]

176. As in Innocent IV, Epist. 150: "Apostolice sedis benignitas sic merita personarum provida discernit deliberatione, ut eos, qui litterarum sciencia et morum nobilitate precellunt, favoris gratia efferat amplioris et maioribus studeat beneficiis honorare." See also Gregory IX, *Decretalium compilatio* 1.7: "Quum in cunctis sacris ordinibus et ecclesiasticis ministeriis sint et aetatis maturitas, et gravitas morum et literarum sciencia inquirenda, multo fortius in episcopo haec oportet inquiri, qui ad curam aliorum positus in se ipso debet ostendere, qualiter alios in domo Dei oporteat conversari." *Corpus Iuris Canonici, Editio Lipsiensis secunda*, Emil A. Friedberg, ed. (Leipzig: Tauchnitz, 1879), 51.

177. See Quintus Aemelianus Cimbriacus, "Post egregiam litteris et moribus operam impensam, sicut decebat Romanorum futurum regem, ne dicam imperatorem...."; Erasmus, Epist. 84: "Quid enim melius, quid praestantius, quid denique divinius, quam virum candidis et litteris et moribus nitentem reperiri..."; and Castiglione cited above, 79.

178. The material would far overflow this note. It would be good to have a history of the term. The Brepols database Library of Latin Texts provides abundant material. A similarity search for *mores et doctrina* yields 121 hits; for *litterae et mores*, 86 hits. Accessed August 8, 2024.

179. Personal communication of Derek Brewer, master of Emmanuel College, Cambridge.

91

This university, proud of its medieval inheritance, a pride visible in its architecture and many other aspects of self-definition, can add to its treasury of medieval forms the description of the undergraduate curriculum as "doctrine and manners," a formula at least two centuries older than its architectural style and its constitution as a university.[180]

"Letters and manners" is not a variant of *docere verbo et exemplo*. The latter is a pedagogy, the former a course of studies. The latter pertains primarily to monastic teaching including regular canons, not to the learning of the cathedral schools. There can be overlap, but decisive is the lack of any significant occurrence of "letters and manners" prior to Ottonian-Salian age. Surveying the material discussed above, it becomes clear that "letters and manners" is the formula of a humanistic education.

Brun's Curriculum: Disciplina Brunonis

The phrase, *disciplina Brunonis*, which would seem to tie the education in eloquence and governing directly to Brun as its originator, is used by Sigebert of Gembloux in describing the education of Dietrich of Metz (964–84), cousin, student, and friend of Brun, member of the royal chapel, appointed bishop by Brun. Steckel[181] and Mayr-Harting[182] question the value of Sigebert's witness to the *disciplina Brunonis* as a new educational form. Sigebert wrote his *Vita* of Dietrich of Metz between 1050 and 1060, nearly a century after Brun's death. He could have "read back" contemporary trends of "the rising schools of France"[183] into a vaguely remembered past. More likely is that he was recalling nostalgically a schooling of an earlier age governed by Brun and Otto. He almost certainly opposed and feared the rising trends in France. That was Anselm of Liège's attitude toward the past and

---

180. A variant of the phrase occurs in the statutes of Merton College, Oxford: "ad proficiendum in moribus et doctrina"; and those of Peterhouse College, Cambridge: "in studio et morum honestate proficiant." See Henry Mayr-Harting, "The Foundation of Peterhouse, Cambridge (1284) and the Rule of St. Benedict," EHR 103 (1988): 318–38. Since the phrases are widely used in educational texts and elsewhere since the eleventh century, but not in the Benedictine Rule, a direct tie to monastic usage is unlikely (*proficiant* is the shared term).

181. Steckel, *Kulturen des Lehrens*, 715–16.

182. *Church and Cosmos*, 60.

183. Mayr-Harting, *Church and Cosmos*, 60.

future of learning, an attitude shared also by Goswin of Mainz and Liège. Goswin saw the old-style professors — Meinhard of Bamberg, Huzman of Speyer, Hermann of Rheims, Drogo of Paris, "and many others" — leaving their teaching profession full of contempt for the abandoning of discipline at the schools and for the intellectual trends introduced by Berengar of Tours, spreading like "poison."

The century separating Sigebert of Gembloux and Metz from Brun and Dietrich of Metz shrinks to half a century if one considers that the bishops planted by Brun were still in office at the end of the tenth century, and that their traditions will have lasted some time beyond their deaths (Wolfgang of Regensburg, d.994, Notker of Liège, d.1008). Furthermore, the divisive trends of the Investiture Controversy were at work separating imperial advocates from adherents of reform. Sigebert was decidedly on the side of imperial traditions. The age of Brun was far from a dim memory, the anticipation of new trends far from a welcome attitude when Sigebert wrote the *Vita* of Dietrich. Imperial traditions were still alive, and Sigebert was trying to save them from extinction, not tout the coming trends from France. Sigebert was rooted in Lotharingian traditions, the area of greatest influence of Brun in episcopal appointments and cathedral-school foundations: Metz, Liège, Verdun, Toul, and Cambrai. Positive aspects of Brun's influence and of Ottonian church and educational governance may have been exaggerated, but a wholesale misstating of Brun's influence seems unlikely.

2. PHILOSOPHY, c.950–c.1150

INTRODUCTION

My purpose in this chapter is to urge some rethinking of the history of philosophy, stringently from the mid-tenth to the mid-eleventh centuries, more expansively to the mid-twelfth. I confess from the outset that philosophy is not my field, that I approach the subject from the point of view of history of education and of aristocratic social ideals, especially of the German imperial courts. I hope that this point of view might add some new perspective on the conception of philosophy, from 950 to 1150 and that the colleagues whose views are discussed here will welcome this outsider's position as a benevolent suggestion for revision and rethinking. I begin by surveying a range of opinion on the nature and context of philosophy in the period.

Marcia Colish's treatment of the tenth and eleventh centuries[1] is a good starting point, since her perspective tends to be broader ("intellectual tradition") than histories of philosophy in the narrower sense. She surveyed intellectual life of the period in question starting with an overview that includes the Normans (special mention of William the Conqueror) and Cluny, the reform activity of Dunstan of Canterbury, and monastic and cathedral schools in France. As she noted,

> Monasteries were the leading centers of religious, artistic and intellectual life. The royal courts rarely provided guidance except through indirect patronage.[2]

By that she meant by and large the French court. She credited the Ottonian dynasty with a peripheral role:

> To the extent that secular rulers patronized culture, the most visible force was the Ottonian court in imperial Germany.[3]

She discussed four figures from the Ottonian courts, Bernward of Hildesheim, Hrotsvitha of Gandersheim, Liutprand of Cremona, and Gerbert of Aurillac. While she credited the imperial obligations of Hrotsvitha's work and its peculiar mix of Christian themes

1. For what follows, see Colish, *Medieval Foundations*, 160–64.
2. Colish, *Medieval Foundations*, 160.
3. Colish, *Medieval Foundations*, 162.

and classical learning, she saw both Hrotsvitha and Gerbert as "product[s] of convent life." She surveyed the range of Gerbert's interests but regards the polymath Gerbert as anomalous: "perhaps the most striking feature of his career is its accidental quality."[4] His patronage by all three Ottos appeared not programmatic for those monarchs but the result of a particular impression Gerbert made on them, which interrupted an embracing indifference, an isolated occasion to which they rose. Finally, Colish credited the language arts with the eventual emergence of speculative thought:

> ...the single development fueling the emergence of speculative thought in the eleventh century was the study of grammar and logic and the emergence of semantic theories that were to take medieval philosophy in creative post-classical directions and to give philosophers and theologians new tools with which to work.[5]

John Marenbon focuses on Gerbert.[6] Like Colish, Marenbon locates Gerbert's intellectual roots and practice in monasteries:

> For the most part these scholars [who carried the intellectual life of the tenth and eleventh centuries] were monks of the great Benedictine houses, such as Fleury on the Loire, and St. Gall. No king made his court the preeminent centre for learning that the palaces of Charlemagne and Charles the Bald had been....[7] The thinkers of the tenth century made their greatest contribution to philosophy through the development of logic, especially formal logic, and by the middle of the eleventh century, these developments in dialectical technique were having an important effect on the manner of theological debate and its philosophical implications.[8]

---

4. Colish, *Medieval Foundations*, 164.

5. Colish, *Medieval Foundations*, 165.

6. John Marenbon, *Early Medieval Philosophy: An Introduction*, 2nd ed. (New York: Routledge, 1988).

7. Marenbon, *Medieval Philosophy: An Historical and Philosophical Introduction* (New York: Routledge, 2007), 114: "Intellectual Activity [around the year 1000] was mainly confined to a few great monasteries."

8. Marenbon, *Medieval Philosophy*, 80.

CHAPTER 2 ✶ PHILOSOPHY, c.950–c.1150

On Gerbert: "Like Notker and Abbo, Gerbert was a monk, first at Aurillac and then, as abbot at Bobbio."[9] Marenbon also mentions that Gerbert served as schoolmaster at Rheims but is silent on his service to Hugh Capet and his attachment to the imperial court as adviser to all three Ottos and tutor possibly to Otto II and certainly to Otto III (a connection that led to his elevation to pope as Sylvester II). For Marenbon and Colish the history of philosophy in the period is monastic first and foremost. It is the history of Aristotelian logic as transmitted by Boethius. He and Colish agree that the importance of the period for philosophy is "the emergence of speculative thought in the eleventh century…" because it generates "the revival of speculative thought that culminates in Anselm of Canterbury." The century experienced a "rising interest in logic and semantics" that prepared the debate over universals.[10] Marenbon notes an "increase in clarity and sophistication and in the range of intellectual reference between Eriugena and Abelard" that he sees "based to no small extent on the unspectacular work of tenth-century scholars," the aforementioned monks of the great Benedictine houses.[11]

The essay on earlier medieval philosophy co-authored by Rosamond McKitterick and John Marenbon[12] gives close attention to library catalogues and the available texts and favors again logic:

In establishing the intellectual context for the study of philosophy in the early Middle Ages, principal considerations are what texts were known and available.[13]

The authors cite the *Timaeus*, the *Consolation of Philosophy*, and Boethius' logical writings; Pseudo-Apuleius' *Perihermenias*; Macrobius' *Commentary on the Dream of Scipio*; and Cicero, *Topics*. So, this list adds the Platonic tradition to the comments of Colish and Marenbon cited above. The authors' summary:

9. Marenbon, *Medieval Philosophy*, 82.
10. Marenbon, *Medieval Philosophy*, 165.
11. Marenbon, *Medieval Philosophy*, 80.
12. "Philosophy and Its Background in the Early Medieval West," *Routledge History of Philosophy* 3: *Medieval Philosophy*, John Marenbon, ed. (New York: Routledge, 1998), 96–119.
13. Marenbon, "Philosophy and Its Background," 99.

There were three main fields of philosophical activity in the early medieval period: the study of logic, the reading and reaction to ancient and late antique philosophical texts and the analytical discussion of problems about Christian doctrine.[14]

McKitterick and Marenbon include the empire and the cathedral schools associated with imperial influence, but they do not associate them with philosophy in the period, and they veer off the mark in identifying the curriculum there with Carolingian models:

> In the episcopal schools of Germany, such as those of Trier, Augsburg, Eichstaett, and Utrecht, Würzburg, Regensburg, Cologne, and Liège, and many more, the Carolingian school curriculum was taught....[15]

They also underplay the role of royal/imperial patronage:

> In the tenth and eleventh centuries on the Continent the Carolingian, Capetian and Saxon kings...were rather less active in the promotion of scholarship and patronage of learning [than the Carolingians of the eighth and ninth centuries].[16]

It is noteworthy that the treatments cited above do not deal at any length with texts supposedly representative of the development of logic and of the "increase in clarity and sophistication and in the range of intellectual reference between Eriugena and Abelard."[17] Of the

---

14. Marenbon, "Philosophy and Its Background," 108.

15. Marenbon, "Philosophy and Its Background," 103. On the changes in the curriculum from the Carolingian to the Ottonian period, see Jeager, *Envy*, 21–52.

16. Marenbon, "Philosophy and Its Background," 107. McKitterick argues the point closely in "Ottonian Intellectual Culture and the Role of Theophano," *Early Medieval Europe* 2 (1993): 53–74. This essay also appeared in *The Empress Theophano: Byzantium and the West at the Turn of the First Millenium*, Adelbert Davids, ed. (Cambridge: Cambridge University Press, 2002), 169–93.

17. The most thorough sifting is Carl Prantl's *Geschichte der Logik im Abendlande* (Graz: Akademische Druk, 1955), 2:49–72, still useful for surveying a range of writings specifically on logic. William Kneale and Martha Kneale, *The Development of Logic* (Oxford: Clarendon, 1984), 199–201, mention Gerbert, Abbo, and Notker but focus on the *Dialectica* of Garland the Computist, whose work is characterized as "confusion" and "a muddle." Garland seems not to distinguish logic from grammar — a significant collapsing of disciplines. On Garlandus, see Eleanor Stump, "*Garlandus Compotista*

CHAPTER 2 ✳ PHILOSOPHY, c.950–c.1150

"thinkers of the tenth century" the only ones mentioned in the studies cited above as representative of the dominant Aristotelianism are Gerbert, Abbo of Fleury, and Notker Labeo. In the second half of the eleventh century, Berengar of Tours, Anselm of Bec, and Roscellinus of Compiègne suddenly emerge as prominent figures worthy of careful consideration, representatives of a strong trend to dialectical studies or at least to speculative philosophy.

But histories of philosophy want to regard the century prior to the second half of the eleventh century as a continuing development from Carolingian trends. Much more likely is that Berengar and Roscellinus, and to some degree, Anselm, represent something radically new (from the perspective of 950–1150), revolutionary and troubling to "philosophy" as practiced in the previous hundred years.[18] The vehemence of the rejection and condemnation of Berengar, especially in the monastic realm, suggests that his thought differed radically from what had preceded, not that Berengar grew out of the work of his older contemporaries.

In these introductory comments, I have surveyed recent opinion of scholars most seriously engaged in the intellectual life of the period, who have contributed distinguished work in the history of philosophy. A survey of handbook treatments and references in general histories of medieval philosophy confirms the picture formed

---

and Dialectic in the Eleventh and Twelfth Centuries," in *History and Philosophy of Logic* (1980): 1:1–18, a revised version in her *Dialectic and Its Place in the Development of Medieval Logic* (Ithaca, NY: Cornell University Press, 1989), which described (68) the *Compotista* as "the earliest complete medieval logic text still extant." Manitius, *Geschichte* 2 treats individual authors in some detail and shares Prantl's perplexity about the primitive state of logic. See also John Marenbon, "Logic Before 1100: The Latin Tradition," in *Handbook of the History of Logic 2. Mediaeval and Renaissance Logic*, Dov M. Gabbay and John Woods, ed. (Amsterdam: North-Holland, 2008), 1–65.

18. Suzanne J. Nelis, I believe, put her finger on the fault line between the old (oratorical/rhetorical, arguing from authority) tradition and the new (dialectics, speculative thought) in contrasting Lanfranc of Bec's learning with that of Anselm: "What Lanfranc Taught, What Anselm Learned," *Haskins Society Journal* 2 (1990): 75–82.

from Colish, Marenbon, and McKitterick.[19] The consensus has it that Aristotelian logic, transmitted and cultivated by Benedictine monks in monasteries like St. Gall, Reichenau, and Fleury, continuing Carolingian traditions and "foreshadowing," or preparing for developments in the later eleventh and twelfth centuries, is the

19. Michael Haren, *Medieval Thought: The Western Intellectual Tradition from Antiquity to the Thirteenth Century* (New York: St. Martin's, 1985), 83: "... the history of thought in the period ca. 1000 to ca. 1150 comprises two main strands. First, there is the Aristotelian contribution, which may be fairly said to be the more distinctive. Nothing is so characteristic of the thought of the eleventh and early twelfth centuries as the way in which Aristotle's logic at once stimulated a desire for intellectual order and was grasped as the means to achieve it. Secondly there is the Platonist contribution. Directly and indirectly it exercised important influences on the intellectual life of the time." Julius Weinberg, *A Short History of Medieval Philosophy* (Princeton, NJ: Princeton University Press, 1964), 58: "Although there was very little philosophy worthy of the name written in Europe from Eriugena to Anselm of Bec, there are some discussions that foreshadow the developments of the twelfth century." Ruedi Imbach, "Philosophy," in *Encyclopedia of the Middle Ages*, André Wauchet, et al., ed. (Chicago: James Clark, 2000) 2:1131: "Until the mid-twelfth century the philosophical corpus was composed of texts of Boethius, Martianus Capella, Macrobius and the *logica vetus*." Dennis Bradley, "Philosophy to the Mid-Twelfth Century," DMA 9:582–90, at 587: "In the tenth century, intellectual life survived in the Benedictine monasteries.... Gerbert [again associated with Benedictine monasticism] taught a full course at Rheims of Aristotle (old logic) such as it could be derived from Boethius." J.P. Beckman, "Philosophie: Western," *Lexikon des Mittelalters* (Munich: Artemis, 1993), 6:2086–92, at 2088–89, passes over the tenth and eleventh centuries as "*Vorscholastik*" and mentions only Berengar of Tours and the monastic resistance to his rationalism. Mariateresa Fumagalli and Massimo Parodi, *Storia della filosofia medievale da Boezio a Wyclif* (Rome: Laterza, 2002), 104–5: "La vita culturale di questo periodo è certamente più povera di quella del secolo precedente: relegata all'interno di scuole episcopali sempre meno numerose e, sopra tutto, nei centri monastici, nei quali tuttavia si delinea, proprio nel secolo X, una prima spinta in direzione di quel processo di renovamento destinato a svilupparsi nel secolo successivo.... Un progresso ulteriore nello studio della logica viene compiuto, tra l'ultimo terzo del X e la prima metà dell'XI secolo, quando si doffondono nei centri di studio I trattati originali di Boezio. [It would be exaggerated to say that at the end of the tenth century the tracts of Boethius were known and absorbed] ...comincia in questo periodo un longo lavoro preparatorio durato un secolo e mezzo."

focus of philosophy and intellectual life in the tenth and eleventh centuries. Philosophical activity is either located in monasteries or flows out from them into other places, which are not their home. The Platonic tradition is mentioned but gets no treatment that suggests its centrality or its parity with Aristotelian logic. Stoic influence receives no mention. Cicero is acknowledged but as the author of the *Topics*, i.e., a work on Aristotelian logic.

The omission of Cicero the philosopher is a blind spot in this eyeing of the two hundred years of philosophy from 950 to 1150. The underplaying of the royal and imperial courts another.

BRUN OF COLOGNE

The evidence both of a dominant Ciceronian/Stoic conception of philosophy and of royal patronage is abundant.[20] I'll start the argument for this claim with a famous passage from 953, a "speech" of Otto the Great to his brother, Brun of Cologne, explaining why the king needs his brother's particular skills in a time of crisis. Brun's biographer Ruotger ascribed the following words to the king:

> I see [in you] a royal priesthood sent by the grace of God Almighty to the aid of our empire. For you combine in your person the religion of a priest and the strength of a king.... And I have long noted that the mother of all noble arts and the virtue of true Philosophy is yours, and it is she who has educated you to modesty and greatness of soul.[21]

The passage is often quoted in the discussion of the "imperial church," for which a "royal priesthood" (1 Peter 2:9) is necessary. The initiative ascribed to the king in placing in his service a man who combines religion, kingliness, and philosophy (at least the benefits of Philosophy)

---

20. It is hard to agree with Colish, *Medieval Foundations*, 162, that "royal courts only rarely engaged in the intellectual life of the period." She credited an "Ottonian Renaissance" in art driven largely by bishops with no secular guidance and support: "an imperially driven agenda was totally absent."

21. *Vita Brunonis* 20: "...video per Dei omnipotentis gratiam nostro imperio regale sacerdotium accessisse. In te namque et sacerdotalis religio et regia pollet fortitudo.... Nec abesse tibi iam dudum perpendi ipsam ingenuarum arcium matrem et *vere* virtutum *philosophie*, que te ad hanc modestiam magnitudinemque animi erudivit." In Kallfelz trans., 206. Emphasis added.

is noteworthy because it defines a context and a role of philosophy quite different from any described in the histories of philosophy cited above. Philosophy gives virtues appropriate to the active life of service to the empire, and philosophy functions in the force-field in which kingliness joins with priestliness, power with religion. His summoning of his brother Brun to the imperial court argues that this essentially philosophical conception of sacred kingship is, if not conceived by, at least put into action by the king and, at the very least, that Ruotger represented the king as dispensing favor and high position (nepotism aside) partly on the basis of preparation by Philosophy.

If we are to believe Ruotger, Brun turned the court into a kind of philosopher's academy, "where through studies, whatever was obscure in the world could be illuminated." The court attracted the learned. In Brun they found an exemplar of wisdom, piety, and justice beyond anything in human memory. Those who came with notions of their own learning left chastened and convinced of their ignorance. God made Brun his vessel, filled him with wisdom and understanding. Brun stimulated thought on philosophical questions, common and abstruse, and atttracted the learned to the court, a group that Folcuin of Lobbes calls *palatini philosophi*.[22] He restored the seven liberal arts, which had long since fallen into neglect, to a place of prominence. All new and grand things that the historians, orators, poets, or philosophers discussed Brun debated with the learned. The court was the stage for disputes between the most learned of the Latin and Greek doctors on the most subtle and highest questions of philosophy. Brun also raised the level of Latin eloquence at court. He was so diligent a reader that he carried a portable library with him when the court traveled.[23]

---

22. Folcuin of Lobbes, writing c.975–80, notes Brun's support for Rather of Verona in language of interest to this study (chap. 22): "Ottho...imperitabat, cujus frater Brun unicum et singulare in Christi ecclesia decus futurum, velut pretiosissimus lapis multiplicibus philosophorum pollebat argumentis. Advocatur Ratherius, et habetur inter palatinos philosophos primus." In *Folcuini Gesta Abbatum Lobiensium*, George Waitz, ed., MGH, SS 4:64. For this writer the term *palatini philosophi* required no explanation.

23. *Vita Brunonis* 5–8. Mayr-Harting, *Church and Cosmos*, 52–63, 131–44, surveys learning at the Ottonian court, though the main focus is the intellectual world of Cologne under Brun.

CHAPTER 2 ★ PHILOSOPHY, c.950–c.1150

There is good reason to think that the origin of the German cathedral schools of the period, some of which were mentioned in the article cited above by McKitterick and Marenbon,[24] lay in the initiative of Otto I and his collaboration with his brother Brun.[25] A new curriculum emerged in cathedral schools in the Ottonian period, most likely shaped by Brun. It leaned heavily on the education of an orator from Roman antiquity. As his students and associates moved into cathedral administration in the empire, the new education was taken into the schools. They flourished and became the major institutions preparing future royal counselors and bishops.[26] The initiative of Otto the Great is well known for recruiting scholars, among them Rather of Verona (also teacher of Brun of Cologne) and Stefan and Gunzo of Novara for his court and for the schools of the north.

The passage from Brun's *Vita* quoting the emperor's summons of his brother is based on a broad conception of philosophy as a tutor of administrators and teacher of virtue. It has Ciceronian roots. Ruotger has placed a passage from the *Tusculan Disputations*, only slightly varied, in the emperor's mouth:

> Philosophy, the mother of all the arts…educated us first for the worship of the gods, then for modesty and greatness of soul.[27]

Striking in Ruotger's adaptation is the restriction to two personal virtues of philosophy's shaping influence on a government minister:

---

24. Marenbon, "Philosophy and Its Background."

25. See Josef Fleckenstein, "Königshof und Bischofsschule unter Otto dem Grossen," *Archiv für Kulturgeschichte* 38 (1956): 38–62; Johannes Staub, "Domschulen am Mittelrhein um und nach 1000," in *Bischof Burchard von Worms, 1000–1025*, Wilfried Hartmann, ed. (Mainz: Gesellschaft für mittelrheinische Kirchengeschichte, 2000), 275–309; Jaeger, *Envy*, 36–43. See also above, 25–27, 83–88.

26. See Jaeger, *Envy*, 36–75.

27. CTD 1.26.64: "…Philosophia…omnium mater artium, quid est aliud nisi…donum…deorum? Haec nos primum ad illorum cultum, deinde ad ius hominum…tum ad modestiam magnitudinemque animi erudivit.…" In King ed., 74. On the importance of the *Tusculan Disputations* in the tenth and eleventh centuries, see Jaeger, *Envy*, 84–85, 121–23.

modesty and greatness of soul, excluding, for instance, mental acumen and speculative thought. Also striking the omission of *cultus deorum*.[28]

By basing the king's words on a Ciceronian conception of philosophy, Ruotger was swimming in the mainstream of philosophy in the second half of the tenth century, both in its historical sources (Cicero) and in its social and political context (the royal/imperial court). Cicero is the major source both for oratory and oratorical studies and for Stoical conceptions of philosophy in the Middle Ages. Of course, that statement should not be taken to suggest the philosophy of ancient Stoicism in the full range of its interests. Cicero's interest was virtually restricted to Stoic ethics[29] and thus focused and limited. His philosophy was available and well received in the Middle Ages.[30] His preoccupations with wisdom, the wise individual, the pursuit of virtue, and the highest good were of intense interest, diffused through the ethics of Christian administration via Ambrose's *De officiis ministrorum*, adapting and expanding Cicero's *De officiis* and in this period prominently informing the curriculum of cathedral-school education. Cicero made the formation of life through discipline the highest activity of philosophy, which "promotes a good and happy life" (*bene beateque vivendum*). Its end is virtue.[31] The *Tusculan Disputations* begins,

28. Ludwig Vones' criticism of claims that Brun instituted an intellectual movement eventually centered in Cologne has merit if "school" is understood as book-learning, classroom teaching, and composition of works. For Vones the Cologne "school" is reduced to "introduction to church administration" and transmission of "practical administrative methods." This ignores the many voices that state clearly that Brun's major influence on future bishops was the transmission of philosophy, virtues, and liberal learning: a Ciceronian program. Unless that process is understood, it is futile to hunt for the curriculum of church administration. See Vones, "Erzbischof Brun," 137.

29. See Michael Lapidge, "The Stoic Inheritance," in *A History of Twelfth-Century Philosophy*, Peter Dronke, ed. (Cambridge: Cambridge University Press, 1988), 81–112, at 88–99.

30. Lapidge, "Stoic Inheritance," 91: "...it was possible for a twelfth-century philosopher to form an accurate and balanced view of Stoic ethics from reading the writings of Cicero and Seneca."

31. *De officiis* 2.5–6, Walter Miller, trans. (Cambridge, MA: Harvard University Press, 1975), 172–73. See also *In L. Pisonem* 71: "Philosophia, ut fertur, virtutis

CHAPTER 2 ★ PHILOSOPHY, c.950–c.1150

...the system and method of instruction in all the arts which have a bearing upon the right conduct of life [*ad rectam vivendi viam pertinerent*] are contained in the study of wisdom which goes by the name of philosophy.... [and in book 5]: Philosophy is the *magistra vitae* and "teacher of manners and of discipline."[32]

Ciceronian ideas and formulations passed to the Middle Ages by the well-known routes.[33] Isidore of Seville defines philosophy as "the knowledge of things human and divine joined to the study of living well" (*cum studio bene vivendi*).[34] Alcuin echoes this:

Philosophy is the investigation of natures, the knowledge of things human and divine.... Philosophy is also proper conduct

---

continet et officii et bene vivendi disciplinam." On Cicero's idea of philosophy, see Josef Mancal, *Zum Begriff der Philosophie bei M. Tullius Cicero* (Munich: Fink, 1982). For any more references to Cicero on philosophy that would be taken up in the Middle Ages, see Jean Leclercq, *Études sur le vocabulaire monastique du moyen âge* (Rome: Herder, 1961).

32. CTD 1.1: "...cum omnium artium, quae ad rectam vivendi viam pertinerent, ratio et disciplina studio sapientiae, quae philosophia dicitur, contineretur, hoc mihi Latinis litteris illustrandum putavi..." (2); 5.5: "O vitae philosophia dux, o virtutis indagatrix expultrixque vitiorum! ...tu magistra morum et disciplinae fuisti." In King ed., 428. Also worth noting in this context is Seneca's virtual identification of philosophy and ethics to the exclusion of "science" in the *Epistulae Morales ad Lucilium* 16.3: "[Philosophy]... animam format et fabricat, vitam disponit, actiones regit, agenda et omittenda demonstrat..." See also his Epistola 89.8: "Philosophia studium virtutis est...."

33. On the idea of philosophy in the earlier Middle Ages, see Leclercq, *Études*, 39–79; Leclercq, "Pour l'histoire de l'expression 'philosophie chrétienne,'" *Mélanges de Science Religieuse* 9 (1952): 221–26; Leclercq, *Love of Learning*, 107–8; Ernst R. Curtius, "Zur Geschichte des Wortes *Philosophia* im Mittelalter," *Romanische Forschungen* 57 (1943): 290–309, at 304–5. Curtius is interested in the wide range of meanings of the word but makes no connection with logic/dialectic other than as one of the seven liberal arts. Von Moos, *Hildebert von Lavardin*, 103–6, lays out the spread of meanings of philosophy in a few lines and analyzes a letter of Hildebert to William of Champeaux clearly indebted to the stoic conception of philosophy.

34. Isidore, *Etymologiae* 2.24.1; Wallace M. Lindsay, ed. (Oxford: Clarendon, 1911) (unpaged).

of life, the study of living well [*honestas vitae, studium bene vivendi*], the meditation of death, contempt of the world.[35]

Hrabanus Maurus repeats Alcuin's definition and swells it to encyclopedic length without adding logic other than to include *logici* as one of the three types of philosophers.[36]

GERBERT OF AURILLAC

That a Ciceronian conception of philosophy, bound to the cultivation of virtue and to service of the state, is not an isolated remnant of ancient learning without contemporary relevance is apparent from many sources, for instance the letters of Gerbert of Aurillac. Gerbert received a letter from the young Otto III inviting the famous scholar — and advisor to both his father and grandfather — to his court in order to provide the young king with instruction and correction "*in scriptis et dictis*" and mathematics, to give counsel in state affairs, and to "banish Saxon rusticity."[37] Gerbert responds enthusiastically. He praises his future pupil for his earlier study of mathematics and moral philosophy: "Unless you embraced the gravity of moral philosophy," Gerbert writes, "humility, guardian of all virtues, would not thus be impressed upon your words."[38] Again one sees the connection of humility with the education of a prince or courtier, and again, philosophy as the discipline of moderation, though limited in this case to *moralis philosophia*. The Ciceronian connection is prominent in Gerbert generally. He articulates the ethical conception of philosophy in a letter asserting a fundamental Ciceronian *habitus* in his life. It is directed to Abbot Ecbert of Tours:

35. Alcuin, *De dialectica* 1: "Philosophia est naturarum inquisitio, rerum humanarum divinarumque cognitio.... Est quoque philosophia honestas vitae, studium bene vivendi, meditatio mortis, contemptus saeculi." In PL 101:952A. See also *De grammatica* PL 101:849C, 852D. Here Cicero meets Cassiodorus, on whose definition of philosophy, see Curtius, "Geschichte."

36. *De universo* 15.1; PL 111:413.

37. Epist. 186, *Die Briefsammlung Gerberts von Reims*, Fritz Weigle, ed., MGH *Briefe der deutschen Kaiserzeit* 2 (Munich: MGH, 1988), 221–23. Again, an indication of the high, or as Otto puts it "supreme," importance of learning for the royal family. He calls the concerns that led to his call to Gerbert "haec summa res" (222, l. 2).

38. Epist. 187, 224: "Nisi moralis philosophie gravitatem amplecteremini, non ita verbis vestris custos omnium virtutum impressa esset humilitas."

CHAPTER 2 ★ PHILOSOPHY, c.950–c.1150

I am not one to separate the Good from the Useful, as does Panaetius, but rather with Cicero I seek to mix the Good with the Useful.... And since Philosophy does not distinguish between the rules of speaking and the rules of conduct, I have always joined the study of eloquence to the study of living well.... For us who are caught up in the affairs of state, both are necessary.[39]

A strong statement: the link of eloquence with the *studium bene vivendi* is necessary for those who administer the affairs of the state. The needs of the *res publica* and the givens of philosophy require it. Gerbert is a Ciceronian far more than an Aristotelian both in his letters and, it seems, in his public life. He once called himself "a diligent executor of the precepts of Marcus Tullius, both in leisure and in public life."[40] He commends Cicero's *Republic* and the *Verrine Orations* to his friend Constantine of Fleury.[41] Weigle's index to Gerbert's letters lists forty-two direct citations of Cicero (none of Aristotle, except a proverb that required no direct knowledge of Aristotle).[42] The name "Aristotle" never occurs in his letters. Of course,

39. Gerbert, Epist. 44: "Cumque ratio morum dicendique ratio a philosophia non separentur, cum studio bene vivendi semper coniuncxi studium bene dicendi, quamvis solum bene vivere praestantius sit eo, quod est bene dicere, curisque regiminis absoluto, alterum satis sit sine altero. At nobis in re publica occupatis utraque necessaria." In Weigle ed., 73.

40. Epist. 158: "...in otio et negotio praeceptorum M. Tullii diligens fui executor." Weigle ed., 187, a claim strengthened by Gerbert's direct borrowings from Cicero. His letter 105, written in the name of Archbishop Adalbero of Rheims, angrily demands the return of borrowed books and begins, "Quousque abutemini paciencia, fidissimi quondam, ut putabatur, amici?" For others, see Weigle's index of citations.

41. Epist. 86; Weigle ed., 114. In Epist. 167 to Abbot Romulf of Sens, he begs, in the tone of a man tortured by care and guilt, for works of Cicero (he does not give titles): "...fluenta M. Tullii sicienti praebete." In Weigle ed., 195.

42. An intense interest in dialectics may well be present without any mention of Aristotle but certainly not without Boethius. Of the seven citations of Boethius in Gerbert's letters, six relate to *De arithmetica*, two to dialectical writings, though the reference to *Dialogues on Porphyry* in Epist. 23, p. 46, ll. 4–6, refers only to the division of philosophy into the active and contemplative life. In Epistola 123, he asks the recipient for an excerpt of Boethius' commentary on *Peri Hermeneias*. The single mention of Boethius by name refers to an unknown *Astrologia* in Epist. 8, p. 31.

he is acquainted with Aristotle as the author of writings on logic, and he includes them in a conception of philosophy also shaped by Boethius' *Consolation of Philosophy*[43] but generally as a form of exercise not as what constitutes philosophy.

Gerbert's teaching of dialectic is attested in one of the most informative documents on education of the period, Richer of St. Remi's *Historiae* 3.46–54. This extensive passage describes Gerbert's teaching at Rheims, stressing dialectics but also poetry, rhetoric, and the quadrivium.[44] It is illuminating both for Gerbert's preoccupation with dialectic and for the position of that discipline within the range of subjects he taught.

Chapter 45 tells of Gerbert's tutelage in *logica* with a master of Rheims, Gerannus (*"in logica clarissimus"*). Taking up teaching duties at Rheims, Gerbert's course of studies begins with *dialectica*. Richer clearly takes "logic" as identical with "dialectic" in the opening of chapter 46. The usage of the schools also applies the term "logic" to mean the language arts in general. Richer follows that more general usage in ending his presentation of the course of studies — beginning in dialectic and ending in oratory — with the comment, "*Sed haec de logica*."[45] Here are chapters 46–48 on the language arts:[46]

43. See his Epist. 45; Weigle ed., 74 and 123; Weigle ed., 151, where he claims that "philosophy alone" is the cure for the cares of public life.

44. Richer von Saint Remi, *Historiae*, Hartmut Hoffmann, ed., MGH, SS 38 (Hannover: Hahn, 2000) 191–98. See Pierre Riché, "L'enseignement de Gerbert à Reims dans le context européen," in *Gerberto: Scienza, storia et mito: Atti del Gerberti Symposium (Bobbio 25–27 Iuglio 1983)*, Michele Tosi, ed. (Bobbio: Salesianum, 1985), 51–69; Gasc, "Gerbert"; Jason K. Glenn, "Master and Community in Tenth-Century Reims," in *Teaching and Learning in Northern Europe, 1000–1200*, Sally N. Vaughn and Jay Rubenstein, ed. (Turnhout: Brepols, 2006), 51–68.

45. 48, p. 195. Cf. Hrabanus Maurus, *De universo* PL 111:414B: "Logica autem dividitur in duas species, hoc est Dialecticam et Rhetoricam"; John of Salisbury, *Metalogicon* 1.10.8–9: "Est itaque logica ut nominis significatio latissime pateat, loquendi vel disserendi ratio." In Hall ed., 28. On the range of meanings of the term, see Mary M. McLaughlin, "Abelard's Conception of the Liberal Arts and Philosophy," in *Arts libéraux et philosophie au moyen âge: Actes du quatrième congrès international de philosophie médiévale* (Montreal: Vrin, 1968), 523–30, at 526–27. In this essay I use "logic," unless further qualified, in the narrower sense, as interchangeable with "dialectic."

46. Richer, *Historiae* 3.46: "Dialecticam ergo ordine librorum percurrens, dilucidis

[46] He clarified dialectic with lucid commentaries, following the course in the order of the books [which follow]. Beginning with Porphyry's *Isagoge*, that is, introductions, in the translation of Victorinus the rhetorician, he proceeded to explain these works according to Boethius. Next, he investigated Aristotle's book of categories, that is, predicates. He elucidated with great acumen the book of Perihermeneias and its difficulties. Next he inculcated in his readers the topics, that is, the loci of arguments, translated by Cicero from Greek into Latin and explicated by the consul Boethius in six books of commentaries.

[47] In addition, he read and explicated, much to the benefit of his students, the four books *De topicis differentiis*, two *De sillogismis cathegoricis*, three *De ypotheticis*, one book of definitions, one also of divisions. After laboring over these, when he wished to advance his students to rhetoric, any effort was suspect to him that did not arrive at the art of oratory without first learning the modes of locution, which are to be gleaned from the poets. For that reason, he clung to the poets of whom he deemed it important to have a close knowledge. Therefore, he read and taught the poets Virgil, Statius, and Terence and the satirists Juvenal, Persius, and Horace, as well

sententiarum verbis enodavit. Inprimis enim Porphirii ysagogas id est introductiones secundum Victorini rhethoris translationem, inde etiam easdem secundum Manlium explanavit. Cathegoriarum id est predicamentorum librum Aristotelis consequenter enucleans. Periermenias vero id est de interpretatione librum, cuius laboris sit, aptissime monstravit. Inde etiam topica id est argumentorum sedes a Tullio de Greco in Latinum translata, et a Manlio consule sex commentariorum libris dilucidata, suis auditoribus intimavit. [47] Necnon et quatuor de topicis differentiis libros, de sillogismis cathegoricis duos, de ypotheticis tres, diffinitionumque librum unum, divisionum eque unum, utiliter legit et expressit. Post quorum laborem, cum ad rhethoricam suos provehere vellet, id sibi suspectum erat, quod sine locutionum modis, qui in poetis discendi sunt, ad oratoriam artem ante perveniri non queat. Poetas igitur adhibuit, quibus assuescendos arbitrabatur. Legit itaque ac docuit Maronem et Statium Terentiumque poetas, Iuuenalem quoque ac Persium Horatiumque satiricos, Lucanum etiam historiographum. Quibus assuefactos, locutionemque modis compositor, ad rhethoricam transduxit. [48] Qua instructis, sophistam adhibuit. Apud quem in controversiis exercerentur, ac sic ex arte agerent, ut preter artem agere viderentur, quod oratoris maximum videtur. Sed hec de logica." In Hoffmann ed., 193–94.

as the historian Lucan. Once these were mastered, he moved on to rhetoric.

[48] To those instructed in this art he assigned a sophist who exercised them in controversies. Thus they would operate within the precepts of the art, while seeming to act without art,⁴⁷ which seems to be the most important thing for an orator. But enough said of Logic.

It is clear that Richer and Gerbert considered logic important in the narrower sense. It is the subject that brought Gerbert to Rheims, garnered him a "leave of absence from the imperial court," and inspired praise from Richer (*dilucidis verbis; aptissime monstravit...utiliter legit*). No other part of his "trivial" teaching is singled out for praise. The longer passage on dialectic stands out in contrast to the brief mention of rhetoric and the omission of grammar. But it is also clear that dialectic is the first step in an orator's education, progressing from that beginning to its final stage in forensic oratory. Richer's presentation places the subjects purposefully in a sequence: first comes the *logica vetus*, then the *modi locutionum*, then the study of the poets, advancing to the "art of oratory."⁴⁸ Logic in the narrower sense was propaedeutic to rhetoric and poetry, and all three subordinated to the oratorical art.⁴⁹

A letter of Gerbert written in 986 or 987 during his stint as *magister scolarum* at Rheims gives some perspective on his teaching there. It is addressed to the monk Bernard of Aurillac. Gerbert responds to the request of Bernard for news of him, and they evidently were not in close touch, since Gerbert fills him in on his departure from Bobbio about

---

47. A difficult passage to translate. Richer posits a kind of oratorical *sprezzatura*: the ability to hide skills gained with great effort and exercise them as though with great ease. Here adapted from Cicero. On 3.48, see Hoffmann ed., 195 n. 3.

48. Richer, *Historiae* 3.47: "...post quorum laborem...ad rhetoricam suos provehere vellet...modi locutionum...[without which there is no advancing] ad oratoriam artem. Poetas igitur adhibuit.... Quibus assuefactos...ad rhethoricam transduxit. Qua instructis, sophistam adhibuit." In Hoffmann ed., 194.

49. Richer's own style exemplifies oratorical training informing the style of historical writing. See Robert Latouche, "Un imitateur de Salluste au Xe siècle: Richer," in Latouche, *Études médiévales* (Paris: Presses Universitaires de France, 1966), 69–81; Hans-Henning Kortüm, *Richer von Saint-Remi: Studien zu einem Geschichtsschreiber des 10. Jahrhunderts* (Stuttgart: Steiner, 1985), 93–112.

CHAPTER 2 ★ PHILOSOPHY, c.950–c.1150

three years earlier. The only other news is that he is teaching "most noble scholars the liberal disciplines" at Rheims. He has composed a booklet on the rhetorical art. Gerbert describes this *opus* as

> admirable to experts, useful to students for the things of rhetors prone to slip the mind, most difficult to comprehend and to fix in the memory.[50]

He offers to send Bernard this booklet and information on music for students. It may be that this passage says nothing about the priority of rhetoric over dialectic, but it is worth noting that Gerbert, asked what he's been doing in the past years, answers in effect, "I've left my abbacy, am teaching the arts and writing about rhetoric." Foregrounding that art says at the very least that he did not anticipate an interest in dialectic at Aurillac.

The discipline of dialectic will maintain its position subordinate to oratory in the course of studies in our period. Walther of Speyer confirms this structure of studies in his *Libellus scolasticus* composed in 984.[51] The *Libellus* introduces his *Life of St. Christopher*. It purports to describe his own education at the cathedral school of Speyer under Bishop Balderich (970–86). After grammar and the poets, an elaborate allegory in all but impenetrable Latin (Vossen's translation is indispensable) introduces Philosophy as a young/old maiden. She is dressed and made up by the five serving girls of Dialectica, then is passed on to Rhetoric for exercise in disputation and legal cases. Finally, the happy crowd of students come to rest at the feet of Logic in its meaning of the language arts in general. They now have mastered these arts. All that remains is left to Cicero: "*Sub pedibus Logice recubabat nexa coaeve / Commissura tibi reliquorum munia, Tulli.*"[52]

This sequence and hierarchy of studies — dialectic leads to rhetoric and poetry; study culminates in legal oratory — was maintained at cathedral schools in Germany and France with gradually weakening foundations up to the time when John of Salisbury will lament its overturning in the twelfth-century schools of Paris.

50. Epist. 92: "...quandam figuram edidi artis rethorice...opus sane expertibus mirabile, studiosis utile ad res rethorum fugaces et caliginossimas comprehendendas...." In Weigle ed., 121.

51. *Der Libellus scolasticus des Walther von Speyer: Ein Schulbericht aus dem Jahr 984*, Peter Vossen, ed. and German trans. (Berlin: De Gruyter, 1962).

52. *Liber scolasticus*, ll. 146–47.

Taken together, Brun at Cologne and Gerbert at Rheims educated a large number of future bishops and abbots. Their influence on politics, church history, and intellectual life in the tenth and eleventh century is vast. Their influence on the history of logic, however, is minor. Logic was a subject of subordinate importance in a culture that educated clergy to positions as royal and ecclesiastical counselors and administrators. As a handmaiden of an orator's education, it was held in prominence more by the great names of its past cultivators — Aristotle, Porphyry, Boethius — than by anything approaching mastery of its intricacies.[53] That lustre may account for the extensive list of texts and authors of the old logic cited by Richer.

GERBERT ON REASON: PHILOSOPHY DEFENDING THE EMPIRE

Gerbert's brief tract *De rationali et ratione uti* (*On the Rational and the Use of Reason*) provides the best evidence for Gerbert's practice of dialectic and the role of Aristotle. It also underscores the role of the king as the muse and instigator of Gerbert's work on logic. In a preface in the form of a letter to Emperor Otto III, the author explains the work's origin. He recalls a time when, at a gathering of scholars in the presence of the emperor, he raised some of the most difficult problems proposed by Aristotle and others:

> While we dwelt in Germany in the hot time of the year, bound to imperial service as we always are and always will be, the impulse of my mind, silently shedding moderation, resolved divine mysteries, I know not how, into words. They brought forward some problems described by Aristotle and the greatest of men in the most obscure utterances, so that it would be remarkable, amidst the exigencies of the wars against the Sarmatians then in preparation, if any mortal might possess such inner chambers of mind, from which things so subtle and so luminous could flow like streams from the purest fount.[54]

53. Cf. Pierre Riché, *Les Écoles et l'enseignement dans l'occident chrétien de la fin du Ve siècle au milieu du XIe siècle* (Paris: Aubier Montaigne, 1979), 261: "[between the eighth and the twelfth centuries] tous les maîtres font...l'éloge de la dialectique... mai ils l'enseignent rarement."

54. "Cum in Germania ferventioris anni tempus demoraremur, imperialibus astricti obsequiis, ut semper sumus, semperque erimus, nescio quid arcana

CHAPTER 2 ★ PHILOSOPHY, c.950-c.1150

In addition to the emperor, many noble scholars and individuals of high learning were present, a fair number of whom were bishops distinguished for their wisdom and famous for their eloquence. But while the profound issues flood to Gerbert almost unexpectedly and certainly without preparation and rehearsal (so his formulation suggests — a good example of *sprezzatura*) and in spite of all the distractions of imperial service, they leave the crowd of *eruditi* speechless. None was able to give a worthy explanation of any of the questions posed by Gerbert. The emperor judged their display of ignorance unworthy of his court,[55] and he ordered Gerbert to prepare a discourse on the various opinions of the rational and the use of reason.[56] The prefatory letter suggests that a great deal is at stake, nothing less than the standing of the imperial court. Gerbert writes his tract lest Italy should think the "sacred palace" sunk in torpor, and lest Greece preen itself as the sole possessor of "imperial philosophy and Roman power." Rome and Byzantium are watching, it seems, as Gerbert is inspired and the others stumped.

This passage deserves a close analysis, but I will just point to the issues it raises. This is the only one of Gerbert's writings where Aristotelian logic is central to a philosophical issue. The questions treated, he says, are "sophistic," and the resolution will be provided by *spinosa dialectica*.[57] This is good confirmation that Gerbert considers some facility with the most difficult problems posed by Aristotle important in philosophy. It looms large in a defense of what Gerbert calls *imperialis philosophia*.

---

divina mensuram secum tacite retractans motus animi in verba resolvit, et quae ab Aristotele summisque viris erant difficillimis descripta sententiis, in medium protulit: ut mirum foret inter bellorum discrimina, quae contra Sarmatas parabantur, aliquem mortalium hos mentis recessus habere potuisse, a quibus tam subtilia, tam praeclara, velut quidam rivi a purissimo fonte profluerent." In PL 139:159A.

55. "Vestra divina providentia ignorantiam sacro palatio indignam judicans...." In PL 139:159B.

56. For a discussion see François Picavet, *Gerbert: Un pape philosophe d'après l'histoire et d'après la légende* (Paris: Leroux, 1897), 150–58. Prantl's judgment of the tract: "eine höchst abenteuerliche Verquickung eines unverdauten Schulwissens." See *Geschichte*, 2:55.

57. PL 139:159D.

The other telling element of this frame narrative is the ignorance of the assembly. Not one of the *eruditi* could give a worthy explanation of the questions raised, though they were "famous for their wisdom and distinguished for their eloquence" (*sapientia praeclari et eloquentia insignes*). We might be justified in inferring from that formulation that those schooled in a Ciceronian education (eloquence joined to wisdom) don't know their Aristotle. Gerbert states outright that their ignorance puts the reputation of the imperial court at risk (or rather he states that sentiment in the words of the emperor). Gerbert is its rescuer. The implied narrative then is, "Thank God that at least one in the emperor's retinue knew his Aristotle."

Of course, Gerbert wrote the narrative to please "sacred ears"[58] and evidently to commend his own talents to them. The problems are the most difficult, they occur to him as if spontaneously, the distractions of looming war can't stop the flow, and the victory of the "inner chambers of the mind" over external cares is nearly miraculous. While he surely did not fabricate the whole report (the emperor had been a witness to the event described), he is reminding the young ruler what kind of a man he is and what kind of intellect he possesses.

The display character of the preface and of the work itself is evident. We see Gerbert casting himself in the role of inspired genius in a world of more limited minds. But the importance for the cultivation of logic is, first, that it happens in isolation. Hence he can assert his credentials for virtuosity in a little-understood discipline. Aristotle is useful because no one else understands him. Second, that Gerbert probably perceived the force of logic to frame arguments that make incontrovertible claims about reality and to approach truth.[59] This implies that Gerbert's understanding of dialectic places it above the role of handmaiden of

---

58. PL 139:168D.

59. This impulse in Gerbert is also indicated in his major scientific preoccupation: mathematics, geometry, astronomy. A couple of verses to Otto III accompanying a work on mathematics admire numbers as realities above falsehood, invention, and ambiguity: "Quocirca gravidi textum rimare libelli / Praesentique vigil vim ratione vide: / Nec locus hic mendis, nec lusum ficta subornant, / Verborumve fidem frivula conciliant, — / Mensuram docet et numerum pondusque remotis / Ambiguis. Tantum mens oculata legat." In Nicolaus Bubnov, ed., *Gerberti Opera Mathematica* (Hildesheim: Olms, 1963), 149, included among *Dubia*.

CHAPTER 2 ✶ PHILOSOPHY, c.950–c.1150

oratory and in doing so rises well outside of the limits within which his contemporaries operate. He also anticipates issues of the controversy over universals in the twelfth century.[60]

What is to be said of its contribution to logic? It survives in two manuscripts, and no one to my knowledge quotes it.[61] Gerbert intended it as an exercise for the emperor to be indulged in between his studies of mathematics: "*Legetis haec inter vestrae matheseos exercitia.*"[62] His prelude to the work suggests his role as an innovator introducing a subject of which most high clerics are ignorant. If many in monasteries mastered the art, the brilliance of his own genius would be dimmed and the imperial court further indicted for its ignorance.

The other important point is the context of this display of philosophy. It is the imperial court. The emperor is credited with high pride in the intellectual level of the court.[63] Gerbert posits something called "imperial philosophy" (*imperialis philosophia*) and positions himself as its defender. His impassioned speech (*Nostrum, nostrum est imperium Romanum!*) makes the emperor into an honorary philosopher joining dominion and learning in his own person:

> Caesar is ours, emperor and Augustus of the Romans, you who born of the highest nobility of the Greeks, surpass the Greeks in dominion [*imperio*], who rule over the Romans by hereditary right, and who lead both in genius and eloquence.[64]

The emperor is the embodiment of philosophy. His "genius and eloquence" are qualities of the kingdom. The intellectual and the

---

60. Picavet, 158.

61. On the manuscripts, see *Oeuvres de Gerbert, Pape sous le nom de Sylvestre II*, A. Olleris, ed. (Hildesheim: Olms, 1963), 297; Manitius, *Geschichte*, 2:737. By contrast, Gerbert's quadrivial works are abundantly transmitted. See Bubnov, passim.

62. PL 139:168D.

63. The same is true of Otto II as represented in Richer's report on the disputation at Ravenna between Gerbert and Ohtric of Magdeburg in late 980 or early 981 in *Historiae* 3.55–65. On disputations and displays of learning and their critical role at an imperial court, see my "Gerbert versus Ohtric."

64. "Noster es Caesar, Romanorum imperator et Auguste, qui summo Graecorum sanguine ortus, Graecos imperio superas, Romanis haereditario jure imperas, utrosque ingenio et eloquio praevenis." In PL 139:159B–C.

political are placed on the same level. The philosophers whose speech and writings are the expression of imperial philosophy are the emperor's speakers and his writing hands. The image implies an imperial obligation to maintain and defend intellectual activity, as in the course of governing he would defend law and justice. The court philosopher is the emperor's champion who must defend the emperor's reputation as embodiment of imperial philosophy. These implications of Gerbert's prologue offer a statement of the commitment to learning as an imperial duty.

At no point in this prologue does Gerbert suggest that the learning on which the reputation of the court depends is monastic in origin or character. The emperor and the empire are the constant points of reference and the prime mover of learning and philosophy for Gerbert.[65] At a glance the figure of Gerbert seems to confirm the consensus view of tenth-century philosophy sketched above: his origins and early career were at the monastery of Aurillac, and he served briefly as abbot of the Benedictine monastery of Bobbio.[66] Richer's report makes clear that Gerbert's early association with the monastery of Aurillac, a religious house touched by the Cluniac reform movement, has no connection to his cultivation of Aristotelian logic, unless the monastery had played the role of whetting his appetite for the subject by its absence. What the young oblate Gerbert studied at Aurillac was grammar.[67]

65. Gerbert's poem in praise of Boethius ("Roma potens dum iura suo declarat in orbe") links the philosophy of Boethius directly with his imperial service and appoints him honorary scholar at the court of Otto III: "Nunc decus imperii, summas qui praegravat artes, / Tertius Otto sua dignum te iudicat aula." MGH, *Poetae* 5:474–75. See also a poem attributed to Gerbert, and attached in PL 139:157–58 (though in no manuscript) to *De rationali*, is studded with language associating learning with the court ("Quisquis opaca velis sophie scandere regna").

66. His abbacy began in late 982 or early 983. By late 983 he had fled the monastery. On Gerbert's rise and fall at Bobbio, see Pierre Riché, *Gerbert d'Aurillac: Le pape de l'an mil* (Paris: Fayard, 2006), 63–74. The rich study of Gerbert as abbot by Michele Tosi, "Il governo abbaziale di Gerberto a Bobbio," in Tosi, ed., *Gerberto*, 71–234, is a treasure trove of material for the history of Bobbio in the tenth century, including a list of its extensive library holdings.

67. Richer, *Historiae* 43: "…in coenobio sancti confessoris Geroldi a puero altus, et grammatica edoctus est." In Hoffmann ed., 191. On the role of Aurillac in Gerbert's development, see Edmond-René Labande, "La Formation de Gerbert à St. Geraud d'Aurillac," in Tosi, ed., *Gerberto*, 21–34, at 25: "Or il semble que Gerbert, s'il y a

CHAPTER 2 ✶ PHILOSOPHY, c.950–c.1150

For further instruction in the arts he travelled to Spain. His introduction to logic came neither in Aurillac, nor in Bobbio, but rather first in Rome at the emperor's court, then at the cathedral school of Rheims. In 970, Gerbert travelled with his two patrons, Bishop Hatto of Vich and Duke Borell II of Barcelona, to Rome, possibly for the marriage of Otto II to Theophanu. Introduced to Pope John XIII, Gerbert impressed him as a young man of high industry possessed of a powerful urge to learn. Italy at that time being impoverished in the areas of music and astronomy, as Richer claims, the pope commended Gerbert to Otto the Great, emperor since 962, as exceptionally learned in the quadrivium and "able to give his [that is, the emperor's] followers a rigorous education in those subjects."[68]

Otto fastens possessively onto the young prodigy and closes all doors to his return to the pope, who then indicates to Bishop Hatto and Duke Borell in the most unassuming tone that the king wished for the time being to retain the young man in his service. These two worthies returned to Spain consoled by the false hope that their charge would soon return to them. When the emperor sounds out the young man on his learning, he finds that he is sufficiently learned in the quadrivium but that now in addition he wished to learn the science of logic.[69] It happened that an archdeacon of Rheims, Gerannus, who enjoyed the highest reputation in the field of logic at the time, was in Rome as the legate of King Lothar to Otto I. The emperor consents to Gerbert's tutelage with Gerannus, and the two eventually head off for Rheims together. From Gerannus Gerbert learned logic and soon was proficient in it.[70]

Twelve or thirteen years passed between Otto's first visit to Rome, his stay in Rheims with Gerannus, and his appointment as Abbot of Bobbio. Therefore, we must exclude both Aurillac and Bobbio as originating sources for Gerbert's knowledge of logic, along with the

---

utilement assimilé cet art [i.e., Grammar], s'il a commencé à s'y former aux procédés de la rhétorique, ignorait encore tout de la dialectique lorsqu'il quitta Aurillac." Also Riché, "L'enseignement," 54–55.

68. Richer, *Historiae* 3.44: "...suos strenue docere valeret." In Hoffmann ed., 192.

69. Richer, *Historiae* 3.44: "...de artibus interrogatus, in mathesi se satis posse, logice vero scientiam se addiscere velle respondit." In Hoffmann ed., 192–93.

70. Richer, *Historiae* 3.45; Hoffmann ed., 66–68.

monastic world generally, though the excellent library of Bobbio will have served him well during his stay there.

Richer's report makes clear also that it was the emperor who was primarily interested in attracting to his service a talented young man and granting him leave of absence to study logic. The pope was the mediator, not the instigator, of Gerbert's pedagogic role. It was Otto the Great who had the largest stake in cultivating a promising young scholar. Far from indicating any kind of indifference of the king to quadrivial and logical studies, we might well infer from Richer's report that the emperor had so intense a concern for cultivating learning that he risked irritating both the pope and the two Spanish gentlemen.

Gerbert maintained close friendships with Abbot Gerald of Aurillac and with other monks of Aurillac and Bobbio, but also with many outside of the monastic life.[71] He defended vigorously the interests of the monasteries and churches he served and ultimately, as pope, of western Christendom. But apart from these ties, he has left few indications in his writings of intellectual obligations to the monastic world.[72] He defined himself as a philosopher in the emperor's service.[73]

71. On Gerbert and the ideal of friendship, see Courtney Demayo, "The Theory and Practice of Friendship in the Middle Ages: Ciceronian *amicitia* in the letters of Gerbert of Aurillac," *Viator* 38 (2007): 319–37.

72. On Gerbert's monastic obligations, see Jean Leclercq, "Interpretazione gerbertiana della vita monastica," in Tosi, ed., *Gerberto*, 677–89; and Michel Sot, "Le Moine Gerbert, l'église de Reims et l'église de Rome," in *Gerbert l'européen: Actes du colloque d'Aurillac, 4–7 juin 1996*, Nicole Charbonnel and Jean-Eric Iung, ed. (Aurillac: Société des Lettres la Haute Auvergne, 1997), 136–49. Both focus on Gerbert's defense of the rights of the Church against lay intrusion. They can show his assimilation of the values of the monastic reform movement and his use of the Rule of St. Benedict and of Scripture in defending rights of the Church, but neither can point to distinct monastic intellectual obligations outside of the polemics of administration. Leclercq, "Interpretazione," 678, says that his study of *grammatica* would have opened the way to the *lectio divina*, but the absence of writings on Scripture by Gerbert and of any mention of scriptural studies in Richer's discussion of his teaching is also worth noting, the more striking since Carolingian studies of the language arts aimed programmatically at the study of Scripture.

73. As asserted, for instance, in the first sentence of *De rationali*: "...imperialibus astricti obsequiis, ut semper sumus, semperque erimus...." In PL 139:159A.

CHAPTER 2 ✷ PHILOSOPHY, c.950–c.1150

A small but telling indication of his sense of self-definition as abbot of Bobbio comes in salutations of his letters during his abbacy. His letter collection begins in his time at Bobbio. While such flourishes are rare in any of Gerbert's letters, six letters dating from Bobbio and the aftermath of his abbacy begin with salutations. They are Epistolae 1: "Domino suo O[ttoni II] cesari semper augusto G[erbertus] quondam liber"; 4: "Divi cesaris G[erbertus] Bosoni in Christo salutem"; 6: "Domine sue Adalaidi semper auguste G[erbertus]"; 7: "G[erbertus] quondam scolasticus Ayrardo suo salutem"; 12: "Hugoni suo G[erbertus] quondam scolasticus"; 14: "Beatissimo pape Johanni G[erbertus] solo nomine officii Ebobiensis cenobii abbas."

The second two express his sense of attachment to his secular lords: "Divine Caesar's Gerbert sends greetings in Christ to Boso"; "To his lady Adelheid, always august, Gerbert." The letter to Boso (whose followers have stolen hay from Bobbio) is pure abbey business, where a formal identification as abbot might seem in order. But Gerbert puts his influence with "Caesar" in the foreground and threatens Boso with the emperor's wrath, not God's. "*Quondam scolasticus,*" "once upon a time a teacher," indicates a nostalgia for the life of study and the schools denied him because of the turmoil of the troubled monastery. The ambiguous, "*quondam liber,*" of Epistola 1, must represent his abbacy as a captive state, his tenuous hold on power also indicated in the letter to the pope, "Abbot in name only." These salutations bespeak a self-identification at odds with that of the abbot dedicated to a spiritual mission.

ABBO OF FLEURY AND OTHERS

By contrast, Abbo of Fleury, neighbor but no friend of Gerbert, regularly precedes his letters with salutations like "A lover of the lovers of Christ, Abbo"; "Servant of the servants of God, Abbo"; "An unworthy servant of the servants of God, Abbo"; "The humble rector of the residents of Fleury, Abbo."[74] Of course, Benedictine monasticism participated in the intellectual life of the period, and Aristotelian logic aroused some interest. But the conviction of the historians of philosophy cited above that that discipline was central to philosophy as the period from 950 to

74. "Amatorum Christi amator Abbo," PL 139:423B; "famulorum Dei famulus Abbo," PL 139:424C; "indignus famulorum Christi famulus Abbo," PL 139:425B; "humilis Floriacensium rector Abbo," PL 139:429A.

1150 conceived and practiced it in the major centers of learning has little basis in the sources.

Abbo of Fleury was a contemporary of Gerbert also prominent for his learning, whose milieu and intellectual commitment are accurately characterized as monastic and Benedictine in contrast to Gerbert's. He was a monk, schoolmaster, abbot, martyr, and saint.[75] His biographer noted his learning in dialectic,[76] but his comments do not privilege dialectic. While Abbo did compose works on conclusions from syllogisms drawing on Boethius,[77] his dialectical studies shrink in his biographer's presentation to the importance of a passing reference. Prantl does not mention Abbo; Grabmann devotes three lines to him.[78] Kneale and Kneale devote part of a sentence to him with appropriately general framing: "Abbo of Fleury and Notker Labeo of St. Gall were other influential teachers of the period."[79]

I question that Abbo, Gerbert, or Notker deserve to be called "thinkers" in the discipline of dialectics. They sought, received, and transmitted an education that prepared them broadly to speak and argue well.[80]

75. See the *Vita Abbonis* of Haimo of Fleury, PL 139:375–414.

76. *Vita Abbonis* 3: "...grammaticae, arithmeticae, nec non dialecticae [artes] jam ad plenum indaginem attigerat...." In PL 139:390B; "...quosdam dialecticorum nodos syllogismorum enucleatissime enodavit...." In PL 139:390C (same passage in 7:394A).

77. *Syllogismorum categoricum et hypotheticorum enodatio*, André Van de Vyver, ed., *Abbonis Floriacensis opera inedita* (Bruges: De Temple, 1966). Also available in a critical edition with German translation: Abbo von Fleury, *De Syllogismis Hypotheticis*, Franz Schupp, ed. (Leiden: Brill, 1996). Schupp argues Abbo's original insight in connecting Boethius' theory of hypothetical syllogisms with the list of such syllogisms known to the Middle Ages through Cicero's *Topics*. But it is also clear from Schupp's scholarship (vi–vii) that Abbo's work had no influence, that the twelfth century took up hypothetical syllogisms without knowledge of Abbo, and the subject was forgotten by the thirteenth century. Remarkable as this insight may have been (9: "In diesem Punkt ist die gesamte mittelalterliche Logik hinter der Leistung Abbos zurückgeblieben"), Abbo's logical writings are like a tree falling in the forest that no one heard.

78. Martin Grabmann, *Geschichte*, 1:212.

79. *Development of Logic*, 199.

80. Anita Guerreau-Jalabert, "Grammaire et culture profane à Fleury au Xe siècle," (Ph.D. diss., University of Paris, 1975), 95, stresses the dual instruction of

CHAPTER 2 ✷ PHILOSOPHY, c.950–c.1150

Dialectic was potentially useful for argumentation; it was also perceived as a mental exercise and an art with the huge authority of Aristotle behind it, but the art itself was obscure and minor in comparison with grammar understood as the arts of language (*litterae*), ranging from grammatical rules to the reading and composing of poetry.[81] Likewise, it may be remarkable that Notker Labeo translated Boethius' Latin translation of *Peri Hermeneias* into German, but that work and other works on dialectics translated by Notker have no particular highlight in the large corpus of works he translated. His accomplishment is, after all, one of translation, not original thought.

My purpose is not in any way to diminish any of the writers discussed but only to question their status as "thinkers" in the discipline of dialectic. Their contributions are elsewhere. Putting Abbo's and Gerbert's cultivation of dialectic in the foreground presents them at their weakest, hence ultimately diminishes them. I believe Pierre Riché has characterized Abbo's relation to dialectic well: "Comme Cicéron et Quintillien, il voit dans la dialectique un auxiliaire de l'art oratoire."[82] The same can be said of Gerbert and of the educated class of the tenth century generally.

The historians of philosophy quoted in the opening of this study would probably not disagree about the stature of dialectic in the period. Few who had studied the tenth century's level of interest in logic would or could disagree. The point here is the definition of philosophy. Privileging dialectic as the defining subject and Benedictine monasticism as its transmitter skews the matter badly. Philosophy between Eriugena and Berengar or Anselm is not "pre-scholastic." It bears hardly any relationship to Scholasticism of any phase. It is not

---

divine and secular letters at the monastery and of the latter "l'apprentissage de la *grammatica* semble être la pierre angulaire."

81. Abbo's *Quaestiones grammaticales*, composed for the monks of Ramsey Abbey, England during his two-year stay there is instructive. He deals with minutiae of pronunciation and prosody. See PL 139:523A-534D. He quotes Virgil fourteen times, Horace eight times, and Aristotle once. Manitius' judgment, *Geschichte* 2:668: "Nirgends zeigt sich besonders tiefes Eingehen oder etwa besondere Gelehrsamkeit."

82. Pierre Riché, *Abbon de Fleury: Un moine savant et combatif (vers 950–1004)* (Turnhout: Brepols, 2004), 97.

dialectical, or at least dialectics was a minor force. If the period is to be understood as insignificant in the history of philosophy, then let it be not because its representatives are mediocre logicians. If they knew little about logic, it was in large part because it did not matter much.

CONSERVATIVE REACTION: PETER DAMIAN

One other set of sources can give sharper focus on the age's conceptualizing of philosophy: the attacks of conservative clergy. Peter Damian's short tract, *De sancta simplicitate scientiae inflanti anteponenda*, is instructive. It is formulated as a letter to a monk named Ariprandus who evidently has expressed a love of learning that he was never able to satisfy by the study of the liberal arts. Peter Damian assures him that a preference of liberal studies to sacred studies is foolishness:

> Having a heart inclined to learning and a very quick mind, you demanded the gateway of the true light rather than the blind wisdom of the philosophers; you preferred to hasten to the desert, following in the footsteps of the fishermen rather than sweating over liberal studies, or I should say, stulties.[83]

His target throughout is grammar: *grammatica, litterae, litterarum studia*.[84] He praises St. Hilary for casting out the "Platonists and Pythagoreans," yet, even though unequipped with *philosophorum studia*, he nonetheless was able to command demons.[85] He gives some

---

83. *De sancta simplicitate, Argumentum*: "...cum docile cor ac facillimum habeas ad discendum, ante veri luminis aditum requisisti quam caecam philosophorum sapientiam disceres; ante ad eremum pervolasti, sequens vestigia piscatorum, quam liberalium artium non dicam studiis sed stultitiis insudares." In PL 145:695A.

84. See *De sancta simplicitate* 3, arguing against eloquence as a preacher's virtue: possessing *copiam scientiae litteralis* is less valuable than living a Christian life (697A); following Christ promotes the faith better than *multiplicitas verborum* (697B); how little Christ needs *nostra grammatica* is evident in that he chose simple men and fishermen to disseminate the faith rather than *philosophos et oratores* (697B). 4: Blessed Benedict, sent *ad litterarum studia*, soon converts to the wise foolishness of Christ (699A); St. Martin cared nothing for *litterae*. Anthony was no rhetorician (*non rhetoricatur*, 699B). He praises Pope Leo IX as *sapienter indoctus*, and that means, no letters: "Litteras non didicerit, grammaticos quoslibet ac mundi philosophos... praecellit" (701A).

85. *De sancta simplicitate*, PL 145:699B.

cautionary tales. A cleric named Ugo of Parma had innumerable "useful" gifts (implying gifts that qualified him for office).[86] So ambitious was he, so bent on attaining a bishopric, that he became a chaplain of Emperor Conrad II but met a bad end before his ambitions were realized. The "study of the arts" (*artium studia*) are for Ugo of Parma the starting point of a career leading through imperial service to a bishopric — and for Peter Damian, the starting point of ambition leading to an untimely death.[87] Another cleric, born of the highest French nobility, whom he does not name in order not to (further) diminish the honor of a man still alive, lacked nothing to qualify him for office (*nescio an aliquid utilitatis desit [ei]*). Peter Damian gives a very illuminating list of the things that make one "useful":

He possessed external goods in full flourishing, noble as an emperor, beautiful in every aspect of his appearance, he speaks like Tullius, writes poetry like Virgil, an eager advocate of the Church, keen and acute in divine law. In scholastic dispute his words flow as if written in a book. Speaking in the vernacular, he does not offend the urbanity of [classical?] Latin grammar [*Romanae urbanitatis regulam non offendit*].

In spite of all his gifts, his life is such that all doors are closed to him.[88] The oratorical aspect of this man's gifts is evident. Even in that activity that comes closest to dialectic, "scholastic disputation," or "school debates," it is flowing speech not ingenious argument or conceptual penetration that distinguishes him. The classical models of this highly learned gentleman are Cicero and Virgil. Aristotle is not mentioned. While *De sancta simplicitate* leaves open the possibility that grammar and oratory are one thing and philosophy another, it is clear that those are the poles within which secular studies unfold. "Philosophy" also serves Peter Damian and others as a designation

86. *Utilitatum dotes*, PL 145:700A. On *utilitas* in the sense of "qualification for office" see Jaeger, *Envy*, 45, 60–61.

87. *De sancta simplicitate* 6, PL 145:700A.

88. *De sancta simplicitate* 6: "Hodie in Romana urbe frater advivit, ortus de summis proceribus Galliarum, cujus nomen taceo, quia fratris ignominiam perhorresco. Cui nescio an aliquid utilitatis desit. Tot siquidem exteriorum bonorum floribus enitescit: nobilis ut imperator, pulcher aspectu quodammodo, sicut Tullius loquitur, ut Virgilius poetatur; tuba vehemens in Ecclesia; perspicax et acutus est in lege divina; scholastice disputans, quasi descripta libri verba percurrit; vulgariter loquens, Romanae urbanitatis regulam non offendit." In PL 145:700C–D.

of the *studia artium* generally. In the mind of the author, studies preparing the orator are inseparable from worldly ambition aimed at high positions in church and secular administration.

Dialectics and Aristotle play a minor or no role in philosophy as Peter Damian conceived and attacked it,[89] even though it is apparent from his *De divina omnipotentia* that he himself had training in dialectics and was willing to use it in argument.[90] In a tract attacking liberal studies and worldly philosophy, only one passage unequivocally recognizes the existence of dialectic: John the Evangelist merits praise, says Peter Damian, because he despised "the cunning subtleties of the orators and the dialecticians" (*spretis oratorum dialecticorumque versutiis*).[91] The tract ends with another cautionary tale: the dream of Jerome, in which the high judge barred him from the gates of heaven and cast him down because "*Ciceronianus es, non Christianus.*"[92]

THE MAINSTREAM: CICERONIANISM

The mainstream of "philosophy" in the period was Ciceronian, and it flowed through the imperial courts. In this configuring of philosophy, oratorical skill and the virtuous governance of life in the context of

89. A survey of the polemics of Otloh of St. Emmeram would lead to the same conclusion. See for instance *De doctrina spirituali*, PL 146:263A–300A, especially 11, 270A–B, *De libris gentilium vitandis et de studio sacrae lectionis*. An interesting passage: "Quid mihi tunc Socrates, vel Plato Aristotelesque, / Tullius ipse rhetor, mundanae dogmatis auctor?" In PL 146:279B. Otloh evidently considered Cicero, not Socrates, Plato, or Aristotle, as the "author of worldly learning."

90. See Toivo J. Holopainen, *Dialectic and Theology in the Eleventh Century* (Leiden: Brill, 1996), 6–43. Also Marenbon's discussion of Damian's tract in *Medieval Philosophy*, 116–18.

91. *De sancta simplicitate*, PL 145:703A. This argument sheds some light on the issue that has long dominated the discussion of philosophy in the period, "dialecticians vs. anti-dialecticians." Holopainen surveys the controversy and summarizes, 157: "it can be doubted whether any eleventh-century thinker maintained a position that would come even close to the 'dialectical' view...there was no significant theoretical controversy between 'dialecticians' and 'anti-dialecticians' in the eleventh century." Peter Damian and Otloh were opposing secular philosophy, not dialectics.

92. *De sancta simplicitate*, PL 145:703B.

CHAPTER 2 ✷ PHILOSOPHY, c.950–c.1150

church or state service are the most prominent elements of "philosophy," and we can extend this to the thinking in cathedral schools in the eleventh century broadly. The ideal of conduct joined to the study of eloquence, as Gerbert, following Cicero, had formulated it, is both a way of life for the public person and a program of studies. Philosophy makes the government minister, and the government minister is a kind of philosopher.[93]

This connection of philosophy and administrative skill continues strong in the eleventh century. A cleric at Worms wrote a letter to his bishop around 1030 commending him for translating Philosophy into acts of public administration: "The schoolmistress of all virtues (*magistra virtutum* = *Philosophia*) has taken up her abode in you, so that in all your undertakings you may follow in her footsteps."[94] The formulation evokes two models of Lady Philosophy: that of Cicero (*magistra virtutum*) and that of Boethius in *The Consolation of Philosophy*. In his complaint to Lady Philosophy, Boethius had reviewed their longstanding relationship and showed Philosophy guiding his investigations of the heavens and shaping his *mores* according to the pattern of celestial harmony. She taught him Plato's dictum that the happy state would be governed by students of wisdom and brought him by that route to devote himself to the service of the state.[95]

The learning of the age is saturated with Ciceronian notions of philosophy. Many considered Cicero the most important philosopher; no one thought Aristotle was. *De officiis* and the *Tusculan Disputations* were the most popular sources. The letter collections from the period of Emperor Henry IV edited by Erdmann and Fickermann contain over 150 direct quotations of Cicero, 99 of them from the *Tusculan Disputations*. The interesting collection of letters from circles of imperial courtiers/clerics, the so-called *Regensburg Rhetorical Letters* (c.1090), often appear as a cento of quotations from the *Tusculan Disputations*. The letters are epistolary philosophizing. They draw on dialectical argumentation and offer one more, late, example of

93. On the trope of the philosopher-king and kingly philosopher, see Seyffert, 109 n. 121.
94. Epist. 52; Bulst ed., *Briefe* 3:89.
95. Boethius, *De consolatione philosophiae*, 1.4.15–16.

dialectic subordinated to rhetoric and to a conception of philosophy as "teacher of manners."[96]

Meinhard of Bamberg, schoolmaster at Bamberg and later bishop of Würzburg, wrote to a former student some time in the 1060s or 70s commending the *Tusculan Disputations* as the most distinguished work of Latin philosophy, whose father is Cicero:

> ...hortor, ut Tusculanis tuis plurimus insideas, quibus Latina philosophia Cicerone parente nichil illustrius edidit.[97]

While prudence warns against declaring a single passage paradigmatic, I think it justified in this case. Meinhard considers "the Tusculans" the most illustrious work of "Latin philosophy." He regards Cicero as its father, and he commends it to a former student on his way to taking up administrative service at the cathedral of Cologne, possibly as its future bishop. There we have the constellation of Ciceronian philosophy at work in the circles of imperial courtier bishops educated at a cathedral school, and philosophy conceived as a guide to the active life of a government minister/bishop. The sentiment is widely enough shared to venture suggesting that Meinhard's words should be regarded as definitive on a central conception of philosophy in the period.

PHILOSOPHIA

Philosophy was a broad concept in the period c.950–c.1150. The word could designate the liberal arts generally, though it often narrowed to mean the quadrivium.[98] But it frequently referred also to the language arts understood as a preparation for oratory in the active life of administration. A *philosophus* could be a teacher of the arts, an advisor to a secular ruler or to an ecclesiastical administrator.[99] *Philosophia* could describe the monastic life, the connection that Jean Leclercq has explored deeply. But used in that context, the term is

---

96. In MGH, BdK 5:274–368. For analysis, see Jaeger, *Envy*, 120–24.

97. "Weitere Briefe Meinhards," Epist. 1 (= M1), in Erdmann ed., MGH, BdK 5: 193.

98. Hrotsvitha's drama "Paphnutius" is a showpiece of quadrivial learning, where "philosophy" is the designation of the quadrivium.

99. Other areas of reference cited in Curtius, "Geschichte."

always antithetical to that which it primarily designates: secular philosophy.

Ciceronian ideas brought with them a conception of philosophy coming to fulfillment in state service, in the active life.[100] Gerbert's confession ("I've always been a follower of Cicero in private and public") manifests a real social and intellectual value. But while the extent to which it was a practiced value is a subject for other studies, the least we can say is that Ciceronian ideals were unquestionably educational ideals to which young men at cathedral schools were trained and that suggests that they at least provided a scenario inculcated and cultivated in future clerical administrators.

CONCLUSIONS

The culture's scant acquaintance with Aristotle and the peripheral use of the *logica vetus* commends the question of how the mouse of logic looms so large in current discussions while the elephant of oratory and lived philosophy hulks unobserved in the same room. Earlier scholars, among them historians of logic and scholastic method, question the significance at least of logic and argue the priority of a "literary culture."[101] Neither Jean Leclercq's study of

---

100. Cicero's contribution to the intellectual world of the Middle Ages is an understudied subject. See Nancy van Deusen, *Cicero Refused to Die: Ciceronian Influence through the Centuries* (Leiden: Brill, 2013).

101. See David Knowles, *The Evolution of Medieval Thought*, 2nd ed., David E. Luscombe and Christopher N.L. Brooke (London: Longman, 1988), 75; and Hans Liebeschütz, "Western Christian Thought from Boethius to Anselm," in *The Cambridge History of Later Greek and Early Christian Philosophy*, Arthur H. Armstrong, ed. (Cambridge: Cambridge University Press, 1967), 587–610. This balanced and gratifyingly specific essay offers a pattern for writing the history of philosophy in the period. Liebeschütz is essentially pursuing the tradition of Boethius, whom he sees as first and foremost a Ciceronian and a "statesman as theologian" and "philosophy as man's guide." According to Liebeschütz, Boethius' interest in dialectic was instrumental, not the goal of studies. He places Gerbert between the poles of Rheims and the imperial court, gives a detailed treatment of the debate at Ravenna with Ohtricus, and a close reading of Gerbert's tract *De rationali et ratione uti*. He does not mention monastic influences. He skips from Gerbert to Berengar of Tours but gives useful readings of Anselm of Besate's *Rhetorimachia* and Manegold of Lautenbach's tract against Wolfhelm of Brauweiler.

the word *philosophia*[102] nor of the "love of learning" in Benedictine monasteries turns up any interest in dialectic, Aristotle, or speculative logic that could compete with the interest in classical literature in the Benedictine houses of the tenth and early eleventh centuries. Leclercq ends a long chapter on "Liberal Studies" with the comment,

> This culture...remains profoundly impregnated by literature. It is more literary than speculative. This characteristic differentiates monastic humanism from...scholastic humanism.[103]

The prominent role assigned to Benedictine monasticism by historians of philosophy is all the more curious, since it occasionally comes with comments downplaying the role of the imperial and royal courts, the major social context of late tenth- and early eleventh-century philosophy. The history of philosophy in the period looks different when viewed from the cathedral schools in their relation to royal, imperial, and ecclesiastical courts. Marenbon and McKitteridge point to eight new cathedral schools that arose in the later tenth century. That number could easily be doubled. They arose primarily because the new or renewed institution served imperial purposes.[104] The quantitative disproportion between these burgeoning institutions and the cultivation of Aristotelian dialectics in monastic communities is evident. Three figures from Benedictine monasticism are made to represent philosophy in the tenth and early eleventh century: Gerbert, Abbo, and Notker; and the appropriation of Gerbert for the monastic realm is questionable.

David Luscombe's essay on "Thought and Learning" is at least a start at recognizing the centrality of cathedral schools. It treats the period circumscribed by the scope of the volume, 1024–98, but ranges necessarily beyond those boundaries on either end. For Luscombe the principal centers of learning in the eleventh century were "episcopal or cathedral schools." He touches on the culture of these schools, the nature and purpose of instruction there, the relevance of this learning to careers in the church and secular courts. He summarizes the character of cathedral-school learning:

102. See n. 33 above.
103. Leclercq, *Love of Learning*, 142.
104. See Fleckenstein, "Königshof und Bischofsschule."

CHAPTER 2 ★ PHILOSOPHY, c.950–c.1150

[Discipline of body and bearing, self-control] as well as the arts and religion were taught; character was formed as well as the mind. Ruotger wrote in his *Life* of Brun, brother of the emperor Otto I, archbishop of Cologne from 953…that Brun had regarded an education in the liberal arts as a vital qualification for rulership of the Church and of the kingdom. Goodness and eloquence were needed. This ideal survived into the eleventh century and beyond.[105]

I would add to Luscombe's observation the importance of classical learning based on various works of Cicero and classical Latin poets and, surprisingly, the composition of Latin poetry, manneristic and obscure in style, its substance cluttered with learning, which various sources claim is the highpoint of education.[106]

It is obvious that institutions as distant and diverse as the cathedral schools at Rheims, Liège, Cologne, Magdeburg, Worms, Würzburg, Regensburg, and Salzburg will also show intellectual diversity and in the period in question the effects of the religious reform movement in varying degrees. The Rheims community since Gerbert showed considerable influence of the Cluniac reform while still offering centrally an education based on the liberal arts, stressing oratorical training. The boundaries between the monastic world and that of secular clergy were porous. Conflict between the two spheres is a guide to the limits of their openness.[107]

A direction of philosophy that combined ideals of the ancient orator with the ethics of late Stoicism as transmitted by Cicero would

---

105. NCMH 4, c.1024–c.1198, 1:463. Mayr-Harting, *Church and Cosmos*, 166, gives striking examples from glossed manuscripts from the second half of the tenth century, where Platonic cosmology is invoked as a model of governing: "There is an almost magical, holistic view of the universe at work at any rate in the tenth century.… If one grasped the intellectual principles of the universe's construction, the moral principles of rule would follow like a quasi-sacramental source of illumination."

106. See Jaeger, "The Status of the Learned Poet in the Eleventh Century," in *Norm und Krise von Kommunikation: Inszenierungen literarischer und sozialer Interaktion im Mittelalter*, Gert Melville, ed. (Tübingen: Lit, 2007), 417–38.

107. The tribulations of Wazo of Liège illuminate claims of secular/imperial clergy asserted against monastic. See Jaeger, *Envy*, 202–3.

seem to deserve a place in history of philosophy from 950 to 1150. It may be that the inclusion of this trend would do little to change the sense that it is a minor period in the history of philosophy. But taking into consideration sources like Ruotger, Walther of Speyer, Gerbert, and Meinhard of Bamberg, the letters, biographies, and poems from cathedral communities would have the advantage of crystallizing a concept of philosophy as the period in question understood, cultivated, and possibly even practiced it.

Greater skepticism of library catalogues, surviving manuscripts, and book patronage as sources for intellectual interests and educational practice would also help focus on what was central in the period. Library holdings are important sources of intellectual tradition, of course, but they can signal something very different than focal points of intellectual interest in a given period, and small libraries do not necessarily signal lack of learning, any more than large ones indicate learning that is broad and deep. Extensive holdings of Carolingian writings do not by themselves indicate continuing influence of Carolingian thought and cultural institutions. Books had to some extent a representative and not merely a practical function in the Ottonian period (and the more splendid, the more representative). Given that fact, less may have been more.[108]

McKitterick and Marenbon recognize clearly that bishops are the main bearers of culture in the period. It is worth considering that bishops themselves are to the Ottonian/Salian era what books were to the Carolingian, the works of art of the period, its philosophy embodied, many of them products of imperial patronage.

I also hope that the idea of intellectual continuity from the Carolingian to the Ottonian/Salian period and from the eleventh century to the twelfth will be revisited. The Carolingian age prepared for Ottonian culture in many ways, above all by creating a high level of Latin literacy. But the philosophy and scriptural studies of the earlier period faded. Beryl Smalley recognized the period 950–1100 as a low point in the

---

108. Mayr-Harting cites the manuscript collections of canon law available in the tenth-century Cologne library and contrasts that collection with the silence of other sources on the study and practice of law. He makes a useful distinction between the book as an "icon [that] symbolizes the archbishop as a fountain source of canon law" and "a book for actual study." See *Church and Cosmos*, 139.

study of the Bible in the Middle Ages. Was there really any continuity joining the logic of the ninth century to that of the tenth? Or that of the tenth and early eleventh to that of the twelfth? The non-reception of the logic of Gerbert and Abbo suggests that continuity in logic happened in the thinnest of trickles. The major response to dialectic, once it asserted itself seriously in Berengar in the second half of the eleventh century, was strong resistance both in monastic and episcopal centers. If the dialectical studies in Benedectine monasteries had prepared for the logic of the late eleventh century, could the resistance to Berengar possibly have polarized the intellectual world as severely as it did?

The stress placed by historians of philosophy on Aristotelian logic is understandable within shared notions of the modern discipline of philosophy: first, that thought becomes philosophical when it becomes speculative; second, that the history of philosophy is the history of written philosophical texts.[109] Those presuppositions enable a perspective that writes the history of philosophy from 950 to 1150, from Carolingian sources forward and from early Scholasticism backwards. I think it is that tendency above all that has directed the historians of philosophy to a subject of minor importance in the philosophy of the period in between and distracted from what that period took to be philosophy. A trend that produced no philosophical writings and had its expression in contemporary administrative, diplomatic, and legal practice, in the scantly recorded education of the cathedral and monastic schools, and in the lives and letters of the philosophers who embodied and lived it has not yet asserted itself in histories of medieval philosophy.[110]

---

109. Ernesto Grassi surveys the opposition of speculative to humanistic philosophy fundamental in modern thought: *Renaissance Philosophy: Studies in Philosophy and Poetics* (Binghamton, NY: Center for Medieval and Early Renaissance Studies, 1988), 1–17.

110. Philosophy as a way of living (rather than strictly a way of thinking and writing) was well known in the ancient world and has a prominent modern commentator in Pierre Hadot. See his *What Is Ancient Philosophy?*, Michael Chase, trans. (Cambridge, MA: Harvard University Press, 2002). Marenbon notes a variant of this conception in *Medieval Philosophy*, 7.

3. MEINHARD OF BAMBERG AND EARLY MEDIEVAL HUMANISM

CARL ERDMANN AND MEINHARD'S LETTERS

Carl Erdmann was one of a distinguished list of German medievalists of the generation of scholars who lived through World War II and worked untainted by Nazi ideology. Some of them survived the war years to realize scholarly plans of great scope, which in individual cases have become the foundations for the study of the Middle Ages since 1945: Ernst Robert Curtius, Erich Auerbach, Erwin Panofsky, Ernst Kantorowicz, Leo Spitzer, Friedrich Ohly, Gerd Tellenbach.

Carl Erdmann did not survive. He died in Zagreb shortly before the end of the war of unknown causes while returning home to Germany from military service as a translator in Albania. His scholarship prior to his death in 1945, even though cut short, established him as the equal of those just named. His *habilitation* was published in 1935 with the title *Die Entstehung des Kreuzugsgedankens*.[1] It is now still a fundamental work on the ideas of holy war, religious knighthood, and the Peace of God movement leading to the Crusades. His *Studien zur Briefliteratur Deutschlands im elften Jahrhundert* (1938) established the letters of German cathedral communities as a major source of political, social, and cultural history in the period; and his edition of those letters (which only appeared in 1950) created the basis for a broad study of the culture.[2]

The recent biography by Folker Reichert has revealed Erdmann's vision of the scope and significance of the letters and of their value for German cultural and intellectual history.[3] In Erdmann's journeyman days as an archivist and paleographer, he worked for the *Monumenta Germaniae Historica* in the position of *wissenschaftlicher Mitarbeiter*. During a stay in Paris in 1930, he uncovered in the Bibliothèque

---

1. English edition as *The Origin of the Idea of Crusade*, Marshall Whithed Baldwin and Walter A. Goffart, trans. (Princeton, NJ: Princeton University Press, 1977).

2. Erdmann, *Studien zur Briefliteratur Deutschlands*. In the following, I refer to individual letters using Erdmann's abbreviations: H45 = *Hannoversche Briefsammlung* 45; M1 = *Weitere Briefe Meinhards von Bamberg* 1, etc.

3. See Reichert, 104–10.

Nationale a collection of thirty-six letters from eleventh-century Bamberg. He recognized an extraordinary importance in this find. Scrupulous archivist and sober stylist though he was, he also had the gift of seeing the wide implications of his discoveries. Inspired by the letters of Codex Parisinus Lat. 2903, he envisioned a far-reaching contribution to medieval intellectual history, especially to the history of education and culture in Germany. A modest man who wrote with the sobriety of a scientist, his excitement at the find overflowed in personal communications. He wrote letters to friends bubbling over with enthusiasm. He was, as his biographer Reichert put it, "intoxicated with the joy of discovery."[4] In letters to Paul Kehr, president of the MGH, Walter Holtzman, and Peter Rassow, he called his find of the Paris codex "the most fortunate/happiest discovery for medieval German history in a long time."[5] He called the three months of his stay in Paris "the age of discoveries."[6]

For Erdmann the letters in Codex Parisinus Lat. 2903 were situated somewhere between diplomatic and literary sources,[7] and he observed how his own interests turned surprisingly to literary history.[8] But what inspired Erdmann most was their relevance to a broader history of ideas showing the roots of high medieval culture in the Salian period. It would trace a path that leads from Ottonian-Salian Germany into twelfth-century humanism and "the renaissance of the twelfth century." In Erdmann's view, the Latin letters from Germany were the best evidence of that course of development. His planned work was ambitious: an extensive history of medieval school and intellectual life with eleventh-century letters as the point of departure.[9] He foresaw that it would take fifteen to

4. Reichert, 110: "Vom Finderglück berauscht."

5. "...der glücklichste Fund, der seit geraumer Zeit für die mittelalterliche deutsche Geschichte gemacht [wurde]." On Erdmann's letters to friends announcing the find, see letters to Paul Kehr, Walter Holtzman, Peter Rassow, Gerd Tellenbach, et al, in Reichert, 110–11 and n. 114.

6. "Zeitalter der Entdeckungen," Reichert, 110.

7. M1, Erdmann ed., MGH, BdK 5:190: "[Parisinus Lat. 2903] eine Absender-Überlieferung von literarischem Charakter...."

8. Letter to Gerd Tellenbach, Sept. 29, 1941. Reichert, 300.

9. Reichert, 302.

CHAPTER 3 ✷ MEINHARD OF BAMBERG

twenty years of work and fill several volumes. At the same time, he suspected, correctly, that that much time was not to be given him. But in the dark years that did remain to him the conception of the project gave him comfort and consolation.

Something of the scope and nature of Erdmann's uncompleted work was preserved through his contacts with Ernst Robert Curtius. Their correspondence is lost,[10] but Curtius recalled Erdmann's plans in his opus magnum, *European Literature and the Latin Middle Ages*. Curtius wrote:

> The intellectual leadership which Germany held under the Ottos could not be maintained. The history of Western culture from Charlemagne to Dante has not yet been comprehended and presented as a coherent whole. Carl Erdmann planned a history of Franco-German culture in the eleventh century, during which French cultural primacy arose in a highly original development and twelfth-century Humanism was prepared to a far greater extent than has been recognized in previous studies. He did not live to carry out this plan.[11]

The letters from the Ottonian-Salian period would be the foundation of this work, and the author of the letters in Parisinus 2903, Meinhard of Bamberg, would play a major role: "A literary history of Germany in the high Middle Ages cannot be written without Meinhard."[12] As Erdmann foresaw, neither can a history of European humanism. Reichert summarizes the potential of Erdmann's proposed work: "Had he actually accomplished this project [it would have become] a fundamental element of the cultural history of the high Middle Ages."[13]

It would also have placed Erdmann in the ranks of other German scholars mounting a counterthrust to fascist intellectual history. That direction of cautious, sometimes coded scholarship[14] of those

10. Reichert, 301–3.
11. At 388 and n. 22.
12. Erdmann, *Studien*, 116.
13. ELLMA, 302.
14. On the anti-fascist undercurrent of Erdmann's *Origin*, see Norman F. Cantor, *Inventing the Middle Ages: The Lives, Works and Ideas of the Great Medievalists of the Twentieth Century* (New York: Morrow, 1991), 398, 403–4.

living under Nazism could travel safely, so to speak, under the topic of humanism. That direction would have taken encouragement from Thomas Mann's turn to a pan-European humanism in his essays of the 20s and 30s and in his radio transmissions from the USA to Germany during the war, especially in his novel tetralogy, *Joseph and his Brothers* (1933–43).

As early as his anti-Nazi polemic in *Deutscher Geist in Gefahr*[15] (1932), Curtius proclaimed a renewed study of the Middle Ages as the path to a "new humanism" that would resist the culture-destroying trends of the time:

> The new humanism must be centered in the study of the Middle Ages [*Mediaevalismus*]. It will be driven by the urge to restoration.... That is the form in which humanistic self-encounter and self-reflection must take place in this day and age."[16]

Whether through Thomas Mann's inspiration or the anti-fascist leaning of German humanists, the topic of a unity of the development of European culture was in the air in the 20s and 30s. The classicist Werner Jaeger published his major work, *Paideia: Die Formung des griechischen Menschen*, beginning in 1934, and Erwin Panofsky's *Iconology: Humanistic Themes in the Art of the Renaissance* originated as the Flexner Lectures at Bryn Mawr in 1937–38, followed by his *Renaissance and Renascences* in its earliest form (1944). Erdmann can only have taken affirmation and encouragement to pursue his own plans of a history of humanism in medieval Europe from those influences, especially from Curtius' encompassing vision and from the trend Curtius championed in the years after World War I, very much against the grain of

---

15. Stuttgart: Deutsche Verlags-Anstalt.

16. *Deutscher Geist*, 126. See Dirk Hoeges, "Emphatischer Humanismus: Ernst Robert Curtius, Ernst Troeltsch und Karl Mannheim. Von Deutscher Geist in Gefahr zu Europäische Literatur und lateinisches Mittelalter," in *"In Ihnen begegnet sich das Abendland": Bonner Vorträge zur Erinnerung an Ernst Robert Curtius*, Wolf-Dieter Lange, ed. (Bonn: Bouvier, 1990), 31–52; Frank Töpfer, "Selbstbegegnung in der Geschichte: Zum Begriff des Humanismus bei Ernst Robert Curtius," *Archiv für Begriffsgeschichte* 54 (2012): 91–117; C. Stephen Jaeger, "Ernst Robert Curtius: A Medievalist's Contempt for the Middle Ages," *Viator* 47.2 (2016): 367–79.

CHAPTER 3 ✷ MEINHARD OF BAMBERG

the time, to assert the unifying factors of French and German cultures. The broader perspective of medieval intellectual history, as Curtius sketched it in *European Literature*, embraced Erdmann's vision, while it also extended it: "The history of Western culture from Charlemagne to Dante... comprehended and presented as a coherent whole." It is not unreasonable to imagine that Erdmann's work would have approximated the foundation-laying impact of the post-war work of Curtius, Kantorowicz, or Auerbach. Erdmann himself foresaw its potential at that level of importance.

It is a pity that the correspondence between Erdmann and Curtius is lost.[17] But the passage from *European Literature and the Latin Middle Ages*, quoted above, shows his appreciation of Erdmann's vision. The enticing idea of a multi-volume study of humanistic education and culture in the Middle Ages centered on the tenth and eleventh centuries with the letters of Meinhard as their point of departure, has not found a successor to Erdmann, though recent work on cathedral schools have furnished a base for it.[18] Münster-Swendsen, Steckel, and Jaeger worked without the unifying vision that Erdmann had projected but not elaborated, though Münster-Swendsen's broad historical framing of the topic comes close.

It is at least clear now that Erdmann's broad view was justified and that his plan to argue the development from Ottonian-Salian Germany to twelfth-century France was well conceived. Considerations that discouraged that direction of studies may be indicated in Curtius' coy formulation, "French cultural primacy arose in a highly original development...." The implication that a flourishing high culture of learning rooted in Germany had preceded that

17. Reichert, 301–3.
18. See Münster-Swendsen, "Masters and Paragons"; Münster-Swendsen, "Medieval 'Virtuosity': Classroom Practice and the Transfer of Charismatic Power in Medieval Scholarly Culture c.1000–1230," in *Negotiating Heritage: Memories of the Middle Ages*, M. Birkedal Bruun, ed. (Turnhout: Brepols, 2009), 43–63; Bruun, "The Model of Scholastic Mastery in Northern Europe c.970–1200," in Vaughn and Rubenstein, 307–42; Steckel, *Kulturen des Lehrens*; Steckel, "Charisma and Expertise: Constructing Sacralized Mastership in Northern and Western Europe, 800–1150," in *Schüler und Meister*, Thomas Jeschke and Andreas Speer, ed. (Berlin: De Gruyter, 2016), 641–79; Jaeger, *Envy*; and above, 15–16.

development in France and contributed to it extensively (Ciceronian ethics, humanistic literary studies, courtliness) required caution in its proclamation lest it appear tinged with German triumphalism. Perhaps something like these hesitations is at work among German medievalist historians since Erdmann.

The Bamberg school has remained of interest to historians, but the main focus has been tracking students, networks of teachers and students, the library holdings, the traffic in manuscripts, the conservatism and steady decline of the school after the mid-eleventh century. The subject is shadowed by the entrenched idea of the preeminence of the French schools, an idea that is ripe for abumbration.[19] Johannes Fried and Claudia Märtl recognized the conservative orientation of the Bamberg school. Both noted the stasis in the school's curriculum into the twelfth century.[20] Bamberg remained conservative and loyal to the emperor. The school prepared students for service to the empire.[21] Bamberg maintained this tradition into the twelfth century.

19. The French orientation to intellectual inquiry, reasoned argumentation, critical thought — undoubtedly a rising trend in France since the mid-eleventh century — has seemed to German scholars the sole defining feature of a successful, flourishing cathedral school. Since this orientation had no place in the German schools, they appeared narrow and mediocre. But something had drawn throngs of students since the mid-tenth century to Würzburg, Liège, Worms, Speyer, Cologne, Bamberg, and some twenty other cathedral schools. It was what the biographer of Benno of Osnabrück called *imperiale studium*. See below, n. 123. The appeal of the German schools was paedeic, humanistic, and literary. That form of education grew increasingly irrelevant in Germany in the wake of the Investiture Controversy. The intellectual trends in France increased in appeal.

20. Fried, "Die Bamberger Domschule," 174–75; Claudia Märtl, "Die Bamberger Schulen: Ein Bildungszentrum des Salierreichs," in *Die Salier und das Reich 3. Gesellschaftlicher und Ideengeschichtlicher Wandel im Reich der Salier*, Stefan Weinfurter, ed. (Sigmaringen: Thorbecke, 1992), 327–45, at 341. "Bamberg scheint einen recht konservativen…Kurs zu steuern, und dabei beharren zu wollen, was bisher seine Grösse bestimmte" (344).

21. Erdmann, "Die Bamberger Domschule," 45: "Die Bamberger Domschule vermittelte ihren Zöglingen eine Ausbildung, die sie nochmals in besonderem Masse für den Dienst am Kaiserhof und in der Reichskanzlei geeignet machte."

CHAPTER 3 ✶ MEINHARD OF BAMBERG

Against this position, Matthias Tischler argued a progressive spirit in Meinhard and his school.[22] Tischler adapted the concept introduced by Jacques Le Goff, "medieval intellectual," and proposed Meinhard as a forerunner of this figure. Tischler's argument is not persuasive. Meinhard's intellectual, political, and social grounding lies in the imperial court and its ties to the network of imperial churches, as Fried and Märtl argued. He is a variant form of the cleric-courtier-diplomat cultivated in the German cathedral schools since the mid-tenth century. Tischler stresses Meinhard's express opposition to the interpretation of the Eucharist by Berengar of Tours.[23] Though Meinhard never mentions Berengar, the reference is pointed and clear.[24] However, Meinhard's rejection of the trend set by Berengar argues against Tischler's siting of the Bamberg schoolmaster as a forerunner of a twelfth-century trend toward critical thought. It also renders improbable Tischler's idea that Meinhard's engagement is evidence of the transformation of Bamberg into "an institution of higher learning of international stature."[25] Meinhard's position is set in opposition to trends towards rational inquiry, and the tract in which it is addressed (*De fide*) shows very little originality or range of thought. Also the circumstances of its composition point to its peripheral position in Meinhard's role as schoolmaster.[26] Bamberg's stature in the eleventh century is established by its relation to the

22. Matthias M. Tischler, "Meinhart von Bamberg: Die Physiognomie eines 'Protointellektuellen' des 11. Jahrhunderts," in *Deutsche Texte der Salierzeit: Neuanfänge und Kontinuitäten im 11 Jahrhundert*, Stephan Müller and Jens Schneider, ed. (Munich: Fink, 2010), 251–85, basing his analysis on Jacques Le Goff, *Intellectuals in the Middle Ages* (Cambridge, MA: Harvard University Press, 1993).

23. Steckel gives a granular analysis of the Eucharist controversy and its influence on the schools: *Kulturen des Lehrens*, 886–961.

24. Tischler, 259–63.

25. Tischler, 261.

26. Meinhard apparently wrote the work as an assignment imposed on him against his own wishes by Bishop Gunther. He remonstrates in the scolding, complaining tone typical of some of his other letters to Gunther. Being burdened with the double task of teaching letters and manners, he is now asked in addition to write a work on theology, which he is loathe to do. He is not a theologian, and it is dangerous for the non-expert to write about the faith. See M39, Erdmann ed., 238–40.

imperial church and the imperial chapel,[27] its intellectual ambition and distinction marked by its adherence to the *imperiale studium*,[28] not by any international reach in its self-conception.

MEINHARD AND HUMANISM: LETTER M1 TO "G"

It is Meinhard's humanism that places him in the line of culture and thought leading into the twelfth century in France and England. His cultural affinities are not with Berengar, Roscellinus, Abelard, the new independent schools of France, or the schools of Paris and Scholasticism but with Brun of Cologne, Gerbert of Aurillac, Bernard of Chartres, Hildebert of Lavardin, William of Conches, Thierry of Chartres, Peter of Blois, and John of Salisbury. A focus on Meinhard's humanism has been blurred by the idea that the purpose of the German cathedral schools was to prepare competent clerks in rhetoric and composition.[29] For Johannes Fried, the orientation to dictamental and stylistic skills is evidence of the narrowness and intellectual mediocrity of the school.[30] It is important to correct this idea and to bring the subject back to the focus Erdmann established.

27. See Herbert Zielinski, *Der Reichsepiskopat in spätottonischer und Salischer Zeit (1002–1125)* (Wiesbaden: Steiner, 1984), 84–86, 145–47.

28. See below n. 123.

29. Märtl, "Schulen," 341: "es geht immer noch [well into the twelfth century] hauptsächlich darum, den Schülern die Feinheiten des Notars- und Diktatorenhandwerks, vor allem vollendete Sprachbeherrschung, beizubringen." Loris Sturlese picks up Fried's view (discussed below) and declares *dictet, declinet* "die Grabinschrift der deutschen Domschulen." See *Die deutsche Philosophie im Mittelalter* (Munich: Beck, 1993), 189; Vones, "Erzbischof Brun," 137. The Cologne "school" is concerned with "practical administrative methods"; its purpose: an "introduction to church administration." Frank Rexroth, *Fröhliche Scholastik: Die Wissenschaftsrevolution des Mittelalters* (Munich: Beck, 2018), 52: "Der Unterricht war...auf die Produktion auch weltlicher Texte ausgerichtet, auf die Kompetenz etwa, Urkunden und Briefe formgerecht auszustellen." Against Joachim Ehlers' argument that a "pragmatic orientation" of studies under the Ottos prepared young men for "administration" and composing documents, Mayr-Harting, *Church and Cosmos*, 33: "[the arrangements for teaching and learning at Cologne cathedral school, second half of the tenth century, are not in accord with] any idea that the 'school' provided a training for (non-existent) 'administration'."

30. Fried, "Bamberger Domschule," 168 on Meinhard.

CHAPTER 3 ✴ MEINHARD OF BAMBERG

The main sources for some widely accepted ideas about imperial cathedral schools have not been deeply examined: the letters themselves. Historians read the letters mainly as sources of historical information, a perspective that more-or-less excludes the riches that Erdmann saw in them. I can offer here a close reading of some of Meinhard's letters and hope that they shed light on medieval humanism in its early phase.

Erdmann claimed that to understand Meinhard, one must see how his role as teacher and his literary judgment flow from his humanism. His relation to ancient literature is intimate. He had absorbed ancient Roman models in ethical values, his written style, and his persona as letter writer. Christian elements in Meinhard's self-conception and his activity as teacher are less prominent than Roman.[31] Of major importance was the alignment of letters with manners, *litterae* with *mores*.[32] In Meinhard's own phrase, Bamberg is above all a school of manners, *schola morum*.[33]

The concept of a medieval humanism has an uneven history. This is not the place to rehearse it.[34] Meinhard's embodiment of ancient humanism has a strong individual character. This cautions against narrower definitions. The purpose of this study is to read closely some of Meinhard's letters to identify that individual character and to observe something of Meinhard's personality and temperament.[35] My point of departure is the first letter of the Parisian codex. M1 (to use Erdmann's numbering) is one of the most remarkable letters in the history of medieval education and of medieval humanism.[36] A

31. As Steckel correctly points out, *Kulturen des Lehrens*, 795–96.

32. Erdmann, *Studien*, 102–3.

33. H78a, Erdmann ed., 127.

34. See introduction, above 4–12; Jaeger, *Envy*, 36–52, 278–91; and von Moos, *Hildebert*, 1–37.

35. Claudia Zey gives a focused view onto Meinhard's political engagement in the relations of Bamberg and the imperial court, and of his close cooperation with Bishop Gunther: "Vormünder und Berater Heinrichs IV. im Urteil der Zeitgenossen (1056–1075)," in *Heinrich IV*, Gerd Althoff, ed. (Ostfildern: Thorbecke, 2009), 87–127.

36. Text and English translation appended at the end of this chapter. See the comments by Jaeger, *Envy*, 96–116; Steckel, *Kulturen des Lehrens*, 797–99; Erdmann, *Studien*, 282.

close reading of the letter as a whole helps clarify its purpose and its context in history of humanist education.

∗

The letter is directed to a student whom Meinhard names only with the initial "G." He is evidently taking his leave from Meinhard and the Bamberg school and is heading for Cologne, where he is either the newly selected archbishop or a candidate for the position.[37] After an extravagant greeting (discussed below), Meinhard dramatizes the dangers of G's calling. He does so in an allegorical scene stressing the need of practicing virtue so as to avoid succumbing to those dangers.[38] Meinhard depicts a contest between two courts, the noble court of virtues opposing the dangerous court of vices. He, G, is the object of this competition. The first has called on him as their "sweet minion"[39] for his exemplary manners (*specimen morum*) and his sharpness of mind. The second lures him with temptations of the flesh:

> Be aware what a tumult of warring emotions will engage in conflict, both for you and against you. For there the noble retinue[40] of virtues calls you for the perfection of your manners, for the sharpness of your genius, as its own minion to the throne of its court and claims you as its courtier. But here also the silken bodies of the Colognese, or rather the Babylonese, that slippery brood, will sollicit you with a face painted with seductions, a smile to flatter, not to hearten you. I fear that such hospitality could turn Juno-like [i.e., treacherous. See *Aeneid* 1.67].

Meinhard makes clear that G is the chosen one. Erdmann had noted the closing words of the letter foreseeing a wedding of G and the church of Cologne, presided over by Christ — meaning the appointment to archbishop.[41] The comment that the "noble retinue

37. M1, Erdmann ed., 192–94.

38. A kind of psychomachia, says Erdmann following a comment by Curtius, *Studien*, 282.

39. *Deliciosum suum* must connect with *domesticum* in the next sentence. "sweet minion" gives the flavor of the original. *Deliciosus* as a noun, *hapax leg.*? The context: it is court/courtly language. The *deliciae* of Bishop Gunther's court included a dwarf beloved of the bishop named Askericus. See M28, Erdmann ed., 226.

40. *Familia* again court language = retinue.

41. Erdmann, *Studien*, 282.

CHAPTER 3 ✶ MEINHARD OF BAMBERG

of Virtue has called him to the throne of their court" declares that he is chosen to lead the church. The term *principatum curie* ("the throne of the court") speaks clearly: the church of Cologne has called him to reign over its court.

The letter has much to reveal about Meinhard's teaching. The most general indication is the letter's character ("genre" would be saying too much) as a letter of admonition, more concisely in the German "*Mahnbrief*," "*Mahnrede*." The former teacher packs his most pertinent ideas and teaching into a short letter of advice. Meinhard feels restricted to the essential minimum by the limits of the epistolary form. He apologizes for forcing the broad subject of virtue into the narrow limits of a letter:

> As you know, such subjects [fame and reputation endangered through insufficient reflection on virtue] are poured forth in the fields of disputation where the reins are loosed, though the narrows of letter-writing cannot contain them.

It is a topic better treated in the give-and-take of a discussion, much reduced by the letter form. He adds, helpfully for defining the topics of his teaching, "This and many things like this you have heard me lecture on/preach."[42] He clearly emphasizes the topic as taken from instruction: "You have often heard me dispute about nobility (*advertisti me de nobilitate...disputantem*) turning into one of two paths, toward glory or toward ignominy." As the model of glory Meinhard holds up G's father. Follow his model, fashion your character and behavior in imitation of his. This description comprises a number of qualities central to the social and ethical ideals of medieval humanism:

> For he is a man instructed in every kind of virtue, a man who enjoys to an astonishing degree all the charm and grace of humanity, qualities visible far and wide not only in his dazzling

---

42. One of the few sources on the classroom component of Meinhard's teaching. Discussion and debate are freewheeling, the "fields of disputation" are opened, "the reins loosened" (193). I have not found a close description of a classroom at a cathedral community in Germany. John of Salisbury's extensive description of the teaching of Bernard of Chartres is exceptional. See *Metalogicon* 1.24.47-98. Also the "evening colloquies" that constituted a part of Fulbert of Chartres teaching, but outside of the classroom. Jaeger, *Envy*, 219-21.

blaze of manners [*flagrantia morum*] but also in the bright good humor [*hilaritas*] which shone most graciously from his eyes.

Being "a man instructed in every kind of virtue" (*omni genere virtutis instructus*), G's father exemplifies the virtues taught. Erdmann stresses a consistent courtesy in Meinhard's language ("*Höflichkeit*") informed more by classical than Christian models: *humanitas, benevolentia, honestas, virtus, magnanimitas, gravitas, modestia, verecundia, industria, constantia, probitas.*⁴³ Embodying them in his own presence no less than his language is the major means of transmitting them to students (charismatic teaching), along with, no doubt also, lecturing and debating. But it is significant that the epitome in this letter is from G's life (his father) rather than his reading.

The individual virtues embodied in G's father are striking for the purity of their Ciceronian pedigree: *lepor humanitatis, hilaritas*. Charm, kindness, bright good humor are also qualities frequently mentioned in the biographies of clerics prior to election to the episcopacy.⁴⁴ Uncommon is *flagrantia morum*. The phrase is unusual; it invites commentary. One might anticipate rather *nobilitas, honestas, probitas* or, most common, *elegantia morum*.⁴⁵ As a descriptor of manners, *flagrantia* is rare in Cicero, where it occurs only in a negative sense: *flagrantia oculorum* is an excessively coquettish look women use to allure men.⁴⁶ Patristic and medieval Christianity, however, used the word abundantly to refer to fervent piety, love of God: *flagrantia caritatis*.⁴⁷ Meinhard clearly intended to lend this pious

---

43. Erdmann, *Studien*, 96–97.

44. Jaeger, *Origins*, 32–48; Jaeger, *Envy*, 76–117; Erdmann, *Studien*, 96.

45. *Elegantia* is more often a term of style rather than behavior for Meinhard (H62, Erdmann ed., 106; H105, Erdmann ed., 176). His usage is ambiguous in the passage in praise of his time of study in Rheims, "than which nothing could be more…exacting of elegance…" (nihil esse potest…ad elegantiam accuratius").… H65, Erdmann ed., 113. See below, 397.

46. *Pro Caelio* 20.49: *Flagrantia oculorum*, describing a loose woman with eyes blazing to attract men. Cf. Horace, *Carmina* 2.12.

47. Augustine, on Psalm 17: "*ignis ex facie ejus exardescit*": *et flagrantia charitatis… inardescit*. In PL 36:149; CCSL 1. Bede, *Commentary on Luke* 3.7: *Fidei flagrantia*; in CCSL 120, D. Hurst, ed. (Turnhout: Brepols, 1960), l. 42.

coloring to the manners of G's father, placing it in a sequence with charm, kindness, good humor that beams gracefully from his eyes.

These qualities are held up in the name of virtue, though they are qualities of the personality, especially social qualities. *Humanitas* is broader. It includes compassion for the condition of humanity itself and at the same time imbues human kindness with charm, grace and amiability. In association with *lepor* and *hilaritas*, it means an excellence of the person, especially in social situations, in charming and in winning the affection of others. Von Moos notes[48] Meinhard's *"heitere Gesittetheit und Sinn für feinen Witz"*: civil behavior and refined wit go together. For Meinhard this winning and charming exterior is the gift of someone who has mastered the inner world of thought, impulse, emotion. Grace and kindness are "ornaments of the soul" (*ornamenta animi*). Mastery of impulse gives aura to the man instructed in virtue. In general, what Meinhard inculcates is a scrupulous judgment of every act, weighing of moral factors in action, both lived and judicial.

So Meinhard taught virtue. But how was it taught? It is a complicated issue, not to be guessed at, still waiting for a detailed treatment. But for the moment, we can follow the two approaches Meinhard commends to G: imitation and reading.

LEARNING BY IMITATION

How does the student learn virtue? First, by "the most exacting imitation of good people" (*accuratissima bonorum imitatio*). Its wisdom is gotten through *convictus*, a life shared by teacher and student.[49] That is, by charismatic learning. Imitation of a model person is the most primal and the most instinctual form of education. Accordingly, it happens with or without a social or conceptual structure to guide and record it. Observed as pedagogic practice and, we might say

---

48. Hildebert, 4.

49. In Meinhard's extravagant praise of his two years spent with Magister Hermannus at the cathedral school of Rheims, probably 1055–57 (H65, Erdmann ed., 112–13), the only specific object of praise is the *convictus* that that life afforded him, not learning and study in the conventional sense. His praise is directed at social qualities. He was received in the most humane manner (*humanissime*) and enjoyed a course of studies optimal for its "usefulness, elegance, and highest a person can attain." (*utilitas, elegantia, sublimitas*).

policy, in the West, it occurs in aristocratic milieux. The Greek and Roman ideals of *paideia* were transmitted by a double system of instruction that relied no less on the living than on the literary model. Seneca envisioned teaching happening most effectively in a shared life of teacher and student:

> The living voice and a life shared [*convictus*] by pupil and master benefit you more than any speech.... Long is the path through precepts; brief and effective through examples.[50]

The pedagogy of teacher imitation was strong in Stoicism. Zeno the founder of the school urged students to shape every act as if they had to account to their teachers for it. Seneca rephrases:

> We must attach ourselves through love to some good man and hold him constantly before our mind's eye, and we should live as if he observed us constantly and do what we do as though he were observing.[51]

Testimonies to the central role of teaching by example in early Christianity, the early Middle Ages, the Carolingian and the Ottonian-Salian periods are abundant.[52] Meinhard's advice to G is widely shared in one form or another. The classroom and a curriculum are secondary to the presence of an admired mentor. The teacher in this form of "instruction" is the lesson itself.[53] The "virtue" cultivated is not primarily bookish. It is seen and observed and inculcated both by the psychology by which we admire good acts and dislike bad and by the teacher admonishing, praising, and rebuking.[54]

The new houses of canons regular that burgeoned in the second half of the eleventh century made teaching the secular and ecclesiastical world by example into their principal spiritual/social

---

50. Jaeger, *Envy*, 77.

51. Jaeger, *Envy*, 77.

52. See Steckel, *Kulturen*, 116–24.

53. See Münster-Swendsen and Steckel on this point.

54. The table arrangements at the court of Thomas Becket, both as chancellor of England and archbishop of Canterbury, are a good illustration of a *schola morum*. See *Envy*, 301–9.

obligation.⁵⁵ For Hugh of St. Victor, imitation of good and holy individuals was a pedagogical principle of the training of novices at St. Victor, and he includes the entire community among those "who seek to be reformed through the example of good people."⁵⁶ At St. Victor in the first half of the twelfth century, the pedagogy of imitation is linked to spiritual goals by the doctrine of the image and likeness of God, to which individuals seek to assimilate when they imitate the actions of good people.

Meinhard has a different model in mind. G's father possesses the virtues of a good man, but his authority comes even more through his noble pedigree. The virtues of G's father descend to him from "the distinguished effort of the ancestors/forebears." Their example urges him to follow the path to "glory" and to shun the other path. The operative forces are nobility, glory, the *mos maiorum*, and the *gloria parentum*. The fame of his most august father (*opinio augustissimi patris*) is the main incitement to vigilance in moral matters. Family descent counts, yes, but even more so membership in a noble class accustomed by long tradition to weigh behavior scrupulously in the balance and cleave to the fine and humane path. That behavior and that practice of exacting judgment is the value urged on G by his teacher. This concept is much closer to ancient Roman ideals of the virtue to which class and family standing obligates the nobility than to Christian communities, clerical or monastic.

Sita Steckel finds in Meinhard's letters to students and colleagues an "increasingly secularizing humanistic tendency."⁵⁷ Erdmann agrees.⁵⁸ It is evident in Meinhard's admonitions to G. The models to imitate proposed to students in other religious communities, clerical and monastic, tend to remain in the scope of Christian precedents, Jesus and the saints, as in the idea of the image of God within the school of St. Victor. But Meinhard is a cleric serving in an episcopal community, commending the *mos maiorum* as the model for self-formation and

55. Bynum, *Docere Verbo et Exemplo*, passim.
56. Hugh of St. Victor, *De institutione novitiorum* 4: "Nos, qui per exemplum bonorum quasi per quoddam sigillum optime exsculptum informari cupimus...." In Feiss and Sicard, ed. 363–64; PL 176:933c.
57. Steckel, *Kulturen*, 795–96.
58. *Studien*, 61–63.

nobilitas and *gloria* as the goals of discipline. Classical, Roman these ideals may be, but they are also the lesson for a high officer of the Church.[59]

MEANINGFUL READING

The second source of learning and virtue Meinhard urges on his student G is reading. Consistent with the Ciceronian Romanness of the virtues of G's father is the second bit of advice for finding and following the path to glory: meaningful reading (*fructuosa lectio*). His praise of Cicero's *Tusculan Disputations* is striking. He acclaims it the "most illustrious work that Latin philosophy, with Cicero as its parent, has produced."[60] Few would place it that high in competition with the rest of "Latin philosophy." It is a book of statesmanship and service to the *res publica*. It is to the end of a state minister's career and life what his *De officiis* is to their beginnings. It was a work of major importance for the eleventh-century cathedral schools. Its great appeal lay in its combining of asceticism and rejection of the world with a stoically courageous affirmation of state service. Cicero faced personal suffering and public tribulation when he wrote this work late in life. The five days of the discussions at Tusculum address five topics: indifference to death, pain, grief, emotional suffering, and the way to a happy life. That path is the cultivation of virtue (*cultus virtutum*). Its message is: persist, suffer through all the tribulations of the active life and make the cult of virtues — identified with philosophy — into your guide.

The appeal of this stance to worldly clergy in the German empire in the second half of the eleventh century should be evident. Torn between parties in the Investiture Controversy, they could find in Cicero's work a rule of life, a philosophy that lent dignity to administrative service while at the same time casting serious doubt on it. It helped to reconcile *contemptus mundi* with service of the state. These are themes of another set of letters of the eleventh century also from the milieu of secular clergy serving the *res publica*: clerics of Regensburg. Norbert Fickermann gave them the title *The Regensburg Rhetorical*

---

59. Steckel, *Kulturen*, 944: Meinhard was less "geistlicher doctor," more "Adelserzieher."

60. M1: "Hortor ut Tusculanis tuis plurimus insideas, quibus latina philosophia Cicerone parente nichil illustrius edidit." In Erdmann ed., 193.

Letters.[61] The authors of these letters find in the *Tusculan Disputations* a Roman model for the identification of philosophy and the active life. It makes philosophy into the teacher and guide of manners[62] and makes the conduct of public life into a form of philosophical discourse, a program of studies, a theater of *mores*.

Well might the "Tusculans" be a guide for G. His entrance into the life of Cologne is freighted with dangers. Meinhard sets G's departure in that frame: his life and his honor are at stake, and to depart so much as an inch from the path of virtue is to risk disaster. It seems that G has a close familiarity with the lessons of Cicero's work, since Meinhard commends it to him as "your Tusculans." Meinhard's lessons are not the stable fixed quantities of virtues, like those of Cicero's *De Officiis* or William of Conche's *Moralium dogma philosophorum*. They convey virtues as endangered qualities, easily overturned. To maintain them requires wisdom, courtesy, and commitment to ancestral custom. Even the splendor of G's father encumbers him with danger as much as distinction (*te tuo periculo gravet*). Ignominy is as likely an outcome as glory. G's "Tusculans" will have brought home in every chapter the lesson of this fraught state that is a bishopric — like a seat in the Roman Senate. To assume the archbishopric of Cologne is not a walk in the park. It is a perilous testing of the one chosen.

The interpenetration of classical literature and learning with Christianity is the idiom of administrative acts and positions taken in the service of a king or bishop. We know from Meinhard's letters that Roman epic, lyric, and comedy loom large in his own usage. An example of his sophisticated use of Horace is discussed below. Much attests to the accuracy of Erdmann's judgment that no history of education and literature in Germany could be written without giving Meinhard a major place.[63]

---

61. Jaeger, *Envy*, 84–85.

62. CTD 5.2.5-6: "O vitae philosophia dux, o virtutum indagatrix expultrixque vitiorum!... Tu magistra morum et disciplinae fuisti." In King ed., 428.

63. Erdmann, *Studien*, 116.

WHY CATHEDRAL-SCHOOL EDUCATION?

Along with the pedagogy of virtue, the letter to G also sits in a distinct social and professional context. The young student G moves from the cathedral school to the archiepiscopal court. The letter is fully aligned with that broader purpose of the Bamberg school to prepare young men for higher office. We glimpse Meinhard's student en route to fill an episcopal position to which he has been chosen. It is a typical instance of calls from school to bishopric (more often via service in the imperial court chapel) expressed with words like "having shown himself suited (*idoneus*), he is called from the school to the court for his elegance of manners and his acute genius."[64] The assumption must be that G's position as archbishop-in-spe will have a critical element of diplomacy, restraint, self-control, good judgment in both personal and legal affairs in which his education will have rendered him *instructus*.

If this is indeed the goal of that education, then that conventional view that it instructs in the preparation of documents in service of church and empire, is far off the mark. Johannes Fried expressed that position with a sharp edge. Arguing for the severe intellectual limits and twelfth-century decline of the Bamberg school, he points precisely to Meinhard as giving emphatic expression to what Fried supposed to be the core of his teaching:

> The reasons [for the mediocrity and ultimate decline of the school] are to be found in the core activity of the school itself. Meinhard of Bamberg, the cathedral school master celebrated far and wide, expressed in a crisp and precise formulation the goal of his instruction: "Persistent composition; repeated conjugation." That was all that was aspired to. Grammar and school rhetoric, still in the early twelfth century, count as the surest proof of a rich intellect.[65]

---

64. Jaeger, *Origins*, 28–48.

65. Fried, "Domschule," 168: "Die Gründe sind im Kern des Schulbetriebs selbst zu suchen. Meinhard von Bamberg, der weithin gefeierte Domscholaster umriss im elften Jahrhundert knapp und präzis das Ziel seines Unterrichts: *dictet instanter, declinet iugiter*. Mehr wurde nicht angestrebt. Grammatik und Schulrhetorik gelten auch im frühen 12. Jahrhundert als sicherster Beweis eines reichen Geistes."

CHAPTER 3 ✶ MEINHARD OF BAMBERG

Fried's reading is a misunderstanding of Meinhard's letter (M69) and hence of his exclamation, *dictet, declinet*. A close reading of the letter gives a clear perspective on the standards that the famous schoolmaster actually advocated and imposed. In that letter Meinhard is scolding an unnamed Bamberg teacher in unusually harsh terms for pulling a young student (*puer, tyrunculus*), hardly into the rudiments of grammar, out of school and allowing him to go off to court, where his manners will be corrupted by courtly laxness (*curiali illa licentia*). This imperious phrase, *dictet, declinet*, is not the "core" of teaching; it is the elementary beginning. Meinhard sees this student fleeing, like others, the feared "discipline" of schooling.[66] It appears also that the teacher receiving this tongue-lashing has allowed the young student's arguments to prevail over the practice of the experienced master:

> It is plainly ridiculous that a teacher like you with deep experience and seniority, still with your wits about you, should be taught by a stupid beginner what needs to be done.[67]

Clearly Meinhard's formulation, *dictet instanter, declinet iugiter*, is a punishment urged on the teacher to treat a "stupid beginner" (*stolidus tyro*) for indolence. Its vehemence (*instanter! iugiter!*), a further goading rebuke to the teacher. Constant grammar and dictamenal

---

66. See also H3, Erdmann ed., 195: Meinhard recalls to Bamberg a student who has run off to Rheims because the "onslaught of severe school discipline is intolerable"; "make an effort" to get him back. No doubt "that horrible vengeance of scorned discipline will seize his mind to abhor sane council like that legendary Orestes driven by furies." M24, Erdmann ed., 221. Evil manners are a plague in such a great kingdom; everywhere discipline is dying out. See also below, 171–74; M19, Erdmann ed., 213. The complaint was widespread: Anselm of Liège (writing c. 1050–56) saw the imperial school of Liège endangered students fleeing "the yoke of discipline," giving themselves over to a life of levity (*levitas*) in the courts of kings and bishops. Anselm longs for a return to the golden age when schools demanded "nothing more than the study of letters along with the discipline of manners." See *Gesta episcoporum Leodiensium* 28, MGH 7:205. Goswin of Mainz, letter to Walcherus 27–28, notes that students flee instruction in the "gravity of moral discipline." Huygens ed., 31–32; Jaeger, *Envy*, 223, 365–66.

67. H 69: "Ridiculum plane est a stolido quodam tyrone experientissimum vos et viridem adhuc veteranum, quod factum opus sit, doceri." In Erdmann ed., 117.

practice is what the master imposes for a student quitting before he has begun the basics. Consistent with this hierarchy of subjects, it is clear that *dictet, declinet* "crisp and precise" though it is *(knapp und präzis)*, is very far from a statement of the core and goal of imperial study. We can focus on that goal in a crisp and precise comment of a student of Würzburg writing around 1030. He praises the school as "a gushing spring out of which flows the doctrine of eloquence and proper conduct of life" (*recte vivendi et dogma loquendi*).[68] Or with clearer focus on the *recte vivendi* or *mores* side of the formula, a letter from the canons of Worms to their colleagues at Bamberg (1115), urging them to support their bishop elect, a former student of Bamberg schooled in the institutes of the Bamberg school from youth on: "knowledge of letters, skill in administrative affairs, the gift of good judgment."[69] Fried's formulation reduces Meinhard's pedagogy to low-level competence (*"Mehr wurde nicht angestrebt"*).

For Fried, grammar and rhetoric, mastery of the notarial art, are the highest intellectual ambition to which one can aspire in eleventh-century Bamberg. Meinhard would emphatically disagree. It is easy to get a clear fix on his assessment of grammar in the hierarchy of studies: he ranks it at the bottom. A letter (M12) to an unnamed colleague states this priority clearly. The letter is directed to a mature, experienced teacher on Meinhard's staff. It begins by showering ironic praise on the flattery with which the colleague opened his letter to Meinhard, then goes on to rebuke him in unvarnished language for requesting a book of grammar:

---

68. *Die ältere Wormser Briefsammlung*, ll. 264–65; Bulst ed., 3:127.

69. Canons of Worms to Bamberg 1115, *Wormser Briefsammlung,* nr. 300: "vestris institutis fundatus a puericia...in litterarum scientia, in rerum agendarum pericia, in honestate morum, in gratia discretionum." In *Codex Udalrici*, Klaus Nass, ed., MGH *Briefe der deutschen Kaiserzeit* 10, 2 vols. (Wiesbaden: Harrassowitz, 2017), 2:505. The phrases *pericia/peritia rerum agendarum* and variants, *experiencia, prudentia, industria, auctoritas,* have an interesting history in the language of ecclesiastical suitability for office, *idoneitas*. A scan of *rerum agendarum peritia* in the Library of Latin Texts and Google testifies to the quality of "business" competence to which it refers and clarifies the context of the phrase in relation to the *instituta* of the Bamberg cathedral school.

CHAPTER 3 ✳ MEINHARD OF BAMBERG

You astonish me by such an urge to study the rules of grammar. Is this an attempt to return to boyhood? What, pray tell, is a fifty-year-old man doing pondering toy rattles and infantile droolings? Good gods above! What monstrosity is this? But while I'm still reeling from astonishment, the comment of Cicero occurs to me that when Socrates and Cato were both at an advanced age, the one studied music [stringed instruments], the other learned Greek. That's nothing [compared to Cicero's accomplishments]. This man left a legacy of great examples to both Greeks and Romans. I have done as you request [i.e., sent the grammar book], but I fear that the texts are distorted from neglect. I for my part have long since bidden farewell to such trivialities.[70]

Grammar by itself is not a measure of intellectual richness, but rather of intellectual immaturity.

M12 gives a clearer measure both of grammar and of the level of intellectual ambition expected of a colleague. Meinhard is not only speaking as the headmaster (as in M 69), but also as a man of letters, a *litteratus*, at a level that might make plausible the predicate of an admiring contemporary who called him *scholasticissimus*.[71] It is a document not only of pedagogic but of cultural importance. He holds a mature colleague up to shame for tinkering with grammar rather than emulating Cicero, Socrates, and Cato. That sets the level of "intellectual richness" that the famous schoolmaster expects. He equates grammar studies with "trivialities," "toy rattles," "infantile droolings." The older teacher's preoccupation with the rudiments of grammar deserves only ridicule. It is a betrayal of the level of literary and philosophical judgment appropriate to his status. Meinhard expresses unvarnished contempt for one who appears to have abandoned

---

70. M12: "Numquidnam repuerescere conatur? Numquidnam crepundia et infantiles salivas homo quinquagenarius meditatur? Dei boni, quid hoc monstri est? Verum in medio hoc stupore dum occurrisset mihi ex Cicerone Socratem et Catonem ambo iam senes, illum fidibus, istum Grece didicisse, id vero est inquam nichil: hic homo magnorum exemplorum vel Grecis vel Romanis reliquum facit. Morem ergo gessi vobis, sed vereor, ne depravata sint pleraque incuria scriptorum. Nam ego iam diu est, quod his neniis valedixi." In Erdmann ed., 205.

71. For this and other contemporary acknowledgments of Meinhard's excellence, see Tischler, 252 n. 5.

that high standard.⁷² He is telling the colleague not only how to teach, but how to think. Yes, not only Meinhard the *litteratus* is speaking but also the school principal. He does not want his staff playing the childrens' games of studies. He wants the colleague to use his time on the highest level of intellectual reflection. By mentioning the examples that Cicero both wrote and embodied, he makes his colleague painfully sensitive of the distance separating him from his Roman predecessor as orator and author.

PAIDEIA: FORMATION OF THE INDIVIDUAL

The view that sees dictatorial/dictamenal competence as the highest goal of learning ignores the humanistic side of cathedral-school education altogether. The formation of the individual, *paideia* in its medieval instantiation, is the object of *mores* and *cultus virtutum* joined to the study of eloquence. To regard administrative duties narrowly defined as the goal of cathedral-school education in the imperial church is like regarding the purpose of the Harvard Business School as the training of accountants, notary publics, and clerks — not entirely wrong but a trivializing of the role of that school in economy and government. Dictamenal duties were a preliminary and a byproduct of cathedral-school education. The creation of a lettered and trained advisor, diplomat, orator was primary.

None of the sources on the school, biography, letters, or poems treat *dictamen* in any other than a cursory way.⁷³ Meinhard himself had nothing to say about those activities in his letters, no advice to give his students on those subjects other than to write an elegant style — on that he was insistent. The lessons in *dictamen* were there in the library's document collection, and for the next generation, in the

---

72. Cicero, *Cato de senectute* 3 tells of Cato's studies of Greek literature late in life. .

73. Ulrich of Bamberg, assembler of the *Codex Udalrici*, composed an *Ars dictaminis*. See *Historischer Verein für die Pflege der Geschichte des ehemaligen Fürstbistums Bamberg,* Franz Bittner, ed., 100 (1964): 145–71. It is a brief introduction to Latin style, elegant (Cicero, Quintilian) and decorative or mannerist (Martianus Capella). His conception of style is classical and humanistic, written style closely linked to lived style. His loving dedication to his friend Gottschalk is fully in line with the cultivation of friendship of the schools (*castus amor*), and he sketches a literary ideal in which it is poetry that fulfills learning and perfects the student for its calming, taming, soothing effect.

CHAPTER 3 ✴ MEINHARD OF BAMBERG

Codex Udalrici[74] discussion of documents and how to prepare them had no place alongside the high-flying ideals of study expressed in letters and poems from the period. Master Pernolf of Würzburg was praised a few decades before Meinhard as a "prince of primates" who explained the mysteries of the poets. He taught poetry, composition, virtue; and this teaching would make his students into the highest pontiffs and candidates for heaven and ultimately for salvation.[75] It seems unlikely that Goswin of Mainz and Liège had dictamenal competence in mind when he referred to students as "those to be formed by artist's hand from wet and malleable clay into vessels of glory on the wheel of discipline."[76] Bernard of Clairvaux in the next century is speaking the same language of humanist ethical ideals when he praises Lady Wisdom as higher than the "glory of angels."[77]

Meinhard summed up his education in the two years he spent at Rheims cathedral school, and which he regarded with great affection, in a letter to his former teacher Hermann. That study was the best imaginable, he wrote, "more effective for utility, or more refined for elegance, or more exquisite for sublimity" than any other.[78] In a few words Meinhard sweeps the range of educational goals: effective in making one "useful" (*ad utilitatem efficacius*), exacting in cultivating "elegance" (*ad elegantiam accuratius*), scrupulous for (in pursuit of?) sublimity (*ad sublimitatem exquisitius*). "Utility" in this context is a broad term meaning suitability for the roles required in serving the Church;

---

74. Erdmann, *Bamberger Domschule*, 450, shows that the school favored the "literary" collecting of letters and documents from the realm of politics and public life. He questions the earlier idea that the collection was aimed at positions taken on the investiture controversy. The *Codex Udalrici* is a good example. The collection is available as models of writing.

75. On Pernolf of Würzburg, see Jaeger, *Envy*, 66–70.

76. The Letter of Goswin to Walcherus, in Jaeger, *Envy*, 365–66. The statement sits in the same context as Meinhard's H 69: stupid and lazy students who think they know much with minimal studies, throw over discipline and live a dissolute life.

77. Epist. 113.5, *Sancti Bernardi Opera*, Jean Leclercq et al., ed., 7:290.

78. H 65: "studio illo nihil esse potest vel ad utilitatem efficacius vel ad elegantiam accuratius vel ad sublimitatem exquisitius." In Erdmann ed., 112–13.

"elegance," disciplined behavior; "sublimity" (a resonant term),[79] the highest one can achieve, leaving open whether it means the highest position in a hierarchy or some vaguer excellence of accomplishment. Both "elegance" and "sublimity" are ethical terms but also style words. Again, in this rising curve of importance, manners and some quintessence of ideal character are at the top.

Cathedral-school education is hard to describe because it is a process of formation defined not by a set curriculum but by the action of the teacher at work in shaping by praise, blame, precept, and example — living and literary — the manners of a student. That process of formation happens in the context of a shared life, *convictus*. This sense of rendering scrupulous judgment of a student's behavior, shaping, molding, correcting, rejecting individual acts as they occur in the performance of public life, comparing lived action with literary models — this is the essence of instruction in *mores*. It is well formulated in the Middle Ages in Hugh of St. Victor's *On the Instruction of Novices* and scripted in the customary *Liber ordinis Sancti Victoris* of St. Victor, Paris. The context of ideals is different at St. Victor from those of an imperial cathedral school, but the process is closely related.

I referred to this process earlier as *paideia*, borrowing the term from Werner Jaeger's study of ancient Greek educational ideals. A discourse like this essay on Meinhard, or any attempt at a historical reconstruction, calls on terms that present themselves as ethical concepts, hence are always reduced when defined narrowly or seen in a single instance. They can be observed in texts like Meinhard's letter to G, M1, and in many portraits of educated clerics.[80] The Middle Ages produced one epic work of literature that offers a comprehensive vision of the human ideal embodied and in action, the *Tristan* romance of Gottfried von Strassburg,[81] which has been called "a courtier romance" as opposed to the chivalric romances of

---

79. See C. Stephen Jaeger, *The Sense of the Sublime in the Middle Ages*. Online at: https://www.academia.edu/72905836; and chapter 1: https://www.academia.edu/72939654.

80. See Jaeger, *Envy*, 76–117.

81. See Jaeger, *Medieval Humanism in Tristan*, passim.

CHAPTER 3 ✳ MEINHARD OF BAMBERG

Chrétien de Troyes, Wolfram von Eschenbach, and others. The ideal also tends towards plastic description in Gothic sculpture, as in the *Wise and Foolish Virgins* of Strassburg Cathedral. Finally, it is fully realized in its infinite richness of nuance and lived dramatic moment, dialectical analysis in narrative, and anecdote in Castiglione's *Book of the Courtier*.

I can point to one moment in the letters of Meinhard when that richness of process and of concepts in action comes partially to expression. It is a letter of congratulation directed to Leopertus of Palestrina on the occasion of his rise to cardinal-bishop (M14).[82] Meinhard enumerates the qualities that account for that rise and places them in an active, lived context:

> Hardly any powers of eloquence are adequate to explain with what gentle and imperious reign your love dominates in our heart through the sweetest condiments of your *humanitas*. For who could distinguish whether you are wiser in condemning or more gentle in correcting, whether you accuse more justly or implore more humbly? You console persuasively as a man of empathy, you exhort fruitfully, and through thick and thin you hold, by the grace of God, to the norm of a catholic doctor, strong in authority, perfected in your person....[83]

The perspective of the writer is also that of the mentor (of students/of bishops) observing the subject and judging his actions ("who could distinguish whether..."), finding ideal response at the extreme of each action performed, a balance of assertion and restraint,

---

82. Leopertus, bishop of Palestrina, friend of Peter Damian and of the abbey of Montecassino, was made cardinal bishop in 1065. He served as papal legate in Germany in 1066.

83. M14: "Quam suavi et imperioso regno caritas tua per dulcissima humanitatis tue condimenta cordi nostro dominetur, vix ullis eloquentie viribus explicetur.... Quis enim interpretetur, utrumnam sis in arguendo discretior an in corrigendo lenior, dum increpas erectior an dum obsecras humilior? Consolaris certe ut qui affectuose, exhortaris ut qui fructuose, denique per omnia catholici doctoris Dei gratia normam tenes, auctoritate polles, personam imples." In Erdmann ed., 206–7. *Personam imples* is an intriguing formulation, something like, "fulfill your person, your role." On the letter and the probability of Meinhard's authorship, see *Studien*, 285.

shaping his actions in rendering judgment, fully in control of the range of calibrations binding justice to mercy and condemnation to forgiveness. Opposites come to equilibrium in Leopertus: he "reigns" but with "love"; his rule is "gentle" but "imperious." The virtues operate in judgment of moral and legal issues, but they are colored by the grace and force of execution (*auctoritas*) and maturity of person (*personam imples*).

These acts of judgment call upon that same sense of scrupulous oversight, refined and nuanced but authoritative that Meinhard's letter M1 to G inculcates. What Meinhard commended to G, what he taught his students, what he transmitted to them by his writing — and we can assume by his personal behavior — and what he praised in Cardinal-Bishop Leopertus, were shadings of an accepted norm of excellence in cathedral communities, especially those loyal to the emperor, and in the elite levels of church administration. The essence of this model is summed up in the word *humanitas*, a human and social ideal not identical with piety or transcendence.

The type of the educated cleric, prepared as bishop or guided through a bishopric by these virtues— affable, well liked by all, all things to all, handsome, beaming a quality through his presence that gives testimony to his inner virtues, humble but with the humility of the "great man" — is the core of moral discipline at the schools of imperial churches into the twelfth century[84] and widely admired in clerical life in general in the period.

The view of a curriculum narrowly focused on grammar, rhetoric, and correctly prepared documents presupposes an organized administration, formulas that need to be mastered, procedures and techniques that need to be learned, men to be fit into narrow slots in a bureaucracy. But Ottonian-Salian administration rested much more on ceremony and ritual.[85] These were transmitted by experience and close relation of the student with teacher, bishop with king, governed ideally by a neo-Ciceronian/Christian ethic. Imperial self-presentation

---

84. Jaeger, *Origins*, 28–48.

85. Gerd Althoff, *Otto III*, Phyllis Jestice, trans. (University Park: Pennsylvania State University Press, 2003), 19; and Althoff, *Die Macht der Rituale: Symbolik und Herrschaft im Mittelalter* (Darmstadt: Wissenschaftliche Buchgesellschaft, 2003). See also Leyser and Mayr-Harting.

counted far more than notarial competence. Bamberg and all the imperial German schools became mediocre and narrow when they lost what most essentially constituted their curriculum: the preparation of the personality and character of the student. That is the discipline of *mores*. When that discipline faded, so did the ideal of individual formation it transmitted. It moved out of German cathedral schools and relocated.[86]

There is good reason for Meinhard and other schoolmasters of the period to stress the ministerial qualities called for in a bishop of the period, and there is good reason, consequently, to call on the system of values from Roman antiquity: the virtues inculcated are constituents of *idoneitas* for the aspiring bishop in the imperial church. Two aspects of this assemblage of virtues stressed in Meinhard's letters are good humor and love.

HILARITAS

As for the first, *hilaritas* is one of the "ornaments of the soul," the one that shines in the eyes of G's father and radiates "ocular grace" (*ocularis gratia*). "Bright good humor" or "joviality" are close in English. The qualities of "grace and charm of humanity" imply humor and affability but also wit and pleasing qualities in social intercourse. Good humor as a quality favored in educated clerics has a long history. Courts and court life, episcopal or secular, are generally its social context. Joviality inspires affection and admiration. Together with a variety of virtues, it holds a high place in the descriptions of qualities that please princes and of the *idoneitas* of aspiring clerics. Meinhard's sense of humor is a special case. His sense of irony, joking, good humor is pronounced. It deserves a study.[87] It is best expressed in his letters to and about his bishop, Gunther (1057–64). The wit is sharp, often caustic and scolding. *Hilaritas* may have shone most graciously/gracefully from the eyes of G's father, but it had a rather different aura in Meinhard's.

Letter H78a berates Bishop Gunther for oversleeping and neglecting his duties to his bishopric, leading a life of self-indulgence

---

86. See below, 171–74.
87. Erdmann, *Studien*, 27 observes the "spöttisch-humoristische Note" common in Meinhard.

at his estate in Carinthia.[88] The letter is especially rich in ironies. Erdmann ascribed the letter to Poppo, *decanus*, but Meinhard's provocative sense of humor dominates and is unmistakable. I think, contrary to Erdmann, for that reason it must be ascribed to Meinhard as primary author.[89] The letter calls on Gunther to return home to tend to his responsibilities. Bamberg needs his action and his authority. The letter opens with a comparison of Gunther to the aged but heroic Greek wise man, Nestor:

> Antiquity in its fables marveled at Nestor for living three lifetimes vigorous and unharmed. This present age can with greater justice marvel at you. At you, I say who number as many ages (*saecula*) as your church has had bishops [five], who in so many years of prudence still with utmost efficacy present so virile, nay rather so youthful a vigor. For if there is anything of truth in that astrological belief, I would by no means rashly [*haud temere*] affirm that Saturn and Mercury, to use the words of that age, saluted each other at your birth. However, I urge you by no means absurdly [*haud absurde*] to look to your own nest and pay attention to its increasingly frail body.

Clearly it is also Gunther's body that worries him. He urges Gunther to practice the strenuous physical exercises of young army recruits and responds sensitively to a suggestion Gunther has made that he, Meinhard, has been lazy, hinting that he, Meinhard, would do well to slim down. Meinhard's reaction, soaked with sarcasm:

> Come now, good corrector, man of utmost vigilance! Just look at yourself, transformed like Polemon. Oh, and if only you could turn down the volume of your snoring, because I find it necessary to steal away into peace and quiet. Furthermore, either

88. The text and English translations are included below at 175–80.

89. The closing two paragraphs refer to judicial cases, normally the responsibility of the dean. The body of the letter however is playful, satiric, caustic. There is a clear break preceding the last two paragraphs. Meinhard calls attention to the break himself by ending his satirical riff with *Sed haec hactenus*, "but enough of this." The final two paragraphs are clearly Poppo's style, straightforward, dour, both about legal proceedings with un-Meinhardian touches of piety and blandishments to Gunther rare in Meinhard but common in Poppo to Gunther. See M 21: "Tu, domne dilectissime et vita quondam dulci longe longeque dulcior...." In Erdmann ed., 216. Probably H78a was co-written by Meinhard and Poppo, as were H81, M6, and M21.

CHAPTER 3 ★ MEINHARD OF BAMBERG

I am a bad prophet, or you, swelling up as you are in laziness and sleep, will have to be lifted and rolled out of Carinthia by hoists and pulleys. But enough for now.

The exchange of jibes — you call me fat and lazy? Look at yourself! — follows flattery raising Gunther to mythological heights of health and vigor. The jibe that he will need machinery to lift him out of his bed follows the flattering comparison with the philosopher Polemon, converted by a lecture of Xenocrates on temperance to a life of discipline guided by nature.[90] The pomposity of the comparisons, the mock-heroic tone is underscored by the repeated *haud temere, haud absurde*. The phrases call attention to the rashness and absurdity of its own empty flattery, as if to say openly, "Believe me, this is neither a rash nor an absurd comparison" but to imply subtly, "it most certainly is." "You snore so much, I have to leave the room!" shows Meinhard stretching for provocative put-downs.

Why did Meinhard feel not just justified but safe in speaking to his bishop in a sarcastic and mocking tone[91] that might well have put him in disfavor with a less tolerant or sensitive bishop? Of course, it was a clerical duty to instruct and correct the behavior of their betters, secular and ecclesiastic, but it was not without dangers.[92] Irony was a mode in which correction could happen behind a veil of flattery. To praise publicly the chastity of a notoriously lascivious king or bishop, especially

90. On Polemon, see Diogenes Laertius, *Lives* 4.3.16.

91. As he himself admits. He ends another letter chiding Gunther for sleeping too much and reading too little with this self-erasing apology: "If you sense any sharp barbs in these letters, please take them in the way they are meant." H62, Erdmann ed., 110. Meinhard to Gunther H71, Erdmann, ed., 118: Hart[wig?] passes on Gunther's opinion that Meinhard says overinflated things with a big mouth. Meinhard responds, Gunther might more aptly say "my words are not so much windy as overflowing with venom" (*non vento plenas sed felle superabundantes*).

92. Abbot Walo of St. Arnulf of Metz repeatedly criticized and worked to correct Archbishop Manasses I of Rheims, who behaved in his office more like a warrior than a pastor in administering the church. In revenge, the bishop reviled and harassed him violently. See Jaeger, *Envy*, 151–52. The relevant letters of Walo to Manasses I are in the Hannover collection, Erdmann, ed., H108 and 109. See Gerd Althoff and Christl Meier, *Ironie im Mittelalter: Hermeneutik, Dichtung, Politik* (Darmstadt: Wissenschaftliche Buchgesellschaft, 2011), 84–89.

161

in court or in councils, or the peace-loving gentleness of a war-like ruler, is licit and effective criticism. John of Salisbury dedicated his treatise on court life and government to the chancellor of England and future archbishop of Canterbury, Thomas Becket: *Policraticus* or *On the Follies of Courtiers and the Footsteps of Philosophers*. Becket is the one courtier in England known to be "above any suspicion of frivolity," he says, then proceeds to criticize the very aspects of court life for which Becket as chancellor of England was notorious.[93]

But Meinhard did not make any attempt to shelter himself by a disguise of irony. His irony is unambiguous. He goes straight into the face of his bishop. While that might indicate *facetia* in a personal friendly relationship, a criticism jokingly magnified, the criticisms levelled at Gunther are meant seriously: his absences and his manners are deleterious to the Church. Gunther seems to have imposed the curse of Proserpina on himself, says Meinhard, again mythologizing Gunther, since he spends half his year in the dark underworld of Carinthia exiling himself from the enlightened world of good manners and people (*hanc lucem morum et hominum*, i.e., Bamberg).[94] The mere mention of Carinthia brings out the satiric strain in him. He writes to a Bamberg cleric accompanying Gunther in Carinthia, begging him to return to Bamberg and asks casually about Gunther:

> But what is our lord up to? What about his battalion of helmeted rabbits? What wars, what battles are they fighting? What triumphs are they celebrating? Gods above, what a mob not of men, but of mosquitoes! How magnificent and meaningless the noise they make! No *gravitas*, no discipline.... Rescue yourself, tear yourself away from this life in a cesspool.[95]

---

93. See Jaeger, "Irony and Role-Playing in John of Salisbury and the Becket Circle," in *Culture politique des Plantagenets (1154–1224)*, Martin Aurell, ed. (Poitiers: Centre d'études supérieures de civilisation médiévale, 2003), 319–31. On irony and satire at the court of Henry II, see Peter J.A. Jones, *Laughter and Power in the Twelfth Century* (Oxford: Oxford University Press, 2019); and Katrin Beyer, *Witz und Ironie in der Politischen Kultur Englands im Hochmittelalter: Interaktionen und Imaginationen* (Würzburg: Ergon, 2012); and, more generally, Althoff and Meier.

94. M22, Erdmann ed., 217.

95. H73, Erdmann ed., 121. Then follows the comment that has gotten much attention from Germanists, that Gunther prefers the stories of Attila

CHAPTER 3 ✶ MEINHARD OF BAMBERG

In a letter to Gunther very much in contrast to that ironic tone — indeed, correcting it — Meinhard congratulates Gunther on his planned pilgrimage to the Holy Land but encumbers it with all kinds of misgivings. Meinhard offers a remarkable take on his own customary mode of speaking with Gunther — excessive criticism:

> What am I doing? What madness seizes me?! [Here you are pressing for the prize of a heavenly calling], while I act the devil's advocate [*Sathane stimulus*] and box your ears, adjuring you and reminding you of these things, I who have constantly been an annoying and often a sharp monitor.[96]

Meinhard regrets, untypically, his own inactivity and admires Gunther's willingness to suffer the difficulties of a long pilgrimage. But the regret is couched in a language appropriate to a parent speaking to a young man used to being scolded (*te colafizo*).

Meinhard's voice can be reverential (M71) or sarcastic. Clearly some special relationship obtains between these two men, in which the lesser in rank has licence to criticize, taunt, and ridicule the higher.[97] Some observations on Bishop Gunther by Lampert of Hersfeld, admirer of Gunther, former Bamberg student, and possibly once Bamberg schoolmaster, cast a special light on Meinhard's criticism. They call into question Meinhard's snide comment about Gunther weighted down by obesity. Lampert praises Gunther's physical beauty

---

and Dietrich to Augustine and Gregory. Erdmann thinks that the "army of helmeted rabbits" refers to the crowds of minstrels Gunther has gathered around him. Erdmann, "*Fabulae curiales*: Neues zum Spielmannsgesang und zum Ezzo-Liede," *Zeitschrift für deutsches Altertum* 73 (1936): 87–98, at 91–92.

96. M23: "Sed quid ago? Que me rapit dementia? Tu…bravium superne vocationis persequeris [2 Cor. 12:7], et ego quasi stimulus Sathane te huiusmodi rerum memoria in inculcatione colafizo, ego inquam, qui tociens tam inportunus, nonnumquam acerbus monitor fui.…" In Erdmann ed., 218. In another letter, he asks Gunther to accept the sharp barbs he is constantly aiming at him in "the right way" "in the way they are meant." H62: "ut si quos in litteris istis senseritis aculeos, illos eo vos recipiatis animo, quo finguntur affectu." In Erdmann ed., 110.

97. Zey gives a picture of Meinhard cooperating closely and on the most personally engaged terms with Gunther on matters of politics, strategy, and even personal conduct. He warns Gunther against the seductive powers of the queen regent Agnes.

to the skies.[98] Gunther so far surpassed all other mortals in elegance of appearance and the overall proportion of his body, he says, that he drew great crowds in Jerusalem who wanted only to marvel at his beauty. Others praised these same qualities in Gunther. No one but Meinhard warns Gunther that mechanical apparatus will be necessary to lift him out of his dissolute life in Carinthia if he continues to swell up (*intumueritis*) from excess. Furthermore Gunther's reported behavior on the crusade during murderous attacks by Muslim raiders showed a heroism that might rival those "courtly fables" of Attila the Hun and Dietrich of Bern of which Gunther was so fond.[99] By a bold and daring gesture, Gunther frees himself from the grip of a Muslim prince who is about to strangle him with his unrolled turban, bashes the man in the face, flattening him with a single blow, and leads a counter-attack that turns the tide in favor of the Christians and in fact rescues the entire enterprise of the crusade from certain disaster.[100]

Nobility, affability, courtesy combined with heroic action — the historical validity of the tales of Gunther's bravado would seem to be confirmed materially by the so-called *Gunthertuch*. It is a Byzantine silk tapestry, once splendid, now rather badly damaged. It represents

98. Lampert, who may have been Meinhard's predecessor as schoolmaster at Bamberg, wrote of Bishop Gunther (1057–65), "This was a man adorned with all the gifts of the body, in addition to the glory of his manners and the wealth of his mind and splendor of body, he was also fully enriched with [worldly] goods. He was born of the leading men of the palace.... He was unhesitating in speech and in council, learned in letters both divine and human, in stature and elegance of figure and the overall build of his body preeminent among all other mortals...." ("...vir preter morum gloriam et animae divicias corporis quoque bonis adprime ornatus... tum statura et formae elegantia a tocius corporis integritate...caeteris eminens mortalibus...." In Lampert, *Annals* (1065), Otto Holder-Egger, ed., MGH, SSR 99; *The Annals of Lampert of Hersfeld*, Ian S. Robinson, trans. (Manchester: Manchester University Press, 2015), 106–7. Here follows the story of his fabled physical beauty, so great that on the crusade of 1064/65 crowds gathered in "field and town" to admire him. For further references to contemporary sources on Gunther's beauty, see Lampert, Robinson trans., 102 and n. 412.

99. H73; and Erdmann, *Fabulae curiales*.

100. Lampert, *Annales* 1065. The same story embroidered with colorful details in *Annales Altahenses*, MGH, SSR 4:69.

CHAPTER 3 ✶ MEINHARD OF BAMBERG

the *triumphus* of a Byzantine emperor returning victorious from a military campaign.[101] The circumstances in which Gunther received it are not certain, but it seems plausible that it was a gift meant to allude to the bishop's heroism on the crusade. Gunther was in possession of the tapestry when he died on the way home from the crusade. His body was wrapped in it, transported to Bamberg and buried with the corpse. It seems unlikely that many contemporaries thought Gunther was a fat and lazy man.

The most likely explanation of this disparity between Lampert's glorifying and Meinhard's belittling Bishop Gunther is that Meinhard's personal goading indicated a joking relationship between the two men. To face an insulting joke and respond with another is a sign of a quick wit, of *facetia*. It was a courtly and admired relationship between men; no offense could be taken, as in the famous anecdote of Charlemagne and Alcuin. Seated across a table from the Scotsman Alcuin, his clerical advisor and favorite, the emperor asks him "What's the difference between a Scot and a sot?" "What separates a Scot from a sot?" (*Quid interest inter Scotum et sotum?*), and he receives the answer "Just this table" (*Tabula tantum*). This is cavilling (*cavillatio*), a jesting duel in which exaggerated criticism is licit.[102] It is also a test of wit. Gunther is not insulted by overblown and witty criticism; he is challenged. Too bad we do not know how he reacted to such goading. But the joking relationship is lent some plausibility given the general preference for a light, humorous atmosphere of converse at court and school.[103] Whatever it indicates of the relationship, it displays how

---

101. Sigrid Müller-Christensen, *Das Gunthertuch im Bamberger Domschatz* (Bamberg: Diözesan-Museum, 1966); G. Prinzing, "Das Bamberger Gunthertuch in neuer Sicht," in V. Vavrinek, ed., *Byzantium and its Neighbors: From the Mid-Ninth to the Twelfth Century* (Prague: Institut Slav, 1993), 218–31.

102. *Cavillatio* is a mode of joking, generally between two men who understand each other very well, though it can also be nasty and destructive. Other examples in Jaeger, *Origins*, 163.

103. Anselm of Liège, writing c.1050s, tells of the practice of Bishop Ebrachar of sending joking letters to his schoolmasters to encourage their work when he was absent: "quos reliquisset scolarum magistros, litteris animare, ipsis crebro dulci carmine alludere solebat...ut caros filios ad studia incendebat." In *Gesta episcoporum Leodiensium*, MGH, SS 7:202, quoted from Münster-Swendsen, *Masters and Paragons*, 107. See also Reiner

wit and irony can feature prominently in the daily affairs of a learned cleric serving a bishop. For a cleric in a position like Meinhard's to speak to his bishop with audacious openness, sheltered thinly in classical references and high diction, wit, and humor can become instruments of correction and of fun.

LOVE AND FRIENDSHIP

Love is not so much one of the virtues commended by Meinhard writing to G as it is the very fabric of his language. While love and friendship are typical, even obligatory, for student–master relations in the cathedral schools in the tenth to the twelfth centuries, Meinhard's idiom is emphatic and forceful, even impetuous in the sense of the quality of expression that Augustine called *impetus*.[104] The letter to G (M1), first letter of the Paris collection, opens with force and flash:

> When I think of you, that singular quality of your inborn genius shakes my concentration like a bolt of lightning and I am swept with exhilaration through sweet fantasies by those pure delights of your nature. I can therefore only wish that you would in like manner focus your attention and attune your ears to full acuity [for what I have to say here].[105]

Erdmann noted the affectionate tone that characterizes Meinhard's letters to students and to dignitaries on particular occasions and characterizes that tone as "polite."[106] But the opening

---

of St. Laurent, *Eraclius of Liège*: "quos reliquerat scholarum magistros provocabat... mittendo scripta vel hilari prosa vel dulci metro composita." In MGH, SS 20:562. *Hilaritas* as an ideal atmosphere of converse among students, masters and lords, deserves a study.

104. Augustine, *De doctrina Christiana* 4.20.42, R.P.H. Green, ed. and trans. (Oxford: Oxford University Press, 1995), 250: A mode of expression that is "forceful with the emotions of the spirit" and "violent with the passions of the soul."

105. "Cum meam de te cogitantis aciem illud singulare indolis tue quasi fulmen perstringit et in illis genuinis nature tue deliciis mecum ipse per dulces fantasias exhilarescere cepi, utinam tu aures attentionis solicite suspensus accommodes!" In Erdmann ed., 192.

106. *Studien*, 96: "Ein weiteres Element der Verkehrsformen ist für den Stilcharakter von spezieller Bedeutung: die Höflichkeit."

CHAPTER 3 ✷ MEINHARD OF BAMBERG

of the letter to G is uniquely vehement. The reader weaves through a complex periodic sentence construction[107] conveying the startled response of the teacher to the memory of the student's excellence: the thought of G's qualities shakes his mind like a bolt of lightning. The violent image is more appropriate as a reaction to prophetic speech or to the experience of ecstasy[108] than to a student's impressive qualities. The sentence continues in the same tone of intoxicated enthusiasm: "...I am swept with exhilaration through sweet fantasies by those pure delights of your nature..." (... *et in illis genuinis nature tue deliciis mecum ipse per dulces fantasias exhilarescere cepi...*). Thoughts turning to "sweet fantasies" is tinged erotic, though the dominant of *fantasia* is negative, as in diabolically inspired thoughts or deceptive images.[109]

So much for the chain of dependent clauses; now follows the result clause. The exuberant tone gives way to the voice of the teacher: now pay attention as closely as I've focused on the thought of your excellence. Meinhard introduces the allegory of the two courts in a contest for the soul of G. The sensuality of the court of vice is evoked obtrusively; its vividness is apotropaic. It urges the rejection of physical love, of seduction by sexual desire in favor of the nobility of virtue. It would have been possible to find other metaphors for corruption, but Meinhard is insistent: slippery bodies and painted faces smiling invitingly are the prostitute's means of seduction. Given the threats just evoked by the parable of the two courts, what can one hope for in G? He is still a young man about whom the ultimate judgment on his person is not yet rendered. The writer stresses his own anxiety at G's parlous situation with some lines from Horace, an allusion that again is colored erotic:

107. Erdmann, *Studien*, 59: "Gerade in der Architektonik des Satzes ist er in den Geist der klassischen Sprache eingedrungen und schreibt ein 'echtes', kein 'übersetztes' Latein."

108. See Jaeger, "*Sermo propheticus*: The Grand Style in the Medieval Sermon from John the Evangelist to Aelred of Rievaulx," *Mittellateinisches Jahrbuch* 55 (2020): 1–39.

109. See Thietmar of Merseburg, *Chronik* 8.16; MGH, SSR n.s. 9, Holtzmann ed., 512; Honorius, *Gemma Animi*, PL 172:592D: *daemonum fantasia*; Guibert, PL 156:397B: *diaboli fantasia*; Hildegard, PL 197:1147C: diabolical; 1182D: erotic. Far and away the dominant implication is false, deceptive thoughts.

> *Do you not be like that Venus-favored Paris, of whom your Flaccus*
>   *[Horace] says in his sapphics:*
> *They say the judge of the contest placed the palm*
> *Beneath his bare foot.*[110]

We must read this allusion from its context in the poem by Horace from which it is taken, *Carmen* 3.20. The poem poses a contest between two claimants vying for possession of a beautiful boy, presumably as lover. The one contender is named Pyrrhus, the other an unnamed "African lioness" (*Gaetula leaena*).[111] Pyrrhus has stolen the boy from the woman, who claims him as her "pup" (*catulus*). While the two combatants prepare for the trial-by-combat, the coveted boy, in the role of judge, places his naked foot on the palm, the badge of victory, signaling that the outcome is undecided. The palm will go to the victor after the battle. Like the tense moment just preceding a decision in dire combat, so also in G's life, the two camps, the court of virtues and the court of vice, are preparing for battle to win over G. He is in the position of the beautiful boy, called by Horace "Nearchus." Meinhard changes the name to "Venus-favored Paris."

The Horace poem also associates the boy Nearchus with Ganymede, kidnapped by Jupiter, and Nireus, the beautiful Greek boy mentioned in *Iliad* 2.673 as "the most beautiful of the Greeks." Both Paris of the myth and the Bamberg student G face struggles between rivals for the ownership of the boy.[112] The comparison equates G with three legendary beautiful and desired boys, makes him into the object of a love rivalry. Why does Meinhard replace Horace's "Nearchus" with "Venus-favored Paris" (*Paridem illum Venerium*)? Surely to stress the erotic destiny of Trojan Paris winning and abducting Helen of Troy as a reward from Venus/Aphrodite. Nearchus is far less renowned.

110. Horace *Carmen* 3.20.11–13: "Arbiter pugne posuisse palmam / Sub pede nudo / Fertur." In *Horace: Odes and Epodes*, Niall Rudd, ed. & trans. (Cambridge, MA: Harvard University Press, 2004), 190–93.

111. *Gaetulia* is a region of North Africa. *Gaetuli*, a Berber tribe inhabiting the region.

112. The Horace poem forecasts the contest for the "lovely" Indian prince in *Midsummer Night's Dream*, nurtured by Titania, claimed by Oberon.

CHAPTER 3 ★ MEINHARD OF BAMBERG

How far these associations are meant to bear on G, to infantilize or eroticize this choice youth, is left to the reader to puzzle out. The allusion evokes "desireable boy courted with passion by competing lovers," and with that the limit of interpreting mythological allusions in this case is reached. But I would caution against underestimating the poetic sophistication of Meinhard and of his student G. What a modern reader can tease out as implications of such subtle allusions is put in place by Meinhard, who was not ignorant of the branchings and affiliations of the plot and characters of the Horatian poem. We should assume that he was aware what his appropriation of it meant. We can claim for certain that Meinhard did not exclude the homoerotic overtones of the Horatian poem,[113] even while warning G against replaying the role of Paris (*ne tu illum Paridem referas*), i.e., warning against a fatal choice for the erotic over wisdom and power. The imagery operates through its erotic energy, even while Meinhard is urging: choose Virtue. The forbidden erotic keeps close company with the licit, as so often in the discourse of clerical friendship relations. In M1 it is erudite playfulness, its erotic undertone in no way at odds with the moral dominant.

Meinhard's use of the poem by Horace also suggests a close and intimate relation between teacher and student on the level of the study of poetry. *Tuus Flaccus* implies familiarity and affection, as does also *Tusculanae tuae*. We must assume that G also was capable of understanding the net of associations the teacher was weaving in this subtle reference. Love between master and student became a norm of discourse in the traditions of the cathedral schools.[114] Meinhard spoke this language of warm emotional ties binding students to master. It is moderated compared to other expressions of love and friendship in the teacher-student relation,[115] except in M1 to G, where his enthusiasm is

---

113. As did one strain of the medieval school tradition on the teaching of this poem. See Tina Chronopoulos, "Ganymede in the Medieval Classroom: Reading an Ode by the Roman Poet Horace," *Medium Aevum* 86.2 (2017): 224–48.

114. See Jaeger, *Envy*, 103–6; Jaeger, *Ennobling Love: In Search of a Lost Sensibility* (Philadelphia: University of Pennsylvania Press, 1999), 59–81; Münster-Swendsen, *Masters and Paragons*, 258–68; Steckel, *Kulturen*, index "Freundschaft."

115. M30 is addressed also to G., as *unice dilecto*, probably the same recipient as M1. It is full of compliments and encouragement, though assurances of love are thin.

evident. However unique M1 may be in its cultured poetic prose, its imagery, and its concentration into a few paragraphs of central topics of cathedral-school instruction, at the same time the letter places its author firmly in contemporary cathedral-school culture.

Love and friendship, whatever they were for personal relations, were also a cultivated atmosphere of instruction and intellectual exchange. Meinhard gives us only a few glances into his classroom. The reference to lecturing and preaching in M1 is as close as he comes. But the affectionate and courteous atmosphere of casual literary discussion is evident in letter M22 to an unnamed friend. His purpose in writing is to bring the friend, presently in Carinthia with Bishop Gunther, back to Bamberg. Meinhard recalls that he owes a debt to the friend, "some kind of literary gift" (*aliquo literario munere*). No form of business is more welcome to Meinhard. Knowing in how many unique ways the friend loves him, in the form of a letter Meinhard sends a down payment or pledge (*arram*) of this gift that he owes:

> While pondering what form of discourse to use in writing, our colloquy springs to mind, the one we held, just the two of us, while strolling like the Peripatetics. I mean the one about vanity, what it is and in how many ways it is to be understood. But while I turn the matter over in my mind prior to developing it fully in writing, I am tossed by a positive tidal wave of ideas, from the shallows of the theme into the heights, and the brevity of a letter won't contain such a flood. I've decided that so great a topic is only to be dealt with in long and untroubled leisure. So, if you will return to me before the images of such great ideas vanish from my mind, I will explain for you the entire range of thoughts so that I can render for you the strongest judgment and the application of all these ideas.[116]

116. M22: "Dum mecum deliberarem, quonam scribendi argumento uterer, occurrit mihi collatio nostra, que proxime inter nos deambulando more Peripatetico habita est: dico de vanitate, quidnam esset et quot modis intelligenda. Verum dum rem animo prius quam stilo experiri et informare vellem, estu quodam rationum sic e vado propositi in altum eiectus sum, ut tantos fluctus epistolaris brevitas non sufferret. ...tante rei nisi multo in liberoque ocio indulgendum non censui. Quodsi te ipsum prius mihi reddideris, quam tantarum rerum notiones in animo evanescant, totam hanc copiam tibi exponam, ut tibi potissimum iudicium ususque horum omnium offeratur." In Erdmann ed., 216–17.

CHAPTER 3 ✷ MEINHARD OF BAMBERG

The colloquy held outside the classroom in a casual, convivial atmosphere, discoursing on philosophical, in this case moral, topics, has a long tradition from the Peripatetics to Erasmus and beyond. The atmosphere of a neo-classical form of intellectual exchange is clearly evoked, and it must have been an agreeable mode of actually dealing with matters brought up in reading and classroom lecture/discussion.[117] The "Cassiciacum Dialogues" of Augustine were available as a model for unconstrained philosophical-theological discussions. Meinhard would have called this atmosphere of ideas freely shared among like-minded friends, *humanitas*.

THE DECLINE OF THE IMPERIAL SCHOOLS

Meinhard of Bamberg is the best early representative of the humanism that developed in the imperial cathedral schools, and he is a figure around whom a history of medieval humanism can crystallize, as Erdmann predicted. But along with humanistic elements in his letters, there is an unmistakable pessimistic tone. Since the mid-eleventh century the imperial cathedral schools were losing their students. Facing the rigors of school discipline, they left to seek a more commodious social atmosphere and a different kind of intellectual discourse. There are repeated references in Meinhard to students fleeing discipline. He pleads with a colleague in Rheims to send back to Bamberg a student who has run off to Rheims because the "onslaught of severe school discipline is intolerable." Meinhard acknowledges with awe that Rheims is favored by "divine auspices" (which he leaves enticingly vague) but begs Archdeacon Odo to persuade him to disabuse him of his most insane resolution (*dementissimi propositi*) and have him return to Bamberg. No doubt "the horrible vengeance of scorned discipline will seize his mind to abhor sane council, as did that legendary Orestes driven by furies."[118] To his friend and fellow master in Liège (Franco?) enlisting his support in circumstances where evil ways are thrust on the entire kingdom, and like a bereaved father, he grieves that the desire for

---

117. A vivid and emotional description of the evening colloquies of Fulbert of Chartres in a letter of Adelman of Liège. See Jaeger, *Envy*, 219–20.

118. M3: "Haut negaverim tetricam illam et horribilem violate discipline vindictam animo illius obversari, usque eum velud Orestem illum poeticum furiis agitatum ab sano consilio abhorrere." In Erdmann ed., 195.

discipline has all but died out (*"discipline desiderium quae ubique sit extincta"*).[119] He complains that half-learned men, persuaded of the fullness of their knowledge, spread their ignorance far and wide. Detestable and miserable masters like these propagate like armies of frogs, bringing the total destruction and death of manners and discipline, replacing them with the immorality of loose living.[120]

The complaint was widespread: Anselm of Liège writing as early as c.1050–56, saw the imperial school of Liège endangered by students shunning "the yoke of discipline," giving themselves over to a life of levity (*levitas*) in the courts of kings and bishops. Anselm longs for a return to the golden age when schools demanded "nothing more than the study of letters along with the discipline of manners."[121] Goswin of Mainz, in a letter to his student Walcherus, complains of students who flee instruction in the "gravity of moral discipline."[122] Gone are the days recalled by the biographer of Benno II of Osnabrück, when crowds of students flocked to Speyer from all ends of the kingdom to devote themselves to the "imperial study," which then burned bright everywhere along with the passionate study of letters.[123] It is clear: the imperial cathedral schools are losing students, and the masters are alarmed. Bamberg held on longer than others, as did Liège. That decline registers clearly also in Meinhard's letter M19. Meinhard accepts a student sent to Bamberg by an unnamed master who had complained of the conditions at his community. Meinhard writes:

> Among those grave and lamentable misfortunes, you deplored as the worst of your calamities that the study and the light of letters had altogether died out, and even more, that the moral discipline so excellently ensconced at your school from early on

119. M24; Erdmann ed., 221.

120. M24, Erdmann ed. 220–21; M19, Erdmann ed., 213.

121. *Gesta episcoporum Leodiensium* 28, MGH 7:205.

122. Gozechin (Goswin) of Mainz, *Epistola ad Walcherum* 27–28, Huygens ed., 31–32; translated in Jaeger, *Envy*, 223, 365–66.

123. *Vita Bennonis II* 4: "Cumque eodem tempore de toto regno illuc undique clericorum turba concurreret, eo quod circumquaque flagrans imperiale studium, studium etiam litterarum inibi ardentissimum florere fecisset [imperator]...." In Harry Breslau, ed., MGH, SS 30.2:873. See Münster-Swendsen, *Masters and Paragons*, 85–92.

CHAPTER 3 ✶ MEINHARD OF BAMBERG

had now dissolved through neglect and was by now dead and buried.[124]

That explains, says Meinhard, why the master has sent this student to Bamberg for an education, so that those two hallmarks of your school, manners and letters, will with God's grace be resuscitated.

The decline of studies coincides with the weakening of the imperial church, of course. The careers students foresaw in studying at an imperial school were drying up. Along with the demands of the old curriculum, the close relationship between cathedral-school education, royal chapel, and promotion to a bishopric was dissolving. In disciplinary terms, then, the imperial cathedral schools grew with the rise of "letters and manners" and fell with their decline. The institutional basis of a humanistic education was being eroded.

The schools of France were one alternative. Some students sought the new schools forming outside of cities with wandering teachers like Roscelinus of Compiègne. Some were drawn by the school of Berengar of Tours or to other cathedral masters like William of Champeaux, who withdrew from Notre Dame in Paris to found the school of St. Victor on the left bank, forced, it seems, out of his position as *magister scolarum* at Notre Dame by his successor Peter Abelard, himself earlier a master of an itinerant school.

Students abandoning the old learning also could seek the courts of kings and nobles. The diaspora of humanistic studies and humanist masters fed into secular courts. Anselm of Liège deplored that route as encouraging lax morality; so did Meinhard. Yet it is the courts of lesser nobility where we must look to follow the survival of medieval humanism. The new independent schools, especially those in Paris, were the mainstream. The old humanist masters like William of Conches and Thierry of Chartres watched their classrooms shrink. But while the German cathedral schools declined into insignificance,

---

124. M19: "Inter alia gravia et luctuosa hunc dolorem quasi capitalem deplorastis studium lumenque litterarum penitus apud vos occidisse nec minus disciplinam moralem egregie apud vos antiquitus institutam situ quodam et negligentia nunc dissolutam iam iamque obisse, immo sepultum esse. Quas ob res adolescente vestrum officine nostre erudiendum informandumque tradidistis, ut duo pignora vestra, mores dico litterasque, per eum vobis Dei gratia aspirante resuscitentur." In Erdmann ed., 213.

the humanistic program they had founded lived on in cathedral communities of France and England, enriched by elements it had lacked in eleventh-century Germany: a speculative Platonism based on the study of the *Timaeus* and in some cases elaborating a vision of Christian and Platonic cosmology reconciled as well as a probing study of the quadrivium, or, to put it more generally, natural science and mathematics. Studies of the quadrivium left no trace at Bamberg in the previous century.[125] The development of the humanistic trends that began in the tenth century flowed into the humanism of the twelfth. It is important to distinguish the humanist strain in twelfth-century culture from the scholastic. The learned culture too often is homogenized into a twelfth-century renaissance. The humanist strain died out as a school discipline in the course of the twelfth century; the scholastic flourished.

---

125. See Märtl, *Bamberger Schulen*, 341.

CHAPTER 3 ★ MEINHARD OF BAMBERG

APPENDIX

Meinhard of Bamberg, Letters. From Weitere Briefe Meinhards Epist. 1 (= M1), Erdmann ed. 192–94.

Unice diligendo G., M. Latin Text

Cum meam de te cogitantis aciem illud singulare indolis tue quasi fulmen perstringit et in illis genuinis nature tue deliciis mecum ipse per dulces fantasias exhilarescere cepi, utinam tu aures attentionis sollicite suspensus accommodes! Deprehendas vero, quanti pro te et contra te pugnantium affectuum misceantur tumultus. Ibi enim hinc generosa virtutum familia te quasi deliciosum suum per morum specimen, per ingenii acumen in curie sue principatum vocat et quasi domesticum vendicat, hinc te etas lubrica, bombicina Colonidum corpora, immo ipsa hospes tue multiformis Colonia seu mavis Babilonia delibuto vodluptatibus vultu blandius te quam salubrius sollicitat. Et vereor quo se Iunonia vertant hospicia. Quidem tu, obsecro, in teatri huius spectaculo quidnam votis et suspiriis nostris polliceris? Ne tu, queso, ne Paridem illum Venerium referas, de quo Flaccus tuus in saphicis suis:

Arbiter pugne posuisse palmam
Sub pede nudo
Fertur.

Sepenumero advertisti me de nobilitate in utramvis partem vel glorie vel ignominie disuptantem, quam grave scilicet onus insignis maiorum industria humeris posterorum imponat, quibus vite honestas morumque observantia non tam gloriosa quam necessaria, qui etsi vigilantissime egerint, non tam laudem merentur quam vitant reprehensionem, utpote quibus in maxima fortuna minima sit licentia. Nam si a via, quam eis gloria parentum editissimo virtutis loco stravit, inde inquam si tantillum quid exorbitaverint, o mi G., in quantum precipicium fame, nominis, honorum ruituri sunt! Hec inquam vel et multa id genus et his similia, que ut nosti in campis disputationis laxis frenis effunduntur, cum epistolares angustie ista non recipiant, me audistis predicantem. Quamobrem etiam atque etiam unicis modis te monitum atque obtestatum velim, ut pro existimatione tua nichil satis exacti arbitreris. Fac queso, ut tui ipse memineris, neu sis quod aiunt *caput sine cerebro*.

Ad quam vigilantiam cum alia tum precipue te augustissima patris opinio debet excitare, que te haut sane sciam utrum magis suo illius splendore illustret an tuo ipsius periculo gravet. Est enim vir ille omni genere virtutis instructus, omni lepore humanitatis mirifice conditus, que in eo non solum flagrantia morum latissime redolet, sed ex ipsa oculorum hilaritate gratiosissime renidet. Atque sic in te animi ornamenta redundent, ut illa ocularis gratia relucet.

Ut vero etiam illa induas, plurimo quidem te meo iudicio tum accuratissima bonorum imitatio tum etiam fructuose lectionis frequens illud et dulcissimum contubernium iuvabit. Unde hortor, ut Tusculanis tuis plurimus insideas, quibus Latina philosophia Cicerone parente nichil illustrius edidit. Per hoc enim studiorum quasi vestibulum ad illud Augustini sacrarium commodissime tibi viam affectabis.

Vix possum ab amplexu tuo avelli, ut aliquando illud raucidum 'vale' subscribam. Unum tamen hoc tibi instillaverim: sic te age, ut quo hoc convictu Coloniam Christo mediante tibi despondeas.

Vale in Christo.

Letter 1: To G., uniquely worthy of love, M.
English Translation
Since, when I think of you, that singular quality of your inborn genius shakes my concentration like a bolt of lightning and I am swept with exhilaration through sweet fantasies by those pure delights of your nature, I can only wish that you would in like manner focus your attention and attune your ears to full acuity [for what I have to say here].

But you are well aware what a tumult of opposed affections, both for you and against you, war with one another. For, here on the one hand, the noble family of virtues calls you as their sweet minion for the beauty of your manners and character, for the sharpness of your mind to reign over their court and claims you as their courtier. Meanwhile, on the other hand, your hostess herself, shape-shifting Cologne, the silken bodies of the Colognese, or rather the Babylonese, that slippery brood, will sollicit you with a face painted with seductions, a smile to flatter, not to hearten you. I fear that

CHAPTER 3 ✴ MEINHARD OF BAMBERG

such hospitality could turn Juno-like.[126] But what about you, pray tell: what can you promise for our vows and sighs in the spectacle of this theater? Do not be like that Venus-favored Paris, of whom your Flaccus [Horace] says in his sapphics:
They say
The judge of the contest placed the palm
Beneath his bare foot.[127]

You have often heard me dispute about nobility turning into one of two paths, toward glory or toward ignominy. I stressed what a heavy burden the distinguished service of our ancestors places on the shoulders of descendants, to whom a morally upright life and careful custody of manners is not so much a virtue as a necessity, and who, even if all their acts were performed with the utmost perspicacity, seek not so much to merit praise as to avoid blame, as with those raised highest by Fortune are held least in licentiousness.[128] For if they stray so much as an inch away from the path leading to the exalted place of virtue, which the glory of their parents paved for them, what a headlong plunge, my G., their fame, reputation and honor will suffer! This and many things like this you have heard me lecture on and preach. As you know, such subjects are poured out in the fields of disputation where the reins are loosened, though the narrows of letter-writing cannot contain them. For that reason, I should wish to admonish and beseech you over and over again in no uncertain terms, that in your judgment you regard no issue as sufficiently weighed in the balance. See to it, I beg you, that you remind yourself lest you become what they call "a head without a brain."

The august fame of your father is one of many factors that should rouse you to vigilance, which in relation to you truly I hardly know whether his splendor raises you up more than it weighs you down. For he is a man instructed in every kind of virtue, a man who enjoys to an astonishing degree all the charm and grace of humanity, qualities

126. That is, treacherous, as in *Aeneid* 1.671.

127. Horace, *Odes* 3.20.11–13. The poem treats a contest between a young man and a girl for the affections of a beautiful youth. The umpire/judge (who is the beautiful youth himself) places his foot on the palm of victory, since the outcome is not yet decided. Why Venus-born Paris? Horace's poem addresses a Pyrrhus.

128. Sallust, *Bellum Catilinae* 51.13. See Erdmann, *Studies*, 62 n. 3.

visible far and wide not only in his dazzling blaze of manners, but also in the bright good humor that shone most graciously from his eyes.

So that you may take on these qualities, the first aid in my judgment is the most scrupulous imitation of good people. Then also the frequent and delightful pastime of meaningful reading. For that reason, I urge you to occupy yourself above all with your *Tusculans*[129] than which Latin philosophy, with Cicero as its parent, has produced nothing more illustrious. For this is the vestibule of studies in which you may most readily find the path to the sacred shrine of Augustine.

Only with great difficulty can I tear myself away from your embrace to finally append that painful word "farewell." But one thing more I must instill in you: behave in such a way that in this communal life you wed yourself to Cologne with Christ officiating.

Farewell in Christ

H78a. Meinhard and Dean Poppo[130] to Bishop Gunther.
Latin Text. Erdmann ed., 126–27.

Nestorem illum, quod tres gradus vegetus et incolomis duraverit, fabulosa miratur antiquitas. Presens hec etas longe meliori iure [vos] obstupescere queat, vos inquam, qui, cum tot secula numeretis quot ecclesia vestra presules, cum tot annorum prudentia virilem adhuc, immo iuvenilem efficacissime presentatis vigorem. Enimvero si quid veri mathematica mentiretur illusio haud temere affirmaverim Saturnum Mercuriumque in vestra se, ut illorum verbis utar, salutasse genitura.

Verumtamen haud absurde vos admonuerim tandem aliquando nidum respicere et fatiscenti consulere corpori. Par quippe est, ut, quemadmodum experientissimi veterani factitarunt, ita vos iam tyronibus aliis munia illa castrensia prescribatis vosque ipsum tam laboriosis eruatis exercitiis. Schola quippe morum, id est, claustrum, vestram sibi amodo poscit operam, vestram requirit auctoritatem. Qua de re monitum vos, etiam atque etiam oratum velim, ut post hoc festum continuo redeatis et vobiscum mihi carissimum, vestri

---

129. Cicero's *Tusculan Disputations*.

130. Like other Bamberg letters, this was most likely co-written by Meinhard and Poppo, though Erdmann takes Poppo to be the author.

CHAPTER 3 ✷ MEINHARD OF BAMBERG

amantissimus, reducatis Hart[wig?]; quam rem etiam omnibus gratam futuram non dubitabit.

Vos me per Arn[old?] de somnolentia accusastis, utque illius aliquanto parcior essem, submonuistis. Pape o bonum correctorem, o virum vigilantissimum! Ecce tibi mutatum Polemonem! Atque utinam tantum vos superflue illi stertitioni demeretis, quantum ego necessarie quieti furari soleo. Profecto aut ego vanus augur sum aut vos, ubi hoc otio et somno intumueritis, mechanicis apparatibus e Carinthia evolvendus eritis. Set hec hactenus.

Frater ille, ubi reversus est, inobedientiam, quam patraverat, disciplina corporali correxit et in infimum locum, quoad nobis visum est, reiectus, est tam in choro quam in refectorio. Reversus vero prepositus diem cause ipsius constituit. Quam cum ipse sub obtentu prepositure subterfugisset [et] diu expectatus non rediisset, communi consilio deliberatum est, ut littere certo die ad eum revocandum mitterentur. Quod se prepositus facturum promisit, eoque modo res adhuc pendet infecta.

Heylice causam, ut precepistis, exsecutus sum. Que cum unum tantum ex viris prenominatis confessa fuisset, publice ipsamet ferrum candens gessit et sine controversia cecidit. Sic tamen pertinacissime adhuc in negando perstitit altioremque a me identidem flagitavit examinationem. Verum ego rem integram vestro reservavi arbitrio.

Letter 2. H78a. Meinhard and Dean Poppo[131] to Bishop Gunther.
English Translation
Antiquity in its fables marveled at Nestor for living three lifetimes vigorous and unharmed. This present age can with greater justice marvel at you — at you, I say, who number as many ages as your church has had bishops [five], who in so many years of prudence still with utmost efficacy present so virile, nay rather so youthful a vigor. For if there is anything of truth in that astrological belief, I would by no means rashly affirm that Saturn and Mercury, to use the words of that age, saluted each other at your birth. However, I urge you, by no means absurdly, to look to your own nest and pay attention to its increasingly frail body.

---

131. Like other Bamberg letters, this was most likely co-written by Meinhard and Poppo, though Erdmann takes Poppo to be the author.

Just as the most seasoned veterans do, you also should develop yourself in exhausting exercises such as [those where] you prescribe the practices of the camp to young recruits. In fact, this school of manners, that is the cloister, now calls out for your efforts and requires your authority. In this regard, I wish to admonish you again and again that you return after this festival and bring back with you my dearest, your most loving Hart[wig?]. His return holds promise of a pleasant future for all.

You accuse me through Arn[old?] of laziness, along with the insinuation that I would do well to slim down somewhat. Come now, good corrector, man of utmost vigilance! Just look at yourself, transformed like Polemon.[132] Oh, and if only you could turn down the volume of your reverberant snoring, because I find it necessary to escape into peace and quiet. Furthermore, unless I am a bad prophet, swelling up as you are in laziness and sleep, you will have to be lifted and rolled out of Carinthia by hoists and pulleys. But enough for now.

After his return, that brother has corrected the disobedience that he perpetrated by corporal discipline and has been thrown back into the bottommost place, as it seemed right to us, both in the chorus and the refectory. When the provost returned, he confirmed the day assigned to this case. Since he fled appealing to the provostship and did not return long after he was expected, it was determined by the general council that on a certain day letters should be sent to him recalling him. The provost then promised he would do it, and in this way the affair remains without closure.

I have carried out the case of Heylica as you ordered. Since she confessed only one of the summoned men, she carried the glowing iron in public and succumbed without controversy. However she still persisted tenaciously in her denial and incessantly demanded from me a more thorough investigation. But I have reserved the entire affair for your judgment.

---

132. See above, n. 90.

4. THE MUSIC OF HUMANITY (MUSICA HUMANA)

INTRODUCTION

"Lost Songs of the Early Middle Ages": the title of this symposium[1] struck me immediately as it must strike anyone concerned with a long period of human culture much of which is lost — not only for asserting things lost as an object of scholarly study but also as a reminder of the advantage of writing. Ancient and medieval music passed away in performance, and so the sense of loss must be greater in your field than in mine, in which, though much is lost, much remains. The joy of recovery is proportionally great. The accomplishments of Sam Barrett, of this group, and others engaged in the project, are impressive not only for unearthing much that was buried but also for making it performable.

What is most arresting for me in your work is the stress on the period from the ninth to the eleventh century. The culture of that period is virtually unknown and little explored. It was what we can call a "charismatic culture." That means heroic in all its aspects, not only warfare and athletics but intellectual life, education, poetry and literature, love and friendship. Others call it a "performative culture,"[2] an expressive term, though narrower. "Charismatic" means a culture of "real presence." The cultural artifact is a person embodying values and expressing aesthetic forms, not a work of art, written or painted. The human presence as a work of art, as an exemplar, to put it more dramatically without leaving the solid ground of what is empirically observable. That means that the human presence is something like a musical performance. Once the diplomat, lawyer, bishop, poet, or musician (or both the latter combined) has performed, the performance vanishes, like any theatrical performance.

---

1. The talk was entitled "The Music of Humanity (*Musica Humana*) and Its Place in Early Medieval Education," delivered at the symposium: "Performing Lost Songs of the Middle Ages: Medieval Latin Song from c.800 to c.1200," Pembroke College, Cambridge University, July 2, 2016.

2. Erika-Fischer Lichte, "Culture as Performance," *Modern Austrian Literature* 42 (2009): 1–10.

And here's the methodological bind: we write history from documents. The documentation of the cultures of literature, music, and education for the period from the ninth to the eleventh century is sparse. It consists largely of poems and letters. The poems preserved represent a minuscule percent of the actual productivity of poets in the period. Therefore reconstructing its literary and pedagogic culture is a job rather like reconstructing its music. Cultural acts were performed, only in very exceptional cases written down.

They have been secured from recovery especially by two factors: First, Carolingian written sources are rich; and written sources from the twelfth century are rich. Those two tended to fill the vacuum left by the dearth of writing from the intervening centuries. Second, Latin poetry was generally written in a purposely obscure, almost riddling style that counted for the period as word wizardry and that gave a special esotericism to its performance. Getting to the heart of the poetry is a job very much like squeezing music out of neumes, though probably not quite that hard.

Rediscovering the system of education that was at work in early medieval Europe is also a job of reconstruction. The two areas, music and learning, can profit from mutual study, and so I am pleased to be invited to speak at this colloquium. I know next to nothing on the subject of medieval music; what I do know is that the study of education has much light to shed on it. I want to start with a musical performance represented in a medieval romance, Gottfried von Strassburg's *Tristan* from the first decade of the thirteenth century. Here music is linked to education. The scene as a whole is a small but lucid entry point into the place of music, human and instrumental, in the education of the earlier Middle Ages.

ISOLDE'S SILENT MUSIC

The education of the young princess Isolde of Ireland is placed in the hands of a minstrel named Tantris, who has impressed the queen by his musical skill. (He is in fact Tristan in disguise, come to get a cure for a poisoned wound from Queen Isolde, a talented druggist — and sister-in-law to the man who died inflicting that wound.) Her daughter, the princess, is already an accomplished lute and harp player and singer, and her study with Tantris goes well beyond music to other school disciplines and languages. Along with musical

CHAPTER 4 ✶ THE MUSIC OF HUMANITY

performance, the main subject he taught her was *moraliteit*, "the art that teaches beautiful manners" (*schoene site*). The "sweet discipline" of morality endears its devotee to God and the world. It is the source of honor and success. *Moraliteit* was Isolde's major subject. It made her "well mannered, of a beautiful and pure temperament"; her gestures were "sweet and good." The whole land spoke of her accomplishments. Her father the king would call her to court to entertain him with her "courtly skills and beautiful manners." She brought joy to the whole court: she fiddled dance tunes, lays, and foreign tunes in the style of Sens and Saint Denis. She composed letters, songs, and poetry. Gottfried lists a host of genres and styles, a list that has provided a feast of musical terminology for students of this romance. She was "a rapturous feast for eyes and ears"; she captured minds and hearts with her sweet singing; "hearts grew full of longing." Gottfried compares this enchanting effect of her music to that of the sirens:

> This charming princess, discreet and courteous Isolde, drew thoughts from the hearts that enshrined them as the lodestone draws in ships to the sound of the Sirens' song.

This virtuoso description of a performance is summed up in one of the great virtuoso passages of the poem:

> She sang openly and secretly, in through ears and eyes to where many a heart was stirred. The song which she sang openly...was her own sweet singing and soft sounding of strings that echoed for all to hear through the kingdom of the ears deep down into the heart. But her secret song was her wondrous beauty that stole with its rapturous music hidden and unseen through the windows of the eyes into many noble hearts and smoothed on the magic which took thoughts prisoner suddenly, and, taking them, fettered them with desire![3]

3. *Tristan with the Surviving Fragments of the Tristan of Thomas*, A.T. Hatto, trans. (London: Penguin, 1967), 148. For the German, see Gottfried von Strassburg, *Tristan und Isolde: Kritische Edition. Textband*, Tomas Tomasek, ed. (Berlin: Schwabe, 2023), 151–52, ll. 8112–31: "Si sanc in maneges herzen muot / offenlîchen unde tougen / durch oren und durch ougen: / ir sanc, den si offenlîche tet / beidiu anderswâ und an der stete, / daz was ir süeze singen, / ir senftez seiten clingen, / daz lûte und offenlîche / durch der ôren künicrîche / hin nider in diu herzen clanc. / so was der tougenlîche sanc / ir wunderlîchiu schoene, / diu mit ir muotgedoene / verholn unde tougen /

183

So as part of her learning she becomes master of instrumental and vocal music. But then there is her second, silent song. It is her beauty, her grace and charm learned in the discipline of *moraliteit*. It is the magical, unheard melody that enters the hearers' mind through the eyes. Her "wondrous beauty stole with its rapturous melody...." Hatto translates the Middle High German *muotgedoene* as "rapturous melody," an inspired rendering of what the term implies. But *muot* means primarily mind and spirit. So "mind-song" or "spiritual song" would be a more literal rendering for the music that is seen, not heard. While I can't connect Gottfried with Keats otherwise, I think it's worth quoting:

> Heard melodies are sweet, but those unheard
>
> Are sweeter. Therefore ye soft pipes, play on;
>
> Not to the sensual ear, but more endear'd,
>
> Pipe to the spirit ditties of no tone.

Isolde's body, her presence by itself, sings a song that surpasses mere audible music. Half a century ago, W.T.H. Jackson connected Gottfried's *moraliteit* with what Boethius called the "morality of music." In his treatise on music, Boethius explains music's power to ennoble or corrupt human conduct. Music is "conjoined to *moralitas*," a means of moral discipline. Boethius cites Plato on music's educating force: good music is an important means of maintaining the republic, since the introduction of "lascivious" modes brings about the corruption of morals. "Music of the highest moral character and modestly composed" is a safeguard of the state's welfare as long as it is "temperate, simple, and masculine, rather than effeminate, violent, or fickle." He tells the well-known anecdotes of music inculcating moderation and virtue and calming anger. Music's effect on human behavior is rooted in the relation of body to soul; they are joined by musical harmonies. Heard music reminds the listener of humanity's inner composition. Our delight in hearing musical harmonies is self-recognition, the congruence of soul music with instrumental. Boethius classified music into three groups, *musica mundana, musica humana,* and *musica instrumentalis*. The music of the world, cosmic

---

durch diu venster der ougen in vil manic edel herze sleich / und daz zouber dar in streich, / daz die gedanke zehant / vienc und vahende bant / mit sene und mit seneder nôt."

music, is related to human as macro- is related to microcosm. The harmonies joining our body and soul are the same that hold the stars in their region and the planets in their courses. The pleasure in music is also discovery of world order.

It follows that an unheard music plays in each human being. The silent music of Isolde's presence becomes perceptible in her well-tempered mind and its relatedness to her elegant bearing, her gestures, her beauty. The "tuning" of mind to body is part and parcel of Platonic/Boethian ideas on music and ethics. Cicero quotes the Greek philosopher Aristoxenus:

> Aristoxenus held the soul to be a special tuning of the body, like what in instrumental or vocal music is called harmony. In the same way, the various motions of the body through its nature and its form are said to sing like the sounds produced in vocal music.[4]

BOETHIUS

The rich ideas of cosmic and human harmonies passed to the Middle Ages largely through the agency of Boethius. His *De institutione musica* is cited in writings from monastic and cathedral schools. In Carolingian texts on human music, the Boethian view is in effect: music has a powerful effect on the mood, but generally it is an effect of the moment aimed at correcting an imbalance, as in the widely known tale of the rescue through music of an endangered maiden. A youth, enraged by envy, anger, and music in the Phrygian (military) mode sets out to burn down the maiden's house, but Pythagoras catches wind of the affair, orders music in a calming mode. A spondee is performed, and it dissolves the young man's anger.[5] Charlemagne wrote a letter to Alcuin in the middle of a terrible and bloody campaign against the Saxons, asking his friend and advisor to compose "a sweet melody of versifying." It will help "amid the horrible

4. *Tusculan Disputations* 1.19: "Aristoxenus, musicus idemque philosophus, ipsius corporis intentionem quamdam, velut in cantu et fidibus quae harmonia dicitur: sic ex corporis totius natura et figura varios motus cieri tamquam in cantu...." King ed., 24.

5. For the sources and variants of the tale, see *Anicius Manlius Severinus Boethius: Fundamentals of Music*, Claude V. Prisca, ed.; Calvin M. Bower, trans. (New Haven, CT: Yale University Press, 1989), 5–6.

din of clashing weapons and the raucous blare of trumpets, since a sweet and gentle musical refrain can mollify the savage impulses of the mind." It is a conception of Orphic music taming savage breasts, an idea with a grand future in eleventh-century clerical circles.

MUSIC AND EDUCATION: TUNING THE BODY

Music became a metaphor for moral training, and the language of music was shared with the language of ethics. It's really the eleventh century where we find a profound penetration of musical language into the description of character and personal presence. Fulbert of Chartres (early eleventh century) uses this language to describe the virtues of the Virgin Mary:

> And so these virtues in her thought and the emotions of her heart brought forth an ineffable harmony; even the wisdom of God, which created her and lived in her, delighted to hear it. They flared forth in the visible form of her speech and action, whence people could glorify God and hold to examples of salvation.[6]

They are so abundant that they produce a harmony that sings from her speech and action, pleasing to God and a model for people.

Fulbert's younger contemporary, Bern of Reichenau (abbot of the monastery of Reichenau, d. 1048, reformer of Gregorian chant), wrote an introduction to his treatise on music, *Tonarius*, in the form of a letter to Archbishop Pilgrim of Cologne (c.1021–36), who had requested the work. He introduced it with this soaring, sounding description of the archbishop:

> The beautiful form of the Christian faith, wonderfully glowing in you, proves that you are the seat of wisdom, since the goodness of moral discipline composes the motions of your mind.... [I understand that you], whom not only the study of the four disciplines of the quadrivium has perfected, but also by divine praises the melody of celestial harmony has rendered unchangingly tuned, you, I say, would order

---

6. Fulbert of Chartres, *Sermon on the Birth of the Virgin Mary*: "Depromebant itaque virtutes in cogitatione et affectu cordis ejus ineffabilem harmoniam, quam ipsa creatrix et inhabitatrix ejus Dei sapientia delectabatur audire; coruscabant foris in superficie sermonis et actus, unde merito possent homines glorificare Deum, et exempla salutis accipere." In PL 141:322D–323A.

CHAPTER 4 ✶ THE MUSIC OF HUMANITY

me, who am half-voiced so to speak, or rather almost mute and tongueless in the arts, to put forward a work on the theory of sung music [?].... I have no doubt that you wanted to request that of me so ardently so that your mind might delight in the sonorous sweetness of this art, since the entire structure of our soul is conjoined by a musical coaptation at the instigation of Nature.[7]

The *honestas* of moral discipline has composed the "natural motions" of Archbishop Pilgrim's soul so that he is progressing rationally to supernal things, as his interest in music shows. The four disciplines of the quadrivium have rendered him "foursquare," i.e., perfect. In addition, the melody of celestial harmony has "tuned" him so fully that he never goes out of tune, in contrast to Bern himself, who is by nature off-key, nearly mute and tongueless in the art. Clearly Bern regarded the music of Pilgrim's body and soul as determined by the music of the spheres: "celestial harmony" is the model for his inner composition to which Pilgrim's interest in music is clearly tied. "Your soul delights more sweetly in the sweetness of this art, since the entire conjoining of our body and soul is effected by a musical coaptation at the instigation of Nature." So, the Platonic idea of the soul as a "tuning" of the body asserts itself here. It reiterates the explanation of our human reaction to music (the soul delights). The explanation lies in the musical construction of the soul. It recognizes itself in "sweet music" because of their shared structure. It is a description formulated with a confident command of the vocabulary of ancient ideas of cosmic and human music, but superimposed on it is the framework of moral education. The *"honestas* of moral discipline" is the composer of the musical composition that is Pilgrim of Cologne.

7. Epist. 17: "Praedara Christianae fidei forma in te splendens egregie probat animam tuam sedem esse sapientiae, cum moralis disciplinae honestas...naturales animi tui motus componat.... [I understand that you] quem non solum quatuor matheseos disciplinarum speculatio quadratum, verum etiam caelestis armoniae melos divinis laudibus iugiter reddit intentum, me, ut ita dicam semivocalem, immo paene in artibus mutum ac elinguem decanora musicae modulatione iuberes aliquid proferre.... Non ambigo te tam ardenter id a me expetere voluisse, ut, quoniam tota animae nostrae corporisque compago musica coaptatione coniungitur, animus quoque tuus sonora artis huius dulcedine suavius delectetur...." In *Die Briefe des Abtes Bern von Reichenau*, Franz-Josef Schmale, ed. (Stuttgart: Kohlhammer, 1961), 30–31.

This idea of the physical presence of a person as music is widely present in the eleventh century. Baudri of Bourgueil (d.1130) was abbot of Bourgueil, bishop of Dol-en-Bretagne. One of his richest and most quoted poems is his lengthy, virtuoso description of the bedchamber of Countess Adela of Blois. On the headboard of her bed is a representation of the arts. *Philosophia* sits at the top of this image. She has commanded Music always to sit at her feet, because "music is the force that holds the other sisters in harmony with each other."

> This student [of philosophy] was named Music. Through her art everything gains in vitality. Philosophy had placed her second only to herself and commanded her always to sit at her feet. In fact, she it was who created unity among the other sisters, and it was her doing that like-mindedness nourished the others.[8]

The ethical aspects of music loom large along with the cosmic. As in Platonic/Boethian tradition, the two are closely linked. But Baudri is more sophisticated than others who make minor variations on Boethius:

> So, watching carefully over the harmonizing phrases, she [Music] charmed humans with such sweetness that she was able to restore the human soul itself. For the status of human life, its vigor and rhythm, is governed by a certain harmony — what it is I don't know — such that it seems to arise from the form of a square, which is greater and more solid than other forms. That is why air is in acord with water, earth with fire, and no single element is dissonant with any other. In addition, a vivifying force harmonizes these four, capable of giving life equally to each one individually. Nor does it seem that this fifth force is random, but rather it is the one that solidifies the tetragon as if by some bond. It is this construct of archetypal harmony and this celestial rhythm that governs our bodies.[9]

8. Baudri of Bourgueil, "Adela's Bedchamber," *Carmen* 134, ll. 999–1004: "Discipulae vero fuit huius Musica nomen, / Officio cuius cuncta magis vigeant. / Fecerat hanc ideo sibi Philosophia secundam, / Iusserat et pedibus semper adesse suis; / Quippe per hanc aliae sibi consensere sorores / Atque per hanc ipsas consona mens aluit." In *Baldricus Burgulianus: Poèmes/Carmina*, Jean-Yves Tilliette, ed. (Paris: Les Belles Lettres, 2002), 2:32.

9. *Carmen* 134, ll. 978–92: "Sic ad concinnos invigilans modulos, / haec demulcebat homines dulcedine tanta / Ut recreare hominis ipsam animam valeat. / Nam status

CHAPTER 4 ✶ THE MUSIC OF HUMANITY

Music has the power to "charm humans with such sweetness that it can recreate and restore the human soul itself." The melody and rhythm of life is governed by a certain harmony, following the form of a square, four being the number of perfection. It harmonizes the four elements among themselves, so that there is no discord among air and earth, fire and water — and that's saying a lot. From this unifying force, music gains its vivifying power and gives vigor to all things. The tetragon contains some strange bonding force (the "fifth force"), which is "the archetypal structure of harmony." Harmony, it implies, has a geometric form that is its Platonic archetype, or an intermediary between the phenomenon and its transcendent source.

Baudri dedicates another poem to the organ of Worcester Cathedral:

When the organs ring out equally in harmonized voice, they are the harmonious modulation of our life, which, compounded of many modes [melodies?] is fused into one. In the same way that you can perceive a variety of voices as a single one, in the same way there is one mode [*modus:* key?] in which we live. Just as by great labor pipes are constructed from brass, in this way may God fuse our manners, characters, and our bodies so that *the mystical symphony of our life* will be pleasing. Fashioned in this way by a divine breathing in its interior, so also from many various characters, a unified single character is formed and seems connected by some secret connection, so that it may sing out the sweet voice from a harmonious breast.[10]

---

humanae vigor et modulatio vite / Quodam concentu, nescio quo, regitur, / Ut de quadrata videatur surgere forma / Quae formis reliquis amplius est solida; / Nanque aer undis, terrae concordat et igni / Et neutrum in quadro dissonat a neutro. / Quattuor his et sic concordat vivificans vis, / Mensura ut parili singula vivificet; / Nec veluti quinta vis adiectiva videtur, / Sed nexu quodam tetragonum solidat. / Hic armoniae typicalis compotus atque / Caelestis rithmus corpora nostra regit." In Tilliette ed., 2:32.

10. *Carmen* 218, ll. 1–13: "Organa, que pariter concordi voce resultant, Sunt quedam nostre concors modulatio vite, / Que variis conflata modis excitur in unum / Et grato regi concentu concinit uni. / Et sicut varias voces intelligis unam, / Sic modus est unus, quo vivimus atque coimus. / Utque labor magnus calamos ex ere coaptat, / Sic Deus et mores et corpora nostra coaptet, / Ut placeat nostrae symphonia mistica vitae, / Quae compacta simul intus spiramine divo / Moribus ex multis morem concurrit in unum / Et nexu quodam secreto nexa videtur, / Ut pangat dulcem concordi pectore vocem." In Tilliette ed., 2:147.

It's a hard text, but the upshot is clear, Harmony of life, behavior, manners, and character are a gift of God in the medium of music. It fills our inner life like the wind that fills the pipes of the organ and emerges as harmonic sound. The mysterious phrase, "the mystical symphony of our life" makes the life lived harmoniously into a large-scale musical composition. But also, the unique formulation suggests a romanticizing of the unheard music of composed behavior. The poet stretched to give allure to the concept.

Bernard of Chartres (d.c.1130) was one of the last great representatives of the humanism of the eleventh and twelfth centuries. John of Salisbury has left a vivid description of this widely admired and influential teacher whose literary teaching was passing out of the schools. In his recently discovered, or rather, recently identified glosses on Plato's *Timaeus*, we see the Boethian model of human music deepened to make of music not only a teacher of manners, behavior, and character, but also a requisite to governing the state (a role assigned to music also by Plato in *The Republic*). It's worth quoting here because Bernard places it so fully in the context of moral discipline:

> Upon hearing the harmonies of music, we ought to be reformed in our conduct [*mores*] according to the harmony of virtues... Music overall is given to humans not for their pleasure but for the composition of their character.[11]

And on music in the education of rulers:

> The country's wardens are to be educated in such a way that they will be eager for labor and hardships and affable to their obedient subjects. Because sport and exercise make them eager...while gentleness comes through music which, through the harmony of its tones, teaches harmony of conduct.[12]

---

11. Bernard of Chartres, *Glosae super Platonem* 7.437–43: "Auditis enim consonantiis musicis, debemus in moribus nostris virtutum consonantia reformari. Licet enim anima secundum consonantias sit compacta, tamen ipsae consonantiae ex corporum coniunctione dissonae fiunt et reformandae sunt per exteriorem musicam. Et hoc est: tota musica data est hominibus non ad delectationem, sed ad morum compositionem." In Paul E. Dutton, ed. (Toronto: Pontifical Institute of Mediaeval Studies, 1991), 216–17.

12. *Glosae super Platonem* 3.64–68: "Ita nutriendi sunt tutores patriae, ut prompti ad laborem et affabiles sint obedientibus. Quod prompti sint per exercitium...quod

Eagerness comes through sport and exercise; gentleness through music. This is no longer the response of the figures in Pythagorean and Boethian anecdotes, who are changed for the moment by a particular strain of music. Rather, Bernard is talking about music as a pedagogic instrument to form character — harmony teaches harmonious conduct. The effects of this teaching are lasting.

The musical education and performance of Isolde would not surprise Bernard of Chartres in any way. He would have recognized music as an educating force at work at a very high level. He, along with numerous other students of the Platonic tradition, would have appreciated the idea of the human presence as silent music, musical harmonies made visible and transformed into an embodied mystical symphony.

PLANETARY MOTION — HUMAN MOTION

Clearly the disciplining of the body was an important part of the fashioning of *mores*. Another important factor in understanding "human music" is motion. The connection between motion and music is ancient. Recall Cicero quoting Aristoxenus: "The various motions of the body through its nature and its form are said to sing like the sounds produced in vocal music."[13] The fact of the motion of the planets persuaded ancient philosophers that unheard music must be playing in the cosmos, blocked from human ears by their muddy vesture of decay. Macrobius can be the spokesman of this widely shared idea. He wrote in his *Commentary on the Dream of Scipio*:

> [Given the rationally ordered functioning of the cosmos]..., it is unquestionably right to assume that harmonious sounds come forth from the rotation of the heavenly spheres, for sound has to come from motion, and Reason, which is present in the divine, is responsible for the sounds being melodious.[14]

---

mites et affabiles, per delinimenta praeparatur musicae, quae per sonorum convenientiam morum docet concordiam." In Dutton ed., 147.

13. See above, 185 n. 4.

14. Macrobius, *Commentary on the Dream of Scipio* 2.1.7, William Harris Stahl, trans. (New York: Columbia University Press, 1900), 186. Macrobius, *Commentaire*, Armisen-Marchetti, ed., 2.1.7: "Ex his inexpugnabili ratiocinatione collectum est

So Reason is the composer of the symphony that is each well-ordered person.

Gottfried von Strassburg does not dwell on motion per se in describing the symphony of Isolde's presence, though he does mention her good gestures, her beauty of manners, her bearing, her educated self, which are the source of her entertainment before the court. But the subject loomed large in the development of harmonious presence. *Motus* can by itself mean "emotion," evident in English. Recall that moral discipline "composed the natural motions" of Archishop Pilgrim's soul and prepared the way for celestial harmonies. When the celestial melodies sounding out from the moving planets penetrates the human senses, the cosmic music reverberates like bowed strings in the soul and sets it in motion. When the *motus animi* orders also the motions of the body, as in a dance or a cultivated, studied way of walking, music becomes visible though not audible.

One who walks, stands, gestures, and carries oneself perfectly shows in this motion what harmony reigns within. According to Ambrose, "The motion of the body is the voice of the soul."[15] Novices at the school of St. Victor, Paris in the early twelfth century were subjected to a rigorous discipline of the body. Hugh of St. Victor defined discipline in reference to that aspect:

> Discipline is good and proper behavior.... It strives to *appear* above reproach in all things that it does well. Discipline is also the governed movement of all members of the body and a seemly disposition in every state and action.... [Hugh's pedagogy begins at the body and works inward.] Little by little the image of virtue is impressed on the mind [and that image] is maintained through outward discipline in the disposition of the body.[16]

The conception of music as a pedagogic force in the cultivation of virtue emerges in a form more sophisticated than in previous ages and at the same time more real, more active in the life of schools,

---

musicos sonos de sphaerarum caelestium conuersione procedere, quia et sonum ex motu fieri necesse est, et ratio quae diuinis inest fit sono causa modulaminis."

15. Ambrose, *De officiis*, 1.18.71: "vox quaedam est animi motus corporis." In PL 16:44D.

16. *De institutione novitiorum* 10. In Feiss and Sicard ed., 450–55; PL 176, 935A–B.

CHAPTER 4 ✷ THE MUSIC OF HUMANITY

courts, and monasteries of the eleventh century. One prominent reason for this rise is the discipline of *moralitas* and *ethica*, which takes on a significance that was unprecedented in the earlier Middle Ages. Human music became part of a musical anthropology, a conception of human harmony and perfection that could be taught, transmitted to students, and that was seen as useful and valuable in affairs of church and state.

An explanation of the shift of this Pythagoreon/Boethian idea from musical healing to musical education is yet to be discovered, but there is a clear difference from Boethius to Bern of Reichenau. Music becomes an ethical subject. From the mid-tenth to the early eleventh century in Germany and France, around twenty-five cathedral schools either rose anew or were revived from their Carolingian decline. Twenty-five! Let me stress it, because it is often wrongly assumed that monastic schools were the main bearers of culture in the period. Clearly something major was afoot in education in western and central Europe and eventually also in England.[17]

In the new schools, the formation of character played a major part, along with the arts of language above all. A standard designation for the new learning was "letters and manners."[18] Its origin is in classical Latin and Ciceronian concepts. It does not occur in the sources documenting Carolingian education (with the notable exception of Alcuin writing to Charlemagne in reference to the education of the king). The phrase was as central to the new curriculum as "letters and sciences" is to ours. It has a long history. Its use swells in the twelfth century and remains in educational texts and in letters of recommendation into the sixteenth century and beyond.

The term that really requires illumination is "manners," *mores*, the art of behavior, the development of character, a discipline also known as *cultus virtutum*, *ethica*, or *moralitas*. We encountered the term transferred into Middle High German in Gottfried's *moraliteit*. Any modern study of education in this period that concentrates exclusively on reading and writing, on books read and ideas studied,

---

17. For the details of the development of cathedral school in the period, see above, 22–27.

18. See above, 27–32, 88–92.

will have bypassed what is essential: *mores*.[19] The classicism of this new cathedral-school culture is one of its most striking and under-appreciated aspects. We are accustomed to saying with Charles Homer Haskins that it was the twelfth century that "rediscovered" the classics. But from the late tenth century on the schools of Germany and France were saturated with the classics of Latin philosophy and literature. Poetry, its study and its composition, played a part in curricula that is hard for us to comprehend. Some sources make the composition of poetry into the fulfillment of studies. Richer of St. Remi described the curriculum of Gerbert of Aurillac, which for the language arts lead from dialectic at the bottom to rhetoric.

Rhetoric begins with the poets: Virgil, Statius, Terence, Juvenal, Persius, Horace, Lucan. Then comes advanced rhetoric, then the argument of legal cases. An orator's education culminated in arguing cases before court or council, directed by what Richer calls a "sophist." The Bible fell into neglect, in stark contrast to its importance in Carolingian education. Beryl Smalley calls the early tenth to mid-eleventh century the lowpoint of biblical studies in the Middle Ages, "a dramatic pause in the history of Bible studies."[20]

I have argued elsewhere that teaching in this period relied to a great extent on the charisma of the teacher and on the admiration and love of the students for their teacher.[21] Wibald of Stablo wrote to a young school master of Trier and urged him, "Let your mere presence be a course of studies for your students." "Your mere presence" (*praesentia tua*) was a major concept in the culture of the schools. It was what was being formed in moral education. This made the schoolmaster into a paragon, even a god. Here a description of a now obscure, once famous master of the school of Würzburg, Pernolf. A student praises him in a poem defending the school and exalting the master, as "the prince of primates who reveal the mysteries of the poets/prophets" (*vatum*). Master Pernolf "blazes bright with the beauty of many poets," also a remarkable phrase. He does not illuminate the poems so much as the poems illuminate him. Poetry becomes a charismatic

19. For closer discussion of *mores*, see above, 32–39; and Jaeger, *Envy*, 76–117.

20. Beryl Smalley, *The Study of the Bible in the Middle Ages* (Notre Dame, IN: Notre Dame University Press, 1964), 44–45.

21. Jaeger, *Ennobling Love*, 11–81.

CHAPTER 4 ★ THE MUSIC OF HUMANITY

aura that glows in his very physical presence. "The living stream of learning flows from his breast. The eternal divinity gives him his flow of speech." It might be justified to call this transfiguring of the school master a "sacral professorship,"[22] a term commensurate with the stature of a master of poetry in the period. In many such portraits we can see a sense of human greatness form around the school master, the bishop, and the poet-singer.

The alliance of poetry and music in this charismatic culture was important, also in the formation of an extravagantly idealized image of the educated person. As with moral training, poetry also combines the language of poetics with the language of music. Baudri of Bourgueil praises Godfrey of Rheims, the poet/chancellor of Rheims (d.c. 1096):

> There stirs in you a certain excellence by which you excel all others who recite poetry. For whatever you recite, you recite in a voice so sonorous that whatever you say pleases all.... Placed among the heaven-dwellers you would be a second god, Apollo, if benevolent fates had made you a god. Among the greatest singers of our age, you came to us as Orpheus, or better.[23]

For Baudri, Godfrey is a singer (*cantor*), and his praise of his skill stresses oral performance. But Godfrey was much more than a musician. He was chancellor of the cathedral, a man of affairs with great influence in the diocese. In this dual role, we see the aggrandizing, the extravagant idealizing of the poet-singer: Godfrey's art "ennobled" his bishop (Manasses I), ennobled all of Rheims, made France flourish. His poetry has the power to make those it favors and break those it disfavors. It is stronger than an armed warrior. Godfrey himself boasted that his poetry could turn rivers back in their courses and change winter to summer. These are more than Orphic effects in

---

22. Jaeger, *Envy*, 68–70.
23. Baudri of Bourgueil, *Carmen* 99, ll. 13–17, 63–66: "In te praeterea viget excellentia quaedam, / Cunctis qui recitant qua superemineas. / Quicquid enim recitas, recitas ita voce sonora / Ut, quicquid dicas, omnibus id placeat. / Nam sic verba sonis verbisque sonos moderaris / Quatenus a neutro dissideat neutrum.... / Inter caelicolas deus esses alter Apollo, / Si te fecissent fata benigna deum. / Inter praecipuos cantores temporis huius, / Venisti nobis Orpheus aut melior." In Tilliette ed., 105, 106.

this Orphic singer. The so called "Renaissance of the Twelfth Century" lives at least in part on left-overs from that fading culture.

THE MUSIC OF POETRY

Poetry was generally sung; that was its main performance mode. The participants in this conference are at work rediscovering the music of poetry in the earlier Middle Ages. It will open a view onto charismatic effects in poetry and song. Indeed, poetry in the period had the aura of a kind of word magic. That aura faded along with many other features of eleventh-century culture. Think of that while you're in the spell of this evening's concert. Professor Barrett and his ensemble would be eligible for the mantle of Orpheus if they could be magically transported to eleventh-century Rheims or Paris.

Or even twelfth-century Durham. Lawrence of Durham, who died in 1154, an undeservedly obscure poet-cantor-courtier-lawyer,[24] gave a self assessment in one of his verse dialogues. It places him firmly in the cult of personality of the poet-singer:

> [1.31–33]: Even when cold, I burned with poetry, was keen to learn the meaning of the universe. Apollo saw and showed the Muses' power and joined them to me in a pious love. Then neither summer nor autumnal heat could dry the Pegasean springs for me.... [1.97]: Almighty music makes greater whatever it lights on.... [3.448–74]: [Why did Grace give her gifts to me?] To whom? To me. Why? I was pleasing. My happy body leapt up to reach the heights. You would think I was climbing to reach my ancestors. I was still beardless, but my lofty head surpassed the height of many tall men. My body, fame and reputation grew. My honour and acceptance were widespread. I only wish my merit matched my fame, for I was highly praised in church and town. In verse I could acomplish all I wished. My poems witness this, in many forms. No less skilled where metric laws don't bind, I'd treat my friends to rhythmic verse as well. See how glad the clergy were in church, how the thronging people showed their joy to hang upon my lips and hear my song: My singing voice provided their delight. It imitated trumpets, if I wished it. It gaily sang with many varied sounds. Like the bells enhanced

24. See the work of Mia Münster-Swendsen cited throughout.

CHAPTER 4 ✶ THE MUSIC OF HUMANITY

by tinsmith's art, alone it often sang three notes at once. Now like a falcon, hurled from hunter's hand, it cleaves the empty air with cutting wings, and as it cuts, it takes the wind, and then with tiny beats it keenly soars aloft.[25]

The various strains of education from the earlier cathedral schools flow into him. A monk of St. Cuthbert's at Durham at a young age, he rose in esteem and moved to the episcopal court where he had the title *cantor* and described himself as "courtier" (*palatinus*). He was a talented poet but complained that his legal duties prevented him from devoting himself to his art as he wished. As a young man he had a surging sense of self-worth (1.31–33). He sought competition with other, older men and did not hesitate to proclaim his own victories. He explained his successes as the favor bestowed on him by Grace. "Why Grace? Why me?" he asks. The answer: "*gratus eram*" ("I was pleasing").

---

25. Lawrence of Durham, *Dialogue* 1 and 3, ll. 31–33: "Fervidus ad musas in frigore, quid simul omnis, / Singula quid possit, nosse paratus eram. Hoc et Apollo videns vires patefecit earum, / Expositasque pio junxit amore mihi. / Nec Pegasaea quidem siccare fluenta vel aestas / Sicca, vel autumnus tunc potuere mihi. 1.97: Musica multipotens plerumque quod invenit auget... 3.448–74: Nam quis, quaeso, daret? Quis? Gratia; quidve / Gratia. Cuine? Mihi, Cur ita? Gratus eram. / Exilit interea mihi corpus in ardua laetum, / Sanguine vel colera plus dominante mihi. / Ad cognata sibi conscendere velle putares / Haec elementa, mihi cursus in alta fuit. / Namque genas implumis eram, celsisque quibusdam / Vertice sublimi celsior ipse fui. / Sic corpus, plus fama tamen, plus gloria laudis, / Plus honor, atque mihi crevit ubique favor; / O utinam meritus! Nam multus ubique putabar, / Multus in ecclesia, multus in urbe mea. / Insuper et poteram versu quaecunque volebam, / Remque probant variis carmina facta modis. / Nec minus ipse potens in carmine lege soluto, / Scripta dabam sociis lege soluta meis. / Conspice praeterea quam laetus ab ore canentis / Clerus in ecclesia, quam vel ad ista frequens, / Et satis exultans populus pendere solebat; / Vox pro deliciis, Petre, canentis erat, / Quae varias imitata tubas, quaecunque volebat / Cantum diverso lusit amoena sono. / Et quasi campanae stagni quibus amplius addit / Fusor, saepe simul tres dabat una sonos. / Nunc etiam quasi falco, manu jaciente sequaci, / Vastum cultellis findit inane suis; / Et cultellando ventus legit, atque minutis / Plausibus insistens acriter alta petit." In "Lawrence of Durham, *Dialogues and Easter Poem*," Arthur G. Rigg, trans., *Journal of Medieval Latin* 7 (1997): 42–126, at 45–46.

Polyphony from a single voice, no mean accomplishment. Asked by his dialogue partner why he confines himself to the episcopal court; why he does not visit the city to see its castle, its gate, its houses, Lawrence replies that as cantor his dignity and respect were such that he could not show himself in town: "Should a mighty man walk through the streets on foot?" (1.479). While his three-toned voice trumpets his own fame in this passage, it is a prelude to his fall from the heights, brought down by the jealousy of fortune. Grace eventually leaves him on his own to float but then snatches away all the gifts it had given him.

Lawrence said earlier in this dialogue: "Almighty music makes great whatever it lights on." Similar to what Baudri of Bourgueil had written some fifty years earlier "Through the art of music, everything gains in vitality." It leads to my next point. Music undoubtedly had a role to play in the creation and heightening of personal presence in this culture of charisma. We've already seen the connection suggested in Bern of Reichenau's description of Archishop Pilgrim of Cologne: the melody of celestial harmony tuned his soul to his body and made his inner music visible in his outer presence. Also, the unheard music of Isolde. But it applies to heard music as well. That is no doubt one reason why poetical and musical performance loom so large up to the twelfth century. It also accounts for the fact that so little poetry has survived from the period in proportion to the amount written and performed: sung poetry fulfilled its purpose in performance. The majestic presence attributed to Godfrey of Rheims owed much to his poetry and music. The heightening and magnifying effect of sung poetry works on the person of the performer, but also on the person sung about, living, fictional or historical, in any given performance.

Almost certainly the neumes that Jan Ziolkowski has studied in the texts of classical poetry in this period indicate music at work in this heightening and magnifying function.[26] Ziolkowski points to the selection of speeches, passages of heightened pathos, and passages with references to the cosmos, descriptive or metaphoric, in which neumes are particularly frequent. Among such passages he points out the long discourse in book 1 of Lucan's *Civil War*, where Caesar

26. *Nota Bene: Reading Classics and Writing Melodies in the Early Middle Ages* (Turnhout: Brepols, 2007), 148, 150.

learns the secrets of the Nile from the priest Achoreus, among them the motion and operation of the planets. I wonder, and ask you, is it possible that passages where style is heightened to match a grand subject might especially attract neuming, and whether that might indicate that such passages were especially heightened by music?

ST. VICTOR'S SWANSONG

The heightening effect of music within narrative is dramatically evident in an episode from Sigebert of Gembloux's saint's legend plus poetic epic, *The Passion of the Theban Legion* (c.1075). The veteran soldier (and here scholar) sings out a "song" in the moments before his martyrdom. It is a remarkable work, a blend of martyr legend and heroic epic with strong Germanic coloring (*Waltharius*) but also with elements that tie it into the life of the schools (Sigebert was a master at St. Vincent of Metz and advocate of the imperial position in the Investiture Controversy).

The action is set in the fourth century during the reign of Emperor Maximian (286–305). A legion of Christian soldiers from Egypt is sent by the emperor to wipe out a rebellious Celtic tribe in the Alps. The legion refuses the command and asserts its Christianness by refusing to worship the Roman gods. The emperor orders them first decimated, then when that doesn't work, wiped out. The legion accepts death with passive resistance. They die nobly, refusing to use their weapons. At the end of the slaughter the aging veteran soldier Victor enters the scene (he was not among the legionnaires) and is filled with wonder for the martyrs. He sees sights that strike him mute and paralyzed with horror. He realizes the noble death of the legion and, sensing the approach of his own death, he decides to join them in martyrdom. He seizes the moment to die well. He announces the decision in a magnificent "oration" or "prayer" (*oratio*), eighty-two lines long. It is a high point of this work and of eleventh-century poetry. This description introduces his song:

> Like the snowy swan singing out with prophetic voice, sensing the final moments of its life, shunning fountains, parks, fields, marshes, with expanded chest and raised vocal tone, showing in this way that death is nothing to be feared, his voice sang out songs so sweet and melodic that the birds themselves, expert singers, were struck dumb with amazement to hear them ring

out. No harpist or flute player could produce such a song. This is how he sang of his desire for his final hour.[27]

He looks back over the "vibrant times" of his life and the constant striving that his "restless, fervid breast" drives him to. He reviews those things that do honor to a man who is both strong and wise. It is an exuberantly optimistic view of a life devoted to studies, to discovery, to wandering. There's a Faustian strain in his vitalism: "I have drunk new wine, felt the frosts of winter, seen spring's flowers…" and watched the unsteady balance of human affairs. In the end he goes astray, leaves the path of virtue, and finds in a noble death a way back to Christ. Here are the final lines. They give a clear impression of the crescendo that ends the oration:

> Realizing these things and pondering them in my mature mind with full emotion and supreme desire — how I wish that I, sighing and aspiring like an athlete, how I wish that I might be a comrade in death to these holy men!… My heart, my soul, my reason, my mind, my senses, my spirit, or rather the sum total of my soul sing out Christ, desire and love Him. In Christ I live, Christ I worship, and now in Christ I shall die.[28]

He turns to face the enemy and in that instant his head is struck off.

I have analysed this passage elsewhere and included it in an essay on the sublime style in the Middle Ages.[29] It fits that category well. But what interests us at the moment is its avowed musicality. Sigebert introduces it as a sung performance. It is a rhapsodic "song" of such sweetness that no harp player or flutist could match it. It is the song of the dying swan. Its tones have a magical prophetic quality.

27. *Sigeberts von Gembloux Passio Sanctae Luciae Virginis und Passio Sanctorum Thebeorum* 3.7, ll. 574–84: "Pectore mellito declamat et ore perito. / Qualis olor niveus, sago clamore canorus, / Impendere sue divinans ultima vite. / Exosus fotes, vivaria, prata, paludes, / Arteriis laxis, aucto modulamine vocis, / Sic monstrans forsan mortem nihil esse timendam. / Edit ab ore modos quam dulces quamque melodos, / Quale canat fidicen vix aut tibicina carmen, / Quod stupeant volucres docet resonare canores: / Talis et hic horam canit exoptando supremam." In Ernst Dümmler, ed. (Berlin: Reimer, 1893), 111.

28. Sigebert von Gembloux, *Passio*, ll. 651–67; Dümmler ed., 113.

29. See also below, 399–402.

CHAPTER 4 ✷ THE MUSIC OF HUMANITY

We even have some technical terms of vocal performance: *Arteriis laxis, aucto modulamine vocis...* "with expanded vocal cords and louder melodic tone." (Do these terms place us in the performance hall, rehearsal hall, music lesson? It's the voice of the teacher: "from the diaphragm, project!"). He gives out a melody of such charm as to strike the birds themselves dumb with amazement, a song of longing for his final moment.

By introducing the "oration" as music, the poet was striving to highlight the emotional intensity of the scene, the climactic character of the noble death of Victor. The introduction is there to lend an operatic aura to the speech. I say that at the risk of anachronism, but I think it's worth it in this case to underscore the uniqueness of the passage. The poet not only quotes the speech of St. Victor, but he also dictates its dynamics. Most likely the whole speech was meant to be sung. The unique manuscript *Passio Thebeorum* is not neumed, as I've learned from a helpful librarian at Leiden University special collections. Nonetheless apart from neumes themselves, it fits neatly what Ziolkowski called the "Pathos hypothesis":

> We find neumed speeches by lovers to their confidantes and lovers,...by heroes when they are killed or prepare to kill others.... Composers or neumators may have gravitated towards such passionate outpourings because they afford outlets for expressivity.[30]

Neumed or not, the poet himself tells us that this passage was sung, and the sign he would have set 600 or 700 years later in modern notation is *forte* or *fortissimo*. It is not disembodied expression: the passion elevates the presence of the hero, who can perform splendidly in the moment preceding his self-chosen death.

CONCLUSIONS

I've just sketched in a few features of a culture that faded and died out in the course of the twelfth century. The charismatic world with its magical-artistic modes of thought and performance moved out of reality and into the realm of fantastic fictions like *Tristan and Isolde*. The relation between cathedral schools and court service came under serious fire. The classics were much reduced in their importance in

---

30. *Nota Bene*, 148, 150.

the curriculum. Those teachers who relied on charisma to establish authority became redundant and faced ridicule.[31] A poetry laden with far-fetched diction and tangled in difficult syntax (like Sigebert's and Godfrey of Rheims') fell out of fashion. The neumes marking music in manuscripts of the classics disappeared. Sung poetry no longer was the way to a career, to personal grandeur, and to popular respect. In the course of the twelfth century poets became very much the way we think of poets: poor and alienated. If we are to believe Roger Bacon, by the mid-thirteenth century the vitality had gone out of music, and he called vehemently for church and university to reform music as it had been, "more expressive, more addressed to the senses, more vivid."[32]

---

31. See above, 60–69.

32. Roger Bacon, *Opus Tertium* 73. In *Fratris Rogeri Bacon Opera quaedam Hactenus Inedita* 1, John S. Brewer, ed. (London: Longman, 1859), 298–99.

5. ORPHEUS IN THE ELEVENTH CENTURY

INTRODUCTION

The learned poetry of the eleventh century wards off broad interest by its obscure diction and its display classicism that brings down on it the characterization of "school poetry" and "rhetorical exercises" with the sober opprobrium those terms convey. In addition, its powerful neighbor, the twelfth century, pulls much that preceded into its orbit. There is a tendency to read Marbod, Baudri, and Hildebert looking forward, not backward, as precursors, not as fulfillers. The "school poetry" had a greater role in learning and society than current perceptions credit: "Why did one write poetry? One was taught to in school."[1] The tone in the master's voice here brooked no contradiction and convicted the sensible question, "Why learn poetry?" in advance of impertinence.

USEFUL POETRY

We can get some impression of the distance that separates the learned eleventh-century poet from the "Vagant" of the twelfth in a satirical portrait of the perfect worldly cleric by Peter Damian:

> Today there lives in the city of Rome a brother, born of the highest nobles of France.... If he lacks anything that qualifies him for office, it escapes me, for he is endowed with so many of the flowers of external goods: noble as an emperor, beauty in his entire appearance. He speaks like Cicero; he writes poetry like Virgil; a sounding trumpet in the church; he is learned and sharp in divine law. When disputing like a scholar his speech rolls as if he were reading it from the page; speaking the common language he offends no rule of Roman urbanity.[2]

1. ELLMA, 468, Excursus 7: "The Mode of Existence of the Medieval Poet."

2. Petrus Damianus, *De sancta simplicitate* 7: "Hodie...in romana urbe frater advivit, ortus de summis proceribus Galliarum.... Cui nescio an aliquid utilitatis desit, tot siquidem exteriorum bonorum floribus enitescit: nobilis ut imperator; pulcher aspectu quodammodo; sicut Tullius loquitur; ut Virgilius poetatur; tuba vehemens in Ecclesia; perspicax et acutus est in lege divina; scholastice disputans, quasi descripta libri verba percurrit; vulgariter loquens, Romanae urbanitatis regulam non offendit." In S. Pier Damiani, *De divina omnipotentia e altri opuscoli* Paolo Brezzi, ed.; Bruno Nardi, trans. (Florence: Vallechi, 1943), 163–201, at 188.

The satirist's point is that these are vain and empty attainments, but his lucid picture places the values and ambitions of worldly clerics in sharp focus. The only quality that gives pause is poetry: *ut Virgilius poetatur*. Is poetry a "useful" quality,[3] parallel to high nobility, physical beauty, forensic eloquence, political influence, and legal training? The apparent anomaly can perhaps be dissolved by regarding Virgil's skill as another expression of the verbal eloquence the passage stresses.

This study argues, against such a reading and its premises, that the writer had a concept of poetry that regarded it as an attainment valuable in public life, possibly parallel to noble birth and definitely to legal skill, a talent closely allied with one of the major missions of educated clergy in western Europe in the period — not merely advanced rhetoric. The learned poet of the eleventh century is more likely to be found in furs and silks in high church positions than wandering homeless and hopeful of patronage for the evening's bread.

The eleventh-century cathedral schools were the nurturing ground of a concept of poetry useful to church and state. The extraordinary status of poetry in the period is evident in the poem *De mensa philosophie* from the *Cambridge Songs*. It sets a rich table of philosophical food and drink, but serves only poetry:

> *Hasten to the banquet of philosophy, you who thirst,*
> *And drink the seven streams of its threefold feast.*
> *Flowing from a single fountain, they go separate ways.*
> *Here flow the rudiments of grammar, here the stream of poetry,*

---

3. The word is used in the sense of *utilitas ecclesiae* or *rei publicae*, that is, personal qualities beneficially engaged in the business and administration of church and state. Both contexts are addressed in Peter Damian's portrait of a certain Ugo of Parma. See *De sancta simplicitate* 6, Brezzi ed., 184 and 186: ... *quot utilitatum dotes habuerit, non enumero*, so ambitious in the arts he had an astrolabe fashioned of pure silver. He aspired to the position of bishop and so, "had himself appointed to the chapel of Emperor Conrad" (*dum spiraret ad episcopale fastigium, Conradi imperatoris se constituit capellanum*). The classical definition is Cicero, *De inventione* 2.168–69. Cf. the adaptation in Bernard of Utrecht, *Accessus ad auctores: Commentum in Theodolum*, Robert B.C. Huygens, ed. (Leiden: Brill, 1970), 68, 245–49.

CHAPTER 5 ✶ ORPHEUS IN THE ELEVENTH CENTURY

Here the platter of the satirists, here the applause of the comics,
And the Mantuan flutes bring joy to the banquet.[4]
This is not a niggardly "let them eat poetry!" It is the best dish the host has to offer. The age had a loose hold on the quadrivium, but it had a sense that in poetry Virgil was not always its equal.[5] There is good testimony to the fervid devotion to poetry in school.[6] A poem written by a student of Würzburg in 1031 as a polemic against the school of Worms also testifies to the stature of poetry in that flourishing but poorly documented school at that early period.[7] The

4. *Carmina Cantabrigiensia* 37: "Ad mensam philosophie sitientes currite / et saporis tripertiti septem rivos bibite, / uno fonte procedentes non eodem tramite, / Hinc fluit gramma prima, / hinc poetica ydra, / lanx hinc satiricorum, / plausus hinc comicorum, / letificat convivia / Mantuana fistula." In Walther Bulst, ed. (Heidelberg: Winter, 1950), 65. *Mantuana fistula* = Virgil's pastoral poetry.

5. The sense of outbidding antiquity is evident in much of the school poetry. It imposed an obligation on the poet that had disastrous effects on his Latin style. See the dedicatory letter of Anselm of Besate, *Rhetorimachia*, in *Gunzo, Epistola ad Augienses und Anselm von Besate, Rhetorimachia*, Karl Manitius, ed., MGH, *Quellen zur Geistesgeschichte des Mittelalters*, ser. 2 (Weimar: Böhlau, 1958), 97–100. Anselm associates the deeds of Henry with Augustus Caesar and himself with Virgil, whose task was to praise the deeds of Augustus. Since Henry's are more famous than Caesar's, it follows — though it is not stated outright — that poetic talents beyond Virgil's are called for, and Anselm is his man. That is stated outright. Anselm was offered a position in Henry III's chapel, presumably as a response to his *Rhetorimachia*. See Carl Erdmann, "Anselm der Peripatetiker, Kaplan Heinrichs III," in *Forschungen zur politischen Ideenwelt des Frühmittelalters* (Berlin: Akademie, 1951), 119–24; Beth S. Bennett, "The Significance of the 'Rhetorimachia' of Anselm de Besate to the History of Rhetoric," *Rhetorica* 5 (1987): 231–50; Bennett, "The Rhetoric of Martianus Capella and Anselm de Besate in the Tradition of Menippean Satire," *Philosophy and Rhetoric* 24 (1991): 128–42.

6. Guibert of Nogent (d.1124) claimed that in his youth he had "immersed [his] soul beyond all measure in poetry so I considered scripture ridiculous vanity." He read Ovid and the *Bucolics* and composed love poetry himself. See Peter Stotz, "Dichten als Schulfach: Aspekte mittelalterlicher Schuldichtung," Mlat. Jb. 16 (1981): 1–16, at 9–13.

7. The poem is edited as supplement to *Die ältere Wormser Briefsammlung*, Walther Bulst ed., MGH, *Die Briefe der deutschen Kaiserzeit* 3 (Weimar: Böhlau, 1949), 119–27; and in *Die Tegernseer Briefsammlung, Carmen XLIII*, Karl Strecker,

master is praised as "The prince of those primates, who expound the poets' secrets" (v. 21: *Princeps primatum, qui pandunt abdita vatum*); he is "refulgent with the light of many poets" (v. 24: *poetarum fulget decus omnigenarum*), a striking formulation that implies a mystification of the self that is built on poetic knowledge. He "beams" poetry as he might exude humanity, grace, and charm. The master teaches composition above all other subjects (v. 26). "He devotes all his care to the study of composition" (*Preter scripture studium nihil est sibi cure*).[8] He qualifies his students for office, and himself and them for heaven, through learning and virtue (vv. 75–82).

Still towards the end of the period (c.1125), when studies and poetry in France had gone new ways, a learned German, Ulrich of Bamberg, could make the skilled composition of verse and prose into the measure of learning:[9]

---

ed., MGH, *Epistolae selectae* 3 (Berlin: Weidmann, 1925), 125–34. For commentary on and historical circumstances, see Georg Schepss, "Zu Froumunds Briefcodex und zu Ruodlieb," ZfdPh 15 (1883): 419–33; Johann Kempf, *Zur Kulturgeschichte Frankens während der sachsischen und salischen Kaiser. Mit einem Excurs: Über einen Schulstreit zwischen Würzburg und Worms im 11. Jahrhundert. Programm der königliches Neuen Gymnasiums Würzburg 1914/15* (Würzburg: Neues Gymnasium, 1915); Elizabeth Haefner, *Die Wormser Briefsammlung des 11. Jahrhunderts* (Erlangen: Palm & Enke, 1935); Manitius, *Geschichte*, 522–23, takes Froumund of Tegernsee to be the poet, the bishop of Würzburg, not the schoolmaster, Pernolf, to be the figure defended. But neither identification is tenable. See also Jaeger, *Envy*, 66–70.

8. The meaning is clearly the study of composition, not of Scripture. Cf. vv. 160–61, where *scriptura* refers to the Worms poem to which the Würzburger is responding: "quod cor non celat, quoniam scriptura revelat / Versibus oblatis. mendacibus inmodulatis." See also *Ältere Wormser Briefsammlung*, Epist. 19, 10: "De scriptura [the outer shell, the written form] non erit curandum, cum magis ad sententie nucleum...sit respiciendum," Bulst ed., 36; and some verses in the Tegernsee *Carmen* XLI: "Me bene scribentem faciat, precor omnipotentem /... / Artem scripture sectandi sit tibi cure," Strecker ed., 122.

9. See Franz Bittner, "Eine Bamberger *ars dictandi*," *Bericht des Historischen Vereins Bamberg* 100 (1964): 145–71, at 156. Here *componere* (v. 33) refers to poetry as well as prose. Cf. vv. 58–59: "Nam versus dulces scribendo pectora mulces, / Mulces egregie scribens metri sine lege." On Ulrich's "*Ars dictandi*" and its two introductory poems, see Ian S. Robinson, "The '*colores rhetorici*' in the Investiture Contest," *Traditio* 32 (1976): 209–38, at 213.

CHAPTER 5 ✷ ORPHEUS IN THE ELEVENTH CENTURY

I believe for my own part, my sweetest friend,
And hope you agree, that no one is thoroughly learned,
Nor perfect, who is unable to compose something
Worth hearing. What greater sign is there,
What stronger argument or more certain testimony
Of abundant genius, dearest brother, than when
A poet can soothe ears and minds gracefully?
Here is what we seek, or nowhere. Here, I say,
Is the fruit of long studies.[10]

ORPHEUS, THE SYMBOL OF POETRY
The period made Orpheus into the representative of its lofty conception of poetry.[11] A close reading of three poems, two from

10. Ulrich of Bamberg. *Ars dictandi*, ll. 31–39: "...Fateor me iudice nemo, / Si concedis idem, carissime, doctus ad unguem / Nec perfectus erit, qui nil componere novit / Auditu dignum; quod maius dic rogo signum / Aut argumentum, quod certius est documentum / Divitis ingenii; frater dulcissime, quam si / Dictator mentes et grate mulceat aures? / Hic est aut nusquam quod quaerimus, hic erit inquam / Fructus longorum, ni fallor ego, studiorum." In Bittner ed., 156.

11. Specifically on the Orpheus figure in the Middle Ages, see Peter Dronke, "The Return of Eurydice," *Classica et Mediaevalia* 23 (1962): 198–15; Klaus Heitmann, "Orpheus im Mittelalter," *Archiv für Kulturgeschichte* 45 (1963): 253–94; John B. Friedman, *Orpheus in the Middle Ages* (Cambridge, MA: Harvard University Press, 1970). Hennig Brinkmann, *Mittelalterliche Hermeneutik* (Tübingen: Niemeier, 1980), 205–6, reads the eleventh-century sources as *integumenta* referring to Christ. A few references to update Brinkmann's extensive bibliography of studies of Orpheus from antiquity to the present: Max Wegner, "Orpheus: Ursprung und Nachfolge," *Boreas* 9 (1988): 177–225; Ella Schwartz, "Aspects of Orpheus in Classical Literature and Mythology," (Ph.D. diss., Harvard University, 1984); *Orpheus: The Metamorphosis of a Myth*, John Warden, ed. (Toronto: University of Toronto Press, 1982); William S. Anderson, "The Artist's Limits in Ovid: Orpheus, Pygmalion and Daedalus," *Syllecta Classica* 1 (1989): 1–11; Detlef C. Kochan, "Literarische Spuren einer Symbolfigur: Orpheus zum Beispiel," *Literarische Symbolfiguren von Prometheus bis Svejk: Beiträge zur Tradition und Wandel*, Werner Wunderlich ed. (Bern: Facetten dt. Literatur, 1989), 37–63; Pierre Prigent, "Orphée dans l'iconographie Chrétienne," *Revue d'histoire et de philosophie religieuses* 64 (1984): 205–21; Ian R. Johnson, "Walton's Sapient Orpheus," in *The Medieval Boethius*, Alistair J. Minnis, ed. (Cambridge: Cambridge University

207

the last two decades of the century, one probably from mid-century, opens this conception to view.¹²

AN ELEVENTH-CENTURY WEDDING OF ORPHEUS (ELOQUENCE) AND EURYDICE (WISDOM)

We start with a text that is broadly conceived and useful for placing Orpheus and the poetry he stands for in the context of learning and amalgamating the Orpheus and Eurydice story with Mercury and Philology. The adaptation of Martianus Capella is by a poet either in or acquainted with the Rheims circle toward the end of the eleventh century. He knew the works of Godfrey of Rheims and Marbod of Rennes. In the two manuscripts that have preserved it his poem

---

Press, 1987), 139–68; C. Munro Pyle, "Le thème d'Orphée dans les oeuvres latines d'Ange Politien," *Bulletin de l'Association Guillaume Budé* 39 (1980): 408–19; Arnfried Edler, "Die Macht der Töne': Über die Bedeutung eines antiken Mythos im 19. Jahrhundert," in *Musik in Antike und Neuzeit*, Michael von Albrecht and Werner Schubert, ed. (Frankfurt-am-Main: Peter Lang, 1987), 51–65. On the two endings of the story (following Dronke, *Return of Eurydice*), see M. Owen Lee, "Orpheus and Eurydice: Myth, Legend and Folklore," *Classica et Mediaevalia* 26 (1965): 402–12; David Sansone, "Orpheus and Eurydice in the Fifth Century," *Classica et Mediaevalia* 36 (1985): 53–64.

12. The best commentaries on these poems develop a powerful consensus that they are to be read as "school poetry" and "rhetorical exercises." See Dronke, "Return," 210: ["*Quid suum*," "*Liège song*, and Godfrey of Rheims' *Orpheus* version are] "more in the nature of literary exercises." Heitmann, 260, gives a broader boundary to the same perspective: "Man muß diese Stücke, wenngleich für die besten von ihnen der Mythos gewiß mehr als ein bloßer Vorwand für die Erprobung dichterischer Geschicklichkeit war, doch ihrer Genesis entsprechend vor allem unter formal-rhetorischem Gesichtspunkt lesen." To which I would certainly add, history of education. Friedman, 164: "exercise poems," "rhetorical elaborations on the myth"; 165: "of minor interest poetically, but they are very important as evidence for the portrait of Orpheus as a romance hero"; 166 ("*Quid suum*"): "more interested, one feels, in the rhetorical possibilities of the myth than in the myth itself." This judgment seems to me to warn off readers from taking them seriously. The mythical poem is integrated into a scheme of the ideal education.

CHAPTER 5 ✶ ORPHEUS IN THE ELEVENTH CENTURY

is confusingly titled *De nuptiis Mercurii et Philologie*.[13] This verse adaptation of Martianus in Leonine hexameters deserves a detailed study. No reading that I know takes seriously its joining of a survey of the liberal arts with the Orpheus figure. Boutemy himself tends to discount the first part and regard the poem as "a version of the Orpheus legend." A close reading reveals the poem as a summary of learning at cathedral schools of the eleventh century. Like Alan of Lille's *Anticlaudianus*, though on less grand a scale, it is an allegory of the ideal education.[14]

As in Martianus Capella, the work begins with the marriage of Mercury and Philology. The wedding feast is presided over by Sapientia. Apollo calls upon the nine muses, who "cling closely to study" (v. 82, *studio cohibente*) in order to "magnify the arts." Then each of the Muses sings the praises of one of the arts. After the celebration of the arts, the "ethereal chorus of philosophy" sings a song praising Sapientia. Next Orpheus appears with his wife Eurydice. No reason is given for his entrance. He simply is "there" (v. 242): "Behold the new poet bringing the latest from the poets" (*Ecce novus vates vatumque ferens novitates*)." He calls for silence and begins to sing. The song he sings is of no particular importance, though it goes on at some length (vv. 242–366). It is a series of "hymns" to gods and heroes, essentially the brief retelling of myths. Eurydice follows and sings of some of the paramours of Jove and is awarded the laurel wreath, gems, and gold for her song.[15] When she ends, the feast is over (v. 402). Now

13. See André Boutemy, "Une version médiévale inconnue de la légende d'Orphée," in *Hommages à Joseph Bidez et à Franz Cumont*, Charles H. Josserand, ed. (Brussels: Latomus, 1949), 43–70.

14. Boutemy's title tends to conceal the broad sweep of the poem. Only in that light is it intelligible that the poem has been omitted in Gabriel Nuchelmans, "Philologia et son mariage avec Mercure jusqu'à la fin du XIIe siècle," *Latomus* 16 (1957): 84–107. I have not found any reference to it in the literature on education in the eleventh and twelfth centuries. One of the major documents on eleventh-century learning is masked as "a version of the Orpheus legend."

15. I know of no other version from any period in which Eurydice herself performs as a singer. The extravagant reward seems to aim at legitimizing praise of women. Cf. vv. 398–400: "The happy cohort of the gods, also approving the praises of women, announce the fame of Eurydice with all their vows: and that she deserves the laurel, they affirm with gold and jewels." ("Leta cohors superum

follows a lament on death and the inevitability of the decrees of Fate. The logic of its inclusion, not evident at once, is that we are now, with no transition, into the story of Orpheus and Eurydice. She is bitten by the serpent. He descends to recover her, softens the flinty hearts of the infernal beings with his song, and, following the Ovidian "unhappy ending," loses Eurydice again by looking back.

What does it mean that a poem celebrating the union of eloquence and wisdom through the Muses and the liberal arts ends in the story of Orpheus and Eurydice? Essentially, the message is that education is fulfilled in poetry and music.[16] It does not place Mercury and Philology at the summit of learning but rather Orpheus and Eurydice. Martianus Capella's work also ended with music. The ninth and final book of his *De nuptiis* is devoted to Harmony. Banished from earth, she (the allegorical figure *Harmonia*) joins the

---

laudesque probans mulierum / Euridicis totis referunt preconia votis: / Utque decet laura, gemmis redimitur et auro.") Possibly because some sources make her into a daughter of Apollo? Cf. *Mythographus Vaticanus* 1.75.1–2, Peter Kulcsar, ed., CCSL 91C (Turnholt: Brepols, 1987), 33: "Orpheus Oeagri et Caliope muse filius, ut quidam putant, Appolinis filiam habuit uxorem Euridicen." This still doesn't explain *laudes probans mulierum*. The article on Eurydice in Pauly Wissowa, RE 6.1:1322–27, does not mention a singing Eurydice or a daughter of Apollo.

16. Some details that confirm the poet was working within a structure where poetry fulfills the arts. The "ethereal chorus of philosophy" sings in praise of *sapientia* (vv. 227–29):"At hominum sensus, duce te, sapiendo remensus / Appetit internas herebi penetrare cavernas, / Discutiens utique secreta polique solisque." This marks the catabasis as symbolic of the continuing quest for understanding. To "penetrate the caverns of the underworld" means to investigate the secrets of the heavens. Boutemy, "Version," 52, points to the lines as foreshadowing the descent of Orpheus, but he regards the Orpheus story as tacked on, not the fulfillment of learning. Likewise, the striking parallel between the role of rhetoric as presented by Calliope (vv. 136–59) and the judicial pleading for Eurydice in the underworld (vv. 593–616) is discussed below. Baudri of Bourgueil assigned the same preeminent role to music. The headboard of the allegorical bed in Countess Adela of Blois' bedchamber is inscribed with a representation of Philosophy and the liberal arts. See *Carmen* 134; Tilliette ed., 2:1–43. Music is located at the right hand (v. 975), or at the feet (v. 1002) of Philosophy herself, who has commanded that music always be present as second only to philosophy, because she is the force that keeps the other sisters in harmony with each other (vv. 1001–2). In Tilliette ed., 2:32.

CHAPTER 5 ★ ORPHEUS IN THE ELEVENTH CENTURY

wedding party to celebrate the union in song. Orpheus is also present, along with Amphion and Arion. His song and his failed rescue are mentioned but with no particular profile. He is one of several emblems of Harmony's working. Martianus Capella's work ends with a long-winded rehearsal of the laws of harmonics and metrics. The overall conception of the two works is comparable: a survey of studies ends in the art that fulfills them. But the eleventh-century poet thoroughly changed his conception. He replaced Mercury and Philology (eloquence and wisdom) with Orpheus and Eurydice. That shift explains why this poem is more than a school exercise, more than an illustration of rhetoric: it redefines the character and purpose of learning.

ORPHEUS, DEFEATER OF CRUELTY, BRINGER OF COMPASSION

The underworld scene is the key to the poem's guiding conceptions. Orpheus meets the harshest, cruelest, and most inflexible beings God and nature have created, and his song softens their hearts and turns them into advocates of compassion. The demons of the underworld are converted. The fates are overcome in short order and beg the king, Dis, to relent and spare Eurydice (v. 571): *Flectuntur Parce, que dicunt:"Rex pie, parce!"* The furies, described as *ferva, trux, torva* themselves are softened. They reproach Dis for his harshness (v. 574): *Sevitiam Ditis reprobant cum murmure litis.* The tortured in hell forget their sufferings (v. 575).

Orpheus' plea to Dis is marked by sensual nostalgia. "Hymen," the god of marriage, has driven him to invade the land of hell (v. 534). Orpheus is "a youth bound by the reins of love" (v. 535); his dead bride had "hardly even in her girlish mind tasted the union with a man, still knew not how to love or be loved" (vv. 538–539). Eurydice, roused from the dark regions by her lover's voice, "desires to embrace him" (v. 559). The romantic pathos seizes even the residents of hell and awakens love and compassion in all of them. A chorus of the Furies and the damned together plead with Pluto for Orpheus (v. 586): "Love presses them all with its urgings, from all sides the clamor for forgiveness rings out" (*Omnibus instat amor, venie sonat undique clamor*). The lord of the underworld is at first irritated and hardens his heart (v. 588: *Pluto cor indurat neque vati parcere curat*). But this love-inspired plea for mercy from a unanimous chorus softens and renders him "modest and placid" (v. 617: *Rex prius infestus placida iam mente modestus*) and "lightens the fatal law" (v. 618). But Orpheus violates his condition imposed on him for his bride's redemption. Eurydice is lost forever, and the poet is left with only the consolation of his song, which retains its power to mitigate coarseness and harshness:

> He mitigates the curses of sorrow and anger
> with the art of his lyre,
> and no matter what grief beset him, art restores him.[17]

The essential moment in the scene is the conversion of the underworld, the remarkable metamorphosis from cold, dead rage and vengeful fury to warmth, compassion, and love. This is the power of Orphic music. Love-inspired music soothes and conquers the fury and anger of the harshest and cruelest. Poetry softens fate and prevails even over the gods and the laws of nature.

A central thought of the poet emerges in the meeting of Orpheus and Dis. It is modeled on a courtroom scene. Orpheus is pleading a case, the chorus of the furies and damned speak in his support. Dis is a king sitting in judgment and enforcing or relaxing laws.[18] This conceit of the poet's makes poetry and judicial rhetoric into allies in legal dealings and reiterates a remarkable passage earlier in the poem, the presentation of rhetoric by the muse Calliope (vv. 138–45):

> This art [rhetoric] teaches kings to hold to moderation in the law,
> It reforms the knighthood, who bear the weapons of Mars,

---

17. Vv. 642–43: "Mitigat arte lyre fera dampna doloris et ire, / Quaque fuit victus lugens redit arte revictus." In Boutemy ed., 63.

18. The judicial nature of the proceedings is quite evident. The chorus gives the "king" advice on the treatment of the accused and convicted in general (v. 594): "Parcere prostratis decus est et honor pietatis." They invoke points of law (vv. 598–99): "ne modo maiora pereant concede minora, / Ne vicio regis titubet sententia legis." They appeal to "the law," itself (v. 599 *sententia legis*; v. 604 *lex tua*). The issue glides from death vs. life over into innocence vs. guilt (vv. 607–8): "Innocuos dure non sit tibi perdere cure / Sitque satis diram pretendere sontibus iram." Eurydice's plight is a *casus* (v. 610) and a *causa* (v. 611). They demand that condemnation be based on proof (v. 609): "Non bene dampnatur qui non meruisse probatur." A near-contemporary text describing (satirically) legal procedures and drawing on the same vocabulary. See *Gozechini epistola ad Walcherum* 30.5.800–801; Huygens ed., 37–38.

CHAPTER 5 ★ ORPHEUS IN THE ELEVENTH CENTURY

With the doctrine of vigilance and study of lordly ways
It instructs youth in manners and guides the mature;
It constantly holds the civil laws close to the rule of moderation....
It moderates everything wisely and gently tempers all things.[19]

The softening, taming effect of Orpheus' song is answered in this passage by the moderating, tempering effect of rhetoric. In both, a king is "held to moderation in exercising the laws." Judicial pleading and poetry meet in the function of urging clemency by softening the emotions of the judge or king. This correspondence shows again that the first and second parts of the poem are knit in a unified conception. It also shows us the remarkable symbolic staging that is the highpoint of the underworld scene: poetry and music join forces with judicial rhetoric to soothe, and this makes allies of Orpheus and the residents of hell.

Orphic poetry has a civilizing mission like that of rhetoric as the educator of warriors and the temperer of royal judgment. It inspires mercy and "brings low impious rage" (v. 600: *Carminibus vatis occidit furor impietatis*). It replaces cruelty and vengefulness with love. The conception of poetry as softening and civilizing force has a long history, and the story of Orpheus and Eurydice was frequently its vehicle.[20] But the eleventh century gave a profile to this role that was not received from classical or earlier medieval sources.[21] *Orpheus and Eurydice* becomes a defining myth for the mission of the educated. Boethius mentions the softening effect of song with the casualness of a

19. "Ars docet hoc, leges tenet in moderamine reges, / Milicie gentem Mavorcia tela gerentem / Doctrina vigili studioque reformat herili, / Hoc iuvenum mores struit, instituit seniores, / Perpete mensura cohibens civilia iura. / Quatuuor ornatur virtutibus et decoratur. / Omnia discrete moderatur, cuncta quiete / Temperat...." In Boutemy, "Version," 50.

20. On Orpheus' song as a civilizing force, see Heitmann, 267–69, and in the Renaissance, Warden, 89–91, with some parallels to the eleventh-century figure. See also Warden, 90: Orphic song in its civilizing capacity is "a social and political program."

21. Ovid has no interest in this aspect of the myth. See *Metamorphoses* 10.1–63, ll.1–66. Nor does Virgil, *Georgics* 4.453–54. Quintilian, *Institutes* 1.10.9, makes of Orpheus a musician, philosopher, and poet in one, who by the power of his song *rudes quoque atque agrestes animos admiratione mulceret*. Horace, *Ars poetica* 391–93, presents him as the primal civilizer: "Silvestris homines sacer interpresque deorum / caedibus et victu foedo deterruit Orpheus, / dictus ob hoc lenire tigris rabidosque leones."

received motif (*Consolation* 3.12), though he was to treat the civilizing aspect of music at length in his *De institutione musica*. For Ovid and other classical authors, Orphic song is a producer of *mirabilia*, not a force aimed at a widely accepted social mission. The more detailed description of his civilizing power in Eusebius[22] suggests that it is a product of Christian modelling of the ancient myth. Still, this aspect virtually disappears from Merovingian and Carolingian sources. Venantius Fortunatus does not develop the civilizing force of Orphic song.[23] *Dulcedo* of poetry is the central idea. Where he exploits the obvious parallel of Orpheus in the underworld to his own mission among the barbarians, it dissolves in irony. Far from taming and civilizing them, he himself is turned into a barbarian.[24]

22. Friedman, 56–57
23. See Godman, *Poets*, 1–37.
24. Godman, *Poets*, 1. But see Cassiodorus, *Variae* 2.40.17, MGH, *Auct. ant.* 12:72: "facturus aliquid Orphei, cum dulci sono gentilium fera corda domuerit." Orpheus in Carolingian poetry has a pale, representative role as emblem of poetic excellence. Cf. Theodulf, *Carmen* 27.24–25, MGH, *Poetae* 1:491: "Rideat Orpheum Tityrus aurisonum. / Orpheus in silvis putridas tu pasce capellas, / Tityrus aulenses delicias sequitur." *Versus de eversione monasterii Glonnensis* 1–2, MGH, *Poetae* 2:147. See also, 2:642.10–11: "Dulces modos et carmina praebe, lyra Treicia, / commota quis cacumina planxere yperborea. / Montes simulque flumina ilia putent nunc Orphea, / respondeantque carmina silvae canant melliflua"; Sedulius Scotus, *Carmen* 49.9–10, MGH, *Poetae* 3:211: "Scriptor sum (fateor), sum Musicus alter et Orpheus / Sum hos triturans...." *Carmen* 68.9–10, MGH *Poetae* 3:222: "Armonicen videas melicas depromere voces, / Quam vix Orpheus Trax similare potest." The learned tradition preserves the poet's civilizing role more than the poetic. Edgar De Bruyne, *Études d'esthétique médiévale* (Bruges: Tempel, 1975), 1:211–12, cites a Carolingian commentary on Horace, *Ars Poetica*: "Cum in scripturis non invenitur Orpheus deterruisse silvestres homines, sed potius lenire tigres, posset videri fictum esse.... Cujus sit figura ostendit [poeta de Amphione]: dictus est saxa i.e., saxea corda et dura movere dulcedine cantus.... Nam fuit intentio primorum dare praecepta de moribus, ut silvestria et saxea corda redderent mollia, ut Amphion." Paschasius Radbertus, *De vita S. Adalhardi* 84; PL 120:1550A–C, gives a full paraphrase of the Orpheus story (as received from Boethius) to illustrate the futility of mourning a lost spouse. The varied and disparate character of this tradition testifies to the eleventh century's more unified conception of Orphic song.

CHAPTER 5 ✷ ORPHEUS IN THE ELEVENTH CENTURY

In short, the Orphic poem called *De nuptiis* is a reinterpreting of the educational allegory of classical Roman and later Roman learning, here representing the learning of the eleventh century. Here as in the ancient world, death is unrelenting. But in the eleventh century, the ruling mythic forces at the pinnacle of studies are lovers and both of them singers, Orpheus and Eurydice. They cannot ultimately overcome death, but they have an instrument to soften its sting, one that both of them operate with skill: poetry and song. Art is the great mitigator.

QUID SUUM VIRTUTIS: THE MONSTERS DANCE

The poem *Quid suum virtutis*[25] places the story of Orpheus between an opening section castigating contemporary vices and the decline of virtue (vv. 1–498) and a closing section offering lessons in virtue (vv. 1025–1190). The poem is a showpiece of the manneristic style of eleventh-century poetry. The placement of the Orpheus story again is significant. It is introduced to illustrate the virtues that the present age has lost. Those are study and hard work that develop art:

> *By sweating and toiling in labor joined to native art,*
> *Orpheus extricated Eurydice from the hands [of Dis].*
> *He would not have controlled the rivers or moved the stones*
> *If he had wished to languish in wanton sloth,*

25. *Quid suum virtutis: Eine Lehrdichtung des 11. Jahrhunderts*, Anke Paravicini, ed. (Heidelberg: Winter, 1980). Variously attributed to Thierry of St. Trond and Hildebert of Lavardin. The most recent editor suggests an anonymous poet writing under the pseudonym of Mamucius (possibly also Kalphurnius) and a date prior to 1043–46, based convincingly on an allusion to the poem in *"Ecbasis captivi."* See Paravicini, 8–9. Its origin remains uncertain. Manuscript distribution suggests it was most popular in southern Germany but also in Belgium and northern France. See Paravicini, 14, who conjectures (10) that it may have been written for the instruction of a prince by a member of a court chapel. It is a significant testimony to the unity of French and German school culture in the mid-eleventh century that this poem has proved so hard to locate. For Barthélemy Hauréau, *Les mélanges poétiques d'Hildebert de Lavardin* (Paris: Pedon-Lauriel, 1882), 41, it was the "most interesting and admirable work of Hildebert." Ernst R. Curtius, "Die Musen im Mittelalter," ZRPh 59 (1939): 129–88, at 183–85, found in it "die echte, wahre, widerspruchsfreie Auffassung Hildeberts von der Aufgabe der Poesie, von der Antike, vom Musendienst." A poem written in mid-century, before Hildebert's birth, possibly in Germany, can be taken by two of his most learned students as the very core of his work.

> But impelled by fervent study he composed the Muses' own odes
> And caressed and soothed all things with their beguiling tones.²⁶

Orpheus is the representative of uncorrupted "study" leading to virtue, that is, he is the embodiment of the instruction the poet offers. The text does not locate this kind of study directly at schools, but the values are those of the cathedral schools.²⁷

The effects of Orpheus' music before the descent to the underworld are described in terms familiar from the *De nuptiis*. It "soothes with its sweetness."²⁸ His muse is "sweet."²⁹ It delights and brings happiness.³⁰ It can create a variety of moods according to the temper of the mode. The "gravity of the spondee" calms anger and brings peace to the soul,³¹ though harsher tones stir rage and belligerence (vv. 795–96).

26. *Quid suum virtutis*, vv. 499–504: "Arti materne iunctum sudando laborem / Manibus extorsit Orpheus Euridicen. / Non hic frenaret fluvios, non saxa moveret, / Vellet si blande se dare desidie, / Sed studio dictante sagax dum temperat odas/ Muse demulcens omnia blandiciis." In Paravicini ed., 62.

27. Stress on "natural talent brought to fruition through learning" since Brun of Cologne. See Ruotger, *Vita Brunonis* 1, Kallfelz ed., 3; Sigebert of Gembloux, *Vita Deoderici episcopi Mettensis*, George H. Pertz ed., MGH, SS (Hannover: Hahn, 1841), 4:464.48–465.16, quoting Horace, *Carmen* 4.4.33: *Doctrina vim promovet insitam*. See also Marbod of Rennes, *Vita Licinii* 1: "bonis omnibus animae et corporis a natura ditatus, felicitatem suam virtutis studio cumulavit." In PL 171:1495B.

28. *Quid suum virtutis*, vv. 675–76: "Quem non invitat, que non precordia mulcet / Musica?"; 749–50: ...dulcedine tali / ...permulcebat; 781–82: ...ira resedit, / ...pax et adest animi; 953–56: Exhilarant umbre frontem presente Megera, / Dum lira permulcet, pena dolore caret. / Ad nectar cantus hilarescit ovans Rhadamantus, / Ridet permulsus carmine trux Eacus." In Paravicini ed., 75, 82, 84, 94.

29. *Quid suum virtutis*, vv. 677: "...pisces muti vocis dulcedine capti; 692: Dulcis eum Muse sofa fames tenuit; 721: Sic Musa dulci dulcis fuit Orpheus orbi; 749–50: Huius Musa viri mundum dulcedine tali / Dum permulcebat; 809–10: ...Musa tui, sacer Orpheu, / Tanti dulcoris extiterat superis." In Paravicini ed., 76, 77, 79, 82, 86.

30. *Quid suum virtutis*, vv. 723–24: "Tot res et tante letantur eo modulante, / Has et que vegetat musica letificat; 829–30: Leta... / Stix, qua nil umquam tristius esse potest; 943–44: Numquam / Leta prius, Charon, tua...senectus / ...gaudet; 991–92: ...Parcet...hilares." In Paravicini ed., 79, 87, 93, 96.

31. *Quid suum virtutis*, vv. 780–82: "Mox, ut spondei succinuit gravitas, / ...ira resedit, /...pax et adest animi." In Paravicini ed., 84.

CHAPTER 5 ★ ORPHEUS IN THE ELEVENTH CENTURY

But the dominant mode of music is conciliating, soothing harmony. The learned author integrates these effects into Boethian ideas of cosmic and human music:[32]

> *This man's muse, soothing and delighting the world with such sweetness,*
>
> *Shows clearly how the power of harmony tempers the essence of things,*
>
> *Reconciling dissonant things in a unanimous bond....*
>
> *And this same law of number in its moderating effect*
>
> *Couples the nature of the greater world [macrocosm] with that of the lesser [microcosm]...*
>
> *She [Harmony] joins body to soul, the things of the lower world to the supernal.*
>
> *She ornaments manners and relieves the body of its pain.*[33]

He goes on to derive humanity's inner constitution from the effect of music:

> *Since the musical temper now soothes, now irritates, and again pacifies*
>
> *The mood of the mind,*
>
> *It is more certain than certainty that humanity as a whole*
>
> *Is aptly conjoined by the tempering effect of number.* [34]

Humanity's harmonious constitution renders it susceptible to the tempering and "educating" influence of music, since the "ornament of

32. Cf. Boethius, *De institutione musica libri quinque* 1.2, Gottfried Friedlein, ed. (Frankfurt-am-Main: Minerva, 1966), 187–89. English translation with commentary and bibliography in *Anicius Manlius Severinus Boethius, Fundamentals of Music*, Calvin M. Bower, trans., introd. (New Haven, CT: Yale University Press, 1989), 9–10.

33. *Quid suum virtutis*, vv. 749–64: "Huius Musa viri mundum dulcedine tali / Dum permulcebat, esse palam dederat, / Vis armonie quia rerum temperet esse / Unanimi nodo dissona concilians,... / Et que maioris eadem moderando minoris / Naturam mundi lex copulat numeri.... / Hec anime corpus, hec federat ima supernis, / Hec mores ornat, membra dolore levat." In Paravicini ed., 82–83.

34. *Quid suum virtutis*, vv. 799–802: "Et cum nunc mulcet, nunc asperat et modo pacat / Affectum mentis musica temperies, / Certo certius est hominis subsistere totum / Apte coniungi temperie numeri." In Paravicini ed., 85.

manners" registers the body's harmonious coherence with the soul, for which song and number are responsible.

The descent to and journey through hell are powerfully described, and the representation is based on a conception as distinct and as fundamental to our topic as the corresponding scene of *De nuptiis*. Everywhere are scenes of sadness, suffering, cruelty, and inhumanity. As Orpheus passes through these dead realms singing, his music casts a magic spell, transforming rage and vengefulness into love and gentleness. The "sweetness" of his music softens hell, "destroys the Stygian law," and brings streams of tears to the eyes of the Eumenides:

> Nor is it a wonder to tell, sacred Orpheus,
>
> That your muse brought such sweet sounds to the gods.
>
> You softened the realms of hell and destroyed the law of death.
>
> At your singing the Eumenides wept.[35]

The stones themselves weep (v. 817). The poet's ebullient imagination produced a scene unique in the Orpheus myth: the music of Orpheus sets the monsters of hell dancing:

> All the monsters housed in the Stygian port
>
> Step from one leg to the other to the instruments' tune.[36]

They do not dance well (*incompositas... choreas*), but then they are not used to music (vv. 931–32). The ferryman Charon, who has never experienced a happy day in his life, grows joyful in his bitter old age and works his pole with renewed pleasure in the task:

> Old man Charon, your rough pole, never having seen a day of happiness,
>
> Now at work takes delight in its service.[37]

The raging waves themselves grow glad (v. 945). Hairy Cerberus now fawns on the poet with wags of his tail and nods of his triple-throated

---

35. *Quid suum virtutis*, vv. 809–12: "Nec mirum dictu, quod musa tui, sacer Orpheu, / Tanti dulcoris extiterat superis: / Tartara flexisti, legem Stigis annichilasti, / Te modulante madent Eumenides lacrimis." In Paravicini ed., 86.

36. *Quid suum virtutis*, vv. 921–22: "Quelibet in portu Stigio stabulantia monstra / Alternis gradibus membra movent fidibus." In Paravicini ed., 92.

37. *Quid suum virtutis*, vv. 943–44: "Numquam leta prius, Charon, tua cruda senectus / indulgens conto gaudet in obsequio." In Paravicini ed., 93.

CHAPTER 5 ✶ ORPHEUS IN THE ELEVENTH CENTURY

maw. He turns sociable and becomes the companion of the Hydra (vv. 951–52). The gloomy aspect of the shades grows cheerful (v. 953), and at the dulcet sounds of the lyre and the "nectar of the voice," pain loses its sting, Rhadamanthus grows cheerful and festive, while cruel (*trux*) Eacus, deeply moved, breaks into smiles (vv. 954–56). The king of the underworld (v. 961: *rex Tartareus*) himself sits, as though on a throne (v. 965: *In cuius media maiestas fulta tyranni*), in the middle of a black fire that overwhelms the vision[38] and leaps as a sulphurous whirlwind into the heights. Attended by Agony, Lamentation, and Horror, he feeds the guilty into his consuming fire. At the sound of Orpheus' music, the tyrant is astonished to feel how his teeth-gnashing fury is calmed, and he is transformed from his former self into a gentle creature.[39]

This remarkable scene shows us the cumulative and outbidding impulse, not merely producing poetic flotsam but engaged in the crucial moment of the poem. The guiding idea is the transformation of this entire society from savage inhumanity to courteous sociability through the agency of music. One monster after another turns into a mild-mannered courtier until the entire underworld is a festive[40] grand ballroom with the guests greeting each other affably, walking arm-in-arm, dancing, smiling, making charming and blandishing comments and gestures. If the model for hell in *De nuptiis* was the king's court dispensing law, in *Quid suum virtutis* it is the king's court as social center. The disparity of monsters behaving like nobles, comical to the modern reader, is high seriousness for the eleventh-century poet.

Finally, in an anticlimactic single line, Orpheus' wish is granted (v. 996): *Odis...empta viro redditur Euridice*. Orpheus leads her out, but

---

38. *Quid suum virtutis*, v. 963: "Excedens visum niger estuat ignis in altum" [or "leaps out of sight"?]. In Paravicini ed., 95. The urge to overwhelm is so prominent in the rest of the passage, the more powerful reading seems preferable.

39. *Quid suum virtutis*, vv. 989–90: "Miratur flecti frendens furor ipsius Orci / Mansuescendo stupens se periisse sibi." In Paravicini ed., 96.

40. Cf. *Quid suum virtutis*, vv. 919–62: "ovans Rhadamantus." In Paravicini ed., 92–94; 955. *Ovans* is the festive mood for the triumphal entry: *ovans urbem ingrederetur* (Livy 5.31); *ovans triumphavit* (Vellius Paterculus, 2.96.3). Glossing *ovo/ovans* from Lewis & Short, *Latin Dictionary*.

in this case, as opposed to the *De nuptiis*, love works against him. It forces him to look back. And so he whom no effort or exertion could conquer, is thwarted by love (v. 1008).⁴¹ Eurydice vanishes, and Orpheus is eager to return and work his marvelous effect again, taking courage from the power of his lyre, but is dissuaded by his revulsion at the thought of petitioning evil.⁴² But the divine power of song has already enabled him to win a great victory over Styx, and this shows how "art, with the mediation of fervent study, conquered nature, proving that all things yield to Lady Virtue."⁴³

LIÈGE SONGS: THE UNDERWORLD CIVILIZED

Our next text is a short poem (60 lines) from the so-called *Liège Songs*.⁴⁴ It dates from the end of the century and was written by that redoubtable "Gautier," who had ties to Marbod, Baudri of Bourgeuil,

41. The motif is from Boethius, *Consolation* 3.12.47–48.

42. *Quid suum virtutis*, vv. 1013–18: "Muse confisus rursum fidicen generosus / Squalores imi mox repetens baratri / Conciliante lira molliret saxea corda, / Placaret Parcas, flecteret Eumenides, / Deflens pulsaret, pulsando preces iteraret, / Sollers effectum nee negat ingenium." In Paravicini ed., 97. Orpheus' urge to return and engage hell again is present in Ovid, *Metamorphoses* 10.72, but is thwarted by the ferryman. The eleventh-century poet places the thwarted return in the context of a moral decision, however improbable or unheroic; the thought of hell's evil deters him. The lines leave some room for seeing here a second descent and successful rescue of Eurydice. Cf. Dronke "Return," 199, an outcome that would be more consistent with the poet's faith in powerful song and genius. It would also eliminate the awkward artifice of an Orpheus ready and willing to return but repelled by the thought of dealing with such monsters, "even bearing gifts." But the subjunctives (*molliret*, *placaret*, etc.) followed by vv. 1019–20: "Sed fugit exosus Stigios.... / Indignans supplex nequitie fieri," seem clear, and the upbeat conclusion of vv. 1022–23: "Fortiter extorsit a Stige, quod voluit. / Sic ars naturam vicit..." probably looks backwards past the poet's failure through love to the initial success through song. Read this way, the conclusion states: "What powerful song accomplished, ungovernable love undid."

43. *Quid suum virtutis*, vv. 1021–24: Numine sic artis fidens industria mentis / Fortiter extorsit a Stige, quod voluit. / Sic ars naturam vicit studio mediante / Virtuti domine cedere cuncta probans." In Paravicini ed., 98.

44. *Carmina Leodiensia* 3, Walther Bulst, ed. (Heidelberg: Winter, 1975), 1:1–47, at 11–12.

CHAPTER 5 ★ ORPHEUS IN THE ELEVENTH CENTURY

and probably was himself active at Rheims.[45] The element of study and education that played such a prominent part in both the other poems is absent. The entire poem is given over to the effects of Orpheus' song on the residents of the underworld. The ideas and the conception — transformation from cruelty to mercy and kindness — differ little from what we have observed so far. It is important for the following analysis to have the vocabulary of this transformation before us, and I will limit the discussion of this poem to pointing out the terms of what I will call from now on "Orphic discourse."

Here also, Orpheus' music is imagined as penetrating all of hell and working its magic on all its denizens (vv. 1–3)[46]: *Carmine leniti tenet Orpheus antra Cocyti /... / Carmine placavit quod quisque mali toleravit.* Where there was fury, at the sound of the song there is deep peace and quiet (c. 4): *Fit, quod erat rabies, carmine summa quies.* Those bound in chains forget their pain and anger at the love that the lyre spreads (vv. 7–8): *Immemores pene quos constrinxere catene Inmemores irae fecit amore lirae.* This Orpheus also changes the laws of hell (v. 13): *Arte lireque sanis mutavit iura Plutonis.* As he proceeds, the "dark faces and loathesome figures" whom he passes "transform their grim countenances and greet him cordially" (v. 41): *Intuitus mutant torvos blandeque salutant.* Facing the gods of the underworld, Orpheus "takes away their raging fury and alleviates the fierceness of their hearts" (v. 56): *Sic rabiem demit, sic fera corda premit.* The god of the underworld is overcome, and his "imperial command" returns Eurydice to the poet. The eleventh-century poets show an interest in representing the underworld that is unprecedented in the Orpheus tradition. They were far less interested in the fate of Eurydice than in the civilizing of hell. The conversion of Dis and his realm to kindness is the basic manifestation of Orphic poetry's functioning.

45. Maurice Delbouille, "Un mystérieux ami de Marbode: Le 'redoutable poète' Gautier," *Le Moyen Âge* 57 (1951): 205–40.

46. The seven-fold repetition of *carmine* and *carmina* in the first eight lines suggests that the poet knew Godfrey of Rheims' poem to Enguerrand of Soissons, in which an anaphora with *carmine* is sustained over five lines, and likewise the power of poetry is the theme. See André Boutemy, "Trois Oeuvres inédites de Godefroid de Reims," RMAL 3 (1947): 335-66, at 342, for vv. 99–103.

ORPHIC DISCOURSE

"Orphic" poetry has two major characteristics: it is the fulfillment of learning — liberal and ethical — and it transforms the cruel and vengeful into gentle, loving, compassionate beings. That it "conquers nature" and is an instrument in the pursuit of virtue, as the *Quid suum virtutis* depicts it, is language focused on cathedral-school learning based in large part on *cultus virtutum*, hence is consistent with poetry's role in education.

We know from sources outside the Orpheus poems that these two aspects of poetry were accepted views of its role in studies and life.[47] In this light, the lines on poetry by Ulrich of Bamberg quoted earlier have programmatic character (vv. 32–37).[48] It is a pithy and emphatic restatement of the conclusion just stated: poetry that can "soothe," "charm," or "delight" *(mulcere)*. It attests to thorough learning *(doctus ad unguem)*, and it is the high point of studies.[49] Ulrich elaborates on the effects of poetry a few lines later. His unnamed friend is known as a man of strong and kind genius:

> Who is ignorant of your brilliance?
> Who would deny the kind strain of your mind?
> For in writing sweet verses you soothe breasts,
> And you soothe as well when writing excellent prose.

47. Cf. *Tegernseer Briefsammlung* 32.9–10: "Nunc facito versus, omnis, qui scribere nosti, / Ut modo pellatur mentibus ira suis." In Strecker ed., 81. Hildebert still cultivated a poetry aimed at calming, soothing and consoling. See von Moos, *Hildebert*, 26–27: "[H.]… sieht den höchsten Sinn der Dichtung in der Vermittlung menschlicher Gunst, im Freundesdienst…. Dichtung soll 'erleichtern', die Sorgen vergessen lassen, das Dasein angenehmer machen…. [Der Dichter] hilft den anderen, beschwichtigt, bringt Ruhe und Ordnung in bedrängte und erregte Herzen."

48. See above, 207 and n. 10.

49. The *vir perfectus* is the fulfillment of moral training. Cf. Martin of Braga, *Formula vitae honestae* 6.1–2, Claude Barlowe, ed. (New Haven, CT: Yale University Press, 1950), 247; and the work of Hildebert dependent on it, *Liber de quatuor virtutibus vitae honestae*: "Quarum [namely the four virtues] se formis si mens humana coaptet, / Perfectum faciet integra vita virum." In PL 171:1055C; 171:1063B: "His… formis virtutes commemoratas / Perfectum constat reddere posse virum." See Petrus Alfonsi, *Disciplina clericalis*, prologue, Alfons Hilka and Wernher Sooerhjelm, ed. (Heidelberg: Winter, 1911), 1; Peter of Blois, Epist. 126, PL 207:377 A–B.

CHAPTER 5 ✶ ORPHEUS IN THE ELEVENTH CENTURY

With your manners you ornament these [verses],
Since your will is always bent to Good.[50]

The structure of thought is essentially the same as in the passage from Ulrich of Bamberg on the high standing of poetry in education: genius *(subtilis)* and virtue *(benignus, prona ad bonum)* are shown in poems and prose compositions that "charm and delight." Skilled poetry and virtue are again closely joined in the phrase *moribus haec ornas.* The statement is close to the basic idea of both *De nuptiis* and *Quid suum virtutis*. Ulrich is defining poetry as "Orphic" without any reference to Orpheus.

MYTH ANALYSES CONFLICT: WÜRZBURG vs WORMS AGAIN

The Würzburg school flourished in Ottonian times under Stefan of Novara, summoned from Italy to the north by Otto the Great and Poppo of Würzburg. Witness the biography of Wolfgang of Regensburg, who challenged the Italian master on interpreting Martianus Capella and caused a flap.[51] In the 1030s a "widely famed" Master Pernolf is attested. Bishop Heribert of Eichstätt called on him to test the qualifications of a school master whose learning he doubted. Apart from the poem in question and a few letters spun off from it in the Worms letter collection, there is total obscurity. That is the condition of the eleventh-century German schools, and a brilliant light like this polemical poem and the responding letters shows that documentation depends on chance, and behind the lack of it is a vital school life. Orphic poetry is not an aesthetic idea separable from social circumstances and moral obligations. The concept as the eleventh-century schools developed it analyses situations of conflict. That is, those who observed and described conflict themselves called on the Orpheus myth to articulate conflict and resolution.

50. Ulrich of Bamberg, *Arts dictandi*, ll. 56–62: "...quis te subtilem nesciat esse? / Ingenii venam tibi quis neget esse benignam? / Nam versus dulces scribendo pectora mulces, / Mulces egregie scribens metri sine lege. / Moribus haec ornas, cum sit tibi prona voluntas / Semper ad omne bonum...." In *Eine Bamberger Ars Dictandi*, Franz Bittner, ed., *Historischer Verein für die Pflege der Geschichte des ehemaligen Fürstbistums Bamberg* 100 (1964): 145–71, at 156.

51. See Otloh of S. Emmeram, *Vita S. Wolfkangi* 4–5, Georg Waitz ed., MGH, SS 4 (Hannover: Hahn, 1841), 528.

The poem glorifying the Würzburg school cited earlier[52] is a response to some students of Worms, who in the autumn of 1030 wrote a poem criticizing the school at Würzburg and its master and extolling their own.[53] It may well have begun as an exercise in composition,[54] but it took the form of a taunt and quickly turned serious. Several other letters in the Worms collection illuminate the aftermath, and they leave no doubt that the poem was at the center of a storm that had unpleasant results (for the Worms perpetrators, it seems), and not merely a literary squabble with no social implications.[55]

The passages that interest us juxtapose the peace of the Würzburg school with the hell of contentiousness at Worms. The poet depicts Würzburg as an Elysian realm of studies, an academy of poetry and virtue, its students and master a harmonious community knit together as if "by a single vow" (v. 46). They lead a *dolce vita* of peacefulness and friendship:

> *Are you not aware of the sweet life we lead here,*
>
> *Everywhere pacified, surpassed by none?*[56]

The students are "happy" about their teacher (v. 49: *de principe letus*); with "subtle care he keeps watch over his flock" (v. 42: *Cura subtili proprio vigilabit ovili*) and makes moderate use of the rod (v. 25). He does not despise the less-gifted in favor of the talented students (v. 44). When the sons of nobles win his love, submission to his tutelage does them no dishonor (vv. 57–58). His word brings the "joys of life" (v. 52). The poet wishes him "who is replete with virtue,"

52. See above, 205 n. 10.

53. *Ältere Wormser Briefsammlung*. Walter Bulst ed., MGH, Bdk 3. On the Würzburg school, in addition to the literature in n. 10 above, see above 23 n. 14; Rudolf Blank, *Weltdarstellung und Weltbild in Würzburg und Bamberg vom 8. bis zum Ende des 12. Jahrhunderts* (Bamberg: Historischer Verein, 1968), 47–75; Zielinski, *Reichsepiskopat*, 86–87.

54. Cf. the comment of the perpetrators at Worms, *Ältere Wormser Briefsammlung*, Epist. 15: "...litem, quam cum Herbipolensibus exercitii causa habuimus." In Bulst ed., 32.

55. Cf. *Ältere Wormser Briefsammlung*. Epist. 15, 25, 26, 42; Bulst ed., 31–32, 46–49, 77–79.

56. Vv. 108–9: "An nos mellitam nescis hic ducere vitam, / Undique pacatos et de nullis superatos?" In Bulst ed., 122.

CHAPTER 5 ★ ORPHEUS IN THE ELEVENTH CENTURY

serenity and prosperity. "May he remain safe from all harm," and may he rejoice, "having shed all sad...things," secure on all sides; and may he enjoy the far-famed joys of true peace:

Replete in virtue let him be serene in prosperity,
The future can bring nothing harmful.
Having shed all sad things, he rejoices in the general peace,
Now let the vaunted joys of true peace be his.[57]

The Worms poet has stormed into this citadel of love as a raging enemy of peace. He is a "sower of wrath and destroyer of friendships" (v. 105: *sator irarum et destructor amicitiarum*), filled with "frenzied rage, mad with the love of Mars" (vv. 141–42: *bacharis... /... / Martis amore furendo*). He has fomented between them the "discord of dire wrath" (v. 130: *ire... discordia dire*). His "message of contention" (v. 107: *nuncia litis*) disturbs the "sweet life of Würzburg" and the peace that rules on all sides (vv. 105–9). The peace-breaker's penchant to anger, rage, and combat is consistent with the studies at his school, the poet claims. At Worms they worship "spiritual monsters" (v. 206). They lack all art and put their faith in the quarrels of Mars (v. 207). They call back to life the gods of the underworld (v. 213: *Inferni divos... redivivos*) and prefer their worship to the society of the living under the "law of instruction" (vv. 211–12: *ius documenti*). They worship the "black demons" who while they live are engaged in "constant contentions" (vv. 224–25). They will never prevail in the present combat, "even though the prince of the underworld himself should leave hell and rush to render them aid."[58]

57. Vv. 64–67: "Virtutum plenus sit prosperitate serenus, / Nil eventurum cui quod maneat nociturum, / Tristibus exutus letetur et undique tutus, / Gaudia veracis sibi sint celeberrima pacis." In Bulst ed., 121.

58. Vv. 269–70: "Nos non devinces, licet Inferni tibi princeps/ Infernum linquat, sic auxiliando propinquat." In Bulst ed., 127. The reproach translates into an attack on the excessive study of the classics at Worms. A student of Mainz, writing to his colleagues at Worms in the following year to refuse the requested support in their continuing conflict with Würzburg, makes an ironic reference to this reproach in his salutation. See *Ältere Wormser Briefsammlung*, Epist. 26: "Eximie iuventuti Wormatiensium, insudanti studiis et artibus Atheniensium, R. Mogontinus non Grecus, sed vix effectus Latinus, amicitiam indivulsam, fidem inconcussam." In Bulst ed., 48. The letter is filled with sarcasm and Schadenfreude at the straits of the Worms students.

We are suddenly in the underworld scene of the Orpheus myth, though there has been no signal of the scene change nor any reference to that story. The "sower of wrath" has chosen to revive the gods of hell, those whom the law of Pluto has condemned to the dragon's jaw, but there is no resonating lyre to soften his (Pluto's) anger. No pleading can rescue those who enter his kingdom:

> *Why will you choose the revived gods of the underworld?*
> *Whom the law of Pluto has damned to the dragon's jaw.*
> *No sounding lyre can soften their anger.*
> *Whoever he admits to this place cannot be redeemed at any price.*[59]

The Worms poet is caught in the hell of contention that he has created and has no soothing lyre and no redeeming Orpheus[60] to soften the rage of the beasts he consorts with. Wrathful contentiousness is stylized as a descent to the underworld. Hell is the place of anger, fury, and war. The poet could evoke the story without telling it. The circumstances themselves called for an Orpheus.[61]

If there is an Orpheus in the poem, it is the Würzburg poet. His foe is in the position of Eurydice, caught in hell and locked into the law of Pluto. It takes an Orpheus with his *Lyra concilians* to redeem him. The poet implies but does not state this interpretation. The roles into which he has cast himself and his adversary suggest that that model guided his conception: he is the peacemaker and reconciler. Having railed against the war-like posture of Worms, he makes an extravagant offer of peace:

> *Now let the discord and cruel anger between us fade.*
> *Let us shun war and become joined as twins in our love.*
> *A bond like that of David and Jonathan will join us.*
> *No cruelty will disturb us now or ever more.*

59. Vv. 213–16: "Inferni divos cur optabis redivivos? / Quos lex Plutonis damnavit fauce draconis, / Non resonante lira cuius mulcebitur ira, / Quicquid hic acceptat, nullius iam prece reddat." In Bulst ed., 126.

60. This may well reiterate the contempt the Würzburger feels for his foe as a poet. Cf. vv. 143–48; Bulst ed., 123.

61. The early date of the poem can put to rest any reservation about the advent of the Orpheus figure in the capacity as restorer of peace and love. The indirectness of the treatment suggests this interpretation of the myth is well known.

CHAPTER 5 ✦ ORPHEUS IN THE ELEVENTH CENTURY

*Those caught up in unending quarrels will marvel
To see such a friendship between us.*[62]

This posture of unquestioning forgiveness of wrongs, overlooking of insults, restoration of peace and friendship with no sense of vengefulness was an admired one. The poet is showing his *mansuetudo*.[63] That is the reconciling oil he pours forth to sooth this dispute. His own poem is the bringer of it. The final lines represent the poet as the redeemer of his wrathful colleague at Worms, sowing seeds of peace in the divine field by his song and praying for aid from God, "by whose gifts I master the melody of reason."[64] This poem shows us actual social circumstances that commended the figure of Orpheus as a representative of peace and conciliation. Peace, friendship, love in cathedral schools was a sacred law. To violate it is serious.[65]

---

62. Vv. 130–35: "Inter nos ire fugiat discordia dire, / Expertes belli nos simus amore gemelli, / Fedus Davidis mecum Ionatheque subibis, / Nil nosmet sevum conturbet nunc et in evum. / Multum mirantur nam, talia cum speculantur, / Sunt qui cum rixis nobis in pignore fixis." In Bulst ed., 123. The last line is confusing. See Strecker's and Bulst's puzzlement in their editions, 130, resp. 123. But the sense is fairly clear: many who are held hostage in their disputes will marvel at the model of conciliatory restraint and loving friendship these two provide, having been transformed from bitter enemies to a David and Jonathan.

63. See Jaeger, *Origins*, 36–42, 149–50, 198–99.

64. Vv. 273–79: "Istic prescriptum metrico modulamine dictum, / Cum precor eius opem necnon venerabile nomen, / De cuius donis modulo fungor rationis, /… / Nobis ductores verbi dum posco satores/ Agrum divinum plantantes semine primum." In Bulst ed., 127.

65. The later letters addressing the conflict at Würzburg suggest some legal action was taken, at least threatened, against the perpetrators. See *Ältere Wormser Briefsammlung*, Epist. 25, Bulst ed., 46–47. Another case of anger reproved is that of Wazo of Liège protesting the tyrannical rule of Provost John at Liège c.1021–25 by quitting his post as schoolmaster and writing a strong letter. But the future bishop was the loser in the conflict. John made representations to Bishop Durandus, calling Wazo a contumacious hot-head (*iracundus, obstinatio iracundiae*) and attributing Wazo's protest to his contentiousness (*studio litigii*). John's position carried the day, even though he was accused of inciting local wine merchants to set the dormitory on fire in order to kill Wazo. See Anselm of Liège, *Gesta episcoporum Leodiensium*, 211–15.

STARVING STUDENTS IN HELL

The Würzburg poem is not the only case in which a breach of claustral tranquility conjured Orpheus as the reconciler. Two letters from the Hannover collection show us the same logic at work. The first is written between 1054 and 1079 by a group of students residing at the Hildesheim cathedral school, evidently as guests *(hospites)*, not members of the chapter. They are starving. In their salutation, they sign themselves "famished men whose flesh barely clings to their bones" and wish Bishop Hezilo "the satiety of celestial grace, full of the bread of life."[66] They play changes on their hunger, describing the physical effects in detail. They compare themselves to the tortured in hell, except that their own tortures are worse:

> ...we see ourselves as more miserable than Tantalus, unable to reach the feasts fit for a king placed before him; more cursed than Ixion bound to an ever-turning wheel; more harshly condemned than Sisyphus pushing his stone uphill again and again only to have it fall back; more gravely punished than Tition whose liver grew back each time an insatiable vulture gnawed on it; and in every way [we see] our bodies delivered over to the pains of hell.[67]

They beg the bishop to release them from "the jaws of hell." Having set up the bishop for the role either of Pluto or Orpheus, they end discreetly by casting themselves as Orpheus pleading for Bishop Hezilo before God. Just as the lyre of Orpheus liberated "Erudicen" from hellish creatures who know no forgiveness, they pray that "the cithara of their devotion" will win from God whatever Hezilo wishes.[68]

66. *Briefsammlungen der Zeit Heinrichs 4*, Epist. 27: "Domno patri et episcoporum dignissimo H. famelici et vix herentes ossibus Hiltinisheimensium scholarum hospites uberem celestis gratie sacietatem, plenam panis vivi, qui est Christi, refectionem." In Erdmann and Fickermann ed., 61. The editors identify *vix herentes ossibus* as an echo of Virgil, *Eclogues* 3.102.

67. Epist. 27: "...videmur nobis Tantalo apud inferos antepositas regales epulas tangere non auso miseriores, Ixione rote volubili astricto calamitosiores, Sisipho saxum iam iamque relapsurum volvente magis damnati, Titione, cuius renascens iecur insaciabilis vultur rodit, gravius puniti et omnino adhuc in corpore Penis infernalibus traditi." In Erdmann and Fickermann ed., 62.

68. Epist. 27: "Si Erudicen ab inferis ignoscere nescientibus Orphei liberaverat lira, quelibet optanda benedictissime tue anime apud Dominum impetrabit nostre devotionis cythara." In Erdmann and Fickermann ed., 63.

CHAPTER 5 ★ ORPHEUS IN THE ELEVENTH CENTURY

A CRUEL BISHOP AND A MEEK ABBOT

A letter written in 1074 from Walo, abbot of St. Arnulf in Metz to Archbishop Manasses of Rheims, is not so discreet.[69] The unhappy abbot heaps vituperation on the archbishop who has wronged him. The substance of his complaints is not relevant, just the phrasing and concepts. He grieves for the errors of Manasses, as is appropriate to anyone moved by the "affection of true love." He has grieved far more for the "ragings" of his injurer than for the injuries done himself. He shudders to recall the misery he has suffered under the archbishop's "barbarous rule" *(barbaro dominio)*. He declines to enumerate the threats and the curses he has received from Manasses. Had he been anything but a simple fool, he would not have come to so "ungentle, so cruel, so violent, so monstrous a beast" *(ad te tam inmitem tam trucem tam violentam tam inmanem bestiam)*.

Manasses has had the nerve to suggest that Walo, being "a peaceful, humble and quiet man" *(pacificum, humilem, et quietum)* and constantly given to reading, is not comfortable with the "French manners" of Manasses. Only a monster barren of all virtue, Walo says, could imagine a life tempered by peace, modesty and sobriety to be lower in virtue than one given to harsh and bold combat. The rehearsal of the archbishop's complaints against Walo continues: peace weakens the spirits of the powerful, while combat strengthens the weak and idle. But, Walo replies, Cicero has shown the superiority of the toga to weapons.

The opposition of peaceful, gentle Walo to fierce and barbarous Manasses gives the structure that invokes Orpheus. Walo says he has tried to mitigate the fury of Manasses by citing Scripture and "celestial words":

> How often have I administered the medicine of the Scriptures to you! How often have I tried to mitigate your fury with, as it were, songs of celestial speech. How often have I striven to expel or placate with the lyre of David rather than that of Orpheus, that demon that vexes you![70]

---

69. Epist. 108; Erdmann and Fickermann ed., 182–85. On Walo's conflict with Manasses, see Manitius, *Geschichte*, 2:724–25, also John R. Williams, "Manasses I of Rheims and Gregory VII," AHR 54 (1949): 804–24, at 809–10.

70. Epist. 108: "O quotiens adhibui tibi medicamina scripturarum! quotiens celestibus verbis quasi quibusdam carminibus tuum temptavi mitigare furorem!

The rejection of the "Thracian cithara" only confirms the appropriateness of Orpheus in the circumstances. It is a gesture, like the "rejection of the muses" in invocations[71] that christianizes a domain legitimately occupied by the classical tradition and in so doing concedes a strong sense of obligation to what it rejects. Through its isolation the reference to the harp of David illustrates how accepted was the jurisdiction of Orpheus in the correction of *furor* and *saevitia*. David curing Saul would have had a higher degree of legitimacy, but the Old Testament singer is seldom invoked as a soother of royal anger, though his poetry is often compared to that of Orpheus.[72]

Sigebert of Gembloux gives us a second example of Christian superseding Orphic opposition to violence and rage in his *Passio Thebeorum* (c.1070).[73] He represents Emperor Maximian as the raging king (1.10, l. 613): *nec civilis multum, nec amicus amicis;* (ll. 617–18); *Est trux ira animos... / Nunquam corde reses, ceu mansuescens leo deses;* (l. 621) *ferox et naturaliter atrox;* (l. 627) *barbaricus sensus.*[74] He commands the (Christian) Theban legion to slaughter the foe (a rebel Gallic tribe and Christians) mercilessly:[75] *nec vos miseratio flectat. / Non sit qui pareat, nullus sit qui miserescat.* In a speech full of fine ironies,[76] the emperor's speaker warns the (converted) legion against the dangers of Christianity: their God is taking over, snatching the

---

quotiens non Treicia sed Davitica cythara conatus sum illud vel expellere vel sedare demonium, quo vexaris!" In Erdmann and Fickermann ed., 183.

71. See Curtius, "Die Musen."

72. On the comparison see Friedman, 148–55; Dronke, "Return," 206–8; Prigent, 205–21; the dense and informative study of Eleanor Irwin, "The Songs of Orpheus and the New Songs of Christ," in Warden, *Orpheus*, 51–62; Fabrizio Visconti, "Un fenomeno di continuita iconografica: Orfeo citaredo, Davide salmista, Cristo pastore, Adamo e gli animali," *Augustinianum* 28 (1988): 429–36. Walo is the only monk quoted so far. It may be that in monastic communities the Old Testament figure was the preferred calmer of rage. Also noteworthy for its omission in favor of Orpheus in hell is Christ harrowing hell. Cf. Dronke, "Return," 208.

73. Dümmler ed., 1–125. See above, 200 n. 27.

74. Dümmler ed., 65–66; cf. *Passio Thebeorum* 3, ll. 204–97 ("*De furore Cesaris*"); Dümmler ed., 101–3.

75. *Passio Thebeorum* 2. ll. 36–37; Dümmler ed., 72.

76. *Passio Thebeorum* 2. ll. 25–159; Dümmler ed., 71–75.

CHAPTER 5 ✷ ORPHEUS IN THE ELEVENTH CENTURY

trident from Neptune, etc. Soon he will command the underworld — rightly so, since Dis, harder than stone, is deaf to the pleas and blind to the tears of the wretched. Dis could not even be softened by the tearful songs of Orpheus and refused to grant the life of Eurydice:

> Pluto, whose hardness rivals stones of diamond,
> Could not be persuaded by the tearful songs of Orpheus,
> Songs that moved tigers, stony cliffs and torrential rivers,
> To give over the life of Euridyce to the singer.[77]

But "this new fellow Jesus"[78] hears the pleas of all and has compassion for all, even to the point of returning the dead to life.

This is the only version known to me in which Eurydice is not saved even once and in which the song of Orpheus fails to soften Dis/Pluto. Sigebert obviously required an inflexible king and a thwarted Orpheus in order to create a space for a Christ whose redeeming mission overcame the ineffectual pagan means of arousing mercy. This shows how casually variable and governed by authorial intention the fate of Eurydice is. The purpose of the individual author can override tradition and the momentum that holds the conventional elements of a story in place ("*Stoffzwang*").

This section looked at the Orpheus story as a structuring myth for conflict in actual social-political circumstances. Sigebert's *Passio Thebeorum* helps establish the point even though it is an imaginative narrative poem. The same narrative metaphor was at the disposal of any learned cleric who conceptualized conflict situations. It gave a powerful analogue to the learned peacemaker, softening the rage of rulers no matter what the ultimate success.

A CIVILIZING FORCE: SOOTHING THE ANGER OF KINGS

The soothing and civilizing role of verse was more than a conceit of school poetry.[79] Orphic discourse formulated important duties

---

77. *Passio Thebeorum* 2. ll. 67–70: "Pluto duritia vincens adamantina saxa, / Non potuit flecti lacrimosis cantibus Orphei, / Quis tygres, rupes, silvas flectebat et amnes, / Ut daret Euridicis vitam pretium modulanti." In Dümmler ed., 72–73.
78. *Passio Thebeorum* 2. l. 64: "hic novus Iesus." In Dümmler ed., 72.
79. See Jaeger, *Envy*, 153–57 for "Orphics."

and ideals of secular clergy: restraining and soothing the anger of princes and rulers, making peace, effecting reconciliations, teaching civilized manners to knights, nobles, kings, and — when the occasion warranted — to archbishops. "Mitigating the fury of kings" is mentioned as a matter of praise in Carolingian sources,[80] though it is not common, and Orpheus is not associated with it. Gerbert of Aurillac formulated the task programmatically. He strikes the Ciceronian posture that the art of speaking well must be inseparable from the art of living well. The necessity for combining good speaking and good living is the "mitigating" task of the government minister:

> For us who are occupied in affairs of state both are necessary, for apposite speech aimed at persuasion and at using soothing oratory to restrain from attack the minds of those who are enraged is of the highest value.[81]

Students of medieval rhetoric would do well, I believe, to take a serious detour into the tenth and eleventh centuries to investigate closely a form of rhetoric of such high standing that it merits a place alongside the ancient purpose of rhetoric: *persuasio* and *suavis oratio* that softens raging minds. That the most prominent intellectual of the tenth century can name that pair as having "the highest value" in "affairs of state" should suffice to stir up interest in understanding it, its context, and the discourse that grows up around it.

The discourse of fury and anger mollified was present in the tenth century, and the one whose charisma had peacemaking force was an admired ideal. Ruotger says that Brun of Cologne was born to be a peacemaker, just at the time when his father had "tamed the savageness of the barbarians" *(perdomita barbarorum sevicia)*, turned back the danger of internal strife," and proceeded to rebuild a relatively peaceful kingdom. Brun always cultivated peace "as if it

---

80. Cf. Walahfrid Strabo, *In Natalem S. Mammetis Hymnus* Stanzas 5–6: "Mitis domans immitia, Adiutus armis spiritus / illisque promens mystica, / vicit furores principum, / Vivebat inter bestias, saevi draconis conterens/ quo cive gaudent angeli. / sacris caput conatibus." In Ernst Dümmler, ed. MGH, *Poetae* 2 (Berlin: Weidmann, 1884), 296.

81. *Briefsammlung Gerberts von Reims*, Epist. 44: "...nobis in re publica occupatis utraque necessaria. Nam et apposite dicere ad persuadendum et animos furentium suavi oratione ab impetu retinere summa utilitas." In Weigle ed., 73.

CHAPTER 5 ✶ ORPHEUS IN THE ELEVENTH CENTURY

were the nourishing force and crown of all other virtues." He believed that tranquillity was the atmosphere that strengthens virtue, while strife weakens it.[82]

The first abbot of Gembloux, Erluin (d.987), was described by his contemporary the monk Richarius in verses transmitted by Sigebert of Gembloux as the embodiment of the peacemaking task:[83]

> Who could possibly tell how patient, how sweet and how kind he was at all times? For being the placid man that he was, he softened the hearts of the irascible, calling them out of their savagery into the manners of peace. Soothing in conversation, modest with amazing gravity, not abrasive, not harsh, not violent.... If he saw someone in grief, or sadness, or mourning, he came to their aid with a father's affection, soothing grieving hearts with sweet words.

It is not likely that this early portrait drew even indirectly on the image of Orpheus doing with his song what the abbot did with his speech and his mere presence. But the language dramatically shows the affinities between a clerical ideal and the Orpheus myth. More likely this language of the civilizing and peace-bringing personality

82. Ruotger, *Vita Brunonis* 2; Kallfelz ed., 182–84. Brun's *pietas* renders battle-hardened men war-shy and timid. See *Vita Brunonis* 25: "...quos nulla umquam acies, nulla inflexit asperitas, hos huius viri pietas inbelles et timidos faciebat. [The mere sound of his name put an end to wars, ushered in peace and established the study of the arts]: ...nominis quoque eius fama, quousque pervenit, bella sedaret, pacem formaret, studium in omnibus bonis artibus firmaret." In Kallfelz ed., 216. *Vita Brunonis* 18 and 19; Kallfelz ed., 202–6, show Brun attempting to pacify and reconcile Otto the Great's rebellious son Liudolf. It is the orator (204: *vir bonus, dicendi peritus*) at its Ottonian best, working to mitigate the fury (Liudolf is possessed by an "Erinye") of princes with the suasions of eloquence — the ideal function of the statesman as Gerbert had formulated it. See above, 35 n. 47, 107 n. 39, 232 n. 81.

83. Sigebert of Gembloux, *Gesta abbatum Gemblacensium* 3, Georg H. Pertz, ed. MGH, SS 8 (Hannover: Hahn, 1848), 524, 32–42. On the text, see Wilhelm Wattenbach and Robert Holtzmann, *Deutschlands Geschichtsquellen im Mittelalter: Deutsche Kaiserzeit* 1 (Tübingen: Matthiesen, 1948), 149 and n. 220. Cf. the commemorative lines by Eugenius Vulgarius (southern Italy, c.911), vv. 104–8: "... Johannes / Inferior nulli veterum probitate priorum, / Cuius in octonis mundus suffragia clamat / Quatinus indomitas evi demulceat iras / Ingentesque animi curarum mitiget estus." In Paul Mayvaert, ed.,"A Metrical Calendar by Eugenius Vulgarius," AB 84 (1966): 349–77, at 364.

233

was pre-formed in clerical and monastic circles close to the Cluny reform[84] and then appropriated in the cathedral schools with their stress on poetry and classical learning to describe the music of Orpheus.

Fulbert of Chartres seems to have radiated the effect of soothing tinged with friendship and love implied in *mulcere*. He received a letter from his disciple Hildegar asking that the master correct his student's vice of anger, since Fulbert "emits the sweetest fragrance of mature holiness" through his virtues.[85] We see Fulbert at work in this capacity in his letter to King Robert the Pious restraining his anger against Bishop Odolricus of Orleans.[86] In Fulbert this clerical obligation connects with engagement in the Peace movement. His poem in praise of peace shows how close the conception of a new civilization based on law, moderation, and restraint was to goals of the Peace movement.[87] It would be surprising if that movement did not call on the image of the soothing, calm-restoring peacemaker mollifying the raging of barbarians. But this language is nowhere in evidence in the legislation of Peace and Truce, though sermons and orations could draw on it.[88] With his rough warrior ways Archbishop

---

84. Odo of Cluny praises Gerald of Aurillac for exercising this influence in Aurillac in his *Vita Geraldi* 4.8: "Incolae autem regionis illius mores valde ferinos habere solebant, sed aliquantulum exemplo vel reverentia sancti hominis esse mitiores videntur." In PL 133:700D. Passage cited by Thomas Bisson, "The Organized Peace in Southern France and Catalonia, c.1140–c.1233," AHR 82 (1977): 290–307, at 292.

85. *Letters and Poems of Fulbert of Chartres*, Epist. 95: "...te propter mores tuos matura sanctitate suavissime redolentes erga tibi subditos eo animo esse intelligo, ut bonos sinceri amoris gratia conplectaris." In Behrends ed., 172.

86. Fulbert, Epist. 94; Behrends ed., 170–71. Peter Damian is going about the same duty in his tract *De frenanda ira et simultatibus exstirpandis*, PL 145:649–60. Cf. also the example of Thierry of St. Hubert and Manasses of Rheims. See n. 69 above.

87. Fulbert, *Carmen* 149: "Ad normam redigit qui subdita secla pravitati, / Potens novandi sicut et creandi, /.../ Iam proceres legum racionibus ante desueti / Quae recta discunt strenue capessunt." In Behrends ed., 262–63.

88. This observation is based on a reading of the sources in Ludwig Huberti, *Studien zur Rechtsgeschichte der Gottesfrieden und Landfrieden* (Ansbach: C. Brügel, 1892); and on the documents in MGH, *Leges* 4, *Constitutiones* 1, Ludwig Weiland, ed. (Hannover: Hahn, 1893), 596–617. That the contemporary commentary on legislation and its ends

CHAPTER 5 ✶ ORPHEUS IN THE ELEVENTH CENTURY

Manasses I of Rheims seems to have brought out this quality in the gentler clergy around him. The biographer of Abbot Thierry of St. Hubert in Ardennes, writing c.1090, describes Thierry's soothing effect on Manasses:[89]

...by nature, and by [acquired] manners he was more fierce than appropriate, but he [Abbot Thierry] behaved to him in so laudable a way that he made him his friend.... So, he put aside his harsh ways to a great extent at his admonitions.... Though to many he was frequently ungentle and truculent, to this man alone...he was always gentle and placid.

This complex of concerns comes together in Bern of Reichenau's letters to Henry III praising him as peacemaker.[90] In a letter written before 1044, he explained to the king the significance of his royal title:

could draw on Orphic discourse is evident in a speech of Archbishop Guido of Vienne in the Council of Langres (1116): *Concilium Lingonense* (Paris: Imprimerie Nationale, 1877), 223; and Joannes Dominicus Mansi, *Sacrorum Conciliorum Nova et amplissima Collectio* 21 (Venice: Zatta, 1776), 159. Guido's speech to open the council lamented the depradations on the Church. The effect of his speech, delivered in *mellita oratione:* "His et huiuscemodi declamatis a viro facundissimo coepere audientium mitescere pectora et in pacis modestiae que velle concurrere sacramenta." In Huberti ed., 430. See also the speech of this same Guido (Pope Calixtus II) at the council of Rheims (1119), after hearing much bickering and contention from a host of complainants in *The Ecclesiastical History of Orderic Vitalis* 12.21, Marjorie Chibnall, ed. and trans. (Oxford: Clarendon, 1978) 6:262; cited also by Huberti, 431–32.

89. *Vita Theoderici abbatis Andaginensis* 20: "...natura et moribus plus quam oporteret ferus, propter laudabilem conversationem eius sibi amicum eum fecerat.... Multum ergo feritatis ab eo admonitus deposuit et cum pluribus esset frequenter immitis et truculentus, huic uni... semper fuit mitis et placidus." In Wilhelm Wattenbach ed., MGH, SS 12 (Hannover: Hahn, 1856), 49.9–14. The biographer wrongly takes Manasses' predecessor Gervasius to be the object of this pacifying activity. On the error, see Williams, "Manasses I," 806 n. 7. Walo, abbot of St. Arnulf in Metz in accepting the abbacy of St. Remi, let his good judgment be overruled by the prospect of "tempering the truculence" of Manasses (cf. PL 150:879–80, at 879D) and sought to transform his "canine manners," "savageness of mind," and "bestiality of manners" into "most gentle charity and charitable gentleness." See above, 229–30; and *Briefsammlungen der Zeit Heinrichs IV.*, Epist. 108, Erdmann and Fickermann ed., 183.

90. Schmale ed., 55–64. For commentary, see Karl Schnith, "Recht und Friede: Zum Königsgedanken im Umkreis Heinrichs III.," *Historisches Jahrbuch* 81 (1962): 22–57.

235

The authority of the ancients states clearly that those who are now called kings once were called tyrants because of the cruel ferocity of their manners. But as their zeal for sacred religion grew, they were called kings [rulers] from "right rule" [*recte regendo*]. They had shown themselves rational by suppressing their bestial passions and showing power of judgment.[91]

This shift to reasonable rule occurs "as the zeal of religion grows" (*crescente sacrae religionis studio*).[92] It is a significant connection. It indicates the clergy's sense of being engaged in a mission of civilizing the laity that registers in many sources in the eleventh and twelfth centuries.[93] Bern's letters in praise of Henry III as peacemaker show the language of the Peace movement and that of instruction in *mores* intersecting. In a later letter,[94] Bern praises the king for uniting in his own heart mercy and truth, justice, and peace (an echo of Ps. 84:11). These unions have created a kingdom so peaceful and harmonious as the world has never seen (57). He compares Henry with King David, who was *mitis, humilis, mansuetus* (59, cf. 60). He addresses the king as *omnium regum... mitissime*. Henry is the imitator of David cutting the piece from Saul's mantle and refusing to raise his sword against his enemy, since, "not only do you love your enemies, you gather together all in your kingdom within a bond of love and peace."[95] The concord of his kingdom invites comparison with the period of Christ's birth, Bern continues. Henry takes no vengeance against those who have wronged him, and with "marvelous charity"

91. Bern, Epist. 26: "Veterum satis declarat auctoritas, quod hi, qui nunc reges dicuntur, olim ob crudelem morum ferocitatem tyranni vocabantur, sed crescente sacrae religionis studio reges appellati sunt a recte regendo, dum bestiales motus comprimunt et per discretionis vim se rationales ostendunt." In Schmale ed., 55.

92. Schmale cites Isidore, *Etymologiae* 9.3.19–20, as Bern's source for this etymology, but it is evident from Isidore's passage that the idea of a transition from barbarity to reason inspired by "sacred religion" is Bern's addition.

93. See Jaeger, *Origins*, 211–35. I now believe that the Peace movement was a vital precursor of medieval courtliness, as has been argued by Georges Duby, *Hommes et structures au moyen âge* (Paris: Flammarion, 1973), 227–40.

94. Epist. 27; Schmale ed., 56–64.

95. "...cum non solum inimicos diligitis, verum etiam omnes in regno vestro sub uno karitatis et pacis vinculo constringitis." In Schmale ed., 59.

CHAPTER 5 ✸ ORPHEUS IN THE ELEVENTH CENTURY

he favors, aids, and restores them. Bern "loves" the king for these qualities "There is nothing in this life more cheerful, more dear, more loveable, since good cheer reigns in the kingdom while peace and concord persist" (60). The monk of Reichenau, Bern, never mentions the peacemaker Orpheus, but the peacemaker David and the Prince of Peace he prefigures play that role. Again, we see that the structure of Orphic discourse is present before that figure entered it, an appropriation that had already taken place at Würzburg.

RUODLIEB

The obligation to soothe and calm the ruler is at work in the Latin romance-epic *Ruodlieb*. This remarkable work, written between 1042 and 1070, survives as an extensive fragment. It has scenes of adventure, court life and manners, court intrigue, romance and love. It is also significantly connected with goals of the Peace movement, including what appears a clear allusion to amnesties given by Henry III.[96] There are scenes of court life and ceremony in which the atmosphere is jovial, free of anger, resentment, and self-assertion. There is gaiety and amiability among members of the court, low and high. Ruodlieb's personal qualities are tailored to this atmosphere. He is *mitis* and *benignus* (v. 400), "ready to serve and in all things well mannered, envious of none, and dear to all," the king's "most beloved" and "dearest of all the retinue" (vv. 419–22).[97] The atmosphere of the king's court is determined by *amor* and *clementia*.[98] The king whom Ruodlieb serves, called *rex maior*, thanks his "kind and gentle" courtier for dispelling his anger (vv. 405–7). Even the tamed wild animals that teem the court become representatives of the civilizing power of virtue. Likewise, the king's generous and merciful treatment of his conquered adversary illustrates the nobility of not seeking revenge but reconciling enemies

96. See Karl Hauck, "Heinrich III. und der Ruodlieb," PBB 70 (1948): 372–419.

97. "...promptus eras et in omni morigerebas; / Hinc habeo grates tibi, dilectissime, grandes. / Invidus es nulli sed plebi karus es omni / ...karissime cunctigenorum" (v. 421). In Vollmann ed., 103. Here *invidus* seems to be preferable to Vollmann's conjecture *gravis*.

98. See Jaeger, *Origins*, 168–73; and Helena M. Gamer, "Studien zum Ruodlieb," ZfdA 88 (1957/58): 249–66.

237

through friendship and love and invites comparison with the court and the legislation of Henry III.[99]

"Soothing the anger of the king" was not a minor bit of personal royal psychological counseling but rather a fundamental way of doing business, accomplishing personal and political goals. This was suggested in Gerbert's comment that the soothing oratory of the government minister is *nobis in re publica occupatis...necessaria* and *summa utilitas*. There is good testimony to Orphic discourse functioning in royal business.[100] In this context it may be that the king's "anger" at its palest is little more than a way of saying that he refuses a request. The language of royal favor or disfavor is a language

---

99. Ruodlieb, *Faksimile-Ausgabe des Codex Latinus Monacensis 19486 der Bayerischen Staatsbibliothek München und der Fragmente von St. Florian 2.1. Kritischer Text*, Benedikt Vollmann, ed. (Wiesbaden: Reichert, 1985), 103.

100. For "placating the king," "soothing his anger" in royal politics, we note that the siege of Troja was lifted when Henry II's rage and anger were softened by the children of the city. See Rodulfus Glaber, *The Five Books of the Histories* 3.4, Neithard Bulst, ed. (Oxford: Clarendon, 1989), 100–102. For peacemaking as "placating his anger," see Anselm of Liège, *Gesta* 34; Köpke ed., 7:208, ll. 11–18: Bishop Wolbodo displeased Henry II. He set out with money to "placate" the king. Wazo of Liège restrains the French king (Henri I, in 1046) from attacking Aix merely by writing an eloquent letter, says his idealizing biographer Anselm. See *Gesta* 61: "Qua sententia viri dei audita, tyrannica rabies confestim est sedata." Köpke ed., 226, l.14. On another occasion Wazo defies a prohibition of Henry III and is solemnly summoned to court to account for it. He is fined 300 pounds of silver, and this mundane act of compensation is described as "softening the indignation of that powerful mind" (*Gesta* 66: "potentis animi indignatio non aliter visa est posse leniri," Köpke ed., 229, l. 36), and "placating the emperor" (*Gesta* 66: "imperator postea placatus," Köpke ed., 229, l. 39). The language of royal business and affairs of state regularly draws on the concept. The Admont collection (mid-twelfth century) has an interesting series of letters. See *Die Admonter Briefsammlung nebst ergänzenden Briefen*, Epist. 55–62, Günther Hödl and Peter Classen ed., MGH, *Briefe der dt. Kaiserzeit* 6 (Munich: Harrassowitz, 1983), 107–16. Frederick I summoned Archbishop Eberhard I of Salzburg (Epist. 55), who refused (Epist. 56), thus arousing the king's anger (Epist. 57, 58, 59). Through intermediaries the king's anger was placated (Epist. 60 and 61), and the archbishop agreed to appear before the king (Epist. 62).

CHAPTER 5 ✶ ORPHEUS IN THE ELEVENTH CENTURY

of the emotions: the king's favor is "love," his disapproval "hate" or "anger."[101]

The task of soothing, pacifying, and instructing princes and moving the lay nobility away from barbarity to *mores compositi* registered in tracts on the obligation to shun anger and cultivate clemency. An early example is Wipo's *Tetralogus*.[102] The last two of the four admonishers of the king in this "tetralogue" are the Law and Grace. *Gratia* urges the softening and moderating of the precepts that *Lex* had urged on him:

> After judgment is rendered, let the softening effect of forgiveness follow.... The law makes the king hated when it punishes offenders savagely. What Grace [*gratia*] urges makes the king beloved.[103]

In showing mercy, Henry imitates Jove himself, who punishes crimes by forgiveness (vv. 243–44: ...*parcendo crimina punit*!). Wipo cites a consecration formula for "...the girding on of the king's sword"[104] built on the antithesis of the king's killing weapon to his preserving mercy:

> [Grace addresses King Henry.] When you are angry, king, season your anger with compassion. Hard things are softened by water; while soft things grow hard in fire, and the rule of moderate reason reverses circumstances. That is why the hard diamond is softened by blood...and the command of nature is that sad things yield to soothing.[105]

101. See above, 231; Gerd Althoff, "*Ira regis*: Prolegomena to a History of Royal Anger," in *Anger's Past: Social Uses of an Emotion in the Middle Ages*, Barbara Rosenwein, ed. (Ithaca, NY: Cornell University Press, 1998), 59–74; and C. Stephen Jaeger, "L'amour des rois: Structure social d'une forme de sensibilité aristocratique," *Annales Économies Sociétés Civilisations* 46 (1991): 547–71.

102. *Die Werke Wipos*, Harry Bresslau ed., 3rd ed. MGH *Script. rer. germ. in us. schol.* (Hannover and Leipzig: Hahn, 1956), 75–86.

103. *Tetralogus*, vv. 225–29: "Et post iudicium veniae mulcedo sequatur /.../ Lex odium regi generat feriendo nocentes; / Ut sit carus item rex idem, Gratia suadet." In Bresslau ed., 83.

104. Evidently Wipo's invention. The admonition to compassion does not occur in any preserved royal ordination. See Bresslau ed., 83–84 n. 6.

105. Wipo, *Tetralogus*, vv. 249–55: "Dum rex iratus fueris, miserando quiesce/ Dura foventur aquis, durescunt lenia flammis, / Alternatque vices moderatae ius rationis. / Hinc adamas durus solvetur sanguine molli /.../ Et natura iubet mutari tristia blandis." In Bresslau ed., 88.

This section of the poem is a verse tract on tempering justice with mercy. The eleventh and twelfth centuries produced a fair number of preceptive writings on the subject.[106]

Clearly the figure of Orpheus is an emblem of this duty of clergy. But is it anything more than an emblem? Did poetry itself actually function in this capacity?[107] Wipo's *Tetralogus* and *Quid suum virtutis* might qualify as "orphic" poems in the sense that we have given the word. Fulcoius of Beauvais wrote poetry advocating the cause of Manasses I of Rheims in his conflict with Rome. Fulcoius has much in common with that ideal cleric whose portrait was quoted at the beginning of this chapter: both were French nobility, lived in Rome, were skilled in law, rhetoric, and poetry.[108] Peter Damian died too early to have had Fulcoius in mind, but he certainly would have recognized in him a representative of the species. Fulcoius wrote several verse epistles to popes Alexander II (Epist. 7) and Gregory VII (Epist. 2) seeking reconciliation. When Manasses was excommunicated by Hugh of Die, Fulcoius wrote a conciliatory letter in verse commending the many good qualities of his patron, arguing against the "hatreds" that beset Manasses and urging him to exercise mercy before justice and lift the excommunication

106. For instance, Peter Damian's tract on suppressing anger: *De frenanda ira*; Hildebert's letter to Countess Adela of Blois (Epist. 1.3; PL 171:144–45), a little treatise on clemency, drawing on Seneca and using the language of Orphic discourse; Bernard of Clairvaux, *Sermones super Cantica Canticorum* 12, Leclerq et al. ed., *Sancti Bernardi Opera* 1:60–67; and Peter of Blois' fictional dialogue against royal anger between Henry II and the abbot of Bonneval in PL 207:975–88.

107. Adam of Bremen, *Hamburgische Kirchengeschichte* 3.39, says that Archbishop Adalbert (d.1072), though not partial to *fidicines*, called on them to "relieve his anxieties": "Raro fidicines admittebat, quos tamen propter alleviandas anxietatum curas aliquando censuit esse necessarios." In Schmeidler ed., 183. But this is probably standard medical practice with little evocation of the Orpheus figure.

108. Cf. one of the epitaphs on Fulcoius: "Legem, consilium, rationem, carmina, linguam / Sparsa quis hospitio colligit huic simili? / Quis queat actorem titulare? Quis anser olorem / Hunc pro tot titulis carminibusque suis?" In Marvin L. Colker ed., "Fulcoii Belvacensis Epistulae," *Traditio* 10 (1954): 191–273, at 192. On Fulcoius, see also Williams, "Manasses I," 808 and 813–14; André Boutemy and Fernand Vercauteren, "Fulcoie de Beauvais et l'intérêt pour l'archéologie antique au XIe et au XIIe siècle," *Latomus* 1 (1937): 173–86; Manitius, *Geschichte*, 3:836–40; and Günter Bernt, "Fulcoius von Beauvais," LexMA 4:1019.

CHAPTER 5 ✷ ORPHEUS IN THE ELEVENTH CENTURY

(Epist. 3). Fulcoius is at work with his poetry mollifying the anger of Manasses' foes. On this model it is not improbable to imagine the gifted and learned serving the interests of their lords through poetry.

This sets forth the broader social context that drew the Orpheus figure into its orbit and made of the ancient singer the prototypical softener of royal anger. We know that learned clerics felt an obligation to perform this function and that poetic composition was part and parcel of their education. One showed one's own *mores compositi* by mitigating the anger of lords, bishops, brothers. If the writer ornamented these *mores* with poetry (or vice-versa in Ulrich of Bamberg's formulation), then the writer gave testimony to excellent moral training and powerful genius. Peter Damian's portrait of the futile perfection of a worldly cleric virtually reiterates the educational ideals of the poem *De nuptiis*. The combination of judicial rhetoric, knowledge of the law, poetic composition, and ethical posture was the best the cathedral schools had to offer.

CONCLUSIONS

We can conclude that the Orpheus figure was an emblem for a certain obligation of clergy in their dealings with lords clerical and secular and that this obligation had wide social and political resonance. This idea of the role of poetry virtually died out at the schools after the end of the eleventh century. The Orpheus myth was dissolved into religious or psychological allegories,[109] and Orpheus' civilizing mission was absorbed into the broader role of Orpheus/Christ or Orpheus/Reason. It hangs on as reminiscences.[110] A passage in the fourth homily on the Virgin Mary by Bishop Amadeus of Lausanne

---

110. Bernard Silvester's treatment in his commentary on Virgil's *Aeneid* is instructive. He develops the myth in the interpretation that became shared by the School of Chartres: Orpheus is Reason, which combines wisdom and eloquence, Eurydice is natural desire, etc. The only trace that remains of the eleventh-century Orpheus is Bernard's comment on his lyre. See *The Commentary on the First Six Books of the Aeneid of Vergil, Commonly Attributed to Bernard Silvester*, 6.119: "Lenimen huius ad aliquod honestum opus pigros excitat, instabiles ad constantiam vocat, truculentos mitigat." In Julian W. Jones and Elizabeth F. Jones, ed. (Lincoln: University of Nebraska Press, 1977), 54. There is a clear reminiscence of the eleventh-century Orpheus in John of Salisbury, *Policraticus* 5.10, Clemens J. Webb, ed. (Oxford: Clarendon, 1909), 1:326.20–27.

(mid-twelfth century) adapts an earlier view of Orpheus to describe creation, conversion, and moral training:

> By the sweetness of his wonder-working song he [God] called to life the sons of Abraham from stones and stirred the trees of the forests, that is the hearts of the Gentiles, to faith. He also composed the wild beasts morally, that is, [humanity's] brutish impulses and uncultivated barbarity, and thus he trained the educated out of their [mere] human state, to enter the ranks of the gods.[111]

Orpheus is not mentioned, but the affinity of ideas is clear. The fate of Orpheus in the twelfth-century schools does not show that the ancient singer has at last reemerged and come into his own. It shows the concept losing the firm contours and the social role it had had in the previous century. In the eleventh century the Orpheus figure bore a vital educational ideal with broad social and political significance and maintained this role in competition with Christ and King David.

---

111. Amédée de Lausanne, *Huit homélies mariales* 4.17–22: "...suavitate mirificae cantilenae suscitavit [deus] de lapidibus filios Abrahae, et ligna silvarum, id est corda gentilium ad fidem commovit. Feras quoque, id est feras motus et incultam barbariem moraliter composuit, et homines ab hominibus eductos in numerum deorum instituit." In Georges Bavaud, ed. (Paris: Cerf, 1960), 110–12.

6. HOMO PERFECTUS

INTRODUCTION

The humanism of the eleventh and twelfth centuries gave expression to an ideal of human perfection that raises up humanity to the level of the divine.[1] Plato's cosmological dialogue *Timaeus*, which influenced Christian philosophy and theology in many ways and reached the Middle Ages in a variety of branchings,[2] is the starting point for the pursuit of this ideal of perfection. The creator god, *demiurge*, conceives of the universe as something good; and without completeness, its goodness is frail: "He wished all things to be as like himself as possible."[3] What lacks goodness is incomplete. What exists in a state of change is threatened by incompleteness. The best safeguard against creation's lapse back into disorder is a universe governed by reason implanted in soul and body. Once the cosmos is formed, God calls together the gods and spirits who will shape the human being and assigns them the role of creating mortal creatures who will complete creation: "Unless they are created the world will be imperfect... [it must have] every kind of living creature if it is to be perfect."[4] The assembled gods, secondary creating spirits, have learned their art from their creator hence will fashion the creatures according to the master creator's technique. They reach into the bowl containing the matter from which God made the soul of the world, and of this matter, slightly thinned so as to withhold full divinity from these created beings,

1. The original title of this paper was "*Homo Perfectus*: Universal Human Nature in the Poetry and Philosophy of the Eleventh and Twelfth Century. Prehistory and Survival of a Humanist Myth." See "Note on the Chapters," above, XVI. On the history and development of the idea *homo perfectus*, see Hans Heinrich Schaeder, "Die islamische Lehre vom vollkommenen Menschen, ihre Herkunft und ihre dichterische Gestaltung," *Zeitschrift der deutschen Morgenländischen Gesellschaft*, n.s. 4.79 (1925): 192–268; Jens Holzhausen, *Der "Mythos vom Menschen" im hellenistischen Ägypten: Eine Studie zu "Poimandres," zu Valentin und dem gnostischen Mythos* (Bodenheim: Athenäum, 1994); Martin Mulsow, "Der vollkommene Mensch: Zur Prähistorie des Posthumanen," *Deutsche Zeitschrift für Philosophie* 51 (2003): 739–60, at 743–44.

2. Most directly in the Latin translation (partial) by Calcidius, of the Greek dialogue, second half of the fourth century CE: Calcidius, *On Plato's Timaeus*, John Magee, ed. and trans. (Cambridge, MA: Harvard University Press, 2016).

3. Plato, *Timaeus* 29e–30a, H.D.P. Lee, trans. (Baltimore: Penguin, 1969), 42.

4. *Timaeus* 41a–c; Lee trans., 56.

the human soul is made. In making the human body, they copy the shape of the universe.[5]

These passages narrow a complex narrative of creation to a few points relevant to the idea of perfection. Perfection means fullness, completion, full attainment of a divinely conceived goal. The aspects of this myth that are woven into the high medieval idea of the perfect human being likewise far exceed in complexity what I can lay out in this essay. The chapter that follows sketches the medieval formation of the idea of human perfection, situating it between its pre-history and afterlife. I am aware how imperfect and incomplete the attempt to capture the nature and history of this particular idea in a few pages must be. But I think the purpose justifies the risk: to give outlines to a medieval humanistic ideal and its place in its larger history. I'll begin by sketching various components of the concept of the ideal human received by medieval humanism.

MICROCOSM-MACROCOSM

The main interpreter of the *Timaeus* for Christianity and the Middle Ages, Calcidius, spells out implications of the model for the interrelationship of the universe to the human being.[6] The human being is a microcosm, a small model of the universe. Its soul comes from the heavens, and its body is constructed of the same matter as the cosmos: four elements, corresponding to four humours. A near contemporary of Calcidius remarked that the human is the world in miniature. The world is the human, it represents in the composition of its body a type of universal harmony. Macrobius writes in his *Commentary on the Dream of Scipio* (c.410 CE): "The universe is an immense human; and the human being is a miniature world."[7] The implications for human life and thought are vast. The human imitates divinity in its soul and represents the harmony of the cosmos in the composition of its body. Knowledge of nature and the universe is necessary to gain knowledge of self: the latter is modeled on the former.[8]

5. *Timaeus* 44d; Lee trans., 60.
6. Calcidius, *Plato's Timaeus* 4.55; Magee ed. and trans., 208–9.
7. Macrobius, *Commentary*; Stahl trans., 224.
8. See Finckh, "Minor mundus homo"; M.D. Chenu, *Nature, Man, and Society in the Twelfth Century: Essays on New Theological Perspectives in the Latin West*, Jerome Taylor and Lester Little, trans. (Chicago: University of Chicago Press, 1968), 28–37.

CHAPTER 6 ★ HOMO PERFECTUS

The idea of humanity as microcosm, frequently cited in the patristic age and the early Middle Ages, came to prominence in the twelfth century, most impressively in the creation allegory of Bernard Silvestris' *Cosmographia* (1145), whose two parts are "Macrocosm" and "Microcosm," the creation of the world, then the creation of the human being following the model of the cosmos.[9] The idea implies a grandeur of humanity mirroring that of the universe; a perfect harmony analogous to the harmonious beauty of the macrocosm. This primal perfection may have been disturbed by original sin or by evil elements inherent in the physical matter from which the human form is constructed (as in *Cosmographia*), but the loss sets in place the fundamental spiritual goal of humanity: the restoration of primal perfection as an approach to God. The *Cosmographia* remained unfinished.

The allegorical poem by Godfrey of St. Victor, *Microcosmus* (c.1180–85) probably answered or at least complemented the work of Bernard Silvester: following on the *Cosmographia* is an *anthropographia*. Bernard's sweeps the whole range of cosmic and human. Godfrey's is about the microcosm, though humanity has a celestial nature formed in the pattern of the macrocosm. This late work of medieval humanism is an extended allegory where the moral development of the human soul unfolds in the structure of the seven days of creation. Human dignity is a central idea. The narrative is conceived as a pilgrimage, like Dante's *Divine Comedy*, though Godfrey's poem exercised no evident influence on Dante's.[10]

The *homo quadratus*, the human being ideally formed according to the number four, is a related idea. The square as the symbol of human perfection, the number four as its prototype, is Pythagorean in its origins. The mathematical determination of perfection has its primary expression in architecture and anthropology. In the eleventh century Abbot Bern of Reichenau can praise his patron, Bishop Pilgrim of Cologne, as "a man who through the four arts of the quadrivium was rendered four-fold, and by the melody of celestial

---

9. Bernard Silvester, *Cosmographia*, Peter Dronke, ed. (Leiden: Brill, 1978); Bernard Silvester, *Poetic Works*, Winthrop Wetherbee, ed. and trans. (Cambridge, MA: Harvard University Press, 2015).

10. See below, 378–401.

harmony was made eternally tuned [attentive to] divine praises."[11] In a virtuoso description of the bedchamber of Adela of Blois, Baudri of Bourgueil (d.1130) explains the musical composition of the human body. Harmony renders the human being "fourfold":

> The status, the energy and the melody of human life is governed by some agreement — I don't know how — so that its form seems to arise from the square, which is greater and more stable than other forms.[12]

In Bernard Silvestris' *Cosmographia* the allegorical figure named *Phronesis* (the mind of God) gives the command to Nature, who is shaping primal humanity: *quadret opus!* "Make the work foursquare!" that is, perfect.[13] Thomas Aquinas, in his commentary on the *Nichomachean Ethics*, uses the Greek term:

> The tetragonal human, that is, the truly good being, is without guilt and flaw, that is, made perfect by the four cardinal virtues.... Aristotle means, the tetragonal human is complete in virtue.[14]

Various elements of the macrocosm linked by the number four are the macrocosmic counterpart of the four-fold human: the four elements, the four arts of the quadrivium, the four cardinal virtues.

THE HERMETIC TRADITION: THE HUMAN BEING, A "GREAT MIRACLE"

The so-called Hermetic writings are a collection of philosophical tracts, mostly in dialogue form, probably composed in the Greek culture of Alexandria, Egypt in the second or third century CE. Their central figure is a legendary philosopher-prophet-ruler, three offices united in one person and therefore "three-times great," Hermes Trismegistus. The core of the Hermetic writings are an important source of central ideas of medieval and Renaissance

11. Epist. 17: "tu, quem non solum quatuor matheseos disciplinarum speculatio quadratum, verum etiam caelestis armoniae melos divinis laudibus iugiter reddit intentum [...]." In Schmale ed., 50–51.

12. *Carmen* 134, ll. 981–85; Tilliette ed., 2:32.

13. *Microcosmos* 4.5, *Cosmographia*; Dronke ed., 126.

14. *Sancti Thomae Aquinatis in decem libros Ethicorum Aristotelis ad Nicomachum Expositio* 1.16.193, Angelo M. Pirotta and Martin M.S. Gillet, ed. (Turin: Marietti, 1934), 65. See also De Bruyne, 357.

CHAPTER 6 ★ HOMO PERFECTUS

humanism.[15] They are products of an elite philosophical community, who thought, taught, and wrote in the fiction or belief that the god Hermes is their philosophical guru. They represented Hermes as a contemporary of Moses. That antiquity lent him a particular authority. Add to antiquity the presence in his writings of a distinct concept of a trinity whose third member was the son of God, and the combination offered to later Christianity the example of a pre-Christian, pagan philosopher who had received basic mysteries of Christianity by natural revelation. The authority of this Hermes remained solid down to the sixteenth century, when the writings ascribed to him and his circle were recognized as composed after the rise of Christianity and so had received their revelation of the Trinity by the usual route.[16]

The short Hermetic tract *Asclepius* was the *locus classicus* of the trope "humanity the great miracle." It is cited widely in the humanism of the eleventh and twelfth centuries and in Renaissance humanism. It is a dialogue between the god Hermes and his pupil or disciple Asclepius. The god explains the nature of humans to his pupil:

> The human being, Asclepius, is a great miracle, a living being that deserves worship and acceptance, for the human approaches the nature of God as if it were a god in its own right.[17]

St. Augustine knew the Hermetic writings. He attacked them vigorously in *The City of God*. He formulated their idea of a miraculous humanity in the context of miracles performed by saints but with a significant addition: the greatest miracle of all is not the acts performed but the essence of the person who performs them.

---

15. See Theodore Silverstein, "The Fabulous Cosmogony of Bernardus Silvestris," *Modern Philology* 46 (1948): 92–116, at 95–96; Frances Yates, *Giordano Bruno and the Hermetic Tradition* (London: Routledge and Kegan Paul, 1964); Brian P. Copenhaver, *Hermetica: The Greek Corpus Hermeticum and the Latin Asclepius in a New English Translation with Notes and Introduction* (Cambridge: Cambridge University Press, 2000), Introduction, xlv-lix; Garth Fowden, *The Egyptian Hermes* (Princeton, NJ: Princeton University Press, 1986), with bibliography.

16. See Yates.

17. Par. 6. *Das Corpus Hermeticum Deutsch* 1. *Die griechischen Traktate und der lateinische "Asclepius,"* Jens Holzhausen, trans. (Stuttgart-Bad Cannstatt: Fromann-Holzboog, 1997), 259.

"Of all the miracles performed by humans, the greatest miracle is the human being themself."[18] The turn of thought became a hagiographic convention: not wondrous deeds, but god-given charisma, the miracle-worker's inner gift from which miracles derive, deserves awe and admiration. Bernard of Clairvaux, in his biography of the Irish saint Malachy, weighed his merit as saint, attested by his many miracles, against his person: "In my judgment the first and greatest miracle that he performed was the man himself."[19] The formula was taken into the memorializing of Bernard himself. His biographer, Geoffrey of Clairvaux, wrote in his *Life of Bernard* that, though he had performed many wonders, "the first and greatest wonder was the man himself" (*primum maximumque miraculum, quod exhibuit, ipse fuit.*)[20]

THE HUMAN BEING AS A WORK OF ART

The idea has a long history. St. Ambrose in the late fourth century gave it an impressive formulation:

> Human creature, know yourself.... Know that you are not formed of earth and clay. God breathed on you and made you a living soul. You are a magnificent work of art [*opus es magnificum*] breathed on by God in the act of creating humanity."[21]

The great hand-craftsman, the artist [*opifex*] God, has created mimetically in humanity a copy of himself, so that in the human creature traces of the artist that created humanity would be visible. The trope comes up in various forms in the high Middle Ages: the teacher is a potter; the students "meant to be formed by artist's hand

---

18. Augustinus, *De civitate Dei* 10.12.291: "omni miraculo, quod fit per hominem, majus miraculum est homo." In PL 41:13–806.

19. *Vita Malachiae* 19.43: "primum et maximum miraculum, quod dedit, ipse erat." In Leclercq et al. ed., 3:348.

20. Geoffrey of Clairvaux, *Vita Prima Sancti Bernardi Claraevallis Abbatis*, 3.1.1–6, Paul Verdeyen ed., CCCM 89B (Turnhout: Brepols, 2011), 133.

21. Ambrose, *In Psalmum David CXVIII Expositio*, Sermo 10: "Cognosce te, anima, quia non de terra, non de luto es, quia insufflavit in te Deus, et fecit te in animam viventem. Opus es magnificum, Dei inspiratione formatum." In PL 15:1332D–1333A. The same formulation in his *Commentarius in Cantica Canticorum* 1.33, PL 15:1864C. See Martino Rossi Monti,"*Opus es magnificum*: The Image of God and the Aesthetics of Grace," in *Magnificence and the Sublime*, Jaeger ed., 17–29.

into vessels of glory on the wheel of discipline."[22] Also in the context of discipline imposed on students, Hugh of St. Victor used the image of a perfectly sculpted statue to define the goal of discipline. [23]

THE DIGNITY OF HUMANITY (DIGNITAS HOMINIS)

The idea that dignity is the essence-forming quality of the human creature is central to the *Cosmographia* of Bernard Silvester. In the second part of his work, *Microcosmos*, the allegory of human creation, the figure named Noys or Providentia, the mind of God, explains her plan of construction of the human soul to her assistant, Nature, the craftsperson who is to carry out the conception of the divine mind:

> Since it befits the careful craftsman to make the final portions of his work a worthy consummation, I have decided to complete the success and dignity of my creation with Humanity. I will bestow upon him abundant favor and abundant resources, that he may excel all my creatures by a certain privilege, as it were a distinctive attribute of dignity.[24]

Charles Trinkaus, in his two-volume study of human dignity in the Italian Renaissance, locates the origin of the idea in Genesis 1:26: God created humanity in his own image and likeness.[25] The human soul may come with the inner image of God encrusted by original sin, which does not, however, efface the existence of the likeness of humanity and God. These Christian aspects are undoubtedly a major element in the medieval idea of human dignity.[26] But

22. Cited in Jaeger, *Envy*, 223.

23. PL 176:933B–C.

24. Bernard Silvester, *Cosmographia: Microcosmos* 3.85: "Quoniam par est diligentem opificem claudentes partes operis digna consumatione finire, visus est mihi in homine fortunam honoremque operis terminare. Inpensioribus eum beneficiis, inpensioribus eum inpleam incrementis, ut universis a me factis animalibus quodam quasi dignitatis privilegio et singularitate concertet." In Dronke ed., 123.

25. Trinkaus, *In Our Image and Likeness*.

26. *De spiritu et anima*: "Ita namque conditum est cor hominis, ut in eo quasi in templo Dominus inhabitaret, et tanquam in quodam speculo suo reluceret.... Magna prorsus dignitas hominis est, portare imaginem Dei, et illius in se iugiter

Hermetic ideas deserve mention prominently in this regard. In this tradition the human being is in origin essentially divine, i.e., not an imitation of God via the "image and likeness" implanted in every soul but rather by its paternity in God. The divinity of humanity is in its family lineage, not just a resemblance.

HUMAN DIVINITY

The boundary dividing humans from gods seemed less strict in antiquity than in Christian times. "Godlike," "equal to the immortals" are well-known Homeric epithets. Pindar reflected on the limited divinity of humans:

> *One race of humanity, one of gods — but we draw breath*
> *Both from a single mother. Yet an utter difference separates the two*
> *In power, such that one is nothing,*
> *while for the other an abode remains unshakable forever*
> *in brazen heaven. Still, we do somewhat resemble the immortals*
> *nonetheless, whether in greatness of mind or in physique....*[27]

In Platonic tradition, the divinity of the human soul was not a distant resemblance but explicit.[28] The Christian idea of the obscured but recoverable divinity of the human soul[29] is strongly colored by Platonic ideas. However, the human soul as divine "in the core of its being" (Pindar) is foreign to both. It is strongly asserted in the Hermetic writings, however. The Latin tract *Asclepius* centers on the composition of humanity from both the human and the divine, its striving for divinity through study and knowledge. A

---

vultum aspicere...." In PL 40:1167. "The heart of humanity was created in such a way that God could live there as in a temple, and radiate thence as from his own mirror.... Thence comes the great dignity of Humanity, that he possesses the image of God, so that he can always contemplate his image in himself." In Rossi Monti, 22. See also below, 398–409.

27. Pindar, *The Odes*, Nemean 6; Andrew M. Miller, trans. (Oakland: University of California Press, 2019), 225.

28. Macrobius, *Commentary on the Dream of Scipio*, 2.12.5–11; Stahl. trans., 222–24. *Commentaire au songe de Scipion*, Mireille Armisen-Marchetti, ed. (Paris: Les belles lettres, 2003), 2:53–54.

29. See Andreas Speer, "Vergöttlichung," LexMA, 8:1531–32.

CHAPTER 6 ★ HOMO PERFECTUS

cosmological myth shared widely in these writings assigns a divine origin to humanity. This was not a god-humanity in the sense of Jesus, whose double nature was not inherited by humans, but rather a humanity whose origin was divine but whose divinity was obscured by entanglement in the physical world.

The first tract of the *Corpus Hermeticum* is a myth of the creation of the world entitled *Poimandres*. It tells of the origin of the gods in three emanations: the first is God; the second the *Demiourgos* or handcrafter-artist, charged with creating the cosmos; the third is the son of God. The name of this third deity was to cause some consternation to theologians and philososphers: *Anthropos*, that is, the Son of God in this trinity was named "humanity," or "man." The human race of which *Anthropos* is the primal father originated in the "fall from grace" of this divine child. Descending from heaven to look on the realm of nature created by the demiurge, he sees his own face reflected in the waters of the earth and falls in love with and is wed to Nature. This is the Hermetic version of the "fall of man." *Anthropos* forfeits its native place in the higher realm, is bound to the lower, Nature, and the offspring of their union is the human race. This fallen demigod and its brood have the duty of administering the earth and of restoring, through *gnosis*, their lost divinity. In Hermetic thought, then, humans descend directly through God. This is not likeness but identity — albeit lost — with God. The goal of ethical striving is to restore lost divinity.[30]

The Hermetic idea of the divine human was available in the eleventh and twelfth centuries through the *Asclepius*. But it emerges much more strongly connected with education. Humans are made divine by cultivating virtue and reason. Benzo of Alba (d.1089, imperial chaplain of Emperor Henry III) wrote an extensive book of instruction (c.1085) for Henry IV, in which he names virtue as the source of dignity and divinity in humans.[31] For Baudri of Bourgueil, it

30. *Corpus Hermeticum* 1, Holzhausen ed., 10–22. See Richard Reitzenstein, *Poimandres: Studien zur griechisch-ägyptischen und frühchristlichen Literatur* (Leipzig: Teubner, 1904); Jörg Büchli, *Der Poimandres: Ein paganisiertes Evangelium. Sprachliche und begriffliche Untersuchungen zum ersten Traktat des Corpus Hermeticum* (Tübingen: Siebeck, 2019); Holzhausen, *Mythos*.

31. Benzo von Alba, *Sieben Bücher an Kaiser Heinrich IV* 7.3: "Virtus est mentis dignitas / Et animi nobilitas, / que homines mirificat / Insuper et deificat." In Hans Seyffert, ed. and trans. MGH, SSR 65 (Hannover: Hahn, 1996), 606.

is philosophy that renders humans divine: "Those whom philosophy nurtures are not humans but gods."[32] In Alan of Lille's grand creation allegory, the *Anticlaudianus* (1183) the shaping of an ideal human aims at recreating its lost divinity. The creating spirits have the task of making a "divine human" (*divinus homo*). God's purpose is to rescue humanity from the corrupt state into which it has fallen by means of this "new human."[33]

THE UNIVERSALITY OF THE HUMAN SOUL

The idea that humans have inherently the gift of universal capacities, to be developed by learning, has an early formulation in the Hellenistic idea of *enkyklios paideia*, all-encompassing knowledge.[34] Cicero imagines the ideal *rhetor* who must study every field and acquire a totality of what is knowable. Quintilian too calls for a comprehensive knowledge in his ideal orator. Roman educational thought aimed at preparation for state service, for which the combining of eloquence and wisdom was vital and constituted the scheme of comprehensive knowledge. Developing an inherent and essential universality of humanity was not the goal. The linkage of educational thought with philosophical thought on the creation of humanity was forged in the syncretistic philosophies of late antiquity. Cosmogonic writings expressed this connection in the motif of the "gifts of the planets," in myths of the creation of humanity. The heavenly origin of the human soul is firm Platonic tradition, as is the motif of the descent of the soul on its way to embodiment. The descent of the soul lent itself to the idea of a cosmic education. In the descent to nature of the god Anthropos in the *Poimandres*, the son of god receives from each of the seven planets in turn the peculiar gifts that that planetary spirit has to give: from Jupiter wisdom, from Mars warlike spirit, from Venus feeling, etc. The primal human possesses the capacities of the planetary gods. The array of talents is literally universal, that is, derived from the

32. Baudri de Bourgueil, *Carmen* 153, ll. 49–50: "Sunt dii, non homines, quos lactat philosophia, / Nec deberent dii vivere sicut homo." In Tilliette ed., 2:60.

33. Alain de Lille, *Anticlaudianus* 6.366–67: "Sic ad nos divinus homo descendat, ut ipsis / Virtutum titulis aliorum moribus instet"; 6.390–92: "'Hoc mihi iampridem Racio dictavit ut uno / Munere respicerem terras mundumque bearem / Numine celestis hominis [...]." In Wetherbee ed., 422–25.

34. On the connection of divinity and universality, see Mulsow, 752–53.

universe. This cosmic bequest is the inheritance of every human. The primal human has a mythological, planetary Ur-education.

The entire cosmos is present in the mind of humans, just as the entire creation was present in the mind of the god who created heaven and earth. It follows that humanity is capable of understanding everything and every aspect of creation. Its inborn destiny is to experience, examine, learn, and so develop an understanding adequate to its capacities, i.e., divinity. Humanity's philosophical life is stated emphatically in *Corpus Hermeticum*, tract 11:

> Unless you make yourself equal to God, you cannot understand God; like is understood by like. Make yourself grow to immeasurable immensity, outleap all body, outstrip all time, become eternity, and you will understand God. Having conceived that nothing is impossible to you, consider yourself immortal and able to understand everything, all art, all learning, the temper of every living thing. Go higher than every height and lower than every depth. Collect in yourself all the sensations of all that has been made, of fire and water, dry and wet; be everywhere at once, on land, in the sea, in heaven; be not yet born in the womb; be young, old, dead, beyond death. When you have understood all these at once, times, places, things, qualities, quantities — then you can understand God.[35]

Macrobius' *Commentary on the Dream of Scipio* gives highlight to the motif, gifts of the planets. He is describing the descent of the soul to the physical realm:

> Having started on its downward course [...], as [the soul] passes through these spheres, it [...] acquires each of the attributes which it will exercise later. In the sphere of Saturn, it obtains reason and understanding [....] In Jupiter's sphere, the power to act [...]; in Mars' sphere, a bold spirit [...]; in the sun's sphere, sense-perception and imagination [...]; in Venus' sphere, the impulse of passion [...]; in Mercury's sphere, the ability to speak and interpret [...] etc.[36]

The planetary education of the soul is clearly related to astrological ideas, where the nature of the individual is determined by a single

---

35. *Corpus Hermeticum* 11, par. 20, Holzhausen ed., 134–35; Copenhaver trans., 41.
36. Macrobius, *Commentary* 1.12.13; Stahl trans., 136.

planetary constellation in the birth hour, that is, a strict selectivity of astrological determinants, narrow indeed compared to the comprehensive character of the primal education of the divine soul. All the planetary spirits transmit their gifts to the soul on its way to earth. All human souls participate in this foundation of learning. It predetermines universal education, and universality of education is the path upon which human beings can reclaim their divine character. Educated primally by the universe, humanity has the potential for universal knowledge. The "gifts of the planets" offers a model in which the macrocosm transmits its qualities actively to the microcosm. The cosmos educates the primal human.

The idea of the human capacity for universal learning is prominent in the educational thought of the twelfth century. The *Didascalicon* of Hugh of St. Victor (c.1125–29) is a theoretical treatment of Christian humanist studies; its subtitle is *De studio legendi (On the Study of Reading)*. The work begins broadly with an analysis of the human soul meant to illuminate the nature and purpose of study. The first characteristic: "A tenet approved by the ancient philosophers has it that the soul is formed from all parts of Nature."[37] The soul can comprehend each substance and every nature, since in its essence it is their image and likeness. Impressed with the likeness of all things, as the seal impresses its face on wax, the human mind at the same time is all things:

> This then is the true dignity of our nature, which all possess by nature in the same measure, but that all do not understand in the same degree."[38]

---

37. 1.1: "Probata apud philosophos sententia animam ex cunctis naturae partibus asserit esse compactam." In Buttimer ed., 4. On Hugh's knowledge of the Hermetic *Asclepius*, see *Didascalicon*, Taylor trans., 225 n. 54; and Taylor's notes, index "Asclepius" and "Hermetic Texts." Also Matthias Heiduk, "Revealing Wisdom's Underwear: The Prestige of Hermetic Knowledge and Occult Sciences among Scholars before 1200," in *Networks of Learning*, Sita Steckel et al., ed. (Berlin: Lit Verlag, 2014), 125–46, at 133–34.

38. *Didascalicon* 1.1: "...sic nimirum mens, rerum omnium similitudine insignita, omnia esse dicitur, atque ex omnibus compositionem suscipere...et haec est illa naturae nostrae dignitas quam omnes aeque naturaliter habent, sed non omnes aeque noverunt." In Buttimer ed., 5–6.

CHAPTER 6 ✶ HOMO PERFECTUS

The immersion in sensuality is a hindrance to understanding our true universality. The way to restore that likeness of the soul to the cosmos is therefore study, learning, reading: "Let us be repaired/restored through learning so that we may recognize our nature."[39] Therefore the search for wisdom is the way to escape our corrupted condition, to return to the true nature that we have forgotten. The name of this search for wisdom is "philosophy." Philosophy recalls the intellect of humanity to itself[40] and enables us to reach what is our true goal: to restore the inner image of God. Two paths lead us to this goal: contemplation of the truth and cultivation of virtue.[41] The role of the disciplines of study is to restore the likeness of God. The closer we assimilate to God, the more we understand.[42]

Bernard Silvester clearly conceives of the universality of the newly created human as a product of a cosmic education. In the *Cosmographia*, the task of educating the primal soul is in the jurisdiction of Urania, goddess of the stars and planets. She consults with Nature to map out her plan for the education of the primal soul:

> The human soul must be guided by me through all the regions of heaven, that she may learn wisdom: the laws of the Fates and inexorable Destiny, and the shiftings of unstable Fortune.... In mind and spirit, she will emulate the gods and the heavens.... As she enters the vessel of the body, she will have experienced what influence the stars, what power the firmament possesses, what vital force is in the starry vault, what force the two luminaries exert by their rays, and the five planets. From the heavens she will derive a comely aspect, stability of mind, and principles of conduct.[43]

39. *Didascalicon* 1.1: "reparamur per doctrinam, ut nostram agnoscamus naturam." In Buttimer ed., 6.

40. *Didascalicon* 1.2: "...haec igitur sapientia cuncto animarum generi meritum suae divinitatis imponit, et ad propriam naturae vim puritatemque reducit." In Buttimer ed., 7. Quoting Boethius. See Buttimer's note on the passage.

41. *Didascalicon* 1.8: "Duo vero sunt quae divinam in homine similitudinem reparant, id est, speculatio veritatis et virtutis exercitium." In Buttimer ed., 15.

42. *Didascalicon* 2.1: "hoc ergo omnes artes agunt, hoc intendunt, ut divina similitudo in nobis reparetur, quae nobis forma est, Deo natura, cui quanto magis conformamur tanto magis sapimus." In Buttimer ed., 23.

43. *Cosmographia, Microcosmos* 4.31–46: "Mens humana mihi tractus ducenda per omnes / Ethereos, ut sit prudentior: / Parcarum leges et ineluctabile fatum /

The reason for creating humanity — so says Noys speaking to the assembled creating spirits — is that there is incompleteness in the universe. Being a model of the spiritual universe, the natural realm must have a divine human to fill the space occupied by God in the higher world; an imbalance between macrocosm and microcosm would be an imperfection, and the universe planned by Noys cannot permit such an imbalance. Therefore humanity, the likeness of God, is necessary to perfect creation.[44]

It is important to understand the radical character of this line of thought, particularly in comparison to monastic tradition. What leads to the rediscovery of dignity of the godlikeness of humanity is not ascetic discipline or mystical contemplation but rather study and reading aimed at universal knowledge driven by an inborn universality seeking its counterpart in nature. There is a Gnostic coloring to this argument: through understanding and knowledge we know ourselves, and we know God in us. Hugh of St. Victor's train of thought is original in that the study of the seven liberal arts is the mediator or at least is an essential element of the search. A systematic humanistic course of study coincides with a high goal of Christian theology: the ascent to God.

The preceding comments have aimed at characterizing briefly some of the central elements of an ideal of human perfection, giving only the briefest sketch of their lines of descent from antiquity. The conception of human perfection that synthesizes these and other elements in the eleventh and twelfth century is in its totality without a precedent. It was enriched by an element peculiar to the medieval period: the creation of the ideal being is an educational process (gifts of the planets); and the restoration of the fallen divine human being also (reading, study, cultivation of virtue). The philosophy that linked cosmology with the creation of humanity annexed the disciplines of

---

Fortunaeque vices variabilis / ... / Ingeniis animoque deos caelumque sequetur, / Ut regina suum vas incolet. / Que virtus stellis, et quanta potentia celo / Et quis sidereis vigor axibus, / Quid valeant radiis duo lumina, quinque planete, / Sentiet ingrediens vas corporis. / De celo speciem vultus, animique tenorem / Et morum causas sibi contrahet." In Dronke ed., 127 ; Wetherbee trans., 95–96.

44. *Cosmographia* 10:1–26; Dronke ed., 140–41; Wetherbee trans., 138–41.

CHAPTER 6 ★ HOMO PERFECTUS

moralitas and the seven liberal arts. Education could be envisioned as a means of recreation of inborn divinity.

The two epic allegories of the creation of the world of the twelfth century, the *Cosmographia* of Bernard Silvester and the *Anticlaudianus* of Alan of Lille, both frame the creation of the perfect human as a process of education. Brian Stock has characterized the *Cosmographia* as "a kind of Bildungsroman."[45] The term fits the *Anticlaudianus* more literally than Bernard's work.[46] It is, among other things, a late summation of the humanistic system of education at cathedral schools of the eleventh and twelfth centuries.[47]

The *Anticlaudianus* is set in a time long past the creation, in a universe that has gone to ruin. Sin, immorality, and neglect have led to a steep decline from the primal state of the world and humanity, the time when the creator declared all of creation good. For Alan of Lille, it is a fallen world. To rehabilitate creation and restore goodness and virtue, Natura convokes a congress of allegorical creating spirits. She proposes the creation of a "new human" as the means to rehabilitate creation and restore goodness and virtue to humanity. She lays out a plan of the new human being and commissions creating spirits to execute it, Concordia, Phronesis (the divine mind, providence), Ratio (Reason). This single work of the creation of a perfect human will expunge the errors into which the first phase of creation has fallen. Reason stipulates that the new human must receive the totality of all gifts and talents given singly by the goddesses to humanity in its previous condition: "Let it alone possess whatever all of us possess; thus one individual will be all humans, all will be resolved into one."[48]

The comprehensive gift-giving and talent implanting is formulated in the *Anticlaudianus* as gifts of creating spirits and virtues, not of planets. However, the greater plan of creating the perfect human

45. Brian Stock, *Myth and Science in the Twelfth Century: A Study of Bernard Silvester* (Princeton, NJ: Princeton University Press, 1972), 164.

46. *Anticlaudianus* 6.428–29; Wetherbee ed., 426.

47. Jaeger, *Envy*, passim; Steckel, *Kulturen des Lehrens*; Münster-Swendsen, "Masters"; Münster-Swendsen, "Model."

48. *Anticlaudianus* 2.50–52: "Possideat solus quicquid possedimus omnes; / Omnis homo sic unus erit, sic omne quod unum: / Unus in esse suo, sed erit virtutibus omnis." In Wetherbee ed., 264.

requires an ascent to heaven, which follows the congress of spirits. Phronesis is the heavenly traveller. It is her task to receive from God an archetypal pattern of the human soul, to bring it to earth and install it in a perfect body, the union represented as a marriage of body and soul. The vehicle that transports Phronesis is a cart or chariot, its frame made by Wisdom (Sophia), constructed by seven workers, the seven liberal arts. Grammar forms the pole; Logic the axle; Rhetoric provides decoration. Those are the assigned role of the trivium, the language arts. The four arts of the quadrivium — music, mathematics, geometry, and astronomy — form the four wheels. Once the five horses of the senses are spanned, Phronesis can begin her journey. The charioteer is Ratio, reason. She guides the cart until it passes the region of the planets and the fixed stars. But once she realizes the height of the ascent, she reels and staggers and must hand the guidance over to another guide, Theology, who leads Phronesis to God. The allegory speaks clearly: virtue combined with the liberal arts bring the god-seeker into heaven. Theology leads on to God. Instead of a planetary education, the new human being receives an education, which is, allegorized, the frame of cathedral school learning.

Once arrived, Phronesis explains her mission to God. Nature wants to use her powers to create a new human, one who will exceed all others "by its beauty of form and the model of its manners."[49] The new creation is to return to earth as a "divine human" (*divinus homo*), whose own presence reveals the traces of its artist.[50] God approves the plan. He calls his helper, Noys (the mind or intellect of God) and sends her into the creator's workshop on the search for an appropriate archetype. After long searching, Noys returns. God goes to work on the archetype like a sculptor, carving on the bare face of a seal, until he has shaped it in the form required for Nature's conception. This is the *exemplaris imago*. This archetype posesses the power to imprint itself on raw material, to make copies of itself. God pours the entire treasury of his own form and of the

---

49. *Anticlaudianus* 6.331–32: "Vult hominem formare novum, qui sidere forme / Et morum forma reliquos transcendat." In Wetherbee ed., 420.

50. *Anticlaudianus* 6.364–67: "…Teque [i.e., deum] tuum fateatur opus, quis fecerit actor [auctor] / Predicet artificemque suum factura loquatur." In Wetherbee ed., 422.

CHAPTER 6 ★ HOMO PERFECTUS

ideals of Old Testament figures into the archetype. It possesses the gift of imprinting itself on matter, as the seal leaves its imprint on wax.[51]

Alan's allegory combines in a way that is original and perplexing the creation of the human soul with a mission of redemption. The idea of the new human postulates a second redeemer, the *homo perfectus*, whose task is the moral renewal of humanity.[52] Christianity of course has its first redeemer at work in salvation history, Jesus. A second redeemer at work in the history of humanity, conceived in heaven and set to work on a mission of earthly redemption, is the contribution of Alan. The surprisingly peripheral role of Jesus in the *Anticlaudianus* has been noted by other readers. Jesus is present in Alan"s epic but not integrated into its action. The travellers on their upwards journey note Jesus' presence in the sphere above the angels, and he is praised in a passage of some fifty lines for virtues tending to the ascetic proper to monks and martyrs.[53] Jesus is a presence, but he has no function in the allegorical system of the *Anticlaudianus*. His role is already fulfilled. In a similar rewriting, or rather extension, of Christian redemption history, the earthly paradise is rediscovered at the end of the work, but its architect is not the original creating God but rather the newly created perfect human. The second redeemer does not function through self-sacrifice and crucifixion but rather through exemplarity. Formed from the *exemplaris imago* working through the charismatic transfer of qualities from their perfect form to their human embodiments. The *homo novus* is the seal; humanity the wax receiving its imprint.[54]

Once entrusted with the newly created soul, Phronesis begins her return journey. She avoids contact with the planets (in contradiction of the Hermetic creation story). She is protected by a heavenly salve from influences that would endanger the impressionable new soul. In the *Anticlaudianus*, the gifts are not administered by the planets but

51. *Anticlaudianus* 6.438–43; Wetherbee ed., 428.

52. Christian theological thought took up the idea of "the new human" for redemption theology soon after Alan's epic appeared. See Christel Meier, "Der ideale Mensch in Alans von Lille 'Anticlaudianus' und seine Verwandlungen," in Exemplaris Imago: *Ideale in Mittelalter und Früher Neuzeit*, Nikolaus Staubach, ed. (Frankfurt-am-Main: Peter Lang, 2012), 137–57, at 153–55.

53. *Anticlaudianus* 5.443–70, 519–43; Wetherbee ed., 392, 396.

54. See the discussion of this metaphor in Brigitte Bedos-Rezak, *When Ego Was Imago: Signs of Identity in the Middle Ages* (Leiden: Brill, 2011), 142–50.

by a parade of allegorical virtues. Once the soul is joined to the body, these virtues perform their task. Seventeen virtues and the seven liberal arts shower their individual qualities on the new human. The gift-giving ends: "Now the heavenly and divine human was perfect in every way."[55] Once fully equipped, it can begin the battle with the vices. The poem ends with the victory of the new human, with the establishing of a utopia of world peace, of love, and of the rule of virtue and law in human life. The virtues make their home amid humanity, the earth become a second paradise.

The *Anticlaudianus* is a great, encyclopedic work that combines the most varied strands of thought and ideas in a systematic allegory of the perfecting of humanity through virtues and wisdom, *mores et litterae*. This grandly conceived work attributes to a systematic education in a particular moral-philosophical-theological system a function that neither Platonic philosophy nor Christian theology had foreseen. Viewed from its background in the history of ideas, the *Anticlaudianus* represents an appropriation of the education of an orator from antiquity and the earlier Middle Ages (cathedral schools) for the Christian philosophical-theological tradition.

Some further consideration of the topic of exemplarity can help illuminate this broad complex of thought and ideas. God commissioned Noys to find and bring the *exemplaris imago* from the storehouse of archetypes of created nature. This primal image of humanity (the *Urbild*) contains the entire treasury of all possible merits and distinctions. The copy of this primal soul, the *Abbild*, contains not only all possible qualities but also the entire universe. This effect of the primal on the natural soul is the central philosophical idea of this creation allegory. The conventional motif of the battle of virtues with vices pales in importance when compared with the idea of heavenly qualities transferred charismatically to humans. A concise statement of Phronesis in her speech to God states this function and its importance:

> Let this divine human come down to us in such a way that it is enabled through the fame of its virtues to exercise an influence on the manners and morals of others.[56]

55. *Anticlaudianus* 8.147–48: "Jam perfectus erat in cunctis celicus ille / Et divinus homo." In Wetherbee ed., 474.

56. *Anticlaudianus* 6.366–67: "Sic ad nos divinus homo descendat, ut ipsis / Virtutum titulis aliorum moribus instet." In Wetherbee ed., 422.

CHAPTER 6 ★ HOMO PERFECTUS

This defines the rescue mission of the new human: it operates through the imprinting effect of its soul.

This places us in the logic of charismatic pedagogy and shows how closely and fully the ideal of human perfection is tied to humanistic education. The transfer of human qualities from a model or exemplary teacher to a malleable student is at the core of the system of education at cathedral schools that had developed since the mid-tenth century, came to fruition and broad influence in the eleventh, and then declined in the course of the twelfth century, forced out of the schools by political trends and the rising influence of scholastic philosophy. The high position accorded the new human in the *Anticlaudianus* is a last, dramatic manifestation of an educational ideal of earlier generations. Alan's allegory has its place in the history of education in the Middle Ages as a late attempt to summarize and revivify a dying educational ideal.[57]

Learning by example — by the diffusion of the personal charisma of a teacher, acquiring presence, virtue, and stature through imitation of the master — is an orientation of moral education inherited from classical antiquity that never fully died out in Christendom. Sita Steckel has shown what a significant role this model of teaching and learning played in Carolingian education and beyond.[58] The cathedral schools of the tenth to the twelfth century enriched this mode by a moral philosophy oriented strongly to Ciceronian thought.[59] Caroline Bynum has shown the central role of "teaching by word and example" among the canons regular of the eleventh and twelfth century. The canon regular and schoolmaster of St. Victor, Paris, Hugh of St. Victor, is one of many who give testimony to charismatic pedagogy, but his statements bear special weight given that he wrote a tract on the education of novices that centered on the charismatic relationship between teacher and student. It is in the nature of a teaching relationship based on personal influence that its pedagogy is embodied in the person of the master as

---

57. This historical position is shared by Godfrey of St. Victor, who wrote his *Microcosmus* at the same time Alan was at work on the *Anticlaudianus*. See below, 377–400.

58. See Steckel, *Kulturen des Lehrens*.

59. See above, 95–131.

opposed to an education based on knowledge acquisition grounded in texts. It unfolds from what we might call the body-magic of the teacher. Qualities like grace, beauty of manners, and *gravitas* are not acquired through reading about them but through contact with a teacher who exudes them. In his tract *On the Instruction of Novices*, he elevated imitation of the teacher to the first principle of education:

> Why do you think, my brothers, that we are enjoined to imitate the life and conduct of good individuals, unless it be that by imitating them we are reformed to the likeness of a new life? For in them the form of the likeness of God is expressed, and when we impress ourselves on them through imitation, then we too are reshaped according to the image of that same likeness.

The terms "express" and "impress" are the language of a seal imprinting in wax. Hugh invokes this metaphor to indicate the process of learning by example. The passage continues:

> We who seek to be reformed through the example of good individuals, as through some marvelously sculpted seal, perceive in them the traces of actions, some of which are sublime and eminent, but others abject and debased.... When [the saintly] act in such a way as to arouse the admiration of human minds, then they appear as exquisite sculptures. What stands out in them should be recreated inwardly in us.[60]

These statements of Hugh of St. Victor are closely related to the grandiose conception of the function of the perfect human

---

60. Hugh of St. Victor, *De institutione novitiorum* 7: "Quare putatis, fratres, vitam et conversationem bonorum imitari praecipimur, nisi ut per eorum imitationem ad novae vitae similitudinem reformemur? In ipsis siquidem similitudinis Dei forma expressa est, et idcirco cum eis per imitationem imprimimur, ad ejusdem similitudinis imaginem nos quoque figuramur.... Quid ergo aliud in isto nobis innuitur, nisi quia nos qui per exemplum bonorum, quasi per quoddam sigillum optime exsculptum reformari cupimus, quaedam in eis sublimia et quasi eminentia, quaedam vero abjecta et quasi depressa operum vestigia invenimus? Sanctorum quippe opera quae...in conversatione eorum...humanas mentes in admirationem sui pertrahunt, quasi quasdam in se eminentes sculpturas ostendunt. Quod ergo in illis eminet, in nobis introrsum recondi debet...." In Feiss and Sicard ed., 339–42; PL 176:932D–933C.

CHAPTER 6 ★ HOMO PERFECTUS

in the *Anticlaudianus*. The exemplarity of Alan's *homo perfectus* is an abstraction of the charismatic educational ideal of the cathedral schools. While Hugh of St. Victor was not a master at a cathedral school, it is evident from a plethora of sources that his educational concepts derived from those broadly shared in cathedral communities.[61] The ideal was not restricted to one milieu. The Abbot Wibald of Stablo gave terse expression to it in describing the effect of the physical presence of Bernard of Clairvaux: "The mere sight of him teaches you; the sound of his voice by itself instructs you; to follow him renders you perfect."[62] The passages quoted above touch the core meaning of the ideal of human perfection in the humanist thinking of the eleventh and twelfth centuries: the new human reshapes others in its own image and likeness. The perfecting of an imperfect world is conceivable because humans are equipped with this ability to transmit their virtues to others.

The idea of the teacher as a model and of the pedagogic relationship of an exemplary teacher to a learning student is an element of social and intellectual life of earlier ages. It is not much credited in the intellectual or social history of the Middle Ages and beyond, great though its role was. The educated class in the Middle Ages, as in the ancient world, saw itself enmeshed in networks of moral interrelationships and influences, of charismatic forces emitted and received, beamed and embodied. Aristocratic society was educated on the basis of such networks.

I have avoided the broader question, why the intellectual life of these two centuries revived, combined, and reinterpreted these elements of a received Platonism and its early Christian transformations. I have concentrated on the engineering, not the conceptualizing of the ideal. But it is clear that an important element of this humanistic direction of thought lies in the optimism grounded in a humanist education, a *Bildungsoptimismus*, the idea

---

61. The case is argued in detail in Jaeger, *Envy*, 284–91. It should also be recalled that Hugh received his early education probably in the heartland of Saxon Germany at Hamersleben, near Halberstadt. See Poirel, "Hugo Saxo," 164: "Maître Hugues est arrivé déja tout formé à St. Victor."

62. *Das Briefbuch des Abt Wibalds*, Epist. 142: "Quem si aspicias, doceris; si audias, instrueris; si sequare, perficeris." Hartmann et al. ed., 1:303.

proclaimed by Sigebert, Baudri, Hugh of St. Victor, and Alan of Lille that a comprehensive education renders the student god-like.[63]

A HUMANIST MYTH

The preceding pages focused on creation myths, Platonic, Hermetic, Christian. While there are plenty of discursive writings on the conception of the human, it is most memorably recorded in myths. Humanity the child or emanation of the creating god; humanity created in the image and likeness of God; the human a microcosm, which also derives from a myth of God designing the universe; the re-creation of a perfect human. A tradition in western humanism continues the various strands of this line of thought. In this sense, it is justified to speak of a myth of the primal, archetypal human, the gift of fullness and perfection, the mirror of the universe, from whom humanity descends, a myth stretching across the various ages of western humanism.

Some years ago, I had envisioned a project of writing the history of this myth in its many formulations from Platonism and Gnostic writings to Thomas Mann. Its main sources would have been the German disputation between death and a ploughman (trope for "writer"), *Der Ackermann aus Böhmen* (c.1401);[64] *The Oration on the Dignity of Man* by Pico Della Mirandola (1486);[65] Shakespeare's *Henry IV*, 1 & 2, and *Henry V*; Grimmelshausen's *Der Abenteuerliche Simplicius Simplicissimus* (1669);[66] various novels of education from

63. A classic statement of this optimism is the speech/oration/prayer of the student and soldier Victor just prior to his death with the martyred Theban Legion on the field of Acaunum. I have treated it above, 199–201, and recommend a reading of it as the most eloquent and emotional statement of a student and professor on the glories and ideals of the old learning. Coming in the late days of German cathedral-school education (c.1075) it frames that idealism nicely with Godfrey of St. Victor's speech to the spirit of humanity (c.1085). See also *Envy*, 182–84.

64. *Der Ackermann Frühneuhochdeutsch und Neuhochdeutsch* 25, Christian Kiening, ed. (Stuttgart: Reclam, 2000).

65. Pico della Mirandola, *Oration on the Dignity of Man: A New Translation and Commentary*, Francesco Borghesi et al., ed. (Cambridge: Cambridge University Press, 2012).

66. Hans J.C. Grimmelshausen, *Grimmelshausens Simplicissimus Teutsch* 3.3–6; J.H. Scholte ed. (Tübingen: Niemeyer, 1954), 207–20.

CHAPTER 6 ★ HOMO PERFECTUS

the eighteenth and nineteenth century; and Thomas Mann's *Joseph and His Brothers* (1926–43). These works build on the myth of the primal human, cite it, satirize it (*Grimmelshausen*), build its ideas of education into the structure of the work with no direct reference to the myth (Shakespeare, Bildungsroman).

Thomas Mann's novel tetralogy *Joseph and His Brothers*[67] begins with a rehearsal of the Hermetic myth of creation most fully developed in the *Poimandres*. Mann announces the myth in his prologue: the myth of the primal human, son of Anthropos. The author sublimates the structure of the myth, its anthropology and educational ideal into the sprawling narrative of the novel. In many ways it is Mann's greatest, certainly his longest, and the work to which he devoted the most time. It is also the most extensive expression of his humanistic ideals in a work of fiction.

A few passages from the prologue to the work will show the link to our topic. The first of the four novels begins with a long and virtuoso prelude, "Descent into Hell" (*Vorspiel: Höllenfahrt*). His purpose is to investigate, more precisely to excavate, the earliest beginning of the idea of humanity, starting from the time of the patriarchs and working backwards in time to the most archaic origins. It is a "search for the mystery of this paradoxical character, the human being," a search for the original basis of "the human" and of "the culture and civilization of humanity" (*die menschliche Gesittung*). He lowers his plumb line into the "fountain of the past," passing the various stages in the development of the idea of humanity. At the very bottom of the well, so to speak, the last and earliest stage of that idea, he finds a myth beyond which he cannot procede, i.e., the beginning. Here is the moment of discovery:

> There can be no doubt that we have arrived at the final step "backward," have gained man's loftiest past, defined Paradise and the story of the Fall, of knowledge and of death, back to its pure and truthful form.

The myth that he finds there runs as follows:

> A long tradition of thought — based on man's truest self-perception and arising early on, to become incorporated as an

---

67. Thomas Mann, *Joseph and His Brothers* 1. *The Stories of Jacob*, John E. Woods, trans. (New York: Knopf, 2005), 27–31.

heirloom into the long succession of religions, prophecies, and epistemologies of the East...deals with the figure of the first or perfect human being...who is to be thought of as a youthful creature of pure light, created before the beginning of the world as the prototype and epitome of humanity.... We hear how this primal human son of God contained within his body of light the seven metals, each corresponding to one of the seven planets, from which the world was formed.... This being descended through the seven planetary spheres and from the ruling power of each sphere received some portion of its nature. But then, as he gazed downward, he noticed his reflection in matter, became enamored of it, descended to it, and thus found himself ensnared in the bonds of lower nature. This explains then man's double nature, whereby the hallmarks of a divine origin and essential freedom are forever entangled beyond unravelment in the heavy fetters of the lower world. It is in this narcissistic image so full of tragic charm that the tradition begins to achieve some refinement of meaning.[68]

Mann is virtually quoting the myth of the primal human from the first tract of the Hermetic corpus, *Poimandres*. At the point where Anthropos, the son of god, falls in love with Nature (or with himself in Nature) and weds Nature, he forfeits his divinity. Humanity is the progeny of this union between a banished human-god and an embodied Nature.

The myth of the primal human forecasts the character of Mann's Joseph, a grace-given, godlike spirit of light, beloved of God. This character's education takes him through a course in which he falls only to rise again, ultimately to the highest position of power and influence as the steward of Pharaoh. The structure of the Joseph novels has its basis in the Hermetic myth of the human. So, this purest example of the German Bildungsroman reached far back along a humanistic tradition to ground the author's longest work in an ancient myth of the primal human. This tradition also experienced a flowering in the reflections and representations of *homo perfectus* in the eleventh and twelfth centuries.

---

68. *Joseph*, 27–31.

7. CHARISMATIC BODY/CHARISMATIC TEXT

INTRODUCTION

Hildebert of Lavardin visited Rome in the last years of the eleventh century. Probably on his return to the north in 1100 he wrote a poem of praise for the city's ancient ruins, *Par tibi Roma nihil*.[1] It is elegiac in both senses: in regretting the loss of greatness and in the elegiac meter (elegiac couplets: one line in dactylic hexameter followed by a line in dactylic pentameter). At the poem's core is an admiration for the art of the ancient Romans so exuberant that it clouds the bishop's Christian loyalties. In one of the most impressive passages of medieval poetry, Hildebert admires the crumbling statues of the ancient gods; he imagines the gods themselves in their full glory appearing bodily before their statues and comparing the original — i.e., themselves — with the copy:

> *The art of men once made a Rome so great*
> *That the art of the gods could not destroy it.*[2]
> *Divinities themselves look awe-struck on divinities sculpted,*
> *And wish themselves the equals of those sembled forms.*
> *Nature could not make gods as fair of face*
> *As man created the awe-inspiring images of gods.*
> *Carved likenesses improve these deities;*
> *They merit worship more for the sculptor's art than their own divinity.*[3]

1. *Hildebertus Cenomannensis Episcopus, Carmina minora* 36; Scott ed., 22–24. For commentaries, see Bruce Gibson, "Hildebert of Lavardin on the Monuments of Rome," in *Word and Context in Latin Poetry: Studies in Memory of David West*, Anthony J. Woodman and Jakob Wisse, ed. (Cambridge: Cambridge University Press, 2017), 131–54; and von Moos, *Hildebert*, 251–58.

2. *Cura hominum/cura deum* is a play on words that cannot be reproduced in English. Implied in the latter is the "worship" of the gods, i.e., a benighted pagan faith. In other words, human art was above religious matters. The worship of false gods could not destroy the human art created to honor them.

3. Hildebert, *Par tibi Roma, Carmen* 36, ll. 29–36: "…cura hominum potuit tantam componere Romam, / quantam non potuit solvere cura deum. / hic superum formas superi mirantur et ipsi, / et cupiunt fictis vultibus esse pares. / non potuit Natura deos hoc ore creare, / quo miranda deum signa creavit homo. / vultus adest his numinibus, potiusque coluntur / artificum studio quam deitate

He invests the gods with aesthetic judgment and sets up a contest of beauty and skill between sublime art and sublime beings. That Nature creates gods — and not vice-versa — is a bold idea.[4] Also bold is the outcome: Nature loses the contest to the human artist. The statues — crumbling though they are — are superior to the living gods, as their artist is superior to the "sculptor" of the gods, Nature. The Roman sculptor's art does not just imitate and represent the gods; it corrects their maker. It shows Nature possibilities beyond her own imagination. As if the Platonic process of imprinting ideas on matter were turned upside down, the copy teaches its archetype what beauty is.

It is enough to make iconoclasts of the gods. Here is the very reason gods forbid graven images: the images and not what they represent become the object of worship (*potiusque coluntur / artificum studio quam deitate sua*). They suffer an envious disquiet at this usurpation of charisma, since they wish themselves, in momentary forgetfulness of their stature and dignity, the equals of their fictions. They gawk at their magnificent copies, which ignore their models and gaze past them in Olympian indifference. If we could also see the bested gods collect their wits and overcome their surprise, we could imagine them challenging the artist: "How dare you depict us more beautiful than we are!" To which the Roman sculptor would reply, "Learn through me to be more god-like."

This passage from Hildebert's poem is a myth of representation, comparable to other myths of representation, like Narcissus or Pygmalion. In all three the created or reflected image produces a kind of enchantment in the maker or model. But in the two ancient myths, the source of astonishment is the interchangeability of life

---

sua." In Scott ed., 22–23. See the exchange on this line between Otto Zwierlein, "Par tibi Roma, nihil," *Mittellateinisches Jahrbuch* 11 (1976): 92–94; and Peter von Moos, "Par tibi, Roma." My translation follows von Moos' reading. See also Monika Otter, "*Vultus adest* (The Face Helps): Performance, Expressivity and Interiority," in *Rhetoric Beyond Words: Delight and Persuasion in the Arts of the Middle Ages*, Mary Carruthers, ed. (Cambridge: Cambridge University Press, 2010), 151–72.

4. For instance, in the grand allegorical poems of creation, Bernard Silvestris' *Cosmographia* and Alan of Lille's *Anticlaudianus* the secondary spirits and minor gods precede nature, at least are not created by her. Nature's work is humanity.

CHAPTER 7 ★ CHARISMATIC BODY/CHARISMATIC TEXT

and art. Narcissus sees an image of himself indistinguishable from the living being it reflects. Pygmalion makes a statue so close to life that his desire is enough to overcome the narrow distance between art and life. Both are myths of mimetic representation. Against this, the hyper-mimesis of the medieval myth posits the victory of representation over nature. It is about overcoming and going beyond mimesis. Hildebert's myth presupposes an art that we can call "charismatic," because it competes with the charismatic beings par excellence, the gods, and surpasses them. It is not enough within this mode of representation for art just to be like life, merely to imitate nature. It wants to be grander and more beautiful than nature.

Hildebert's myth of representation has a general aesthetic aspect, which this essay touches on but does not take as its focus. Its subject is the interaction of personal and textual[5] charisma as a historical dynamic at work in the transition from the eleventh to the twelfth century. Hildebert's Rome poem dramatizes aesthetic change as cultural change. The superseded gods — this is the argument — stand for the passing age, the charismatic statues for the coming one. The gods stand for a declining mode of representation, the statues for an ascending one. The date c.1100 is a significant perch from which the poem looks in two directions in time and intellectual history and reflects on the cultural transformation in progress.

The period is in many ways the watershed between the ancient and the modern world. Its transitional nature has been the focus of critical attention. Charles Radding used Jean Piaget's model of the growth of consciousness to understand a whole variety of phenomena like the abolition of the ordeal in the twelfth century.[6] The discussion of the transition in media has made use of the categories, oral culture vs. literate culture.[7] I want to offer a reading of the passage from Hildebert's Rome poem based on the fundamental opposition of bodies and texts,

5. Here and throughout I use "text" to mean any form of representation. This is a convenience, not a deconstructionist extension of textuality to any form of experience.

6. Radding, *A World Made by Men*.

7. See, for instance, Brian Stock, *The Implications of Literacy: Written Language and Models of Interpretation in the Eleventh and Twelfth Centuries* (Princeton, NJ: Princeton University Press, 1983); Ivan Illich, *In the Vineyard of the Text: A Commentary to Hugh's Didascalicon* (Chicago: University of Chicago Press, 1993).

a relationship that is central for culture generally, not only for medieval culture. The lines are a paradigmatic metaphor for a transitional moment in the relations of bodies and texts.

Paul Zumthor has urged the rediscovery of the voice in literary texts.[8] Courtly literature, he suggests, contains a voice that has fallen silent and implies a performance that preceded textualizing, a performance that becomes sublimated in the text. But voice and performance are aspects of a greater act of sublimation on which art in a certain phase rests. At a level hardly accessible to critical excavation and altogether blocked by post-structuralist aesthetics, the foundation of the charismatic text is the charismatic body.

FROM BODIES TO TEXTS

The goal of this essay is to locate Hildebert's image along the trajectory of the body–text dynamic in its development in the eleventh and twelfth centuries.[9] The shift from bodies to texts in that age[10] is close to the transformation of consciousness that Walter Benjamin observed in "The Work of Art in the Age of Mechanical Reproduction."[11] Benjamin compares the work of art in two phases. Prior to mechanical reproducibility, it is characterized by "authenticity" and "aura." The mode of reception — even of wholly secularized art — is "the cult." But given mechanical reproduction, it experiences "the decay" and the

8. See for instance, Paul Zumthor, *Oral Poetry: An Introduction*, Kathryn Murphy-Judy, trans. (Minneapolis: University of Minnesota Press, 1990); Zumthor, "Körper und Performanz," *Materialitaet der Kommunikation*, Hans-Ulrich Gumbrecht et al., ed. (Frankfurt-am-Main: Suhrkamp, 1988), 703–13; Zumthor, "The Text and the Voice," NLH 16 (1984/85): 67–92.

9. Since this essay first appeared, the problem of presence, will, and agency in texts has gotten much attention. See Alfred Gell, *Art and Agency: An Anthropological Theory* (Oxford: Oxford University Press, 1998); William J.T. Mitchell, *What do Pictures Want?: The Lives and Loves of Images* (Chicago: University of Chicago Press, 2006); Jacqueline Jung, *Eloquent Bodies: Movement, Expression, and the Human Figure in Gothic Sculpture* (New Haven, CT: Yale University Press, 2020).

10. These ideas are developed in more detail in Jaeger, *Envy*.

11. In *Selected Writings 4, 1938–1940*, Howard Eiland and Michael Jennings, ed.; Harry Zohn and Edmund Jephcott, trans. (Cambridge, MA: Harvard University Press, 2003), 251–83.

CHAPTER 7 ✷ CHARISMATIC BODY/CHARISMATIC TEXT

"withering of its aura." The reproducible work of art can only emerge and gain legitimacy at the cost of "a tremendous shattering of tradition," which undermines the authority and authenticity of art.

This scheme links aesthetic change to historical change, and its terms apply well to the transition underway in the twelfth century. This transition plays out a contest between two stages of culture that is not restricted to a particular historical setting but recurs at various points in western history: in fifth- and fourth-century BCE Athens, in Rome from the republic to the empire,[12] in the European Middle Ages from the eleventh to the twelfth centuries, and again from the late Middle Ages to the Renaissance. We can call the two stages "charismatic" and "intellectual." Their relationships are basically agonal, but also dynamic and productive.

Charismatic cultures are familiar to us almost exclusively as heroic, warrior cultures, tribal societies with a powerful sense of clan identity and aristocratic honor and an authoritarian hierarchic structure, at the top of which is a charismatic leader.[13] But the warrior aspect of charismatic culture is one of many. "Heroism" is a modality that takes in other aspects of life: intellectual, sexual, romantic, poetic, and artistic. In a charismatic culture the scholar, intellectual, and artist — and not just the warrior — operate in a heroic mode. This is not to turn poets, monks, and schoolmasters into titans. "Heroic" means action and not reflection, presence and not representation, the glorifying of the lived moment, the *kairos*, and of the elegant human response to it — not art. The idealizing of representation is the realm of intellectual, textual culture, a restorative phase when real and present charisma is passing out of existence and artists and poets are struggling to rescue and preserve it in texts, pictures, and statues, as the disciples of Socrates and Christ tried to hold firm the physical

12. On this shift from charismatic to intellectual in Hellenic culture, see Eric A. Havelock, *Preface to Plato* (Cambridge, MA: Harvard University Press, 1963). Cicero's sketch of the history of early Roman philosophy is based on a transition from charismatic (embodying the moral life) to intellectual (written works). See *Tusculan Disputations* 4.2.3.5–6; King ed., 332–33.

13. See *Max Weber on Charisma and Institution Building: Selected Papers*, S.N. Eisenstadt, ed. (Chicago: University of Chicago Press, 1968); and Clifford Geertz, "Centers, Kings and Charisma," in Geertz, *Local Knowledge: Further Essays in Interpretive Anthropology* (New York: Basic Books, 1983), 121–46.

and spiritual presence of the dead master. Prior to the stage where representation becomes a cult, there is a mode of art, poetry, learning, whose effect is tied to the charisma of personal presence, not to the allure of the artifact. We fetichize texts and artifacts, and we are so suspicious of personal charisma, justifiably in the twentieth century, that it takes careful excavation to recover the mentality of an age that derived its values from the charismatic presence.

The irreplaceable center of charismatic culture is the human body, and the memorializing text or artifact is a fairly indifferent item. The body and the physical presence are the mediators of cultural values; they have pedagogic, curricular force. The controlled body with all its attributes — grace, charm, sensuality, beauty, authority — is the work of art of a charismatic culture.

The school life of the eleventh century is particularly rich in examples.[14] The person and physical presence of the teacher played a role in the culture of the eleventh-century cathedral schools that is hard to overestimate. A poem from the school of Wüzburg in the early century uses an oddly mystical formula to praise the master for his teaching of poetry: "He beams with the light of many poets."[15] This reverses the normal relationship of teacher to curriculum. The Würzburg master does not illuminate the texts that he reads and explains. The texts illuminate him. This poem has a clear conception of a sacral professorship; the master teaches by divine right.[16] The living presence of the teacher is the curriculum.[17] The personal aura is the locus of pedagogy, and the language of the body is its medium.[18] The charismatic teacher attracts the student into the force field of his personality and transforms that student, demiurge-like, into a little copy of that teacher. Hugh of St. Victor used the image of a seal and

14. See Guy Beaujouan, "The Transformation of the Quadrivium," in Benson and Constable, 463–87; Horst Wenzel, *Hören und Sehen, Schrift und Bild: Kultur und Gedächtnis im Mittelalter* (Munich: Beck, 1995).

15. *Die ältere Wormser Briefsammlung*, l. 24; Bulst ed., 119.

16. For instance, ll. 28–30: "He retains his power of mind by the gift of the Almighty. / The living stream of learning flows from his breast. / The eternal divinity gives him his flow of speech." In Bulst ed., 120.

17. See Jaeger, *Envy*, 76–83; Wenzel, *Hören und Sehen*, 25–37.

18. Jaeger, *Envy*, passim; Jung, *Eloquent Bodies*.

wax to describe this relationship: the master impresses the stamp of his character on the soft wax of the student.[19] The school of St. Victor offered a curriculum in "manners" — one of the attractions of that school — in which the learning of virtue began in the disciplining of the body to ideals of elegant gait and gestures, posture, and speech.[20]

This is the central conception of an education oriented to the body: it identifies control of the body with virtue. The controlled, disciplined self is defined as a work of art, described with the vocabulary of aesthetics, conceived as parallel to well-made statues.[21] Aesthetics and ethics coalesce in the cultivation of external presence. Bernard of Clairvaux is a good witness to this cult of the person. His description of a beautiful young woman of high nobility, whom he calls only the virgin Sophia, mixes the vocabulary of sculpture with the language of moral pedagogy to articulate the ideal of virtue made visible in the well-governed body:

How well-composed does discipline render every posture not only of the virginal body, but even more so of the mind! It sets the angle of the head, orders the eyebrows, composes the facial expression, masters the set of the eyes, suppresses laughter, moderates speech, reins in appetite, controls anger, and shapes the way of walking. What splendor can compare with this? The splendor of angels? An angel has virginity, but no body. It has happiness, certainly, but not strength. Best and most desirable is that distinction that angels themselves might envy.[22]

This is not primarily praise of virginity, something that any angel can have. Sophia has something they never can have: a body. That is what

19. Hugh of St. Victor, *De institutione novitiorum* 7; Feiss and Sicard ed., 363–67; PL 176.932D–933A.

20. See Jean-Claude Schmitt, *La Raison des gestes dans l'occident médiéval* (Paris: Gallimard, 1990); Jaeger, *Envy*, 244–68.

21. For Bernard of Clairvaux' praise of the virgin Sophia, see Jaeger, *Envy*, 269–70 and n. 2. Hugh of St. Victor makes the equation explicit, *De institutione novitiorum* 8: "We long to be perfectly carved and sculpted in the image of good people, and when excellent and sublime qualities...stand out in them, which arouse astonishment and admiration in people's minds, then they shine forth in them like the beauty in exquisite statues, and we strive to recreate these qualities in ourselves." In Feiss and Sicard ed., 363–67; PL 176:933B–C.

22. Bernard of Clairvaux, Epist. 113; Leclercq et al. ed., 7:290.

the angels envy, and not her virtue. She possesses in her body the theater and staging ground of self-control, and her staging of virtue gives her a heroism (strength, *fortior*) that the angels in their wan eternal "happiness" (*felicior*) can never attain. Virtue disembodied cannot exercise the demiurgic function of shaping others in its image and likeness. The angels envious of the charismatic body (the living virgin Sophia) are like the gods envious of charismatic art (their statues in Hildebert's Rome poem). The parallel shows how the image of astonished supernatural beings works as a device to highlight the age's ethical and aesthetic values.

These are some reflections on a charismatic culture. It is oriented to the body to the extent that the physical presence becomes the medium for aesthetic and educational ideals. In eleventh-century secular culture, the body was the work of art of the inner world, its text, statue, and poem. It was meant to be read, interpreted, imitated.

How well-composed does discipline render every posture not only of the virginal body, but even more so of the mind! It sets the angle of the head, orders the eyebrows, composes the facial expression, masters the set of the eyes, suppresses laughter, moderates speech, reins in appetite, controls anger, and shapes the way of walking. What splendor can compare with this? The splendor of angels? An angel has virginity, but no body. It has happiness, certainly, but not strength. Best and most desirable is that distinction that angels themselves might envy.[23]

This is not primarily praise of virginity, something that any angel can have. Sophia has something they never can have: a body. That is what the angels envy, and not her virtue. She possesses in her body the theater and staging ground of self-control, and her staging of virtue gives her a heroism (strength, *fortior*) that the angels in their wan eternal "happiness" (*felicior*) can never attain. Virtue disembodied cannot exercise the demiurgic function of shaping others in its image and likeness. The angels envious of the charismatic body (the living virgin Sophia) are like the gods envious of charismatic art (their statues in Hildebert's Rome poem). The parallel shows how the image of astonished supernatural beings works as a device to highlight the age's ethical and aesthetic values.

23. Bernard of Clairvaux, Epist. 113; Leclercq et al. ed., 7:290.

CHAPTER 7 ✷ CHARISMATIC BODY/CHARISMATIC TEXT

These are some reflections on a charismatic culture. It is oriented to the body to the extent that the physical presence becomes the medium for aesthetic and educational ideals. In eleventh-century secular culture, the body was the work of art of the inner world, its text, statue, and poem. It was meant to be read, interpreted, imitated.

FROM REAL TO SYMBOLIC PRESENCE

Whatever area of twelfth-century culture we compare with its counterpart in the eleventh, we see a move in orientation from "real presence" to symbolic. This is most evident in the area from which I have borrowed the terms: the Eucharist Controversy.[24] The belief in the real presence of Christ's body and blood in the sacrament yields to the conception of bread and wine as *symbols* of body and blood. The shift registers also in the dispute about universals: the move from realism to nominalism abolishes universal archetypes or places them in a realm inaccessible to human reason, and it changes language from god-given, thing-like signifiers into a human-made symbolic code. In secular rule, the change from itinerant kingship (real presence of the king) to administrative kingship (the king "represented" through documents, contracts, bailiffs, etc.) is part of the same transformation of consciousness.[25] Procedures for electing bishops and abbots change from a system based on charismatic selection (virtue, personal authority, miracle) to one based on bureaucratic selection (canonical procedure formulated in texts and

---

24. See Radding, *World*, 165–72; J. de Montclos, *Lanfranc et Bérenger: La controverse eucharistique du XIe siècle* (Louvain: Spicilegium Sacrum Lovaniense, 1971); R.W. Southern, "Lanfranc and Berengar," in *Studies in Medieval History Presented to Frederick Maurice Powicke*, Richard W. Hunt et al., ed. (Oxford: Oxford University Press, 1948), 27–48; and a number of studies in *Auctoritas und ratio: Studien zu Berengar von Tours*, Peter Ganz, ed. (Wiesbaden: Harrasowitz, 1990).

25. Warren C. Hollister and John Baldwin, "The Rise of Administrative Kingship: Henry I and Philip Augustus," AHR 83 (1978): 867–905. For work correcting the conventional progressive, evolutionary view of the period, R.I. Moore, *The Formation of a Persecuting Society: Power and Deviance in Western Europe, 950–1250* (Oxford: Blackwell, 1987); and Ute-Renate Blumenthal, *The Investiture Controversy: Church and Monarchy from the Ninth to the Twelfth Century* (Philadelphia: University of Pennsylvania Press, 1991).

documents).²⁶ We can add to these various oppositions the opposing pair — body and text — and the shift from a charismatic to an intellectual culture. The direction of change in each case is towards textualizing. From the eleventh to the thirteenth century, charisma passes, as in a massive transfusion, from the body and the real presence to the text and the symbolic presence.

The twelfth century learned to transpose body into text without knowing initially that it was setting into motion a process that could not be reversed. A visible symptom of this process is the gradual fading from the scene of the dominant genres of the eleventh century, the biography and the personal letter, both of which presuppose real presence, and the emergence of a welter of new forms of artistic expression that do not. By the second half of the twelfth century a new form of narrative is popular among the aristocracy, the courtly romance. In charming and flowing narratives knights are shaped, educated, formed into models of chivalrous conduct, and tested at the hands of charismatic damsels, whose mere presence infuses virtue.²⁷

The new narrative creates a new fashion of imitating romances among the nobles, expressed in pageantry and ceremony, in fashions of clothing and naming. At the same time a new mode of representing the human body in sculpture is on the rise. It creates supple, clinging garments, gives to the curve and posture of the body a grace and elegance not seen in representation since classical antiquity and to the facial expression a life-like realism and a supernatural serenity and beauty. It reproduces remarkably the very features and virtues that Bernard of Clairvaux admired in the body of the virgin Sophia.

Credit for these trends in literature and art is often given either to a "renaissance" spirit or to the "discovery" of new styles. Both explanations are formed in the spell of a progressive conception of

26. Hayden F. White, "The Gregorian Ideal and Saint Bernard of Clairvaux," Journal of the History of Ideas 21 (1960): 321–48; and John Sommerfeldt, "Charismatic and Gregorian Leadership in the Thought of Bernard of Clairvaux," in *Bernard of Clairvaux: Studies Presented to Dom Jean Leclercq*, M. Basil Pennington, ed. (Washington, DC: Cistercian Publications, 1973), 73–90; Blumenthal.

27. On the parallel of schoolmaster and courtly damsel as administrators of virtue, see Georges Duby, *Love and Marriage in the Middle Ages*, Jane Dunnett, trans. (Chicago: University of Chicago Press, 1994), 33.

CHAPTER 7 ✷ CHARISMATIC BODY/CHARISMATIC TEXT

cultural change; they presuppose that nothing, or nothing significant, went before to which the artistic modes respond. The model of charismatic body–charismatic text, however, suggests a different explanation: the emergence of charismatic literature and art occurred in a historical moment in which a rising intellectual culture came to terms with a fading charismatic culture. The heroism of the passing age entered a textual contract with the scribes, clerics, storytellers, sculptors, and stonemasons of the scholastic age. Charisma of the body, which had previously defined itself as sculpture-like and imagined gods and angels envying it, now was re-incorporated in courtly literature and Gothic sculpture.

The sublimated presence of body in the art and literature of the twelfth century results from a nostalgic relation to the passing age. Its literature and sculpture are attempts to capture and restore the fading charisma of a "heroic" culture of personal presence. Hildebert's image of the gods shame-faced and embarassed at seeing their charisma usurped by statues is a metaphor for this development. What Walter Benjamin referred to as "a tremendous shattering of tradition" is happening, and it takes the form of a transference of "aura and authenticity" from human beings to art.

TEXTUAL CONTRACT

The general aesthetic at work here is a big subject, but it might be worthwhile to articulate briefly the term "textual contract" and the contest between body and text of which this is the resolution. Bodies need texts. The living human presence has vitality, emotion, sexuality, authority, charisma, and fate. But these qualities weaken, play themselves out, fade, and die. Of course, "it" (if I may generalize the agent of this wish and locate it in the body itself) wants to maintain these desirable but perishable qualities. To this end the body seeks textualizing, and it goes to the artist to get it, not awed by art's grandeur — a comparatively modern and unheroic sensibility — but as a down-at-the-heels prince goes to a moneylender.

This negotiation works smoothly, because the interests of the text coincide with those of the body: texts also need bodies. They have their own form of incompleteness. They have no substance. They are nothing in themselves but words and sounds, weaving and patching, ink and paper, stone and canvas. They are not alive but also not exactly dead. They are worthless unless they can persuade humans that they are sublime, immortal, permanent. That is the agony of texts: their condition of life is illusion, imitation, artifice. They need the qualities of body, which can never arise naturally from within the work of art. The unique and exclusive originating place of voice, authority, sensuality is the body. Even if the artist produced by great rhetorical skill the semblance of a heroic human being and the whole drama of the heroic existence, it remains a form of cheating. The work of art is a beggar with pretensions to glory. Its existence is based on a long-term lease. It is nothing without life, a state it always longs for[28] but can never attain.

The textual contract arises from this mutual insufficiency of bodies and texts. Because each has what the other lacks, they enter an agreement. The body says to the text: "Give me permanence, and I may have something you want." The text answers the body: "If you give me life and life-likeness, I will make you immortal." This is the birth of the charismatic work of art from the charismatic presence. The desiccated word- and sign-magic of the text is pumped full of the charisma of the body and takes on the appearance of life.

The working of the textual contract in western art is evident by contrast to charismatic cultures that refused to enter such an arrangement:[29] the stiff, hieroglyphic character of Egyptian art, the hieratic, symbolic codes of Native American art, the runic-hieroglyphic character of Scandinavian art of the Viking age. The art of heroic cultures shows in its sparseness a refusal to inject life into images, an unwillingness to profane the mysteries of the precious flesh by showing them forth, publicizing them in substitute signs and

28. Therefore the persistence of myths and folktales of the statue's awakening to life. See , for example, Pygmalion, Thomas' Tristan (the cave of statues), *The Winter's Tale, Pinocchio, One Touch of Venus*.

29. It is also evident in its unravelling in the twentieth century: the loss of representation in art, the "withering of aura" in literature, the return of charismatic forms (cinema, rock concerts, performance art), and in the academic discussions of literature and language's inability to convey reality. The grand panorama of these developments was formulated by Michel Foucault in *The Order of Things: An Archaeology of the Human Sciences* (New York: Vintage, 1973).

CHAPTER 7 ✶ CHARISMATIC BODY/CHARISMATIC TEXT

symbols. Texts may be important for such cultures, but they, and not the charismatic body, are the beggars and petitioners.

Not all cultures enter a textual contract, because the cost of it is high. This cost registers in the development of art compared with the "progress" of culture in the European Middle Ages. Some paradigm texts can mark the stages of this development. They show charismatic presence giving way to representation. The first is a description of Bernard of Clairvaux by his biographer Geoffrey of Clairvaux:

> Through numerous signs and miracles God raised his loyal servant, the abbot, to glory. But the first and greatest miracle was the man himself. Serene of face, modest in his bearing, cautious in speech, pious in action.... In his body there was a certain visible grace and charm [or gift, talent — *gratia*], which was spiritual and not physical. His face beamed with light, in his eyes there shone an angelic purity. His inner beauty was so full that it broke forth in visible external signs.[30]

Charisma of person is intact in this passage and unchallenged by representation. The element of symbolic representation rests in the "signs and miracles" the man performs. They are the text narrating the story of his inner virtue via the medium of his body. But the writer warns the reader away from overvaluing either physical (*gratia spiritualis, non carnalis*) or performed charisma. The great miracle is the man himself, not any medium of expression or representation, miracles included. That inner core of the human being creates its perfection, according to Geoffrey. It is marvelously infused into the human body and inadequately expressed in any mediating code. The writer insists on the priority of the body over its "narrated" expression.

The structure of thought here implies a contest between charisma of person and representation. It is the agonal relationship of body

---

30. *Vita prima Sancti Bernardi Claraevallis Abbatis*, 3.1.1–6, Paul Verdeyen, ed., CCCM 89B (Turnhout: Brepols, 2011), 133; PL 185:303C. Various sources confirm Bernard's charismatic force. Hildebert of Lavardin, Epist. 18, PL 171:294C, addressed him in the salutation of a letter as "the one in the church with the ability to educate others to virtue, in word as in example." Wibald of Stablo, Epist. 167, gave a dithyrambic praise of Bernard: "The mere sight of him educates you; the mere sound of his voice refines you; merely following him perfects you." In Jaffé ed., 286; *Das Briefbuch*, Epist. 142; Hartmann ed., 1:303.

and text that also is at work in Hildebert's Rome poem. The same biographer regularly drew on this logic to praise Bernard. At one point he regrets the inadequacy of his attempts to explain what Bernard was and refers the reader to Bernard's own writings:

> We have treated in a few words the sacred manner of living of our father, but it emerges much more clearly from his own writings; and in his letters, you will recognize the man. His own image is as easy to read out of them as if you saw him in a mirror.[31]

Bernard's writings have this effect not because he represented himself in them, but because his person, voice, and presence have passed naturally over into them, as into a second body, and his writings exist in that state of primary dependence on real presence, not in that restorative mode the biographer himself writes in. Bernard's writings are his second self. At one point Geoffrey shows the future saint musing over his own mission of sanctity in terms that suggest a half-serious, half-playful reflection on the interactions of body and text. Bernard ruminates:

> Signs are sometimes made through holy and perfect individuals and sometimes through fictitious ones. I for my part am neither aware of my perfection nor my fiction.[32]

A remarkable formulation. It amounts to saying, "as far as I know, I am not literature," and that disclaimer may owe more to the rhetoric of humility than to his conviction of his non-fictional character. Moving towards "holiness and perfection," he was living in the condition of textuality while in the flesh.

The second text shows physical and textual charisma in balance. It is from Gottfried von Strassburg's *Tristan*, the description of Princess

---

31. *Vita prima* 3.29; Verdeyen ed., 154; PL 185:320B. See an example of a similar logic with priority given to presence over text in Herbert of Bosham, *Vita Thomae*, James Craigie Robertson, ed., Rolls Series 67.3 (London: Longman, 1877), 208: "Let us now open the pages of our exemplar [Becket himself] and continue to read in it. For acts of virtue are certainly read more fruitfully in men themselves than books, just as deeds speak more effectively than words."

32. *Vita prima* 3.20. ll. 510–12: "facta sunt aliquando signa per sanctos homines et perfectos, facta sunt et per fictos. Ego mihi nec perfectionis conscius sum, nec fictionis." Verdeyen ed., 147; PL 185:314D–315A. The word play, *perfectos/per fictos*, repeats the glide from the living to the textual.

CHAPTER 7 ★ CHARISMATIC BODY/CHARISMATIC TEXT

Isolde playing the harp and singing before the court of Dublin.[33] This virtuoso description speaks the language of the agonal relationship between charismatic body and charismatic text. Her playing was a double performance, the poet says. Isolde sang two songs at once, one public and the other private, one audible and the other visible. The public song was the one that all heard, the music of her voice and instrument. The private song was the singer herself, her presence:

> her secret song was her wondrous beauty whose spiritual melody stole hidden and unseen through the windows of the eyes into many noble hearts and smoothed on the magic which took thoughts prisoner suddenly....[34]

There is no competition between person and text. Song and singer appear as equivalent conveyors of beauty and inspirers of desire. Body and text are both divided and united by the stark parataxis of the thought: here audible, here visible music; here performed, here embodied melody. The song is represented as something in itself, perhaps separable, at least imaginable separated from the body that produces it. But at the same time the poet makes it into a quality of Isolde's body, that quality that stirs the erotic imagination and creates desire: the body's beauty and the harmonic interaction of physical form and gesture, of motion and line. Her physical presence is inaudible music.[35] Gottfried's image implies an aesthetic of the physical presence, shared by music and body. The body becomes music, and the music becomes a body. Isolde's double song continues the logic of the agonal relationships between body and text, but representation and presence achieve balance.

The passage from Hildebert that was our point of departure shares the basic premises of those just discussed: they posit a contest

---

33. See also above, 182–85.

34. Gottfried von Strassburg, *Tristan und Isolde*, ll. 8122–31; Tomasek ed., 152. Hatto's translation, with some liberties taken here. *Muotgedoene* = mind song, spiritual ditty, spirit-tune. Hatto translates "rapturous music."

35. The well formed presence as an embodiment of musical harmonies was a trope of ethical instruction. See above, 190–96; and Jaeger, *Envy*, 165–72. Baudri of Bourgueil takes the musical instrument as a metaphor of harmonious self-government. The well modulated life is lived in a single key, and this is the way that God "harmonizes our manners and our bodies, so that the mystical symphony of our life will be pleasing." *Carmen* 218, Tilliette ed., 2:147.

between presence and representation, and they show the text superior to the body. Hildebert confronts charismatic presence (the gods) with charismatic texts (their statues) — and gives precedence to representation. The gods long to be like their statues because their statues are greater, more impressive, more beautiful. Symbolic presence is superior to real presence. This reading of Hildebert's lines locates them in the body–text relationship: the charisma of representation, having appropriated personal charisma, takes precedence over it. In this stage the charismatic text emancipates itself from its ties to a single individual and embodies abstract virtue. The biography is no longer the dominant form, but rather the fictional narrative. The charismatic text still presupposes the human body and charismatic presence as its grounding (no statues without gods), but neither immediate presence nor the memorializing motive are involved.

The fundamental mode of literature in this phase is the fictionalizing of virtue and the enfabulation of charisma. It is projected into the realm of the "marvelous," the *merveilleux*. The courtly romance in its origins is a product largely of clerical authors who shared the education of Hildebert of Lavardin, a humanistic, cathedral-school education. This is the point of contact between Latin and vernacular culture. At the very moment when an old, humanist program is collapsing and being forced out of the schools of Paris, a new narrative form created by humanists displaced from the schools and seeking employment at worldly courts develops into a "novel of education," a "Bildungsroman" — the courtly romance. This narrative form makes courtly virtue accessible through *aventure*.

The courtly romance presupposes charisma and virtue but not a human being who embodies these qualities, in contrast to the biography, letter, or portrait. The charismatic text renders the charismatic presence secondary and lives from it at the same time. It is independent from models but not from what they represent. This train of thought suggests the relevance for the twelfth and thirteenth centuries of a formula of Hans Ulrich Gumbrecht, that literature begins "in the leave-taking from the body."[36]

36. Hans-Ulrich Gumbrecht, "Beginn der 'Literatur' / Abschied vom Körper?", in *Der Ursprung von Literatur: Medien, Rollen, Kommunikationssituationen zwischen 1450 und 1650*, Gisela Smolke-Koerdt et al., ed. (Munich: Fink, 1988), 15–50.

CHAPTER 7 ✷ CHARISMATIC BODY/CHARISMATIC TEXT

It would be possible to develop an aesthetic of the courtly romance from the body–text dichotomy. It is an aesthetic of hyper-mimesis.[37] A hyper-mimetic literature is beyond and above nature while retaining realistic representation. It wants to do for the reader or viewer what the Roman statues do for the gods: astonish them, put them to shame by showing them a world that is theirs but higher, bigger, purer, more perfect. It wants to draw them into that higher world and inspire them to imitate it.

The charismatic text operates on an aesthetic that injects life into the work of art. The representation re-establishes in illusion the properties of presence. It simulates voice, impersonates physicality, enacts presence, counterfeits authority, performs charm, insinuates sexuality. The world evoked through the abstract and wholly unsensual letters of the text is sensual in the highest degree possible for the conceptual, ideal, but its sensuality is holo-, hollow-graphic, like Helen of Troy in part 2 of Goethe's *Faust*.

The charismatic text is functioning when it makes the viewer or reader want to be like it. The reader wants to live in the work of art and according to its laws. The romances had this effect on Don Quixote, in whom we have an approximate counterpart of Hildebert's gods vis-à-vis their statues. The living human being senses its inferiority to the fiction and wants to be like the counterfeit: *cupiunt fictis vultibus esse pares*. Don Quixote has no resistance to this wish. His

37. That is one reason for the serious problems in Auerbach's analysis of romance's representation of reality in *Mimesis*. He posited a purposelessness of the knighthood in social and political life that generated the unreality of romance. Later research has shown that knighthood was just gaining a role as a self-conscious social group in the late twelfth century, not losing it. See Joachim Bumke, *The Concept of Knighthood in the Middle Ages*, W.T.H. Jackson and Erika Jackson, trans. (New York: AMS Press, 1982); John Gillingham, "1066 and the Introduction of Chivalry into England," in *Law and Government in Medieval England and Normandy: Essays in Honour of James Holt*, John Garnett and George Hudson, ed. (Cambridge: Cambridge University Press, 1994), 209–31; Gillingham, "Kingship, Chivalry and Love: Political and Cultural Values in the Earliest History Written in French: Geoffrey Gaimar's *Estoire des Engleis*," in *Anglo-Norman Political Culture and the Twelfth-Century Renaissance*, C. Warren Hollister, ed. (Woodbridge: Boydell, 1997), 33–58; David Crouch, *The Birth of Nobility: Constructing Aristocracy in England and France, 900–1300* (Harlow: Longman, 2005).

identity submerges in the more powerful identity of the narratives. Something like that happens to the viewer of the statue of Apollo in Rilke's poem "Archaic Torso of Apollo." He looks at a headless classical statue in the Louvre, and some magnetism suffusing the work takes command of him. It is watching him more powerfully than he is watching it, and the poet loses the contest of gazing. The marble torso, headless though it is, has eyes and vision and light in its every contour, because the missing head has sublimated itself and diffused vision through the remaining parts. Though you don't see them, it is all eyes: "There is no point that does not see you." The cryptic final line, "You must change your life," is understandable within the logic of the charismatic text: the museum visitor is in the force-field of the statue. It has imposed its will and authority on the weaker living presence. The missing head symbolizes lost or hidden presence sublimated and working through the charismatic work of art. The headless, eyeless body gazes more powerfully just because it has performed that act of sublimating vision into the body.[38]

Mimesis is humble by comparison with charismatic representation. The basic impulse of imitation is to create a world that is the reader's equal and by similarity compel the reader to love it as the reader's self. What is not possible in the affection of like-for-like that mimesis aims at is transformation. There is only stagnation — remaining the same — and loving it. Narcissus is the defining myth of mimesis for that reason. The basic impulse of hyper-mimetic art is to create a world that is greater and grander than the reader's or viewer's, a world of supernaturally beautiful bodies and faces, sublime emotions, motives and deeds, grand and magnificent fates — chains of destiny that are romantic or heroic or both at the same time — in order to draw the humbled viewer up into its realms, dazzle, educate, and transform that viewer through the vision of the higher being one could become — as the romances took control of Don Quixote, as the statue asserted its authority over Rilke.

The image of the dazzled gods in Hildebert's Rome poem is located at the very point in the historical unfolding of charismatic aesthetics where representation emerges from its subservient

---

38. See C. Stephen Jaeger, *Enchantment: On Charisma and the Sublime in the Arts of the West* (Philadelphia: University of Pennsylvania Press, 2012), 267–87.

CHAPTER 7 ✷ CHARISMATIC BODY/CHARISMATIC TEXT

position and takes control, asserts its authority over charismatic presence. Texts appropriate the representing force that had resided in bodies. The aura of the gods, of the divine human, of the charismatic, fades. The aura of the work of art intensifies.

This development has a final stage. "Classical" and "charismatic" art are bought at a price to the culture that produces them. Texts, having bargained for charisma, overstep their contract. Their humble threadbare presence turns into a demoniacal Uriah Heap. What characterizes this late phase of the body–text dynamic is that texts suffocate bodies. To keep to the terms of the textual contract by which representation can promise immortality, texts become body snatchers. They take over force, authority, and sensuality. They are shams, frauds, and counterfeits, elegant and bedazzling. But fakes too want dominance, and they can get it by taking it. Textualization is a threat to embodied charisma.

A phase in the dynamics of body and text in which texts usurp life is a historical experience and not just a critical or theoretical construct. The connection between the loss of a culture's vitality and growing textualization is observable for instance at the turn of the nineteenth to the twentieth century. The artists of European decadence were well aware that brilliance of art coincides with a culture's loss of vitality. Nietzsche invented the term "Alexandrine man" to describe the person or culture that surrenders life to the book.

There is a full awareness of this dynamic in the modern period. Faust in the beginning of Goethe's play desperately seeks release from the intellect and from suffocation through texts, buying, at the cost of his soul, the return to life in its vitality and immediacy. Examples include "Burckhardtianism" fashioned around the vision of Renaissance Italy in *The Civilization of the Renaissance*; the contest of Dionysian vitalism and Apollonian formalism in Nietzsche's *The Birth of Tragedy*, the opposition of woman (dynamic, vital) to man (intellectual) in Shaw's *Man and Superman*; the "wasteland" of an old, paralyzed, sick culture superseded by a new vitality, an idea shared by T.S. Eliot and German Expressionists and appropriated by National Socialist "vitalism" opposing a "degenerate" intellectual culture.

The twelfth and thirteenth centuries were presented with the same bill for their artistic flourishing. We can witness the culture's capitulation to representation by comparing two texts, one from the late eleventh, the other from the late twelfth century that address the relative value of living presence and symbolic presence. The first is from a remarkable but little read work by Sigebert of Gembloux, *The Passion of the Theban Legion*.[39] Written around 1075 by a schoolmaster with imperial leanings after his retirement from teaching at Metz to the monastery of Gembloux,[40] the work is a blend of heroic epic and martyr legend. It takes its peculiar character partly from a series of highly polished and interesting orations that precede, comment on, and follow the martyrdom of a legion of Christian warriors who refuse an order from the Roman emperor Maximian. One of the speeches is delivered by the warrior saint and officer of the legion, Maurice. He begins by urging his comrades to nonviolent resistance and martyrdom, quoting sayings and stories of Christ. But then he interrupts the biblical examples with the cry, "There is no need for examples [from books]: you yourselves are the example."[41] He develops the opposition of written history to living, embodied history and ends:

> We have read this; we have heard that. So many triumphs of the saints are reported throughout the world. But here I see with my very eyes those deeds I have read about.... Are not those whom I should imitate and those at whom I should marvel right here in front of me?[42]

A very different attitude to the living as opposed to the textual presence registers in the beginning of Hartmann von Aue's *Iwein*, written in the last decade of the twelfth century. He describes a springtime festival at King Arthur's court with its intense joy, then turns to a lament about the lack of joy in the present. But he takes the

39. See also Jaeger, *Envy*, 181–90.

40. Still the best general appraisal of Sigebert is Manitius, *Geschichte* 3:332–50: "Einer der vielseitigsten und bedeutendsten Schriftsteller des 11. und beginnenden 12. Jahrhunderts" (332).

41. Sigebert of Gembloux, *Passio* 2.448: "Non opus exemplis: exemplum vos magis estis." In Dümmler ed., 83.

42. 2.505–13; Dümmler ed., 85.

CHAPTER 7 ★ CHARISMATIC BODY/CHARISMATIC TEXT

stories of the ancient heroes as compensation for the mournfulness of the contemporary world:
> I would not want to have lived then if I had to give up the present and their *stories* that give us such pleasure. In those days it was *deeds* that gave satisfaction.[43]

Hartmann's verses are the full antithesis of Sigebert's St. Maurice lives the heroic moment and renounces the recorded and reported words of Christ himself, the Christian hero of the past, in favor of the heroic deeds of the living. Hartmann is willing to trade the heroic age of deeds and intensely lived pleasures for the dreary contemporary world with its alluring stories of the past. The narrated is preferable to the experienced past. The contemporary world may be unheroic, but it has what the heroic past never had: stories about their great ones. It is a gesture that, for this reader at least, has the aura of resignation from life in the writers of European decadence: "As for life, I leave it to whoever wants it; I would rather live in stories." For Sigebert, or St. Maurice, truth is in the immediate presence of an exemplary human being. The living presence, equipped with the weapons of virtue, outdoes even sacred history. For Hartmann, the stories have become the bearers of exemplary force and givers of pleasure. Virtue is enfabulated.

CONCLUSIONS

The culture and intellectual life of the thirteenth century experienced the collapse of immediacy and vitality and sensed that one of its symptoms was its text-boundness. An anecdote of Jacques de Vitry must stand here in place of a full summation of the topic.[44] A

43. Hartmann von Aue, *Iwein*, ll. 54–58: "ichn wolde dô niht sîn gewesen, / daz ich nû niht enwaere, / dâ uns noch mit ir *maere* / sô rehte wol wesen sol:/ dâ tâten in diu *werc* vil wol." In Wilhelm Benecke et al., ed. 7th ed. (Berlin: De Gruyter, 1974), 2. Emphasis added. The passage (not in Chrétien) had not attracted commentary until Walter Haug recognized it as central to the "consciousness of fictionality" developing among authors of the twelfth century. See *Literaturtheorie im deutschen Mittelalter: Von den Anfängen bis zum Ende des 13. Jahrhunderts. Eine Einführung* (Darmstadt: Wissenschaftliche Buchgesellschaft, 1985), 124–25.

44. See C. Stephen Jaeger, "Charisma and the Transformations of Western Culture, 12th to 13th Centuries," *Religions* 14 (2023). Online at https://doi.org/10.3390/rel14121516.

master of a Paris school, so the story runs, was visited one night by an apparition. It was the ghost of a former student, recently dead. The ghost wore a winding-sheet, "heavy as a stone tower." Its shroud was a large piece of parchment, covered at every point with tinsy letters and characters. The teacher asked what the writings meant, and the student answered that they spelled out the sophisms and vain questionings on which he had wasted his time as a student. The ghost sweated profusely from his burden, and the teacher felt its sufferings when a drop of sweat fell onto the back of his hand. Acid-like, it ate a hole in his hand that remained as a permanent reminder of the visit. The next morning the professor resigned his chair and entered a Cistercian monastery.[45]

The anecdote captures a cultural malaise in the air in mid-thirteenth century and depicts suffocation through metastasizing texts as its cause. This ghostly "man of letters," human presence fully textualized, can serve as a paradigm image of an age that has surrendered its vitality to representation and the book.

---

45. Jacques de Vitry, Crane ed., 12.

8. HILDEBERT OF LAVARDIN ON MURIEL OF WILTON

INTRODUCTION

In an earlier publication I posed a question to which this short essay[1] is a partial response: "What if medieval writing, discourse, literature, poetry, music, and art were much bigger than we credit in our largely mechanical view of their aesthetics? Suppose we had been reading through the tunnel vision of critical perspectives that reduced it, calmed it, tamed it? What if sublimity, grandeur, poetic inspiration, beauty, passion, poetic genius, its ability to enrapture and transform, were powerfully active but gone undetected, diminished, or shunted aside by the current shared presuppositions that sent them to the closet to lurk in the dark?"[2]

The work of Caroline Bynum, Paul Binski, Jacqueline Jung, Bissera Pentcheva, Caroline van Eck,[3] and others has done much to draw attention to the elements of wonder, amazement, vitality in medieval art and literature. Yet a fortress of presuppositions fortifies the idea of medieval art as rule-bound, workshop art. Here is a further assault on that fortress.

MURIEL OF WILTON, A VATIC POET

Hildebert of Lavardin (c.1056–1133) celebrated a poet who was famous at the end of the eleventh and early twelfth century, a nun of Wilton Abbey named Muriel. His poem to Muriel is an example of a sophisticated aesthetic response of a medieval poet-cleric-humanist-bishop, a response deriving ultimately from his strong sense of the sublime in another poet's work. None of her poems have survived. Here is Hildebert's encomium:

1. This chapter was originally published as "Hildebert of Lavardin on Muriel of Wilton, a Vatic Poet: Medieval Poetry and Modern Aesthetic Response." See "Notes on the Chapters," above, xvi–xvii.

2. Jaeger, *Sense*, 10.

3. Caroline Bynum, "Wonder" AHR 102.1 (1997): 1–26; Paul Binski, *Gothic Wonder: Art, Artifice and the Decorated Style 1290–1350* (New Haven, CT: Yale University Press, 2014); Jung, *Eloquent Bodies*; Bissera Pentcheva, *The Sensual Icon: Space, Ritual and the Senses in Byzantium* (University Park: University of Pennsylvania Press, 2010); Caroline van Eck, *Art, Agency, and the Living Presence: From the Animated Image to the Excessive Object* (Boston: De Gruyter, 2015).

The ancient world boasted ten sibyls,
And great was the glory of your sex.
The present age, barren but for a single virgin sage,
Enjoys just one genius,
Even in this age humans have some communion with gods.
Unless I'm wrong, they speak through this virgin's voice.
The gods have entrusted to your mind their awesome mysteries
And have appointed your sacred voice their own prophet.
What flows [spontaneously] from your speech — inferior only to the gods —
Surpasses all that the ancients labored at over midnight oil.
Your every breath is immortal,
And all the world marvels at your work as if it were divine.
By your genius you humble the prophets and the famous poets.
Men and women alike are awe-struck at your eloquence.
The poems you sent me I have read and pondered ten times over,
And still I marvel, thinking that they come from sacred shrines deep within.
Skill in such sacred works is beyond human capacities,
Nor do I believe that it is you who speak, but rather the gods speak through you.
The gravity of your thoughts, the deep meaning, their beautiful harmony
Have the face of the divine.[4]

4.   *Hildeberti Carmen* 26: "Tempora prisca decem se iactavere sibillis, / et vestri sexus gloria multa fuit. / unius ingenio prasentia secula gaudent, / et non ex toto virgine vate carent. / nunc quoque sunt homini quedam commercia divum, / quos puto, nec fallor, virginis ore loqui. / mente tua posuere dei penetrale verendum, / osque sacrum vatem constituere suum. / ore tuo quecumque fluunt vigilata priorum / transcendunt, solis inferiora deis. / quicquid enim spiras est immortale, tuumque / tanquam divinum mundus adorat opus. / deprimis ingenio vates celebresque poetas, / et stupet eloquio sexus uterque tuo. / carmina missa mihi decies spectata revolvens / miror, et ex aditis illa venire reor. / non est humanum tam sacros posse labores, / nec te, sed per te numina credo loqui. / pondera verborum, sensus gravis, ordo venustus / vultum divine condicionis habent...." In Scott ed., 17–18.

CHAPTER 8 ✶ HILDEBERT ON MURIEL

Hildebert was not alone in recognizing her genius. Two other contemporaries lavished praise on her work.[5]

I read this poem for the first time about forty years ago. Peter von Moos' important book was my guide through Hildebert's writings. Von Moos envisioned an episcopal bishop-poet with strong classical influence writing at the beginning of the age of courtliness, set against the cultural background of a medieval Christian-*humanitas*. He directed my thinking in a course that I would follow for many years. The praise of Muriel had to be impressive against that background. But what I saw in the poem at that time was narrowly framed: classical learning, an epideictic rhetoric that cultivated hyperbole as part of a rhetoric of show and spectacle. Von Moos gives this clear-eyed definition of Hildebert's self-conception as educator and poet:

> The core of Hildebert's creative work is not to honor God but to elevate and harmonize humanity. An ancient attitude sets the poetic ideal for Hildebert. We sense in him something of the self-conception of Virgil and Horace as pious prophets, as priests teaching the wisdom of the muses.[6]

It was still possible to read Hildebert's poems in the framework of Curtius' dictum that in the Latin Middle Ages one wrote poetry because one learned it at school. Poetry was a learnable skill, useful and practical, acquired for purposes of praising and other occasions calling on elaborate rhetoric. Probe its sources and forms, and you've got its core. I read it with an unstated, maybe unconscious presupposition that Hildebert probably meant less than he said. Take apart the materials that constitute the poem, so I believed — topoi, borrowed diction, rhetorical formulations — and you come closer to an adequate understanding.

---

5. See Baudri de Bourgueil, *Carmen* 137, Tilliette ed., 2:46–47, with extensive note on the poetess and bibliography. For Serlo of Bayeux's poem to Muriel, see *The Anglo-Latin Satirical Poets and Epigrammatists of the Twelfth Century*, Thomas Wright, ed., Rolls Series 59, 2 vols. (London: Longman, 1872), 2:233-40. Muriel moved from the Loire convent of Le Ronceray to Wilton. For discussion of Muriel in the cult of male-female friendship and poetry in the circle of Loire poets, see Holle Canatella, "*Scripsit amica manus*: Male-Female Spiritual Friendship in England and France ca. 1050–1200" (Ph.D. diss., University of Houston, 2010), 149–77.

6. *Hildebert von Lavardin*, 28.

Von Moos' perspective is more sophisticated than that critical position on Hildebert's poetic art. His reading embraces the poetry of praise and education, a higher inspiration, poetic genius, a creative force in the heart and mind of the poet. But rhetoric and the Latin classics were still the measure of things and yielded a reading of the poem to Muriel commensurate with its various elements: the *laudatio temporis acti*. They had ten sibyls, we have one; they had sacred poetry galore, we have little; they had many who trafficked with the gods, we have only one. Of course, the loss of greatness of the present age in general was the gain of Muriel. All remaining classical sanctity centered in her. Ten sibyls in the ancient world were not adequate to match the creative power of this virgin prophetess in the present age. All the prophets and famed poets of the ancient world cannot measure up to the creations of her *ingenium*.

The reader of medieval Latin poetry in 1980 had to be cautious with the term *ingenium*: it was important to see it as less than "genius," closer to "ability," "talent," or "aptitude." The divine breath and appearance, the flow of inspired poetry, the poetry superior to the ancients and the prophets, just below the gods, fit with the hyperbole of the genre *encomium*. These elements constitute the poem's elevating, aggrandizing force. In short, the poem seemed fashioned from a scheme that was highly rhetorical, reducable to classical influence remodeled with minimal Christian coloring.

MURIEL AND THE SUBLIME

What, if anything, is gained by reading this poem against the background of the sublime in the Middle Ages?[7] Essential features of the poem emerge clear and vigorous when read within that framework — Muriel's voice and its effect on Hildebert. The poem is rife with prophetic elements. Her voice is the voice of divinities.[8] They have entrusted her with their deepest secrets, drawn from the secret inner sanctuaries (*ex aditis*) inaccessible to mortals. Her poetic voice is vatic and sibylline. Her mere breath is poetry, it flows as if spontaneously composed. Her words are godlike, beyond human capacities to create or to understand. Her eloquence, her diction,

7. See Jaeger, *Sense*.
8. While Hildebert stresses the beauty of her language, Baudri of Bourgueil lifts up the quality of her singing voice. See *Carmen* 137. In Tilliette ed., 2:46–47.

her ideas, the structure of her poems all bespeak the work of the gods; they even look like the gods, having "the face of the divine condition." If we take this poem as anything more than a product of school learning, then Hildebert is reacting to a real quality of Muriel's poetry, a real effect on the audience, not just making a poetic arrangement of pre-given matter of praise. Its prophetic character lifts it above whatever conventions arrange its parts.

"Prophetic" describes a mood and an atmosphere. Secrets, mysteries, things above nature are conveyed in this mode. That voice enthralls the audience. Recall the awe-struck fear of the monks of Rievaulx when they supposed that their abbot was conversing behind closed doors with beings from the beyond: "The place became very dreadful." "Prophetic" in the parlance of pre-scholastic culture does not mean predictive. It means mysteries revealed, spoken, expressed in the mode of the inspired prophet.

There is something of this awe at the preternatural in Muriel's poetry. Baudri also rates her poetry at the level of the most famous poet-prophets (*praeclari vates*).[9] It is received with astonishment, that is, in the way appropriate to the presence of God, or the gods, or spoken in the voice of the gods. Male and female alike are struck with amazement (*stupet eloquio tuo*). Hildebert himself, after reading them ten times, is in wonder (*miror*) at their divine quality. The mysteries she conveys are in themselves awe-inspiring (*verendum*), coming as they do from deep within divine minds (*dei penetrale, ex aditis*), still redolent of the communion with gods reserved for this unique sybil.

Prominent also is the stress on the sacral character of her poetry. Her *os sacrum* persuades the gods to appoint her their proclaimer. A convocation of gods is implied. It chooses Muriel as the single sacred poet (*suum sacrum vatem*) worthy to transmit their secrets to the world of humans. Such works (her poems) transcend the mortal. They are worshiped or revered as a creation of gods (*mundus adorat tanquam divinum opus*). The mystery spoken by a god or a god's voice gives mortals assurance that they can sense and perceive the ineffable, that they can hear things *quae non licet homini loqui*. Muriel in her own physical presence, her words, her music must project the aura of the numinous: awe, rapt admiration, perhaps even dread.

9. See *Carmen* 137, l. 12.

Hildebert's poem to Muriel is a reader's response to the sublime. There are various divisions among writers who aim at the sublime. Some want to dazzle and captivate (Honorius, Herbert of Bosham, Adam of Dryburgh, Lawrence of Durham). Others (Anselm, Bernard, Aelred, Gottfried, Dante) create a higher world that, like a work of music, plays in its own individual key, that enfolds the listener in the atmosphere of a realm beyond and above nature and yet is seemingly real, that is, a prophetic atmosphere. Works like this can transport the audience into the *status sublimitatis*. Muriel belongs in the latter group. We cannot identify and enter into the epic or lyric tone of her works — which are only realized in performance and hence lost — but we can infer it from Hildebert's response. Her every breath utters something immortal. It is not middle style with occasional surges into the sublime but rather a world separate and above human experience. If this consideration has weight, then we have come well beyond school learning, rhetoric, and classical allusiveness. Hildebert's elevation of Muriel and her poetry to the divine speaks a language stretching to give expression to what is beyond human fathoming.

In this context the quality of *ingenium* has to be understood as bigger and more lustrous than "ability," "skill," or "aptitude." It is the quality by which Muriel surpasses the *vates* and famous poets of ancient times and creates the prophetic mood peculiar to her own work. Baudri agrees with Hildebert on this point. Muriel's compositions place her in the ranks of the "most famous poet/prophets" (*praeclaris vatibus*)[10] and "the wealth of her rich genius bestows on her great treasures" (*Divitis ingenii tibi copia dives abundat*).[11] The etymology of *dives* relates it to *divinus*, and something of that relationship may be present in Baudri's phrase. However, the term *ingenium* would seem to require something larger than the conventional translations.[12] "Genius" or "creative spirit" comes closer. Terms from the workshop conception of poetry clearly are not adequate, and both translators just cited avoided them.

10. *Carmen* 26, ll. 11–12.

11. *Carmen* 26, l. 43.

12. Baudri, *Carmen* 137, l. 1; Tilliette ed., 2:46: "*intelligence*"; Joan Ferrante, ed., *Epistolae: Medieval Womens' Letters*. Online at: https://epistolae.ctl.columbia.edu/letter/26108.html): "wit."

HILDEBERT'S MAGNIFICAT

Finally, the perspective of the sublime applied to this poem, but also in general, teaches us something about the character of hyperbole. Extravagant praise is in part, of course, the purpose of Hildebert's poem, but "hyperbole" is a term from a hermeneutic of suspicion. It diminishes what it describes. It implies inflation. It invites, in fact demands, reduction to the banal and ordinary. It appeals to the reader to shrink the words and the subject before they can sense that the proportion between the two is adequate. "Aggrandizing" is more apt. Hildebert's poem enlarges Muriel or, to use the language of Baudri of Bourgueil's praise of Muriel, "magnifies" her.[13] These are terms from the language of sublime rhetoric. The poet must stretch for words that always fall short of the thing or person described, and the rhetoric must ascend to approach her status. When the Virgin Mary tells the Archangel Michael that her soul "magnifies" the Lord, she means "praises" in the sense of elevating the boundary of the divine, extending language to reach to something beyond magnitude.

In that sense also, Hildebert's praise of Muriel is the magnificat of a poet seen as semi-divine. The praise operates in an emotional and cultural framework more complex and more profound than rhetoric, school learning, and craft-guild artistry. The poet/bishop himself worked and wrote in an atmosphere that valued powerful, creative, transformative language. If he imitated classical formulations, it was in order to activate in his work the pith and force of Horace and Virgil, not to create a showpiece of learning. But as much as he and his culture admired classical style, they admired even more the work of John the Evangelist, beautiful, mystery-filled and awe-inspiring. Hildebert, along with writers and audiences who shared his culture, understood that the aesthetic effect of Muriel's poetry was more prophetic than mimetic, more like that of the Virgin Mary magnifying the Lord than that of a sober observer exaggerating the virtues of an ordinary person.

To what extent might Hildebert and his contemporaries have taken seriously the claim of divinity in the poetry of Muriel, or in any poetry? Is the poem exaggeration for effect? Or an expression of high aesthetic-religious *gravitas*? His use of the language of divine

---

13. Baudri, *Carmen* 137, ll. 1–2: "Olim te fama satis magnificarat apud nos, / Quam modo magnificat gratia colloquii." In Tilliette ed., 2:46.

prophecy elsewhere bears out the high seriousness of the elevation of Muriel's poetry. Hildebert only applies the language of the Muriel poem to one other contemporary, Anselm of Canterbury. In a letter to Anselm, Hildebert praised the archbishop for his tract on the Holy Spirit, declaring that the author's heart (*pectus*) is blessed by the "congress of virtues." They have consecrated Anselm's mind as a shrine for their innermost mysteries. "From thence as from the inner sanctum divine oracles proceed, and sacred lips proclaim [you] nothing less than the interpreter of the divine will."[14] The overlap is considerable, the divergences minor. He puts the major theologian of contemporary Europe in the same frame as the poet Muriel. The period had a concept of the "divine poet." Gerald of Wales half a century later, in lamenting the decline of literature and moral teaching, lamented also that there are no more "divine poets" in his age.[15]

Are there many poets like Muriel, who once inspired awe-struck admiration but were reduced for the modern reader by a critical perspective that diminished much that it touched? I think so. The fervent cultivation of poetry around the end of the eleventh century especially by women suggests to me that that entire piece of learned, creative culture is lost, or at least waiting for rediscovery.[16] In many cases the works are lost, but in others the real impact of the writing that has survived is hard to judge given the lost element of performance and the lack of interpretive tools. Critical perspectives focus on interpretation and aesthetic response. The critic, philologist, and historian speak and write as the dominant critical perspectives allow. To depart from those perspectives risks appearing out of touch or eccentric. The critical

---

14. Hildebert, Epist. 13 to Anselm, PL 171:220B; also in Anselm's Epist. 240: "Beatum sane pectus, quod virtutum conventus reverendum sibi penetrale consecravit. Inde velut ex aditis divina prodeunt oracula, nihilque aliud sacra labia profitentur quam coelestis interpretem voluntatis." In Schmitt ed., 4:149.

15. See above, 82 and n. 153.

16. See the important inroads in Peter Dronke, *Women Writers of the Middle Ages* (Cambridge: Cambridge University Press, 1984); and Alison I. Beach, *Women as Scribes: Book Production and Monastic Reform in Twelfth-Century Bavaria* (Cambridge: Cambridge University Press, 2009), which analyzes the eager study of poetry composition among German religious communities.

language of topoi and conventions, traditions and cultural inheritance flattened a great deal that it touched in the later twentieth century, including Hildebert's poem to Muriel, the concept of the divine poet, and the concept of the medieval sublime. The perspective of the sublime contours the poem to Muriel with a reading adequate to the awe-struck wondering admiration of Muriel's admirer.

OPPROBRIUM AND GLORY

This chapter started with the suggestion that my generation might have been reading medieval literature "through the tunnel vision of critical perspectives that reduced it, calmed it, tamed it." In returning to the point, I would only revise the phrase "tunnel vision." The influence of widely shared critical perspectives is not narrow. An atmosphere of aesthetic evaluation has rather the authority of panoptic vision, which embraces culture broadly in a given period, however briefly or durably.

Can critical perspectives really impinge on aesthetic reception so broadly as to shrink or magnify, darken or brighten a later culture's shared responses to the art of a previous age? The answer must certainly be yes. An era-determined critical atmosphere set in place the indifference to or disdain of much great poetry. Medieval vernacular heroic poetry looked primitive in the Enlightenment. Frederick the Great, having pondered an edition of the *Nibelungenlied* offered to him by a philologist hopeful of patronage, responded that the whole thing was not worth "a single shot of gunpowder." Goethe and Hegel more or less agreed. But the aesthetic climate changed, and a composer in the nineteenth century would write a series of grand operas lifting the work and others from that heroic milieu into a sublimity that few in an earlier age had imagined possible and that shaped a passionate devotion to the world of Nordic myth that is still alive and well.[17] Similarly, Shakespeare had to be introduced to France in the eighteenth century with the coarse language and vulgar scenes removed, translated into Alexandrine verse and the language of French classical drama, that is, starkly diminished.

---

17. It is however, experiencing a return to barbarism, brutality and crude nationalism, as in twentieth-century fascism, so also in the fascism of the twenty-first century.

It is the fate of the art and culture of the Middle Ages to be valued little by one age only to be discovered with enthusiasm by the next. The change of critical perspective from the Enlightenment to Romanticism is a dramatic case, as is the change from Romanticism to — let's call ourselves — Modernism. The opprobrium of "Gothic" changed to glorification. Medieval studies in the twentieth century labored under a large-scale misapprehension. While popular and high culture in the romantic era took inspiration in many forms, mainly aggrandizing, from the Middle Ages, it became a sign of good form in post-romantic academic medievalism to sense something ungenuine and derivative in the literature of the age, to strike a cautious and skeptical attitude, to peel back an idealizing surface and reveal darker things beneath it. If Hildebert praised Muriel's poetry as godlike, the critic's task was in part to expose the lesser things that he probably meant. The perspective of the sublime pushes back against that misapprehension.

9. JOHN OF SALISBURY, A PHILOSOPHER OF THE LONG ELEVENTH CENTURY

INTRODUCTION

Modern historians of twelfth-century culture agree that many phenomena that are new in that age begin early in the preceding century. It is also now fairly common to talk about "the long twelfth century," which may extend as far back as 1029 (the range of the new *Cambridge Medieval History*, 1029–1199) and as far forward as mid-thirteenth century. It is common to judge eleventh-century figures as forerunners of an age yet to come. But since the intellectual roots of poets like Marbod, Baudri, and Hildebert are deep in the eleventh century, the judgment of them as twelfth-century poets arrived early on the scene, or at least poets foreshadowing developments yet to reach fruition needs to be tempered by some knowledge of the traditions they both cultivated and gradually moved away from. Marbod was born c.1035, Baudri in 1046, and Hildebert in 1056. They lived on into the twelfth century (d. respectively 1123, 1130, and 1133). While their poetry may look in both directions, modern scholarship has credited only the forward glance.

The history of philosophy represents eleventh-century monks who write about dialectic as transmitters of the ninth and preparers of the twelfth century. The Latin poem *Ruodlieb* becomes a "proto-romance" popped like a mushroom out of the ground that hasn't yet set in beneath its stem. Meinhard of Bamberg, schoolmaster in the second half of the eleventh century, writes a strikingly pure Ciceronian style and so anticipates the "rediscovery" of the Latin classics in the twelfth century, and so on. The tenth and eleventh centuries are regularly invaded by their more powerful neighbors, like some small principality set between two ambitious royal kingdoms. The shrouded glories of that culture play little role in current assessments of the twelfth century. They live the life of a conquered folk.

This study aims at partially reclaiming John of Salisbury, one of the best-known figures of the twelfth century, for the age that is his real intellectual context. Engaged up to his eyeballs in the affairs and conflicts of his own time, he thought, felt, and wrote in modes that were outdated and passing from the scene. He swam against the tide of the age — at least the educational and intellectual climate

— he lived in, pulling hard to drag it back into the age of his own intellectual origins.

Admittedly the term "the long twelfth century" is a useful one. The Eucharist Controversy and the figure of Berengar of Tours in the previous century, the Scholasticism of the following, and the origins of the university as an institution are single examples of the roots and branches of a twelfth-century flowering. Since historical developments do not accommodate themselves to the calendar, the stretched century insists that the calendar accommodate itself to the developments. But the hegemony of concepts needs as careful minding as the spillage of events over time boundaries. The "long twelfth century" and the "twelfth-century renaissance" have discouraged questions of continuities, masked off persons, events, and modes of thought still hanging on in the twelfth century which, like John of Salisbury, represent not the rising twelfth century but survival of the eleventh.[1] This is especially evident in the milieu of cathedral schools and the independent schools of Paris. To quote from an earlier article:

> Alongside all that is new in the twelfth century an older culture was in a state of decline and collapse. It is the confluence of the dying and the rising cultures and the tensions and conflicts which that confluence spawned that account for the peculiar energy and creativity of the age. But what culture? What was it that John of Salisbury saw ending in his day? The historical study of the twelfth century has had no eyes for the humanism (and the educational structures and ideas supporting it) that began in the mid-tenth and came to an end in the course of the twelfth century. Indeed, most medievalists would be hard pressed to say anything at all about the secular culture of Europe

---

1. See Rodney Thomson, "The Place of Germany in the Twelfth-Century Renaissance," in *Manuscripts and Monastic Culture: Reform and Renewal in Twelfth-Century Germany*, Alison I. Beach, ed. (Turnhout: Brepols, 2007), 19–42. Thomson argues cultural continuity in Germany in contrast to transformation in France. Thomson's essay and others in the same volume show the vitality and energy of intellectual life in twelfth-century Germany. But the imposition of "renewal" and "renaissance" on the period as a whole binds Thomson to defensive arguments that the complexion of Germany was not "more backward-looking and conservative than in the rest of Europe" (41).

in the years 950–1100.... Hildebert, Hugh of St. Victor, John of Salisbury, Otto of Freising, Walter of Châtillon, Alan of Lille thought of themselves as late representatives of a culture that was coming to an end. The passing culture is hidden to our view partly because of the nature of its documentation, partly because of the concepts which structure our thinking.[2]

It seems sensible to propose a "long eleventh century" to accommodate the conservative resistance to the main trends of twelfth-century school life in Paris.

While John's conservatism has not gone unnoticed, his splendid latinity and vast reading of the classics have tended to make him into a representative of the "classical revival of the twelfth century."[3] His humanism and its sources are the subject for another study, but here I want to look at his position in the intellectual trends of the first half of the century.

THE METALOGICON, A CATCHY TITLE

The key to that issue is his *Metalogicon* (1159). The title represents his work as a "defense of logic." That title beams the claim that this is a progressive work, plugged into the mainstream of his time and pushing forward at the cutting edge of twelfth-century thought. But the title is misleading. John starts out with a definition of Logic that embraces all the language arts: "Logic in its broadest sense is the science of verbal expression and argumentative reasoning."[4] While John recurs regularly to the narrower definition of logic — the art of shaping arguments that admit no refutation — this broader framing clearly serves his overriding intention of insisting on the indivisible unity of the trivium.[5] The passage just quoted continues: "Sometimes 'logic' is used with more restricted extension, and limited to rules of

2. "Pessimism in the Twelfth-Century 'Renaissance,'" *Speculum* 78 (2003): 1151–83, at 1181–82.

3. Haskins, 100: John the "highest representative."

4. Ioannis Saresberiensis, *Metalogicon* 1.10.8–9: "Est itaque logica ut nominis significatio latissime pateat, loquendi vel disserendi ratio." In Hall ed., 2; McGarry trans., 32.

5. The same spectrum of meaning in "logic" is maintained by John's teacher Abelard. See McLaughlin, 526–27.

reasoning."[6] He recognizes and accepts the common equating of logic and dialectic. But the predominant position of dialectic in the schools of Paris suggest that this art needs no defense.

John studied in Paris during the period of the high flourishing of dialectical studies. His objection is to the hypertrophy of that discipline, which has severed the study of dialectic from its broader context in language studies generally. What is necessary in John's view is the reestablishing of the broader definition: logic is the art of eloquent speech. It cannot be mastered unless the three arts of the trivium combine to educate to eloquence. It is the embattled arts of grammar and rhetoric that John is rescuing from neglect and trying to reestablish in their proper position in the course of studies. Dialectic flourishes but in a form so trivial as to represent in itself an argument against its separation from grammar and rhetoric. The crumbling position of rhetoric and grammar in the arts of language is what requires shoring. For the purposes of his polemic in the first two books, the broader definition serves him better than the narrower:

> For the present let us concede to logic its widest meaning, which includes all instruction relative to words....[7]

John posits an enemy of grammar — necessary after all if he is to defend it — and gives him the name "Cornificius." Many identifications of Cornificius have been proposed, but none has found consensus.[8] It is probably best to see in this figure a fiction created by John to encompass a variety of positions that can be represented as opposed to "logic" understood as "the science of verbal expression

---

6. *Metalogicon* 1.10.9–11: "Contrahitur enim interdum, et dumtaxat circa disserendi rationes, vis nominis coartatur." In Hall ed., 2.

7. *Metalogicon* 1.10.15–17:"...ut quam latissime protendatur significatio, ei [i.e., to logic] ad praesens sermonum omnium magisterium tribuatur...." In Hall ed., 2.

8. Master Gualo of Paris is one candidate for Lambertus M. De Rijk,"Some New Evidence on Twelfth-Century Logic: Alberic and the School of Mont Ste. Geneviève," *Vivarium* 4 (1966): 1–57, at 4–8. Reginald the Monk is another, according to Prantl, *Geschichte*, 2:230. More recent literature on "Cornificius" is cited in Cary J. Nederman, *John of Salisbury* (Tempe: Arizona Center for Medieval & Renaissance Studies, 2005), 66 n. 3. Nederman adds to the list of possible identifications: Arnulf of Lisieux and Bernard of Clairvaux.

CHAPTER 9 ✴ JOHN OF SALISBURY

and argumentative reasoning."[9] There were indeed foes of logic in the narrower sense. Abelard had polemicized against them. They seem to be theological purists who want to banish human reasoning from the understanding of the faith.[10] John's defense of logic against its attackers remains strictly within the realm of the trivium and has no particular interest in epistemology and theology. While he claims to be defending logic, he is really defending the position of grammar and rhetoric in the disciplines of studies.

There is a captiousness and coyness about the title *Metalogicon*, which I find commonly in John's writings. He is a slippery rhetorician,[11] a polemicist who hurls sharp barbs at opponents and wards off counterattack with rhetoric. In the *Policraticus* he assures readers that none of them is his target of this vehement polemic against the frivolities of court life. He has only one target: himself and others like him. Of course, anyone whom the shoe fits should wear it: "*mutato nomine, de se fabula narratur.*"[12] He dedicated the *Policraticus* to Chancellor Thomas Becket. His explanation: since he wishes to give no offense to anyone, he dedicates his book on the frivolities of courtiers to the one man in England above any suspicion of frivolity, Becket. Then he proceeds to skewer those very courtier vices for which Becket himself had become famous and notorious. We will not understand much of John's polemics in *Metalogicon* unless we penetrate the layers of irony and ironic praise in which much of it is swathed.

9. Cf. Ferruolo, *Origins*, 141–43.

10. See Abelard's Letter 13, "To an Ignoramus in the Field of Dialectics," in *Peter Abelard, Letters IX–XIV*, Edmé R. Smits, ed. (Groningen: University of Groningen, 1983), 271–77.

11. See Jaeger, "Irony." Christopher Brooke observed this aspect of John's judgments of his contemporaries: "In his writings he loves to play with complex irony on the two sides of an issue or a person.... He enjoyed...cutting everybody down to size, while preserving a reasonable respect and sympathy for almost all the men he describes." See "John of Salisbury and His World," in *The World of John of Salisbury*, Michael Wilks, ed. (Oxford: Blackwell, 1984), 1–20, at 2.

12. *Policraticus* 1, prol., ll. 79–80. In Katharine S.B. Keats-Rohan, ed., CCCM 118 (Turnholt: Brepols, 1993), 23. One finds the same claim at the end of the work: *Ioannis Saresberiensis Episcopi Carnotensis Policratici sive De Nugis Curialium et Vestigiis Philosophorum Libri VIII* 8.25, Clemens Webb, ed. (Oxford: Clarendon, 1909), 2:425.7–8. See also Jaeger, "Irony," 323–24.

Metalogicon: our publishers of academic books have a useful term, "the hook of the book." Where is its hook? What is in it that will lure anyone to buy and read it? The hook of John's book is big and sharp. A large part of the *Metalogicon* is specifically a defense of Aristotle against the dialecticians who misuse and misunderstand him. This *intentio operis* should have guaranteed him interested readers. It promises engaged and combative polemics. The title and its explanation call on buzzwords and refer to popular trends in the schools. But once into the book, the reader sees that what is being defended is a humanistic education that subordinates dialectic to the other language arts, and that this education is being forced out of the Paris schools.

An analogy to current trends in academic thought in America suggests itself. Conservative colleagues, especially in the fields of classics and medieval studies, have tended to resist the trends in critical theory that recently thrived in English and foreign-language departments, in the USA anyway. They see young scholars besotted by high-fallutin' French theorizing full of beguiling verbiage, grown indifferent to literature itself, interested only in theory of representation. They complain that students nowadays don't need to read the classics; they only need to read Derrida and Foucault. If any such conservative attempted to re-route the mainstream by writing an intricate and learned treatise on Kant, Nietzsche, and Heidegger entitled, say, *Meta-Anarchitektikon*, "A Defense of Deconstruction," or "A Defense of Post-Modern Critical Theory," with fulsome polemics against Jacques Derrida and his followers — all of which are prefaced with praise — he would be very much in the position of John of Salisbury "defending" logic. By placing himself among the defenders of logic, he placed himself in the majority, but in fact he has infiltrated that majority as the representative of a minority position, namely that logic tends to nonsense when separated from grammar and rhetoric.

THE LURE OF DIALECTIC

If we look at the personalities he discusses who represent the practice of dialectics, we get a clearer view of his object. He begins his review of his studies in Paris in *Metalogicon* 2.10 with Peter Abelard, one of two teachers for whom John has only praise (the other is Gilbert

CHAPTER 9 ✷ JOHN OF SALISBURY

de la Porée). Then he moves on to Master Alberic, "who among others shone forth as a most highly celebrated dialectician."[13] Then after two years, he had as instructors in dialectic "Alberic and Master Robert of Melun." The formulation is a little misleading. It seems to indicate two Alberics, neither identified by a cognomen. But most likely the two are the same. He retained Master Alberic and took on Robert. This Alberic, now identified as Alberic of Paris, is certainly to be distinguished from Alberic of Rheims, mentioned by John in *Metalogicon* 1.5 as an object of attack of the Cornificians. After mentioning his glowing reputation, John moves on to ambiguous praise. Alberic can find problems where you would least suspect them:

> For him, not even a plain surface that was polished smooth could be entirely free from objectionable roughness. According to the saying, for him "the very bulrush would not be free of nodes." For even in the bulrush, he would be sure to discover knots in need of untying.[14]

After praising Robert of Melun as "penetrating, concise, and to-the-point in his replies," John observes that the qualities of the two combined in a single person would have produced a superb disputant. Both "had keen minds and were diligent scholars, persistent in their efforts" (*"ambo acuti erant ingenii, et studii pervicacis"*) — faint praise muted further by the comment that they would have been great scholars,

> had they but possessed a broad foundation of literary learning and kept to the footsteps of their predecessors as much as they took delight in their own inventions.[15]

13. *Metalogicon* 2.10.9–10: "…adhaesi magistro Alberico qui inter ceteros opinatissimus dialecticus enitebat…." In Hall ed., 71; McGarry trans., 95: "…who had a very high reputation as the best of the other dialecticians." "*Inter caeteros*" hangs there oddly. Are the "*ceteri*" those who celebrate Alberic? Or are they other dialecticians rated less than him?

14. *Metalogicon* 2.10.16–17: "…quamvis polita planities offendiculo non careret, et ut aiunt ei scirpus non esset enodis. Nam et ibi monstrabat quod oporteat enodari." In Hall ed., 71. McGarry trans., 96, offers an explanatory note: "That is, difficulties would be conjured up where they did not actually exist."

15. *Metalogicon* 2.10.27–28: "…magni praeclarique viri in philosophicis studiis enituissent, si de magno litterarum niterentur fundamento, si tantum instituissent vestigiis maiorum, quantum suis applaudebant inventis." In Hall and Keats-Rohan ed., 71.

Alberic, John's narrative continues, later went to Bologna, where he "unlearned" what he had formerly taught. He then returned to "unteach" it ("...*dedicit quod docuerat...et reversus dedocuit*"). So, John's recollection of Alberic moves from praise at first apparent, then questionable, then faint, to end with ridicule. Along the way he drops suggestions of vanity ("*suis applaudebant inventis*"), lack of thorough learning, and isolation in dialectic. Robert of Melun comes off somewhat better, possibly because he moved to theological studies.

His judgment of the studies with Alberic and Robert of Melun on the Mt. Ste. Geneviève registers clearly in the report of his own development as a dialectician. Through the teachings of those two, he mastered the basics of the subject so well that he knew "the topics, rules, and other elementary principles" like the back of his hand. The result:

> I had learned the subject so thoroughly that, with childish levity, I unduly exaggerated my own knowledge. I took myself to be a young sage, inasmuch as I knew the answers to what I had been taught.[16]

THE CURE OF GRAMMAR

John is constructing a cautionary tale out of his own career. His studies in dialectic made him think himself an expert in the discipline. His head swelled with self-satisfaction. These are the dangers of dialectical studies practiced in isolation from other disciplines. As in good cautionary tales, there is a conversion. He sobers up:

> However, I recovered my senses, and took stock of my powers. I then transferred, after deliberation and consultation and with the approval of my instructors, to the grammarian of Conches.[17]

His escape and refuge from the dangerous pride of dialectical studies is grammar. He studied grammar for the next three years

---

16. *Metalogicon* 2.10.39–40: "Hoc enim plane didiceram, ut iuvenili levitate pluris facerem scientiam meam quam erat. Videbar mihi sciolus, eo quod in his quae audieram promptus eram." In Hall and Keats-Rohan ed., 71; McGarry trans., 97, minor liberties taken.

17. *Metalogicon* 2.10.42–43: "Deinde reversus in me et metiens vires meas, bona praeceptorum meorum gratia consulto me ad grammaticum de Conchis transtuli...." In Hall and Keats-Rohan ed., 71.

with William of Conches. Then he moved on to quadrivial studies, rhetoric, and finally theology.

This narrative of the author losing himself in dialectic and rescuing himself in broader studies resonates with his earlier report of the path that his most prominent teachers had followed. Gilbert of Poitiers, Thierry and Bernard of Chartres, William of Conches, and Abelard had all struggled against the foolishness of the "Cornificians," and they

> became insane themselves in combating insanity, and for quite a time floundered in error while trying to correct it. The fog, however, was soon dispelled.... The arts regained their own and were reinstalled in their earlier seat of honor.[18]

In setting his own development within this pattern, John has shaped a story of metanoia and conversion. He has made himself embody the dangers of excessive dialectical studies and the escape from them to the refuge of grammar, quadrivial studies, and theology. The narrative has exemplary quality, and he expressly invests it with a moral lesson. While he eluded the pride that excessive dialectic breeds, it claimed his colleagues and teachers at the Mont. When he returned to the Mt. Ste. Geneviève twelve years later, he found that they had succumbed to the dangers he avoided:

> I found them just as and where they were when I had left them. They did not seem to have progressed as much as a hand's span. Not a single tiny [new] proposition had they added toward the solution of the old problems.[19] [The one bit of change he can register is a moral decline.] ...they had unlearned moderation; they no longer knew restraint. [And from the experience he draws the lesson that] just as

---

18. *Metalogicon* 1.5.15–16: "...se omnes opposuerunt errori, sed nec universi insanientibus resistere potuerunt. Insipientes itaque facti sunt dum insipientiae resistebant, et erronei diutius habiti dum obviare nitebantur errori. Verumtamen fumus ille cito evanuit, et praedictorum opera magistrorum et diligentia redierunt artes, et...honorem pristinum nactae sunt..." In Hall and Keats-Rohan ed., 20–21; McGarry trans., 22.

19. *Metalogicon* 2.10.87–88: "Inventi sunt qui fuerant et ubi. Neque enim ad palmum visi sunt processisse. Ad quaestiones pristinas dirimendas, nec propositiunculam unam adiecerant." In Hall and Keats-Rohan ed., 73; McGarry trans., 100.

dialectic expedites other studies so, if left alone by itself, it lies powerless and sterile.[20]

I am not suggesting that the account of his move from dialectic to grammar, because moralized, is also fictionalized. But it does smack of the rhetorical posture he takes in the *Policraticus*. He has much criticism of courtiers, but no one should take offense, because the courtier who embodies all the vices of the court is he himself.[21] In the *Metalogicon* his personal experience is fashioned into a paradigm of the trap of dialectic and redemption through "the broader foundation of liberal studies."

ADAM OF BALSHAM

We should look closely at his praise of another teacher of dialectic, Adam du Petit Pont, Adam of Balsham.[22] John had a curious relationship with this master. The two men became close friends while John taught the rudiments of logic to beginning students in Paris in that period of his studies in grammar, the quadrivium, and theology.[23] He brought Adam questions from his students and received help from the senior master. John stresses that he was not Adam's student. He helped John because of their familiarity, even though Adam had a reputation for jealousy. He praises Adam as a man of "very keen intellect and also of very wide learning" but adds, "whatever others may think" and so tips the reader off that another shoe will drop.[24] Later the mask of praise falls, the bonds of intimacy reveal their weakness, and John charges his former friend with the worst faults of excessive dialecticians:

> Those who follow Aristotle in a confusing babel of names and verbs and subtle intricacies blunt the mental faculties of others

20. *Metalogicon* 2.10.91–92: "Profecerunt in uno dumtaxat, dedidicerant modum, modestiam nesciebant... Expertus itaque sum quod liquido colligi potest, quia sicut dialectica alias expedit disciplinas, sic si sola fuerit iacet exanguis et sterilis...." In Hall and Keats-Rohan ed., 73; McGarry trans., 100.

21. See above, 303 n. 12.

22. See the DictMA 1:51–52, "Adam of the Little Bridge."

23. *Metalogicon* 2.10.61: "familiaritatem contraxi ulteriorem." In Hall ed., 72; McGarry trans, 98: "with whom I became very intimate."

24. *Metalogicon* 2.10.59–60; Hall ed., 72; McGarry trans., 98.

in their effort to show off their own intellectual capacity and, to me, seem to have chosen the worse part. It is my belief that our own English Adam especially fell into this vice in the book that he entitled *The Art of Reasoning*. Would that he had expressed well the good things that he has said! Although his friends and followers attribute his obscurity to subtlety, many have judged that it stems from the folly or envy of vanity. For Adam has presented Aristotle in such involved language that a judicious listener may well comment, "Is not this as frothy, with thick and puffed-up bark, as the shrivelled old branch of a superannuated cork tree?"[25]

John — generously — cites Adam's friends defending him (his obscurity comes from subtlety) and — ungenerously — that of his enemies (it comes from folly or envy of a vain man). John seems to throw fuel on the critics' flames by high-color abuse quoted from the satirist Persius (*Satires* 1.96–97): "frothy, thick, puffed up, the shrivelled old branch of an old cork tree." May all the powers that be protect us from this kind of appraisal in our student evaluations! Or from friends who invent "sober auditors" and quote their withering comments with such relish! John ends this passage with a gesture of anemic diplomacy: "Nevertheless we should be grateful to the authors, for their works are a fountain from which we may drink...."

We can get another perspective on John's relation to logic as practiced and taught in Paris by considering his own teaching. John says that he "took as pupils the children of nobles, who in return provided for my material necessities" "...*mihi...alimenta praestabant*..." does not suggest he was well paid, while other teachers

---

25. *Metalogicon* 4.3.11–23: "Unde qui Aristotelem sequuntur in turbatione nominum et verborum, et intricata subtilitate ut suum venditent, aliorum obtundunt ingenia, partem pessimam mihi praeelegisse videntur. Quo quidem vitio Anglicus noster Adam mihi prae ceteris visus est laborasse, in libro quem artem disserendi inscripsit. Et utinam bene dixisset, bona quae dixit. Et licet familiares eius et fautores hoc subtilitati ascribant, plurimi tamen hoc ex desipientia vel invidentia vani ut aiunt hominis, contigisse interpretati sunt. Adeo enim expressit Aristotilem intricatione verborum, ut sobrius auditor recte subiungat: 'nonne hoc spumosum et cortice pingui, ut ramale vetus praegrandi subere coctum?' Habenda est tamen auctoribus gratia, quia de fonte eorum haurientes, labore ditamur alieno." In Hall ed., 142; McGarry trans., 206–7.

became wealthy from student fees. He relied on Master Adam to help with the questions of his students, a statement that on the one hand puts forward his credentials for a close and trusting alliance with a senior master, on the other projects a junior position for John. Try to imagine Peter Abelard, Gilbert de la Porée, or William of Champeaux admitting that they turned to a more advanced dialectician for help in teaching the rudiments to beginning students.

In her essay on John of Salisbury and twelfth-century education, Keats-Rohan looks closely at the circumstances of John as teacher.[26] He probably took students after his "conversion" from dialectic during the period of his studies with William of Conches and Richard Bishop. That would explain his statement that "I was frequently obliged to recall what I had earlier learned" and that he must lean on a current master of logic, Adam, for help in dealing with questions about dialectic. Clearly the students were not asking him questions related to grammar and theology, which presumably occupied him at the time he took students. He evidently did not teach happily but out of necessity: "...*nobilium liberos...instruendos susceperam, ex necessitate officii et instantia iuvenum....*"[27] Keats-Rohan sees an unwilling teacher revealed in the phrase "*ex necessitate officii*" ("'*Officium*' with its onerous implication of duty rather than vocation...").

WILLIAM OF SOISSONS' LOGIC MACHINE

John mentions only one of his students by name. That is a certain William of Soissons. What we learn about him is that he later devised a logic machine, evidently designed to construct fallacies, or paradoxical or impossible or imponderable conclusions, and to deconstruct the opinions of the ancients. Its purpose was to conquer old-fashioned logic. In other words, the one student John felt impelled to mention by name was the inventor of a mechanical logician.[28] Is this a joke? Is it really a logic machine? With a crank, a

26. Katharine S.B. Keats-Rohan, "John of Salisbury and Education in Twelfth-Century Paris from the Account of his *Metalogicon*," *History of Universities* 6 (1986): 1–45.

27. *Metalogicon* 2.10.55–56; Hall and Keats-Rohan ed., 72.

28. Varied opinions on William of Soissons include Clement C.J. Webb, *John of Salisbury* (London: Methuen, 1932), 9: "a paradoxical innovator in logical theory";

CHAPTER 9 ✶ JOHN OF SALISBURY

barrel, and independently revolving registers on tumblers that form paradoxical utterances every time their revolutions cease? Modern opinions vary. Here is the difficult passage:

> Interim Willelmum Suessionensem, qui ad expugnandam, ut aiunt sui, logicae vetustatem et consequentias inopinabiles construendas et antiquorum sententias diruendas machinam postmodum fecit, prima logices docui elementa....[29]

There is wide disagreement on the meaning of *machina* in the modern English translations I have consulted.[30] Some hold to

---

Jan Van Laarhoven, *John of Salisbury's Entheticus Maior and Minor* (Leiden: Brill, 1987), 1:4: "William...the later 'destroyer'of logic..."; Keats-Rohan, "John of Salisbury," 16: "Perhaps John's pupil was that William of Soissons whom William of Tyre later found expounding Euclid in Bologna, and of whom he observes that he was "impeditioris lingue virum, sed acute mentis et ingenii subtilioris hominem" ("a man of rather unclear speech, but with a penetrating and quite subtle intelligence.") See William of Tyre, *Historia rerum in partibus transmarinis gestarum* (*History of Deeds Done Beyond the Sea*) 39–41; Emily Babcock and August C. Krey, trans. (New York: Columbia University Press, 1943), 823.

29. *Metalogicon* 2.10.64–68; Hall ed., 72.

30. Lynn Thorndike, *University Records and Life in the Middle Ages* (New York: Columbia University Press, 1949), 13: "Meanwhile William of Soissons — who later made an engine to lay siege, as his adherents say, to old-fashioned logic and reach unexpected consequences and destroy the opinions of the ancients — was teaching [sic] the first elements of logic...." In *Metalogicon*, McGarry trans., 98: "Meanwhile I taught the first principles of logic to William of Soissons. William later, according to his followers, invented a device to revolutionize the old logic by constructing unacceptable conclusions and demolishing the authoritative opinions of the ancients." Kneale and Kneale, 201: "...William of Soissons...later produced an engine for capturing, as his friends say, the citadel of the old logic, building up unexpected links of argument, and demolishing the opinions of the ancients"; Keats-Rohan, "John of Salisbury," 16: [commentary, not direct translation] "...William was a disappointment who afterwards devised a system of false logic, *machina*." Klaus Guth, *Johannes von Salisbury: Studien zur Kirchen-, Kultur- und Sozialgeschichte Westeuropas im 12. Jahrhundert* (St. Ottilien: Eos Verlag, 1978), 37: "...er hat, wie seine Schüler sagen, bald darauf eine Maschine (System) konstruiert, um die alte Logik zu erobern, unwahrscheinliche Folgerungen zusammenzustellen, und dadurch logische Sätze der Alten zu vernichten...." Christopher Martin, "William's Machine," *Journal of Philosophy* 83 (1986): 654–72, at 565: "He invented a machine for the purpose of

machina = machine in the literal sense. Others read it as metaphor ("device to lay siege") or abstractly ("a system of false logic"). The latter position seems to me less persuasive than the literal reading. McGarry hedges his bets with "device" but glides over into the camp of the abstractionists in a footnote.[31] The Kneales likewise cover both possibilities with "engine" but then come down solidly on the side of the abstractionists:

> ...almost certainly his invention was some novel pattern of argument which his friends likened to a siege engine, much as a general method of intellectual attack might be called in our time a bulldozer.[32]

It seems to me that Christopher Martin has come closest to identifying the element of logic referred to here. He places William's machine in "theory of entailment," inference-drawing from conditional statements. He also confirms the machine-ness of William's invention by reference to the logic machine of Stanley Jevons (with reference to the Kneales). Most likely, says Martin, William's machine operated on a principle learned from his teacher Adam du Petit Pont, "that anything follows from an impossibility and a necessity follows from anything."[33]

The machine functions within the common practice in dialectical instruction of proposing fallacious arguments to students and insisting on exposure of the fallacy (a significant element of the art of *discrimen veri et falsi*). "*Consequentiae inopinabiles*" are untestable

---

subduing by force the old established principles of logic, for constructing unbelievable consequences and destroying the theories of the ancients." R.W. Southern, *Scholastic Humanism*, 1:216: "...William of Soissons, who had constructed a kind of logical machine for teaching the elements of argument." Carl Scharschmidt quotes the entire passage on John's time in Paris, including the mention of his student William, but omits the lines about the logic machine. See *Johannes Saresberiensis nach Leben und Studien, Schriften und Philosophie* (Leipzig: Teubner, 1862), 12.

31. McGarry, 98 n. 183: "*machinam*, an artificial method of argumentation or reasoning, called a 'machine' because it was devised to construct and to demolish...a device, system, or [reasoning] process."

32. *Development of Logic*, 201.

33. "William's Machine," 571.

claims that defy any empirical knowledge, for instance "the sky is eight times larger than the earth."[34]

But the exact nature of William's machine is less important here than John's take on it. The clues are in the phrase *ad expugnandam... logicae vetustatem...et antiquorum sententias diruendas*. There can be little doubt of what John would make of an invention, be it machine or system, devised to attack "the antiquity of logic" and undermine the opinions of the ancients. He follows the description of the machine with a decided refutation of the premise on which it is based with reference to Aristotle's rejection of the same premise. Keats-Rohan senses irony, not a teacher's pride, in John's comments, and I believe she is right. William of Soissons comes across as, if not a crackpot, then a clever man whose genius has run off the tracks. We might formulate John's subtext: "That's all the schools need, a mechanical logician cranking out fallacious arguments to destroy ancient authority." John's depiction of William of Soissons calls to mind William Butler Yeats' nightmare vision of his countryman George Bernard Shaw. The loquacious Shaw appeared to the sleeping poet Yeats in the form of a sewing machine, unstoppably clicking and smiling.[35]

We can say with some assurance that John of Salisbury did not have a distinguished career as a teacher.[36] What he knew was not what students wanted. The same applied to some of his teachers. William of Conches and Richard Bishop, who had taught in the manner of Bernard of Chartres, both "quit" or "retired" (*"cesserunt"*) when they were "conquered by the onslaught of the ignorant mob" (*impetu multitudinis imperitae victi*), students content to seem rather than be philosophers, John says, content with the appearance of truth, demanding the entire arts course in two to three years.

34. The collection of logical texts published by Lambertus M. De Rijk as *Summe Mettenses*, in *Logica Modernorum* lists *inopinabiles* as one of five categories of fallacious conclusions: "Inopinabile est quod est extra opinionem plurium, ut *celum octies esse maius terra*. Ad quam metam ducitur aliquis cum cogitur concedere quod est extra opinionem suam." In De Rijk, *Logica Modernorum*, 473.

35. Edmund Wilson, *Axel's Castle* (New York: Scribner's, 1935), 60.

36. Nederman, 12, agrees but puts the best face on it: "John may not have been a very popular teacher because he demanded too much from his students."

Parisian masters who taught in the manner of Bernard of Chartres were in danger from the early twelfth century on. The fate of William of Champeaux and his two successors in the chair of Notre Dame, Paris, fits this model. Though they were not students of Bernard of Chartres, they tried their hand at dialectic and were no match for their nemesis, Abelard. If Abelard's account is reliable, they also "retired" when their lectures fell into disregard and Abelard's were in demand. It seems likely that John's own career followed this pattern. He never indicates that he lacked students, but how much enthusiasm could he rouse for the task of teaching men like William of Soissons? Nederman suggests also that the prosecution of Abelard (1140) and Gilbert (1147 and 1148) may have been a factor in his quitting the schools.[37]

We should also stress that John departed Paris of necessity, not because a brighter future beckoned elsewhere. His next stop after Paris was probably some form of temporary employment with his friend Peter of Celle, more a shelter than a firm post. He finally found gainful employment and work suited to his talents at Canterbury on the staff of Archbishop Theobald, either in late 1147 or early 1148.

So, the *Metalogicon* is, indeed, a "defense of logic" but in a special sense: it defends the discipline when joined to the other language arts. John defends dialectic by putting it in its place: at the beginning of studies. "By itself logic is practically useless. Only when it is associated with other studies does logic shine."[38] In particular, he defends the discipline against virtually everyone who practices it in Paris, at least anyone who makes it into the single central discipline. The trend towards dialectical studies separated from the other arts and completable in a short time is in danger of overwhelming the schools. The same trend had possibly also overwhelmed John of Salisbury himself. He is stemming himself against a flood tide or trying to turn back the flood that has already — in his opinion — devastated learning as he knew and valued it.

Now, it is true that John had extensive knowledge of Aristotle and Aristotelian logic, that is, what was available up to the earlier twelfth century. He had studied it for years with excellent teachers,

37. Nederman, 12.
38. *Metalogicon* 4.28.4–6; Hall ed., 164; McGarry trans., 244.

first with Peter Abelard, then with Master Alberic, Robert of Melun, and Gilbert of Poitiers. After an interlude of grammar, rhetoric, and theology, he returned to teach logic with refresher sessions provided by Adam du Petit Pont. But even in his presentation of Aristotle, he both defends the ancient master against the abuses of the moderns and cites him in order to chasten the immoderate indulgences of his contemporaries.

We cannot fault John as an expert in dialectic. He knows what he is talking about, and if he stresses that his teaching reached no further than what is appropriate for beginners, it is because the entire subject is the entry into studies for beginners. Still, his mastery of Aristotle is far from qualifying him as a progressive thinker or as a reformer, a term Nederman applies to him.[39] John's praise of logic and Aristotle recurs to a fading norm. He was defending the logic that William of Soissons' logic machine sought to destroy. In the practice of the Paris schools the predominant moving forces are shallowness, venality, immodesty, arrogance contemptuous of tradition, and what John calls insanity. His harsh views often register only in irony or indirectness in the *Metalogicon* or as masked by the unidentifiable "Cornificius." In other works, he speaks more bluntly:

> Consider the leading teachers of philosophy of our own day, those who are most loudly acclaimed, surrounded by a noisy throng of disciples. Mark them carefully; you will find them dwelling on one rule, or on two or three words...on which to exercise their talents and waste their life.... The points of dispute of our modern Proteus...are as useless as they are trivial.[40]

And in the long poem called *Entheticus* he depicts himself as a young student seduced by the trends in the schools to believe that one can "read little to learn much" and that dialectic is the only discipline that counts:

---

39. Nederman, 63: "The *Metalogicon* is the work of a sympathetic reformer, who is accepting of the general outlines of scholastic learning, while still critical of some of the more extreme or invidious conceptions of advanced education on display in his time." There is a sharper focus in Nederman's comment, "John's was a style of philosophy that was largely out of vogue in the schools of his time..." (74).

40. *Policraticus* 7.9; Webb ed., 2:123. English cited from *Frivolities of Courtiers and Footprints of Philosophers*, Joseph B. Pike, trans. (New York: Octagon, 1972), 244.

> He [i.e., this misguided student] praises Aristotle alone; he scorns Cicero.... He spits upon laws, physics comes to seem worthless, all literature filthy, logic alone pleases, but not to the point where learning it costs work. If they think you're a logician, that's enough. This is not philosophy; it's insanity.[41]

So John's defense of logic cannot stand, I believe, as a progressive work of educational reform. If intended as such, it was a sad failure. It was very little read. Keats-Rohan, collaborator on the *Corpus Christianorum* edition, notes only four reliable manuscripts and contrasts that reception with the abundant copies of the *Policraticus*.[42] The work was overtaken by the influx of new translations of Aristotle. But it also died of its own conservatism.

THE ROOTS OF JOHN'S HUMANISM

The preceding was prologue to my main argument. My point has been to confirm the opinion of John as a humanist resisting contemporary trends. What I offered was not a new interpretation of the *Metalogicon* but a detailed reading that fixes more closely than heretofore on the irony of his title and that puts his criticism of his contemporary masters and fellow students, barely concealed by a gloss of praise, in clearer highlight.

Now I can turn to the roots of John's humanism in the previous centuries. Many aspects of his indebtedness to an earlier system of education, by c.1159 fading fast, register in the *Metalogicon*. While his praise of Abelard and Gilbert of Poitiers show his indebtedness to progresssive masters of the previous generation, his heart clearly is with the old-style humanists. This is clear in his praise of Bernard of Chartres in *Metalogicon* 1.24. Bernard was a grammarian of the previous generation, a specialist in literature who stressed reading of the classics and composition in verse and prose, the poets being, John states, the cradle of philosophy — and grammar its foundation. In

---

41. *Entheticus Maior*, ll. 111–17; Van Laarhoven ed., 1:112. The poem as a whole is dated generally c.1157, though the satire on the schools may derive from John's student days. Van Laarhoven dates it 1141–45, Nederman 1141–47.

42. Hall's edition of the *Metalogicon*, vii–ix, lists eight manuscripts, of which only three are accurate or complete enough to weigh heavily in the edition. See also Keats-Rohan, "John and Education."

CHAPTER 9 ★ JOHN OF SALISBURY

John's opinion (*Metalogicon* 4.35), he was also the greatest Platonist of the age. We have already noted that his own teachers William and Richard followed Bernard's methods and quit the schools, "when popular opinion veered away from the truth," which presumably is what, in John's opinion, Bernard and they taught, or at least sought.

We do not know when Bernard was born. The first mention of him is in a land grant issued by Ivo of Chartres in 1108, of which one of the signers is "Bernardus subdiaconus."[43] His date of death is given in two necrologies of Chartres as June 2, between 1124 and 1130. Dutton conjectures that he will have died not long after 1124. Let us imagine that he died in 1127 as an old man. John refers to him as *"Carnotensis senex Bernardus,"* "the old man of Chartres." His date of birth then must have fallen between c.1050 and c.1070. In any case, the greater part of his life was lived in the period prior to Abelard's besieging of Paris, and his teaching indicates clearly that he is an old-fashioned master of literature and Platonic philosophy.[44] The main thread I would like to follow that leads from John of Salisbury backwards into the eleventh and late tenth century is his conception of philosophy.

John has a broad, widely shared understanding of philosophy that embraces all studies. Hence the Cornificians are trying to banish eloquence from "philosophical studies" (*Metalogicon* 1.1). He regularly assigns poetry and grammar originating roles in the quest for wisdom, the essence of philosophy. Once, "poetry is the cradle of philosophy" (1.22), another time, "grammar is the cradle of philosophy" (1.13). He insists throughout on the necessary connection between philosophy and ethics:

> Any profession of philosophy is useless and false that does not open up into the cultivation of virtue and the shaping of an exemplary life....[45] The preeminent part of philosophy I call ethics, without which philosophy does not deserve the name. In its combined grace and beauty, it excels all other [parts of philosophy.] Open Virgil or Lucan, and there, no matter

---

43. See Bernard of Chartres, *Glosae super Platonem*; Dutton ed., 239.
44. See the discussion in Jaeger, *Envy*, 128–31.
45. *Metalogicon*, Prol. 76–78: "Est quaelibet professio philosophandi inutilis et falsa, quae se ipsam in cultu virtutis et vitae exhibitione non aperit." In Hall ed., 11. My translation.

what field of philosophy you profess, you will find its sweetest savor.[46]

He connects philosophical inquiry with the "practice and cultivation of virtue." Reading, learning, and meditation — the main aids to philosophical inquiry — must precede the cultivation of virtue.[47] The calling of philosopher requires preparation by those three aids (reading, learning, and meditation) and by "the performance of good works."[48] In the *Entheticus:* "Philosophy...brings forth and nourishes virtues and drives out the cruel stepmother vice, and allows no place to error."[49] He also insists on the connection between philosophy and religion: "If the true God is the true wisdom of humanity, then Philosophy is love of the true God."[50] The theme recurs throughout book 4 of the *Metalogicon*.

Apart from the connections between Grace, God, and faith, John's language and concept of philosophy are basically stoic and Ciceronian, though he also owes formulations to Boethius. Cicero is the major source for medieval humanism of a concept of philosophy tied to ethics.[51] A look back will clarify John of Salisbury's debt. Cicero made the formation of life through discipline the highest activity of philosophy, which "promotes a good and happy life" *(bene beateque vivendum)*. Its end is virtue. Philosophy is "the knowledge of things both human and divine." Either Philosophy is "the method of

---

46. *Metalogicon* 1.24.41–45: "Illa quae ceteris philosophiae partibus praeminet ethicam dico, sine qua nec philosophi subsistit nomen, collati decoris gratia, omnes alias antecedit. Excute Virgilium, aut Lucanum, et ibi cuiuscumque philosophiae professor sis, eiusdem invenies condituram." In Hall ed., 52; McGarry trans., 67.

47. *Metalogicon* 1.23.15–16: "Ceterum operationem cultumque virtutis scientia naturaliter praecedit...." In Hall ed., 50.

48. *Metalogicon* 1.24.3–4; Hall ed., 51.

49. *Entheticus* ll. 245–46: "Muneribus cunctis praecellit Philosophia, /.../ virtutes parit et nutrit, vitiumque noverca / pellit, et errori non sinit esse locum." In Van Laarhoven ed., 1:120. See *Entheticus* ll. 235–310; Van Laarhoven ed., 1:120–25 for a full discussion of philosophy.

50. *Entheticus*, ll. 305–6; Van Laarhoven ed., 124–25.

51. See above, chapter 2, passim.

CHAPTER 9 ✷ JOHN OF SALISBURY

obtaining virtue and constancy, or there is none." It is the "discipline of virtue."[52] The *Tusculan Disputations* begin:

...the system and method of instruction in all the arts which have a bearing upon the right conduct of life [*"ad rectam vivendi viam pertinerent"*] are contained in the study of wisdom which goes by the name of philosophy [1.1].... As to philosophy, mother of all the arts, what else is it except,... the gift or the discovery of the gods.... It instructed us first in the worship of the gods, then in the justice of mankind... and next taught us the lessons of temperance and greatness of soul" [1.26.64].... Philosophy is the *magistra vitae* and "teacher of manners and of discipline." (*"O vitae philosophia dux, o virtutis indagatrix expultrixque vitiorum! ... tu magistra morum et disciplinae fuisti"*) [5.5].[53]

Ciceronian ideas and formulations passed to the Middle Ages by the well-known routes.[54] Isidore of Seville defines philosophy as "the knowledge of things human and divine joined to the study of living well" (*cum studio bene vivendi*).[55] Alcuin echoes this:

Philosophy is the investigation of natures, the knowledge of things human and divine.... Philosophy is also proper conduct

52. Cicero, *De officiis* 2.5–6, Walter Miller, trans. (Cambridge, MA: Harvard University Press, 1975), 172–73. Cf. also Cicero, *In L. Pisonem* 71, in *Various Orations*, Neville H. Watts, trans. (Cambridge, MA: Harvard University Press, 2000), 224: "...Philosophia, ut fertur, virtutis continet et officii et bene vivendi disciplinam...." On Cicero's idea of philosophy, see Mancal, *Zum Begriff*, 1:39.

53. CTD, King ed., 3, 74, 428. Also worth noting in this context is Seneca's virtual identification of philosophy and ethics: "Philosophy...moulds and constructs the soul, it orders our life, guides our conduct, shows us what we should do, and what we should leave undone...." *Epistola* 16.3, *Epistles*; Richard M. Gummere, trans. (Cambridge, MA: Harvard University Press, 1917), 104; *Epistola* 89.8: "Nec philosophia sine virtute est nec sine philosophia virtus. Philosophia studium virtutis est...." In Gummere trans., 2:382.

54. On the idea of philosophy in the earlier Middle Ages, see above, chapter 2, passim; Jean Leclercq, *Etudes sur le vocabulaire monastique du moyen âge* (Rome: Herder, 1961), 39–79; Leclercq, "Pour l'histoire"; Leclercq, *Love of Learning*, 100–101; Curtius, "Zur Geschichte," 304–5; von Moos, *Hildebert*, 103–5.

55. Isidore, *Etymologiae* 2.24.1.

319

of life, the study of living well [*honestas vitae, studium bene vivendi*], the meditation of death, contempt of the world.[56]

Hrabanus Maurus repeats Alcuin's definition and swells it to encyclopedic length.[57]

The late tenth and eleventh centuries received Ciceronian notions of philosophy abundantly. Cicero loomed large in a new curriculum of cathedral-school education based on the double instruction of "letters and manners," reading the ancients, studying composition in prose and poetry, and the disciplining of behavior that went by the name of "cultivation of virtue" (*cultus virtutum*).[58]

In a passage that has become central to defining the "imperial church system," Otto the Great addressed his brother, Brun of Cologne, explaining why he needs his brother's diplomatic skills in a time of crisis:

> I see [in you] a royal priesthood sent by the grace of God Almighty to the aid of our empire. For you combine in your person the religion of a priest and the strength of a king.... And I have long noted that the mother of all noble arts and the virtue of true Philosophy is yours, and it is she who has educated you to modesty and greatness of soul.[59]

Gerbert of Aurillac replied to a letter of Otto III inviting the famous scholar — and advisor to both his father and grandfather — to his court in order to "banish his Saxon rusticity." Gerbert praises his future pupil for his earlier study of mathematics and moral philosophy:

> Unless you embraced the gravity of moral philosophy, humility, guardian of all virtues, would not thus be impressed upon your words.[60]

56. Alcuin, *De dialectica* 1; PL 101:952A. Cf. also *De grammatica*, PL 101:849C, 852D.

57. Hrabanus Maurus, *De Universo* 15.1; PL 111: 413.

58. Jaeger, *Envy*, passim.

59. Ruotger, *Vita Brunonis* 20: "...video per Dei omnipotentis gratiam nostro imperio regale sacerdotium accessisse. In te namque et sacerdotalis religio et regia pollet fortitudo... Nec abesse tibi iam dudum perpendi ipsam ingenuarum arcium matrem et vere virtutem philosophie, que te ad hanc modestiam magnitudinemque animi erudivit." In Kallfelz trans., 206. See also above, 84.

60. Epist. 187: "Nisi moralis philosophie gravitatem amplecteremini, non ita verbis vestris custos omnium virtutum impressa esset humilitas." In Weigle ed., 224. See also above, 106 and n. 38.

CHAPTER 9 ★ JOHN OF SALISBURY

Here again we see the connection of humility with the education of a public figure, a prince. Again, philosophy is the discipline of moderation. The Ciceronian connection is prominent in Gerbert generally. In a letter to Abbot Ecbert of Tours, he asserts a fundamental Ciceronianism that has guided his entire life:

> I am not one to separate the Good from the Useful, as does Panaetius, but rather, with Cicero, I seek to mix the Good with the Useful.... Since Philosophy does not distinguish between the rules of speaking and the rules of conduct, I have always joined the study of eloquence to the study of living well.... For us who are caught up in the affairs of state, both are necessary.[61]

A cleric of Worms wrote a letter to his bishop around 1030 commending him for translating Philosophy into acts of public administration:

> The schoolmistress of all virtues [*magistra virtutum* = *Philosophia*] has taken up her abode in you, so that in all your undertakings you may follow in her footsteps.[62]

The formulation evokes two models of Lady Philosophy: that of Cicero (*magistra virtutum*) and that of Boethius in *The Consolation of Philosophy*. In his complaint to Lady Philosophy, Boethius had reviewed their longstanding relationship and showed Philosophy guiding his investigations of the heavens and shaping his *mores* according to the pattern of celestial harmony. She taught him Plato's dictum that the happy state would be governed by students of wisdom and roused in him the urge "to practise that by public administration that I had learnt of thee in private conference."[63]

---

61. Gerbert, Epist. 44: "Non is sum, qui cum Panetio interdum ab utili seiungam honestum, sed potius cum Tullio omni utili admisceam... Cumque ratio morum dicendique ratio a philosophia non separentur, cum studio bene vivendi semper coniuncxi studium bene dicendi, quamvis solum bene vivere praestantius sit eo, quod est bene dicere, curisque regiminis absoluto, alterum satis sit sine altero. At nobis in re publica occupatis utraque necessaria." In Weigle ed., 73.

62. Epist. 52; Bulst ed., 89.

63. I, Prose 4.15–16; Stewart trans., 142–45.

Still in the mid-twelfth century Wibald of Stablo could invoke this Ciceronian and Boethian model of philosophy as *magistra morum*. He wrote a letter to a cleric at Liège, excusing himself from important peace negotiations by referring to the greater philosophical training of the recipient:

> That teacher and liege-lady of yours, Philosophia, the *magistra* and instructor of things human and divine, has not shaped and informed our manners as she has yours.[64]

The practical governance of life in the context of state service figures here as a prominent element of "philosophy," and we can extend this to the thinking in cathedral schools in the eleventh century broadly. This ideal of conduct joined to the study of eloquence is both a way of life for the public figure and a program of studies. Philosophy makes the state minister, and the minister is a kind of philosopher.[65]

The dominant voice from antiquity is that of Cicero, though it joins with that of Boethius. Philosophy for these and many other writers is Stoic, practical, hard to distinguish from ethics. Meinhard, schoolmaster at Bamberg from c.1065 to 1085, wrote to a former student commending the *Tusculan Disputations* as the most important work of Latin philosophy, whose father is Cicero.[66] The letter collections from the period of Henry IV edited by Erdmann and Fickermann contain over 150 direct quotations of Cicero, 99 of them from the *Tusculan Disputations*. The interesting collection of letters from circles of imperial courtier clerics, the so-called Regensburg Rhetorical Letters (c.1090), often appear as a cento of quotations from the *Tusculan Disputations*.

CONCLUSIONS

An educational ideal based on ancient notions of philosophy crystallized at cathedral schools and may well have found their way there from the higher instance of the imperial court. An ideal of

---

64. *Wibaldi Epistolae* 331, Jaffé ed, 462; *Das Briefbuch abt Wibalds von Stablo und Corvey*, Epist. 304, Hartmann, Zatschek, and Reuter ed., 2:643.

65. Sigebert of Gembloux alludes to Plato's idea of the philosopher king in referring to the wise men serving Otto I: Brun, Dietrich of Metz, and others of Brun's students. See *Vita Deoderici* 7; MGH, SS 4:467, ll. 38–39.

66. See above, 148 and n. 60.

service to the state by ministers trained to humility and greatness of soul must have been useful to the emperors in whose administration the Church played such a central role.

There can be no doubt that it is this conception of philosophy that John is defending in the *Metalogicon*. The passages quoted earlier make evident his obligation to Ciceronian ideals but also to a notion of philosophy as a doctrine that guides the active life of state ministers according to an ideal called "virtue." The program of philosophy and the system of education that John defended was not an invention of the twelfth century. It was an old program, at least two hundred years old by the time he wrote. While the sources seem to indicate its prominence in the tenth and eleventh centuries, it is also present in earlier periods. Indeed, it seems plausible to postulate its survival in a line that is only occasionally broken since Roman antiquity. By the twelfth century it had outlived its day. The fact that a great work of civic philosophy like the *Policraticus*, decked out in a stunning array of classical references, could still arise from it and have a grand future is a testimony to John's skill as a writer but not to the vitality of the system in which he had been educated. John's two great works are, along with a few other works of poetic philosophy from the twelfth century, final resting places of the humanism of the eleventh and early twelfth century.

10. PESSIMISM IN THE TWELFTH-CENTURY "RENAISSANCE"

INTRODUCTION

The term "twelfth-century renaissance" has proven usable against all opposition.[1] Its hold on medievalists is firmer than that of its

---

1. Literature from the last two decades calling on the term with acceptance, and at the same time referencing the controversy, includes Hans-Werner Goetz, *Geschichtsschreibung und Geschichtsbewusstsein im hohen Mittelalter* (Berlin: Akademie, 1999), 57–61 and n. 84 for previous literature on the controversy; Peter Damian-Grint, *The New Historians of the Twelfth-Century Renaissance* (Rochester, NY: Boydell, 1999); various essays in *Aufbruch- Wandel-Erneuerung: Beiträge zur "Renaissance" des 12. Jahrhunderts. 9. Blaubeurer Symposion vom 9.- 's. Oktober 1992*, Georg Wieland, ed. (Stuttgart: Frommann-Holzboog, 1995); and in *Anglo-Norman Political Culture and the Twelfth-Century Renaissance: Proceedings of the Borchard Conference of Anglo-Norman History 1995*, C. Warren Hollister, ed. (Woodbridge: Boydell, 1997); *Renovacion intelectual del Occidente europeo (siglo XII): XXIV Semana de Estudios Medievales Estella, 14 a 18 de julio de 1997* (Pamplona: Gobierno de Navarra, 1998); Stephen C. Ferruolo, "The Twelfth-Century Renaissance," in *Renaissances before the Renaissance: Cultural Revivals of Late Antiquity and the Middle Ages*, Warren Treadgold, ed. (Stanford, CA: Stanford University Press, 1984), 114–43; Winthrop Wetherbee, "Philosophy, Cosmology, and the Twelfth-Century Renaissance," in Dronke, ed., *History of Twelfth-Century Philosophy*, 21–53; and R.N. Swanson, *The Twelfth-Century Renaissance* (Manchester: Manchester University Press, 1999). On the other hand, Moore, *First European Revolution*, gives a magisterial overview of developments from the tenth to the thirteenth century, seeing the developments of the period in the kind of differentiated and nuanced interrelationships that become visible beyond the conception of a "renaissance." Peter Godman argues against the obscuring force of the terms "renaissance" and "humanism" in *The Silent Masters: Latin Literature and Its Censors in the High Middle Ages* (Princeton, NJ: Princeton University Press, 2000). See also Benson and Constable, *Renaissance and Renewal*; Rodney M. Thomson, "England and the Twelfth-Century Renaissance," *Past and Present* 101 (1983): 3–21; and Thomson's review essay, "Richard Southern and the Twelfth-Century Intellectual World: Review of R.W. Southern, *Scholastic Humanism*," *Journal of Religious History* 26 (2002): 264–73. For earlier literature, see also Chris D. Ferguson, *Europe in Transition: A Select, Annotated Bibliography of the Twelfth-Century Renaissance*

progenitor on our colleagues in fifteenth- and sixteenth-century studies, among whom "early modern period" has asserted itself against, or at least alongside, the time- and usage-hallowed "Renaissance."[2] Whatever anyone may think of the congruence of twelfth-century and Italian renaissances, or of the dignity borrowed by the earlier century from the later, or even simply of its historical "fit" with the twelfth century, the term has found a home in medieval scholarship, and consciences more exacting than my own have approved it. Like "dead as a doornail," the wisdom of our ancestors is by now in the phrase (as it is even more so in the term "Middle Ages"). My purpose is not to belabor a point accepted more by inertia than conviction but rather to show what is obscured in conceiving the social and intellectual revolutions of the twelfth century as a "renaissance" and what might be gained by scrapping the term.

The term rests — legitimately — on the argument from grandeur. And who will refute that argument? The twelfth century is a great and fascinating age, probably of the long stretch of the "Middle Ages" the period whose remarkable individuals and high accomplishments have provoked and inspired the most and best scholarship: its exhilarating intellectual life, the growth of independent schools and famed teachers in Paris, the rise of the universities of Bologna and Paris; the great Gothic cathedrals and abbey churches of England; the Gothic style in architecture, book illustration, and handcraft design; a new classicism, plasticity, humanity in the representation of the human body in sculpture; the grand poetic-philosophical-ethical visions of Bernard Silvester, Alan of Lille, and John of Hanville; the Latin poems of the Archpoet, Walter of Châtillon, Primas of Orleans, and many of the songs of the *Carmina Burana*; the culture of courtly chivalry, a charming and elegant literature glorifying it; and the new fashion in loving that it represents, "courtly love." We have

---

(New York: Garland, 1989). Rodney Thomson, ed., *England in the Twelfth Century Renaissance* (Aldershot: Variorum, 1998); and Alex Novikoff, ed., *The Twelfth-Century Renaissance: A Reader* (Toronto: University of Toronto Press, 2016). A search (5/21/2024) of the term "twelfth-century renaissance" on the Internet turns up more references than it is worth citing. Particularly striking is the number of university courses with that title.

2. A prominent example: *The Journal of Medieval and Renaissance Studies* was renamed *Journal of Medieval and Early Modern Studies*.

CHAPTER 10 ✳ PESSIMISM IN THE TWELFTH CENTURY

credited the age with the "discovery" or the rediscovery, or even the "invention" of individuality, philosophical rationalism, and romantic love. And we have recognized the twelfth-century formation of important new social groups: the knighthood, a ministerial class, and a class of urban citizens, merchants, intellectuals, patricians.

In counterpoint to all these developments, which formed the focal point of Charles Homer Haskins' great study of the period,[3] the continuing church and monastic reform movements registered vitality in the religious life and produced or favored dramatic clashes in which the historical tendencies of the period incarnate seem to engage in single combat: Abelard and Bernard of Clairvaux, Henry II and Thomas Becket. There is something grand and operatic about characters like Suger of St. Denis, Eleanor of Aquitaine, William Marshal, Heloise,[4] Rainald of Dassel. Even at its worst, the age seems bigger than life. Its parasites beg, its fanatics rave, its egotists boast, and its bores bore us on a grand scale (Archpoet, Tanchelm, Peter Abelard, and Peter Lombard). Because of all this grandness, we reward the age with the grand title "Renaissance." Never mind that this term does not occur in any variant in any contemporary appraisal of the worldly culture of the age.

Gerhart Ladner remarked emphatically on the lack of terms of renewal among twelfth-century philosophers in characterizing their own age:

> it is very remarkable that philosophers of nature and natural scientists of the twelfth century, such as Adelard of Bath and Herman of Carinthia — while they considered nature as an innovating force under God in generation and conservation — do not seem to have designated their own time as an age of either rebirth or reform.[5]

---

3. *The Renaissance of the Twelfth Century*.
4. A quality that may well be most fully realized in the early twenty-first century. A notice in the *New York Times* (April 21, 2002) announced a then-new opera "Heloise and Abelard" by Stephen Paulus. At the same time the Slovak composer Juraj Benes was at work on an opera with Heloise and Abelard among its characters.
5. "Terms and Ideas of Renewal," in *Renaissance and Renewal*, 7.

Ladner finds that the terms for renewal occur abundantly in plant metaphors and were applied to the church reform movement and to the growth of monastic orders, just not to the realm in which a "renaissance" is supposed to have occurred. Never mind that its real embodiment is in the future or that its appropriation for the earlier century "disembodies" it, so to speak. It is like a ghost accepted in our presence (the ghost of a renaissance yet to come), an apparition that does not bring even the most empirical historians out of countenance — because it has become such a familiar specter.

But my purpose in this study is not to doubt the greatness of the age and its accomplishments or to apply and test any of the criteria by which earlier scholars — most famously Erwin Panofsky[6] — have questioned or ruled out "renaissance" as a term that applies to the twelfth century. My purpose is to study the self-conception of the age as formulated by those who lived, wrote, and studied in its secular culture. From the most famous to the least, a pessimism prevails that is very much at odds with the tendency of modern scholars to make it into a "renaissance." There is a large discrepancy between the *Zeitgeist* and the *Zeitghost*.

By "secular culture" here and throughout I mean the various cultural spheres of secular clergy. The range is broad. It includes clerics at worldly courts from royal and imperial, to courts of lower nobility, cathedral communities, the papal curia, cathedral schools, the independent schools of Paris, and the early universities. It also includes the culture of courtly literature in the vernacular whether composed by clerics, knights, counts, dukes, or kings. It excludes monastic communities, though not necessarily monastic writers commenting on the culture of "the world" (*saeculum*).

The predominant categories available to us from that culture's language of self-conception are quickly surveyed: "decline," "decay," "senility," "corruption," and "collapse." I begin with a survey of some of the topoi the period called on to assess its relation to the past. It will introduce us both to the terms and concepts of historical self-assessment and to the methodological problems of analyzing them.

---

6. Erwin Panofsky, *Renaissance and Renascences in Western Art* (Stockholm: Almquist & Wiksell, 1960).

CHAPTER 10 ✶ PESSIMISM IN THE TWELFTH CENTURY

TOPOI OF HISTORICAL CHANGE

We have to look critically at self-sitings of the twelfth century in its contemporary character and in its relations to the past.[7] All claims available to writers for rise or decline, youth or moribundity, grandeur or decadence are topoi that may have little value to indicate the actual sentiments in twelfth-century courts, schools, monastic and cathedral communities, or the real observations of their inhabitants. The documentary value of topoi of historical change requires close scrutiny. In what follows I cite all the materials I have gathered in the course of my research, both negative and positive estimations of the period. They establish clearly the imbalance in favor of pessimism.

A problem in the rhetoric of this study is that it appears to critical readers that I have cited sources selectively so as to register a pessimistic bias. In lectures and seminars I have asked critics for suggestions of sources I have not considered. And many colleagues received an inquiry from me: "Who in the twelfth century speaks positively about the culture of the age?" This study contains all the sources suggested by recipients of my inquiry. The answer from skeptics tended to take the form, "What about architecture? What about courtly literature?" and so confused the monuments of the age with the self-assessment of their creators.

The World Grown Old

Senility and old age are the predominant metaphors in the self-conception of the twelfth century: "Almost everyone in the eleventh and twelfth centuries thought that the world was growing old and that things were going from bad to worse as the end approached."[8] Of the six ages of the world predicted in the prophecy of Daniel,

---

7. How malleable the view of the past was, how high-handedly the contemporary "memory" treated the remembered past, is evident from Patrick Geary, *Phantoms of Remembrance: Memory and Oblivion at the End of the First Millennium* (Princeton, NJ: Princeton University Press, 1994).

8. Giles Constable, *The Reformation of the Twelfth Century* (Cambridge, MA: Harvard University Press, 1996), 162. See also James M. Dean, *The World Grown Old in Later Medieval Literature* (Cambridge, MA: Harvard University Press, 1997).

contemporaries regarded themselves as living in the last.[9] The sentiment is double-edged: it may express Christian optimism (it is a distinction, a state approaching the perfection of the Christian age: Augustine) or disillusionment and cynicism (it predicts the senility and decay in the present generation). Observers of secular culture in the twelfth century were unanimously of the disillusioned and cynical bent, as we will see in the next section. It would be shallow analysis to assume that several generations defined their present condition and position in Christian history as senility and decline only because they were under the intractable influence of a historical topos — and that no path leads from that topos to their actual views of the contemporary world — and more shallow yet to imagine that a far more positive and optimistic attitude might have flourished unregistered beneath the solemn surface of near-unanimous gloom.

There were, after all, topoi of historical optimism at the disposal of twelfth-century writers. For instance, the golden age of politics and of studies was a topos known from both the Carolingian and the Ottonian periods. Some lines by the poet known as the "Irish Exile" (*Hibernicus exul*), written on the occasion of the imperial coronation in 800, set the present decisively above the past:

> *Former ages are celebrated with glowing praise,*
> *And all that is past finds favor.*
> *This is the way people used to think.*
> *False rumors of the ancients outweighed the true fame*
> *of contemporaries.*
> *The way we think and act, however, has changed.*
> *We prefer everything from the present age to the past.*[10]

---

9. On the "six ages of the world," see Rocderich Schmidt, "'Aetates mundi': Die Weltalter als Gliederungs prinzip der Geschichte," *Zeitschrift fur Kirchengeschichte* 67 (1955/56): 288–317.

10. Hibernicus Exul, *Carmen* 5, ll. 1–10: "Laudibus eximiis celebrantur saecula prisca, / Omneque praeteritum gratificare solet, /.../ Hoc homines inter passim contingit haberi, / Rumori veterum cedere fama nova. / Nobis econtra ordo est commutatus et usus, / Priscis quaeque extant tempora praeferimus." In MGH, *Poetae* 1:400. For comments on the lines, see Godman, *Poets*, 662–63.

CHAPTER 10 ✷ PESSIMISM IN THE TWELFTH CENTURY

The lines are remarkable for their boldness and self-confidence: whatever others may think of the past, "we" (it is a shared sentiment) have revalued values; "we" prefer the present. The lines are remarkable also for finding much resonance in two generations of intellectuals associated with the court and in the empire generally.[11] That distinguishes the passage from the topos as it occurs in the twelfth century, where there is praise of individual rulers that invokes the golden age.[12] But apart from the praise of rulers, the twelfth century did not draw on the topos of the golden age to express its own self-conception, whereas the Carolingian age did.

If a period tends generally to represent itself as a period of decline, and there are not decisive voices contradicting that pessimism, then surely the expressions of pessimism can be taken as registering a felt sentiment. Topoi show forth attitudes and postures; they do not, or only in exceptional cases, create them. They may preform or predispose thought, but they do not (unless some threat hides behind them) silence opposite opinions and force unpredisposed thought into their ready-made mold. Topoi of pessimism certainly do not tie the hands and tongues of those filled with enthusiasm for the age they live in. The period that actually thought of itself as an age of renaissance and renewal easily overrode the topos, "the world is senile." As Leon Battista Alberti wrote to Filippo Brunelleschi in the dedication of his treatise *On Painting and Sculpture*:

> I used to marvel and to regret that so many excellent and divine arts and sciences, which...were possessed in great abundance by the talented of antiquity, have now disappeared. Consequently

---

11. See the often quoted verses by Modoin (Naso), ll. 24–27: "Prospicit alta novae Romae meus arce Palemon, / Cuncta suo imperio consistere regna triumpho, / Rursus in antiquos mutataque secula mores. / Aurea Roma iterum renovata renascitur orbi." In MGH *Poetae* 1:385. See also Alcuin, *Epistola* 178 to Charlemagne (closing verses): "Tempora concedat Christus felicia regni / Huius et aeterni, David amate, tibi." In MGH, Epp 4:296; and Alcuin, *Epistola* 170: "si, plurimis inclitum vestrae intentionis studium sequentibus, forsan Athenae nova perficeretur in Francia, immo multo excellentior." In MGH, Epp 4:279. For the Ottonian period, see Brun of Cologne's dedication poem to his brother Otto I, MGH, *Poetae* 5.2:378; and Schramm.

12. See below, 343, for Theobald of Canterbury and John of Salisbury on Henry II, and Petrus Riga on the birth of Philip Augustus.

> *I believed what I heard many say that Nature had grown old and weary, and was no longer producing intellects...on a vast and wonderful scale. But after I came back here to this most beautiful of cities [Florence],... I recognized in many, but above all in you...a genius...in no way inferior to any of the ancients.... For the ancients...it was less difficult to master those noble arts which for us today prove arduous; but it follows that our fame should be all the greater.*[13]

In one of the paradigmatic statements of a "renaissance" in Italy Giorgio Vasari writes that he has given a brief history of art since its origins in order to show:

> how the arts resemble nature as shown in our human bodies, and have their birth, growth, age, and death; and I hope by this means they will be enabled more easily to recognize the progress of the renaissance of the arts, and the perfection to which they have attained in our own times.[14]

It was possible for Alberti and others to revise the view that dominated the statements of earlier centuries (the twelfth included) because, clearly, their enthusiasm and optimism about their own age overrode the momentum of that conventional judgment of the present. The humanist view exemplified in the passage just cited represents not a topos paraded in celebration of a single occasion

13. Leon Battista Alberti, *On Painting and Sculpture: The Latin Texts of "De pictura" and "De statua,"* Cecil Grayson, ed. and trans. (London: Phaidon, 1972), 32–33 (emphasis mine).

14. Giorgio Vasari, *The Lives of the Painters, Sculptors and Architects*, William Gaunt, ed. and trans. 4 vols. (London: Phaidon, 1963), 1:18. See also Vasari, "Life of Michelangelo," ed. Gaunt, 4:111, on Lorenzo de' Medici's founding a school to end the dearth of sculptors living in his own day. He wanted his age to rival the great painters of earlier days. Erasmus also recognized the superiority of the arts in his age to that which had preceded: "...in our age again [i.e., as in ancient times], the diligence of craftsmen has once more achieved every effect of art." In *Antibarbari – The Antibarbarians*, Craig R. Thompson, ed., in Collected Works of Erasmus, 23 (Toronto: University of Toronto Press, 1978), 90. He framed the argument for the vitality of his own age precisely in opposition to the idea of "the world grown old" (*Antibarbarians*, 26), cited and discussed in Istvan Bejczy, *Erasmus and the Middle Ages: The Historical Consciousness of a Christian Humanist* (Leiden: Brill, 2001), 3. See also Ferguson, *Renaissance*, 43–44.

CHAPTER 10 ★ PESSIMISM IN THE TWELFTH CENTURY

but an experience of the observer, one widely shared, that developed into a "new conception of cultural history."[15] Classical antiquity was followed by dark ages, giving way to a "rebirth" of ancient literature and art. That new conception is the decisive break with earlier historical models.[16] The fifteenth century could produce it; the twelfth could not. It was very far from considering itself the end of "middle ages" and the rebirth of the ancient world.

Antiqui and Moderni

The topos of the ancients versus the moderns, which informs the passage from Alberti just quoted, is also instructive. It is fairly common in the twelfth century but almost exclusively favors the ancients. R.W. Southern made this change into an indication of "a new sense of the superiority of the present over the past." Far from showing "the scholastic vigor of contemporary Europe," the passage he cites[17] from Otto of Freising's *Chronicle* says the opposite. Otto praises wise men of previous generations — Berengar of Tours, Manegold of Lautenbach, and Anselm of Laon — as *divinitus inspirati* in contrast to the philosophers of Otto's own day *(Nos vero)*, whose dreary job is to observe "how the world, contemnible for its inconstancy, is already failing *(deficientem)* and drawing the last breath of extreme senility." This is far from Southern's reading: "

> At last the men of the schools are beginning to be identified by their contemporaries as giving a culminating place in world history to the present.[18]

15. Ferguson, *Renaissance*, 40. Numerous enthusiastic self-assessments of the Renaissance are cited in Panofsky, *Renaissance and Renascence*, 29–36.

16. Now we can add to this inventory of "renaissance" historical models the dedication poem of Brun of Cologne (mid-tenth century) declaring the advent of Otto I the dawning of a new age after the barbaric "dark age" and the restoration of the study of the ancients. See above, 87–88.

17. Southern, *Scholastic Humanism*, 1:189.

18. Southern, *Scholastic Humanism*, 1:188. See also Curtius, ELLMA, 119–20, 251–55; Elisabeth Gossmann, Antiqui und Moderni im Mittelalter: Eine geschichtliche Standortbestimmung (Munich: Schöningh, 1974); Wilfried Hartmann, "'Modernus' und 'Antiquus': Zur Verbreitung und Bedeutung dieser Bezeichnungen in der wissenschaftlichen Literatur vom 9. bis zum 12. Jahrhundert," in Antiqui und Moderni: Traditionsbewusstsein und Fortschrittsbewusstsein

Southern's claim that "even the most conservative writers found grandeur in the present" applies to monks admiring the revival of monastic houses but not to secular culture.

A representative example is William of Conches' letter to Geoffrey the Fair of Anjou, introducing his reworked *Philosophia mundi* with the new title *Dragmaticon*. It begins with the author's answer to a question put to him by the duke: why the masters of the present age have less authority than the ancients. In part the masters are to blame, he replies, in part the students, and in part the bishops. The masters lack knowledge and justice, the students lack discipline, and the bishops scorn the learned and seek only wealth. Therefore, "all dignity and authority have perished."[19]

---

im späten Mittelalter, Albert Zimmermann, ed. (Berlin: De Gruyter, 1974), 21–39; Elisabeth Gossmann, "'Antiqui' und 'Moderni' im 12. Jahrhundert," in Zimmermann, *Antiqui und Moderni*, 40–57; and Goetz, *Geschichtsschreibung*, 59–60. See also some observations in Southern's *Scholastic Humanism* 1:185–89, especially his important point that "...in the early years of the twelfth century... scholars even of the last generation came to be referred to as *antiqui*...." He interprets this to mean "old-fashioned" (186).

19. *Guillelmi de Conchis Dragmaticon philosophiae* 1, prol., Italo Ronca, ed., CCCM 152 (Turnhout: Brepols, 1997), 3–4. See also glosses on Macrobius, quoted in Edouard Jeauneau, "'Nani gigantum humeris insidentes': Essai d'interpretation de Bernard de Chartres," *Vivarium* 5 (1967): 79–99, at 86: "Antiqui multo meliores fuerunt modernis: quod in operibus eorum apparet, quorum expositione semper laborant moderni." Adelard of Bath's scathing satire on contemporary philosophers appears in *De eodem et diverso*, in *Conversations with His Nephew: On the Same and the Different, Questions on Natural Science, and On Birds*, Charles Burnett, ed. and trans. (Cambridge: Cambridge University Press, 1998), 8–11. See also 2–3 for its dedicatory letter (the moderns are silent out of fear of envy, while the ancients were eloquent); Walter of Châtillon, *Moralisch-satirische Gedichte Walters von Chatillon*, Karl Strecker, ed. (Heidelberg: Weidmann, 1929), 7a.2–3: "Nescimus vestigia veterum moderni," and "Cur per carnis vitium peccant sic moderni?" Strecker ed., 97; 7.3: "Dicta fuit aurea vita proavorum, / quando nec simonia vendicabat chorum / nec regnabant scismata, set vi modernorum / effodiuntur opes irritamenta malorum," Strecker ed., 91; and 7.11, Strecker ed., 113–15; Alan of Lille, *Anticlaudianus*, prose prologue: "nullos reprehensionis morsus sustineat [opus meum], quod modernorum redolet ruditatem," Wetherbee, ed., 222. Some time prior to 1180, Nigel Wireker laments in his *Speculum stultorum*, prologue,

CHAPTER 10 ★ PESSIMISM IN THE TWELFTH CENTURY

John of Salisbury appears to sing a very different tune at the beginning of the *Metalogicon:*

> I have not been ashamed to cite moderns, whose opinions in many instances I unhesitatingly prefer over the ancients. I trust that posterity will honor our contemporaries, for I have profound admiration for the extraordinary talents, diligent studies, marvelous memories, fertile minds, remarkable eloquence, and linguistic proficiency of many of those of our own day.[20]

And yet in the body of the work he repeatedly condemns an extreme form of this attitude in language typical of the conventional rejection of the *moderni:*

> If anyone applied himself to studying the ancients [in the schools dominated by 'Cornificians'], he became a marked man and the laughingstock of all. Everyone enshrined his own and his master's inventions.[21]

---

ll. 17–22: "Saepius admiror, dum tempora lapsa revolvo, / Quam fuerint nobis quamque notanda tibi. / Nil cum praeterito praesens mihi tempus habere / Cernitur, in caudam vertitur omne caput. / Fit de nocte dies, tenebrae de luce serena, / De stulto sapiens, de sapiente nihil." Then follows a complaint well known among the conservative critics of the Paris schools: that "beardless boys" take the place of wise men. See *Speculum stultorum,* John H. Mozley and Robert R. Raymo, ed. (Berkeley: University of California Press, 1969), 31. See also Johannes de Alta Silva, *Dolopathos, sive De rege et septem sapientibus:* "[h]arum autem exemplo modernorum quidam incitati, sed eorum dicendi modum nequaquam sequentes, animum et studium ad mendacia converterunt, malueruntque falsas laudes vel vituperia commentari, quam puram in properaculo positam dicere veritatem." In H. Oesterley, ed. (Strassburg: Trübner, 1978), 2–3. The ancient authors earned immortality by their honesty and truth.

20. *Metalogicon* 1, prologue: "Nec dedignatus sum modernorum proferre sententias, quos antiquis in plerisque praeferre non dubito. Spero equidem quod gloriam eorum qui nunc sunt posteritas celebrabit, eo quod multorum nobilia mirer ingenia, investigandi subtilitatem, diligentiam studii, felicitatem memoriae, fecunditatem mentis, et oris facultatem, et copiam verbi." In Hall ed., 11; McGarry trans., 6.

21. *Metalogicon* 1.3: "siquis incumbebat laboribus antiquorum, notabatur, et omnibus erat in risu. Suis enim aut magistri sui quisque incumbebat inventis." In Hall ed., 16; McGarry trans., 15. John's preference for the ancients and contempt for the moderns is explicit in the poem *Entheticus [Maior] de dogmate philosophorum,*

It also becomes clear that "those of our own day" whom he admires are the old guard (Abelard included) now being forced out, their teaching neglected, by a new generation.[22]

It is also possible to find affirmation of the moderns in the period. Matthew of Vendôme points out features of narration and versifying in which the moderns are held to higher norms than the ancients and says that rather than imitating, the moderns should apologize for the ancients.[23] John of Hauville cites an ancient opinion on the static position of the earth, then praises the opinion of an unnamed contemporary writer as superior: "The astuteness of our modern youth, though less renowned, is superior."[24] Such individual appraisals must be weighed carefully against the negative assessment of the moderns. The two just cited are lightweights. Matthew's comments come in a few lines in the middle of his treatise. They have no particular profile, and the sentiment does not register elsewhere in the work. John may praise a single "modern youth," but he speaks very differently when assessing the moderns as a whole. He prefaces the same book of his *Architrenius* 8 with a sharp attack on the *moderni*:

> All good doctrine flows from the lips of the ancients. It is an earlier age that gave rise to the Pegasean stream. The world [at present], though it shows the outward signs of age, is childish in understanding, and does not mature.[25]

---

in van Laarhoven, *John of Salisbury's Entheticus Maior and Minor*, 1.107–9, ll. 39-66; 1.115, ll. 145–46; 1.129, ll. 347–56. Also see below, 355 and n. 73.

22. *Metalogicon* 1.24. 2.10: "[Alberic of Rheims and Robert of Melun] would have been outstanding...had they but kept to the footsteps of their predecessors as much as they took delight in their own inventions." In McGarry trans., 96: "... magni praeclarique viri in philosophicis studiis enituissent, si de magno litterarum niterentur fundamento, si tantum institissent vestigiis maiorum, quantum suis applaudebant inventis." In Hall ed., 54.

23. *Ars versificatoria* 4.5 and 4.8, in Edmond Faral, *Les arts poétiques du XIIe et du XIIIe siècle: Recherches et documents sur la technique littéraire du moyen âge* (Paris: Champion, 1924), 181; cited and discussed in Janet Martin, "Classicism and Style in Latin Literature," in Benson and Constable, 565–66.

24. Johannes de Hauvilla, *Architrenius* 8.8; Winthrop Wetherbee, ed. and trans. (Cambridge: Cambridge University Press, 1994), 216–17.

25. *Architrenius* 8.1; Wetherbee ed., 198–99.

CHAPTER 10 ✷ PESSIMISM IN THE TWELFTH CENTURY

Occasionally advocacy of the *moderni* reveals more about the ambitions of the author than about his assessment of his contemporaries. It can take the form of a *captatio benevolentiae*. John of Hauville complains at the beginning and end of the *Architrenius*, in tirades against envious and carping readers, that the preference for the *antiqui* is a mask for resentment against anyone who writes:

> through [envy's] cruelty the renown of modern writers languishes.... As I enter the dark night of shadowy fate, let this book emerge into daylight: let it know a favor as enduring as the fame of the ancients and be cherished by all people to eternity and beyond![26]

And Walter Map complains that the *moderni*, his contemporaries, are not sufficiently respected:

> When I have begun to rot, [my] book will begin to gain savour... and in the remotest generations my ancientness will gain me dignity: for then, as now, old copper will be of more account than new gold. Every century has disliked its own modernity; every age...has preferred the previous one to itself.[27]

This seems to prepare the way for a defense of the *moderni*. But far from it: that coming age of recognition will be "an age of apes (as it now is)." The passage is a plea for recognition of his own works, not a defense of his generation. Similarly, William of Malmesbury praises an Irish historian of the previous century, Marianus Scotus, for redating the life of Christ but then muses on the fact that modern scholars are not celebrated no matter how much they may know or what discoveries they may make:

> I often wonder why such misfortune should befall the learned of our time, that in so great a number of scholars and students, pale with studying night and day, hardly anyone responds with

26. *Architrenius* 1.3; Wetherbee ed., 8–9; 9.25, Wetherbee ed., 252–53.

27. Walter Map, *De nugis curialium* 4.5: "Cum enim putuerim, tum primo sal accipiet, totusque sibi supplebitur decessu meo defectus, et in remotissima posteritate michi faciet auctoritatem antiquitas, quia tunc ut nunc uetustum cuprum preferetur auro nouello Omnibus seculis sua displicuit modernitas, et queuis etas preteritam sibi pretulit." In Walter Map, *De nugis curialium / Courtiers' Trifles*, Montague R. James, ed. and trans.; Christopher N.L. Brooke and Roger A.B. Mynors, rev. (Oxford: Clarendon, 1983), 312–13.

unqualified praise for knowledge. So much does ancient custom please, and so little encouragement, though deserved, is given to new discoveries, even very respectable ones. All strive with all their might to grovel in the way of the ancients, and everything modern appears vile. And so, because favor nourishes genius, once favor ceases, all genius grows numb.[28]

This vision of his contemporaries shows a potential for genius in a generation of epigones. Studies proliferate, but genius is numbed, and the striving for greatness is stymied by a consensus of inferiority to the ancients.

Dwarves and Giants

The trope of "dwarves on the shoulders of giants," which John of Salisbury attributed to Bernard of Chartres, is related. It is ambiguous praise at best. Both Alan of Lille and William of Conches interpreted it to the disadvantage of the moderns. The latter wrote:

> We do not know more than the ancients, though we see more. For we have their writings and, in addition, a natural genius by which we perceive anything new. For we are dwarves on the shoulders of giants, seeing much because of someone else and little on our own.[29]

My point is not that no one speaks up for the moderns but rather that it is impossible to carve unambiguous affirmation of the age out of

28. William of Malmesbury, *Gesta regum Anglorum* 3.292: "sepe mirari soleo cur nostri temporis doctos hoc respergat infortunium, ut in canto numero discentium, in tam tristi pallore lucubrantium, vix aliquis plenam scientiae laudem referat: adeo inveteratus usus placet, adeo fere nullus novis, licet probabiliter inventis, serenitatem assensus pro merito indulget. Totis conatibus in sententiam veterum reputatur, omne recens sordet; ita, quia solus favor alit ingenia, cessante favore obtorpuerunt omnia." In William of Malmesbury, "*Gesta regum Anglorum*": *The History of the English Kings* 3.292, Roger A.B. Mynors, Rodney M. Thomson, and Michael Winterbottom, ed. and trans. (Oxford: Clarendon, 1998), 1:526. See also Adelard of Bath, *Questiones naturales*, Burnett ed. and trans., 82.

29. "Non enim plura scimus quam antiqui, sed plura perspicimus. Habemus enim illorum scripta et, praeter hoc, naturale ingenium quo aliquid novi perspicimus. Sumus enim nani super humeros gigantum, ex alterius qualitate multum, ex nostra parvum perspicientes." In Jeauneau, "Nani gigantum," 85. See also Alan of Lille, prose prologue 3 to the *Anticlaudianus*; Wetherbee ed., 222.

CHAPTER 10 ★ PESSIMISM IN THE TWELFTH CENTURY

the advocacy of the *moderni*. This structure of thought, the moderns versus the ancients, in fact provided the twelfth century with another scheme in which it could have glorified itself, its personalities, and its accomplishments, if it wished to do so, as the Irish Exile, Alberti, Erasmus, and others did for their own ages. But the only use made of it was to affirm the moderns as minor and occasional. "The moderns preferred to the ancients" cannot supply testimony to anyone's sense of living in a grand age in the twelfth century. The small tail (praise of the moderns) requires added bulk and muscle (a scholarly consensus of a "renaissance" in the period) in order to wag the big dog (rejection of the moderns). Again, it seems unlikely that mute self-affirmation reigns, while self-criticism, audible but empty of documentary value, dominates the records. The age generally represented its intellectual life as minor and mediocre compared with the ancients.

HISTORIOGRAPHY

I turn now to specific areas of twelfth-century culture. I have limited my survey to four: historiography, the life of the schools, poetry, and the culture of love. These are areas in which scholars have traditionally located the vitality of the age and planted the banner of renaissance. While this selection limits the range of commentary, I should reiterate that I have excluded no area of secular culture where optimism reigns. The voices quoted in what follows are representative.

The writing of history proliferated in the twelfth century.[30] One of its most prominent historians was Otto of Freising. Otto was for Haskins a perfect example of a philosophizing historian[31] in the mainstream of his time, educated in Paris, in touch with trends in philosophy and theology, Cistercian abbot, powerful Bavarian bishop, uncle of Frederick Barbarossa. He seems to touch all the bases — or most of them — of the twelfth-century renaissance. So how did this representative figure regard his age? In a word, darkly. A profound and cynical pessimism characterizes Otto's *Chronicle of the Two Cities* written (in its first version, now lost) between 1143 and 1146, then

30. See Goetz, *Geschichtsschreibung*; M.-D. Chenu, "Theology and the New Awareness of History," in his *Nature, Man and Society*, 162–201; Damian-Grint, *New Historians*; and Nancy Partner, *Serious Entertainments: The Writing of History in Twelfth-Century England* (Chicago: University of Chicago Press, 1977).

31. Haskins, 224–75 on historical writing, 241–44 on Otto of Freising.

reworked and sent to Frederick Barbarossa in 1152. The work is unique because it develops something approaching a philosophy of history and applies it consistently to analyzing events.[32]

While historians of the Gentiles (Greeks and Romans) imagined their task as reporting the virtues and strengths of their peoples, the task of the Christian historian, Otto says,[33] is to tell the history, not just of one, but of the "two cities," from which history emerges as a chronicle of human miseries and a retelling of the "tragedies of mortal woes."[34] This is part of the plan of a wise God to scare humans away from transitory things. The present age requires the

32. The literature on Otto's conception of history is extensive. See the fundamental work by Josef Koch, "Die Grundlagen der Geschichtsphilosophie Ottos von Freising," in *Geschichtsdenken und Geschichtsbild im Mittelalter*, Walther Lammers, ed. (Darmstadt: Wissenschaftliche Buchgesellschaft, 1961), 321–49; Hans-Werner Goetz, *Das Geschichtsbild Ottos van Freising: Ein Beitrag zur historischen Vorstellungswelt und zur Geschichte des 12. Jahrhunderts* (Cologne: Böhlau, 1984), 62–98, 300–28; and Nikolaus Staubach, "Geschichte als Lebenstrost: Bemerkungen zur historiographischen Konzeption Ottos von Freising," *Mittellateinisches Jahrbuch* 23 (1988): 46–75.

33. Prologue to book 1, in *The Two Cities: A Chronicle of Universal History to the Year 1146 A.D. by Bishop Otto of Freising*, Charles Christopher Mierow, trans. (New York: Columbia University Press, 1928), 93–95; original text with German translation in *Chronik oder die Geschichte der zwei Staaten*, Walther Lammers, ed.; Adolf Schmidt, trans. (Darmstadt: Wissenschaftliche Buchgesellschaft, 1974), 10–14. A few comments on the present age: ll. 2–5: "Nos autem, tanquam in fine temporum constituti ex ipsis nostri temporis experimentis eas [i.e., erumpnas mortalium] in nobis invenimus," Lammers ed., 12; ll. 5–9: "regnum Romanorum...maxime diebus nostris ex nobilissimo factum est pene novissimum," Lammers ed., 12; ll. 12–16: "non solum antiquitate senuit [regnum], sed etiam ipsa mobilitate sui...sordes multiplices ac defectus varios contraxit ipsiusque occasus toti corpori minatur interitum." Lammers, ed., 7.34, ll. 1–2: "ex tumultuosissimi temporis feculenta improbitate haut diu stare posse mundum putaremus."

34. On the conception of the *Chronicle* as "tragedy," see Peter von Moos, "Lucans *tragedia* im Hochmittelalter: Pessimismus, *contemptus mundi* und Gegenwartserfahrung (Otto von Freising, 'Vita Heinrici IV.', Johann von Salisbury)," *Mittellateinisches Jahrbuch* 14 (1979): 127–86.

CHAPTER 10 ✷ PESSIMISM IN THE TWELFTH CENTURY

lessons of history less than earlier periods, he continues, because his generation lives amidst vivid examples of the miseries of existence in the city of Babylon, the Roman Empire. The empire in its wanderings, its *translatio*, has not grown better: it has declined. It has, by Otto's days, sunk to the last position instead of rising to the noblest and foremost. It has become senile and decrepit, marred with innumerable stains and defects, as it passed from Babylon to Greece to Rome to Germany. The fate of the chief world power is living testimony to the tragedies of mortal woes, and its present state foretells the imminent fall of the whole structure. Therefore, living experience renders the need for mere stories of tragic decline less than in earlier days.

Otto wrote the *Chronicle* during the turbulence prior to the election of his nephew as emperor Frederick I in 1152. His view of the present age brightened in his later work, the *Gesta Friderici*, which he began in 1157 and left as a fragment of two books at his death in 1158. Happy are those who write in the present, he says, for now the turbulence of war is ended with glorious peace. The time of weeping has given way to a time of laughing.[35] His conception of a worldly history doomed to steady decline through a series of tragic events gives way to a new age of exemplary deeds of the emperor. But this is a temporary change brought about by the advent of Frederick, not a fundamental shift in Otto's thinking on the nature of history, certainly not a transformation of Otto from "the greatest pessimist of his age" into "the greatest optimist."[36] In other respects, the skepticism remains.[37] Frederick's

35. Otto of Freising, *The Deeds of Frederick Barbarossa* 1, prologue, Charles Christopher Mierow, trans. (New York: Columbia University Press, 1966), 24–25, 27. See also Otto of Freising and Rahewin, *Die Taten Friedrichs oder richtiger Chronica*, ll. 6–11: "hoc tempore scribentes quodammodo iudico beatos, dum post turbulentiam preteritorum non solum pacis inaudita reluxit serenitas, sed et ob victoriosissimi principis virtutes tanta Romani imperii pollet auctoritas, ut et sub eius principatu gens vivens humiliter silendo conquiescat." In Franz-Josef Schmale, ed.; Adolf Schmidt, trans. (Darmstadt: Wissenschaftliche Buchgesellschaft, 1974), 114; ll. 12–13: "post tempus flendi tempus ridendi," Schmale and Schmidt ed., 118.

36. Justus Hashagen, *Otto von Freising als Geschichtsphilosoph und Kirchenpolitiker* (Leipzig: Teubner, 1900), 31–32.

37. Goetz reviews the long tradition of conjecture on the reasons for Otto's changed attitude and argues for a change of circumstance, not an abandoning of the pessimism of the *Chronicle*. See *Das Geschichtsbild Ottos*, 275–76; likewise

reign is an interruption of the comprehensive and predetermined development of history, not a reversal of it. Fortune, Otto says, has "not yet turned its malign aspect on you,"[38] implying a fundamental malice of Fortune and a temporary respite under Frederick's reign. In sending a revised version of the *Chronicle* to Frederick in 1156 or 1157, half a decade into his nephew's reign, Otto confirmed that the dark vision of that work was still in effect for that part of world history not lifted temporarily from its misery by Frederick's reign.

Otto's *Chronicle* calls on a number of models and tropes of history that are — or would seem — inherently positive and optimistic. He adapts the historical scheme of Augustine's *City of God*, with its great polemical energy and fundamental Christian optimism.[39] He calls on the ideas of *translatio imperii* and *translatio studii* as one frame of development in universal history. He draws on the scheme of *moderni* versus *antiqui* and the image of dwarves on the shoulders of giants (indirectly alluded to), only to turn all of them negative.[40] Nowhere in his works is the high-soaring optimism of an age of spiritual and intellectual renewal in sight. They are characterized rather by the resignation of a man embittered by the world he inhabits, the one exception being the limited optimism — dynastically motivated — about the reign of Frederick Barbarossa.

Turning from Otto of Freising to other histories and *vitae* from the period, we find few positive and many negative judgments of

---

Staubach, "Geschichte als Lebenstrost," 64–65 (the new optimism of *Gesta* does not represent a change in his fundamental pessimism). Elisabeth Megier, "*Tamquam lux post tenebras*, oder: Ottos von Freising Weg von der *Chronik* zu den *Gesta Friderici*," *Mediävistik* 3 (1990): 131–267, elucidates the shift by reference to genre considerations, the change of rhetoric appropriate to praise of a ruler. on the motif of "mutability" in Otto, see also Megier, "*Fortuna* als Kategorie der Geschichtsdeutung im 12. Jahrhundert am Beispiel Ordericus Vitalis und Ottos von Freising," *Mittellateinisches Jahrbuch* 32 (1997): 49–70.

38. *Die Taten Friedrichs*, ll. 20–21: "obscenum tibi nondum vultum fortuna verterit." In Schmale and Schmidt ed., 118; Mierow trans., 27.

39. On Augustine's influence on Otto, see Goetz, *Das Geschichtsbild Ottos*, 235–42.

40. See above, 333, 338.

CHAPTER 10 ✶ PESSIMISM IN THE TWELFTH CENTURY

the present. Where writers register praise and optimism about the present, they focus on individuals, not on the period itself. Suger of St. Denis praises a stratagem of Louis the Fat above anything ever accomplished by ancients or moderns.[41] Walter Map has high praise for Louis VII of France.[42] William the Breton lauds Philip Augustus for his patronage of the schools of Paris.[43] Theobald of Canterbury (given voice by John of Salisbury) praises Henry II for creating a new golden age;[44] and Otto of Freising praises Frederick Barbarossa for bringing peace and renewed authority to the Roman empire. These personalities may suspend briefly the badness of their times, but the praise ordinarily focuses on the person of the ruler and is occasional praise, which finds little or no echo in the worldly culture of France, Germany, or England generally. And personal praise can easily be muted into an occasion for scourging rather than exalting the present. Herbert of Bosham praises Thomas Becket in this sense:

> Such virtue joined with decorum will be admired by all future ages but imitated by few, perhaps none. Though such virtue lived in our time, it was not of our tepid age, which brings forth only the self-loving and self-seeking.[45]

41. Suger of St. Denis, *Vie de Louis VI le Gros*, Henri Waquet, ed. and trans. (Paris: Champion, 1929), 230.

42. *De nugis curialium*, James et al., ed. and trans., 442–57.

43. *Oeuvres de Rigord et de Guillaume le Breton, historiens de Philippe-Auguste*, Henri François Delaborde, ed., 2 vols. (Paris: Renouard, 1882–85), 1:230; Baldwin, "Masters at Paris," 140–42. William the Breton, however, wrote his praise of the Paris schools shortly before 1220, referring to a time just before 1210. A short poem by Petrus Riga celebrates the dawning of a new age with the birth of Philip Augustus. See William Chester Jordan, "*Quando fuit natus*: Interpreting the Birth of Philip Augustus," in *The Work of Jacques Le Goff and the Challenges of Medieval History*, Miri Rubin, ed. (New York: Boydell and Brewer, 1997), 171–88.

44. Letter 101. *The Letters of John of Salisbury* 1. *The Early Letters (1153–1161)*, W.J. Millor, Harold E. Butler, and Christopher N.L. Brooke, ed. (Oxford: Clarendon, 1986), 161.

45. Herbert of Bosham, *Vita Thomae* 6.9: "Virtus quidem cum decore suo omnibus post futuris saeculis admirabilis, sed imitabilis paucis; utrum vero cuiquam, nescio. Eo quidem admirabilior virtus haec, quod etsi in nostro tempore,

Aelred of Rievaulx praises St. Ninian:

> When I think of the saintly ways of this saintly man, I am ashamed of our own inane stupidity and of the spinelessness of this wretched generation.[46]

This is a consistent strain: individuals may be good, but the age is bad. Orderic Vitalis undertakes to write his *Historia ecclesiastica* in order to record

> the deeds of the good and evil leaders of this wretched age [*huius nequam seculi*].... Since now is the time when "the love of humanity waxes cold and iniquity abounds" [Mt. 24:12], miracles grow rarer whilst crimes...are multiplied all over the world.... The time of Antichrist draws near preceded by drying up of miracles and a growing frenzy of vices.[47]

Against this, note Orderic's enthusiasm for the crusade: "a tremendous movement is taking place in our own day, and a noble and marvellous theme for exposition is unfolded for writers to study."[48]

Things look different in the monastic reform movement. Giles Constable's book with the resonant title *The Reformation of the Twelfth Century* has plenty of evidence of a sense of a dawning new age. Orderic Vitalis contrasts the worldliness of his age to its religious progress:

> Although Evil predominates in the world, the devotion of the faithful grows in greater proportion. A rich harvest grows in the field of the Lord. Everywhere monasteries are built and the crowds of monks spread throughout the world.[49]

---

haec non tamen nostri temporis est vel teporis, quo homines se ipsos amantes et solum quaerentes quae sua sunt." In James Craigie Robertson, ed., Rolls Series 67.3 (London: Longman, 1877), 509.

46. Aelred of Rievaulx, *Lives of S. Ninian and S. Kentigern* 9: "Cogitantem me sanctissimi viri morem sanctissimum pudet socordie nostre, pudet hujus misere generationis ignavie." In Alexander Forbes, ed. (Edinburgh: Edmonston and Douglas, 1874), 150. See Brian Patrick McGuire, *Brother and Lover: Aelred of Rievaulx* (New York: Crossroad, 1994), 44.

47. 1, prologue; Chibnall ed., 1:130–31. See also 5, prologue; Chibnall ed., 3:8–9; and 6, prologue, Chibnall ed., 3:214–15.

48. 9, prologue; Chibnall ed., 5:4–5.

49. 2.26; Chibnall ed., 4:310.

CHAPTER 10 * PESSIMISM IN THE TWELFTH CENTURY

Otto of Freising agrees. One of the only bright spots in his *Chronicle* is his description of monks, anchorites, and solitaries at the end of book 7, whom he praises for their "pure and holy lives."[50] Otto gives what we can take as a paradigm of historical optimism in the twelfth century:

> Because of the multitude of our sins and the stinking immorality of this most war-torn of times, we would think the world imminently doomed, were it not sustained by the merits of the holy citizens of the true city of God, whose variously abundant and beautifully distinguished communities flourish throughout the entire world.[51]

Similarly, Anselm of Havelberg develops an optimistic view of historical progress based exclusively on the advance of the church and religion, not secular studies.[52]

Historical consciousness itself arose in the twelfth century not from any sense of dawning and rebirth but rather as a response to decline. Twelfth-century historians wrote history to overcome a perceived crisis of the present through a nostalgic evocation of the past. This is the striking conclusion of Hans-Werner Goetz in his study of the historical awareness of the high Middle Ages.[53] This

---

50. Otto, *Chronicle* 7.34–35; Lammers ed., 558–67; Constable, *Reformation*, 49.

51. 7.34; Lammers ed., 560.

52. See Constable, *Reformation*, 48–49; and Karl Morrison, "Anselm of Havelberg: Play and the Dilemma of Historical Progress," in *Religion, Culture and Society in the Early Middle Ages: Studies in Honor of Richard E. Sullivan*, Thomas F.X. Noble and John J. Contreni, ed. (Kalamazoo, MI: Medieval Institute Publications, 1987), 219–56. See Anselm of Havelberg, *Dialogus* (*Dialogi*) 1.10, Gaston Salet, ed. (Paris: Editions du Cerf, 1966), 94, on Norbert of Xanten: "religio per eum renovata maxima coepit habere incrementa." Similarly, monastic authors could make Lanfranc into a reviver of studies. See Guitmund of Aversa, *De corporis et sanguinis Christi veritate in eucharistia*, PL 149:1428B–C; and Milo Crispin of Bec, *Vita Lanfranci*, PL 150:29B.

53. Goetz, *Geschichtsschreibung*, 396: "Das Geschichtsbewusstsein entsprang... einer *Krise* der eigenen Zeit oder der eigenen Institution in der Gegenwart, die Geschichtsschreibung wollte an den Glanz der Vergangenheit erinnern. Die Krise der Gegenwart sollte durch ein Vergangenheitsbewusstsein gemeistert werden." See also Timothy Reuter, "Past, Present and No Future in the

conclusion is consistent with my survey of the historical sources: historiography in the twelfth century is ordinarily testimony to a sense of decline, not to the glory of the present.

LEARNING AND STUDY

It was among monastic reformers and their advocates that we find enthusiasm and optimism about the present age for the spread of the reformed monastic orders.[54] It should be said that "crowds of monks," burgeoning monasteries, and growing asceticism are not what support the twelfth century's reputation for "renewal," "reawakening," and "rebirth." The growth of schools, secular learning, and worldly culture do, as a look at the table of contents of Haskins' *Renaissance of the Twelfth Century* and of any of the studies mentioned above will confirm. The movement called "renaissance" is generally regarded as a rebirth of learning. I can cite one prominent voice that is enthusiastic about the state of learning in his own age.

The classically trained cleric Chrétien de Troyes uses the scheme *translatio studii* in the prologue to his romance *Cligès* to sketch the history of chivalry and learning, *chevalerie et clergie*. Both arose in Greece, then wandered to Rome. Now they have found a new homeland in France:

> God grant it may be kept here and find such a pleasing home that the honor now arrived may never depart from France![55]

Twelfth-Century *Regnum Teutonicum*," in *The Perception of the Past in Twelfth-Century Europe*, Paul Magdalino, ed. (London: Hambledon Press, 1992), 15–36.

54. John Gillingham, "A Historian of the Twelfth-Century Renaissance and the Transformation of English Society, 1066–c.1200," in *European Transformations: The Long Twelfth Century*, Thomas F.X. Noble and John Van Engen, ed. (Notre Dame, IN: University of Notre Dame Press, 2012), 45–74.

55. Chrétien de Troyes, *Cligès*, ll. 30–44: "Ce nos ont nostre livre apris / qu'an Grece ot de chevalerie / Le premier los et de clergie. / Puis vint chevalerie a Rome / et de la clergie la some, / qui or est en France venue. / Dex doint qu'ele i soit maintenue / et que li leus li embelisse / tant que ja mes de France n'isse / l'enors qui s'i est arestee. / Dex l'avoit as altres prestee, / car des Grezois ne des Romains / ne dit en mes ne plus ne mains: / D'ax est la parole remese / et estainte la vive brese." In Laurence Harf-Lancner ed. (Paris: Champion, 2006), 62–64.

CHAPTER 10 ✷ PESSIMISM IN THE TWELFTH CENTURY

Enthusiastic optimism indeed. It sets the learning and chivalry of France in a line of descent from that of the Greeks and Romans, whose ashes are now cold, while the fires burn bright in France. The sense of historical movement is transference and inheritance, not awakening, restoration of something lost. The tropes of decline and senility have no place in Chrétien's praise of his age. Others not so enthusiastic for the present might well contest the claim that "nothing more is heard of Greeks and Romans." Chrétien's use of *translatio* does not make common cause with the idea of the "six ages of the world" and makes no mention of culture's senility. On the contrary, the present age in France seems to have come into its own in an upward curve, peaking in France, its apogee projected hopefully into the future. But anyone who quotes this passage as testimony to a sense of grand intellectual fulfillment in France of the twelfth century should bear in mind how isolated the sentiment is.

Here are some other positive assessments of secular learning in the twelfth century. The poet Hugh Primas of Orleans has high praise for the school of Rheims under Master Alberic in the 1130s:

> Rheims has always enjoyed a high reputation, but now, under Alberic, it has most profitably increased the treasure received from the ancients....[56]

But he wards off the inference that "Greeks and Romans" are the givers of the ancient treasury. The school's distinction consists in despising the works of the pagans in favor of Christian writers:

> It is not the poets who are read here but St. John and the prophets; not Socrates but the eternal Trinity stands in high repute.[57]

Praise of the new schools of Paris in the period of their formation, c.1100–1150, is rare indeed.[58] A notable exception is William of Tyre.

---

56. Poem 18, ll. 31–71. In *Hugh Primas and the Archpoet*, Fleur Adcock, ed. and trans. (Cambridge: Cambridge University Press, 1994), 44–46.

57. Poem 18:49–54: "Non leguntur hic poete, / Sed Iohannes et prophete. / Non est scola vanitatis, / Set doctrina veritatis./ Ibi nomen non Socratis / Sed eterne trinitatis." In *The Oxford Poems of Hugh Primas and the Arundel Lyrics*, C.J. McDonough, ed. (Toronto: University of Toronto Press, 1984), 63.

58. There is abundant praise of the school of St. Victor. See Jaeger, *Envy*, 244–68. This school, however, founded by Abelard's adversary, William of Champeaux, represents a throwback to an older curriculum now deeply Christianized, letters and manners leading to theology. The enthusiasm of its students cannot be taken

He recalls the days of his studies in Paris, starting c.1146, with warmth, enthusiasm, and high praise for his teachers and for teachers of the previous generation. He studied letters with "excellent teachers, venerable men, worthy of cherished memory, vessels of learning." He then cites a host of Parisian and Chartrian masters with pure admiration. Of Peter Lombard, with whom he studied theology, he says,

> he was unique; the chorus of the wise embrace his surviving works with veneration and study them with reverence.... All of these live in blessed memory and illustrious writings down to the present day, for they illuminated learning and rendered it manifold it passing on.[59]

Guido of Bazoches (b.1146) belonged to the next generation. His studies in Paris are not exactly datable, but they will not have commenced earlier than 1160. Sometime in the course of his studies he wrote to a friend praising the city and its studies in glowing terms and inviting the friend to join him:

> On this island Philosophy has since ancient times located her throne. She alone, with her sole companion, Studies [*studium*], though despised, possesses a perennial fortress of light and immortality, from which she treads underfoot the withering

---

as affirmation of the new schools of dialectic, rather the opposite. It raises the question, if it was possible for the students of this school to praise it warmly, why was the same not true of the independent schools of Paris, or of the long-standing school of Mont Ste. Geneviève?

59. William of Tyre, *Chronique* 19.12: "literarum studiis etatis nostros dedicavimus dies, in liberalibus artibus doctores precipui, viri venerabiles et pia recordatione digni, scientiarum vasa, thesauri disciplinarum." On Peter Lombard: "In theologia autem virum in ea scientia singularem, cuius opera que exstant prudentum chorus cum veneratione amplectitur et colit cum reverentia, ... magistrum videlicet Petrum Lonbardum." [William's summary] "Horum omnium usque hodie in benedictione vivit memoria et permanet inclita recordatio, qui elucidaverunt scienciam et pertranseuntes fecerunt eam multiplicem, multos erudientes ad iusticiam in quibus perhenniter vivunt oblivionis dispendia non sensuri." In Robert B.C. Huygens, ed., CCCM 63A (Turnhout: Brepols, 1986), 880–81. On this passage, see Huygens, "Guillaume de Tyr étudiant: Un chapitre (XIX, 12) de son 'Histoire' retrouvé," *Latomus* 21 (1962): 810–29. On the reference to the prophecy of Daniel 12:4 (*pertranseuntes fecerunt eam multiplicem*), see below, 350–51.

CHAPTER 10 ✶ PESSIMISM IN THE TWELFTH CENTURY

flower of this long-since aging world. On this island the seven sisters, that is, the liberal arts, have built themselves a perpetual mansion.[60]

By the beginning of the thirteenth century, the reigns of Louis VII and Philip Augustus are credited with patronage of flourishing studies.[61]

THE CRITICS

The voices of critics abound.[62] The humanists, whose roots lie in the old learning of cathedral schools, are a chorus of disapproval of the new and contemporary. Their voices are abundant and shrill and include John of Salisbury, Peter of Blois, William of Conches, Thierry of Chartres, Otto of Freising, Gerald of Wales. To survey some of these views, we can again start with Otto of Freising. Studies and learning in the twelfth century are for Otto witnesses of the universal decline. True, he says in the *Chronicle of the Two Cities*, all learning originated in the East and moved west, but that development occurs because knowledge is destined to end here.[63] Otto ignores the invitation to progressive thinking inherent in the trope *translatio studii*. He agrees with modern historians of

---

60. Epistola 4: "In hac insula regale sibi solium ab antiquo filosofia collocavit, que sola solo comite contempta studio perhemnem lucis et immortalitatis possidens arcem victorioso pede calcat mundi iam pridem senescentis aridum florem. In hac insula perpetuam sibi mansionem septem pepigere sorores, artes videlicet liberales." In *Liber epistularum Guidonis de Basochis*, Herbert Adolfsson, ed. (Stockholm: Almquist and Wiksell, 1969), 14–15.

61. Alexander Neckham, writing in 1211, quotes what appears to be a common wordplay ("Parisius/Paradisus") and praises the schools under Louis VII warmly in *De laude divinae sapientiae*, Thomas Wright, ed., Rolls Series 34 (London: Longman, 1863), 453. On the wordplay and this text, see Ferruolo, *Origins*, 12–13. William the Breton, chaplain of Philip Augustus, writing c.1220, praises Paris as superior to Athens and Rome in the number of students. See above, 343 n. 43.

62. See Ferruolo, *Origins*.

63. *Chronicle* 1, prologue: "omnis humana potentia seu scientia ab oriente cepit et in occidente terminatur." In Lammers ed., 12–14; 5, prologue: "omnis humana...sapientia ab oriente ordiens in occidente terminari cepit." In Lammers ed., 372.

the twelfth-century schools on one point: he sees a burgeoning of studies and learning in the early century, but he understands this trend as fulfilling the prophecy of Daniel 12:4 that a proliferation of studies would mark the period of decline before the Last Judgment: "Many shall run to and fro and knowledge will be manifold."[64] The prophesied running to and fro is inane busy-ness. The increase of knowledge is growing insight into the obvious: things are so bad that the end is near. Growth of knowledge is a function of the world's old age. Those who come later know more than those who precede. It follows that they acquire knowledge in amounts not available to sages in earlier times. The upshot is clear: Otto's idea of intellectual "progress" is far from a positive, hopeful, and optimistic one. He sees the learned of his age not as bold and energetic innovators but rather as immature but well-informed observers of decline. All

64. Dan. 12:4: "Pertransibunt plurimi et multiplex erit scientia." There is a problem in understanding the line in the Bible. See the commentary in *The Interpreter's Bible: The Holy Scriptures in the King James and Revised Standard Versions*, George A. Buttrick, ed. (New York: Abingdon-Cokesbury, 1956), 6:544–45. But decisive for our context is Otto's understanding of the line. He clearly understood *pertransire* as "scurrying" and the "multiplicity" of knowledge as a phenomenon of final decline, as his elucidation of the passage in 5, prologue indicates: "Hanc in senio mundi ex his, quas dixi, causis sapientiam fore multiplicandam propheta previdit, qui ait, 'Pertransibunt plurimi.'" In Lammers ed., 372. "The Prophet foresaw this growth of wisdom in the old age of the world for the reasons I have cited [namely, corruption and senility], and so he said 'Many shall hurry to and fro....'" In Mierow, trans., 322. Schmidt's German translation in Lammers' edition privileges one of the accepted readings of the line from Daniel, but the one that does not make sense in the context of Otto's work: "Pertransibunt plurimi" becomes "Viele werden bis in die Endzeit kommen." Mierow's translation (322) comes closer to Otto's intention: "The prophet foresaw that, in the old age of the world (for the reasons which I have mentioned), wisdom must be multiplied; and so he said: 'Many shall run to and fro, and knowledge shall be increased.'" William of Tyre integrated the same passage from Daniel into his praise of his teachers (above, 348 n. 59), interpreting it as a prophecy of an admirable spread of knowledge: "Horum omnium usque hodie in benedictione vivit memoria qui elucidaverunt scienciam et pertranseuntes fecerunt eam multiplicem" and ignoring the context: an indication of the coming Last Judgment.

CHAPTER 10 ✶ PESSIMISM IN THE TWELFTH CENTURY

the intellectual energy of his age is but a look back to the dreadful tragedies of the road just traveled. The sum product of its "wisdom" is that its wise ones recognize the decrepitude of the Roman Empire, which earlier writers, who knew less, tended to idealize.

The prologue to his fifth book[65] is a history of learning according to the scheme of *translatio studii*.[66] Here Otto is explicit in his judgment. Knowledge has passed from the Romans to the "French and Spanish," and "most recently" (*nuperrime*) it appeared in the days of

> ...the most illustrious doctors, Berengar, Manegold, and Anselm [of Laon]. [These] divinely inspired men were able to foresee the causes of these things. We however are in a position not merely to believe but also actually to see the things that were predicted, since we behold the world (which, they predicted, was to be despised for its changeableness) already failing and, so to speak, drawing the last breath of extremest old age.[67]

65. *Chronicle* 5, prologue: "Proinde Romanum imperium, quod pro sui excellentia a paganis aeternum, a nostris pene divum putabatur, *iam ad quid devenerit*, ab omnibus videtur" [emphasis added]. In Lammers ed., 372. There is a tendency to press a positive attitude toward intellectual progress out of this passage. See Verena Epp, "Ars und *scientia* in der Geschichtsschreibung des 12. Jahrhunderts," in *Scientia und ars im Hoch- und Spätmittelalter*, Ingrid Craemer-Ruegenberg and Andreas Speer, ed. (Berlin: De Gruyter, 1994), 829–45, at 840.

66. On this motif, see Franz Josef Worstbrock, "*Translatio artium*: Über die Herkunft und Entwicklung einer kulturhistorischen Theorie," *Archiv für Kulturgeschichte* 47 (1965): 1–22; and Werner Goez, Translatio imperii: *Ein Beitrag zur Geschichte des Geschichtsdenkens und der politischen Theorien im Mittelalter und in der frühen Neuzeit* (Tübingen: Mohr, 1958).

67. Book 5, prologue, ll. 8–12: "nuperrime a diebus illustrium doctorum Berengarii, Managaldi et Anshelmi translatam [i.e., humanam sapientiam]. Quarum rerum previdere et quasi somniare divinitus inspirati homines causas potuere. Nos vero non solum credere, sed et videre quae premissa sunt possumus, dum mundum, quem pro mutatione sui contempnendum predixerunt, nos iam deficientem et tanquam ultimi senii extremum spiritum trahentem cernimus." In Lammers ed., 374; Mierow trans., 323. Who are the "divinitus inspirati homines"? Mierow takes them to be the aforementioned sages, Berengar, Manegold, and Anselm (of Laon). Schmidt leaves it open ("Diese Entwicklung

Now it is odd — and not easily explainable by the category "twelfth-century renaissance" — that Otto makes a previous generation of philosophers and theologians into the heirs of wisdom and excludes his own generation. Berengar of Tours, Manegold of Lautenbach, and Anselm of Laon he seems to credit with divine inspiration, at least with praise for which no contemporary sage is singled out, and he sets them distinctly against the present age as paragons of a fading wisdom. They and not the present generation are the recipients of the knowledge handed down from the Greeks and Romans. Not Bernard and Thierry of Chartres, not the famous and controversial Peter Abelard, not the extremely learned and widely famed Hugh of St. Victor, not Bernard Silvester, Gilbert of Poitiers, or Peter Lombard. None of the famed doctors and poets of twelfth-century France receives mention from Otto — only three scholars from the eleventh century, one of whom lived into the twelfth, about whom we know comparatively little. (I will come back to this point later.) The passage quoted asserts clearly that the destiny of learning in its present phase is to predict, observe, and describe its collapse from decrepitude, not to exercise wisdom in reform, renewal, or active realization of progress in the world.

Otto's observations of school life at mid-century are more sober in the *Gesta Friderici*. His presentation is more restrained and nuanced. The pessimism of the *Chronicle of the Two Cities* is less evident, but it is not revoked. He issues no judgments of the schools and learning in general but also no praise. But his juxtaposition of Abelard and Gilbert of Poitiers makes his position on the dominant trends clear. Whereas Abelard despised his teachers and persuaded himself of the brilliance of his own thought,

> [Gilbert] from his youth subjected himself to the instruction of great men and put more confidence in the weight of their authority than in his own intellect: such men as, first, Hilary of Poitiers [fourth century]; next Bernard of Chartres; finally, the brothers Anselm and Ralph of Laon. From them he had

haben von Gott inspirierte Männer vorauswissen...können"). Otto could have made it clearer if he wished to refer to the three sages, but that seems to me the most probable construction of the reference. In either case, the stark adversative, "Nos vero," excludes Otto's own generation from the category of the divinely inspired.

CHAPTER 10 * PESSIMISM IN THE TWELFTH CENTURY

secured not a superficial but a solid education. His moral sense and the seriousness of his living were not at odds with his intellectual attainments. He was dignified in bearing and in utterance.[68]

Certainly, we would assign Gilbert a prominent place among the *moderni* along with Abelard. But what counts here is Otto's opinion that Gilbert respected authority, led a moral life, and credits an earlier generation of humanist scholars and theologians for his a solid grounding in learning. He also behaved and spoke with dignity. Otto agrees with John of Salisbury,[69] both of them championing solid, methodical learning based on letters and morals (*doctrina et mores*) leading to theology. Both glorify the previous generation of teachers and see the present generation leading students to shallowness and arrogance.

While Otto did revise his attitudes toward empire in the *Gesta*, he did nothing comparable for studies. There is certainly no trace of a sentiment like "happy are those who study in this age!" Otto's voice is one in a mighty chorus of blame. Wherever we turn in the twelfth century, we find criticism and a dire pessimism about the direction of the schools. I will limit my discussion to a few texts and point to the mass of evidence collected by Stephen C. Ferruolo.[70]

John of Salisbury is the most extensive and energetic of many sources. His *Metalogicon* (1159) is a reaction against the new trends in the schools in the second quarter of the century. After studying and teaching in Paris in the thirties and forties, he returned at some point after 1148 to visit his old friends on the Mont Ste. Geneviève, only to find that they had stagnated in the study of dialectic and were arguing the same propositions and posing the same questions to their students. His main adversary, to whom he gives the fictive name "Cornificius," is the representative of what John sees as the most dangerous trend. Cornificius despises the arts of language and advocates a facile, empty dialectical argumentation. John sees civilization itself threatened by this trend:

68. *Gesta Friderici* 1.52; Schmale and Schmidt ed., 236; Mierow trans., 88.
69. See above, 299–324.
70. *Origins of the University.*

> One who would eliminate the teaching of eloquence from philosophical studies wrests from Philology's arms her beloved Mercury. Although he may seem to attack eloquence alone, he undermines and uproots all liberal studies, assails the whole structure of philosophy, tears to shreds humanity's social contract, and destroys the means of brotherly charity. Deprived of their gift of speech men would degenerate to the condition of brute animals.... It may thus be seen that our 'Cornificius' attacks not merely one, or even a few persons, but all civilization and political organization.[71]

John sees the intellectual, social, and political scene of his day as fraught with crisis and beset by an instability that threatens to engulf all human intercourse, and this perspective asserts itself from beginning to end of the *Metalogicon* and more strongly yet in other of his writings on the schools.[72] The wars, deaths, and schism to which he refers at the end of the *Metalogicon* as the mark of his age seem, by their very inclusion, allied with the atmosphere of the schools and the collapse of communication and morals, the inevitable result of the direction of studies.

John's hostility to the schools is less concealed and more openly satirical in the *Policraticus*, finished in the same year as the *Metalogicon*:

> Consider the leading teachers of philosophy of our own day, those who are most loudly acclaimed, surrounded by a noisy throng of disciples. Mark them carefully; you will find them dwelling on one rule, or on two or three words...on which to

71. *Metalogicon* 1.1; Hall ed., 13–14; McGarry trans., 11–12. See also above, 299–324.

72. John invokes the pleasant prospect of "reviving golden yesterdays and returning to happier years" but realizes it is impossible, since his soul is "oppressed by a bitter sadness owing partly to fear and partly to other disturbing thoughts." See *Metalogicon* 4, prologue: "Iucundum enim fuerat in antiqua redire tempora, et ad annos respicere meliores, nisi amaritudo quae partim ex metu partim ex alia sollicitudine incumbit, animum praegravaret." In Hall ed., 140. McGarry, 203 translates, "owing to the realization that the good old days have gone." See also the final chapter, 4.42: "Iam enim flere magis vacat quam scribere, et visibili argumento doceor quod mundus totus subiacet vanitati." In Hall ed., 183; McGarry trans., 273–74, where John summarizes: "The present day is more suited to weeping than to writing. What I see about me convinces me that the world is subject to vanity."

CHAPTER 10 ✶ PESSIMISM IN THE TWELFTH CENTURY

exercise their talents and waste their life The points of dispute of our modern Proteus are as useless as they are trivial.[73]

John represents and advocates not new, but old learning. His *Metalogicon* is a conservative, rearguard action to resuscitate an old and dying humanistic curriculum by amalgamating it with the newly fashionable art of dialectic. His chapter reviewing his own education (2.10), one of the major sources on masters and schools in the first half of the twelfth century, is framed with a bias that, to my knowledge, has gone unnoticed. John casts himself in the exemplary role of a student seduced by the dangers of dialectic, who rescues himself by a return to grammar:

> I had learned the subject [dialectic] so thoroughly [after studies with Abelard, Alberic of Rheims, and Robert of Melun] that, with youthful lack of reflection, I unduly exaggerated my own knowledge. I took myself to be a young sage, inasmuch as I knew the answers to what I had been taught. However, I recovered my senses and took stock of my powers. I then transferred...to the grammarian of Conches.[74]

The trajectory of his own intellectual development mirrors that of the few "lovers of letters" (Gilbert of Poitiers, Thierry of Chartres, William of Conches, and Abelard) who — made temporarily "foolish" by the foolishness of hyperlogicians — recovered their sanity long enough to reestablish a brief recrudescence of the arts.[75] His teachers Alberic and Robert were at that time one-sided men stagnating in

---

73. *Policraticus* 7.9; *Frivolities*, 244–45; *Policratici*, Webb ed., 2:123–24. See also John's explicit criticism of the new schools in *Entheticus* 1.4–12, van Laarhoven ed., 1:104–17. These passages are also interesting for making "logic" the object of John's attack and clearly show the rhetorical irony and hidden agenda behind calling his work *"Metalogicon,"* a "defense of logic." See also above, 301–4.

74. *Metalogicon* 2.10: "Hoc enim plane didiceram, ut iuvenili levitate pluris facerem scientiam meam quam erat. Videbar mihi sciolus, eo quod in his quae audieram promptus eram. Deinde reversus in me et metiens vires meas...me ad grammaticum de Conchis transtuli." In Hall ed., 71; McGarry trans., 97. See also above, 306–8.

75. *Metalogicon* 1.5: "...fumus ille cito evanuit, et...redierunt artes, et...honorem pristinum nactae sunt." In Hall ed., 20–21; McGarry trans., 21–23. But the trend was quickly resisted by the Cornificians.

dialectic who could have become great scholars and teachers "had they but possessed a broad foundation of literary learning and kept to the footsteps of their predecessors."[76]

The decline of an older, humanistic educational system is evident in both the curricular and the biographical details of his work. Like Otto of Freising, John looks back to an earlier master of the schools for a model of learning and teaching, not to his own days and — perhaps more tellingly — not to his own teachers. In a much-quoted passage, John describes the teaching methods of the great master of grammar Bernard of Chartres, who died approximately thirty years before the composition of the *Metalogicon*. Bernard is for John a representative of a civilized and civilizing curriculum, in which the arts of language and manners (*mores*) are joined to the reading of the classical poets and to poetic composition. John also reports the early retirements of two of his teachers, William of Conches and Richard the Bishop. They were forced from their positions "by the onslaught of the ignorant mob."[77] Students in droves rushed to masters who promised them competence in easy and short studies.

Another famous master of the old humanistic curriculum, Thierry of Chartres, observed the same change and reacted with a gesture of elite exclusivity. By his own account, in his commentary on Cicero's *De inventione*, he banished the ignorant rabble and the chaos of the schools from his "palace" of learning. "No counterfeiters of genius, who despise studies" are eligible for his teaching.[78] Another of Thierry's students praises him as "the immovably fixed anchor in this turbulent time of changing studies" — which also indicates that the rush of change boded no good for that system in which he was immovably fixed.[79] From the complaints of humanist masters against the decline of studies there also emerges a clear picture of schools being overwhelmed by crowds of students eager to get a

76. *Metalogicon* 2.10.26–30: "...magni praeclarique viri in philosophicis studiis enituissent, si de magno litterarum niterentur fundamento, si tantum instituissent vestigiis maiorum." In Hall ed., 71; McGarry trans., 96.

77. *Metalogicon* 1.24.124; Hall ed. 54; McGarry trans., 71.

78. Cited in Peter Dronke, "Thierry of Chartres," in *History of Twelfth-Century Philosophy*, Dronke, ed., at 362.

79. Dronke, "Thierry of Chartres," 363.

CHAPTER 10 ★ PESSIMISM IN THE TWELFTH CENTURY

quick education in a narrow area of study, a trend that was counter to the curricula that John of Salisbury, Hugh of St. Victor, and Thierry of Chartres championed, a curriculum that united the two divisions of the liberal arts.[80] The times were indeed changing fast. No anchor held firm, and no one, whether old- or new-fashioned, student or master, welcomed the future and renounced the past. At least none that I know of has left written testimony to that attitude.

It appears that the old system of humanistic education was in decline. Works of poetic philosophy burned bright for a short time, then went out and disappeared altogether.[81] The great age of episcopal biography was past, experiencing a late flare-up in the *vitae* of Thomas Becket. A classic or late-classic poetic style in Latin, slightly baroque and with an affected obscurity, ceded to a sober, scholastic prose style in philosophical discourse. The art of letter-writing declined from its high point in the eleventh and early twelfth centuries to give way to the banalities of the *ars dictaminis*. Rhetoric and poetry disappeared from the curriculum of the schools, and with them went the reading of the classical authors.[82] The Parisian

80. I have found such complaints since the second half of the eleventh century, but the trend they observe clearly came to a head in the French schools of the early twelfth century. For earlier instances, see Jaeger, *Envy*, 217–26. See also Hugh of St. Victor, *Didascalicon* 3.3: "...in that time [the days of 'the ancients'] there were so many learned men that they alone wrote more than we are able to read. But the students of our day, whether from ignorance or from unwillingness, fail to hold to a fit method of study, and therefore we find many who study but few who are wise." In Taylor trans., 87. John of Salisbury reports that Gilbert of Poitiers predicted for such students a career as bakers, since acording to him that was the one trade that required no skill: *Metalogicon* 1.5.2–7; Hall ed., 20.

81. That is, poems in that genre, philosophical allegories, were no longer composed. Alan's *Anticlaudianus* remained a popular and important work. See Christel Meier, "Die Rezeption des *Anticlaudianus* Alans von Lille in Textkommentierung und Illustration," in *Text und Bild: Aspekte des Zusammenwirkens zweier Künste in Mittelalter und früher Neuzeit*, Christel Meier and Uwe Ruberg, ed. (Wiesbaden: Reichert, 1980), 408–549. On the philosophical poetry of the age, see Wetherbee, *Platonism*.

82. On the decline of the arts, see Walter of Chatillon 1.14, Strecker ed., 8; 4.20, Strecker ed., 67; 11, Strecker ed., 113–15; 13.13–14, Strecker ed., 125–26; and Gerald of Wales, *Itinerarium Kambriae*, in *Giraldi Cambrensis Opera*, John

schools of dialectic and theology swelled, and the centers of literary/ philosophical studies — Chartres, Tours, and Orleans — shrank. The decline of the school of St. Victor in Paris is consistent with this trend, though the immediate cause of its decline is the figure of its rigorous reform abbot, Walter of St. Victor.

In the course of the twelfth century the general view of the schools turned darker, not lighter.[83] We can end this survey of the dominant pessimism with a letter of Stephen of Tournai, a canon regular, abbot of the monastery of St. Geneviève, and bishop of Tournai from 1192 to 1203. His letter about the decline of the schools is directed to a pope, either Celestine III or Innocent III (the letter is not more exactly datable).[84] A sickness plagues the schools, he warns, and unless treated, it will turn incurable. Every discipline is distorted: the study of Scripture, theology, philosophy, and the liberal arts. In the open street, the Holy Trinity is torn apart and dissected. For every master there is a host of errors, for every schoolroom a scandal, for every back street a blasphemy. The so-called liberal arts have lost their liberality and are so enslaved that beardless youths usurp the chairs of old masters to teach half-baked learning. They reject all the rules and all the authentic masters in order to catch the flies of their ridiculous phrases in the spiderwebs of their sophistic argumentation. The situation calls out urgently for the hand of apostolic correction.

This letter is generally credited with some influence in the founding of the University of Paris.[85] It gives support to Stephen Ferruolo's thesis that the university arose as a solution to the problems of the

---

S. Brewer et al., ed., Rolls Series 21, 8 vols. (London: Longman, 1861–91), 6:4. On these developments see John O. Ward, "Gothic Architecture, Universities and the Decline of the Humanities in Twelfth-Century Europe," in *Principalities, Powers and Estates: Studies in Medieval and Early Modern Government and Society*, L.O. Frappell, ed. (Adelaide: Adelaide University Press, 1979), 65–78; Knowles, *Evolution*, 72–84; and Jaeger, *Envy*, 217–36.

83. Again I would refer the reader to the abundant materials in Ferruolo, *Origins*.

84. Stephen of Tournai, *Epistola* 251. *Chartularium Universitatis Parisiensis*, Heinrich Denifle, ed. (Paris: Delalain, 1889), 1:47–48.

85. See Ferruolo, *Origins*, 269–77.

burgeoning schools and metastasizing dialectic studies in Paris, a reaction to complaints about the miserable condition of the Paris schools. While the letter can be read as indicating — through a negative perspective — the burgeoning of studies and the vitality of the schools,[86] it also underscores my point: the growth of studies roused little fanfare and much harsh criticism.

POETRY

Perhaps one of the most persistent complaints of participants in the Latin culture of the twelfth century is the decline of poetry. I want to highlight this topic for good reason: all the complaints about decline noted so far have the character of language, not substance. Tweaked and kneaded, they can be forced from behind a rhetorical posture of pessimism to reveal something positive, some disguised optimism or some masked will to reform and improve consistent with an age of renaissance. (Particularly difficult to wrestle down is the "dwarves on the shoulders of giants" image.) But the actual decline in the social and intellectual status of poetry lamented by contemporaries is documentable to a standard of proof acceptable, I think, to a rigorous empiricist. This particular complaint therefore has a high documentary value.

We should begin by observing the height from which poetry declined. In the cathedral schools of the preceding century, poetic composition in Latin, not the Bible, was the most important subject of study. Poetry in that age is represented as the high point and fulfillment of learning in the arts, a role regularly linked to its utility. Poetry was not only in itself a lucrative area of study but also good for a career.[87] A fair number of bishops from the eleventh century came into their office with reputations also as poets, and it is quite possible that that talent helped them into the bishop's chair.[88] Two bits of testimony from many will have to suffice here. Guibert of Nogent confessed in his autobiography that in his youth (c.1065–75) "[I] had immersed my soul beyond all measure in poetry so that I considered Scripture ridiculous vanity." His friends had encouraged

---

86. As Haskins, 381, reads it.
87. See Jaeger, *Envy*, 139–64.
88. See Jaeger, "Stature."

him to stick with poetry because with his talent he could become an important and wealthy man, but he rejected such rewards in favor of the monastic life.[89] He gave up poetry for religion. The story of his conversion would have had much less weight if Guibert had not preferred the religious life to something of great value in secular life. It had to be plausible to his readers that a gift for poetry was something that someone smart could parlay into fame and fortune.

Peter Damian, ardent reformer and critic of worldly learning from the second half of the eleventh century, wrote a satirical portrait of a Frenchman of high aristocracy suited for all church offices. Eloquence is the overriding qualification: "He speaks like Cicero and composes poetry like Virgil."[90] This passage places poetry on a level with forensic eloquence, political influence, legal training, high birth, and physical beauty as a qualification for high office in the Church. The passage gives us an idea of the heights from which poetry had fallen by the twelfth century. No one in the twelfth either praises or attacks poetry as a qualification for high church office. No one imagines that fame, wealth, and stature are available through Latin poetry, though many lament that they no longer are. Poetic composition shed its utility and retained only its aesthetic and satiric value. It became a marginal accomplishment, a relic of an outmoded educational system.

As early as the turn of the century, complaints of the neglect and decline of poetry proliferate. An anonymous nun and poet, who evidently has insulted a prince or king in her compositions, complained around 1100 that the gift of the Muses and the well of Pegasus no longer have any worth.[91] She herself, like Ovid, has

89. Guibert of Nogent, *Autobiographie: De vita sua*, Edmond-Rene Labande, ed. (Paris: Belles Lettres, 1981), 112; *Self and Society in Medieval France: The Memoirs of Abbot Guibert of Nogent (1064?–c.1125)*, C.C. Swinton Bland, trans.; John F. Benton, rev. (New York: Harper & Row, 1970), 79.

90. *De sancta simplicitate* 7, in *De divina omnipotentia e altri opuscoli*, Brezzi and Nardi ed. (Florence: Vallecchi, 1943) 188; PL 145:700C–D. See Jaeger, *Envy*, 140.

91. Constant Mews argued with some energy that the author of the poem may be Heloise and the powerful man who has wronged her Suger of St. Denis. See *The Lost Love Letters of Heloise and Abelard: Perceptions of Dialogue in Twelfth-Century France*, Constant J. Mews, ed. and trans. (Basingstoke: Palgrave, 2001), 163–69.

CHAPTER 10 ★ PESSIMISM IN THE TWELFTH CENTURY

been forced into exile. Composing poems and studying philosophy were virtues in earlier times, she says, but not now: "Poems count for nothing in this age, nor do philosophical debates and rhetorical compositions."[92] A poem by Hildebert of Lavardin written shortly after the beginning of the century sounds the same theme. There was a time, he says, when "divine poets" were valued for fine compositions, good manners, and firm faith and could win fame and wealth, but no longer.[93] Rodulfus Tortarius warns a friend in the early twelfth century that his confidence in his poetry is misplaced. Gone are the days when poetry was valued. If Virgil lived now, he would starve. Now neither high birth nor good manners nor poetic talent is rewarded.[94] Sometime in the first third of the century a canon of St. Omer, Petrus Pictor (Peter the Painter), complains:

I see how the world is transformed in our times.

The wisdom of the ancients is dying out altogether as modern times advance.

Once it was the glory of clerics to master the arts.

To seek out dishonor and to seek out levity,

To flee good manners — this is what the tribe of the present day strives for.

To know the good arts is now the lowest priority.

It takes greater effort to learn the arts of composition and poetry,

To learn grammar and to philosophize wisely

Than to pile up coins upon coins.[95]

Mews also provides the edition by André Boutemy and an English translation of the poem. Gerald Bond also includes Boutemy's text, with translation and discussion, in *The Loving Subject: Desire, Eloquence, and Power in Romanesque France* (Philadelphia: University of Pennsylvania Press, 1995), 167–69.

92. Lines 47–48, quoted in Bond, *Loving Subject*, 168: "Ista vetus probitas, nil carmina tempore vestro, / Nil genus aut species rethoricusve color."

93. Hildebert, *Carmen* 17, ll. 21–22; Scott ed., 7.

94. *Rodulfi Tortarii Carmina*, Epist. 1, Marbury B. Ogle and Dorothy M. Schullian, ed. (Rome: American Academy, 1933), 251–56, at 251.

95. *Petri Pictoris Carmina* 3.47–65: "Temporibus nostris mutari secula cerno, / Omne vetus studium perit accedente moderno. / Artes scire bonas fuit olim gloria cleri, / ... / Nunc inhonesta sequi, nunc sectari levitatem / Gens hodierna studet

361

Laments like these increase in the course of the century. The poems of Walter of Châtillon are full of them,[96] and the topic is represented in the *Carmina Burana*.[97] Gerald of Wales complains in his *Journey through Wales* that few study the liberal arts, while many flock to logic only to get lost in its labyrinths and whirlpools:

> Where are the divine poets? Where are the noble professors of manners? Where are the masters of the Latin tongue? Who nowadays in his writings, be it poetry or history, can hope to add new luster to the art of letters? Who in our time, I ask, either teaches manners or captures for eternity deeds nobly done in the lasting bonds of literature? In earlier times the man of letters stood on the topmost step of the hall of fame. Now those who devote themselves to study, which is toppled deep in ruin and sunk in disrepute, are no longer there to be imitated and venerated, but rather they are despised.[98]

---

morumque fugit probitatem. / Artes scire bonas modo pro minimo reputatur, / ... / Est gravius studium bene scribere, versificari, discere grammaticam, prudenter philosophari / Quam nummos nummis, libras libris cumulare / Aut ex usuris usuras multiplicare." In Lieven Van Acker, ed., CCCM 25 (Turnhout: Brepols, 1972), 50–51.

96. Walter of Châtillon 11, "Felix erat studium," Strecker ed., 113–15; 1.14–15: "Quid dant artes nisi luctum / et laborem? vel quem fructum / fert genus et species? / Olim plures, nec est mirum, / provehebant 'Arma virum' / et 'Fraternas acies.' / Antiquitus et studere / fructus erat et habere / declamantes socios.," Strecker ed., 8; 9.8: "iam mendicat misere chorus poetarum, / nulli prodest imbui fonte litterarum," Strecker ed., 106; 13.13: "Profuit antiquitus litteratum esse, / cum floreret studium copiosa messe, / set modernis fodere magis est necesse / quam vatum Parisius scolis interesse." In Strecker ed., 125. See Verena Epp, "Sicht der Antike und Gegenwartsbewusstsein in der mittellateinischen Dichtung des 11./12. Jahrhunderts," in *Hochmittelalterliches Geschichtsbewusstsein im Spiegel nichthistoriographischer Quellen*, Hans Werner Goetz, ed. (Berlin: Akademie, 1998), 295–316, at 302–4.

97. *Carmina Burana* 6, "Florebat olim studium," Benedikt Vollmann, ed. (Frankfurt: Suhrkamp, 1987), 6.

98. *Itinerarium Kambriae*: "ubi divini poetae; ubi nobiles morum assertores; ubi linguae Latinae moderatores? Quis hodie scriptis, sive poeticis seu historicis, literatam adornat eloquentiam? Quis, inquam, nostri temporis, vel mores astruit, vel indite gesta perpetuis literarum vinculis aeternitati ascribit? Adeo literarum

CHAPTER 10 ✶ PESSIMISM IN THE TWELFTH CENTURY

In his autobiographical reminiscence, *De rebus a se gestis*, Gerald gives a report on his self-sponsored three-day festival at Oxford of readings from his *Journey through Ireland*, a report so glowing as to imply that he himself may rank among the "divine poets" and "masters of the Latin tongue." The reading produced such an effect that it seemed

> that in a sense this event renewed the genuine and ancient times of the poets, nor does the present age or any previous age recall something similar done in England.[99]

Renewal of the ancient times of the poets was wishful thinking, it appears. In the middle of the next century a French poet, Henri d'Andeli, would lament the decline of the arts and poetry in France and express the hope that this neglect would last no more than thirty years. In his satirical poem of the mid-thirteenth century, "The Battle of the Seven Arts," part allegory, part mock-heroic epic, poetry and eloquence suffer decisive defeats from the armies of logic.[100] In fact, Europe had to wait not thirty but a hundred years between Henri and Petrarch for the first breath of a revival of the Latin language according to classical models.

The history of Latin poetry in the Middle Ages was virtually over by the end of the twelfth century. Religious poetry in Latin survived, and England produced a fair number of political poems from the fourteenth century on. But essentially the Latin secular lyric ended

---

honor, in summis olim gradibus constitutus jam proclivis in ruinam, ad ima devolvi videtur, ut earum addicti studiis non solum hodie non imitabiles, non venerabiles, verum etiam odibiles reperiantur." In Brewer, ed., 4. The same theme is developed more broadly and in the context of the various warring disciplines of the schools in the preface to *Speculum ecclesiae*, in *Giraldi Cambrensis Opera*, Brewer et al., ed., 4:3–12. The passage is badly transmitted, and many lines are missing, but Brewer has reconstructed the train of thought.

99. *De rebus a se gestis* 2.16: "renovata sunt quodammodo in authentica et antiqua in hoc facto poetarum tempora; nec rem similem in Anglia factam vel praesens aetas vel ulla recolit antiquitas." In *Opera* 1:72–73.

100. *The Battle of the Seven Arts: A French Poem by Henri d'Andeli, Trouvère of the Thirteenth Century*, Louis John Paetow, ed. and trans. (Berkeley: University of California Press, 1914).

with the *Carmina Burana*, some songs of which may derive from the thirteenth century, but its contents are largely from the twelfth.[101] This observed decline of poetry in the twelfth century does not mean that there were no great poets: Hildebert, Baudri of Bourgueil, Bernard Silvester, the Archpoet, Alan of Lille, and the anonymous poets of the *Carmina Burana* represent a remarkable flowering of poetry. But none of them — good, bad, or mediocre — felt this was an age that favored poetry. On the contrary, they wrote from a general awareness of the decline and gradual extinction of poetry and rhetoric, a sense that Virgil and Horace would have starved if they had lived in the twelfth century. The general awareness of decline also does not mean that there were no voices praising contemporary poetry. But Matthew of Vendôme's brief and casual ranking of the moderns as superior to the ancients in their avoidance of narrative digression and of certain metrical errors is far from adequate to drown out that ground tone of complaint.[102] Nor is it at all surprising that a brilliant flourishing of poetry should occur in an epoch that defined itself as aged, corrupt, and in decline. The same was true of the flourishing of poetry, literature, and the arts in Europe in the years c.1890–1910.

101. See Jan Ziolkowski, "History of Medieval Latin Literature," in *Medieval Latin: An Introduction and Bibliographical Guide,* Frank A.C. Mantello and Arthur George Rigg, ed. (Washington, DC: Catholic University of America Press, 1996), 505–36, at 510; and Christopher J. McDonough, "Lyric," in Mantello and Rigg, 589–96. The basic surveys of Latin poetry in the Middle Ages set the end of secular Latin poetry in the twelfth century, though it trails off to an end point in Philip the Chancellor, who died in 1236. See Max Manitius, *Geschichte der lateinischen Literatur des Mittelalters,* 3 vols. (Munich: Beck, 1973); Frederick J.E. Raby, *A History of Secular Latin Poetry in the Middle Ages,* 2nd ed., 2 vols. (Oxford: Clarendon, 1957); Joseph de Ghellinck, *L'essor de la littérature latine au douzième siècle* (Brussels: Desclée, 1955); Joseph Szövérffy, *Secular Latin Lyrics and Minor Poetic Forms of the Middle Ages: A Historical Survey and Literary Repertory from the Tenth to the Fifteenth Century* (Concord, NH: Classical Folia Editions, 1992). Szöverffy's ambitious three-volume survey held firm to the plan stated in the subtitle in volume 2, only to change it in volume 3 to read *"to the Early Thirteenth Century."* Fourteenth- and fifteenth-century Latin poetry on political and military occasions from England is collected in *Political Poems and Songs Relating to English History,* Thomas Wright, ed., Rolls Series 14, 2 vols. (London: Longman, 1859).

102. See above, 336.

CHAPTER 10 ✳ PESSIMISM IN THE TWELFTH CENTURY

Grandeur in the arts, be it ever so brilliant, does not a renaissance make — it may even be a symptom of decline and decadence.

LOVE

Finally, let us turn to another great theme of the twelfth century: love. We cannot start with the optimistic and positive statements of contemporaries on this topic. There are none. Neither courtly love nor spiritual friendship inspired praise of love as experienced in the age. But the state of love inspired much criticism.

What we call courtly love appears in the twelfth century as something uniquely new in vernacular literature. Yet the classical authors of courtly romance present love as in a state of decline in the present day. Chrétien de Troyes laments at the beginning of *Yvain* that "Nowadays...[love] has few adherents, since almost all have abandoned [it], leaving it much debased." In earlier ages love was done nobly and courteously, but now it has become "a laughing-stock."[103] Gottfried von Strassburg echoes the sentiment: They are right who say that

> love is hounded to the ends of the earth. All that we have is the bare word, only the name remains to us; and this we have so hackneyed, so abused, and so debased that the poor, tired thing is ashamed of her own name.[104]

---

103. Chrétien de Troyes, *Arthurian Romances*, Douglas D.R. Owen, trans. (London: Dent, 1993), 281; Chrétien, *The Knight with the Lion, or Yvain (Le Chevalier au Lion)*, ll. 18–28: "or i a molt po des suens, / qu'a bien pres l'ont ja tuit lessiee; / s'an est Amors molt abessiee, / car cil qui soloient amer / se feisoient cortois clamer / et preu et large et enorable; / or est Amors tornee a fable/ por ce que cil qui rien n'en santent / dïent qu'il aiment, mes il mantent, / et cil fable et mançonge an font/ qui s'an vantent et droit n'i ont." In William W. Kibler, ed. and trans. (New York: Garland, 1985). Similarly later in *Arthurian Romances*, ll. 5398–5400: "People no longer fall in love nor do they love any more as they used to, and so they do not even want to hear about it." In Owen trans., 353–54. The troubador Giraut de Borneil, "Per solatz revelhar," 1:412–20 complains that all pleasure has passed from the world and "worthiness" (*pretz*) is banished. He has given up his attempt to rescue these values. Minstrels no longer praise noble ladies; therefore their "worthiness" (*pretz*) is in ruins. Their lovers now prefer to practice deceit than to praise them. See *Sämtliche Lieder des Trobadors Giraut de Borneil*, Adolf Kolsen, ed. (Halle: Niemeyer, 1910), 65.

104. Gottfried von Strassburg, *Tristan*, ll. 12280–86: "Minne ist getriben unde gejaget / in den endelesten ort. / wirn haben an ir niuwan das wort. / uns ist

Heinrich von Veldeke, who originated the tradition of courtly romance in Germany, says the same:

> When love was honored, so, too, was honor. Now day and night evil habits are taught. If one could see both the present and the past at the same time, how he would lament the present! Now virtue is perverted.[105]

Of course, these statements are also topoi; they represent golden-age thinking and *laudatio temporis acti*. But it does seem odd that they would sound this attitude that love is in decline in their time, given that they are among the earliest poets to express this love in poetry. Also telling is Hartmann von Aue's statement at the beginning of his translation or adaptation of Chretien's *Yvain* that in the present day all joy that they knew back in Arthur's day has passed out of the world, but the present, which also has a life to lead, must console itself with the ancient tales of Arthur and his knights. Given the choice, he would prefer the dreary present with its stories to the past age when deeds glorified men.[106]

Given that the originator of Arthurian romance himself tended to irony and satire of love, this may be a statement of a real sense of loss. Again, these writers had a set of topoi of optimism at their disposal

---

niuwan der name beliben / und hân ouch den alsô zetriben, / also verwortet uncle vernamet, / daz sich diu müede ir namen schamet." In Tomasek ed., 230; Hatto trans., 203.

105. "Do man der rehten minne pflac, / dô pflac man ouch der êren. / nu mac man naht uncle tac die boesen site leren. / swer diz nu siht und jenez dô sach, / owê, waz der nu klagen mac!/ tugende weln sich nû verkêren." In *Des Minnesangs Fruhling*, Karl Lachmann et al., ed.; Hugo Moser and Helmut Tervooren, rev., 3 vols. (Stuttgart: Hirzel, 1977–82), 1:120.

106. Hartmann von Aue, *Iwein*, ll. 48–58; Patrick M. McConeghy, ed. and trans. (New York: Garland, 1984), 4. It sounds very much like the self-definition of a decadent poet. There is something effete and self-deprecating about preferring the dreary age of words to the glorious age of deeds. See Wirnt von Gravenberc, *Wigalois*, ll. 10259–66: "The world has changed. Its joy is wretched. Justice has fled, violence is rising. Loyalty is brittle, disloyalty and hatred prevail. Times have changed and every year it gets worse." Cited in Joachim Bumke, *Courtly Culture: Literature and Society in the High Middle Ages*, Thomas Dunlap, trans. (Berkeley: University of California Press, 2000), 574.

CHAPTER 10 ✶ PESSIMISM IN THE TWELFTH CENTURY

("Now at last we love again as in the golden age"; or "the lewd pagan Ovid loved falsely; we in the Christian era [or in the courtly era] do it well"). But no one made use of such affirmative turns of thought. I know of no courtly poet writing in any European language in the twelfth century who agrees with C.S. Lewis' idea that what they depicted was "an entirely new way of feeling," or with Peter Dinzelbacher's that they were the discoverers of love between man and woman in the West.[107] Lewis and Dinzelbacher may be, in strictly historical perspective, completely right. In fact, I believe that they are. So much the greater our curiosity should be as to why no one living in that society, writing a great literature of courtly love, thought of praising the experience they had discovered. Gottfried and Chrétien thought of themselves as galvanizing the corpse of a dead ideal, and the modern image of them creating an ideal ex nihilo does not correspond to what they claimed to be doing.

If this feeling of decline registered only in literary sources, we might think that the poets' claims of what they were doing does not matter much against what they actually did in creating a new and highly original literature of love. In fact, however, a sense of the decline of love and friendship registers broadly throughout the culture. Cicero had already claimed that true friendships are rare,[108] and the attitude found echo in the Middle Ages:

That love that Pylades felt for Orestes
And Laelius for Scipio does not exist today.
Confidence or loyalty in either partner is rare.[109]

But the twelfth century took the comment seriously and personally and created or at least stoked a nostalgia for a kind of friendship that had passed from the earth. Aelred of Rievaulx puts a particular spin on this topos by turning it into an indictment of the Christian era. One of the speakers in his dialogue on friendship complains that there never were many friends, but

107. Lewis, *Allegory*, 4 and 11; Peter Dinzelbacher, "Uber die Entdeckung der Liebe im Hochmittelalter," *Saeculum* 32 (1981): 185–208.

108. *De amicitia* 4.15 and 5.20.

109. Hugo Sotovagina, in *The Anglo-Latin Satirical Poets and Epigrammatists of the Twelfth Century*, Thomas Wright, ed., Rolls Series 59.2 (London: Longman, 1872), 219: "Non amor est hodie quo se Pylades et Orestes, / Quo se amaverunt Laelius et Scipio. / Fidens vel fidus rarus in alterutrum."

> in this age of Christianity, friends are so few, it seems to me that I am exerting myself uselessly in striving after the virtue that I, terrified by its admirable sublimity, now almost despair of ever acquiring.[110]

Aelred himself answers with a spirited defense of Christian friendship, but he refers only to the Apostles and the martyrs of the early Church, not to his own age. Peter Abelard's student, wife, and lover, Heloise, does note the decline of love in the present age. She laments the loss of love and "natural vigor" in men. In a letter to her husband and founder of the religious house of which she was abbess, she calls for a new rule of the religious life, one that would take into account male frigidity over against the Rule of St. Benedict, written in a time when men could still love:

> We see that the world has now grown old, and that with all other living creatures men too have lost their former natural vigour; and...amongst many or indeed almost all men, love itself has grown cold.[111]

She is of course generalizing from her own castrated husband and measuring the difference that separates the passion of their early days from the frigid consolations of theology and the religious life. The god of love himself would raise a similar complaint in a poem from the *Carmina Burana*. In a dream-vision dating from the end of the twelfth or early thirteenth century, the god Cupid appears to the sleeping poet. The god is shabby and downcast because of the present state of love, and he complains:

110. Aelred of Rievaulx, *De spirituali amicitia*, 1.25: "Cum tanta sit in amicitia vera perfectio, non est mirum quod tam rari fuerunt hi quos veros amicos antiquitas commendavit. Vix enim, ut ait Tullius, tria vel quatuor amicorum paria in tot retro saeculis fama concelebrat. Quod si nostris, id est christianis temporibus, tanta est raritas amicorum, frustra, ut mihi videtur, in huius virtutis acquisitione desudo, quam me adepturum, eius mirabili sublimitate territus, iam pene despero." In Hoste and Talbot ed., 293; Aelred of Rievaulx, *Spiritual Friendship*, Mary Eugenia Laker, trans. (Kalamazoo, MI: Cistercian Publications, 1977), 56.

111. Heloise, Letter 5 to Abelard; Luscombe, ed.; Radice, trans., 167. The reference in Mt. 24:12: "because iniquity shall abound, the love of many shall wax cold," is changed so that senility and not "iniquity" is responsible for frigidity, gendered masculine in Heloise's text. On the cooling of charity with reference to Heloise's statement, See Dean, 62–66; as a literary motif, Dean, 99–102.

CHAPTER 10 ★ PESSIMISM IN THE TWELFTH CENTURY

> *The ancient vigor has passed away [from love], its virtue has vanished;*
> *My strength has failed me, and Cupid's bow shoots no more!*
> *The arts of love no longer are taught.*
> *Handed down by Ovid, they are everywhere perverted.*
> *Wherever these arts are practiced by the moderns,*
> *love is a foul abuse of this custom of behaving.*

The poet makes his lament also into an indictment of the present age. The nature of love is betrayed in the present. Its art as formulated by Ovid is no longer a subject of instruction, and if anyone applies that art "the way the moderns do," it is a foul abuse of tradition. The moderns glory in love's shame."[112]

Bernard of Clairvaux recalls the days when the Patriarchs "burned with desire for the presence of Christ in the flesh" and can hardly hold back his tears "for the lukewarmness and frigid apathy of these times."[113] Peter of Blois explains why he has written his book *On Christian Friendship*:

> Since truths have lost their value among people and love itself has grown cold, hardly anyone can find perfect loyalty in another, hardly any love can be found that is not bought and sold."[114]

---

112. *Carmina Burana* 105.6–7: "vigor priscus abiit, evanuit iam virtus. / Me vis deseruit, periere Cupidinis arcus! / Artes amatorie iam non instruuntur / a Nasone tradite, passim pervertuntur; / nam siquis istis utitur more modernorum / Turpiter abutitur hac assuetudine morum." In Vollmann ed., 198.

113. *Sermones in Cantica canticorum* 2.1.1: "Ardorem desiderii patrum suspirantium Christi in carne praesentiam frequentissime cogitans, compungor et confundor in memetipso. Et nunc vix contineo lacrimas, ita pudet teporis torporisque miserabilium temporum horum." In *Sancti Bernardi Opera*, Leclercq et al. ed, 2:8.

114. *De amicitia Christiana*, prologue: "Quoniam diminutae sunt veritates a filiis hominum, et refrigescente charitate multorum, vix aliquis in alio integritatem fidei experitur, vix invenitur dilectio, quae non sit quaestuaria et venalis" In PL 207:871A.

Richard of St. Victor compares the time of the apostles, when all lived together in harmony, one heart and one mind, with the world of the present:

> Alas, to what ends, or rather cesspools, those of the world have descended! But even apart from those of the world who are blinded by ambition, religion itself is so scattered by division in our wretched age that hardly anyone works in harmony with any other. I confess, it disgusts me to be here; let us go hence.[115]

It would certainly be fair to object that the lives of Abelard and Heloise, the sermons of Bernard, Richard of St. Victor's writings on love, and others from the community of St. Victor refute their comments on the miserable state of love. But whatever we may think about the level of passion experienced or expressed, these unparalleled lovers of God and each other saw good love and friendship in their own age as wretched in comparison with the past.

PESSIMISM AS A HISTORICAL CATEGORY

So, was the twelfth century an age of renaissance and renewal or an age of decline? Was it the best of times or the worst of times? What does it mean that so much apparent pessimism bubbled up from the heart of so ebullient and creative an age? Pessimism is a notoriously difficult concept to apply as a historical category. It is polyvalent.[116] It

---

115. *De gradibus charitatis* 4: "Heu in quos fines, imo faeces saeculorum homines devenerunt! Cum, ut de saeculi hominibus taceamus quos excaecavit ambitio, ipsa religionis electio nostro miserabili tempore tanta divisione spargatur, ut vix unus alteri conveniat in unum. Fateor, taedet hic esse; exeamus hinc." In PL 196:1204C–D.

116. See for instance Huizinga's thoughts in the chapter of the 1924 English translation of *Waning of the Middle Ages* entitled "Pessimism and the Sublime Ideal of Life." Further citation uses the newer translation, *The Autumn of the Midlde Ages*, Rodney J. Payton and Ulrich Mammitzsch, trans. (Chicago: University of Chicago Press, 1996). For general reflections on pessimism, see Matei Calinescu, *Five Faces of Modernity: Modernism, Avant-Garde, Decadence, Kitsch, Postmodernism* (Durham, NC: Duke University Press, 1987), 151–56; and Bernard A. Van Groningen, *In the Grip of the Past: Essay on an Aspect of Greek Thought* (Leiden: Brill, 1953). There is no entry for "Pessimismus" in the reference work *Geschichtliche Grundbegriffe*, an extensive and interesting one, however, in the *Historisches Wörterbuch der Philosophie*.

CHAPTER 10 ✴ PESSIMISM IN THE TWELFTH CENTURY

may be an entirely subjective attitude out of which one imposes one's own failures on the world as a whole.

Sir Walter Raleigh depicted history with bitter disillusionment in a language nurtured by *contemptus mundi* in his *World History*.[117] But Raleigh wrote that work while confined in the Tower of London awaiting execution, and this perspective narrows the scope of his pessimism to his own circumstances, however broadly he may have projected it. One man's ill fortune foisted onto world history cannot cancel out the vitality of the Elizabethan age, any more than one Jaques can diminish the exuberant energy, self-confidence, and optimism of the world of *As You Like It*, a world that finds adversity sweet, restores oppressed good people to their rightful position, overcomes evil, and allows love to triumph.

Pessimism may also be a form of social criticism, aiming at reform and revolution.[118] We know (my generation at least knows) the dynamic by which criticism of the contemporary world emerges from a will to reform, not from pessimism and resignation. That may well describe a dynamic built into the historical scheme of Hugh of St. Victor, based on two phases of world history: the period of creation and the period of restoration.[119] This scheme also provides the structure of moral development of the world in Alan's *Anticlaudianus*: nature and humanity are, in the poem's "present," so corrupted from their original state that it requires a "new human" to set it right. In both, the present corruption of the world represents an appeal to reformation, and this dynamic is very different from the inevitability of decline and end in Otto of Freising.

Melancholy world-weariness is often a fashionable pose conferring an aura of superior wisdom on its sufferer and of ignorance on those who are content, who must not understand the world if they can be happy. Huizinga points to the "sentimental need" of the late-medieval Flemish nobility for "a dark costume of the soul"[120] The intelligentsia

---

117. Sir Walter Raleigh, *The History of the World*, Constantine A. Patrides, ed. (London: Macmillan, 1971), 45–81.

118. See Arthur Herman, *The Idea of Decline in Western History* (New York: Free Press, 1997), 13–45.

119. See Southern, "Aspects."

120. *Autumn*, 33–34.

of the Italian and northern Renaissance also affected gloom as an intellectual posture and wore their melancholy as a badge of genius. Melancholy is a psychic precondition to world-rejecting pessimism.[121] At least the two keep close company.

But there is a specific historical context in which pessimism has documentary value for an age's self-assessment.[122] Change and transition, the fading of old values and the advent of new, are real and concrete historical categories. The trends, styles, fashions, even the great accomplishments of one age are superseded by the next. The experience of transition divides a culture into two camps: old and new. In periods of radical change, both voices will be raised.[123] These are the circumstances we are dealing with in the first half of the twelfth century. The voices registered in this study are for the most part those of unhappy conservative critics of new trends. Naturally they viewed the new with deep misgivings. They saw a culture they admired — in which they had grown up and labored, whose teachers they loved and revered — threatened, indeed, overwhelmed by a new culture that appeared to them shallow, corrupting, vulgar, irreverent, immodest, and self-important.

Those misgivings surface as "pessimism."[124] The entrenched values of an earlier culture are being replaced, and those with vested and sentimental interest in the passing culture lament their passing. A peculiar circumstance of the twelfth century is that the representatives of the old culture are virtually the only voices that appraised the

121. Raymond Klibansky, Fritz Saxl, and Erwin Panofsky, *Saturn and Melancholy: Studies in the History of Natural Philosophy, Religion and Art* (London: Nelson, 1964).

122. See the model proposed by Melville, "Zur geschichtstheoretischen Begründung."

123. That includes a period as ensconced in self-affirmation as the Renaissance of the sixteenth century. See Don Cameron Allen, "The Degeneration of Man and Renaissance Pessimism," *Studies in Philology* 35 (1938): 202–27; and William J. Bouwsma, *The Waning of the Renaissance, 1550–1640* (New Haven, CT: Yale University Press, 2000).

124. Embedded in the same context of change, conflict, and anxiety is the genre of satire, which came into its own in the twelfth century. See Rodney M. Thomson, "The Origins of Latin Satire in Twelfth Century Europe," *Mittellateinisches Jahrbuch* 13 (1978): 73–83.

CHAPTER 10 ✶ PESSIMISM IN THE TWELFTH CENTURY

trends of the time. The winners write history, whether intellectual or political. Certainly, the humanists of the fifteenth and sixteenth century were loud in glorifying what they represented and mocking what they sought to supersede. They were, in the stingy logic of winners and losers, the winners. But it is a puzzle of twelfth-century intellectual life that the humanists are the "losers," and yet they are the main observers of transition and change. Where are the voices of all those masters and students of the Mont Ste. Geneviève and other new Parisian schools, the logicians, lawyers, doctors, and theologians who created a new intellectual world and a great institution (the university) to accommodate it? They must have toiled oblivious of the shrill criticism that beat around their ears, while leaving it to all those cultural conservatives cited above to formulate a judgment of the age. The only mockery directed by the *moderni* at the old fogies bewailing decline registers in the writings of the fogies themselves (John of Salisbury). We cannot find advocates of the new age — scholars, philosophers, poets, or lovers — who will call it a new age and mean it as praise, though we know it had many representatives.

Alongside all that is new in the twelfth century, an older culture was in a state of decline and collapse. It is the confluence of the dying and the rising cultures and the tensions and conflicts that confluence spawned that account for the peculiar energy and creativity of the age. But what culture? What was it that John of Salisbury saw ending in his day? The historians of literature, history and philosophy studying the twelfth century have had no eyes for the humanism (and the educational structures and ideas supporting it) that began in the mid-tenth and came to an end in the Latin culture of Germany, France, and England in the course of the twelfth century.[125] Above all, there was no understanding of the forces that connected 950 to 1150 and established humanism in the Middle Ages as a movement. Most medievalists would be hard-pressed to say anything at all about the secular culture of Europe in the years 950 to 1100.[126] We think of the poets and scholars of the early twelfth century always as forerunners,

125. For a discussion of earlier opinions on the subject, see above, 1–12.

126. A situation was somewhat alleviated, or at least addressed by *Latin Culture in the Eleventh Century: Proceedings of the Third International Conference on Medieval Latin Studies*, Michael W. Herren, Christopher J. McDonough, and Ross G. Arthur, ed. (Turnhout: Brepols, 2002).

never as fulfillers of an intellectual tradition. But Marbod, Baudri, Hildebert, Hugh of St. Victor, John of Salisbury, Otto of Freising, Walter of Chatillon, and Alan of Lille thought of themselves as late representatives of a culture that was coming to an end. The passing culture is hidden to our view partly because of the nature of its documentation, partly because of the concepts that structure our thinking.

CONCLUSIONS

That brings me to my final point, the harm done by the term "renaissance." Is "renaissance" a useful term for the twelfth century? That term and its large family — "rebirth," "renascence," "renewal," "origin," "emergence," "the rise of" "the discovery of" — imply preceding darkness, posit ground earlier sterile, now at last fertile, in which the new can be born and flourish. Of course, it makes it unnecessary to ask what immediately preceded, because it masks the coinciding of a dying and a rising culture, makes the dying appear as part of the new along with what is rising. These two conditions have made it possible for modern scholars looking at the twelfth century to turn old conservatives into new reformers. To make Hugh of St. Victor, Otto of Freising, and John of Salisbury (to mention only the most prominent voices) into representatives of a "renaissance," we have to ignore or "correct" their own conceptions of their place in the intellectual history of their time. Among their deepest sentiments is nostalgia toward the passing of the old culture.

Otto of Freising made not Abelard, Gilbert of Poitiers, Adam of Balsham, and Peter Lombard, not even Bernard of Clairvaux but rather Berengar of Tours, Manegold of Lautenbach, and Anselm of Laon into models of inspired intellects, a priority that is incomprehensible if Otto is to represent renaissance and renewal. Current conceptions of philosophy and theology in the twelfth century provide no categories that would explain why Otto or anyone at all would rank Manegold of Lautenbach above Peter Abelard. John of Salisbury glorified Bernard of Chartres, a representative of old-style humanistic education typical of the eleventh-century cathedral schools, while issuing divided judgments on all of his own contemporaries, with the qualified exception of Peter Abelard. Yet John of Salisbury and Otto of Freising are regularly made into representatives of a "renaissance"

CHAPTER 10 ✶ PESSIMISM IN THE TWELFTH CENTURY

in their age.[127] Those two would certainly have been astonished and appalled at the contemporary view of them as aligned with a "new" age, when they had expended so much effort, ingenuity, and moral commitment to oppose the new or (in John's case) to refashion it in the image of the old.

R.W. Southern recognized that John cannot be mustered as an adherent of the new intellectual trends:

> In the midst of the remarkable advances in scholastic projects during these years [1136–47] we might have expected that a scholar of John of Salisbury's monumental learning, with his determination to give all branches of knowledge their due place, would have found inspiration in the growing systematization of knowledge that was going on round him. He held himself aloof.[128]

It is, to put it mildly, unfair to the author of the *Metalogicon*, the *Policraticus*, and the two poems entitled "Entheticus" to state that "he held himself aloof." The argument shows Southern under the spell of his progressive view of twelfth-century intellectual life. Far from aloof, John was powerfully engaged in a widespread action to reject precisely the growing systematization of knowledge. It was for him a drastic narrowing of thought.

"Renaissance" was a useful term in the nineteenth and twentieth centuries. It served the purpose of calling attention to the energy and productivity of the twelfth century. It was never historically accurate, but it was powerfully heuristic, and a research agenda developed from it whose riches are only meagerly indicated above. But it is time to scrap it. It is now more trouble than it is worth. It obscures more than it illuminates. In the nostalgia of twelfth-century humanists for the past, in their laments for the decline of the world and the passing of history, learning, poetry, and love we sense the shadow of eleventh-century culture, heavy and dark, largely invisible and badly in need of illumination. If we knew more about it, we would understand the twelfth century much better. Before we can do so, we should change the default setting of our thinking that makes the twelfth century into exclusively an age of origins.

127. Southern, *Scholastic Humanism*, 167.
128. Above, 333.

11. VICTORINE HUMANISM

Since humans are by nature social animals, it is only natural that they have mutual obligations and that they show each other the sociability by which, joined together as it were by a bond of nature, they lead a life at once peaceful and happy. Only through this can they lead a blessed life.[1]

INTRODUCTION

A union of spiritual and intellectual trends current in twelfth-century France constituted the peculiar character of the culture of the abbey of St. Victor, Paris. This amalgam was sharply formulated by Dominique Poirel:

Among the secular and monastic schools, often given to privileging now profane, now sacred studies, the Parisian abbey [of St. Victor] chose to harmonize them in the core of a program as complete as possible in the conviction that they form the two components, indispensable and complementary, of a comprehensive wisdom, indissolubly Christian and humanist.[2]

The present chapter affirms Poirel's view of St. Victor's commitment to a comprehensive pursuit of knowledge — Christian and humanist — and adds to it an essential third element alongside spiritual and literary studies: manners and social ideals. These play a major role in the life of St. Victor and in the broader trend characteristic of its intellectual and cultural life prior to the stricter reform after mid-century. It is the aggregation of the three, spiritual, intellectual and social ideals, of Christianity with humanism, that creates the universality of the program of studies in that community

---

1. Godfrey of St. Victor, *Microcosmus* 3.172, 3.192. Quoted again and discussed below, 399–402.

2. Dominique Poirel, "Aux sources d'une influence: les raisons du rayonnement victorin," in *L'école de Saint-Victor de Paris: Influence et rayonnement du moyen âge à l'époque moderne*, Dominique Poirel ed. (Turnhout: Brepols, 2010), 5–25, at 18: "Entre les écoles séculières et monastiques, souvent tentées de privilégier soit les études profanes, soit les études sacrées, l'abbaye Parisienne choisit de les accorder à l'intérieur d'un programme aussi complet que possible, dans la conviction qu'elles forment les deux volets indispensables et complémentaires d'une sagesse totale, indissolublement chrétienne et humaniste."

and sets it decisively apart from the culture of monastic, cathedral, and court communities.

If we had to point to a single work that most fully displays the range of Victorine humanism, it would have to be its last major work, Godfrey of St. Victor's *Microcosmus*.³ Godfrey's work was not prominent in his own time and has found little interest down to the present. Neither of his major works, the *Fons philosophiae* and the *Microcosmus*, has inspired much commentary and debate. His contribution was in the formal elements of his epic allegory. He had a good imagination and a talent for developing commonplace tropes into extensive allegorical ideas but did not succeed in integrating them into a coherent narrative. His skill lies in comprehensive (if not always clear or consistent) organizational schemes and vivid narrative realization of ideas, especially ideas received from Augustine and earlier Victorines. Viewed from the perspective of history of ideas, his originality consists in amalgamating the theme of microcosm/macrocosm with Victorine theology. The lack of any reception by Godfrey's contemporaries suggests that neither the imaginative conception nor the link to philosophy had much impact.⁴ But it says nothing about the usefulness of the work as a mirror of the beliefs and practices that governed his studies and his life at St. Victor prior to running afoul of the conservative reforming abbot, Walter of St. Victor (d.c.1180).

3. *L'oeuvre de Godefroid de Saint-Victor* 1. *Le Microcosme (Microcosmus)*, Françoise Gasparri, ed. (Turnhout: Brepols, 2020). Consistent with an earlier version of this article I will cite both Gasparri ed., and the earlier edition by Delhaye. For a broader view of Godfrey's life and activity, see Françoise Gasparri, "Philosophie et cosmologie: Godefroid de Saint-Victor," in *Notre-Dame de Paris: Un manifeste Chrétien (1160–1230)*, Michel Lemoine ed. (Turnhout: Brepols, 2004), 119–42. Gasparri is the best guide to humanistic elements in the whole of *Microcosmus*: affirmation of the human condition, the dignity of humanity, the divinity of humanity, the primacy of free will as the source of dignity. She mentions the importance of Seneca in the work (second only to the Gospels, says Godfrey) and moral teaching.

4. The *Microcosmus* survives in a single manuscript. The threadbare reception is probably connected with the conditions under which the author composed: exile and alienation from the community. Loss of interest in allegorical epic as a literary--philosophical form cannot explain it. By contrast one hundred manuscripts transmit the *Anticlaudianus* of Godfrey's contemporary Alain of Lille.

CHAPTER 11 ★ VICTORINE HUMANISM

Influential or not, his writings qualify him as broadly representative of the humanism of the abbey of St. Victor. He wrote the *Microcosmus* towards the end of the century, c.1173–85. He lived in exile from the abbey in a priory after being banished by Abbot Walter. The intellectual energy that had produced the first generations of Victorine writers, scholars, and poets was in stark decline. Godfrey was alone among his contemporary Victorines in penning a sprawling allegory full of enthusiasm for the values of the earlier phase of its life and full of optimism for the ideas of medieval humanism. As sometimes happens in intellectual history, a latecomer to a movement is the one who makes the most encompassing summing up of the thought world that has preceded. Dante stands in this relationship to the Christian Middle Ages generally. Godfrey is the summarizer and last representative of Victorine humanism. He is no Dante, but it also happens that in mediocre writing a traditional form reverts to type. Its shared contours become sharply focused because they are not complicated by originality or versatility of mind.

MICROCOSMUS AND OTHER CREATION ALLEGORIES

The basic idea of Godfrey's *Microcosmus* was in the air in the twelfth century, most impressively represented in the creation allegory of Bernard Silvester's *Cosmographia* (unfinished, mid-twelfth century).[5] Its two parts are "Macrocosm" and "Microcosm," the creation of the world, then the creation of the human being upon the model of the cosmos. The idea implies a grandeur of humanity mirroring that of the universe: a perfect harmony of humanity analogous to the harmonious beauty of the macrocosm. It also implies the universality of the human mind, an idea spelled out in detail in the opening chapters of Hugh's *Didascalicon*. This primal perfection may have been disturbed by original sin or by evil elements inherent in the physical matter from which the human form is constructed (as in *Cosmographia*). But the tarnishing flaw sets in place the fundamental spiritual goal of humanity: the restoration of primal perfection as an approach to God. Bernard's *Cosmographia* remained unfinished, at least has not been transmitted in finished form. It is not unlikely that

5. See above, 249–57.

Godfrey answered or complemented Bernard Silvester in naming his own work *Microcosmos*: the answer to a *cosmographia* is an *anthropographia*.

The *Anticlaudianus* of Alan of Lille (c.1180–85) is in a similar position in poetic form and history of ideas, also closely tied to Victorine humanism. In this grand allegory of the creation of a perfect human, a platoon of allegorical creating spirits undertake the formation of the new human, which is itself the means of restoring fallen humanity, the necessary antidote to the disordering of humanity through sin. Godfrey's *Microcosmus* overlaps in many points with the *Anticlaudianus*, though the work of the Victorine is neither so grand nor so verbose. Whereas Alan foresees the redemption of humanity through virtue, a life of happiness in a kind of new paradise, Godfrey's allegorical pilgrimage ends in the realm of charity. An allegory of the creation of humanity in analogy to the universe sets love as the endpoint and goal of life in this society. Love as *telos* of a creation allegory is to my knowledge unique within the traditions of medieval humanism but not in the idea world of St. Victor.

THE WAYSIDE INN OF CHARITY

Godfrey's work fits three perspectives, philosophy/theology/society, into a unified scheme. An episode at a critical moment in the narrative of *Microcosmus* shows the linking of these elements. I will spare the reader a summary of the narrative. Hugh Feiss' summary provides a good guide through the work.[6] I move on to a critical passage that illustrates the importance of social ideals as the entry into theology.

After chapters on Christology and human emotions, the allegory has advanced to the sixth day. The trope of a difficult journey now takes on a role in the narrative it had not had previously. The narrator and fellow pilgrims (not mentioned earlier) are walking a road alongside the "lower waters" of creation. At this border crossing, there is a change of guides. Grace had led them to this point; their new guide is *caritas*, love. The travelers interrupt their journey to rest at an inn, the "wayside inn of Charity" (*diversorium charitatis*). The way

6. See Feiss' introduction to his partial translation of the *Microcosmus* in *On Love: A Selection of Works of Hugh, Adam, Achard, Richard and Godfrey of St. Victor* (Turnhout: Brepols, 2011), 305–14.

CHAPTER 11 ✳ VICTORINE HUMANISM

has been long and difficult, the sun is hot, the travelers seek rest from the summer heat and the difficulties of the path and find it in this inn on the border between the land of Grace and the land of Charity. It is a passage that has not stirred interest among commentators, but it deserves a close reading. It is central to that social aspect of Victorine humanism,[7] situated between the two lands of the border crossing.

The wayside inn is amply supplied, pleasant, and safe. Therefore, they enter this inviting "mansion":

> We had traveled the entire path to the wayside inn with Grace as our guide. Here we found a well-supplied and pleasant place to take our rest. We were at pains to relieve what we had previously suffered from the summer sun and to evade the difficulties of the coming winter that threatened. Hardly had we entered the resting place of this house, as comfortable as it was amiable, than we saw before us kind Charity with her happy face.[8]

Lady Charity in person greets them with a welcoming smile (*hilari vultu*) and gracious words. "She showed us an affability it would be impossible to describe" (*se nobis ineffabiliter affabilem prebuit*). Then she continued to serve them in a way that anticipated their every wish. Her gifts of hospitality were so abundant that a hundred tongues would not suffice to recount them. It seemed like paradise with its full supply of heavenly delights. Once they are seated at the table of spiritual foods, she personally washed their hands with water, offered bread and wine to each of the guests. Eventually she introduces herself as the "mother of all that is delightful and delicious," and ultimately as the queen of the realm they are about to enter.

Lady Charity first tends to the companions of Godfrey who are suffering badly, nearly broken with labor, weariness, and despair.

---

7.   Julie Kerr, *Monastic Hospitality: The Benedictines in England, c.1070–c.1250* (Woodbridge: Boydell & Brewer, 2007), places Victorine hospitality in the context of humanism.

8.   *Microcosmus* 3.143, ll. 2–7: "ad usque diversorium caritatis duce gratia pervenimus, ubi et amplo et ameno et tuto loco repausandi invento, preteritos estivi solis ardores mitigare et imminentes future hiemis asperitates declinare curavimus. Ingressi igitur tam commode tamque ioconde stationis mansionem, mox obviam nobis habuimus hylari vultu benignam caritatem." In Gasparri ed., 302; Delhaye ed., 158.

381

One look at them and she knew what was in their hearts, and with a compassion born of sweet affability, she first refreshed those most in need. She takes Godfrey by the hand and leads him and his companions into an upper room redolent of grandeur and sweetness, of marvelous size and beauty, filled with astonishing abundance and fragrance.

The idyll of the inn of Charity continues at length. It follows the travelers' progress through the house and is lavish with details of the sensitive kindness and considerateness of Lady Charity. Especially striking is the hostess' instinctual compassion: she spares guests the embarassment of asking for anything but knows at a glance what they need and proceeds to serve them accordingly. She conducts them through two "meals," the *refectio* and *collatio*. The first happens in silence, the initial refreshment after travel. The second is a full meal, guests recumbent and engaged as at a philosophical symposium[9] in civil discussions of topics related to charity. Boisterous contention is banished. That the first collation is allegorically an introduction to Scripture, and the *refectio* an advanced seminar, is mentioned but very much in the background during the welcoming sessions (chaps. 143–46).

No member of the Victorine community would have failed to recognize this idyllic moment in the allegory as broadly patterned on the courtesy that was an integral part of the social life of the house. Lady Charity's speech welcoming the travelers into her realm resonates clearly with the entry into a life based on vows and profession. The tavern's hostess speaks:

> "[In your trek through the lower waters you have fortunately found your way to me], and it was a happy turn that brought you to my wayside inn, that is, assuming that you won't be drawn away from me again. For it is just as good for you not to be drawn away from me, as it was for you to pay me this visit."... Gazing on her I wondered what her intention might be, for I feared lest she might perhaps wish to thwart my plans. But this lady quickly perceived my thoughts and commented: "You should know that unless you

---

9. Defined by John of Salisbury in connection with the banqueting customs of Thomas Becket. See Jaeger, *Envy*, 301–8 on banqueting customs at Becket's Canterbury. Kerr, *Monastic Hospitality*, draws a clear distinction between Victorine hospitality and monastic customs.

CHAPTER 11 ✳ VICTORINE HUMANISM

yourself stray from your purpose and unless you wish to withdraw from your intended course, you will, in following your decision [*propositum*], no longer depart from my kingdom."[10]

Propositum can refer to any kind of binding decision, but it is also a technical term for monastic profession.[11]

Godfrey has imagined this whole social setting as a kind of royal court. Lady Charity reveals herself as queen of the realm.[12] Queen though she is, commanding many servants, or rather sons and daughters, she takes it upon herself to wait on guests personally, a sign of her humble, courteous willingness to serve. The narrator is the *dux* of his *comites*. While these terms can mean simply leader and companions, they are also technical terms of an aristocratic hierarchy, in modern English, a duke and his counts. Likewise, Lady Charity's following is referred to as her *familia* — again, perfectly well understood as generic "family," but also "retinue" as of a king's court.[13] In other words "the land of charity" is ruled metaphorically by a royal court with a queen welcoming a duke and his counts into her retinue.

SOCIAL IDEALS

The rich overlay of associations related to the actual life at St. Victor is evident if we compare the allegorical reception into the kingdom

10. 3.145, ll. 28–39: "me...non infauste reperisti et ad meum huc diversorium feliciter divertisti, si tamen de cetero a me ultra non diverteris. Eque enim tibi expedit a me ultra non divertere sicut tibi expedit ad me divertisse." His postremo dictis, aliquantulum turbatus sum, cum precedentia verba eius satis me exhylarassent, sed nichil adhuc ausus sum interrogare, intuitus eam cogitabam quid intenderet. Metuebam enim ne forte intentionem meam vellet inpedire. Ipsa vero mox videns cognitionem meam subiunxit dicens: "Scias autem quod nisi tu ipse sic deliraveris ut ab intencione tua recedere volueris, propositum tuum prosequendo, a meo regno ultra non egredieris." In Gasparri ed., 308; Delhaye ed., 161. Cf. the stipulation in the *Liber ordinis* 22, ll. 71–73: "unusquisque in ea vocatione, qua vocatus est et qua coepit, constanter usque in finem Domino servire studeat et placere." In Jocqué and Milis ed., 99.

11. Abundantly represented in the combination *propositum monachi* parodied in the Archpoet's "meum est propositum, in taberno mori."

12. *Microcosmus* 3.145, l. 39: "Ego sum regina huius, quem tu perambulas, mundi." In Gasparri ed., 308; Delhaye ed., 161.

13. *Microcosmus* 3.143; Gasparri ed., 302–4; Delhaye ed., 159.

of charity with the welcoming ceremony into the abbey of St. Victor as prescribed in the *Liber ordinis Sancti Victoris Parisiensis*. It sets out explicitly a reception based on ideals of courtesy.[14] The duties of officials receiving guests are described in detail. The courtyard porter or gatekeeper *(portarius curiae)* must be a person of known and proven character, affable and kind *(probatus moribus, affabilis et benignus)*, instructed in the discipline of speech and manners since he must be an example to all and embody the reputation of the entire house. If the community is a body, he is its face. He lives in the *mansio* at the entry gate. His office is important. The moment of reception, the mood of good humor and humane kindness, the *Liber* explains, is not just external etiquette, not just "manners," but rather a revelation of the character of the entire institution:

> Those who come from outside are especially to be received with great kindness and humanity [*cum magna benignitate et humanitate*] from the first moment of reception…so that from their first impressions of the exterior they form an estimate of the things concealed within.[15]

If the first gesture toward guests and travelers is one of love, they will feel strengthened.

This seems to have been precisely the impression the approach to St. Victor made on Godfrey. In his poem *Fons philosophiae* he recalled his first impression of the community. It had favored his entrance into the Victorine life: "By the very face of things I was compelled

---

14. *Liber ordinis* 15–17; Jocqué and Milis ed., 55–69. See Jaeger, *Envy*, 244–68; and Jaeger, "Humanism and Ethics at the School of St. Victor in the Early Twelfth Century," *Mediaeval Studies* 55 (1993): 51–79. The contrast to the prescriptions for receiving guests in the Benedictine Rule is telling. While the rule likewise stresses a humane and compassionate reception, the mood and gestures are different. The Benedictine Rule prescribes that all guests be received as if they were Christ. The priors or the brothers welcome them *cum omni officio caritatis*. The welcomers and the newcomers then pray together. They show their humility either by bowing their heads or by lying prone before the guest.

15. *Liber ordinis* 15, ll. 18-20: "hii, qui deforis adveniunt, praecipue primo occursu cum magna benignitate et humanitate recipiendi sunt, non solum ut ex his, quae extrinsecus vident, eorum, quae intrinsecus latent, existimationem colligant, set ut prima quoque caritate confirmati." In Jocqué and Milis ed., 55–56.

CHAPTER 11 ★ VICTORINE HUMANISM

to sit at the master's feet and hold to him with rapt attention...."[16] Certainly the new church building, completed by 1150, no doubt a magnificent structure, spreading wider and probably rising higher than the abbey of St. Denis,[17] will have been part of that "face." That first impression wins him for the instruction of the master, which inspired in him a rapture and began the repair of his earlier state.

Godfrey's reminiscence accords well with the prescriptions for manner and mood of reception in the *Liber*. Those who receive guests, visitors, and postulants must epitomize Victorine courtesy. The reception and instruction of novices require "the maximum of care and affection."[18] Someone who troubles arriving guests with questions and delays is not suited as porter, especially if his rejoinders are abrasive or wounding. If he turns people away for any reason, he must beg their pardon humbly and explain himself, "lest they be hurt by his repulse." Guests arriving for the first time must be met *cum magna benignitate et humanitate*. If they arrive on horseback, the porter is to approach the one he takes to be the superior and with a smiling face *(hilari vultu)* receive his reins and stirrup and say, "May our lords be welcome."[19] It might be a reception scene from a courtly romance. When the knight Calogrenanz arrives at an unknown castle in Chrétien de Troyes' *Yvain*, he sees the master of the castle himself coming towards him:

---

16. *Fons philosophiae*, ll. 761–62: "Ipsa rerum facie cogor assidere / Et magistri pedibus pronus adherere...." In Pierre Michaud-Quantin, ed. (Namur: Éditions Godenne, 1956), 61.

17. William W. Clark, "The Twelfth-Century Church of St. Victor in Paris: A New Proposal," in *From Knowledge to Beatitude: St. Victor Twelfth-Century Scholars and Beyond. Essays in Honor of Grover A. Zinn, Jr.*, E. Ann Matter and Lesley Smith, ed. (Notre Dame, IN: Notre Dame University Press, 2013), 68–85. According to Clark, the church of 1130–50 was "of grander proportions than its Parisian rivals, St. Denis and St. Germain des Prés, second only to the cathedral of Notre Dame." The twelfth-century building was partly destroyed in the sixteenth century and altogether in the wake of the French Revolution. Clark, 79, argues plausibly that the great size of the building implies the grandeur of the finished structure, now lost to recovery.

18. *Liber ordinis* 22, ll. 1–2; Jocqué and Milis ed., 96.

19. *Liber ordinis* 15, l. 29; Jocqué and Milis ed., 56.

No sooner had I saluted him than he came forward to hold my stirrup and invited me to dismount.... Then he told me more than a hundred times at once that blessed was the road by which I had come thither.[20]

The ethic of kindness and compassion does not end when the guest or postulant novice enters the community. All those accepted as novices should demonstrate "good manners" (*boni mores*), especially "gentleness, willingness to learn, and patience with correction."[21] After a new brother's perseverance and the sincerity of his profession is tested, he is led by the *hospitarius* to the abbot in the chapter, at whose feet he prostrates himself and seeks indulgence. "What is your request, brother?" asks the abbot. "I seek God's mercy and your society." The abbot responds, "May the lord grant you the society of his elect."[22] The stress on acceptance into society is, I believe, deeply engaged in the social thought of the early Victorines. Hugh of St. Victor had written a memorable homily on the Ecclesiastes passage, "To everything there is a season" (Eccl. 3). On "a time to embrace and a time to refrain from embraces" (3:5), he commented:

> There are the embraces of those who are dear and the life together of amicable society, in which, putting aside the experience of the flesh, a sweet life shared meets with the most gracious and delightful consent. They [those who are dear, *chari*] will however pass away at their time, lest the heart of humanity should find its rest [solely] in humanity, while the pact of eternal love remains unfulfilled. So there is a time of embracing and a time of refraining from embraces, so that humanity will not seek in time what belongs to eternity, and so that the one who loves the society of the living will bear in mind at all times the departure of one destined to die.[23]

20. *Ivain*, ll. 197–98; Chrétien de Troyes, *Arthurian Romances*, William W. Comfort, trans. (London: Dent, 1975), 182.

21. *Liber ordinis* 22, ll. 17–19; Jocqué and Milis ed., 97.

22. *Liber ordinis* 22, ll. 102–7: "Usque ante pedes abbatis statim procedens, toto corpore extento, se prosternet, veniam petens. Tunc abbate interrogante: 'Quae est petitio tua, frater?', ita iacens respondebit: 'Dei misericordiam et vestram societatem requiro, et abbas respondebit: 'Dominus det tibi societatem electorum suorum.'" In Jocqué and Milis ed., 101.

23. Hugh of St. Victor, *Homiliae in Ecclesiasten*, 15: "Sunt et amplexus charorum et contubernia societatis amicae, in qua praeter carnis experientiam, convictus dulcis

CHAPTER 11 ✷ VICTORINE HUMANISM

To find the heart's rest in a dear friend is a sanctioned act — it is a reminder of the "pact of eternal love" — and the thought of death does not warn against but rather sweetens the pact of love in the present moment. The postulant's words to the abbot prescribed in the *Liber*, "I seek God's mercy and your society," seem formulated to convey this message: of course, rejoice in the society of brothers, but remember the greater society of the elect.

Godfrey also wrote a memorable passage in the *Microcosmus* attesting to and affirming the social character of the shared life. He is explaining "ordered love":

> Since humans are by nature social animals, it is only natural that they have mutual obligations and that they show each other the sociability by which, joined together as it were by a bond of nature, they lead a life at once peaceful and happy. Only through this can they lead a blessed life [*vita beata*].[24]

This sense of a loving community joined by a commitment to sociability is codified in the many prescriptions of loving kindness, goodness, and humanity that should link one brother to the next. Virtually every act respecting another brother is to be performed "gently, affably, considerately" *(benigne, affabiliter)*. If the *vestiarius* needs to discourage the use of superfluous garments, he should do it *amicabiliter et caritative*.[25] Members of the community are to greet

---

gratissimo foederatur consensu qui et ipsi solvuntur tempore suo, ne cor hominis in homine requiescat, donec veniat quod non solvitur pactum charitatis aeternae. Propter haec omnia tempus est amplexandi, et tempus longe fieri ab amplexibus: ut in tempore non quaerat homo quod aeternum est, et qui hominis viventis societatem diligit, cogitet semper morituri separationem." In PL 175:222C–D.

24. *Microcosmus* 3.172, 3.192: "Cum naturaliter homo *sociale animal* sit, naturaliter sibi invicem debent et exhibent homines societatem qua velud quodam naturali vinculo sibi devincti pacificam et iocundam simul vitam ducant.... Per hanc solam ad beatam vitam pervenitur." In Delhaye ed., 192. Delhaye identifies the source of *sociale animal* as Seneca, *De beneficiis* 7.1.7. The phrase is famous from Aristotle, and a medieval reader might well have translated "political" with "social" without a sense of changing the meaning. Is this a divergence from the values of canons regular? Certainly *naturaliter animal sociale* diverges from a strict religious definition of human nature.

25. *Liber ordinis* 18, l. 117; Jocqué and Milis ed., 75.

guests with good cheer *(laetam faciem demonstret)* and speak to them courteously *(benigne eos alloquatur)*.[26] Guests arriving at mealtime are to be treated *largiori humanitate*.[27] The hospitaler should attend to the needs of the sick *cum omni humanitate et caritate*.[28]

The *Liber ordinis Sancti Victoris* has a distinctive character compared with other works of the genre. Its recent editor, Ludo Milis, characterizes the Victorines, as they represent themselves in the *Liber*, as "more original in fashioning the mode of their life, more courteous (even in the literal sense of the word) and more urbane."[29] I agree and have supported this characterization in earlier publications.[30] The passages just cited bear comparison with Andreas Capellanus' precepts to courtly ladies for the courtly reception of their lovers: "Greet whomever you receive with an urbane and cheerful manner"; "when someone arrives whoever it is, receive them with a cheerful manner and be at hand to serve them with charming conversation" [defining the *opus curialitatis*]; "Receive those who come to you with a cheerful greeting and exchange words of courtesy with them...."[31]

I do not mean to imply overlap in any other sense than the language and manners of courtesy. But the sharing of that common language and form of conduct, called by name *curialitas* or *urbanitas* among educated clergy — secular, religious, or monastic — is a fact of the history of manners.

The allegory of the Inn of Charity arose from an essential Victorine course of development, which Godfrey himself had experienced. His

26. *Liber ordinis* 17, ll. 221–22; Jocqué and Milis ed., 68.

27. *Liber ordinis* 17, l. 118; Jocqué and Milis ed., 64.

28. *Liber ordinis* 17, ll. 177–78; Jocqué and Milis ed., 66–67.

29. *Liber ordinis* avant propos, Jocqué and Milis ed., vi: "plus originaux dans la formation de leur genre de vie, plus courtois (même au sens littéral du mot) et plus urbains."

30. "Humanism and Ethics at the School of St. Victor," *Mediaeval Studies* 55 (1993): 51–79; Jaeger, *Envy*, 247–52.

31. *De Amore* 1.410: "hilari...facie et urbanitatis quemlibet receptu suscipiant"; 1.414: "hilari vultu in suo quemlibet adventu suscipere et suavia sibi responsa praestare"; 1.417: [defining the *opus curialitatis*] "ad vos venientes hilari receptione suscipitis et curialitatis verba secum adinvicem confertis." In *Andreas Capellanus on Love*, Patrick G. Walsh, ed. and trans. (London: Duckworth, 1982), 160, 162..

CHAPTER 11 ★ VICTORINE HUMANISM

description of his arrival at St. Victor quoted above is programmatic: entrance to St. Victor was a return to the self of those who have gone astray in the world and who seek repair and restoration of their primal goodness. The intoxicating liquor of instruction is the first dose of medicine to restore the novice to his primal state:

The very appearance of things forced me to sit
And cling, attentive, to the master's feet.
His speech was resonant with such things
That snatched me away, or rather, restored me to myself.
For, rapt at first and made alien from myself,
And drunken by the streams I had until then traversed,
I am restored to myself, refreshed by a new liquor,
And the repair of my ancient state begins.[32]

The resonance of these lines with the scheme of cosmic and human history, put forward by Hugh of St. Victor and widely influential, is audible here in the personal life of a convert to St. Victor. The age of creation translated into a social context means microcosmic "development." It mirrors that of the macrocosm, the first entry into the world and fall from grace, followed by the age of restoration. Godfrey's vision of his formation/reformation within the program of education of St. Victor may well point to a more general conception of the purpose of the Victorine life. It has a special attraction and a special course of development for those who commit to that life.

The house did not accept oblates. The normal minimum age was fifteen. The house's commitment was to the reeducation of young men with at least a minimum background in learning and experience. Godfrey himself had spent about ten years in the schools of Paris before his entry into the Victorines. Novices at St. Victor were conceived by the *Liber* and by Godfrey's *Microcosmus* not as boys or even as mature men on a rising arc in their lives, with St. Victor at the summit, but as men whose lives were broken in the

---

32. *Fons philosophiae* 2.765–72: "Ipsa rerum facie cogor assidere / Et magistri pedibus pronus adherere, / Ore cuius talia mihi sonuere, / Que me mihi raperent, imo reddidere. / Raptus enim primitus et alienatus, / Et quod circuiueram rivis debriatus, / Reddor mihi, temeto novo recreatus, / Et antiquus incipit reparari status." In Michaud-Quantin ed., 61.

world. Godfrey conveys this aspect allegorically in the condition of the travelers who find shelter and rest at the wayside Inn of Charity. They are exhausted, wearied from their travels, urgently in need of restoration.[33] The *Liber* and other documents conceive the work of the house as rehabilitation, re-creation,[34] restauration of those who renounce a previous life perceived as ruinous or failed, as embodying the vanity, confusion, and turbulence inevitable given the nature of life in "the world."

This career that led through disappointment or failure to rehabilitation outside of the Paris schools was followed by well-known figures: William of Conches, Richard Bishop, John of Salisbury.[35] Within the Victorine community we can mention a number of figures rebounding from troubles or failures in the world. Hugh of Champfleury was a disgraced ex-royal-chancellor who "retreated" to St. Victor.[36] We can add Etienne de Senlis, bishop of Paris (d.1142), and somewhat later in the century, Étienne de la Chapelle, archbishop of Bourges, Thomas Becket, and Arnulf of Lisieux, both of the latter received at St. Victor at various stages of their life after losing the favor of the English king. While not members of the community, the latter sought and found refuge there. Finally, of course, was St. Victor's founder himself, William of Champeaux. In his new foundation he had established, among other things, a haven for students, teachers, scholars, some new, some broken or bent, many well educated and of noble standing.[37] For men in Godfrey's situation, it offered refuge from

33. *Microcosmus* 3.143, ll. 19–20: "itineris mei comites, longioris me seu labore seu tedio seu et desperatione fractos...." In Gasparri ed., 302; Delhaye ed., 158.

34. Godfrey, *Fons philosophiae*, 2, ll. 767–68: "reddor mihi, recreatus; antiquus incipit reparari status." In Michaud-Quantin ed., 61.

35. See above, 67, 71–72. For an earlier generation of teachers/scholars disgusted with the rise of dialectic in the schools, see Jaeger, *Envy*, 221–26.

36. Stephen of Garland, also a disgraced ex-royal chancellor, was thought to have retired to St. Victor, but that is in doubt. He made gifts to St. Victor seven years before his death in 1147 (Charter of Notre-Dame, Paris, c.1140) but is not mentioned in the necrology of St. Victor.

37. Robert of Torigni would observe that during the abbacy of Gilduin, "multi clerici nobiles saecularibus et divinis litteris instructi, ad illum locum habitaturi convenerunt." In *De immutatione ordinis monachorum* 5, PL 202:1313B.

the life of the Paris schools. This career was allegorized by Godfrey as the move away from the realm of Nature into the realm of Grace.[38] St. Victor offered rehabilitation and re-creation to novices, as did the wayside Inn of Charity to the pilgrims of Godfrey's *Microcosmus*.

One other element of the Inn of Charity allegory that links with the social context of entry into St. Victor is the prohibition of any raucous contention in discussions.[39] Any novice who had followed a career like that of Godfrey would understand that the contentiousness has a real social referent: the schools of Paris, especially their dominant discipline, dialectics. Godfrey represented the nature of that art as akin to warfare.[40] He confesses that his ethical training had quieted his previously "strident and restless tongue."[41] The disputatious character of studies at the Parisian schools had created an agonistic culture. Conflict, contention, disputation, and self-assertion dominated the atmosphere of studies. The young Abelard is a good example. The founding of St. Victor in Paris was among many other things a rejection of that culture.

Conservative critics of the Paris schools complained[42] that the reliance of dialectics on doubt, the defense of theses put forward

38. The speech of Lady Charity to the wanderer stresses this course of development. *Microcosmus* 3.147, ll. 30–35: "[tu] a corporalibus ad spiritualia per naturalia et gratuita tendens, in difficilibus mandatorum dei semitis, non contentus publica strata, te exercere cupis. Et quia omnem ornatum tuum inefficacem esse sine me comperisti, prudenti consilio ad meum domicilium...divertisti." In Gasparri ed., 314; Delhaye ed., 164. On "rehabilitation," *Microcosmus* 3.148: The study of sacred Scripture recalls the humiliation of humanity after the fall from grace and teaches humanity of the things which are natural to the dignity of their condition. See Gasparri ed., 315; Delhaye ed., 165. On the transformation from old to new humanity, =*Microcosmus* 3.151; Gasparri ed, 320; Delhaye ed., 168–69.

39. *Microcosmus* 3.144, ll. 10–12: "Neque enim inter epulas verborum colluctationes aut clamosas disputationes admittebat, volens omnes suos sub silentii quiete panem suum manducare." In Gasparri ed., 304; Delhaye ed., 159. It has a precedent in Hugh's *De institutione novitiorum* 6, Feiss and Sicard ed., 268–94; PL 176:931B.

40. *Fons philosophiae* 2.145–88; Michaud-Quantin ed., 40–41.

41. *Fons philosophiae* 2.773; Michaud-Quantin ed., 62.

42. On Godfrey's conversion, see Ferruolo, *Origins*, 42: "He had become unsatisfied with the unnourishing disputations over the profound mysteries of the divinity

for debate, the self-assertiveness that engendered an arrogant contentiousness and contempt for tradition posed a real threat to clarity and seamlessness of doctrine. The "noisy throngs of disciples" that followed Abelard became an argument against his orthodoxy. Though Godfrey clearly admired his own teacher, Adam of Balsham, John of Salisbury presented him as an arrogant, self-important purveyor of obscurities, however much he may have valued him as a friend.[43] It is probable that Lady Charity's banishing of contentious disputation from her wayside inn responded to a real situation at the schools of Paris. St. Victor, just outside the city, was positioned as the haven of quiet, restfulness, moral, and intellectual clarity, and the living model of the peace and amical love of a well-governed life.

The ethical training that drew Godfrey and other students to St. Victor exercised a function central and fundamental to the whole conception of St. Victor.[44] Indeed, its ethical training is one cornerstone in the founding of the order by William of Champeaux. William's retreat from the schools of Paris was a retreat to an older form of ethical training still widely practiced at cathedral schools, on the wane and virtually abandoned by the independent schools of Paris. Hildebert of Lavardin congratulated William for his move from Notre Dame to the new foundation of St. Victor. While others criticized him for continuing his teaching, Hildebert commended it as a return to "true philosophy." In his new life, Hildebert wrote, William's teaching would bring forth "beauty of conduct" like honey from the comb.[45] This and other witnesses make clear that *venustas morum* was central to William's teaching at the new foundation, and that means central to the whole conception of the house.[46]

---

that preoccupied theologians in the schools and had chosen to retire to the tranquility of the cloister."

43. Above, 308–10.

44. See Jaeger, *Envy*, 244–45.

45. Hildebert of Lavardin, *Epistolae* 1.1; PL 171:141A.

46. Bynum's studies have made clear that precisely the teaching role of regular canons, teaching their own brothers and others "by word and example," distinguished them from monks. See Bynum, *Docere Verbo*; Bynum, "The Spirituality of Canons Regular in the Twelfth Century: A New Approach," *Mediaevalia et Humanistica* n.s. 4 (1973): 3–24.

CHAPTER 11 ✶ VICTORINE HUMANISM

William of Champeaux retreated from new learning back into the old. "Philosophy" regained its ancient and early medieval meaning of *bene vivendi disciplina*.[47]

It is not surprising for several reasons that the *Liber Sancti Victoris* lays particular stress on the ethical training of novices, that it enjoins an ethic of "kind and humane" treatment, affable and courteous conduct to all alike. These are examples of the honey of *venustas morum*. It is also not surprising that one of Hugh of St. Victor's major works, and one of his most influential, is his tract *On the Instruction of Novices*.[48] It is a work on the cultivation of virtue, and as such it borrows in full cloth from the ethical training in "elegance of manners" at home in the cathedral schools of the empire, well known and practiced in the homeland of Hugh of St. Victor.

Hugh's tract presents itself as an introduction to spiritual formation for novices of St. Victor, men "to whom all earthly glory and beauty is as a heap of dung."[49] The substance of the work is however very different from what this introduction leads the reader to expect. It is centrally about the discipline of manners and gestures.[50] The ethical and pedagogical focal point of the work is "discipline": *disciplina virtutis, morum disciplina* are some of the formulations. The singularity of Hugh's usage is apparent in the definition he gives in the *De institutione*:

> Discipline is good and proper behavior, to attain which it is not enough just to avoid evil. It strives also to *appear* above reproach in all things that it does well. Discipline is also the governed movement of all members of the body and a seemly disposition in every state and action.[51]

---

47. Misfortune still dogged him for what remained of an intellectual approach to his teaching, however. It was at St. Victor, in a course on rhetoric, that Abelard dealt him his hardest blow, documented in the *Historia calamitatum* 1.6; Luscombe ed., 8–10.

48. On the influence of the work see Rudolf Goy, *Die Überlieferung der Werke Hugos von St. Viktor: Ein Beitrag zur Kommunikationsgeschichte des Mittelalters* (Stuttgart: Hiersemann, 1976), 340–67.

49. *De institutione novitiorum*, prologue. Feiss and Sicard ed., 51–54; PL 176:926B–C

50. Schmitt recognized the work as essentially concerned with comportment and connected to both humanism and courtly manners. See *La raison*, 193–94, 197.

51. *De institutione novitiorum* 10: "Disciplina est conversatio bona et honesta, cui parum est, malum non facere, sed studet etiam in his que bene agit per cuncta

This peculiar form of ethical education insists on the body and its disciplining to elegance, beauty, and propriety as the original locus of moral formation. The composition of the inner world begins with the body:

> Just as inconstancy of mind brings forth irregular motions of the body, so also the mind is strengthened and made constant when the body is restrained through the process of discipline. Little by little, the mind is composed inwardly to calm, when through the custody of discipline its bad emotions are not allowed free play outwardly. The perfection of virtue is attained when the members of the body are governed and ordered through the inner custody of the mind.[52]

Exterior disciplina and *usus corporis* become identical with *cultus virtutis* at an early stage of training. Hugh makes the connection explicit:

> The members of the body are to be restrained outwardly, therefore, through discipline, so that the condition of the mind may be firmed up within and strengthened.... Little by little, as it becomes habitual, that same image of virtue is impressed on the mind that is maintained through outward discipline in the disposition of the body.[53]

The first step on the path to God is governance of the body. The mastery of external things leads to mastery of the inner world, and the composed and mastered body gives testimony to the virtuous

---

irreprehensibilis apparere. Item disciplina est membrorum omnium motus ordinatus et dispositio decens in omni habitu et actione." In Feiss and Sicard ed., 450–55; PL 176:935A–B.

52. *De institutione novitiorum* 10: "Sicut enim de inconstantia mentis nascitur inordinata motio corporis, ita quoque, dum corpus per disciplinam stringitur, animus ad constantiam solidatur. Et paulatim intrinsecus mens ad quietem componitur, cum per discipline custodiam mali motus eius foras fluere non sinuntur. Integritas ergo virtutis est, quando per internam mentis custodiam ordinate reguntur membra corporis." In Sicard ed., 460–67; PL 176:935B–C.

53. *De institutione novitiorum* 10: "Liganda sunt ergo foris per disciplinam membra corporis, ut intrinsecus solidetur status mentis.... Paulatimque eadem virtutis forma per consuetudinem menti imprimitur, que foris per disciplinam in habitu corporis conservatur." In Sicard ed., 476–85; PL 176:935D.

CHAPTER 11 ✶ VICTORINE HUMANISM

soul. It follows that the body can be read like a book for the signs of virtue. Elegant bearing registers a well and virtuously composed mind. The well-ordered functioning of all members of the body produces *concordia universitatis*, harmony of the whole being.[54] Its external sign is moderation, order, and beauty.

We should recall the duties of the porter laid out in the *Liber Ordinis*. A good humored, kind, and humane conduct is especially important, since "from their first impressions of the outside [visitors] form an estimate of the things concealed within." The parallel is evident. St. Victor is conceived as a community where the visible surface testifies to the character of the house itself, in the same way that the composed and mastered body of the members of the community gives testimony to the virtuous soul. Just as Godfrey of St. Victor, after reading the "very face of things," professed the order, the observer reads the body of the Victorine canon for signs of virtue. This suggests a conceptual unity underlying the life of St. Victor, Hugh's ethical thought, and no doubt also that of William of Champeaux. Just as the exterior behavior of disciplined individuals gives testimony to the virtues composing their minds, so also the behavior of the "outer human," the person on the outside of the house, the porter, symbolizes the ideals within: *benignitas, humanitas, caritas*. Also bound up in this conceptual unity are aspects of Hugh's theology. The duty of the porter resonates with Hugh's definition of a sacrament:

Pupil: Why is a sacrament called a sign of something sacred?

Master: Because through what one sees outwardly, something inward and invisible is signified.[55]

It follows that seeing a well-instructed member of the Victorine community is like seeing a sacrament, parallel, for instance, to looking at the water in the baptismal font or the wine and wafer of the Eucharist.

The comparison also points to the energy and pedagogic force of the personal presence, and the humanistic, aristocratic character of

54. *De institutione novitiorum* 12; Feiss and Sicard ed., 826; PL 176:943A.

55. *De sacramentis legis naturalis et scriptae*: "Discipulus: Quare dicitur sacramentum sacrae rei signum? Magister: Quia per id quod foris visibile cernitur, aliud interius invisibile significatur." In PL 176:34A.

Victorine ethics. This character is nowhere more strikingly evident than in the pedagogy of teaching by example.[56] Virtue is acquired by the imitation of good people. Hugh clearly conceived of this process of formation as a parallel to human artworks, handcraft, and sculpture:

> We who seek to be reformed through the example of good people, as through some marvelously sculpted seal, perceive in them the traces of actions, some of which are sublime and outstanding, but others abject and depressed....[57] When [the saintly] behave in such a way as to arouse the admiration of human minds, then they appear as exquisite sculptures.[58]

Again, the pedagogy of imitation is linked to spiritual goals by the doctrine of the image and likeness of God, which people seek to imitate when they imitate the actions of good individuals. By this route ethical training merges with theology, the same route that would link reading to pursuit of the image of God in the *Didascalicon*.

It is easy to distinguish the training of novices as conceived by Hugh of St. Victor from both monastic and canonical traditions. Caroline Bynum has drawn that distinction sharply.[59] What can be added here is the dependence of ethical training at St. Victor on traditions of medieval humanism. *Disciplina morum* and other terms for ethical training in Hugh's *De institutione* form part of the ethical tradition inherited from classical antiquity and taught in royal courts at least since Carolingian times and at courts and cathedral schools since Ottonian. Hugh of St. Victor, and presumably the community

---

56. Bynum, "Spirituality"; Jaeger, *Envy*, 258–60.

57. An intricate word play on the surface contours of a seal, expression, impression, depression: the image is articulated by rises (*sublimia et eminentia*) and depressions (*deorsum pressa*); *introrsum signata – exterius figurata*.

58. *De institutione novitiorum* 7: "Nos, qui per exemplum bonorum quasi per quoddam sigillum optime exsculptum informari cupimus, quedam in eis sublimia et quasi eminentia, quedam vero abiecta et quasi depressa operum vestigia invenimus.... Quando vero talia operantur que humanas mentes in admirationem sui pertrahunt, quasi quasdam in se eminentes sculpturas ostendunt." In Feiss and Sicard, ed. 363–64; PL 176:933C.

59. In Bynum, "Spirituality."

CHAPTER 11 ★ VICTORINE HUMANISM

of St. Victor, were the beneficiaries of the *disciplina morum* of eleventh-century cathedral schools.

The ideals of beautiful manners and the congruence of inner world and outer appearance are central to the ethical teachings of those schools. The ideals of Victorine ethics reflect the classical origins of the code of refined, beautiful manners conveyed in the terms *venustas* and *elegantia morum*. The founders and early teachers at the school of St. Victor superimposed an ethic of gentle, refined, "courtly and urbane" bearing onto the ideals of the apostolic life and those of the rule of St. Augustine: equality of manners and renunciation of possessions. In doing so they also eliminated the cult of personality that had been such an important factor in the old humanist learning, while retaining the charismatic pedagogy that was its concomitant.[60] The result was an extraordinary code that stressed sociability along with religion,[61] an aristocratic, quasi-monastic courtesy,[62] an ascetic Ciceronianism, which had a degree of legitimacy that the old imperial program of cathedral school education with its more worldly Ciceronianism could never again attain in the wake of the Investiture Controversy and religious reform movement. It occupies a middle position between the worldly ethic of the secular courts (courtliness) and the asceticism of the new monastic movements. This combination must have had strong appeal to precisely the kind of men who converted from worldly life to canonical, men of high aristocracy like Stephen of Garland and Hugh of Champfleury.

---

60. Hugh's pedagogy is structured around principles at work in the ethics of cathedral schools. Theology is far more closely integrated with ethical training than at more worldly cathedral schools, but the structures of ethical learning remain consistent. See Donna R. Hawk-Reinhard, "Hugh of Saint Victor's Pedagogy," in *A Companion to the Abbey of Saint Victor in Paris*, Hugh Feiss and Juliet Mousseau, ed. (Leiden: Brill, 2018), 123–28.

61. That Victorine postulants begged "God's mercy and your society" from the abbot is consistent with this code. The words of admission to the order in the Benedictine Rule 58.21 are the verses from Ps. 118:116: "Receive me, Lord, as you have promised, and I shall live; do not disappoint me in my hope."

62. Poirel, *Hugo Saxo*, 168: "...les leçons de bonnes manières du *De institutione novitiorum* et le ton général de courtoisie qui distingue les oeuvres du Victorin se comprennent bien mieux si notre auteur est issu d'une haute lignée...."

HUMANISTIC THEOLOGY

ANTHROPOLOGY

It was important to begin this essay with ethics and spiritual-social values in order to establish those aspects along with the intellectual and religious as part of that "program as complete as possible...of a comprehensive wisdom, indissolubly Christian and humanist."[63] Now we can turn to the scholarly and intellectual aspects of Victorine humanism. These are best approached via its anthropology. An extravagantly ideal view of the human being, its origins, capacities, and destiny, is a striking and embracing concept of Victorine anthropology.[64] It owes much to the humanism of the eleventh and twelfth centuries out of which the Victorine school in part developed. It has much in common with the idealizing of the human in the humanism of the fifteenth and sixteenth centuries.

We can start again with Godfrey's *Microcosmus*. Early in his work Godfrey pleads for the dignity of the human body. The very fact that the human being is called a "world" (*mundus*, the human being a *minor mundus*) shows the great dignity of humanity by analogy to the greater world.[65] Godfrey rejects as shallow and carnal the view of the individual as "a worm, a leaf, a blade of grass." This ascetic view detracts from the true dignity that humanity possesses, even in its body, sanctified because God himself took on a human body. Through that act the human being has been exalted to a god.[66]

His chapter 79 is a virtual hymn to the human condition, including even mortality among the sources of human dignity. The passage begins by comparing human beings with angels. While humans are burdened by a frail body, they can be blessed with grace greater than that of angels. Mortality means struggle for humans, something

---

63. See Poirel, "Aux sources."

64. Gasparri, 122: [*Microcosmus* is] "une véritable manifeste en faveur de la nature humaine"; 124: "au fond la science à laquelle les Victorines sont le plus attachés est celle de l'homme"; [Godfrey's work is] "une étude de la nature de l'homme," [which represents a "theological humanism."] Feiss, *On Love*, 305, points to Godfrey's "resounding affirmation of human dignity."

65. *Microcosmus* 1.12, ll. 3–14; Gasparri ed., 74; Delhaye ed., 31.

66. *Microcosmus* 1.16; Gasparri ed., 84; Delhaye ed., 44–45.

angels are spared, and "where the struggle is greater, the crown after victory is also greater."[67] Virgin women embody this glorifying contest. They have virtue, while angels have only happiness.[68] The virgin wins by her strength what the angel has by nature. Thus humans are inferior to angels by nature but superior by grace. Human superiority is apparent in this: that through grace humanity becomes not only ruler of the world (*dominus mundi*) in a role like that of a god, but also similar to God, a god. Never has any angel experienced the god-like state, nor ever will. What wonder then that theologians call the human *mundus*, since humanity was seen also as worthy of the name "God."[69] Most forget the state in which they were created, but their primal nature gives them access to celestial things.[70]

The journey of Godfrey's pilgrims through the six days of creation ends with its consummation in the creation of humanity. Humanity was made as a "divine work of art" (*opus dive artis*), with the creator joining a celestial and imperishable spirit to perishable matter. This being merits the eternal habitation of God. But an even greater measure of divine art was the idea of placing the mystery of the spiritual world, i.e., of the microcosm, into this being, which God himself had decided to inhabit. The human is a being "formed fully and perfectly in the image and likeness of God."[71]

Godfrey ends his work with a remarkable passage addressing "the human spirit" directly (*apostrophus ad spiritum humanum*), summing up humanity's nature and urging it to become how it was created:

> "Listen now, spirit of humanity! We have written and spoken so much and so long about you.... We have held you up to view for yourself, so that by seeing yourself you would know

67. *Microcosmus* 2.78–79; Gasparri ed., 172–74; Delhaye ed., 90–91. With reference to 1 Cor. 9:24–25.

68. Godfrey has adapted letter 113 of Bernard of Clairvaux to "the Virgin Sophia." In *Sancti Bernardi Opera*, Jean Leclercq et al., ed., 7:287–91.

69. *Microcosmus* 2.79, ll. 1–22; Gasparri ed., 172–74; Delhaye ed., 91–92.

70. *Microcosmus* 1.22, ll. 1–12; Gasparri ed., 92; Delhaye ed., 48.

71. *Microcosmus* 202. 3-10: "Hic est novissimus et maximus ornatus terre, scilicet homo factus in terra et de terra ad imaginem et similitudinem Dei, quod nulli alii terrene creature collatum est, quod nullo alio precedentium dierum consummatum est." In Gasparri ed., 422; Delhaye ed., 222.

> yourself and knowing, would marvel at yourself. And how should you not wonder at yourself, if you once see yourself as we have depicted you? Would you not awaken to see yourself with open eyes? Or are you still asleep, oblivious to all the storms that have beat around you this whole time? Listen then: philosophically we have configured you for the world in the things of nature. Theologically in respect to Grace we have preferred to show you to be a microcosm, that is the eternal habitation of God. [We have done this] not only for you as yourself but also as divided into yourself and the habitation of God. Your body is that habitation, and in that body God is to reside in you and through you for eternity. That means that your body will participate in eternal goods with you and through you. Spiritually you will see your body your creator through all eternity, and it will see in you bodily its eternal redeemer. Through this your redeemer and the redeemer of your body will reform you not only "in the image and likeness of its divinity" but also "the body of your humility will configure to the body of his glory." [Phil. 3:21] That way, not only you but all humanity will be a microcosm, that is, the eternal kingdom of God. No creature is so suited to this role as the human." [72]

Until this point, Godfrey's Latin usage had favored the use of the masculine referring to all humans. As if Godfrey recognized the injustice of the grammar, he now specifically addresses women in his praise, and in doing so raises women to a position of preeminence unusual in monastic and secular/monastic communities:

> In both regards [nature and grace] you are united to God personally, and no angel is. In both regards you are set above every other creature, and no angel is: not only in the masculine sex — but also, a source of greater wonder to the holy angels and the envy of reprobate men — in the feminine sex. [This is

72. *Microcosmus* 3.236: "Eia nunc o spiritus humane de quo hactenus tot et tanta locuti sumus, de quo tot et tanta scripsimus... cui hactenus temetipsum proposuimus, ut videndo te, agnoscas te et agnitum admireris te... Redemptor tuus et suus non solum te reformabit ad ymaginem et similitudinem divinitatis sue sed et corpus humilitatis tue configurabit corpori claritatis sue ita un non solum tu sed et totus homo sit microcosmus, id est eternum regnum dei. Quod utique nulli alii creature tam excellenter collatum est ut homini." In Gasparri ed., 488; Delhaye ed., 258.

because both the angels and the reprobates], the former to their greatest wonder, the latter to their confusion, see the female exalted above the choruses of angels. With the king her son, she is constituted the queen of the world. Thus nothing among creatures made pure by grace can be more eminent than woman, whom God has chosen for himself as a singular vessel of grace, so that every creature will show her honor....[73]

As a celebration of humanity with the stress on the male this work as a whole deserves to take its place among others of its kind, like the *Cosmographia* and the *Anticlaudianus*.[74] It also looks ahead to the speech in tribute to humanity as the great miracle in chapter 25 of the Middle High German work *Der Ackermann aus Böhmen* and to Pico della Mirandola's *Oration on the Dignity of Man*. As a paen to the female, it has no parallel, to my knowledge.

Both of the grand twelfth-century allegorical epics, *Cosmographia* and *Anticlaudianus*, are creation allegories in the tradition of the *Timaeus*. Both center on the creation of a perfect human being, arguable doctrinally for Adam before the fall. But in his *homo novus* Alan posits a redeeming figure who will provide the moral redemption of a fallen world, and so proposes an alternative to or perhaps an ally of Christ in his redeeming mission. Christ is very much on the periphery and inactive in the process of re-creation of humanity. Bernard's *Cosmographia* moved Curtius to suggest a survival of beliefs associated with the kind of primitive fertility cults studied by James Frazer and introduced to the study of medieval romance by Jessie Weston.[75]

Another unusual aspect of the "speech to humanity" is the elevation of the body to a role in the here rather more complex process of human redemption. The human body is sanctified by Christ's use

---

73. *Microcosmus* 237; Delhaye ed., 259.

74. In contrast to Alanus' work, the core of Godfrey's thinking on human dignity is the humanity of Christ.

75. Curtius, "Zur Literarästhetik des Mittelalters 2," ZfRPhil 58 (1938): 185–90; ELLMA, 112; Jessie Weston, *From Ritual to Romance* (Princeton, NJ: Princeton University Press, 1920); James Frazer, *The Golden Bough: A Study in Magic and Religion* (New York: Macmillan, 1922).

of it. He chose it as his place of habitation during his mission to the created world. Godfrey grants it the role of the everlasting place of residence of Christ. The human soul is of course the major beneficiary of redemption through being the image and likeness of God. But now the human body has a parallel role. It has its own redemption in which its used, abused earthly form will be recreated to match the heavenly form of Christ's. Only that transcendent fate of the body can explain and furnish the microcosmic basis of humanity.

How should one read this unusual glorification of body and soul? Human self-aggrandizement? That is far off the mark. This and the other texts glorifying humanity, the human mind and spirit, are best understood in the context in which they occur. They are teaching texts of a community. Positing a high ideal says to the student that this is the creature as which you are created; now become the man or woman you are. That motive sounds clearly in Godfrey's *Apostrophus*. It is a wake-up call to a human spirit given to indolence. Wake up and realize the goal that your maker has set for you. By elevating humanity into transcendental heights, he means to dazzle and astonish — not just to inform — his reader. Gaining self-knowledge by sober insight, mere understanding, does not do the job. The spirit must be shaken and spellbound by the thought of his nature. For that reason this and other humanists project a sublime image of humanity to their readers. This authorial intention registers in the lines:

> We have held you up to view for yourself, so that by seeing yourself you would know yourself and knowing, would marvel at yourself. How could you fail to strike awe in yourself, if you see yourself as we have depicted you?[76]

The same logic of rhetorical persuasion by grandiosity is at work throughout the community addressed, however broad it might be. It is central not just to the philosophy but to the pedagogy of medieval humanism.

Human Universality

Eleventh- and twelfth-century humanism had developed a broad and varied ideal of the human. Appropriations of the creation myth of Plato's *Timaeus* established an intellectual free zone where

---

76. *Microcosmus* 3.236; Gasparri ed., 488; Delhaye ed., 258.

conceptions of an ideal human, a universal human[77] could develop bound loosely or not at all to the creation story of Genesis. This ideal in its many different forms must be seen as central to humanism in general, however different in its details, especially its Christian remodeling. The human ideals listed earlier are prominent in Victorine writings: the individual as microcosm, the universality of humanity, human perfection, the human being as a work of art and "a great miracle," the dignity of humanity, the divinity of humanity. Godfrey of St. Victor was continuing lines of thought inherited from his predecessors. Hugh of St. Victor formulated an ideal of the primal human and the making of the human soul in a number of works. He sweeps across the range of concepts mentioned above. Here Hugh's wedding of humanism with Christian theology is most evident. The major non-Victorine works of poetic theology — Bernard Silvester's *Cosmographia* and Alain of Lille's *Anticlaudianus* — leave the reader wondering about the degree of their author's obligation to Christianity. Curtius issued a decided judgment on the question for Bernard: "It is not possible to claim Bernardus Silvestris for orthodoxy."[78]

That question cannot arise with Hugh of St. Victor. Rather the fascination of Hugh's humanistic thought is in part the seams and joints by which he connects humanistic glorification of humanity with Christian theology. His treatment of the creation of humanity bears comparison with the attempt of Thierry of Chartres to harmonize the creation story of the *Timaeus* with that of Genesis. God's purpose in creating humanity was, in part, so that "He might make it a sharer in that good that He himself was." His greater goal was to glorify this creature tenuously put together out of body and spirit. The joining of body and soul, far from representing a curse and a burden on the primal human, was the demonstration and proof to the created being of God's will and ability to elevate humans to participation in His own glory. So this great virtuoso act of joining and harmonizing opposites was not just architectonics. It was a display of awesome power. We might say transgressive power, since

---

77. See above, 243–66.
78. Curtius, "Zur Literarästhetik," 189.

God dared join what was pure, rational, and virtuous to a medium that by nature resisted those qualities.

If God can do something as wildly improbable as fit the soul into earthly matter, think what more He could do, and take this virtuosity as a promise of coming glorification. The joy and pleasure of earthly life is there as a promise and prediction of a future life even more joyous. The greater purpose of humanity in the eyes of God is to rise to glory out of abasement and by that route prove the wisdom of God's complex creation of humanity:[79]

> The soul is the vessel of the image and likeness of God. The image is reason, the likeness, love; the image is knowledge and wisdom, the likeness love of virtue.[80]

Humanity was given two goods immediately upon its creation, one material, the other spiritual. Humanity was lord of material things but had no obligation to serve temporal things. Such service would have reduced "the dignity of humanity's foundation." But through its need of material things, it recognizes the insufficiency of its nature. This insufficiency was an especially wise gift of the creator God, since it directed humanity to the things that are the source of its true good. In other words, the creation of humanity out of spirit and matter set in place productive tensions designed by God aimed at moving this creation toward the highest spiritual things and towards glorification. "Great indeed was the dignity of humanity's foundation, because it was made such that no good would suffice it except the highest."[81] Insufficiency of humanity, its urgent need to develop and mature, was a central idea of God's design. The contest of spiritual against material was a dynamic intended to activate humanity's striving to achieve the highest good. This justification of the body, the locus of insufficiency, as an instrument of God to push humans on to discover their divinity and live by it clearly influenced Godfrey's idea. The body has its own, microcosmic, role in the greater drama of redemption.

79. *De Sacramentis* 1.6.1. In *Hugh of Saint Victor on the Sacraments of the Christian Faith (De sacramentis)*, Roy J. Deferrari, trans. (Cambridge, MA: Medieval Academy of America, 1951), 94.

80. *De Sacramentis* 1.6.2; Deferrari trans., 95.

81. *De Sacramentis* 1.6.6; Deferrari trans., 99.

Humanity then develops along an arc where reason seeks knowledge, knowledge generates wisdom. That dynamic assures that after the fall humanity can rise again to reawaken its awareness of its primal origin and purpose. The first human being was made perfect in body and soul. It possessed perfect knowledge and full understanding of truth. Humanity required knowledge of all things since it was destined to rule over all things. Humanity did not lose plenary knowledge by original sin. What it lost was something higher: knowledge of its soul, and that had to be recovered by an instrument that had not existed and was not necessary prior to the fall: study.[82]

Hugh's *Didascalicon* is the handbook of that study, aimed in its general intent precisely at restoring the lost knowledge of the soul. This treatise is a complete program of reading in the arts and theology. It opens with an explanation of the construction of the human soul, an important statement of a bold attempt to integrate ancient philosophical views of human nature into Christian doctrine. Knowledge of the soul is the key to self-knowledge without which humanity cannot understand its mental and spiritual capacities. Hugh cites an opinion "approved among philosophers," that the soul is constructed of all the parts of nature. It contains in itself the entire cosmos and all its forms. It recognizes and understands all things in the universe because it contains them in itself: "One and the same mind, having the capacity for all things, is fitted together out of every substance and nature...."[83] That means that every human soul contains potentially the entire universe in itself.

The idea is consistent with the model of the individual as microcosm, its own structure mirroring that of the greater universe. (Hugh does not refer to this comparison, but Godfrey was to pick it up and take it as the plan of his allegorical work.) It is consistent with Hugh's later view of humanity's plenary knowledge and

---

82. *De Sacramentis* 1.6.11–15; Deferrari trans., 101–3.

83. *Didascalicon* 1.1: "Eadem mens, quae universorum capax est, ex omni substantia atque natura, quo similitudinis repraesentat figuram, coaptatur." In Buttimer ed., 5; Taylor trans., 46.

understanding prior to original sin. It follows that humanity has by its inborn nature the capacity for understanding everything:[84]

> The mind, imprinted with the likenesses of all things, is said to be all things and to receive its composition from all things, and to contain them not as actual components, or formally, but virtually and potentially. ... This all-comprehending universality of the soul accounts for the native dignity of humanity: "This then is the dignity of our nature that all possess in equal measure...."[85]

HUMAN DIVINITY

But humanity has lost the knowledge of itself and its soul because of the corrupting influence of sensuality. Therefore it is given the means of restoring this marred perfection: study and learning: *Reparamur per doctrinam ut nostram agnoscamus naturam*.[86] The ultimate goal of study is to restore the image and likeness of God in humanity, obscured because of original sin, restorable through "contemplation of truth and the practice of virtue."[87] The value that Hugh places on reading and study establishes a redemptive narrative of the growth of the human soul, a rise propelled by study, reflection, and contemplation to self-recognition (*ut nostram agnoscamus naturam*).[88] It is fueled by that inborn compulsion of the human to rebel against its own insufficiency, generated by the God-given tension between body and soul. Learning is the means to reactivate all those capacities

---

84. Hugh may well have taken the idea that the human soul contains all parts of nature, all of nature, in itself, from the Hermetic tract *Asclepius*, which he knew well. The *Didascalicon* ends with a quotation from *Asclepius* 6.13. See Taylor trans., 225 n. 54. Taylor notes other reminiscences of the *Asclepius* throughout the *Didascalicon*. See also Heiduk, 133–34.

85. *Didascalicon* 1.1: "Mens, rerum omnium similitudine insignita, omnia esse dicitur, atque ex omnibus compositionem suscipere, non integraliter, sed virtualiter atque potentialiter continere, et haec est illa naturae nostrae dignitas quam omnes aeque naturaliter habent...." In Buttimer ed., 5–6.

86. *Didascalicon* 1.1; Buttimer ed., 6.

87. *De Sacramentis* 1.8; Deferrari trans., 54–55.

88. Franklin Harkins, *Reading and the Work of Restoration: History and Scripture in the Theology of Hugh of St. Victor* (Toronto: Pontifical Institute of Mediaeval Studies, 2009).

CHAPTER II ✶ VICTORINE HUMANISM

muddied over by the influence of the flesh after being joined to the soul in its descent from the spiritual to the physical realm. The idea has a Gnostic flavor, since the means to partial redemption is knowledge (*gnosis*).

Comprehensive study and reading are commensurate with the universal composition of the soul, hence a duty for anyone sensible of the ability to recharge all the capacities in the mind, to reconstruct the entire universe within and by that means ultimately to restore the image and likeness of God. So Hugh's admonition repeated throughout the *Didascalicon* to "study everything" has its justification in the structure of the soul, created to be or to resemble everything, hence also to strive to know everything.[89]

The Hermetic tradition saw in humanity a creature divine by nature: the child of God, hence like Christ, of divine origin. In the Victorines, as in Christian humanism generally, the idea of the divine human is muted to a resemblance, the "image and likeness" of the Genesis creation story.[90] Humanity is divine by imitation of its maker — in part an artistic conception of God the creator[91] — but only by likeness, not identity.

Hugh of St. Victor's opening of the *Didascalicon* joins a strand of thought from the Platonic-Hermetic tradition with the idea of divinity regained through study inherited from cathedral-school traditions, where study is represented as a means to regain humanity's divinity. Sigebert of Gembloux (c.1075) roused himself to write the second book of his *Passion of the Theban Legion* by the thought that "mind and reason" have made him god-like.[92] Benzo of Alba says that understanding of virtues and vices makes the human a miracle or

89. Dominique Poirel, "Apprend tout': Saint-Victor et le milieu des victorins à Paris, 1108–1330," in *Lieux de Savoir: Espaces et communautés*, Christian Jacob ed. (Paris: Albin Michel, 2007), 302–22.

90. See Trinkaus, *In Our Image and Likeness*.

91. Martino Rossi Monti, "*Opus es magnificum*: The Image of God and the Aesthetics of Grace," in *Magnificence and the Sublime in Medieval Aesthetics: Art, Architecture, Literature, Music*, C. Stephen Jaeger, ed. (New York: Palgrave-Macmillan, 2010), 17–29.

92. Prohem. 2.21–22: "Nos quoque laudemus, qui plus laudare valemus, / Quos similes domino mens facit et ratio." In Dümmler ed., 69. See also above, 263–64.

407

even a god: "Virtue is dignity of mind and nobility of soul, which miraclifies, even more, deifies, humans."[93] Baudri of Bourgeuil claims that philosophy makes those whom it nourishes gods: "*Sunt dii, non homines, quos lactat philosophia.*"[94] The thought is still strong in the twelfth century. William of Conches, explaining Boethius' Lady Philosophy, states:

> Philosophy makes humanity rise above human nature, that is, humanity is deified.... Humanity rises above itself [i.e., experiences *ecstasis*] when it becomes immortal through wisdom and virtue.... This is because it is found that the wise are deified when they rise to what is of God.[95]

Divinization is an intellectual accomplishment, a work of philosophy consistent with Hugh's claim that study restores the image and likeness of God. The *novus homo* of Alan's *Anticlaudianus* — its body shaped by cosmic virtues and the seven liberal arts — is also conceived as a "divine human," "a human and a god."[96] Accordingly human universality also is a characteristic of the "new human being" in that poem.

The modern reader of the Victorines and other early Christian humanists must reflect carefully on their ideas of divinization as attitudes toward learning and the image of the learned they may imply. They may have functioned primarily to motivate learning. They may have had little more effect on the self-fashioning and

---

93. *Ad Heinricum IV* 7.3: "Qui virtutes et vicia / Et virtutum officia / Recte novit discernere, / Non est ex bruto genere. / Virtus est mentis dignitas / Et animi nobilitas, / Que homines mirificat / Insuper et deificat." In Benzo of Alba, *Ad Heinricum IV, imperatorem libri VII: Sieben Bücher an Kaiser Heinrich IV.* Hans Seiffert, ed. and trans. (Hannover: Hahn, 1996), 606.

94. *Carmen* 153; Tiliette ed., 60.

95. Guillelmi de Conchis, *Glosae super Boetium* 1, Prose 1.1, ll. 62–69: "Philosophia facit supra naturam hominis hominem ascendere, id est hominem deificari.... In hoc excedit homo, cum per sapientiam et virtutem fit immortalis.... Et hoc est quod invenitur sapientes homines deificari cum ad hoc quod dei est ascendunt...." In Lodi Nauta ed., CCCM 158.2 (Turnhout: Brepols, 1999), 20. For more on the subject, see John Howle Newell, "The Dignity of Man in William of Conches and the School of Chartres in the Twelfth Century" (Ph.D. diss., Duke University, 1978), 172.

96. *Anticlaudianus* 1.236, 6.366–67; Wetherbee ed., 242, 422.

the self-presentation of a student like G of Bamberg, Meinhard's student, or Walcherus of Liège, the student of Goswin, than the Latin mottos of modern universities. But there can be no doubt that divinization of a sort through study was a held ideal of Victorines and of students and masters and of cathedral schools from the eleventh to the mid-twelfth century. Hugh of St. Victor was a central figure in articulating that ideal. His works were significant for integrating humanist ideas so closely into Christian doctrine, making study the route to restoring the image and likeness of God.

RICHARD OF ST. VICTOR ON FREE WILL

Richard of St. Victor had less interest in secular studies and their role in restoring lost human perfection, but he retained the fervent optimism and affirmation of the human condition we find in Hugh and Godfrey. For Richard, human dignity derives most directly from humanity's gift of free will. His tract *De statu interioris hominis* focuses on this theme:

> Among all the good things of creation, nothing in humanity is more sublime, nothing confers greater dignity than free will.... What is there, I ask you, more sublime in humanity, what can be found that has greater dignity, than that in which it is created in the image of God. For free will has the image not just of eternity, but also of divine majesty.[97]

He rhapsodizes on the subject of free will and touches on the topic that played a major role in Victorine ethics, control of the inner and outer human being:

> Seek in the microcosm, I beg you, for humanity is called by this name, that is, a lesser world. Seek in the human heart what it is that is formed in the image and likeness of God, what is preferred to all others in the privilege of dignity...and you will find, I believe, nothing other than free and rational consent.... It governed all things [in humanity's primal condition], distributed all things, commanded all things. Nothing was done contrary to

[97]. *De statu interioris hominis* 1.3: "Inter omnia creationis bona, nihil in homine sublimius, nihil dignius libero arbitrio.... Quid, quaeso, in homine sublimius, quid dignius inveniri potest, quam illud in quo ad imaginem Dei creatus est? Habet sane libertas arbitrii imaginem non solum aeternitatis, sed et divinae majestatis." In PL 196:1118C–D.

its will.... Every motion of the body, every sense, every desire, every affection, every thought was stirred according to its will, directed, reigned in, restrained. What sublime power! What powerful sublimity![98]

Richard of St. Victor did not take up Hugh's assertion that study is the prior means of restoring the image and likeness of God. For Richard the power of free will is the force that must govern all human actions in moving fallen humanity towards the lost primal perfection. Richard uses the metaphor of a king commanding his subjects:

> Does it not seem to you that the human soul bears in itself a kind of royal person when it has begun to preside strongly over its emotions and passions...and to command them with authority and to keep control in a vigorous way over the kingdom of the heavens within us?[99]

In other words, the force of virtue, working in mind and body, moves humanity towards the perfection of the primal state. But Richard is decisive in denying humanity's ability ever to recreate this state:

> Little by little and bit by bit each day the king has restored the kingdom in his chosen ones. But never in this life will he restore

---

98. *De statu interioris hominis* 1.14: "Quaere, obsecro, in microcosmo, nam et sic dictus est homo; quaere, inquam, in microcosmo, hoc est in minore mundo; quaere in corde humano quid sit illud quod ad imaginem et similitudinem Dei formatur, quod aliis omnibus dignitatis suae privilegio praefertur...et invenies, ut arbitror, nihil aliud quam liberum rationalemque consensum de quo hoc rectius intelligatur. Nihil quod in homine erat ejus imperio contradicebat. Omnia gubernabat..., omnia disponebat, omnibus imperabat. Nihil movebatur contra ejus voluntatem.... Omnis motus corporeus, omnis sensus, omnis appetitus, omnis affectus, omnis cogitatus ad ejus nutum movebatur, dirigebatur, refrenabatur, reprimebatur. O quam sublimis potestas! O quam potens sublimitas, imperare bestiis terrae, volucres coeli et pisces maris sub potestate habere! O dignitas sublimitatis! O sublimitas potestatis!" In PL 196:1126C.

99. *De eruditione interioris hominis*, 1.1: "Nonne tibi videtur animus humanus in se regiam quodammodo personam gerere, cum coeperit affectibus et passionibus... fortiter praesidere, et cum auctoritate imperare, et illud quod intra nos est regnum coelorum viriliter vendicare?" In PL 196:1232B–C.

it to that peace and security that humanity possessed in paradise prior to sin.[100]

He proposes a double route to restoration of the image and likeness of God: Reason governing thought aligns with and aims at the image. Love aligns with, and aims at, the likeness.[101]

CONCLUSIONS

The subject of Victorine humanism has appeared occasionally on the surface of scholarship but skipped along like a flat rock on a lake only to sink after a skip or two. While my study has not penetrated deeply into the remarkable humanist-intellectual-theological world of St. Victor in the first three quarters of the twelfth century, I hope to have added a skip or two, and I hope others will take up further work on this rich subject.

The humanism of the abbey of St. Victor is of course an intellectual or philosophical movement closely integrated into theology but also a moral, ethical, and perhaps first of all, a social humanism. Françoise Gasparri has observed that the science to which the Victorines are most closely bound is "the science of humanity."[102] I could only agree more enthusiastically if she had added "science and discipline of humanity." The ideas of Victorine humanism and of medieval humanism generally are reduced to an apparatus of thought when separated from an ethical discipline that aims at realizing intellectual ideals in human action.

---

100. *De statu interioris hominis* 1.16: "Hoc quotidie regnum paulatim et per partes in suis electis rex regnum restituit, nunquam tamen in hac vita ad eam pacem vel securitatem quam ante peccatum homo in paradiso habuit." In PL 176:1127D.

101. Hugo Feiss, ed., *On Love: A Selection of Works of Hugh, Adam, Achard, Richard and Godfrey of St. Victor* (Turnhout: Brepols, 2011), 83.

102. Gasparri, 124: "Au fond la science à laquelle les Victorins sont le plus attachées est celle de l'homme." Godfrey's *Microcosm* is "une étude de la nature de l'homme."

12. ODYSSEUS, PARZIVAL, AND FAUST

INTRODUCTION

"The trouble with the Germans," Nietzsche once said, "is the way they use the word 'and.'" "Goethe and Schiller" was his target. The harmless connective shrinks oceans of separation to rivulets and levels mountain ranges of contradictions to plains — so Niezsche thought. I suspect that he — and many readers — would see big trouble ahead in my title.

There is a logic that links Odysseus, Parzival, and Faust and justifies the risky use of the great equalizer, "and." That logic is rooted in the mode — both of being and of representing — that antiquity would have called *megethos, megaloprepeia, hypsos* in Greek and *magnificentia, grandiloquentia, sublimitas* in Latin and would be rendered in English as "magnificence," "greatness," "grandeur," or in the context of style, "sublime."[1] A more general claim grounds the connection as well. It is that the exalting mode is far more embracing than its much-studied highpoints in western tradition might suggest. While each of my figures and each term of grandiosity is culturally bound, the mode of thought and representation is not. What Odysseus, Parzival, and Faust share is a mode of depiction that I will call "charismatic." My three characters are charismatic figures in the general acceptance of the word. In the specific sense I want to develop here, the works that brought them to life infuse that quality into the world of the narrative and create a higher world that operates by laws as far above the real and normal as the hero himself is.

This vantage point — a medieval work viewed from the perspective of an ancient and a modern work — allows me to highlight, question, criticize two paradigms deeply embedded in the thinking of medievalists on their subjects generally and on medieval romance in particular. The one is a negative judgment of medieval art, literature, architecture, and culture generally when compared to antiquity and modern. The other is the paradigm of the real vs. the ideal as an approach to romance.

---

1. See "Sublime," *Encyclopedia of Aesthetics*, Michael Kelley, ed. (New York: Oxford University Press, 1998), 4.322–23.

The seed of this essay was an informal reading group on medieval literature at University of Washington a few years ago. At one of the meetings, we read Erich Auerbach's essay, "Camilla, or the Rebirth of the Sublime." Comparing scenes from Virgil's *Aeneid*, the Old French *Roman d'Eneas* (with a glance at Veldeke's *Eneit*), and Dante's *Divine Comedy* (not Camilla but the arrival of the divine messenger in Canto 9 of *Inferno*), Auerbach argues that courtly literature bypassed the sublime style, which was reborn in Dante. Dante's reverence for Virgil commended elements of the sublime in the master's style and pointed forward to the reverence of classical antiquity among the early humanists and ultimately to the Renaissance.[2] Auerbach is at pains to rescue the medieval narratives by stressing the charm of their style, the middle, not the high or grand style. But the condescension is unmistakeable,[3] and Auerbach's reluctance to entertain the question, "which passages are more impressive, Virgil's, the Old French poet's, or Dante's?" does not matter. The answer is clear: "ancient sublimity" was not available to courtly literature.

At that session of the reading group a guest from Germany, Andreas Krass objected to Auerbach's framing of the topic. It makes the high courtly tradition appear as a dwarf between two giants. My question to him: "Well, isn't it? Isn't that a reasonable description of courtly literature in comparison with ancient and Renaissance?" This essay is, on its margins and in its subtext, a fumbling attempt to answer my own question.

There is a level at which a "rescue" attempt of the Middle Ages vis à vis antiquity can only be puerile — perhaps the first level that occurs to the reader. Who would want to engage in comparisons of Aristotle and Thomas Aquinas or classical Greek and high Gothic sculpture? Not I, if it happens at the level of "My age is just as good as yours." But I do object to the uncritical view of the Middle Ages as a dwarf between two giants. There is a casual acceptance of a dwarfish Middle Ages, a tendency of its students to build miniaturizing views

---

2. Erich Auerbach, "Camilla, or, The Rebirth of the Sublime," in his *Literary Language and its Public in Late Latin Antiquity and in the Middle Ages*, Ralph Mannheim, trans. (New York: Pantheon, 1965), 181–233.

3. "Camilla," 216–17.

CHAPTER 12 ✶ ODYSSEUS, PARZIVAL, AND FAUST

of the period into historical judgments, and that uncritical posture distorts. It is a default setting of judgement, at work at a level below consciousness — like embedded commands in software — that tends to weigh diminishing more heavily than aggrandizing views of any given phenomenon of the period.[4] It hardly matters how gross the diminution or how faint the aggrandizing. When looking at the Middle Ages from the view of the ancient world or the Renaissance, condescension to medieval literature is practically good form.

That attitude has strong representatives: Erich Auerbach, Ernst Robert Curtius, and Johan Huizinga.[5] Medieval literature emerges from the great study by Curtius a borrower, its plumage plucked from other, bigger, and brighter birds. Huizinga's *Waning of the Middle Ages* puts forward, vehemently at times, the view of medieval people as juvenile, silly, self-deceiving, living in overwrought illusions closer to children's fairy tales than to epic grandeur. *Waning*, great book though it is, is paternalistic and condescending to the period it studies. It has shaped a paradigm for conceiving aristocratic culture in the Middle Ages down to the present. Reality was crass and brutal, the sensibilities iron. It follows that the gentle, sublime vision of noble knights, obediently serving beloved women and trembling at their displeasure, must have been a howling lie, a palliative, a drug to numb the awareness of the truly "medieval" conditions of real life — or worse, a cover-up, masking its gross brutality as sublime humanity.

I believe that this view is as mistaken as the romantic fallacy it rejects that reads courtly literature as a representation of feudal realities.[6]

---

4. Two earlier studies aim at showing the social reality of phenomena widely held to be the product of overwrought idealizing, courtliness and love. See Jaeger, *Origins* and *Ennobling Love*.

5. See Bibliography.

6. For the ways courtly and chivalric ideals penetrated beyond the surface of noble life, shaped values, tastes and social practices, and motivated behavior, see Maurice Keen, *Chivalry* (New Haven, CT: Yale University Press, 1984); Elspeth Kennedy, "The Knight as Reader of Arthurian Romance," in *Culture and the King: The Social Implications of the Arthurian Legend. Essays in Honor of Valerie Lagorio* (Albany, NY: SUNY Press, 1994), 70–90; Malcolm Vale, *The Princely Court: Medieval Courts and Culture in North-West Europe, 1270–1380* (Oxford: Oxford University Press, 2001); Richard F. Kaeuper, *Chivalry and Violence in Medieval*

It is troublesome that the courtly romance, which has probably had a longer and greater success in transmitting an extravagantly idealistic set of values, can be debunked and stripped of that status by several generations of scholars — the best of their generations among them. Essentially, medievalists tend to share the popular view, however differently nuanced, of their period as brutish and small, its hygiene wretched, its living conditions primitive. No one points out this sort of thing for ancient Greece and Rome, at least not by way of diminishing its art. It is possible to threaten people (in the U.S. anyway) by saying, "I'm gonna get medieval on you!" But no threat at all radiates from "I'm gonna get Homeric on you!" There is a kind of medievalist self-contempt at work here. That variant of a term in use in sociology and ethnic studies seems to me not inappropriate. It describes a minority's acceptance of the discrediting prejudices thrust on them by the dominant social groups.[7]

A factor that supports medievalist self-contempt, subtly, not intentionally, is the representation of the human form in medieval book illumination. Book illumination remains the most popular means for scholars and publishers to make the Middle Ages visible to a broader public. As a decorative art, it is hardly surpassable for richness, but its representation of the human figure is schematizing, cartoonish, and reductive. Figures from illuminated manuscripts are virtually ubiquitous to supply the visual appetite with images of "medieval man," what we might call "visual" or "imagined anthropology."

THE MINIATURIZED MIDDLE AGES

The translation of the letters of Abelard and Heloise by Betty Radice in the Penguin Classics series is one of the most widely read Latin works from the Middle Ages.[8] The cover features "portraits"

Europe (Oxford: Oxford University Press, 1999); Mark Girouard, *The Return to Camelot: Chivalry and the English Gentleman* (New Haven, CT: Yale University Press, 1981); and Aurell, *Lettered Knight*. These seem welcome correctives to a debunking posture riding too high.

7. See Sander L. Gilman, *Jewish Self-Hatred: Anti-Semitism and the Hidden Language of the Jews* (Baltimore, MD: The Johns Hopkins University Press, 1986).

8. *Letters of Abelard and Heloise*, Radice trans.

CHAPTER 12 ✱ ODYSSEUS, PARZIVAL, AND FAUST

of the two lovers from the fourteenth-century Chantilly manuscript — one of the few visual representations of the couple available from the Middle Ages, thus the standard aid to the imagination of specialist and general reading public alike. We see two puppet-like, gesticulating munchkins, wide-eyed, their individuality submerged in a design style and in the coded representations of class, their eloquence reduced to stylized hand signals. We need only open the book to see the incongruence between the emotional power of the letters of Heloise and the homuncula representing her on the cover.

The comparison of ancient, medieval, and Renaissance art makes the Middle Ages a period of curiosities and charming miniatures, the childhood of the West, indeed a "middle" age, strung like a rickety bridge between two tall mountains, an age when Christianity gave all the glory to God and left none for humans. Even that form of medieval art that does glorify the human figure, high Gothic sculpture, plays no part in imagined anthropology. The scholarly literature on it derives the plasticity of Gothic sculptural style from classical Roman/Greek sculpture. Curtianism transfers comfortably to that medium. If there is glory to give, then we give it either to God or to antiquity.

The glorification of the human form in Gothic sculpture and the chivalric idealism of courtly literature operate in the charismatic mode. If that mode is our point of comparison, it helps us to see a stature in medieval art and literature not visible in the dwarf-between-two-giants model. I would suggest that the programmatic and automatic diminution of the Middle Ages in the minds of scholars creates an important task for critical scholarship. The task is to restore medieval conceptions and representations to the size in which they appeared to their own age and so rescue them from artificial miniaturization. The assumption, which makes this enterprise coherent, is that each period had its own charismatic mode and its own aggrandizing representation. They are quite different in many ways but similar and comparable in others. Understanding how charismatic effects are achieved by literature gives us a ground for comparison. I will approach Odysseus, Parzival, and Faust via four points: charismatic representation, the fantastic, the structural element of "the hero rising," and defiance of the gods.

CHARISMATIC REPRESENTATION

I am not talking about themes and ideas. I want to look at a level of the text I will call its "dynamics." Dynamics in literature, as in music, involve change, tensions of various sorts, kinetics and might best be regarded as crescendo and diminuendo in character, mood, or tone. In literature as in music, dynamics register in their emotional impact on the reader or listener. Dynamics are accordingly very different from "meaning," more elemental, more bound to the emotions and emotional responses — again, as in music. Dynamics are one factor that draws the reader into the work, stimulates identification, participation, and imitation. The dynamics of a work of art or literature operate when exemplary figures charged with charismatic force exercise a magnetism, a gravitational pull on the mind and imagination of the reader — the urge to be like the hero, to live in the hero's world, to act like he or she acts. They operate when the reader's mind and imagination are captivated by the values the model embodies and makes them the reader's own. Although that formulation suggests conscious choice, it is more accurate to say that the reader is absorbed into the world and the values of the model. The dynamics of exemplarity, imprinting, and the psychology of the diminished boundary between reality and illusion are far more important to ordinary readers than something as intellectually highfalutin as "meaning." Meaning generates understanding; the dynamics of a work produce transformation.

The basic impulse of charismatic art is to create a world greater and grander than the one the reader or viewer lives in, a world of sublime emotions, heroic motives and deeds, godlike bodies and actions, and superhuman talents — a world of wonders, miracles, and magic — in order to dazzle and astonish the humbled viewer. That astonishment overwhelms the narrow rationalism that sees in the work of art only illusion, not higher or heightened reality. The artwork exerts a force on the viewer and reader parallel to the force of a charismatic personality in life. As the charismatic person can cast a spell over us, so also the work of art. That spell diminishes the viewer's will and the critical sense that insists on the barrier between art and life.

CHAPTER 12 ✶ ODYSSEUS, PARZIVAL, AND FAUST

The ability of charismatic art to captivate constitutes its "educating force."[9] It offers an education in human qualities: the superhuman, supernatural qualities of the hero come to life (however briefly) in the reader by a transformative miracle, and readers live the heroic life vicariously. Charismatic art is functioning when it makes the reader want to live in the higher world it depicts, to think and behave according to its laws.

The higher the epic world is elevated above reality, the stronger the magnetism that draws the reader upwards out of the everyday into the ideal pattern. Mimesis (understood as verisimilitude) and realism work very differently on the reader. Those modes ordinarily tend to alienate and distance the reader rather than captivate and enthrall. The process of elevating the reader by absorption into the epic world is better understood by students of classical literature than by medievalists. Here is Werner Jaeger's eloquent description of this thrust of Homeric epic:

> The epic with its exalting, ennobling and transfiguring power, affects more than the use of epithets: the same nobility appears in the epic descriptions and portraits. Everything low, contemptible, and ugly is banished from the world of the epic. The ancients themselves observed how Homer transports everything, even ordinary objects and common events, to a higher plane.[10]

The ancients also understood the educating force of a literature of exaggerated idealism. Werner Jaeger goes on to claim that criticism is a rarity, because its implied pessimism is "directly opposed to the educational principles of the old aristocracy and its cult of great examples represented by Homer...." Homer does in an epic mode what poems of praise do in a lyrical or choric mode. "Exaltation" and "ennobling" are the main activities in nurturing a "cult of great examples," because it charges the exalted hero with imitability, and that accounts for its "transfiguring" and "transporting" force.

---

9. See C. Stephen Jaeger, "Bookburning at Don Quixote's: Thoughts on the Educating Force of Courtly Romance," in *Courtly Arts and the Art of Courtliness*, Keith Busby and Christopher Kleinhenz, ed. (Cambridge: D.S. Brewer, 2006), 3–28.
10. *Paideia*, 1:42.

The greatness of characters and grandness of narrative worlds are inseparable from charismatic literature generally. The exalted hero rising to glory in an enchanted world took the reader along with him. Longinus (or the author of the first-century treatise *On the Sublime*) chided an earlier writer for not explaining how the sublime style "develops our natures to some degree of grandeur."[11] That dynamic is not at all limited to ancient writings or any age of the aristocracy. In a longer study[12] I quote witnesses to this sense of aggrandizement that comes to the reader through charismatic figures both real and fictional. Heightening, enlarging, elevating, magnifying become part of the vocabulary of charismatic effects. Hans-Georg Gadamer provided a marvelously compact German term for the effect: "*Zuwachs an Sein*," something like "growth in being," "increase of being."[13]

This link formed between model and imitator by the enthralling and captivating force of the model is a fundamental element of human psychology and anthropology, observable still in rock concerts, political rallies, religious revival meetings, churches, and occasionally high school and university classrooms. We imitate people we admire; we want to participate in the kind of life they lead. Fictional characters exert that influence perhaps more powerfully than real ones.[14]

An educating effect, in the sense just defined but also in the conventional usage of the word, is one of the qualities my three characters possess in common. They exerted a powerful shaping force on readers, in fact helped fashion in each of the three cases a sense of national identity. Homer became known as the "educator of Greece." Wolfram's *Parzival* is regularly referred to as the first "Bildungsroman." Goethe's *Faust* profoundly influenced the formation of a German national character, in its heights and depths.

11. Longinus, *On the Sublime* 1; Fyfe and Russell trans., 160–61.

12. *Enchantment*.

13. *Die Aktualität des Schönen* (Stuttgart: Reclam, 1977); English translation as *The Relevance of the Beautiful and Other Essays*, Nicholas Walker, trans. (Cambridge: Cambridge University Press, 1986).

14. See Bryan R. Warnick, *Imitation and Education: A Philosophical Inquiry into Learning by Example* (Albany: SUNY Press, 2008).

CHAPTER 12 ★ ODYSSEUS, PARZIVAL, AND FAUST

In the nineteenth century both Parzival and Faust were regularly invoked in the mythmaking of German nationalism looking to give definition to a German identity. It is no coincidence that Richard Wagner's youthful ambition to write a Faust opera was fulfilled in his *Parsifal*.

Medieval romance in general exerted a charismatic influence on readers that sets it apart from and above virtually any other narrative form in the West. That effect is evident in the imitation of the Arthurian world in court ceremony, tournaments, in the adaptations of chivalric ideals borrowed from romance by manuals of chivalry, in the founding of chivalric orders, in the vogue of chivalry in the late Middle Ages and early modern period and in the nineteenth and twentieth centuries.[15]

THE FANTASTIC

The fantastic has a vital role in charismatic literature. More than perhaps any other element, it lures the reader into participation and imitation. If the "presence" in the work of art is not greater than that of the reader, if the fictional world is not more magical, mysterious, and miraculous than the experienced world, then the charismatic effect is absent. A fantasy world and a charmed destiny exercise a high degree of fascination and enchantment. The critical sense is lulled to sleep. We shed it gladly as if we were entering a happy dream. The reality principle is just a nuisance. We embrace fantasy to silence its cavilling, complaining, and reproaching voice.

In all three of the works discussed here, the fantastic has free reign. Plausibility may be stretched like taffy and never break. At the beginning of *Faust 2*, Act 2, Mephisto shakes out Faust's old fur coat. A passel of bugs, beetles, lice, and grasshoppers come flying out and sing a welcoming chorus, in excellent German, singing of their sadness at the long absence of their master and of the time given them to settle into his coat. It would be juvenile nonsense if we hadn't already entered an agreement with the imagined world to suspend skepticism. Faust wants access to the mysteries of nature and gets it (and ultimately stiffs the provider with whom he's contracted for it). That is precisely the enchantment of *Faust 2*, that it seems to remove the veil that separates us from nature. Nature speaks our language,

15. See above, 276–77.

and so we ride for free through a world to which the entry fee was the main character's soul. We hear nature and its creatures speak in many forms. Why not singing insects? In Homer gods, spirits, and enchanted objects are present in every critical moment to help and hinder. In Wolfram's *Parzival* the hero's destiny is guided through dangers towards the kingship of a mysterious castle devoted to a mysterious object (the Grail) to a pre-determined resolution that combines repentance, transformation, and redemption.

Homer and Wolfram von Eschenbach both faced the charge of being fantasy-mongering liars. Homer virtually asked for it. His hero is a great liar. Whopping fabrications help protect him — as part of a disguise — and they help construct charisma. The exaggeratedly fantastic parts of the *Odyssey* are part of the hero's own first-person narrative, as open to doubt as the tall tales he tells on his arrival in Ithaca. Homer took no pains, or few, to ward off the reproach. He has King Alcinous validate the truth of Odysseus' stories:

> "Odysseus, we are far from regarding you as one of those imposters and cheats whom this dark world brings forth in such profusion to spin their lying yarns which nobody can test."[16]

The fantastic parts of Odysseus' narration are confirmed in their truth elsewhere in the story (e.g., his crew members refer to the fabulous adventures) but only casually and without highlight. Homer clearly did not particularly fear the accusation of lying. He no doubt knew the value of hooking the audience into the fantastic: if the lie is great enough, it silences criticism or even turns it into praise. Some lines of Pindar, a great admirer, softly hurl the reproach of lying at Homer:

> ...*I think the tale*
> *of Odysseus is greater than his deeds, all through the grace of Homer.*
> *Upon his lies and the winged intelligence*
> *there is a kind of majesty; genius persuasive in speech deceives us; blind*
> *Is the heart in the multitude.*[17]

---

16. 11:362–69. In Homer, *The Odyssey*, Emile V. Rieu, trans. (Baltimore, MD: Penguin, 1964), 181.

17. Nemea 7, *The Odes of Pindar*, Richmond Lattimore, trans. (Chicago: University of Chicago Press, 1947), 114–15.

CHAPTER 12 ✶ ODYSSEUS, PARZIVAL, AND FAUST

Pindar's gratitude for Homer's lies is barely concealed. Behind the harshness of the last line is the plea, if these are lies, don't stop.

The magical charge on the world is at work in even more extravagant forms in courtly romance. The concocting of wonders and marvels is part-and-parcel of the romance-making imagination. The accusation that romances are full of lies accompanies that form from Geoffrey of Monmouth to *Amadis of Gaul*. Wolfram's contemporary rival, Gottfried von Strassburg, called him an "inventor of wild tales, one of those who can dupe dullards and children into thinking they can turn base matter to gold."[18] The didactic poet Thomasin von Zirclaere (c.1215) attacked romances in general with as much ambiguity in his attitude as Pindar: the romances are a pack of lies, but the lies contain truth, though it's clothed in falsehoods. They are good for educating children and the unlearned.[19] Again, lies ward off discrediting by their positive value. Romantic falsehoods are good for educating the young and unlearned laity, and that includes presumably most of the knightly class.

In the *Odyssey* and *Parzival*, the fantastic happens to be real. That is, the narrative never suggests that the fantastic elements are illusions that will fade. In *Parzival* the Holy Grail is built into the Christian cosmos as a kind of para-orthodox means to salvation. The hero's response to its wonders becomes part of the theme of his development, one that strongly validates the fantastic elements. Something like the rejection of the sceptical position (it's all lies) is thematized in Parzival's first visit to the Grail castle. As the spectacle of the Grail ceremony unrolls before his eyes, the young hero sits like a stump and watches, stifling wonder in favor of good manners. He sees the silver knives that miraculously cut steel ("made marvelous," or "made for astonishment" — *ze wunder gemachet*). He sees the young squire run through the hall carrying a bleeding lance. He sees the Grail perform the miracle of serving up whatever food the guest desires. The wonders are genuine, and the real ones conspire with

---

18. Gottfried von Strassburg, *Tristan*, ll. 4665–66; Tomasek ed., 87–88; English translation, *Tristan, with the Surviving Fragments of the "Tristan" of Thomas*, A.T. Hatto, trans. (Harmondsworth: Penguin, 1982), 105.

19. Ll. 1089–90, 1118–62. In *Der Welsche Gast des Thomasin von Zirclaria*, Heinrich Rückert, ed. (Berlin: Walter De Gruyter, 1965), 30, 31–32.

the staged ones in the Grail ceremony to rouse astonishment and shake Parzival loose from his captivity in the ordinary. Instead, he sits there in silence refusing to let the trivial lessons in manners he has learned from his teacher in courtesy, Gurnemanz, be overridden by the miraculous. Parzival "noted well the splendor and the great wonders," Wolfram says, "and yet for courtesy's sake was embarassed to ask."[20]

After he leaves the Grail castle in disgrace, he meets his cousin Sigune, who hears of his failure and exclaims:

> You saw such great wonders, and yet you failed to ask?!... You saw the cutting silver and the bloody spear? What do you want with me, disgraced and cursed man!"[21]

And so, his moral failing consists of equal parts lack of compassion and insensitivity to the marvelous. The salvation of a king and his realm, and his own salvation, depends in the critical moment on the hero's ability to be provoked to pity and wondering astonishment — and it doesn't happen. He sacrifices humanity — and imagination — to decorum.

But the scene doesn't only reproach Parzival for captivity in the mundane. It also models an affirming reader's response to marvels. Lest the point go past the reader, Wolfram conjures a fictive listener, some anonymous representative of skepticism in his audience, only to put him down:

> "There's no such thing [as a food-providing Grail]," many a one will claim. There's malice in that answer. The Grail was the fruit of salvation, nearly the equivalent of the kingdom of heaven."[22]

That sort of affirmation and modelling of the reader's response happens on a much grander and more dramatic scale in *Faust* 2. A big difference in *Faust* is that the fantastic elements are recognized as fantasy and illusion — and nonetheless powerfully affirmed, in fact played out positively against an empirical mindset that rejects them

---

20. Wolfram von Eschenbach, *Parzival*, 239.8–10; Karl Lachmann, ed.; Eberhard Nellmann, rev. & comm.; Dieter Kühn, trans. (Frankfurt-am-Main: Deutscher Klassiker, 1994), 398.

21. Wolfram von Eschenbach, *Parzival*, 255.5–6.

22. Wolfram von Eschenbach, *Parzival*, 238.18.

as nonsense. Goethe makes rationalism that scoffs at fantasy into an object of scorn. The court of the emperor watches the phantom of Helen of Troy in the first act with reactions that range from cynicism to amazement. But one old scholar averts his eyes because

> "her presence seduces us to extravagance. I'll rely on books. There it says, she pleased all the greybeards of Greece. It fits perfectly. I'm not so young, and still she pleases me."[23]

The pedant doesn't deny the reality of the phantom. He just wants to authenticate it by the means in which he places his faith. The reproach of lying, directed at the fantastic, has shriveled to pettifogging source-citing and consulting the relevant secondary literature on the subject, even though the primary prodigy/fantasy-in-itself is available. In this way the author justifies the fantastic against narrow rationalism. The acceptance, not the rejection, of fantasy, is faustian. In *Faust 1*, the world appears natural. There are no (or few) mysteries on its surface, as there are in the *Odyssey* or any courtly romance. They are present in the world of Faust nonetheless — mysteries, phantoms, and fantasies as extravagant as anything romance has to offer. But ordinary mortals have no access to them, and that includes highly learned ones like Faust himself. The museum character, the crypt-like, life-deprived atmosphere of Faust's study in the opening scene of *Faust 1* is the very image of a desiccated world of pure rationality, where human beings shrivel to scraps of curled paper. All the books, papers, experimental apparatus, the bric-a-brac of conventional learning, far from revealing nature, have closed down access to her secrets. Faust quotes some wise man:

> "The way to the spirit world is open. It's your mind that is closed; your heart that is dead.... Mysterious in the full light of day, Nature holds its veil tight. No levers and wrenches will force out what it doesn't reveal."[24]

It was fully accessible in the world of *The Odyssey*. Access in courtly romance was restricted to those who could enter the realm of adventure. The price of admission has gone sky high in *Faust*. He pawns his soul to get beyond confinement in the Immanent.

---

23. *Faust 2*, 1.6533–34. Author translations.
24. *Faust 1*, Night, 443–44.

But having sold it, he has full access. The gates are opened, the veil removed.

The earliest parts of the play turn on this breakthrough from a fantasy-deprived reality to a spirit-haunted world full of life and danger. But the real triumph of the fantastic is reserved for the central moments of *Faust 2*, Acts 2 and 3, which are an allegory of fantasy gripping the observer, pulling in and seducing the reader, the enchantment by the illusion, ending in the fading of the illusion. Faust's pursuit of Helen of Troy assimilates the quest motif to an allegory of the workings of the imagination. The urge to accomplish the impossible, to make fantasms real, is affirmed repeatedly, once in Act 2, in Faust's conversation with the centaur Chiron, who transports him on his back to the entrance of the underworld. Chiron is a hard-headed realist and ancient tutor of heroes. He is bored with Faust's quest for a phantom woman, thinks he must be sick. Faust objects. The accomplishment of conquering a resisting woman is greatest when reality opposes it. Anyone can love when circumstances cooperate, he implies.

"And should I not draw this peerless body [Helen] into life by the force of powerful longing?... Now my imagination [*mein Sinn*] and my whole being are captivated."[25]

Chiron suggests medicine for his insanity and deposits him with the Sybil Manto, doctor and prophetess.

Faust: "I don't want to be cured. My imagination is charged. Cure me and I'd be as vulgar as all the rest."

Manto [siding with Faust]: "I love anyone who desires the impossible."[26]

She sends him off to the underworld with the admonition not to bungle it as did Orpheus, whose quest of the impossible she had also favored. Faust's success with Helen is stunning. It certainly outdoes that of Orpheus, even if in the end the illusion fades and the phantom Helen of Troy returns to her own realm (like the shade of Eurydice) and Faust is left holding only her dress and her veil.

25. Act 2, Klassische Walpurgisnacht: Am unteren Peneios, ll. 7438–44. In *Goethe, Faust: Der Tragödie erster und zweiter Teil*, Erich Trunz, ed., (Munich: Beck, 1998), 227.

26. Act 2, ll. 7459–60, 7488; Trunz ed., 227–28.

CHAPTER 12 ★ ODYSSEUS, PARZIVAL, AND FAUST

Manto, who loves seekers of the impossible, is the spirit of an alliance between fantasy and the quest. It is worthwhile reflecting on the logic of that alliance. Questing heroes need fantasy landscapes. No one quests for the everyday. If Odysseus, Hercules, or Parzival lived in a world without gods, monsters, and enchantments, they would be Don Quixotes or Leopold Blooms. The union of quest and fantasy is an important element of the dynamics of romance and adventure. The distance that separates the quest from stasis, high ambitions from low, the unattainable from the attainable, is one of those factors that generates magnetism, pulls the reader into that forcefield. The formula for the highest level of charismatic charge in the world of the questing hero is to take the unknown, add the mysterious, and combine it with the impossible.

STRUCTURE: THE HERO RISING

The Odyssey, *Parzival*, and *Faust* share a plot structure with a common underlying dynamic. That structure is another element, along with exaltation and fantasy, drawing the reader into the hero's destiny. Odysseus rising is the prime example. His first appearance in the *Odyssey* is in book 5: he washes up on a beach in the land of the Phaecians, naked, scum-crusted, and half alive, looking more like some primeval sea-creature crept from the deep to die, than a king, sacker of cities, and hero of the Trojan War. The princess Nausicaa and her attendants discover him and are appropriately terrified. Yet after a few cunning speeches and Athena's magical sprucing up, he is so transformed that the princess can say,

> "When we first met, I thought him repulsive, but now he looks like the gods who live in heaven. I wish I could have a man like him for my husband."[27]

In short order he rises from monstrous to magnificent.

The same dynamic is at work in his arrival at the palace of King Alcinous and Queen Areté in book 6. Athena smuggles him into the palace of the Phaecian king. He seats himself like a beggar in the ashes of the fire. But King Alcinous calls him to a place of honor not because of any sense of who he is but just because of the obligation of guest-friendship. Odysseus is escorted to a polished silver chair.

---

27. *Odyssey* 6.229–45, Rieu trans., 108.

Called upon to tell his story, he tells of his stay with Calypso and his release, he lets slip that the goddess so desired him that she offered him immortality and eternal youth — and he turned them down. He establishes that gods vie for and against him. Alcinous is so impressed as to say to the still anonymous guest,

> "I wish that a man like you, like-minded with myself, could have my daughter and remain here as my son-in-law. I would give you a house and riches."[28]

So, he has risen literally from the ash heap to potential wealth and stature, made himself a candidate for heir to the throne. That's only the start. They still don't even know who he is. At the banquet the next evening Odysseus reveals his identity (9.16–17.) and tells the fabulous stories of his adventures on his travels — Cyclops, the Sirens, the visit to the land of the dead. When he finishes, his audience sits in stunned silence, "held by the spell of his words" (11.333). Queen Areté breaks the silence with a speech that voices the beguiled admiration that all feel: "Phaeacians, what do you think of this man, his looks, his presence, and the quality of his mind?" (11.336–37). An odd summation: Odysseus talks fantastic adventures, and the queen praises his appearance! The object and the response are out of joint:

> Odysseus: "I overcame the Cyclops and Circe and traveled to hell."
>
> Areté: "What a body, what looks, what a mind!"[29]

The phrase *eidos te megethos* is one of the formulae for charismatic presence in the *Odyssey*, applied elsewhere only to gods and goddesses. It implies radiance, godlike qualities. (Cf. 5.217 and 6.152). *Eidos* and *megethos* both indicate the shape and overall appearance but imply beauty. E.V. Rieu comes close to the variegated meaning: "his looks, his presence, and the quality of his mind." Alongside his individual excellences — his godlikeness, his long-suffering, his cunning and machinations — there is some big thing that is not exhausted by a listing of his qualities and his deeds. It is whatever Queen Areté sees when, having heard his story, she calls on the Phaeacians to admire his body, his presence, his mind. It is a composite quality we might

---

28. *Odyssey* 7.312–14; Rieu trans., 120.
29. Author paraphrase.

CHAPTER 12 * ODYSSEUS, PARZIVAL, AND FAUST

call aura. He *is* what he tells. Adventures overcome appear somehow written on his surface, as though tattooed there or transmuted into stature and beauty. Books 5–12 of the *Odyssey* are built on the rising curve of honor along which Odysseus moves from the ashes to a stature above other mortals.

The same dynamic is at work when he changes from the limping old man to the greatest discus thrower in Scheria in the athletic games of the Phaecians (8.14–15); and repeatedly when he changes from grimy beggar to Odysseus on his return to Ithaca. Telemachus in book 16 virtually repeats the words of Nausicaa: "Only a moment ago you were an old man in shabby clothes. Now you look like one of the gods who live in the wide heavens" (16.198). The overarching intention of books 5–12 is to create the drama of the emergence of Odysseus from nothing, from naked, natural man, from "the thing itself" to a man endowed with every feature of honor and distinction, making gradually visible the stature that is his. It is not adventure that these books are primarily about. Adventure and combat are present but subordinated to the theme of the obscure piece of flotsam who rises to the stature of the fabulous man. We can call this dynamic, "enter abject — emerge exalted." Notice that it is the opposite of the structure of Sophocles' King Oedipus, who enters exalted and exits wretched. Alongside the well-known narrative structure, the fall of the great, *casus virorum illustrium*, is the less observed "rise to glory of the insignificant-seeming." Both are techniques of charismatic representation. In both, the main character is pumped full of the qualities most valued by the audience: wisdom, cunning, courage, luck. The hero's failure in the tragedy and success in the epic both affirm in different ways that set of values. That affirmation maximizes the participation of the reader and facilitates an uncritical identification, though the effects of tragedy on the viewer clearly caution rather than inspire the audience.[30]

The comparison with Wolfram's *Parzival* and more generally with the narrative structure at work in Chrétien de Troyes' major romances, which the Germans call *"doppelter Kursus,"* shows the

---

30. This is a big subject to broach in passing, but since it is not germane to my main point, I refer the reader to the tour de force of a study by Terry Eagleton, *Sweet Violence: The Idea of the Tragic* (Oxford: Blackwell, 2003).

dynamic of the hero's rise common to charismatic narrative. In the Parzival romance even more than in Homer, the author maximizes the distance and heightens the tension that separates the hero at his debut from his final exaltation. Parzival rises from bumbling fool to Grail king. But the romance does something Homer does not: it joins tragic fall to heroic exaltation. The knight sets out on a first course, a first quest, and fails miserably, tragically, then works his way back up the scale of honor to succeed brilliantly and enter into a grand destiny, which in any case was preordained.

Faust also calls on the dynamic of "rise" and operates on a double course that begins with tragedy and ends with triumph. The Faust of the opening scenes is an old man, wearied by the pedantries of a life of shallow learning, trapped in culture and striving for nature, experience, and knowledge not available in books and university courses. The pact with the devil gets him youth and freedom. It opens a backdoor to the titanism or semi-divine stature he covets, since the front door was closed by the Earth spirit. It also gets him a love that ends tragically but that in the end facilitates his redemption after the adventures of the second part of the drama.

DEFYING THE GODS

Charismatic art affirms the human condition. It might not be too much to say that is why it exists. Here again, art and literature operate on the same psychology as embodied charisma. In our three works this registers most strongly in the relations of the heroes with the gods or with God. The presence of gods and spirits, the working of the supernatural in human life, creates awe and enchantment. Actions of the gods for or against the hero elevate his role, place him in the same league — if not on the same level — with the gods. This is too obvious to need illustration. There is no human excellence and no significant act in the *Odyssey* that is not either magical, god-given, or both. Hero figures can become great because gods exist. Without them they would be ordinary. Odysseus can maintain his godlike presence, excel, show greatness, and survive because the balance of divine favor allows it. In Hellenic literature and thought, human greatness is inseparable from piety, at least a belief in the gods. Individuals can become like gods (because the gods give them that gift temporarily), and they can actually become gods, as did Hercules.

CHAPTER 12 ★ ODYSSEUS, PARZIVAL, AND FAUST

Now it is one thing to face dangers of the unknown, to do combat with giants and monsters. But vying with gods is adventure of a different order. Odysseus' heroism is heightened both by the favor of Athena and by the hate of Poseidon. But the real exaltation comes from his refusal of immortality. Calypso offers it directly: he will have eternal youth if he will stay with her. The invitations of Circe and Alcinous are comparable, though lower on the scale of value. But he turns them down and instead heads on into suffering to regain his comparatively modest position as island king, husband, and father and to remain a mortal man. If a thing's value is in proportion to the sacrifice it takes to keep it, then Odysseus' sacrifice of immortality highlights dramatically the value of humanity. That act of renunciation had to seem greater to a Greek aristocracy that Werner Jaeger could describe as "god-intoxicated" than its casual treatment in the *Odyssey* seems to indicate. That is the most powerful affirmation of the human condition in Homer's work: that a hero courted by divinity prefers humanity.

The insistence on the human condition rises to defiance of God in Wolfram's *Parzival*. After Parzival is denounced and disgraced at King Arthur's court for his early foolishness and failure at the Grail castle, he wanders for four years in a state that he himself calls "hate of God" (*goteshaz*). God has treated him badly, he thinks, because he allowed him to lose all honor, whereas Parzival had served him loyally, Parzival claims, deludedly. God has violated his feudal obligations — the master supports the loyal vassal — so Parzival's thinking. On Good Friday of the fourth year, he meets a penitent knight who chides him for wearing armour on a sacred day and reminds him of God. Then Parzival realizes the depth of misery to which he has sunk, recalls how powerful God is, and remorse wells up in his heart. It is like a conversion. He asks himself,

> "What if God can give help that could overcome my sadness. But if he ever loved knights, if any knight ever earned his keep from God, or if shield and sword and true manly combat can be worthy of his help, so that his help could dispel my gloom, if today is his day for helping, then let him help, if help he can!"
> [9.451, ll. 13–22]

It is one of the high points of the romance. But it is clear also that at the moment of *metanoia*, when his alienation from God is overcome, he is far from surrendering his will and his ego. On the contrary, Parzival dictates terms to God. Those conditions are: if knighthood and combat are worthy in the eyes of God, then he is God's man again. Then he will accept God's help. The clear implication is, otherwise forget it. His speech to God is one part remorse and three parts challenge. It says — and I am paraphrasing broadly but very much in the sense of Parzival's retort to God:

> "I am a knight and nothing else. I do not give up my weapons and armor; I do not perform suicidal penances [like Hartmann von Aue's Gregorius in similar straits], I do not go mad [like Chrétien's Yvain]. I am what I am. Take me, take a soldier. If that is good enough for God, then let him help. If not, then I'll be damned on my own terms."[31]

The hermit Trevrizent validates this challenge to God by initially misunderstanding it. He tells Parzival in the Good Friday scene, his catechizing of Parzival, that anger against God is senseless. Parzival can get nothing from God by defiance, says the wise old man. But the end of the romance proves the wise man wrong. Parzival meets Trevrizent again when he is called to be Grail king, and his teacher admits that he was wrong on that point:

> "Hardly ever has a greater marvel come to pass.... You have forced God's eternal trinity by anger to grant your will."[32]

This arrangement between God and Parzival is not in Wolfram's source, Chrétien de Troyes. Chretien's Perceval is seized by remorse and does penance on Good Friday. That is, the conventional sacraments are adequate for his salvation. Wolfram's Parzival, on the contrary, sets conditions. In effect, he puts his redemption and his calling as Grail king on the line to force God's recognition of the dignity of knighthood — and God relents. So in the end Parzival has it all: worldly honor, God's grace, wife, and family. He is Grail king and close friend of Arthur and his court. Loyalty to his knightly calling and to his wife have gained a sacramental, redemptive force, and the conventional means of redemption fade far into the background.

31. *Parzival* 9.451.13–22. In Wolfram von Eschenbach, *Parzival*, Eberhard Nellmann, ed.; Dieter Kühn, trans. (Frankfurt-am-Main: Deutscher Klassiker, 1994), 1:748.

32. *Parzival*, 16.798.2–5; Nellmann ed., 2:360.

Parzival's insistence on knighthood is a parallel to Odysseus' commitment to mortality. Odysseus gives up more; Parzival risks more and gains more. Wolfram's vision is more extravagant than Homer's since Odysseus, in renouncing immortality, also does not get it. Parzival risks everything and gains it all back. In both cases human obligations override reverence for God or the gods and the ambition to be like them.

The idea of human divinity based on skill, talent, excellence, apart from grace loomed in the eleventh and twelfth centuries, loomed large in the fifteenth and sixteenth. It is a humanistic idea. It played a major role in Goethe's *Faust*. Faust's pretensions to divinity — his frustrated efforts to attain to god-like understanding — add to his growing despair in the opening scenes. Faust senses his godlike-ness, but the limits on his penetration of nature refute the intimation. He tries everything in the opening scenes to maintain his titanic self-conception. He conjures spirits to prove that he is their equal. Failing that, he finds the alternate route in suicide, a way to prove that "human dignity does not shrink from the height of gods" (712–13). But the final insight of the scenes leading up to the devil's pact is that escape from the human and flight to the other world are not what will satisfy Faust. That rather is life, of which his stifling intellectual world has robbed him. The heights are closed to him, but the depths are a backdoor to divinity. If divinity is available to Goethe's titans, then only through the world, with the devil leading the way. That means the rejection of God.

I promised earlier not themes, ideas, and meaning, just charisma-making and dynamics. I seem to have come perilously close to the ideas in Faust. But it only seems that way. My point is that the aura of the hero is increased by a defiance of God that forces God's capitulation. That defiance makes Faust a titan. The idea that the deepest sin and rejection of God is a way to redemption works to affirm the human. It is the dynamic that creates the magnetism, constructs Faust's charisma.

CONCLUSIONS

In each of the three cases we have a god scorned, challenged, defied. Yet the human protagonist does not forfeit the favor of the gods for it. The dynamic at work here is rising above or outside of divinity to affirm humanity. Parzival, Gawain, Tristan, and Lancelot become comparable to Odysseus and Faust on the level of charismatic representation. The comparison requires that the medievalist rescuing the literature from medievalist self-contempt make large concessions on the score of language and eloquence. With the exception of Gottfried von Strassburg's *Tristan*, medieval romance makes only minor and occasional use of one of the most effective instruments of charismatic representation: the sublime style. But that leaves a lot. The question is not, "How do modern scholars judge their language and style in comparison with Homer and Virgil?" but rather, "How powerfully did works move and inspire readers?" The dynamics of courtly romance were capable of stirring reactions the equivalent of the sublime style through characterization, scene, and action. Romance's influence on chivalric education and on courtly culture is the measure of its impact.

The distance separating the ideal in romance from "the real" in the society of the twelfth and thirteenth centuries is an essential element of the dynamics of romance, probably also of the *Odyssey* and *Faust*. What an odd idea: that any literary work becomes more genuine and truthful the closer it comes to mirroring the reality from which it arose. Suppose it arose to change that reality? Goethe did not begin *Faust* because the world around him seemed Faustian. He wrote it because the world seemed so trivial, unpoetic, convention-bound, so dominated by a sterile rationality as to stifle a faustian self-conception. He wrote *Faust* not to hide the banality of life, but to correct it.

Something like that is probably true of chivalric idealism in general. It arose as an answer to a perceived corruption of the warrior class. That was at least one major influence. Richard F. Kaeuper[33] and others have argued that the founding of French chivalric orders in the fourteenth century, with their extravagant idealism, is a response to crushing French losses in the Hundred Years War, to a loss of self-confidence in the warrior nobility, even to the reproaches of cowardice and failure. I suspect that like the chivalric orders of the fourteenth century, the chivalric romances of the twelfth arose as instruments of reform and education. But whatever the forces that produced them, they exercised that influence from their beginning to the twentieth century.

33. *Chivalry and Violence*.

BIBLIOGRAPHY

PRIMARY SOURCES

Abbo of Fleury (Abbonis Floriacensis). *De Syllogismis Hypotheticis.* Franz Schupp, ed. Leiden: Brill, 1996.

—. *Opera Inedita.* André Van de Vyver, ed. Bruges: De Temple, 1966.

Abelard, Peter. *Carmen ad Astralabium.* Juanita Feros Ruys. ed. and trans. In *The Repentant Abelard: Family, Gender and Ethics in Peter Abelard's Carmen ad Astralabium and Planctus.* New York: Palgrave, 2014.

—. *Dialogus inter Philosophum, Iudaeum et Christianum.* Rudolf Thomas, ed. Stuttgart: Frommann, 1970.

—. *Historia calamitatum: Texte critique avec une introduction.* Jacques Monfrin, ed. Paris: J. Vrin, 1959.

— and Heloise. *The Letter Collection of Peter Abelard and Heloise.* David Luscombe, ed.; Betty Radice, trans. Oxford: Clarendon, 2013.

—. *Letters IX–XIV.* Edmé R. Smits, ed. Groningen: University of Groningen, 1983.

—. *The Letters of Abelard and Heloise.* Betty Radice, trans. with intro. London: Penguin, 2003.

Der Ackermann Frühneuhochdeutsch und Neuhochdeutsch. Christian Kiening, ed. Stuttgart: Reclam, 2000.

Adam of Bremen. *Hamburgische Kirchengeschichte.* Bernhard Schmeidler, ed. MGH, SSR 2. Hannover: Hahn, 1977.

Adelard of Bath. *Conversations with His Nephew: On the Same and the Different, Questions on Natural Science, and On Birds.* Charles Burnett, ed. and trans. Cambridge: Cambridge University Press, 1998.

Die Admonter Briefsammlung nebst ergänzenden Briefen. G. Hool and Peter Classen, ed. MGH, *Briefe der deutschen Kaiserzeit* 6. Munich: MGH, 1983.

Aelred of Rievaulx. *Aelredi Rievallensis Opera Omnia.* Anselm Hoste and Charles H. Talbot, ed. CCCM 1.1. Turnhout: Brepols, 1971.

—. *Lives of S. Ninian and S. Kentigern.* Alexander Forbes, ed. Edinburgh: Edmonston & Douglas, 1874.

—. *Spiritual Friendship.* Mary Eugenia Laker, trans. Kalamazoo, MI: Cistercian Publications, 1977.

Alan of Lille. *Anticlaudianus: Texte critique avec une introduction et des tables.* Robert Bossuat, ed. Paris: J. Vrin, 1955.

—. *Literary Works.* Winthrop Wetherbee, ed and trans. Cambridge, MA: Harvard University Press, 2013.

Alberti, Leon Battista. *On Painting and Sculpture: The Latin Texts of "De pictura" and "De statua."* Cecil Grayson, ed. and trans. London: Phaidon, 1972.

Alcuin of York. *De dialectica.* PL 101:949–68.

—. *De rhetorica et virtutibus.* PL 101:919–46.

Alexander Neckham. *De laude divinae sapientiae.* Thomas Wright, ed. Rolls Series 34. London: Longman, 1863.

Die altere Wormser Briefsammlung. Walther Bulst, ed. MGH, *Die Briefe der deutschen Kaiserzeit* 3. Weimar: Böhlau, 1949.

Ambrose of Milan. *Commentarius in Cantica Canticorum.* PL 15:1851–1962.

—. *De officiis ministrorum.* PL 16:23A–184B.

—. *In Psalmum David CXVIII Expositio.* PL 15:1197–1526.

Amédée de Lausanne. *Huit homélies mariales.* George Bavaud, ed. Paris: Cerf, 1960.

Andreas Capellanus. *Andreas Capellanus on Love.* Patrick G. Walsh, ed. and trans. London: Bloomsbury, 1982.

The Anglo-Latin Satirical Poets and Epigrammatists of the Twelfth Century. Thomas Wright, ed. Rolls Series 59.2. London: Longman, 1872.

Annales Magdeburgenses. George H. Pertz, ed. MGH, SS 16. Hannover: Hahn, 1859, 107–69.

Anselm of Besate. *Rhetorimachia in Gunzo, Epistola ad Augienses und Anselm von Besate, Rhetorimachia.* Karl Manitius, ed. MGH, *Quellen zur Geistesgeschichte des Mittelalters.* Ser. 2. Weimar: Böhlau, 1958.

Anselm of Canterbury. *Opera omnia Anselmi.* 5 vols. Franciscus Schmitt, ed. Edinburgh: Nelson, 1946–52.

Anselm of Havelberg. *Dialogus (Dialogi).* Gaston Salet, ed. Paris: Editions du Cerf, 1966.

Anselm of Liège. *Gesta episcoporum Leodiensium.* Rudolf Köpke, ed. MGH, SS 7. Hannover: Hahn, 1846.

Aquinas, Thomas. *Sancti Thomae Aquinatis in decem libros Ethicorum Aristotelis ad Nicomachum Expositio.* Angelo M. Pirotta and Martin M.S. Gillet, ed. Turin: Marietti, 1934.

Augustine of Hippo. *De civitate Dei.* PL 41:13–806.

—. *De doctrina Christiana.* R.P.H. Green, ed. and trans. Oxford: Oxford University Press, 1995.

Bacon, Roger. *Opus Tertium.* In *Fratris Rogeri Bacon Opera quaedam Hactenus Inedita* 1. John S. Brewer, ed. London: Longman, 1859.

Baudri de Bourgueil. *Baldricus Burgulianus: Poèmes/Carmina*. Jean-Yves Tilliette, ed. Paris: Les Belles Lettres, 2002.

—. *Carmina*. Karlheinz Hilbert, ed. Heidelberg: Winter, 1979.

Bede, the Venerable. *Commentary on Luke*. P. Hurst, ed. CCSL 120. Turnhout: Brepols, 1960.

Benzo of Alba. *Ad Heinricum IV, imperatorem libri VII: Sieben Bücher an Kaiser Heinrich IV*. Hans Seiffert, ed. and trans. MGH, SSR 65. Hannover: Hahn, 1996.

Bern of Reichenau. *Die Briefe des Abtes Bern von Reichenau*. Franz-Josef Schmale, ed. Stuttgart: Kohlhammer, 1961.

—. *Vita S. Udalrici*. PL 142:1183C–1204C.

Bernard of Chartres. *Glosae super Platonem*. Paul E. Dutton, ed. Toronto: Pontifical Institute of Mediaeval Studies, 1991.

Bernard of Clairvaux. *Sancti Bernardi Opera*. Jean Leclercq et al., ed. 8 vols. Rome: Editiones Cistercienses, 1957–77.

Bernard of Utrecht. *Accessus ad auctores: Commentum in Theodolum*. Robert B.C. Huygens, ed. Leiden: Brill, 1970.

—. *Bernard d'Utrecht, Conrad d'Hirsau, Dialogus super auctores*. Robert B.C. Huygens, ed. Leiden: Brill, 1970.

Bernardus Silvestris. *The Commentary on the First Six Books of the Aeneid of Vergil*. Julian W. Jones and Elizabeth F. Jones, ed. Lincoln: University of Nebraska Press, 1977.

—. *Cosmographia*. Peter Dronke, ed. Leiden: Brill, 1978.

—. *Poetic Works*. Winthrop Wetherbee, ed. and trans. Cambridge, MA: Harvard University Press, 2015.

Bernward of Hildesheim. *Vita Bernwardi*. Georg H. Pertz, ed. MGH, SS 4. Hannover: Hahn, 1841, 754–82.

Boethius, Anicius Manlius Severinus. *The Consolation of Philosophy*. Hugh F. Stewart, trans. & rev. Cambridge, MA: Harvard University Press, 1968.

—. *De institutione musica libri quinque*. Gottfried Friedlein, ed. Frankfurt-am-Main: Minerva, 1966.

—. *Fundamentals of Music*. Calvin M. Bower, trans., introd., and comment. New Haven, CT: Yale University Press, 1989.

Boutemy, André. "Trois Oeuvres inédites de Godefroid de Reims." RMAL 3 (1947): 335–66.

—. "Une version médiévale inconnue de la légende d'Orphée." In *Hommages à Joseph Bidez et à Franz Cumont*. Charles H. Josserand, ed. Brussels: Latomus, 1949, 43–70.

Briefsammlungen der Zeit Heinrichs IV. Carl Erdmann and Norbert Fickermann, ed. MGH, *Briefe der deutschen Kaiserzeit* 5. Weimar: Böhlau, 1950.

Calcidius. *On Plato's Timaeus.* John Magee, ed. and trans. Cambridge, MA: Harvard University Press, 2016.

—. *Timaeus a Calcidio translatus commentarioque instructus.* J.H. Waszink, ed. London: Warburg, 1975.

Carmina Burana. Benedikt Vollmann, ed. Frankfurt-am-Main: Suhrkamp, 1987.

Carmina Cantabrigiensia. Walther Bulst, ed. Heidelberg: Winter, 1950.

—. *Cambridge Songs (Carmina Cantabrigiensia).* Jan Ziolkowski, ed. and trans. Cambridge, MA: Harvard University Press, 1994.

Carmina Leodiensia. Walther Bulst, ed. Heidelberger Akademie der Wissenschaften. Philosophisch-Historische Klasse 1. Heidelberg: Winter, 1975.

Castiglione, Baldesar. *The Book of the Courtier.* Charles Singleton, trans. Garden City, NY: Doubleday, 1959.

Chartularium Universitatis Parisiensis 1. Heinrich Denifle, ed. Paris: Delalaine, 1889.

Chrétien de Troyes, *Arthurian Romances,* William W. Comfort, trans. London: Dent, 1975.

—. *Arthurian Romances.* Douglas D.R. Owen, trans. London: Dent, 1993.

—. *Cligès.* Laurence Harf-Lancner ed. Paris: Champion, 2006.

—. *Cligès: Edition critique du manuscrit B.N. fr.* 12560. Charles Mela and Olivier Collet, ed. and trans. Paris: Livres de Poche, 1994.

—. *The Knight with the Lion, or Yvain (Le Chevalier au Lion).* William W. Kibler, ed. and trans. New York: Garland, 1985.

Cicero. *De officiis.* Walter Miller, trans. Cambridge, MA: Harvard University Press, 1975.

—. *Tusculan Disputations* J.E. King, ed. and trans. Cambridge, MA: Harvard University Press, 1971.

Conrad of Hirsau. *Accessus ad auctores.* In *Bernard d'Utrecht, Conrad d'Hirsau, Dialogus super auctores.* Robert B.C. Huygens, ed. Leiden: Brill, 1970.

—. *Dialogus de mundi contemptu vel amore.* Robert Bultot, ed. Louvain: Nauwelaerts, 1966.

Das Corpus Hermeticum Deutsch 1. *Die griechischen Traktate und der lateinische "Asclepius."* Jens Holzhausen, trans. Stuttgart-Bad Cannstatt: Fromann-Holzboog, 1997.

★ BIBLIOGRAPHY

Corpus Iuris Canonici, Editio Lipsiensis secunda. Emil A. Friedberg, ed. Leipzig: Tauchnitz, 1879.
Epistolae: Medieval Womens' Letters. Joan Ferrante, ed. At: https://epistolae.ctl.columbia.edu.
Erasmus of Rotterdam. *Antibarbari. The Antibarbarians*. Craig R. Thompson, ed. Toronto: University of Toronto Press, 1978.
Feiss, Hugo, ed. *On Love: A Selection of Works of Hugh, Adam, Achard, Richard and Godfrey of St. Victor*. Turnhout: Brepols, 2011.
Folcuin of Lobbes. *Folcuini Gesta Abbatum Lobiensium*. Georg Waitz, ed. MGH, SS 4:52–74.
Fowden, Garth, ed. and trans. *The Egyptian Hermes*. Princeton, NJ: Princeton University Press, 1986.
Fulbert of Chartres. *The Letters and Poems of Fulbert of Chartres*. Frederick Behrends, ed. and trans. Oxford: Clarendon, 1976.
Fulcoius of Beauvais. Marvin L. Colker, ed. In "Fulcoii Belvacensis Epistulae." *Traditio* 10 (1954): 191–273.
Geoffrey of Clairvaux. *Vita Prima Sancti Bernardi Claraevallis Abbatis*. Paul Verdeyen, ed. CCCM 89B. Turnhout: Brepols, 2011.
Gerald of Wales. *Instruction for a Ruler: De principis instructione*. Robert F. Bartlett, ed. Oxford: Oxford University Press, 2018.
—. *De principis instructione liber*. George F. Warner, ed. Rolls Series 21.8. London: Eyre & Spottiswoode, 1891.
—. *Itinerarium Kambriae*. In *Giraldi Cambrensis Opera*, J.S. James Dimock, ed. Rolls Series 6. London: Longman, 1861–91.
Gerbert of Rheims. *Die Briefsammlung Gerberts von Reims*. Fritz Weigle, ed. MGH, *Briefe der deutschen Kaiserzeit* 2. Weimar: Böhlau, 1966.
—. *Gerberti Opera Mathematica*. Nicolaus Bubnov, ed. Hildesheim: Olms, 1963.
—. *Oeuvres de Gerbert, Pape sous le nom de Sylvestre II*. A. Olleris, ed. Hildesheim: Olms, 1963.
Giraut de Borneilh. *Sämtliche Lieder des Trobadors Giraut de Bornelih*. Adolf Kolsen, ed. Halle: Niemeyer, 1910.
Glaber, Rodulfus. *The Five Books of the Histories*. Neithard Bulst, ed. Oxford: Clarendon, 1989.
Godfrey of Saint Victor. *Fons Philosophiae*. Pierre Michaud-Quantin, ed. Namur: Éditions Godenne, 1956.
—. *L'oeuvre de Godefroid de Saint-Victor* 1. *Le Microcosme (Microcosmus)*. Françoise Gasparri et al., ed. and trans. Turnhout: Brepols, 2020.

—. Godefroy de Saint-Victor. *Microcosmus.* Philippe Delhaye, ed. Lille: Facultés catholiques, 1951.

Goethe, Johann Wolfgang von. *Faust: Der Tragödie erster und zweiter Teil.* Erich Trunz, ed. Munich: Beck, 1998.

Gottfried von Strassburg. *Tristan.* Friedrich Ranke, ed. 11th ed. Berlin: Weidmann, 1967.

—. *Tristan und Isolde: Kritische Edition. Textband.* Tomas Tomasek, ed. Basel: Schwabe, 2023.

—. *Tristan, with the Surviving Fragments of the Tristan of Thomas.* Arthur T. Hatto, trans. London: Penguin, 1967.

Gozechinus (Goswin) of Mainz. *Gozechini epistola ad Walcherum VI.* Robert B.C. Huygens, ed. CCCM 62. Turnholt: Brepols, 1985.

Grimmelshausen, Hans J.C. *Grimmelshausens Simplicissimus Teutsch.* J.H. Scholte ed. Tübingen: Niemeyer, 1954.

Guibert of Nogent. *Autobiographie: De vita sua.* Edmond-Rene Labande, ed. Paris: Les belles lettres, 1981.

—. *Self and Society in Medieval France: The Memoirs of Abbot Guibert of Nogent (1064?–c.1125).* C.C. Swinton Bland, trans.; John F. Benton, rev. New York: Harper Torchbooks, 1970.

Guido of Bazoches. *Liber epistularum Guidonis de Basochis.* Herbert Adolfsson, ed. Stockholm: Almquist and Wiksell, 1969.

Guitmund of Aversa. *De corporis et sanguinis Christi veritate.* PL 149:1427A–1494D.

Häring, Nikolaus M, ed. *Commentaries on Boethius by Thierry of Chartres and His School.* Toronto: Pontifical Institute of Mediaeval Studies, 1971.

—. "The Creation and the Creator of the World according to Thierry of Chartres and Clarenbaldus of Arras." AHDLMA 22 (1955): 137–216.

Hartmann von Aue. *Iwein.* 7th ed. Wilhelm Benecke, et al., ed. Berlin: De Gruyter, 1968.

—. *Iwein.* Patrick M. McConeghy, ed. and trans. New York: Garland, 1984.

Helmold of Bosau. *Chronica Slavorum.* J.M. Lappenberg, ed. MGH, SS 21. Hannover: Hahn: 1868.

Henri d'Andeli. *The Battle of the Seven Arts: A French Poem by Henri d'Andeli, Trouvère of the Thirteenth Century.* Louis John Paetow, ed. and trans. Berkeley: University of California Press, 1914.

Herbert of Bosham. *Vita Thomae.* James Craigie Robertson, ed. Rolls Series 67.3. London: Longman, 1877.

BIBLIOGRAPHY

Hermetica: The Greek Corpus Hermeticum and the Latin Asclepius in a New English Translation with Notes and Introduction. Brian P. Copenhaver, ed. and trans. Cambridge: Cambridge University Press, 2000.

Hildebert of Lavardin. *Carmina minora.* A. Brian Scott, ed. Leipzig: Teubner, 1969.

—. *Epistolae.* PL 17:141A–312C.

—. *Liber de quatuor virtutibus vitae honestae.* PL 171:1055C–1064C.

—. *Les mélanges poétiques d'Hildebert de Lavardin.* Barthélemy Haureau, ed. Paris: Pedon-Lauriel, 1882.

Homer. *The Odyssey.* Emile V. Rieu, trans. Baltimore, MD: Penguin, 1964.

Horace. *Odes and Epodes.* Niall Rudd, ed. & trans. Cambridge, MA: Harvard University Press, 2004.

Hrabanus Maurus. *De clericorum institutione.* PL 107:293–420A

Hugh of Saint Victor. *De institutione novitiorum.* PL 176:925–51.

—. *De institutione novitiorum.* In *L'oeuvre de Hugues de St. Victor.* Hugh Feiss and Patrice Sicard, ed. Turnhout: Brepols, 2000.

—. *De sacramentis Christiane Fidei.* Rainer Berndt, ed. Münster: Aschendorff, 2008.

—. *The Didascalicon of Hugh of St. Victor: A Medieval Guide to the Arts.* Jerome Taylor, trans. New York: Columbia University Press, 1961.

—. *Hugh of Saint Victor on the Sacraments of the Christian Faith (De sacramentis).* Roy J. Deferrari, trans. Cambridge, MA: Medieval Academy of America, 1951.

—. *Hugonis de Sancto Victore Didascalicon de Studio Legendi: A Critical Text.* Charles H. Buttimer, ed. Washington, DC: Catholic University Press, 1939.

Hugh Primas of Orleans. *Hugh Primas and the Archpoet.* Fleur Adcock, ed. and trans. Cambridge: Cambridge University Press, 1994.

—. *The Oxford Poems of Hugh Primas and the Arundel Lyrics.* Christopher J. McDonough, ed. Toronto: University of Toronto Press, 1984.

Isidore of Seville. *Etymologiae.* Wallace M. Lindsay, ed. Oxford: Clarendon, 1911.

Jacques de Vitry. *The Exempla or Illustrative Stories from the Sermones Vulgares of Jacques de Vitry.* Thomas F. Crane, ed. New York: Franklin Reprint, 1971.

Johannes de Alta Silva. *Dolopathos, sive De rege et septem sapientibus.* Hermann Oesterley, ed. Strassburg: Trübner, 1873.

Johannes de Hauvilla. *Architrenius.* Winthrop Wetherbee, ed. and trans. Cambridge: Cambridge University Press, 1994.

John of Salisbury. *Frivolities of Courtiers and Footprints of Philosophers.* Joseph B. Pike, trans. New York: Octagon, 1972.

—. *Ioannis Saresberiensis episcopi Carnotensis Metalogicon.* Clemens J. Webb, ed. Oxford: Clarendon, 1929.

—. *Ioannes Saresberiensis Metalogicon.* John Barrie and Katherine Keats-Rohan, ed. CCCM 98. Turnhout: Brepols, 1991.

—. *John of Salisbury's Entheticus Maior and Minor.* Jan Van Laarhoven, ed. Leiden: Brill, 1987.

—. *Johannes Saresberiensis episcopi Carnotensis Policratici sive de nugis curialium et vestigiis philosophorum libri VIII.* Clemens J. Webb, ed. 2 vols. Oxford: Clarendon, 1909.

—. *The Letters of John of Salisbury 1. The Early Letters (1153–1161).* W. J. Millor, Harold E. Butler, and Christopher N.L. Brooke, ed. Oxford: Clarendon, 1986.

—. *The Metalogicon of John of Salisbury: A Twelfth-Century Defense of the Verbal and Logical Arts of the Trivium.* Daniel McGarry, trans. Berkeley: University of California Press, 1962.

—. *Policraticus.* Clemens J. Webb, ed. Oxford: Clarendon, 1909.

—. *Policraticus.* Katharine S.B. Keats-Rohan, ed. CCCM 118. Turnholt: Brepols, 1993.

Lampert of Hersfeld. *Annales.* Otto Holder-Egger, ed. MGH, SSR 38. Leipzig: Hahn, 1894.

—. *The Annals of Lampert of Hersfeld.* Ian S. Robinson trans. Manchester: Manchester University Press, 2015.

Lawrence of Durham. *Dialogi Laurentii Dunelmensis Monachi et Prioris.* James Raine, ed. Durham: Andrews, 1880.

—. "Dialogues and Easter Poem." Arthur G. Rigg, trans. *Journal of Medieval Latin* 7 (1997): 42–126.

Liber ordinis Sancti Victoris Parisiensis. Lucas Jocqué and Ludovicus Milis, ed. CCCM 61. Turnhout: Brepols, 1984.

Longinus. *On the Sublime.* W. Hamilton Fyfe, ed. and trans.; Donald Russell, rev. Cambridge, MA: Harvard University Press, 1995.

Macrobius. *Commentaire au songe de Scipion.* Mireille Armisen-Marchetti, ed. Paris: Les Belles Lettres, 2003.

—. *Commentary on the Dream of Scipio.* William Harris Stahl, trans. New York: Columbia University Press, 1952.

Manegold von Lautenbach. *Liber contra Wolfelmum*. Wilfried Hartmann, ed. MGH, *Quellen zur Geistesgeschichte des Mittelalters* 8. Weimar: Böhlau, 1972.

Mann, Thomas. *Joseph and his Brothers*. John E. Woods, trans. New York: Knopf, 2005.

Mansi, Johannes Dominicus. *Sacrorum Conciliorum Nova et Amplissima Collectio*. 53 vols. Venice: Zatta, 1692–1769.

Marbod of Rennes. "Liebesbriefgedichte Marbods." Walther Bulst, ed. In *Liber Floridus: Mittellateinische Studien: Paul Lehmann zum 65. Geburtstag gewidmet am 13. Juli 1949 gewidmet von Freunden, Kollegen und Schülern*. Bernard Bischoff, ed. St. Ottilien: Eos Verlag, 1950, 287–302.

—. *Vita Licinii*. PL 171:1493B–1504C.

Martin of Braga. *Formula vitae honestae*. Claude Barlowe, ed. New Haven, CT: Yale University Press, 1950.

Matthew Paris. *Historia Anglorum. Historia minor*. Frederic Madden, ed. London: Longman, 1866.

Mayvaert, Paul, ed. "A Metrical Calendar by Eugenius Vulgarius." AB 84 (1966): 349–77.

Meinwerk of Paderborn. *Das Leben des Bischofs Meinwerk von Paderborn*. Franz Tenckhoff, ed. MGH, SSR 59. Hannover: Hahn, 1921.

Milo Crispin of Bec. *Vita Lanfranci*. PL 150:19D–58C.

Des Minnesangs Fruhling. Karl Lachmann et al., ed.; Hugo Moser and Helmut Tervooren, rev. 3 vols. Stuttgart: Hirzel, 1977–82.

Mythographus Vaticanus. Peter Kulcsar, ed. CCSL 91C. Turnholt: Brepols, 1987.

Novikoff, Alex, ed. *The Twelfth-Century Renaissance: A Reader*. Toronto: University of Toronto Press, 2016.

Odo of Cluny. *Vita Geraldi*. PL 133:639A–710C.

Onulf of Speyer. *Colores rhetorici*. Wilhelm Wattenbach, ed. Berlin: Sitzungsberichte der Preussischen Akademie der Wissenschaften, 1894, 361–86.

—. "Die 'Rethorici colores' des Magisters Onulf von Speyer." Cornelia Linde, ed. *Mittellateinisches Jahrbuch* 40 (2005): 333–81.

Orderic Vitalis. *The Ecclesiastical History of Orderic Vitalis*. Marjorie Chibnall, ed. and trans. 6 vols. Oxford: Oxford University Press, 1968–80.

Otloh of S. Emmeram. *Vita S. Wolfkangi*. Georg Waitz, ed. MGH, SS 4. Hannover: Hahn, 1841, 521–42.

Otto of Freising. *Chronik oder die Geschichte der zwei Staaten*. Walther Lammers, ed.; Adolf Schmidt, trans. Darmstadt: Wissenschaftliche Buchgesellschaft, 1974.

———. *The Deeds of Frederick Barbarossa*. Charles Christopher Mierow, trans. New York: Columbia University Press, 1966.

———. *The Two Cities: A Chronicle of Universal History to the Year 1146 A.D. by Bishop Otto of Freising*. Charles Christopher Mierow, trans. New York: Columbia University Press, 1928.

———, and Rahewin. *Die Taten Friedrichs oder richtiger Chronica*. Franz-Josef Schmale, ed.; Adolf Schmidt, trans. Darmstadt: Wissenschaftliche Buchgesellschaft, 1974.

Paravicini, Anke, ed. Quid suum virtutis: *Eine Lehrdichtung des 11. Jahrhunderts*. Heidelberg: Winter, 1980.

Paschasius Radbertus. *De vita S. Adalhardi*. PL 120:1507–1556C.

Peter of Blois, *Epistolae*. PL 207:1A–560C.

Petrus Alfonsi. *Disciplina clericalis*. Alfons Hilka and Werner Söderhjelm, ed. Heidelberg: Winter, 1911.

Petrus Damianus. *De frenanda ira et simultatibus exstirpandis*. PL 145:649–60.

———. *De sancta simplicitate*. Paolo Brezzi, ed., Bruno Nardi, trans. In *S. Pier Damiani, De divina omnipotentia e altri opuscoli*. Florence: Vallecchi, 1943.

———. *De sancta simplicitate scientiae inflanti anteponenda*. PL 145:695A–704B.

Petrus Pictor. *Petri Pictoris Carmina*. Lieven Van Acker, ed. CCCM 25. Turnhout: Brepols, 1972.

Pico della Mirandola. *Oration on the Dignity of Man: A New Translation and Commentary*. Francesco Borghesi et al., ed. Cambridge: Cambridge University Press, 2012.

Pindar. *The Odes*. Andrew M. Miller, trans. Oakland: University of California Press, 2019.

———. *The Odes of Pindar*. Richmond Lattimore, trans. Chicago: University of Chicago Press, 1947.

Plato. *Timaeus*. Desmond Lee, trans. Baltimore: Penguin, 1969.

Poeta Saxo. *Annales*. Paul Winterfeld, ed. MGH, *Poetae* 4.1. Berlin: Weidmann, 1899, 1–71.

Political Poems and Songs Relating to English History. Thomas Wright, ed. Rolls Series 14. 2 vols. London: Longman, 1859.

Raleigh, Walter. *The History of the World*. Constantine A. Patrides, ed. London: Macmillan, 1971.

* BIBLIOGRAPHY

Regensburger rhetorischen Briefe. Norbert Fickermann, ed. *Briefsammlungen der Zeit Heinrichs IV.* Munich: MGH, 1981, 259–382.
Richard of St. Victor. *De statu interioris hominis.* PL 196:1115C–1160B.
Richer of St. Rémy. *Historiae.* Hartmut Hoffmann, ed. MGH, SS 38. Hannover: Hahn, 2000.
—. *Histories.* Justin Lake, ed. 2 vols. Cambridge, MA: Harvard University Press, 2013.
Rodulfus Tortarius. *Rodulfi Tortarii Carmina.* Marbury B. Ogle and Dorothy M. Schullian, ed. Rome: American Academy in Rome, 1933.
Ruotger of Cologne. *Ruotgers Lebensbeschreibung des Erzbischofs Brun von Koln.* Irene Ott, ed. MGH, SSR, n.s. 10. Cologne: Böhlau, 1951.
—. *Vita Brunonis. Lebensbeschreibungen einiger Bischöfe des 10.–12. Jahrhunderts.* Hatto Kallfelz, trans. Darmstadt: Wissenschaftliche Buchgesellschaft, 1973.
Seneca. *Epistolae.* Richard M. Gummere, trans. 3 vols. Cambridge, MA: Harvard Univesity Press, 1917–25.
Sigebert of Gembloux. *Chronographia cum continuationibus.* Ludwig Bethmann, ed. Continuatio Praemonstratensis. MGH, SS 6.
—. *Gesta abbatum Gemblacensium.* Georg H. Pertz, ed. MGH, SS 8. Hannover: Hahn, 1848, 523–42.
—. *Passio Sanctae Luciae Virginis und Passio Sanctorum Thebeorum.* Ernst Dümmler, ed. Berlin: Royal Academy, 1893.
—. *Vita Deoderici episcopi Mettensis.* Georg H. Pertz, ed. MGH, SS 4. Hannover: Hahn, 1841, 461–83.
Simplicius Simplicissimus. *Der abenteuerliche Simplicius Simplicissimus.* Hans J.C. Grimmelshausen, ed. Norderstedt: Vero, 2015.
Suger of St. Denis. *Vie de Louis VI le Gros.* Henri Waquet, ed. and trans. Paris: Champion, 1929.
Die Tegernseer Briefsammlung. Karl Strecker, ed. MGH, *Epistolae selectae* 3. Berlin: Weidmann, 1925.
Thangmar. *Vita Bernwardi Episcopi Hildesheimensis.* MGH, SS 4.
Thomasin von Zirclaere. *Der Welsche Gast des Thomasin von Zirclaria.* Heinrich Rückert, ed. Berlin: De Gruyter, 1965.
Thietmar of Merseburg. *Die Chronik des Bischofs Thietmar von Merseburg und ihre Korveier Überarbeitung.* MGH, SSR, n.s. 9. Robert Holtzmann, ed. Berlin: Weidmann, 1935.
Ulrich of Bamberg. *Codex Udalrici.* Klaus Nass, ed. 2 vols. MGH, *Briefe der deutschen Kaiserzeit* 10. Wiesbaden: Harassowitz, 2017.

—. "Eine Bamberger *ars dictaminis*." Franz Bittner, ed. *Bericht des Historischen Vereins Bamberg* 100 (1964): 145–71.

Vasari, Giorgio. *The Lives of the Painters, Sculptors and Architects*. William Gaunt, ed. and trans. 4 vols. London: Phaidon, 1963.

Vincent of Beauvais. *De eruditione filiorum nobilium*. Arpad Steiner, ed. Cambridge, MA: Harvard University Press, 1938.

Vita Theoderici abbatis Andaginensis. Wilhelm Wattenbach, ed. MGH, SS 12. Hannover: Hahn, 1856, 36–57.

Vollmann, Benedikt, ed. *Faksimile-Ausgabe des Codex Latinus Monacensis 19486 der Bayerischen Staatsbibliothek München und der Fragmente von St. Florian 2.1. Kritischer Text.* Wiesbaden: Reichert, 1985.

Walahfrid Strabo. *In Natalem S. Mammetis Hymnus*. Ernst Dümmler, ed. MGH, *Poetae*. Berlin: Weidmann, 1884, 2:259–423.

Walter Map. *De nugis curialium / Courtiers' Trifles*. Montague R. James, ed. and trans.; Christopher N.L. Brooke and Roger A.B. Mynors, rev. Oxford: Clarendon, 1983.

Walter of Châtillon. *Moralisch-satirische Gedichte Walters von Chatillon*. Karl Strecker, ed. Heidelberg: Weidmann, 1929.

Werner of Basel. "Warnerii Basiliensis Paraclitus et Synodus." AHDLMA 8 (1933): 261–429.

Wibald of Stablo. *Das Briefbuch des Abt Wibalds von Stablo und Corvey*. Martina Hartmann et al., ed. MGH, *Briefe der deutschen Kaiserzeit* 9. 3 vols. Hannover: Hahn, 2012.

—. *Wibaldi Epistolae*. Bibliotheca Rerum Germanicarum 1. Monumenta Corbeiensia. Philipp Jaffé ed. Aalen: Scientia, 1964

William Fitzstephen. Vita Sancti Thomae: *Materials for the History of Thomas Becket, Archbishop of Canterbury*. Rolls Series 67.3. James C. Robertson, ed. London: Longman, 1875.

William of Conches. *Das Moralium dogma philosophorum des Guillaume de Conches: Lateinisch, Altfranzösisch, Mittelniederfränkisch*. J. Holmberg, ed. Uppsala: Almquist and Wiksells, 1929.

—. *Dragmaticon philosophiae*. Italo Ronca, ed. CCCM 152. Turnhout: Brepols, 1997.

—. *Glosae in Iuvenalem*. Bradford Wilson, ed. Paris: Vrin, 1980.

—. *Glosae super Boetium*. Lodi Nauta, ed. CCCM 158.2. Turnhout: Brepols, 1999.

—. *Glosae super Platonem: Texte critique avec introduction, notes et tables* 3. Edouard Jeauneau, ed. Paris: Vrin, 1965.

★ BIBLIOGRAPHY

—. *Philosophia mundi*. Gregor Maurach, ed. Pretoria: University of South Africa, 1980.

William of Malmesbury. *"Gesta regum Anglorum": The History of the English Kings*. Roger A.B. Mynors, Rodney M. Thomson, and Michael Winterbottom, ed. and trans. Oxford: Clarendon, 1998.

William of Tyre. *Chronique*. Robert B.C. Huygens, ed. CCCM 63A. Turnhout: Brepols, 1986.

—. *Historia rerum in partibus transmarinis gestarum (History of Deeds Done Beyond the Sea)*. Emily Babcock and August C. Krey, trans. New York: Columbia University Press, 1943.

William the Breton. *Oeuvres de Rigord et de Guillaume le Breton, historiens de Philippe-Auguste*. Henri Francois Delaborde, ed. 2 vols. Paris: Renouard, 1882–85.

Willigis of Mainz. *Libellus de Willigisi consuetudinibus*. MGH, SS 15.

Wipo. *Die Werke Wipos*. 3rd ed. Harry Bresslau, ed. MGH, SSR, Separatim editi 61. Hannover and Leipzig: Hahn, 1915.

Wireker, Nigel. *Speculum stultorum*. John H. Mozley and Robert R. Raymo, ed. Berkeley: University of California Press, 1969.

Wolfram von Eschenbach. *Parzival*. Karl Lachmann, ed.; Eberhard Nellmann, rev. & comm.; Dieter Kühn, trans. Frankfurt-am-Main: Deutscher Klassiker, 1994.

Worms Briefsammlung. *Die ältere Wormser Briefsammlung*. Walther Bulst, ed. MGH, *Briefe der deutschen Kaiserzeit* 3. Weimar: Böhlau, 1949.

SECONDARY WORKS

Allen, Don Cameron. "The Degeneration of Man and Renaissance Pessimism." *Studies in Philology* 35 (1938): 202–27.

Althoff, Gerd. *Die Macht der Rituale: Symbolik und Herrschaft im Mittelalter*. Darmstadt: Wissenschaftliche Buchgesellschaft, 2003.

—. "*Ira regis*: Prolegomena to a History of Royal Anger." In *Anger's Past: Social Uses of an Emotion in the Middle Ages*. Barbara Rosenwein, ed. Ithaca, NY: Cornell University Press, 1998, 59–74.

—. *Otto III*. Phyllis Jestice, trans. University Park: Pennsylvania State University Press, 2003.

—, and Christl Meier. *Ironie im Mittelalter: Hermeneutik, Dichtung, Politik*. Darmstadt: Wissenschaftliche Buchgesellschaft, 2011.

Anderson, William S. "The Artist's Limits in Ovid: Orpheus, Pygmalion and Daedalus." *Syllecta Classica* 1 (1989): 1–11.

Auerbach, Erich. "*Camilla*, or, The Rebirth of the Sublime." In Erich Auerbach, *Literary Language and its Public in Late Latin Antiquity and in the Middle Ages*. Ralph Mannheim, trans. New York: Pantheon, 1965, 181–233.

—. *Mimesis: The Representation of Reality in Western Literature*. Princeton, NJ: Princeton University Press, 2013.

Aurell, Martin. *Le chevalier lettré: Savoir et conduite de l'aristocracie aux XII et XIIIe siècles*. Paris: Fayard, 2011.

—. *The Lettered Knight: Knowledge and Aristocratic Behaviour in the Twelfth and Thirteenth Centuries*. Jean-Charles Khalifa and Jeremy Price, trans. Budapest: Central European Press, 2017.

Baldwin, John W. *The Government of Philip Augustus: Foundations of Royal Power in the Middle Ages*. Berkeley: University of California Press, 1986.

—. "Masters at Paris from 1179 to 1215: A Social Perspective." In Benson and Constable, 138–64.

Beach, Alison I. *Women as Scribes: Book Production and Monastic Reform in Twelfth-Century Bavaria*. Cambridge: Cambridge University Press, 2009.

Beaujouan, Guy. "The Transformation of the Quadrivium." In Benson and Constable, 463–87.

Beckman, J.P. "Philosophie: Western." *Lexikon des Mittelalters*. Munich: Artemis, 1993, 6:2086–92.

Bedos-Rezak, Brigitte. *When Ego Was Imago: Signs of Identity in the Middle Ages*. Leiden: Brill, 2011.

Bejczy, Istvan. *Erasmus and the Middle Ages: The Historical Consciousness of a Christian Humanist*. Leiden: Brill, 2001.

Benedetto, L.F. "Stephanus grammaticus da Novara." *Studi Medievali* 3 (1908–11): 499–508.

Benjamin, Walter. *The Work of Art in the Age of its Technological Reproducibility*." In *Walter Benjamin: Selected Writings* 4, *1938–1940*. H. Eiland and M. Jennings, ed. Cambridge, MA: Harvard University Press, 2003, 251–83.

Bennett, Beth S. "The Rhetoric of Martianus Capella and Anselm de Besate in the Tradition of Menippean Satire." *Philosophy and Rhetoric* 24 (1991): 128–42.

—. "The Significance of the 'Rhetorimachia' of Anselm de Besate to the History of Rhetoric." *Rhetorica* 5 (1987): 231–50.

Benson, Robert L., and Giles Constable, ed. *Renaissance and Renewal in the Twelfth Century*. Cambridge, MA: Harvard University Press, 1982.

Bernt, Günter. "Fulcoius von Beauvais." LexMA 4 (1989): 1019.

Beyer, Katrin. *Witz und Ironie in der Politischen Kultur Englands im Hochmittelalter: Interaktionen und Imaginationen.* Würzburg: Ergon, 2012.

Bezzola, Reto R. *Les origines et la formation de littérature courtoise en occident (500–1200)* 1. *La tradition impériale de la fin de l'antiquité au Xie siècle.* Paris: Champion, 1944.

Binski, Paul. *Gothic Wonder: Art, Artifice and the Decorated Style 1200–1350.* New Haven, CT: Yale University Press, 2014.

Bischoff, Bernard. *Mittelalterliche Studien: Ausgewählte Aufsätze zur Schriftkunde und Literaturgeschichte.* 3 vols. Stuttgart: Hiersemann, 1966–81.

Bisson, Thomas. "The Organized Peace in Southern France and Catalonia, c.1140–c.1233." AHR 82 (1977): 290–307.

Bittner, Franz. "Eine Bamberger *ars dictaminis*." *Bericht des Historischen Vereins Bamberg* 100 (1964): 145–71.

Blank, Rudolf. *Weltdarstellung und Weltbild in Würzburg und Bamberg vom 8. bis zum Ende des 12. Jahrhunderts.* Bamberg: Historischer Verein, 1968.

Blumenthal, Ute-Renate. *The Investiture Controversy: Church and Monarchy from the Ninth to the Twelfth Century.* Philadelphia: University of Pennsylvania Press, 1991.

Bond, Gerald. *The Loving Subject: Desire, Eloquence, and Power in Romanesque France.* Philadelphia: University of Pennsylvania Press, 1995.

Boutemy, André, and Fernand Vercauteren. "Fulcoie de Beauvais et l'intérêt pour l'archéologie antique au XIe et au XIIe siècle." *Latomus* 1 (1937): 173–86.

Bouwsma, William J. *The Waning of the Renaissance, 1550–1640.* New Haven, CT: Yale University Press, 2000.

Bradley, Dennis. "Philosophy to the Mid-Twelfth Century." DMA 9:582–90.

Brinkmann, Hennig. *Mittelalterliche Hermeneutik.* Tübingen: Niemeier, 1980.

Brooke, Christopher N.L. "John of Salisbury and his World." In *The World of John of Salisbury.* Michael Wilks, ed. Oxford: Blackwell, 1984, 1–20.

Brunhölzl, Franz. "Der Bildungsauftrag der Hofschule." In *Karl der Grosse: Lebenswerk und Nachleben 2. Geistiges Leben.* Bernard Bischoff, ed. Düsseldorf: Schwan, 1965, 28–41.

Büchli, Jörg. *Der Poimandres: Ein paganisiertes Evangelium. Sprachliche und begriffliche Untersuchungen zum ersten Traktat des Corpus Hermeticum.* Tübingen: Siebeck, 2019.

Bumke, Joachim. *The Concept of Knighthood in the Middle Ages*, W.T.H. Jackson and Erika Jackson, trans. New York: AMS Press, 1982.

—. *Courtly Culture: Literature and Society in the High Middle Ages*. Thomas Dunlap, trans. Berkeley: University of California Press, 2000.

Bynum, Caroline. *Docere verbo et exemplo: An Aspect of Twelfth-Century Spirituality*. Missoula, MT: Scholars Press, 1979.

—. "The Spirituality of Canons Regular in the Twelfth Century: A New Approach." *Mediaevalia et Humanistica* n.s. 4 (1973): 3–24.

—. "Wonder." AHR 102.1 (1997): 1–26.

Calinescu, Matei. *Five Faces of Modernity: Modernism, Avant-Garde, Decadence, Kitsch, Postmodernism*. Durham, NC: Duke University Press, 1987.

Canatella, Holle. "Scripsit amica manus: Male-Female Spiritual Friendship in England and France ca. 1050–1200." Ph.D. diss., University of Houston, 2010.

Cantin, André. *Les sciences séculières et la foi: Les deux voies de la science au jugement de S. Pierre*. Spoleto: Fondazione CISAM, 1975.

Cantor, Norman F. *Inventing the Middle Ages: The Lives, Works and Ideas of the Great Medievalists of the Twentieth Century*. New York: Morrow, 1991.

Chenu, M.D. *Nature, Man, and Society in the Twelfth Century: Essays on New Theological Perspectives in the Latin West*. Jerome Taylor and Lester Little, trans. Chicago: University of Chicago Press, 1968.

Chronopoulos, Tina. "Ganymede in the Medieval Classroom: Reading an Ode by the Roman Poet Horace." *Medium Aevum* 86.2 (2017): 224–48.

Clark, William W. "The Twelfth-Century Church of St. Victor in Paris: A New Proposal." In *From Knowledge to Beatitude: St. Victor, Twelfth-Century Scholars, and Beyond. Essays in Honor of Grover Z. Zinn, Jr.* E. Ann Matter and Lesley Smith, ed. Notre Dame, IN: Notre Dame University Press, 2013: 68–85.

Clerval, A. *Les écoles de Chartres au Moyen-Âge (du Ve au XVIe siècle)*. Frankfurt-am-Main: Minerva, 1965.

Colish, Marcia. *Medieval Foundations of the Western Intellectual Tradition 400–1400*. New Haven, CT: Yale University Press, 1997.

—. *The Stoic Tradition from Antiquity to the Early Middle Ages*. 2 vols. Leiden: Brill, 1985.

Combridge, Rosemary. "Ladies, Queens and Decorum." *Reading Medieval Studies* 1 (1975): 71–83.

Constable, Giles. *The Reformation of the Twelfth Century*. Cambridge, MA: Harvard University Press, 1996.

Cotts, John D. *The Clerical Dilemma: Peter of Blois and Literate Culture in the Twelfth Century*. Washington, DC: Catholic University Press, 2009.

Cowdrey, Herbert E.J. "Anselm of Besate and Some North-Italian Masters of the Eleventh Century." *Journal of Ecclesiastical History* 23 (1972): 115–24.

Crossnoe, Marshall. "Introduction." *A Companion to the Abbey of Saint Victor, Paris*. Juliette Mousseau and Hugh Feiss, ed. Leiden: Brill, 2018, 3–51.

Crouch, David. *The Birth of Nobility: Constructing Aristocracy in England and France, 900–1300*. Harlow: Pearson/Longman, 2005.

Curtius, Ernst Robert. "Zur Literarästhetik des Mittelalters 2." ZfRPhil. 58 (1938): 129–232.

—. "Die Musen im Mittelalter." ZRPh 59 (1939): 129–88.

—. *European Literature and the Latin Middle Ages*. Willard R. Trask, trans. Princeton, NJ: Princeton University Press, 1990.

—. "Zur Geschichte des Wortes *Philosophia* im Mittelalter." *Romanische Forschungen* 57 (1943): 290–309.

Damian-Grint, Peter. *The New Historians of the Twelfth-Century Renaissance*. Rochester, NY: Boydell, 1999.

Darlington, Oscar G. "Gerbert the Teacher." AHR 52 (1946/47): 456–76.

Davids, Adelbert, ed. *The Empress Theophano: Byzantium and the West at the Turn of the First Millenium*. Cambridge: Cambridge University Press, 2002.

Dean, James M. *The World Grown Old in Later Medieval Literature*. Cambridge, MA: Harvard University Press, 1997.

De Bruyne, Edgar. *Études d'esthétique médiévale*. 2 vols. Bruges: Tempel, 1946–75.

Delbouille, Maurice. "Un mystérieux ami de Marbode: Le 'redoutable poète' Gautier." *Le Moyen Âge* 57 (1951): 205–40.

Delhaye, Philippe. "Grammatica et ethica au XIIe siècle." RTAM 25 (1958): 59–110.

—. "L'enseignement de la philosophie morale au XIIe siècle." *Mediaeval Studies* 11 (1950): 77–99.

—. "L'organisation scolaire au XIIe siècle." *Traditio* 5 (1947): 211–68.

—. "La place de l'ethique parmi les classifications scientifiques au XIIe siècle." *Miscellanea moralia in honorem E.D.A. Janssen*. Louvain: Nauwelaerts, 1949, 19–44.

Demayo, Courtney. "The Theory and Practice of Friendship in the Middle Ages: Ciceronian *amicitia* in the letters of Gerbert of Aurillac." *Viator* 38 (2007): 319–37.

De Montclos, Jean. *Lanfranc et Bérengar: La controverse eucharistique du XIe siècle*. Louvain: Spicilegium Sacrum Lovaniense, 1971.

De Rijk, Lambertus M. *Logica Modernorum: A Contribution to the History of Early Terminist Logic.* Assen: Van Gorcum, 1962.

—. "Some New Evidence on Twelfth-Century Logic: Alberic and the School of Mont Ste. Geneviève." *Vivarium* 4 (1966): 1–57.

Detten, Georg von. *Über die Dom- und Kloster schulen des Mittelalters, insbesondere uber die Schulen von Hildesheim, Paderborn, Münster und Corvey.* Paderborn: Junsermann, 1893.

Dinzelbacher, Peter. "Uber die Entdeckung der Liebe im Hochmittelalter." *Saeculum* 32 (1981): 185–208.

Dronke, Peter. "The Return of Eurydice." *Classica et Mediaevalia* 23 (1962): 198–15.

—. "Thierry of Chartres." In *A History of Twelfth-Century Philosophy.* Peter Dronke, ed. Cambridge: Cambridge University Press, 1988, 358–85.

—. *Women Writers of the Middle Ages.* Cambridge: Cambridge University Press, 1984.

Duby, Georges. *Hommes et structures au moyen âge.* Paris: Flammarion, 1973.

—. *Love and Marriage in the Middle Ages.* Jane Dunnett, trans. Chicago: University of Chicago Press, 1994.

Dutton, Paul Edward. "The Uncovering of the *Glosae super Platonem* of Bernard of Chartres." *Medieval Studies* 46 (1984): 192–221.

Eagleton, Terry. *Sweet Violence: The Idea of the Tragic.* Oxford: Blackwell, 2003.

Eck, Caroline van. *Art, Agency, and the Living Presence: From the Animated Image to the Excessive Object.* Boston: De Gruyter, 2015.

Edler, Arnfried. "'Die Macht der Töne': Über die Bedeutung eines antiken Mythos im 19. Jahrhundert." In *Musik in Antike und Neuzeit.* Georg von Albrecht and Werner Schubert, ed. Frankfurt-am-Main: Peter Lang, 1987, 51–65.

Ehlers, Joachim. "Deutsche Scholaren in Frankreich." In Joachim Ehlers, *Ausgewählte Aufsätze.* Martin Kintzinger and Bernd Schneidmüller, ed. Berlin: Duncker & Humblot, 1996, 163–90.

—. "Dom und Klosterschulen in Deutschland und Frankreich im 10. Und 11. Jahrhundert." In *Schule und Schüler im Mittelalter.* Martin Kintzinger et al., ed. Cologne: Böhlau, 1996, 29–52.

Endres, Joseph A. *Petrus Damiani und die weltliche Wissenschaft.* Münster: Aschendorff, 1910.

Epp, Verena. "*Ars* und *scientia* in der Geschichtsschreibung des 12. Jahrhunderts." In *Scientia und ars im Hoch- und Spätmittelalter.* Ingrid

Craemer-Ruegenberg and Andreas Speer, ed. Berlin: De Gruyter, 1994, 829–45.

—. "Sicht der Antike und Gegenwartsbewusstsein in der mittellateinischen Dichtung des 11. /12. Jahrhunderts." In *Hochmittelalterliches Geschichtsbewusstsein im Spiegel nichthistoriographischer Quellen.* Hans Werner Goetz, ed. Berlin: Akademie, 1998, 295–316.

Erdmann, Carl. "Anselm der Peripatetiker, Kaplan Heinrichs III." In *Forschungen zur politischen Ideenwelt des Frühmittelalters.* Berlin: Akademie, 1951, 119–24.

—. "Die Bamberger Domschule im Investiturstreit." *Zeitschrift fur bayerische Landesgeschichte* 9 (1936): 1–46.

—. "*Fabulae curiales*: Neues zum Spielmannsgesang und zum Ezzo-Liede." *Zeitschrift fur deutsches Altertum* 73 (1936): 87–98.

—. "Onulf von Speyer und Amarcius." In *Forschungen zur politischen Ideenwelt des Frühmittelalters.* Friedrich Baethgen, ed. Berlin: Akademia Verlag, 1951, 124–34.

—. *The Origin of the Idea of Crusade.* Marshall Whithed Baldwin and Walter A. Goffart, trans. Princeton, NJ: Princeton University Press, 1977.

—. *Studien zur Briefliteratur Deutschlands im elften Jahrhundert.* MGH, *Schriften* 1. Leipzig: Hiersemann, 1938.

Evans, Gillian. *Old Arts and New Theology: The Beginnings of Theology as an Academic Discipline.* Oxford: Clarendon, 1980.

Faral, Edmond. *Les arts poétiques du XIIe et du XIIIe siècle: Recherches et documents sur la technique littéraire du moyen âge.* Paris: Champion, 1924.

Ferguson, Chris D. *Europe in Transition: A Select, Annotated Bibliography of the Twelfth-Century Renaissance.* New York: Garland, 1989.

Ferguson, Wallace K. *The Renaissance in Historical Thought: Five Centuries of Interpretation.* Cambridge: Cambridge University Press, 1948.

Feros Ruys, Juanita. *The Repentant Abelard: Family, Gender and Ethics in Peter Abelard's* Carmen ad Astralabium *and* Planctus. New York: Palgrave, 2014.

Ferruolo, Stephen C. *The Origins of the University: The Schools of Paris and Their Critics, 1100–1215.* Stanford, CA: Stanford University Press, 1985.

—. "The Twelfth-Century Renaissance." In *Renaissances before the Renaissance: Cultural Revivals of Late Antiquity and the Middle Age.* Warren Treadgold, ed. Stanford, CA: Stanford University Press, 1984, 114–43.

Finckh, Ruth. "*Minor mundus homo*": *Studien zur Mikrokosmus-Idee in der mittelalterlichen Literatur.* Göttingen: Vandenhoeck and Ruprecht, 1999.

Fleckenstein, Josef. *Die Bildungsreform Karls des Grossen als Verwirklichung der norma rectitudinis*. Bigge-Ruhr: Josefs, 1953.

—. *Die Hofkapelle der deutschen Könige*. 2 vols. MGH, *Schriften* 16. Stuttgart: Hiersemann, 1959–66.

—. "Königshof und Bischofsschule unter Otto dem Grossen." *Archiv für Kulturgeschichte* 38 (1956): 38–62.

Forschner, Maximilian. *Die stoische Ethik: Über den Zusammenhang von Natur-, Sprach- und Moralphilosophie im altstoischen System*. Stuttgart: Clett-Cota, 1981.

Forse, James H. "Bruno of Cologne and the Networking of the Episcopate in Tenth-Century Germany." *German History* 9 (1991): 263–79.

—. "Religious Drama and Ecclesiastical Reform in the Tenth Century." *Early Theater* 5 (2002): 47–70.

Foucault, Michel. *The Order of Things: An Archaeology of the Human Sciences*. New York: Vintage, 1973.

Frazer, James. *The Golden Bough: A Study in Magic and Religion*. New York: Macmillan, 1922.

Fried, Johannes. "Die Bamberger Domschule und die Rezeption von Frühscholastik und Rechtswissenschaft in ihrem Umkreis bis zum Ende der Stauferzeit." In *Schulen und Studium im sozialen Wandel des hohen und späten Mittelalters*. Johannes Fried, ed. Sigmaringen: Thorbecke, 1986, 163–201.

—. "Der Archipoeta, ein Kölner Scholaster?" In Ex Ipsis Rerum Documentis: *Beiträge zur Mediävistik. Festschrift für Harald Zimmermann*. Klaus Herbers et al., ed. Sigmaringen: Thorbecke, 1991, 85–90.

Friedman, John B. *Orpheus in the Middle Ages*. Cambridge, MA: Harvard University Press, 1970.

Fumagalli, Mariateresa, and Massimo Parodi. *Storia della filosofia medievale da Boezio a Wyclif*. Rome and Bari: Laterza, 2002.

Gadamer, Hans Georg. *Die Aktualität des Schönen*. Stuttgart: Reclam, 1977.

—. *The Relevance of the Beautiful and Other Essays*. Nicholas Walker, trans. Cambridge: Cambridge University Press, 1986.

Gamer, Helena M. "Studien zum Ruodlieb." *ZfdA* 88 (1957/58): 249–66.

Ganz, Peter, ed. Auctoritas *und* ratio: *Studien zu Berengar von Tours*. Wiesbaden: Harrasowitz, 1990.

Gasc, Hélène. "Gerbert et la pédagogie des arts libéraux à la fin du dixième siècle." *Journal of Medieval History* 12 (1986): 111–21.

★ BIBLIOGRAPHY

Gasparri, Françoise. "Philosophie et cosmologie: Godefroid de Saint-Victor." In *Notre-Dame de Paris: Un manifeste Chrétien (1160–1230)*. Michel Lemoine, ed. Turnhout: Brepols, 2004, 119–42.

Geary, Patrick. *Phantoms of Remembrance: Memory and Oblivion at the End of the First Millennium*. Princeton, NJ: Princeton University Press, 1994.

Geertz, Clifford. "Centers, Kings and Charisma." In Clifford Geertz, *Local Knowledge: Further Essays in Interpretive Anthropology*. New York: Basic Books, 1983, 121–46.

Gell, Alfred. *Art and Agency: An Anthropological Theory*. Oxford: Oxford University Press, 1998.

Gibson, Bruce. "Hildebert of Lavardin on the Monuments of Rome." In *Word and Context in Latin Poetry: Studies in Memory of David West*. Anthony J. Woodman and Jakob Wesse, ed. Cambridge: Cambridge University Press, 2017, 131–54.

Gibson, Margaret T. "The *artes* in the Eleventh Century." In *Arts libéraux et philosophie au moyen âge: Actes du quatrième congrès international de philosophie médiévale*. André Cantin, ed. Montreal: Institut d'études médiévales, 1969, 121–26.

—. "The Continuity of Learning circa 850–circa 1050." *Viator* 6 (1975): 1–13.

—. "The Study of the 'Timaeus' in the Eleventh and Twelfth Centuries." *Pensamiento* 25 (1969): 183–94.

Gillingham, John. "1066 and the Introduction of Chivalry into England." In *Law and Government in Medieval England and Normandy: Essays in Honour of James Holt*. John Garnett and George Hudson, ed. Cambridge: Cambridge University Press, 1994, 209–31.

—. "A Historian of the Twelfth-Century Renaissance and the Transformation of English Society, 1066–c.1200." In *European Transformations: The Long Twelfth Century*. Thomas F.X. Noble and John Van Engen, ed. Notre Dame, IN: University of Notre Dame Press, 2012, 45–74.

—. "Kingship, Chivalry and Love: Political and Cultural Values in the Earliest History Written in French: Geoffrey Gaimar's *Estoire des Engleis*." In *Anglo-Norman Political Culture and the Twelfth-Century Renaissance*. C. Warren Hollister, ed. Woodbridge: Boydell, 1997, 33–58.

Gilman, Sander L. *Jewish Self-Hatred: Anti-Semitism and the Hidden Language of the Jews*. Baltimore, MD: Johns Hopkins University Press, 1986.

Gilson, Etienne. "L'humanisme médiévale et renaissance" In Etienne Gilson, *Les idées et les lettres*. Paris: Vrin, 1955, 171–96.

—. *The Mystical Theology of St. Bernard*. Kalamazoo, MI: Cistercian Publications, 1990.

Girouard, Mark. *The Return to Camelot: Chivalry and the English Gentleman.* New Haven, CT: Yale University Press, 1981.

Glauche, Günther. "Die Rolle der Schulautoren im Unterricht von 800 bis 1100." In *La scuola nell' occidente latino dell' alto medioevo* 2. Spoleto: Presso la Sede del Centro, 1972, 617–36.

Glenn, Jason K. "Master and Community in Tenth-Century Reims." In *Teaching and Learning in Northern Europe, 1000–1200.* Sally N. Vaughn and Jay Rubenstein, ed. Turnhout: Brepols, 2006, 51–68.

Godman, Peter. *Poets and Emperors: Frankish Politics and Carolingian Poetry.* Oxford: Oxford University Press, 1987.

—. *The Silent Masters: Latin Literature and its Censors in the High Middle Ages.* Princeton, NJ: Princeton University Press, 2000.

Goetz, Hans-Werner. *Das Geschichtsbild Ottos van Freising: Ein Beitrag zur historischen Vorstellungswelt und zur Geschichte des 12. Jahrhunderts.* Cologne: Böhlau, 1984.

—. *Geschichtsschreibung und Geschichtsbewusstsein im hohen Mittelalter.* Berlin: Akademie, 1999.

Goez, Werner. *Translatio imperii: Ein Beitrag zur Geschichte des Geschichtsdenkens und der politischen Theorien im Mittelalter und in der frühen Neuzeit.* Tübingen: Mohr, 1958.

Gombrich, Ernst. *In Search of Cultural History.* London: Oxford University Press, 1969.

Gossmann, Elisabeth. "'Antiqui' und 'Moderni' im 12. Jahrhundert." In *Antiqui und Moderni im Mittelalter: Eine geschichtliche Standortbestimmung.* Albert Zimmermann, ed. Munich: Schöningh, 1974, 40–57.

Goy, Rudolf. *Die Überlieferung der Werke Hugos von St. Viktor: Ein Beitrag zur Kommunikationsgeschichte des Mittelalters.* Stuttgart: Hiersemann, 1976.

Grabmann, Martin. *Geschichte der scholastischen Methode.* 2 vols. Graz: Akademischer Druck- und Verlagsanstalt, 1957.

Grassi, Ernesto. *Renaissance Humanism: Studies in Philosophy and Poetics.* Walter F. Veit, trans. Binghamton, NY: Center for Medieval and Early Renaissance Studies, 1988.

Guerreau-Jalabert, Anita. "Grammaire et culture profane à Fleury au Xe siècle." Positions des thèses, University of Paris, 1975.

Gumbrecht, Hans-Ulrich. "Beginn der 'Literatur' / Abschied vom Körper?" In *Der Ursprung von Literatur: Medien, Rollen, Kommunikationssituationen zwischen 1450 und 1650.* Gisela Smolka-Koerdt et al., ed. Munich: Fink, 1988, 15–50.

★ BIBLIOGRAPHY

Guth, Klaus. *Johannes von Salisbury: Studien zur Kirchen-, Kultur- und Sozialgeschichte Westeuropas im 12. Jahrhundert.* St. Ottilien: Eos, 1978.

Hadot, Pierre. *What Is Ancient Philosophy?* Michael Chase, trans. Cambridge, MA: Harvard Belknap, 2002.

Haefner, Elizabeth *Die Wormser Briefsammlung des 11. Jahrhunderts.* Erlangen: Palm & Enke, 1935.

Haren, Michael. *Medieval Thought: The Western Intellectual Tradition from Antiquity to the Thirteenth Century.* New York: St. Martin's, 1985.

Harkins, Franklin. *Reading and the Work of Restoration: History and Scripture in the Theology of Hugh of St. Victor.* Toronto: Pontifical Institute of Mediaeval Studies, 2009.

Hartmann, Wilfried. "Manegold von Lautenbach und die Anfänge der Frühscholastik." *Deutsches Archiv für Erforschung des Mittelalters* 26 (1970): 7–149.

—. "'Modernus' und 'Antiquus': Zur Verbreitung und Bedeutung dieser Bezeichnungen in der wissenschaftlichen Literatur vom 9. bis zum 12. Jahrhundert." In Zimmermann, *Antiqui und Moderni*, 21–39.

Hashagen, Justus. *Otto von Freising als Geschichtsphilosoph und Kirchenpolitiker.* Leipzig: Teubner, 1900.

Haskins, Charles Homer. *The Renaissance of the Twelfth Century.* New York: Meridian, 1975.

Hauck, Karl. "Heinrich III. und der Ruodlieb." PBB 70 (1948): 372–419.

Haug, Walter. *Literaturtheorie im deutschen Mittelalter: Von den Anfängen bis zum Ende des 13. Jahrhunderts. Eine Einführung.* Darmstadt: Wissenschaftliche Buchgesellschaft, 1985.

Havelock, Eric. *Preface to Plato.* Cambridge, MA: Harvard University Press, 1963.

Hawk-Reinhard, Donna R. "Hugh of Saint Victor's Pedagogy." In *A Companion to the Abbey of Saint Victor in Paris.* Hugh Feiss and Juliet Mousseau, ed. Leiden: Brill, 2018, 123–28.

Heiduk, Matthias. "Revealing Wisdom's Underwear: The Prestige of Hermetic Knowledge and Occult Sciences among Scholars before 1200." In *Networks of Learning*, Sita Steckel et al., ed. Berlin: Lit, 2014, 125–46.

Heitmann, Klaus. "Orpheus im Mittelalter." *Archiv für Kulturgeschichte* 45 (1963): 253–94.

Herman, Arthur. *The Idea of Decline in Western History.* New York: Free Press, 1997.

Herren, Michael W., et al., ed. *Latin Culture in the Eleventh Century: Proceedings of the Third International Conference on Medieval Latin Studies.* Publications of the *Journal of Medieval Latin* 5.1–2. Turnhout: Brepols, 2002.

Hexter, Jack G.H. "The Education of the Aristocracy in the Renaissance." In *Reappraisals in History.* Jack G.H. Hexter, ed. Evanston, IL: Northwestern University Press, 1962, 45–70.

Hoeges, Dirk. "Emphatischer Humanismus: Ernst Robert Curtius, Ernst Troeltsch und Karl Mannheim. Von Deutscher Geist in Gefahr zu Europäische Literatur und lateinisches Mittelalter." In *In Ihnen begegnet sich das Abendland: Bonner Vorträge zur Erinnerung an Ernst Robert Curtius.* Wolf-Dieter Lange, ed. Bonn: Bouvier, 1990, 31–52.

Hollister, C. Warren. *Anglo-Norman Political Culture and the Twelfth-Century Renaissance: Proceedings of the Borchard Conference of Anglo-Norman History 1995.* Woodbridge: Boydell, 1997.

—, and John Baldwin. "The Rise of Administrative Kingship: Henry I and Philip Augustus." AHR 83 (1978): 867–905.

Holopainen, Toivo J. *Dialectic and Theology in the Eleventh Century.* Leiden: Brill, 1996.

Holzhausen, Jens. *Der "Mythos vom Menschen" im hellenistischen Ägypten: Eine Studie zu "Poimandres," zu Valentin und dem gnostischen Mythos.* Bodenheim: Athenäum, 1994.

Huizinga, Johan. *The Autumn of the Midlde Ages.* Rodney J. Payton and Ulrich Mammitzsch, trans. Chicago: University of Chicago Press, 1996.

—. "John of Salisbury: A Pre-Gothic Mind." In *Men and Ideas: History, the Middle Ages, and the Renaissance.* James S. Holmes and Hans Van Marle, trans. Princeton, NJ: Princeton University Press, 1959, 159–77.

—. *The Waning of the Middle Ages: A Study of the Forms of Life Thought and Art in France and the Netherlands in the 14th and 15th Centuries.* Fritz Hopman, trans. London: Arnold, 1924.

Huberti, Ludwig. *Studien zur Rechtsgeschichte der Gottesfrieden und Landfrieden.* Ansbach: C. Brügel, 1892.

Huygens, Robert B.C. "Guillaume de Tyr étudiant: Un chapitre (XIX, 12) de son 'Histoire' retrouvé." *Latomus* 21 (1962): 810–29.

—, ed. "Textes latins du XIe au XIIIe siècle." *Studi Medievali,* ser. 3.8 (1967): 476–89.

Illich, Ivan. *In the Vineyard of the Text: A Commentary to Hugh's Didascalicon.* Chicago: University of Chicago Press, 1993.

Imbach, Ruedi. "Philosophy." In *Encyclopedia of the Middle Ages.* André Wauchet, et al., ed. Chicago: James Clark, 2000, 2:1131.

The Interpreter's Bible: The Holy Scriptures in the King James and Revised Standard Versions. New York: Abingdon-Cokesbury Press, 1956.

Irwin, E. "The Songs of Orpheus and the New Songs of Christ." In Warden, *Orpheus*, 51–62.

Jaeger, C. Stephen. "Beauty of Manners and Discipline *(schone site, zuht)*: An Imperial Tradition of Courtliness in the German Romace." In *Barocker Lust-Spiegel: Festschrift for Blake Lee Spahr.* Martin Bircher et al., ed. Amsterdam: Rodopi, 1984, 27–46.

—. "Bookburning at Don Quixote's: Thoughts on the Educating Force of Courtly Romance." In *Courtly Arts and the Art of Courtliness.* Keith Busby and Christopher Kleinhenz, ed. Cambridge: D.S. Brewer, 2006, 3–28.

—. "Charisma and the Transformations of Western Culture, 12th to 13th Centuries." *Religions* 14 (2023). Online at https://doi.org/10.3390/rel14121516.

—. "The Courtier Bishop in *Vitae* from the Tenth to the Twelfth Century." *Speculum* 58 (1983): 291–325.

—. *Enchantment: On Charisma and the Sublime in the Arts of the West.* Philadelphia: University of Pennsylvania Press, 2012.

—. *Ennobling Love: In Search of a Lost Sensibility.* Philadelphia: University of Pennsylvania Press, 1999.

—. *The Envy of Angels: Cathedral Schools and Social Ideals in Medieval Europe.* Philadelphia: University of Pennsylvania Press, 1994.

—. "Ernst Robert Curtius: A Medievalist's Contempt for the Middle Ages." *Viator* 47.2 (2016): 367–79.

—. "Gerbert von Aurillac versus Ohtric von Magdeburg: Spielregeln einer akademischen Disputatio im 10. Jahrhundert." In *Spielregeln der Machtigen: Mittelalterliche Politik zwischen Gewohnheit und Konvention. Festschrift Gerd Althoff.* Claudia Garnier and Hermann Kamp, ed. Darmstadt: Wissenschaftliche Buchgesellschaft, 2010, 95–120.

—. "Humanism and Ethics at the School of St. Victor in the Early Twelfth Century." *Mediaeval Studies* 55 (1993): 51–79.

—. "Irony and Role-Playing in John of Salisbury and the Becket Circle." In *Culture politique des Plantagenêt (1154–1224).* Martin Aurell, ed. Poitiers: CNRS, 2003, 319–31.

—. "L'amour des rois: Structure social d'une forme de sensibilité aristocratique." *Annales Économies Sociétés Civilisations* 46 (1991): 547–71.

—. *Medieval Humanism in Gottfried von Strassburg's* Tristan und Isolde. Heidelberg: Carl Winter, 1997.

—. *The Origins of Courtliness: Civilizing Trends and the Formation of Courtly Ideals, 939–1210.* Philadelphia: University of Pennsylvania Press, 1985.

—. "*The Origins of Courtliness* after Twenty-Five Years." *Haskins Society Journal* 21 (2009): 187–216.

—. *The Sense of the Sublime in the Middle Ages.* Online at: https://www.academia.edu/72905836.

—. "*Sermo propheticus:* The Grand Style in the Medieval Sermon from John the Evangelist to Aelred of Rievaulx." *Mittellateinisches Jahrbuch* 55 (2020): 1–39.

—. "The Stature of the Learned Poet in the Eleventh Century." In *Norm und Krise von Kommunikation: Inszenierungen literarischer und sozialer Interaktion im Mittelalter.* Gert Melville, ed. Tübingen: Lit, 2007, 417–38.

Jaeger, Werner. *Paideia: The Ideals of Greek Culture.* Gilbert Highet, trans. 2nd ed. 3 vols. Oxford: Oxford University Press, 1969.

Jeauneau, Edouard. "'Nani gigantum humeris insidentes': Essai d'interpretation de Bernard de Chartres." *Vivarium* 5 (1967): 79–99.

Johanek, Peter. "Klosterstudien im 12. Jahrhundert." In Fried, *Schulen und Studium*, 35–68.

Johnson, Ian R. "Walton's Sapient Orpheus. In *The Medieval Boethius.* Alistair J. Minnis, ed. Cambridge: Cambridge University Press, 1987, 139–68.

Jones, Peter A. *Laughter and Power in the Twelfth Century.* Oxford: Oxford University Press, 2019.

Jordan, William Chester. "*Quando fuit natus:* Interpreting the Birth of Philip Augustus." In *The Work of Jacques Le Goff and the Challenges of Medieval History.* Miri Rubin, ed. New York: Boydell and Brewer, 1997, 171–88.

Jung, Jacqueline. *Eloquent Bodies: Movement, Expression, and the Human Figure in Gothic Sculpture.* New Haven, CT: Yale University Press, 2020.

Kaeuper, Richard F. *Chivalry and Violence in Medieval Europe.* Oxford: Oxford University Press, 1999.

Kallendorf, Craig W., ed. and trans. *Humanist Educational Treatises.* Cambridge, MA: Harvard University Press, 2002.

Keats-Rohan, Katharine S.B. "John of Salisbury and Education in Twelfth-Century Paris from the Account of his *Metalogicon*." *History of Universities* 6 (1986): 1–45.

Keen, Maurice. *Chivalry.* New Haven, CT: Yale University Press, 1986.

Kempf, J. *Zur Kulturgeschichte Frankens während der sachsischen und salischen Kaiser. Mit einem Excurs: Ober einen Schulstreit zwischen Würzburg und Worms im 11. Jahrhundert. Programm der königliches Neuen Gymnasiums Würzburg 1914/15.* Würzburg: Neuen Gymnasiums, 1915.

Kennedy, Elspeth. "The Knight as Reader of Arthurian Romance." In *Culture and the King: The Social Implications of the Arthurian Legend. Essays in Honor of Valerie Lagorio.* Martin B. Schichtmann, ed. Albany: SUNY Press, 1994, 70–90.

Kerr, Julie. *Monastic Hospitality: The Benedictines in England, c.1070–c.1250.* Woodbridge: Boydell & Brewer, 2007.

Klewitz, Hans W. "Königtum, Hofkapelle und Domkapitel im 10. und 11. Jahrhundert." *Archiv für Urkundenforschung* 16 (1938): 102-56.

Klibansky, Raymond F., Fritz Saxl, and Erwin Panofsky. *Saturn and Melancholy: Studies in the History of Natural Philosophy, Religion and Art.* London: Nelson, 1964.

Kneale, William, and Martha Kneale. *The Development of Logic.* Oxford: Clarendon, 1984.

Knowles, David. *The Evolution of Medieval Thought.* 2nd ed. David E. Luscombe and Christopher N.L. Brooke, ed. London: Longman, 1988.

—. "The Humanism of the Twelfth Century." In David Knowles, *The Historian and Character and Other Essays.* Cambridge: Cambridge University Press, 1963, 16–31.

Koch, Josef. "Die Grundlagen der Geschichtsphilosophie Ottos von Freising." In *Geschichtsdenken und Geschichtsbild im Mittelalter.* Walther Lammers, ed. Darmstadt: Wissenschaftliche Buchgesellschaft, 1961, 321–49.

Kochan, Detlef C. "Literarische Spuren einer Symbolfigur: Orpheus zum Beispiel." In *Literarische Symbolfiguren von Prometheus bis Svejk: Beiträge zur Tradition und Wandel.* Werner Wunderlich, ed. Bern: Haupt, 1989: 37–63.

Köhn, Rolf. "Schulbindung und Trivium im lateinischen Hochmittelalter und ihr möglicher praktischer Nutzen." In Fried, *Schulen und Studium,* 203–84.

Kortüm, Hans-Henning. *Richer von Saint-Remi: Studien zu einem Geschichtsschreiber des 10. Jahrhunderts.* Stuttgart: Steiner, 1985, 93–112.

Kurth, Godefroid. *Notger de Liège et la civilisation au Xe siècle.* Paris: Picard, 1905.

Labande, Edmond-René. "La Formation de Gerbert à St. Geraud d'Aurillac." In *Gerberto: Scienza, storia et mito: Atti del Gerberti Symposium. Bobbio 25–27 Iuglio 1983.* Michele Tosi, ed. Bobbio: Salesianum, 1985, 21–34.

Ladner, Gerhart. "Terms and Ideas of Renewal." In Benson and Constable, *Renaissance and Renewal,* 687–726.

Lapidge, Michael. "The Stoic Inheritance." In Dronke, *History,* 81–112.

Latouche, Robert. "Un imitateur de Salluste au Xe siècle: Richer." In Robert Latouche, *Études médiévales*. Paris: Presses Universitaires de France, 1966, 69–81.

Leclercq, Jean. *Études sur le vocabulaire monastique du moyen âge*. Rome: Herder, 1961.

—. "Interpretazione gerbertiana della vita monastica." In Tosi, ed., *Gerberto*, 677–89.

—. *The Love of Learning and the Desire for God: A Study of Monastic Culture*. Catharine Misrahi, trans. New York: Fordham University Press, 2003.

—. "Pour l'histoire de l'expression 'philosophie chrétienne'." *Mélanges de Science Religieuse* 9 (1952): 221–26.

Lee, M. Owen. "Orpheus and Eurydice: Myth, Legend and Folklore." *Classica et Mediaevalia* 26 (1965): 402–12.

Le Goff, Jacques. *Intellectuals in the Middle Ages*. Teresa L. Fagan, trans. Cambridge, MA: Harvard University Press, 1993.

Leonardi, Claudio. "Intellectual Life." In NCMH 3. Timothy Reuter, ed. Cambridge: Cambridge University, 1999, 186–211.

Lerner, Robert. "Literacy and Learning." In *One Thousand Years: Western Europe in the Middle Ages*. Richard de Molen, ed. Boston: Houghton-Mifflin, 1974, 165–223.

Lèsne, Emil. *Histoire de la propriété ecclésiastique en France* 5. *Les écoles de la fin du VIIIe siècle à la fin du XIIe*. Lille: Champion, 1940.

Lewis, C.S. *The Allegory of Love: A Study in Medieval Tradition*. Oxford: Oxford University Press, 1977.

Lichte, Erika-Fischer. "Culture as Performance." *Modern Austrian Literature* 42 (2009): 1–10.

Liebeschütz, Hans. "The Debate on Philosophical Learning during the Transition Period (900–1080)." In *The Cambridge History of Later Greek and Early Medieval Philosophy*. Arthur H. Armstrong, ed. Cambridge: Cambridge University Press, 1970, 587–610.

—. *Medieval Humanism in the Life and Writings of John of Salisbury*. London: Warburg Institute, 1950.

—. "Western Christian Thought from Boethius to Anselm." In Armstrong, *Cambridge History of Later Greek and Early Christian Philosophy*, 535–639.

Linde, Cornelia. "Die 'Rethorici colores' des Magisters Onulf von Speyer." *Mittellateinisches Jahrbuch* 40 (2005): 333–81.

Lindgren, Uta. *Gerbert von Aurillac und das Quadrivium: Untersuchungen zur Bildung im Zeitalter der Ottonen*. Wiesbaden: Steiner, 1976.

Lutz, Cora. *Schoolmasters of the Tenth Century*. Hamden, CT: Archon, 1977.

Mancal, Josef. *Zum Begriff der Philosophie bei M. Tullius Cicero*. Munich: Fink, 1982.

Märtl, Claudia. "Die Bamberger Schulen: Ein Bildungszentrum des Salierreichs." In *Die Salier und das Reich* 3. *Gesellschaftlicher und Ideengeschichtlicher Wandel im Reich der Salier*. Stefan Weinfurter, ed. Sigmaringen: Thorbecke, 1992, 327–45.

Manitius, Max. *Geschichte der lateinischen Literatur des Mittelalters*. 3 vols. Munich: Beck, 1976.

—. *Philologisches aus alten Bibliothekskatalogen. Rheinisches Museum für Philologie*. Frankfurt-am-Main: Sauerländer, 1892.

Marenbon, John. *Early Medieval Philosophy: An Introduction*. 2nd ed. London: Routledge, 1988.

—. "Logic before 1100: The Latin Tradition." In the *Handbook of the History of Logic* 2. *Mediaeval and Renaissance Logic*. Dov M. Gabbay and John Woods, ed. Amsterdam: North-Holland, 2008, 1–65.

—. *Medieval Philosophy: An Historical and Philosophical Introduction*. London: Routledge, 2007.

—. "Philosophy and Its Background in the Early Medieval West. *Routledge History of Philosophy* 3: *Medieval Philosophy*. John Marenbon, ed. New York: Routledge, 1998, 96–119.

Marshall, Linda. "The Identity of the 'New Man' in the 'Anticlaudianus' of Alan of Lille." *Viator* 10 (1979): 77–94.

Martin, Christopher. "William's Machine." *Journal of Philosophy* 83 (1986): 654–72.

Martin, Janet. "Classicism and Style in Latin Literature." In Benson and Constable, 565–66.

Mayr-Harting, Henry. *Church and Cosmos in Early Ottonian Germany: The View from Cologne*. Oxford: Oxford University Press, 2007.

—. "The Foundation of Peterhouse, Cambridge (1284) and the Rule of St. Benedict." *EHR* 103 (1988): 318–38.

McCarthy, Joseph. "Clement of Alexandria and the Foundation of Christian Educational Theory." *History of Education Society Bulletin* 7 (1971): 11–18.

—. *Humanistic Emphases in the Educational Thought of Vincent of Beauvais*. Leiden: Brill, 1976.

McDonough, Christopher J. "Lyric." In *Medieval Latin: An Introduction and Bibliographical Guide*. Frank A.C. Mantello and Arthur G. Rigg, ed. Washington, DC: Catholic University of America Press, 1996, 589–96.

McGuire, Brian Patrick. *Brother and Lover: Aelred of Rievaulx*. New York: Crossroad, 1994.

McKinney, Loren C. *Bishop Fulbert and Education at the School of Chartres*. Notre Dame, IN: Notre Dame University Press, 1957.

McKitterick, Rosamond. *The Frankish Kingdom under the Carolingians, 751–987*. London: Longman, 1983.

—. "Ottonian Intellectual Culture and the Role of Theophano." *Early Medieval Europe* 2 (1993): 53–74.

—. "The Palace School of Charles the Bald." In *Charles the Bald: Court and Kingdom*. Margaret Gibson and Janet Nelson, ed. Oxford: B.A.R., 1981, 385–400.

—, and John Marenbon. "Philosophy and Its Background in the Early Medieval West." In *Medieval Philosophy. Routledge History of Philosophy 3*. John Marenbon, ed. London: Routledge, 1998, 96–119.

McLaughlin, Mary M. "Abelard's Conception of the Liberal Arts and Philosophy." In *Arts libéraux et philosophie au moyen âge: Actes du quatrième congrès international de philosophie médiévale*. André Cantin, ed. Montreal: Institut d'études médiévales, 1969, 523–30.

Megier, Elisabeth. "*Fortuna* als Kategorie der Geschichtsdeutung im 12. Jahrhundert am Beispiel Ordericus Vitalis und Ottos von Freising." *Mittellateinisches Jahrbuch* 32 (1997): 49–70.

—. "*Tamquam lux post tenebras*, oder: Ottos von Freising Weg von der Chronik zu den *Gesta Friderici*." *Mediavistik* 3 (1990): 131–267.

Meier, Christel. "Der ideale Mensch in Alans von Lille 'Anticlaudianus' und seine Verwandlungen." In Exemplaris Imago: *Ideale in Mittelalter und Früher Neuzeit*. Nikolaus Staubach, ed. Frankfurt-am-Main: Peter Lang, 2012, 137–57.

—. "Die Rezeption des *Anticlaudianus* Alans von Lille in Textkommentierung und Illustration." In *Text und Bild: Aspekte des Zusammenwirkens zweier Künste in Mittelalter und früher Neuzeit*. Christel Meier and Uwe Ruberg, ed. Wiesbaden: Reichert, 1980, 408–549.

Melville, Gert. "Zur geschichtstheoretischen Begründung eines fehlenden Niedergangsbewusstseins im Mittelalter." In *Niedergang: Studien zu einem geschichtlichen Thema*. Reinhart Koselleck and Paul Widmer, ed. Stuttgart: Klett-Cotta, 1980: 103–35.

Mews, Constant J. "Cicero and the Boundaries of Friendship in the Twelfth Century." *Viator* (2007): 369–84.

—. *The Lost Love Letters of Heloise and Abelard: Perceptions of Dialogue in Twelfth-Century France*. Constant J. Mews, ed. and trans. Basingstoke: Palgrave, 2001.

Mitchell, William J.T. *What do Pictures Want?: The Lives and Loves of Images*. Chicago: University of Chicago Press, 2006.

Moore, R.I. *The First European Revolution, c.970–1215*. Oxford: Oxford University Press, 2000.

—. *The Formation of a Persecuting Society: Power and Deviance in Western Europe, 950–1250*. Oxford: Blackwell, 1987.

Morrison, Karl. "Anselm of Havelberg: Play and the Dilemma of Historical Progress." In *Religion, Culture and Society in the Early Middle Ages: Studies in Honor of Richard E. Sullivan*. Thomas F.X. Noble and John J. Contreni, ed. Kalamazoo, MI: Medieval Institute Publications, 1987, 219–56.

Müller, Jan-Dirk. *Gedechtnus: Literatur und Hofgesellschaft um Maximilian I*. Munich: Fink, 1982.

Müller-Christensen, Sigrid. *Das Gunthertuch im Bamberger Domschatz*. Bamberg: Diözesan-Museum, 1966.

Mulsow, Martin. "Der vollkommene Mensch: Zur Prähistorie des Posthumanen." *Deutsche Zeitschrift für Philosophie* 51 (2003): 739–60.

Münster-Swendsen, Mia. "Masters and Paragons: Learning, Power and the Formation of a European Academic Culture, c.900–1230." Ph.D. diss., University of Copenhagen, 2004.

—. "Medieval 'Virtuosity': Classroom Practice and the Transfer of Charismatic Power in Medieval Scholarly Culture c.1000–1230." In *Negotiating Heritage: Memories of the Middle Ages*. Mette Birkedal Bruun, ed. Turnhout: Brepols, 2009, 43–63.

—. "The Model of Scholastic Mastery in Northern Europe c.970–1200." In *Teaching and Learning in Northern Europe, 1000–1200*. Sally N. Vaughn and Jay Rubenstein, ed. Turnhout: Brepols, 2006, 307–42.

—. "Regimens of Schooling." In *The Oxford Handbook of Medieval Latin Literature*. Ralph J. Hexter & David Townsend, ed. Oxford: Oxford University Press, 2012, 403–22.

Nederman, Cary J. *John of Salisbury*. Tempe: Arizona Center for Medieval & Renaissance Studies, 2005.

Nelis Suzanne J. "What Lanfranc Taught, What Anselm Learned." *Haskins Society Journal* 2 (1990): 75–82.

The New Cambridge Medieval History 3. 900–1024. Timothy Reuter, ed. Cambridge: Cambridge University Press, 1999.

Newell, John Howle. "The Dignity of Man in William of Conches and the School of Chartres in the Twelfth Century." Ph.D. diss., Duke University, 1978.

Norden, Eduard. *Die Antike Kunstprosa vom VI. Jahrhundert vor Christus bis in die Zeit der Renaissance*. 2 vols. Leipzig: Teubner, 1909.

Nuchelmans, Gabriel."Philologia et son mariage avec Mercure jusquà la fin du XIIe siècle." *Latomus* 16 (1957): 84–107.

Ohly, Friedrich."*Deus Geometra*: Skizzen zur Geschichte einer Vorstellung von Gott." In *Tradition als historische Kraft: Interdisziplinäre Forschungen zur Geschichte des früheren Mittelalters*. Manfred Balzer, et al., ed. Berlin: De Gruyter, 1982, 1–42.

Otten, Willemien. *From Paradise to Paradigm: A Study of Twelfth-Century Humanism*. Leiden: Brill, 2004.

—. "Medieval Latin Humanism." *Encyclopedia of Mediterranean Humanism*. Houari Touati, ed. Online at: http://www.encyclopédie-humanisme.com/?Medieval-Latin-Humanism.

Otter, Monika."*Vultus adest* (The Face Helps): Performance, Expressivity and Interiority." In *Rhetoric Beyond Words: Delight and Persuasion in the Arts of the Middle Ages*. Mary Carruthers, ed. Cambridge: Cambridge University Press, 2010, 151–72.

Panofsky, Erwin. *Renaissance and Renascences in Western Art*. New York: Harper & Row, 1972.

Paré, Gerard, Pierre Tremblay, and Adrian M. Brunet. *La renaissance du XIIe siècle: Les écoles et l'enseignement*. Paris: Vrin, 1933.

Partner, Nancy. *Serious Entertainments: The Writing of History in Twelfth-Century England*. Chicago: University of Chicago Press, 1977.

Pentcheva, Bissera. *The Sensual Icon: Space, Ritual and the Senses in Byzantium*. University Park: University of Pennsylvania Press, 2010.

Picavet, François *Gerbert: Un pape philosophe d'après l'histoire et d'après la légende*. Paris: Leroux, 1897.

Poirel, Dominique. "'Apprend tout': Saint-Victor et le milieu des Victorins à Paris, 1108–1330." In *Lieux de Savoir: Espaces et communautés*. Christian Jacob, ed. Paris: Albin Michel, 2007, 302–22.

—. "Aux sources d'une influence: Les raisons du rayonnement victorin." In *L'école de Saint-Victor de Paris: Influence et rayonnement du moyen âge à l'époque moderne*. Dominique Poirel, ed. Turnhout: Brepols, 2010, 5–25.

———. "*Hugo Saxo*: Les origines germaniques de la pensée de Hugues de Saint-Victor." In *L'histoire des idées au temps de la réforme: Contribution des échanges entre l'Empire et ses voisins européens (850–1150)*. T. Lesieur, ed. *Francia* 33 (2006): 163–74.

Poole, Reginald Lane. *Illustrations of the History of Medieval Thought and Learning*. 2nd ed. New York: Dover, 1920.

Prantl, Carl. *Geschichte der Logik im Abendlande*. Graz: Akademischer Druck, 1955.

Prigent, Pierre. "Orphée dans l'iconographie Chrétienne." *Revue d'histoire et de philosophie religieuses* 64 (1984): 205–21.

Prinzing, G. "Das Bamberger Gunthertuch in neuer Sicht." In V. Vavrinek, ed., *Byzantium and its Neighbors: From the Mid-Ninth to the Twelfth Century*. Prague: Institut Slav, 1993, 218–31.

Pyle, C. Munro. "Le thème d'Orphée dans les oeuvres latines d'Ange Politien." *Bulletin de l'Association Guillaume Budé* 39 (1980): 408–19.

Radding, Charles. "Evolution of Medieval Mentalities: A Cognitive-Structural Approach." *AHR* 83 (1978): 577–97.

———. "Superstition to Science: Nature, Fortune and the Passing of the Medieval Ordeal." *AHR* 84 (1979): 945–69.

———. *A World Made by Men: Cognition and Society, 400–1200*. Chapel Hill: University of North Carolina Press, 1985.

Rashdall, Hastings. *The Universities of Europe in the Middle Ages*. 3 vols. Oxford: Oxford University Press, 1997.

Reichert, Folker. *Fackel in der Finsternis: Der Historiker Carl Erdmann und das "Dritte Reich."* 2 vols. Darmstadt: Wissenschaftliche Buchgesellschaft, 2022.

Reitzenstein, Richard. *Poimandres: Studien zur griechisch-ägyptischen und frühchristlichen Literatur*. Leipzig: Teubner, 1904.

Renardy, Charles. "Les écoles Liègoises du XIe et XIIe siècle." *Revue Belge de philologie et d'histoire* 57 (1979): 309–28.

Renovacion intelectual del Occidente europeo (siglo XII), XXIV Semana de Estudios Medievales Estella, 14 a 18 de julio de 1997. Pamplona: Gobierno de Navarra, 1998.

Reuter, Timothy. "Past, Present and No Future in the Twelfth-Century *Regnum Teutonicum*." In *The Perception of the Past in Twelfth-Century Europe*. Paul Magdalino, ed. London: Hambledon Press, 1992, 15–36.

Rexroth, Frank. *Fröhliche Scholastik: Die Wissenschaftsrevolution des Mittelalters*. Munich: Beck, 2018.

Riché, Pierre. *Abbon de Fleury: Un moine savant et combatif (vers 950–1004)*. Turnhout: Brepols, 2004.

—. *Les Écoles et l'enseignement dans l'occident chrétien de la fin du Ve siècle au milieu du XIe siècle*. Paris: Aubier Montaigne, 1979.

—. *Education et culture dans l'occident barbare, 6–8 siècles*. 3rd ed. Paris: Editions de Seuil, 1972.

—. "L'enseignement de Gerbert à Reims dans le context européen." In *Gerberto: Scienza, storia et mito. Atti del Gerberti Symposium, Bobbio 25–27 Iuglio 1983*. Michele Tosi, ed. Bobbio: Salesianum, 1985, 51–69.

—. *Gerbert d'Aurillac: Le pape de l'an mil*. Paris: Fayard, 2006.

Robinson, Ian S. "The 'colores rhetorici' in the Investiture Contest." *Traditio* 32 (1976): 209–38.

Rossi Monti, Martino. "*Opus es magnificum*: The Image of God and the Aesthetics of Grace." In *Magnificence and the Sublime in Medieval Aesthetics: Art, Architecture, Literature, Music*. C. Stephen Jaeger, ed. New York: Palgrave-Macmillan, 2010, 17–29.

Sansone, David. "Orpheus and Eurydice in the Fifth Century." *Classica et Mediaevalia* 36 (1985): 53–64.

Schaeder, Hans Heinrich. "Die islamische Lehre vom vollkommenen Menschen, ihre Herkunft und ihre dichterische Gestaltung." *Zeitschrift der deutschen Morgenländischen Gesellschaft* n.s. 4.79 (1925): 192–268.

Scharschmidt, Carl. *Johannes Saresberiensis nach Leben und Studien, Schriften und Philosophie*. Leipzig: Teubner, 1862.

Schauwecker, Helga. "Otloh von St. Emmeram: Ein Beitrag zur Bildungs- und Frömmigkeitsgeschichte des 11. Jahrhunderts." Ph.D. diss., University of Würzburg, 1962.

Schepss, Georg. "Zu Froumunds Briefcodex und zu Ruodlieb." *ZfdPh* 15 (1883): 419–33.

Schieffer, Rudolf. "Bleibt der Archipoeta anonym?" *MIÖG* 98 (1990): 59–79.

Schmidt, Roderich. "'Aetates mundi': Die Weltalter als Gliederungs prinzip der Geschichte." *Zeitschrift für Kirchengeschichte* 67 (1955/56): 288–317.

Schmitt, Jean-Claude. *La Raison des gestes dans l'occident médiéval*. Paris: Gallimard, 1990.

Schnell, Rüdiger. "Die höfische Kultur des Mittelalters zwischen Ekel und Ästhetik." *Frühmittelalterliche Studien* 39 (2005): 1–100.

Schnith, Karl. "Recht und Friede: Zum Konigsgedanken im Umkreis Heinrichs III." *Historisches Jahrbuch* 81 (1962): 22–57.

Schramm, Percy Ernst. *Kaiser, Rom und Renovatio: Studien zur Geschichte des römischen Erneuerungsgedankens vom Ende des karolingischen*

Reiches bis zum Investiturstreit. 2nd ed. Darmstadt: Wissenschaftliche Buchgesellschaft, 1984.

Schwartz, Ella. "Aspects of Orpheus in Classical Literature and Mythology." Ph.D. diss., Harvard University, 1984.

Silverstein, Theodore. "The Fabulous Cosmogony of Bernardus Silvestris." *Modern Philology* 46 (1948): 92–116.

Silvestre, Hubert. "Notice sur Adelman de Liège, évèque de Brescia (d.1061)." *Revue d'Histoire Ecclésiastique* 56 (1961): 855–71.

Simon, Joan. *Education and Society in Tudor England.* Cambridge: Cambridge University Press, 1966.

Smalley, Beryl. *The Becket Controversy and the Schools.* Oxford: Blackwell, 1973.

—. *The Study of the Bible in the Middle Ages.* Notre Dame, IN: Notre Dame University Press, 1964.

Somfai, Anna. "The Eleventh-Century Shift in the Reception of Plato's 'Timaeus' and Calcidius's 'Commentary'." *Journal of the Warburg and Courtauld Institutes* 65 (2002): 1–21.

Sommerfeldt, John. "Charismatic and Gregorian Leadership in the Thought of Bernard of Clairvaux." In *Bernard of Clairvaux: Studies Presented to Dom Jean Leclercq.* Basil Pennington, ed. Washington, DC: Cistercian Publications, 1973, 73–90.

Sot, Michel "Le Moine Gerbert, l'église de Reims et l'église de Rome." In *Gerbert l'européen: Actes du colloque d'Aurillac, 4–7 juin 1996.* Nicole Charbonnel and Jean-Eric Iung, ed. Aurillac: Société des Lettres la Haute Auvergne, 1997, 135–49.

Southern, R.W. "Aspects of the European Tradition of Historical Writing 2. Hugh of St. Victor and the Idea of Historical Development." *Transactions of the Royal Historical Society,* ser. 5.21 (1971): 159–79.

—. "Lanfranc and Berengar." In *Studies in Medieval History Presented to Frederick Maurice Powicke.* Richard W. Hunt et al., ed. Oxford: Oxford University Press, 1948, 27–48.

—. *The Making of the Middle Ages.* New Haven, CT: Yale University Press, 1953.

—. "Medieval Humanism." In R.W. Southern, *Medieval Humanism and Other Studies.* Oxford: Oxford University Press, 1970, 29–60.

—. "The Place of England in the Twelfth-Century Renaissance." *History* 45 (1960): 201–16.

—. *Platonism, Scholastic Method, and the School of Chartres: The Stenton Lecture 1978.* Reading: Reading University Press, 1979.

—. *Scholastic Humanism and the Unification of Europe*. 2 vols. Oxford: Blackwell, 1995.

Sprandel, Rolf. *Ivo von Chartres und seine Stellung in der Kirchen Geschichte*. Stuttgart: Hiersemann, 1962.

Specht, Franz A. *Geschichte des Unterrichtswesens in Deutschland von den ältesten Zeiten bis zur Mitte des dreizehnten Jahrhunderts*. Stuttgart: Cotta, 1885.

Speer, Andreas. "Vergöttlichung." LexMA 8:1531–32.

Staub, Johannes "Domschulen am Mittelrhein um und nach 1000." In *Bischof Burchard von Worms, 1000–1025*. Wilfried Hartmann, ed. Mainz: Gesellschaft für mittelrheinische Kirchengeschichte, 2000, 279–309.

Staubach, Nikolaus. "Geschichte als Lebenstrost: Bemerkungen zur historiographischen Konzeption Ottos von Freising." *Mittellateinisches Jahrbuch* 23 (1988): 46–75.

Steckel, Sita. "Charisma and Expertise: Constructing Sacralized Mastership in Northern and Western Europe, 800–1150." In *Schüler und Meister*. Thomas Jeschke and Andreas Speer, ed. Berlin: De Gruyter, 2016, 641–79.

—. *Kulturen des Lehrens im Früh- und Hochmittelalter: Autorität, Wissenskonzepte und Netzwerke von Gelehrten*. Cologne: Böhlau, 2011.

Steinen, Wolfram von den. "Humanismus um 1100." *Archiv für Kulturgeschichte* 46 (1964): 196–214.

Stock, Brian. *The Implications of Literacy: Written Language and Models of Interpretation in the Eleventh and Twelfth Centuries*. Princeton, NJ: Princeton University Press, 1983.

—. *Myth and Science in the Twelfth Century: A Study of Bernard Silvester*. Princeton, NJ: Princeton University Press, 1972.

Stotz, Peter. "Dichten als Schulfach: Aspekte mittelalterlicher Schuldichtung." Mlat. Jb. 16 (1981): 1–16.

Struve, Tilman. "'Vita civilis naturam imitetur': Der Gedanke der Nachahmung der Natur als Grundlage der organologischen Staatskonzeption Johannes von Salisbury." *Historisches Jahrbuch* 101 (1981): 341–61.

Stump, Eleanor. *Dialectic and Its Place in the Development of Medieval Logic*. Ithaca, NY: Cornell University Press, 1989.

—. "*Garlandus Compotista* and Dialectic in the Eleventh and Twelfth Centuries." *History and Philosophy of Logic* 1 (1980): 1–18.

Sturlese, Loris. *Die deutsche Philosophie im Mittelalter*. Munich: Beck, 1993.

Saint Giron, Baldine. "Sublime." *Encyclopedia of Aesthetics*. Michael Kelley, ed. New York: Oxford University Press, 1998, 4:322–26.

★ BIBLIOGRAPHY

Swanson, Robert N. *The Twelfth-Century Renaissance*. Manchester: Manchester University Press, 1999.

Szöverffy, Josef. *Secular Latin Lyrics and Minor Poetic Forms of the Middle Ages: A Historical Survey and Literary Repertory from the Tenth to the Late Fifteenth Century*. 3 vols. Concord, NH: Classical Folia, 1992–94.

Taylor, Henry Osborn. *The Classical Heritage of the Middle Ages*. New York: Columbia University Press, 1901.

Thomson, Rodney M. "England and the Twelfth-Century Renaissance." *Past and Present* 101 (1983): 3–21.

—. "The Origins of Latin Satire in Twelfth-Century Europe." *Mittellateinisches Jahrbuch* 13 (1978): 73–83.

—. "The Place of Germany in the Twelfth-Century Renaissance." In *Manuscripts and Monastic Culture: Reform and Renewal in Twelfth-Century Germany*. Alison I. Beach, ed. Turnhout: Brepols, 2007, 19–42.

—. "Richard Southern and the Twelfth-Century Intellectual World: Review of R.W. Southern, *Scholastic Humanism*." *Journal of Religious History* 26 (2002): 264–73.

Thorndike, Lynn. *University Records and Life in the Middle Ages*. New York: Columbia University Press, 1949.

Tischler, Matthias M. "Meinhart von Bamberg: Die Physiognomie eines 'Protointellektuellen' des 11. Jahrhunderts." In *Deutsche Texte der Salierzeit: Neuanfänge und Kontinuitäten im 11. Jahrhundert*. Stephan Müller and Jens Schneider, ed. Munich: Fink, 2010, 251–85.

Töpfer, Frank. "Selbstbegegnung in der Geschichte: Zum Begriff des Humanismus bei Ernst Robert Curtius." *Archiv für Begriffsgeschichte* 54 (2012): 91–117.

Tosi, Michele. "Il governo abbaziale di Gerberto a Bobbio." In *Gerberto: Scienza, storia et mito. Atti del Gerberti Symposium, Bobbio 25–27 Iuglio 1983*. Michele Tosi, ed. Bobbio: Salesianum, 1985, 71–234.

Traube, Ludwig. *Einleitung in die lateinische Philologie des Mittelalters: Vorlesungen und Abhandlungen* 2. Paul Lehmann, ed. Munich: Beck, 1911.

Trinkaus, Charles. *In Our Image and Likeness: Humanity and Divinity in Italian Humanist Thought*. 2 vols. Notre Dame, IN: Notre Dame University Press, 1995.

Vale, Malcolm. *The Princely Court: Medieval Courts and Culture in North-West Europe, 1270–1380*. Oxford: Oxford University Press, 2001.

Van Deusen, Nancy, ed. *Cicero Refused to Die: Ciceronian Influence through the Centuries*. Leiden: Brill, 2013.

Van Groningen, Bernard A. *In the Grip of the Past: Essay on an Aspect of Greek Thought.* Leiden: Brill, 1953.

Verbeke, Gerard. "Aux origines de la notion de 'loi naturelle'." In *La filosofia della natura nel medioevo: Atti del terzo congresso internazionale di filosofia medioevale.* Milan: Vita e Pensiero, 1966, 164–73.

Visconti, Fabrizio. "Un fenomeno di continuita iconografica: Orfeo citaredo, Davide salmista, Cristo pastore, Adamo e gli animali." *Augustinianum* 28 (1988): 429–36.

Vones, Ludwig. "Erzbischof Brun von Köln und seine 'Schule'." In *Köln: Stadt und Bistum in Kirche und Reich des Mittelalters: Festschrift für Odilo Engels.* Hanna Vollrath and Stefan Weinfurter, ed. Cologne: Böhlau, 1993, 125–37.

Von Moos, Peter. *Hildebert von Lavardin 1056–1133: Humanitas an der Schwelle des höfischen Zeitalters.* Stuttgart: Hiersemann, 1965.

—. "Lucans *tragedia* im Hochmittelalter: Pessimismus, *contemptus mundi* und Gegenwartserfahrung (Otto von Freising, 'Vita Heinrici IV', Johann von Salisbury)." *Mittellateinisches Jahrbuch* 14 (1979): 127–86.

—. "*Par tibi, Roma, nihil*: Eine Antwort." *Mittellateinisches Jahrbuch* 14 (1979): 119–26.

Vossen, Peter. *Der Libellus scolasticus des Walther von Speyer: Ein Schulbericht aus dem Jahr 984.* Berlin: De Gruyter, 1962.

Wallach, Liupold. "Education and Culture in the Tenth Century." *Mediaevalia et Humanistica* 9 (1955): 18–22.

—. "Onulf of Speyer: A Humanist of the Eleventh Century." *Medievalia et Humanistica* 6 (1950): 35–56.

Walsh, Patrick G. "Alan of Lille as a Renaissance Figure." *Studies in Church History* 14 (1977): 117–35.

Ward, John O. "Gothic Architecture, Universities and the Decline of the Humanities in Twelfth-Century Europe." In *Principalities, Powers and Estates: Studies in Medieval and Early Modern Government and Society.* L.O. Frappell, ed. Adelaide: Adelaide University Union Press, 1979, 65–78.

—. *The Rhetoric of Cicero in its Medieval and Early Renaissance Commentary Tradition.* Virginia Cox and John O. Ward., ed. Leiden: Brill, 2006.

Warden, J., ed. *Orpheus: The Metamorphosis of a Myth.* Toronto: University of Toronto Press, 1982.

Warnick, Bryan R. *Imitation and Education: A Philosophical Inquiry into Learning by Example.* Albany: SUNY Press, 2008.

★ BIBLIOGRAPHY

—. "Learning from the Lives of Others: A Social Analysis of Human Exemplarity and Imitation." Ph.D. diss., University of Illinois, Urbana, 2005.
Wattenbach, Wilhelm, and Robert Holtzmann. *Deutschlands Geschichtsquellen im Mittelalter: Deutsche Kaiserzeit* 1. Tübingen: Matthiesen, 1948.
Webb, Clement C. J. *John of Salisbury*. London: Methuen, 1932.
Weber, Max. *Max Weber on Charisma and Institution Building: Selected Papers.* S. N. Eisenstadt, ed. Chicago: University of Chicago Press, 1968.
Wegner, Max. "Orpheus: Ursprung und Nachfolge." *Boreas* 9 (1988): 177–225.
Weinberg, Julius. *A Short History of Medieval Philosophy*. Princeton, NJ: Princeton University Press, 1964.
Wenzel, Horst. *Hören und Sehen, Schrift und Bild: Kultur und Gedächtnis im Mittelalter*. Munich: Beck, 1995.
Weston, Jessie. *From Ritual to Romance*. Princeton, NJ: Princeton University Press, 1920.
Wetherbee, Winthrop. "Philosophy, Cosmology, and the Twelfth-Century Renaissance." In Dronke, *History*, 21–53.
—. *Platonism and Poetry in the Twelfth Century*. Princeton, NJ: Princeton University Press, 1972.
White, Hayden F. "The Gregorian Ideal and Saint Bernard of Clairvaux." *Journal of the History of Ideas* 21 (1960): 321–48.
Wieland, Georg. *Aufbruch- Wandel-Erneuerung: Beiträge zur "Renaissance" des 12. Jahrhunderts. 9. Blaubeurer Symposion vom 9.–11. Oktober 1992.* Stuttgart: Frommann-Holzboog, 1995.
Wilks, Michael. "Alan of Lille and the New Man." *Studies in Church History* 14 (1977): 137–57.
Williams, John R. "The Cathedral School of Rheims in the Eleventh Century." *Speculum* 19 (1954): 661–77.
—. "The Cathedral School of Rheims in the Time of Master Alberic, 1118–36." *Traditio* 20 (1964): 93–114.
—. "Manasses I of Rheims and Gregory VII." *AHR* 54 (1949): 804–24.
Wilson, Edmund. *Axel's Castle*. New York: Scribner's, 1935.
Woodward, William Harrison. *Studies in Education during the Age of the Renaissance, 1400–1600*. New York: Columbia University Teacher's College Press, 1967.
—. *Vittorino de Feltre and Other Humanist Educators*. New York: Columbia University Teacher's College Press, 1963.

Worstbrock, Franz Josef. "Translatio artium: Über die Herkunft und Entwicklung einer kulturhistorischen Theorie." *Archiv für Kulturgeschichte* 47 (1965): 1–22.

Yates, Frances. *Giordano Bruno and the Hermetic Tradition*. London: Routledge and Kegan Paul, 1964.

Zey, Claudia. "Vormünder und Berater Heinrichs IV. im Urteil der Zeitgenossen (1056–1075)." In *Heinrich IV.* Gerd Althoff, ed. Ostfildern: Thorbecke, 2009, 87–127.

Zielinski, Herbert. *Der Reichsepiskopat in spätottonischer und salischer Zeit (1002–1125)*. Wiesbaden: Steiner, 1984.

Zimmermann, Otto. "Brun I.: Erzbischof von Cöln und die in den Schulen seiner Zeit gepflegte Wissenschaft." Ph.D. diss., University of Leipzig, 1871.

Ziolkowski, Jan. "History of Medieval Latin Literature." In *Medieval Latin: An Introduction and Bibliographical Guide*. Frank A.C. Mantello and Arthur G. Rigg, ed. Washington, DC: Catholic University of America Press, 1996, 505–36.

—. *Nota Bene: Reading Classics and Writing Melodies in the Early Middle Ages*. Turnhout: Brepols, 2007.

—. "Twelfth-Century Understandings and Adaptations of Ancient Friendship." In *Medieval Antiquity*. Andries Welkenhuysen, et al., ed. Louvain: Louvain University Press, 1995, 59–81.

Zumthor, Paul. "Körper und Performanz." In *Materialitaet der Kommunikation*. Hans-Ulrich Gumbrecht et al., ed. Frankfurt-am-Main: Suhrkamp, 1988, 703–13.

—. *Oral Poetry: An Introduction*. Kathryn Murphy-Judy, trans. Minneapolis: University of Minnesota Press, 1990.

—. "The Text and the Voice." NLH 16 (1984/85): 67–92.

Zwierlein, Otto. "Par tibi Roma, nihil." *Mittellateinisches Jahrbuch* 11 (1976): 92–94.

INDEX

A
Abbo of Fleury, abbot 33, 97, 98, 99, 119, 120, 121, 128, 131; Aristotle 121; Boethius 120; letters 119–121
Abelard, Peter: Anselm of Laon 44–45; Astralabe 66; *Historia calamitatum* 45, 66, 393; John of Salisbury 301, 304, 307, 336; logic 303, 310, 314–17, 355; love 370; new learning 60–62, 65, 67, 140, 327, 352–53, 391–93; Paris 173; scholarship 97–98; *Sic et non* 66; *Theologia Christiana* 20; humanism 7, 10,
Adalbero of Rheims, archbishop 107
Adalbert, archbishop of Hamburg/Bremen 25, 240
Adalbold of Utrecht 47
Adam du Petit Pont 308, 312, 315
Adam of Balsham 308, 374, 392; *The Art of Reasoning* 309
Adam of Bremen 25, 240
Adam of Dryburgh 294
Adela of Blois, countess 188, 210, 240, 246
Adelard of Bath 327, 334
Adelman of Liège, bishop 25, 41, 62, 63, 64, 171
Ademar of Chabannes 61
Aelred of Rievaulx 7, 167, 294, 344, 367, 368
aesthetics 7, 15, 181, 223, 268, 269, 271, 273–75, 277, 281, 283, 289, 295–97, 360
Alan of Lille 19, 264, 301, 326, 364, 374; *Anticlaudianus* 14, 39, 58, 59, 69, 77, 79, 87, 209, 252, 257, 259, 260, 261, 263, 268, 334, 338, 371, 378, 380, 401, 403, 408
Alberic of Paris, master 304, 305, 306, 315, 336, 347, 355
Alberic of Rheims 305, 336, 355

Alberti, Leon Battista 331, 332, 333, 339
Alcuin of York 13, 52, 105, 106, 165, 185, 319, 320; *On Rhetoric and the Virtues* 89
Alexander II, pope 240
Amadeus of Lausanne, bishop 242
Amadis of Gaul 423
Ambrose of Milan 40; *De officiis min* 192; *In Psalmum David CXVIII Expositio* 248
Amphion 211, 214
Andreas Capellanus 388
Angelram of St. Riquier, abbot 41
Anselm of Bec/Canterbury 97, 99, 100, 121, 294, 296
Anselm of Besate, *Rhetorimachia* 47, 127, 205
Anselm of Havelberg 345
Anselm of Laon 21, 45, 61, 65, 66, 90, 333, 351, 352, 374
Anselm of Liège 90, 92, 151, 165, 172, 173
Apostles 368
Aquinas, Thomas 246, 414
Aquitaine 61
Archpoet 326, 327, 364, 383
Arion 211
Ariprandus, monk 122
Aristotle 8; aesthetics 414; Aristotelianism 39, 97, 99, 100, 101, 113, 116, 119, 128, 131, 316; categories 109; empiricism 39; logic 97, 100, 101; *Nichomachean Ethics* 246; *Peri Hermeneias* 107, 121
Aristoxenus 185, 191
Arnulf of Lisieux 302, 390
Arthurian romance 366
Arthur, king 286, 366
Asclepius 247, 250, 251, 254, 406
Astrologia 107
astronomy 37, 38, 39, 114, 117, 258
Attila the Hun 162, 164

auctores 28, 46
auctoritas: ancients 236, 341; "force" 150; history 152
authority: artistic 271, 272, 297; historical 10, 121, 236, 247, 313, 334, 343; personal 43–44, 60–67, 74, 81, 147, 157, 160, 180, 201, 275–78, 353; political 353, 410; textual 283–85
Auerbach, Erich 133, 137, 283, 415; "Camilla, or the Rebirth of the Sublime." 414
Augsburg: cathedral school 98
Augustine of Hippo, St. 162; *Cassiciacum Dialogues* 171; *City of God* 247, 342; *De doctrina Christiana* 166; *impetus* 166–70; optimism 330, 342; rule 397; St. Victor 378
Aulus Gelius 89
Aurell, Martin 16
Aurillac, abbey 116
Azecho of Worms, bishop 47
Azelinus, bishop 32

B
Babylon 55, 341
Bacon, Roger 202
Balderich of Speyer, bishop 42, 50, 111
Balderich of Trier 42, 50
Bamberg: cathedral school 24, 25, 31, 138, 139, 141, 142, 150–52, 158, 160, 163, 165, 168, 174, 176; letters 134
Barrett, Sam 181, 196
Baudri of Bourgueil, abbot: humanism 6, 264, 373; Muriel 293–95; music 198, 210, 246, 281; philosophy 251, 408; poetry 9, 188–89, 195, 203, 220, 291, 299, 364
Becket, Thomas, archbishop 73, 74, 146, 161–62, 303, 327, 343, 357, 382, 390
Benedictines 96, 97, 100, 116, 119, 120, 121, 128, 384, 397; dialectic 131; *Rule of St. Benedict* 92, 118, 368
Benedict of Chiusa 61

Benes, Juraj 327
Benjamin, Walter 270, 277
Benno II of Osnabrück, bishop 32, 138, 172
Benzo of Alba, imperial chaplain 251, 407
Berengar of Tours 25, 45, 46, 62, 63, 64, 93, 99, 100, 121, 127, 139, 140, 173, 300, 333, 351, 352, 374; dialectic 131
Bernard of Aurillac 110
Bernard of Chartres 19, 68, 71, 140, 143, 190, 191, 307, 313, 314, 316, 317, 338, 352, 356, 374
Bernard of Clairvaux 43, 57, 58, 60, 81, 155, 248, 263, 273–74, 276, 279, 280, 294, 302, 327, 369–70, 374, 399; *Sermones super Cantica Canticorum* 240
Bernard Silvester 5, 19, 241, 326, 352, 364; *Cosmographia* 39, 79, 245, 246, 249, 255, 257, 268, 379, 401, 403; *Microcosmos* 249
Bern of Reichenau 81, 186–87, 193, 198, 235–37, 245
Bernward of Hildesheim 29, 86, 95
Bible 26, 42, 87, 118, 131, 194, 206, 229, 358, 359, 382, 391; Carolingians 89, 194; Gospels 378
Bildungsroman 257, 265, 266, 282, 420
Binski, Paul 289
Bishop, Richard 310, 313, 390
Bobbio, abbey 97, 110, 116, 117, 118, 119
Boccaccio, Giovanni 6
Boethius, Anicius Manlius Severinus 8, 21, 47, 48, 100, 109, 112, 116, 121, 127, 184, 188, 193, 255, 318, 322, 408; *Consolatio philosophiae (Consolation of Philosophy)* 37, 38, 97, 108, 125, 214, 220, 321; *De arithmetica* 107; *De institutione musica libri quinque* 185, 214, 217; *Dialogues on Porphyry* 107; music 185, 213
Bologna 306, 311, 326

INDEX

Bond, Gerald 361
Bonneval, abbey 240
Borell II, duke 117
bounteousness 58
Boutemy, André 209, 210
Brewer, Derek 91
Brixen 41
Brunelleschi, Filippo 331
Brun of Cologne 10, 12, 19, 21, 23, 25, 26, 70, 72, 83, 84, 85, 86, 112, 140, 216, 232, 320, 331, 333; appointments 89; *Dedication Poem* 87; philosophy 101–5
Burchard II, bishop 31
Burckhardt, Jacob 10; *Civilization of the Renaissance in Italy* 19, 285
Bynum, Caroline 261, 289, 392, 396

C

Caesar, Julius 198
Calcidius 243, 244
Calliope 210, 212
Cambrai, cathedral school 93
Cambridge Medieval History 3, 299
Cambridge Songs (Carmina Cantabrigiensia) 204
canons regular 146, 261, 387
Canterbury 73, 74, 146, 161, 314, 382
Capetians, education 98
Carmina Burana 326, 362, 364, 368, 369
Carolingians: biblical studies 194; court schools 70; education 13, 34, 83, 85, 86, 89, 98, 146, 193; libraries 130; music 185; poetry 214, 232; sources 182
Castiglione, Baldassare 16, 91; *Book of the Courtier* 42, 78, 157
cathedral schools 19–94; German 90, 264; numbers 193. *See also* Augsburg, Bamberg, Cambrai, Chartres, Cologne, Eichstaett, Hildesheim, Liège, Mainz, Metz, Paris, Regensburg, Rheims, Salzburg, Toul, Trier, Utrecht, Verdun, Worms, Würzburg.

Cato 33, 153; *Distichs* 40
Celestine III, pope 358
Cervantes, Miguel de, *Don Quixote* 283, 284, 427
Chantilly manuscript 417
charisma (charismatic): artistic 430–32; bodily 270, 274, 277, 279, 281; cultural 201; divine 260; heroic 413–34; literary 277, 420, 421; monastic 85; pedagogic 83, 86, 144–45, 261, 263; personal 44, 46, 52, 64, 67, 71, 194, 198, 201, 232, 248, 259, 261, 268, 269, 271, 272, 275–82, 285, 422, 430, 433; physical 267–88; poetic 194, 196; representational 418–20; textual 270–87
Charlemagne, emperor 12, 13, 17, 52, 89, 96, 135, 137, 165, 185, 193
Charles the Bald, emperor 96
Chartres: philosophical studies 358; cathedral school 5, 20, 24, 33, 41, 42, 62, 71, 241, 317, 408, 450, 463, 465, 469
Chrétien de Troyes 156, 347, 367, 385, 429; *Cligès* 346; *Yvain* 365, 366, 385, 432
Cicero 30, 37; *Cato de senectute* 153; *De amicitia* 367; *De inventione* 204, 356; *De legibus* 337; *De officiis* 40, 42, 51, 53–64; 104, 125, 148, 319; *De oratore* 51; dialectic 121; *Epistolae* 44; Gerbert 109–11, 320–21; *In L. Pisonem* 104, 319; John of Salisbury 316, 318, 320–22; *litterae et mores* 89; Meinhard 30, 144, 153–54; Peter Damian 123–24, 203, 360; philosophy 105–6, 127–28, 229; *Pro Caelio* 144; *Republic* 107; rhetoric 252; Stoicism 86, 89, 129–30, 318; *Topics* 97, 101, 120; *Tusculan Disputations* 37, 48–51, 56, 84, 103, 104, 125, 126, 148, 149, 178, 185, 191, 271, 319, 322; *Verrine Orations* 107; Walo 229

477

Cistercians 288, 339, 368
Cluny 1, 81, 95, 234; reform movement 116, 129
Codex Parisinus Lat. 2903 134, 141
Codex Udalrici 152, 154, 155, 207
Colish, Marcia 95, 96, 97, 100
Collodi, Carlo, *Pinocchio* 278
Cologne 21, 23, 26, 55, 86, 89, 102, 104, 126, 129, 138, 142, 143, 176, 178; archbishopric 149; cathedral school 98, 140; library 130
compositio morum 54, 76
Conrad II, emperor 123, 204
Constable, Giles 344
constancia (constancy) 58, 59
Constantine of Fleury 107
contemptus mundi 49, 148, 371
convictus 15, 40, 41, 63, 145, 146, 156, 387
Cornificius 302, 305, 307, 315, 317, 335, 353, 354
Corpus Christianorum 316
cosmogonic writings 252
courtly literature 80, 270, 276, 282, 283, 326, 365, 366, 385, 415, 416, 423, 425, 434
courtly love 365–69
courts 159; royal 69–78
Crusades 133
cultus virtutum (cultivation of virtue) 13, 32–40, 37, 46, 50–52, 58, 69, 73, 76–77, 79, 81, 106, 148, 154, 192–93, 222, 255–56, 317–18, 320, 393
curiales 50–59
curiositas 46
Curtius, Ernst Robert 5, 13, 17, 55, 105, 133, 291, 401, 403, 415; *Deutscher Geist in Gefahr* 136; *European Literature and the Latin Middle Ages* 12, 135, 137

D
Dante Alighieri 12, 17, 135, 137, 245, 294, 379, 414
David, king 236, 242

decor animae 57, 60, 76
Della Mirandola, Pico, *Oration on the Dignity of Man* 264, 401
De nuptiis Mercurii et Philologie 209, 210, 215, 216, 218, 219, 220, 223, 241. See also Mercury and Philology.
Der Ackermann aus Böhmen 264, 401
Derrida, Jacques 304
De sillogismis cathegoricis 109
De topicis differentiis 109
De ypotheticis 109
dialectic 131, 390; Abelard 314; Abbo 120–22; *Dialectica* 98, 111; Gerbert 108–14, 194; John of Salisbury 302–10, 315; monasteries 127–28, 299; new learning 36; Paris 358; Peter Damian 122–24; Regensburg letters 125–26; William of Champeaux 33, 67–68, 347–48; William of Conches 71–72
dictamen 140, 151, 154, 155
Dictionary of Medieval Latin from British Sources 88
Dietrich of Bern 92, 93, 162, 164, 322
Dietrich of Metz 92, 93, 322
dignitas hominis 249
Dinzelbacher, Peter 367
Dis 211, 212, 215, 221, 231
disciplina 39, 43, 54, 65, 70, 90, 92, 105, 179, 393, 394, 397; *vivendi* 32, 47–49, 50
disputation 23, 36, 62, 64, 70, 111, 115, 123, 143, 264, 391, 392
divinus homo 252, 258, 260
doctrina et mores 12, 13, 82, 89, 91, 92, 353
Drogo of Paris 65, 93
Dunstan of Canterbury 95
Durandus of Liège, bishop 227
Durham: music 196; St. Cuthbert's 197
Dutton, Paul Edward 317

E
Ebalus of Rheims, archbishop 33

* INDEX

Eberhard I of Salzburg, archbishop 238
Ebrachar, bishop 165
Ecbert of Tours, abbot 106, 321
Ehlers, Joachim 83, 84, 87, 140
Eichstaett, cathedral school 98
Eleanor of Aquitaine 327
elegantia 34, 37, 41, 44, 53, 144, 145, 164, 397
Eliot, T.S. 285
enlightenment 10
Enlightenment, the 297, 298
Erasmus, Desiderius 7, 91, 170, 332, 339
Erdmann, Carl 11, 12, 15, 16, 17, 140, 322; *Die Entstehung des Kreuzugsgedankens (The Origin of the Idea of Crusade)* 133; Meinhard's Letters 133–39, 141, 147, 149, 159, 178, 179; *Studien zur Briefliteratur Deutschlands im elften Jahrhundert* 30, 133, 135, 141–42, 144, 147, 149, 159, 166–67
Eriugena, John Scotus 8, 97, 98, 100, 121
Erluin of Gembloux, abbot 233
ethics (*ethica*) 41, 44, 50, 59, 60, 78, 104, 105, 129, 138, 185, 186, 192–93, 398; Abelard 66; aesthetic 273; cathedral school 22, 29, 33–38; classical 72, 73, 104, 105, 129, 138, 185; courtly 16; John of Salisbury 68, 317–19, 322, 398; literature 13; music 186; Victorine 396, 397, 409
Étienne de la Chapelle, archbishop 390
Etienne de Senlis, bishop 390
Eucharist Controversy 45, 62, 139, 275, 300
Eurydice 207–15, 220, 231, 241, 426
Eusebius of Caesarea 214

F
facetia 162, 165
fantastic 421–26
Faust 413–34. *See also* Goethe, Johann Wolfgang von, *Faust*.
Feiss, Hugh 380

Ferruolo, Stephen C. 353, 358
Fickermann, Norbert 125, 148, 322
Fitzstephen, William 73, 74
Fleckenstein, Josef 25, 26, 27, 83
Fleury, abbey 96, 100
Folcuin of Lobbes 102
forma vivendi 32
Forse, James H. 86
Foucault, Michel 2, 278, 304
Franco of Liège 171
Frazer, James 401
Frederick I Barbarossa, emperor 238, 339, 340, 341, 342, 343
Frederick the Great 297
Fried, Johannes 138, 139, 140, 150, 152
Frontinus: *Strategemata (On the Art of Warfare)* 87
Froumund of Tegernsee 206
Fulbert of Chartres 19, 24, 25, 33, 41, 42, 46, 62–64, 68, 143, 171, 186, 234
Fulcoius of Beauvais 240, 241
Furies 211

G
Gadamer, Hans-Georg 420
Gasparri, Françoise 411
Gautier 220, 221
Gawain 433
Geistesgeschichte 6
Geisteshaltung 7, 9
Geoffrey of Clairvaux 248, 279, 280
Geoffrey of Monmouth 423
Geoffrey the Fair of Anjou 334
geometry 114, 258
George, Stephan 6
Gerald of Aurillac, abbot 118, 130, 234
Gerald of Wales 53, 81, 82, 296, 349, 357; *De principis instructione* 77; *De rebus a se gestis* 363; *Journey through Ireland* 363; *Journey through Wales* 362
Gerannus of Rheims 108, 117
Gerbert of Aurillac 10, 19, 23, 24, 35, 44, 95–100, 106–21, 128–29, 131, 140, 194, 232, 233, 238, 320, 321;

479

Aristotle 108, 112–14; Cicero 125–27; *De rationali et ratione uti* 112–18, 127; imperial philosophy (*imperialis philosophia*) 113, 115, 116; letters 119; *magister scolarum* 110; philosophy 106–17; Spain 117; Sylvester II, pope 97
Gerhard of Seeon, abbot 25
Gervasius of Rheims, archbishop 235
Gilbert de la Porée 304, 310, 314
Gilbert, Humphrey 78
Gilbert of Poitiers 307, 315, 316, 352, 353, 355, 357, 374
Gilson, Etienne 9, 17
Godfrey of Rheims, chancellor 195, 198, 201, 221; Orpheus 208
Godfrey of St. Victor 264, 382, 383, 392, 395; *Address (Apostrophus) to the Spirit of Humanity* 14, 388–402; *Fons philosophiae* 378, 384, 389, 390, 391; free will 409–10; *Microcosmus* 1, 14, 245, 246, 249, 255, 256, 261, 377–80, 383, 387, 389–91, 398–405; wayside inn of Charity 380–381
Goethe, Johann Wolfgang von 283, 297, 413; *Faust* 200, 283, 285, 420, 421, 424, 425, 426, 427, 430, 433, 434
Goetz, Hans-Werner 345
Gombrich, Ernst 2, 17
Gothic 80, 156, 277, 298, 326, 414, 417
Gottfried von Strassburg 76, 77, 192, 294, 367, 423; *moraliteit* 183, 184, 193; *Tristan und Isolde* 75, 81, 156, 182, 201, 278, 280–81, 365, 433, 434.
Gottschalk 154
Gozechin (Goswin) of Mainz 25, 42, 43, 44, 65, 93, 151, 155, 172
Grabmann, Martin 4
grammar 74, 111, 116, 121; Bernard of Chartres 356; *Cambridge Songs* 204; dialectic 110; Gerbert 118; northern grammarians 61; John of Salisbury 302–8, 310, 315–17, 355–56;

Meinhard 151–53; *mores* 34–35; Peter Damian 122–23; Petrus Pictor 361; speculative thought 96–98
gravitas 42, 44, 53, 91, 144, 162, 216, 262, 295
Greeks: Aquinas 246; Cato 153; Cicero 109; historians 340; *imperium* 115, 347; model 49–50; *paideia* 146, 156; scholarship 84–85, 102, 352; sculpture 417
Gregory I, pope 162
Gregory VII, pope 240
Grimmelshausen, H.J.C. 264, 265
Guibert of Nogent 205, 359, 360
Guido of Bazoches 348
Guido of Vienne, archbishop 235
Guitmund of Aversa 45, 46, 345
Gumbrecht, Hans Ulrich 282
Gunther of Bamberg, bishop 30, 53, 139, 159, 162, 163, 178, 179
Gunzo of Novara 103

H
Hannover letter collection 40, 133, 161, 228
Hariulf 41
Harmonia 210
Hartmann von Aue 286, 287, 366, 432
Hartwig 180
Harvard Business School 154
Haskins, Charles Homer 19, 28, 194, 327, 339, 346; *Renaissance of the Twelfth Century* 5, 195
Hatto, A.T. 117, 184, 281
Hatto of Vich, bishop 117
Heap, Uriah 285
Hegel, Georg Wilhelm Friedrich 2, 297
Heidegger, Martin 304
Heinrich von Veldeke 366
Helen of Troy 168, 283, 425, 426
Heloise 7, 327, 368, 370, 416, 417; poetry 360. See also Abelard.
Henri d'Andeli, *Battle of the Seven Arts* 363

★ INDEX

Henri I, king 238, 239
Henry II, emperor 53, 72, 162, 238, 240, 327, 331, 343
Henry III, emperor 47, 205, 235, 236, 237, 238, 251
Henry IV, emperor 125, 251
Herbert of Bosham 280, 294, 343
Hercules 68, 427, 430
Heribert of Eichstätt, bishop 223
Herman of Carinthia 327
Hermann of Rheims 40, 65, 93, 155
Hermes Trismegistus 246, 247
Hermetic tradition 14, 246, 247, 250, 254, 259, 264, 406, 407; *Corpus Hermeticum* 251, 253; *Poimandres* 251, 252, 265, 266
Herod, king 49
heroic cultures 160–61, 164, 181, 199, 271, 277, 278, 284, 286, 287, 297, 363, 418, 419, 430
Hezilo of Hildesheim, bishop 228
hilaritas 159–65
Hilary of Poitiers, St. 122, 352
Hildebert of Lavardin 203, 299, 301, 373, 392; Adela of Blois 240; Berengar 46; Bernard of Clairvaux 279; humanism 5, 6, 8–10, 81–82; *Magnificat* 295–96; Meinhard 140; Muriel of Wilton 289–98; *Par tibi Roma nihil* 267, 269, 270, 274, 277, 280–84; poetry 222, 361, 364; *Quid suum virtutis* 215
Hildegar of Chartres 41, 42, 234
Hildesheim 23, 26, 32; cathedral school 228
Hincmar of Rheims 70
Holtzman, Walter 134
Holy Grail 422, 423, 424, 430, 431, 432
Holy Land 163
Homer: epic 419; epithets 250; fantasy 422–27; *Iliad* 168; *Odyssey* 422, 423, 425, 427, 428, 429, 430, 431, 434
homo novus 259, 401
homo perfectus 243–66

honestas 12, 38, 39, 54, 58, 65, 106, 144, 175, 187, 319
Honorius 167, 294
Horace 109, 121, 149, 167, 194, 291, 295, 364; *Ars Poetica* 213, 214; *Carmen Saeculare* 168, 169, 216; *Odes* 177
Hrabanus Maurus 89, 106, 320
Hrotsvitha of Gandersheim 95, 96; *Paphnutius* 126
Hugh Capet, king 97
Hugh of Champfleury, chancellor 390, 397
Hugh of Die 240
Hugh of St. Victor 249, 263, 264, 352, 356, 371, 389, 403; charismatic teaching 261; *De institutione novitiorum (On the Instruction of Novices)* 42, 58, 65, 77, 147, 156, 185, 192, 214, 217, 262, 273, 391–96 *De sacramentis legis naturalis et scriptae* 395; *Didascalicon* 254, 255, 379, 396, 405–7; free will 409–10, 410; *Homiliae in Ecclesiasten* 386; human divinity 406–7; imitation 64, 146, 272–73; liberal arts 256, 356–57; old learning 14, 73, 81, 301, 373–74, 393; nature 39
Huizinga, Johan: *Waning of the Middle Ages* 370, 371, 415
human dignity 8, 14, 51, 249, 398, 401, 409, 433
human divinity 250–52
humanist creation myths 264–65
humanitas 6, 56, 144, 157, 158, 171, 291, 395
human universality 252–63
Huzmann of Speyer 65, 93

I
imitatio 145–47, 176
imperial bishops 26, 44, 52
imperial cathedral schools (*imperiale studium*) 83, 87, 138, 140, 141, 151,

481

172–73; decline 171–72
imperial church system 11, 27, 51, 101, 140, 154, 159, 173, 320
ingenium et mores 12, 29
Innocent III, pope 358
Investiture Controversy 49, 93, 138, 148, 199, 397
Irish Exile 330, 339
Isidore of Seville 105, 319; *Etymologiae* 236
Isolde of Ireland 75, 76, 183, 185, 191, 192, 198, 281; music 182–84
Isolde, queen 182
Israel the Irish Bishop 85
Ivo of Chartres 317

J
Jackson, W.T.H. 184
Jacques de Vitry 287
Jaeger, Werner 136, 137, 156, 419, 431
Jerome, St. 124
Jerusalem 53, 164
Jevons, Stanley 312
John of Hauville 326; *Architrenius* 336–37
John of Liège, provost 227
John of Salisbury 80, 299–324; Adam of Balsham 308–9, 392; Becket 382; Bernard of Chartres 190, 338; courtier 16; education 65–66, 68–69, 71; *Entheticus* 315, 318, 335, 354, 375; ethics 35, 37, 41, 76; Henry II 331, 343; humanism 4–5, 10, 11; 316–21; *Metalogicon* 35, 68, 79, 108, 143, 301–5, 308, 311, 314–18, 323, 335, 353–57, 375; old learning 111, 140, 349, 373–74, 390; *On the Follies of Courtiers and the Footsteps of Philosophers* 161; *Policraticus* 79, 161, 242, 303, 308, 315, 316, 323, 354, 375; William of Soissons 310–15
John Scot Eriugena 8
John, St. the Evangelist 124, 295, 347
John XIII, pope 117

Jotsald of Cluny 81
Jung, Jacqueline 289
Juvenal 109, 194

K
Kaeuper, Richard F. 434
Kallendorf, Craig W. 77
Kant, Immanuel 304
Kantorowicz, Ernst 133, 137
Keats, John 184, 310, 313, 316
Kehr, Paul 134
Kneale, William and Martha 120, 312
Knowles, David 7
Krass, Andreas 414

L
Ladner, Gerhart 327
Lady Charity 381, 382, 383, 391, 392
Lady Philosophy 37, 125, 321, 408
Lampert of Hersfeld 163
Lancelot 433
Lanfranc of Bec 46, 99, 345
Langres, council of 1116 235
Lawrence of Durham 196, 197, 294
Leclercq, Jean 7, 126, 127
Le Goff, Jacques 139
Leiden University 201
Leo IX, pope 54, 122
Leonardi, Claudio 2, 3
Leopertus of Palestrina 157, 158
letters and manners (*litterae et mores*) 12, 13, 27–32, 45, 51, 53, 55, 76, 78, 91, 141; Castiglione 79; Cicero 89, 320; Fulbert of Chartres 41; imperial schools 173; Meinhard 139; new learning 193; Ottonians 88–92. William of Champeaux 347. *See also litterae et mores; ingenium et mores; sapientia et mores; mores et doctrina; morum honestas et litterarum eruditio.*
levitas 151, 172
Lewis, C.S. 367
liberales doctrinae 29

library catalogues 28, 97, 130
Library of Latin Texts 88, 91, 152
Liebeschütz, Hans 127
Liège 24, 25, 29, 62, 89, 90, 92, 129, 138, 171, 220; cathedral school 65, 93, 98, 321; imperial school 151, 172; school 65
Limoges 61
Linde, Cornelia 35
Liudolf, prince 233
Liutprand of Cremona 95
logic 96, 98, 112, 121, 122; Aristotelian 97, 100, 101, 113, 116, 119, 128, 131, 314; Berengar 64; *Compotista* 99; Gerbert 108–9, 114–18; Gerald of Wales 362; Hrabanus Maurus 106; John of Salisbury 301–9; *logica vetus* (old logic) 100, 110, 127; machine 310–15. *See also* dialectic.
Loire poets 6, 9, 291
London, schools 74
Longinus, *On the Sublime* 420
Louis the German, king 70
Louis VI, the Fat, king 343
Louis VII, king 343, 349
Lucan 109, 194, 317; *Civil War* 198
Luscombe, David 3, 128

M

Macrobius 8, 21, 100, 334; *Commentary on the Dream of Scipio* 97, 191, 244, 250, 253
Magdeburg 23, 26, 115, 129
magnificentia 413
Mainz 24, 26, 93, 172; cathedral school 225; synod of 1049 54
Malachy, St. 248
Manasses I of Rheims, archbishop 161, 195, 229, 234, 235, 240
Manegold of Lautenbach 20, 21, 33, 38, 42, 127, 333, 351, 352, 374
Manitius, Max 4, 72, 99
Mann, Thomas 264, 266; *Joseph and His Brothers* 136, 265

mansuetudo 53, 227
Marbod of Rennes 6, 9, 10, 203, 208, 220, 299, 373; *Vita Licinii* 216
Marenbon, John 96, 97, 98, 100, 103, 124, 128, 130, 131
Marianus Scotus 337
Marshall, Linda 59
Martial, St. 61
Martianus Capella 21, 60, 67, 100, 154, 208, 211, 223; *De nuptiis Mercurii et Philologie* 209, 210
Martin, Christopher 312
Märtl, Claudia 138, 139
Mary, Virgin 186, 242, 295
mathematics 106, 114, 115, 174, 258, 320
Matthew of Vendôme 336, 364
Matthew Paris 74
Maurice, St. 286, 287
Maximian, emperor 199, 230, 286
Mayr-Harting, Henry 21, 86, 88, 92, 102, 129, 130, 140
McGarry, Daniel 312
McKitterick, Rosamond 97, 98, 100, 103, 128, 130
Medici family 7
Meinhard of Bamberg 10, 46, 53, 65, 93, 130, 133–80; cathedral schools 149–52; Cicero 48–49, 58, 299, 322; courtliness 16; *De fide* 139; *hilaritas* 159–65; humanism 15, 56; imperial schools 171; letters 11, 19, 29–32, 40, 55, 60, 126, 175–79; love and friendship 166–70; *mores* 33–34
Meinwerk of Paderborn 53
melancholy 371, 372
Mercury and Philology 36, 208–11, 354
Metz: cathedral school 93; St. Vincent abbey 199, 201
Mews, Constant 360
Michael, archangel 295
microcosm/macrocosm 39, 244–45, 378
Milis, Ludo 388

483

mimesis 269, 283, 284, 295, 419
Modesty 58
monastic schools 22, 27, 131, 185, 193, 377
Montecassino, abbey 157
Monumenta Germaniae Historica 88, 133
morales disciplinae 29
moralitas 9, 16, 33, 34, 73, 74, 76, 77, 78, 184, 192, 193, 257
moraliteit 75, 76, 183, 184
mores 39, 81, 85, 189, 191, 213, 217, 234, 331, 362; Alan 260; Anselm of Laon 66; Bern 236; Bernard of Chartres 190, 356; Boethius 37, 125, 321; Cicero 149; courtly 9, 16, 70; education 33–34, 40, 44, 51–52, 54, 57, 152, 154, 159; Gerbert 239; governance 59, 73–74, 156; *mores et doctrina* 12, 91, 353; *moribus etiam instituendus* 29; *morum elegantia* 41, 53; *morum honestas et litterarum eruditio* 12; Victorine 386. *See also* letters and manners (*litterae et mores*).
Münster-Swendsen, Mia 15–16, 137
Muriel of Wilton 289–93
music 181–202; Boethian 188, 190, 191, 193; celestial harmony 125, 186, 187, 198, 245, 321; David, king 230; education 186–90; Gregorian chant 186; human motion 191–95; *musica humana* 184; Orpheus 196; Orphic 186, 195, 212, 213, 214, 215, 221, 223, 230, 231, 235, 237, 238, 240; planetary 191–195; Platonic 187, 189; polyphony 197; Pythagorean 191, 193; St. Denis 183; Sens 183

N

Narcissus 268, 269, 284
narrative structure 427–29
Natura 39, 257, 267
Nazism 136, 285

Nebuchadnezzar, king 49
Nederman, Cary 314
Nero, emperor 49
Nestor 160, 179
"new human" (*novus homo*) 39, 58, 59, 60, 252, 257–63, 371, 380, 408
"new learning" 36, 62, 65, 68, 193, 393
Nibelungenlied 297
Nietzsche, Friedrich, *Birth of Trajedy* 285, 304, 413
Ninian, St. 344
Norden, Eduard 4
Notker, imperial chaplain 89, 90, 93, 97, 98, 120, 121, 128
Notker Labeo of St. Gall 99, 120, 121
Notre Dame. *See* Paris, Notre Dame.
Noys 249, 256, 258, 260

O

Odolricus of Orleans, bishop 234
Odo of Cluny, abbot 234
Odysseus 413–34
Ohly, Friedrich 133
Ohtricus, master 23, 25, 115 127
"old learning" 36, 45, 46, 51, 52, 58, 59, 60, 62, 64, 65, 66, 67, 68, 69, 71, 72, 73, 74, 77, 79, 173, 264, 349, 355
Onulf of Speyer 37, 41; *Colores rhetorici* 34, 47
Orderic Vitalis 344
Orleans 358
Orpheus 195, 196, 203–42, 426; and Eurydice 208–15; Carolingians 214; compassion 211–14, 226; eloquence 208–10; Merovingians 214; study 216. *See also* Eurydice.
Otloh of St. Emmeram 21, 33, 124
Otto I, the Great, emperor 333; Brun of Cologne 88, 92, 101–3, 320, 331, 333; cathedral schools 12, 23, 25, 61, 83–90, 223; court 70, 322; Gerbert 117–18; Liudolf 233
Otto II, emperor 23, 97, 115, 117

INDEX

Otto III, emperor 53, 97, 106, 112, 114, 116, 320
Ottonians: culture 11, 83, 95, 102; education 70, 88–93, 103, 223, 396; governance 51, 158; imperial church 27; libraries 130; "renaissance" 101. *See also* Henry II, emperor; Otto I; Otto II; Otto III.
Otto of Bamberg 57
Otto of Freising 301, 333, 340, 343, 351, 356, 371, 374; *Chronicle of the Two Cities* 339, 341, 342, 345, 349, 352; *Gesta Friderici* 341, 352
Ovid 205, 214, 360, 367, 369; *Metamorphoses* 213, 220

P

paideia 146, 154–58, 252
Panaetius 107, 321
Panofsky, Erwin 133, 328; *Iconology: Humanistic Themes in the Art of the Renaissance* 136
Paris: Bibliothèque Nationale 133; Louvre 284; Notre Dame, cathedral school 67, 111, 173, 288, 314, 385, 392; Mt. Ste. Geneviève 306, 307, 348, 353, 373; music 196; St. Germain des Prés 385; university 301, 304, 308, 309, 314, 326, 328, 347, 358, 391, 392
Parzival 413–34
Paulus, Stephen 327
Peace of God 133, 234, 236, 237
pedagogy, charismatic 44, 83, 86, 137, 144, 145, 147, 259, 261, 272, 397
Pentcheva, Bissera 289
Perihermeneias 109
Pernolf of Würzburg, magister 155, 194, 206, 223
Perseus Project 89
Persius, *Satires* 109, 194, 309
pessimism 325–376, 370–373
Peter Damian 21, 157, 204, 241, 360; Aristotle 124; *De divina omnipotentia* 124, 203; *De frenanda ira* 234, 240; *De sancta simplicitate scientiae inflanti anteponenda* 122–24, 203, 204, 360; dialectics 124; philosophy 122–23; Platonists 122
Peter Lombard 327, 348, 352, 374
Peter of Blois 5, 10, 140, 240, 349; *On Christian Friendship* 369
Peter of Celle 314
Petrarch, Francesco 6, 363
Petrus Pictor 361
Petrus Riga 331, 343
Philip Augustus, king 59, 331, 343, 349
Philology and Mercury 36
philosophy: Alexandrian 246; Boethian 321; Cassiodorus 106; Ciceronian 9, 13, 37, 39, 56, 58, 86, 87, 101, 103, 104, 105, 106, 107, 114, 124, 124–125, 125, 126, 127, 137, 144, 148, 158, 193, 232, 261, 299, 318, 319, 320, 321, 323; Gnostic 256, 264, 407; Hermetic 246–247; Isidore of Seville 105; John of Salisbury 299–324; *palatini philosophi* 102; Peripatetics 170; *Philosophia* 39, 46, 71, 72, 95–131, 188, 318, 319, 321, 322, 334, 408, 210; Platonism 21, 72, 97, 101, 129, 173, 185, 187, 188, 189, 191, 250, 252, 260, 263, 264, 268, 317, 407; Pythagorean 191, 245; Realism 62; scholastic 261; Stoic 9, 25, 37, 38, 39, 86, 87, 101, 104, 129, 146, 322
phronesis 246, 257, 258, 259, 260
Piaget, Jean 269
Pilgrim of Cologne, archbishop 186, 187, 192, 198, 245
Pindar 250, 422, 423
Plantagenets 59, 72
Plato 8, 63, 124, 125, 184, 243, 321, 322; Academy 25; Platonism 97, 100, 101; *Republic* 190; *Timaeus* 20, 21, 38, 39, 69, 72, 97, 173, 190, 243, 244, 401, 402, 403

Pluto 211, 226, 228, 231
poetry 320, 339, 375; 12th-century 359–65; academic 28, 154–55, 203, 206; Alexandrine 285, 297; Bernard of Clairvaux 81; civilizing force 231–36; composition 296, 360; court 59; decline 359–64; education 223; France 21; Gerald of Wales 82; Gerbert 108, 110–11; heroic 297; Hildebert 9, 267–75; Isolde 194; Italian 79; Latin 5, 129, 182, 183, 194, 292, 360, 363, 364; Liège songs 220–21; Loire Valley 6; love 366; Meinhard 169; Muriel 281–98; music 181–202; old learning 64; Orphic 203–42; Peter Damian 123; philosophical 317, 357; political 363; religious 363; sacred 292; scholastic 28, 203, 205, 208, 231; secular lyric 363; useful 204; Virgilian 205
Poirel, Dominique 377
Polemon 160, 161, 180
Poppo, decanus 159, 160, 178, 179
Poppo of Würzburg, bishop 23, 223
Porphyry, *Isagoge* 109
Primas of Orleans 326, 347
Proserpina 162
prudence 126, 160, 179
Prudentius 87
Pseudo-Apuleius: *Perihermenias* commentry 97
pulchritudo morum 53
Pygmalion 268, 269, 278
Pythagoras 185; Pythagoreans 122

Q
quadrivium 108, 117, 126, 174, 186, 187, 205, 245, 246, 258, 308
Quid suum virtutis 215–20, 222, 223, 240
Quintilian 30, 89, 154, 252; dialectic 121; *Institutes of Oratory* 51, 213

R
Radding, Charles 269
Radice, Betty 416
Rainald of Dassel 327
Raleigh, Walter 371
Ralph of Laon 45, 352
Ramsey Abbey 121
Rashdall, Hastings 4
Rassow, Peter 134
Rather of Verona 102, 103
Ratio (Reason) 58, 59, 112, 191, 192, 241, 257, 258, 411
Ravenna 23, 115, 127
recte vivendi dogma 32
reform and reformation 1, 26, 87, 89, 93, 95, 116, 118, 129, 202, 234, 316, 327, 328, 344, 352, 358, 359, 371, 377, 389, 397, 400, 434
Regensburg 24, 25, 125, 129, 148, 223; cathedral school 98
Regensburger rhetorischen Briefe 37, 38, 48, 49, 322
Reichenau, abbey 81, 100, 186
Reichert, Folker 11, 12, 17, 133, 134, 135
Reiner of St. Laurent 165
renaissance 276; 12th-century 2, 5, 11, 19, 27, 174, 195, 300, 325–76, 339, 352; 15th-century 4, 10, 14–16, 42, 77, 213, 246–47, 249, 271, 285, 326, 371, 414–15, 417; term 374
renewal 19, 22, 25, 87, 259, 300, 327, 328, 331, 342, 346, 352, 370, 374
Reuter, Timothy 3
Rheims 33, 127, 144, 171, 221, 347; cathedral school 124, 97, 117, 129 145, 151, 155; council of 1119 235; music 196; poetry 208
rhetoric 140, 150, 152, 158, 204, 211, 232, 240, 258, 280, 294, 329; dialectic 126; epideictic 291–92, 342; ethics 29, 34–35, 52; Gerbert 100, 108–12; John of Salisbury 302–4, 307, 315; judicial 210, 212, 213, 241; old learning 64, 66–67, 357, 364, 393; Ornulf 37, 41; poetry 194; sublime 295

Richard of St. Victor 51, 317, 369, 370; *De statu interioris hominis* 409; free will 409–10
Richard the Bishop 67, 356
Richarius, monk 233
Riché, Pierre 121
Richer of St. Remi 108–11, 194; *Vita of Gerbert* 115–18
Rieu, E.V. 428
Rilke, Rainer Maria 284
Robert of Hereford 51
Robert of Melun 305, 306, 315, 336, 355
Robert of Torigni 390
Robert the Pious, king 234
Rodulfus Tortarius 361
Roman d'Eneas 414
romanticism 10, 298
Rome: arts 35, 268, 417; education and learning 146, 215, 252, 346–47, 349, 351–52, 423, 434; empire 115, 341–43, 351; ethics 72, 141, 159; governance 44, 48, 50–51, 103, 113; Hildebert 267–88; humanism 74; literature 4, 149; model 49–50; papal 117, 203, 240; philosophy 49–50, 85, 148–49; religion 199; "second" 25; Senate 149
Romulf of Sens, abbot 107
Roscellinus of Compiègne 99, 140, 173
Ruodlieb 237–40, 299
Ruotger of Cologne 26, 70, 71, 81, 84, 85, 86, 87, 101–4, 129, 130, 216, 232

S

Salians 11, 70, 92, 130, 134, 135, 137, 146, 158
Salzburg, cathedral school 129
Sapientia 209
sapientia et mores 12, 29
Saul, king 230, 236
Saxon dynasty, education 98
Scaglione, Aldo 13, 16
Scharschmidt, Carl 312
Schiller, Friedrich 413
Schnell, Rüdiger 83
schola morum 141, 146
Scholasticism 6, 15, 22, 121, 131, 140, 300; criticisms 69; prose style 357
sculpture, Gothic 156, 277, 414, 417
Seneca 40, 104, 105, 146, 240, 319; *De beneficiis* 387
Shakespeare, William 54, 265, 297; *As You Like It* 371; *Henry IV* 125, 251, 264, 322; *Henry V* 264; *Midsummer Night's Dream* 168; *Winter's Tale* 278
Shaw, George Bernard 285, 313
Sigebert of Gembloux 92, 233, 264, 322; *Passio Thebeorum (Passion of the Theban Legion)* 199–200, 201, 230, 231, 286, 287, 407; *Vita of Dietrich* 93
Smalley, Beryl 130, 194
Socrates 25, 63, 124, 153, 271, 347
Sophia 64, 258, 273, 274, 276, 399
Sophocles 429
Southern, R.W. 8, 19, 40, 312, 333, 334, 375
Spartans 49
Speyer 24, 111, 138, 172
Spitzer, Leo 133
Statius 109, 194
St. Denis, abbey 61, 385
Steckel, Sita 15, 17, 22, 26, 83, 92, 137, 139, 141, 147–48, 261
Stefan of Novara 23, 60, 61, 67, 71, 72, 103, 223
Stephen of Garland, chancellor 390, 397
Stephen of Tournai 358
St. Gall, abbey 61, 96, 100
Stock, Brian 257
Stoics. *See* philosophy.
St. Omer 361
Strassburg, *Wise and Foolish Virgins* 156
studium bene vivendi 32, 106, 107, 319
St. Victor, abbey: anthropology 398–405; Ciceronianism 397; community 370, 382, 390, 395; human divinity 406–7; human universality 402–5;

Liber ordinis Sancti Victoris 156, 384, 385, 387, 388, 389, 390, 395; school 33, 67, 73, 147, 156, 173, 192, 199, 261, 273, 347, 358, 377, 378, 379, 380, 403; social ideals 383–97
sublimitas 410, 413; Meinhard 34, 41
Suger of St. Denis 327, 343, 360
Sylvester II, pope 97

T

Tanchelm 327
Taylor, Henry Osborne 6
Tellenbach, Gerd 133, 134
Terence 109, 194
textual contract 277–86
Thangmar of Hildesheim 81
Theobald, archbishop 314
Theobald of Canterbury, archbishop 73, 331, 343
theology 34, 65, 358, 368, 374; Alan of Lille 258–60; arts 34; Hugh of St. Victor 256; humanistic 398–409; John of Salisbury 303, 307, 308, 310, 315, Meinhard 139; Otto of Freising 339, 353; Peter Lombard 348; Plato, *Timaeus* 243; Victorine 378, 380, 395–96, 411; William of Champeaux 347
Theophanu, princess 117
Thierry of Chartres 10, 20, 140, 173, 307, 349, 352, 355, 356, 403
Thierry of St. Hubert 234, 235
Thierry of St. Trond 215
Thomasin von Zirclaria 77, 423
Tischler, Matthias 139
topoi of change 329–38; *Antiqui and Moderni* 333–37; dwarves and giants 338, 359; world grown old 329–32
Toul, cathedral school 93
Tournai, St. Geneviève 358
Tours, philosophical studies 358
translatio imperii 342
translatio studii 342, 346, 349, 351
Traube, Ludwig 4, 5

Trier 24, 29, 90, 98; cathedral school 194
Trinkaus, Charles 249
Tristan und Isolde. See Gottfried von Strassburg.
trivium 27, 34, 36, 258, 301, 302, 303
Trojan War 427
Truce of God 234
Tudors 78

U

Ugo of Parma 123, 204
Ulrich of Bamberg 206, 207, 222, 223, 241; *Ars dictaminis* 154
University of Cambridge 82; Emmanuel College 91; graduation ceremony 91; Peterhouse College 92
University of Oxford, Merton College 92
University of Washington 414
utilitas 34, 41, 123, 145, 155, 204, 232, 238
Utrecht, cathedral school 98

V

van Eck, Caroline 289
Vasari, Giorgio 332
Veldeke's *Eneit* 414
Venantius Fortunatus 214
venustas morum 33, 53, 392, 393
Verdun, cathedral school 93
Vicelin, student 45
Victorinus, rhetorician 109
Vincent of Beauvais: *De eruditione filiorum nobilium* 77
Virgil 364, 434; Abbo 121; *Aeneid* 142, 177, 241; *Bucolics* 205; Dante 414; *Eclogues* 228; *Georgics* 213; Gerbert 109, 194; Hildebert 291, 295; John of Salisbury 317; Peter Damian 123, 203–5, 360; Rodulfus 361
virtues: Alan of Lille 257–60; bodily 273–74, 394–95; cardinal 246; civic 38, 59–60, 74, 323, 340; courtly and chivalric 275–76, 282, 287; Gerbert 106; inner 35, 54, 58, 279; love

166–71; manners 53–54; Meinhard 142–80; moral education 13, 33, 40, 43, 46, 51, 56, 69, 84–85, 145–48, 206, 251, 263, 406–7; Muriel 295–97; music 184, 186–90, 192, 200; old learning 59, 366–68; peacemaking 231–42; philosophy 48–49, 78, 101–4, 125, 318–19, 321, 408–10; rhetoric 52; virginity 398–99. *See also cultus virtutum; hilaritas; honestas; Quid suum virtutis.*
von den Steinen, Wolfram 6, 7, 9
Vones, Ludwig 83, 84, 104
von Moos, Peter 8, 9, 145, 291, 292

W

Wagner, Richard 421
Walcherus of Liège 44, 65, 151, 155, 172, 409
Walo of St. Arnulf of Metz, abbot 161, 229, 235
Walter Map 337, 343
Walter of Châtillon 301, 326, 334, 357, 362, 374
Walter of St. Victor 358, 378, 379
Waltharius, epic 199
Walther of Speyer 130; *Libellus scolasticus* 111; *Life of St. Christopher* 111
Wazo of Liège 29, 129, 227, 238
Weigle, Fritz 107
Weill, Kurt, *One Touch of Venus* 278
Werner of Basel 64
Weston, Jessie 401
Wibald of Stablo 33, 42, 46, 50, 64, 194, 263, 279, 321
Wilks, Michael 59
William Marshal 327
William of Champeaux 21, 33, 66–67, 72, 105, 173, 310, 314, 347, 390, 392–93, 395
William of Conches 10, 71–73, 140, 317, 349, 355, 390, 408; *Dragmaticon* 72, 334; John of Salisbury 68, 307, 310, 313, 338, 356; humanism 4, 173; *Moralium dogma philosophorum* 40, 72, 149; *Philosophia mundi* 39, 46, 72, 334; Plato, *Timaeus* 38
William of Malmesbury 52, 81, 337
William of Soissons 310–15
William of Tyre 311, 347, 348, 350
William the Breton 343, 349
William the Conqueror, king 95
Willigis of Mainz 43, 90
Wilton Abbey 289
Wipo, *Tetralogus* 239, 240
Wittig, Claudia 13
Wolbodo, bishop 238
Wolfgang of Regensburg, bishop 29, 60, 61, 90, 93, 223
Wolfhelm of Brauweiler 21, 127
Wolfram von Eschenbach 6, 9, 156; *Parzival* 413, 417, 420–24, 427, 429–33
Woodward, William Harrison 77
Worcester, cathedral 189
Worms 24, 29, 31, 47, 125, 129, 138, 206; cathedral chapter 152; cathedral school 205, 224, 225; letter collection 223, 224, 321; poet 225, 226, 227
Würzburg 23, 26, 29, 60, 90, 129, 138, 152, 223, 226, 272; cathedral school 98, 205, 224, 225, 227, 237, 272

X

Xenocrates 161

Y

Yeats, William Butler 313

Z

Zeno 146
Zey, Claudia 141, 163
Ziolkowski, Jan 198, 201
Zumthor, Paul 270

✶✶✶

*Production of This Book Was Completed on
2 October 2024 at Italica Press in
Clifton, Bristol, United Kingdom.
It Was Set in Adobe Jenson Pro
and MS Gothic Dingbats and
Printed on 55-Pound
Natural Paper.*

✷ ✷ ✷
✷ ✷
✷